Health Care USA
Understanding Its Organization and Delivery

Fourth Edition

Harry A. Sultz, DDS, MPH
Professor Emeritus
Social and Preventive Medicine
School of Medicine and Biomedical Sciences
Dean Emeritus
School of Health Related Professions
State University of New York at Buffalo
Buffalo, New York

Kristina M. Young, MS
Clinical Assistant Professor
Social and Preventive Medicine
School of Medicine and Biomedical Sciences
State University of New York at Buffalo
Buffalo, New York

JONES AND BARTLETT PUBLISHERS
Sudbury, Massachusetts
BOSTON   TORONTO   LONDON   SINGAPORE

World Headquarters

Jones and Bartlett Publishers
40 Tall Pine Drive
Sudbury, MA 01776
978-443-5000
info@jbpub.com
www.jbpub.com

Jones and Bartlett Publishers
Canada
2406 Nikanna Road
Mississauga, ON L5C 2W6
CANADA

Jones and Bartlett Publishers
International
Barb House, Barb Mews
London W6 7PA
UK

Library of Congress Cataloging-in-Publication Data

Sultz, Harry A.
   Health care, U.S.A. : understanding its organization and delivery / Harry A. Sultz,
Kristina M. Young.—4th ed.
      p. ; cm.
   Rev. ed. of: Health care USA / Harry A. Sultz, Kristina M. Young. 3rd ed. 2001.
   Includes bibliographical references and index.
   ISBN 0-7637-2571-4
     1. Medical care—United States. 2. Medical Policy—United States. I. Title: Health care,
USA. II. Young, Kristina M. III. Sultz, Harry A. Health care USA. IV. Title.
    [DNLM: 1. Delivery of Health Care—United States. 2. Health Policy—United States. W
84 AA1 S96h 2003]
   RA395.A3S897 2003
   362.1'0973—dc21

                         2003047493

Production Credits
Publisher: Michael Brown
Associate Editor: Chambers Moore
Production Manager: Amy Rose
Associate Production Editor: Karen C. Ferreira
Associate Marketing Manager: Joy Stark-Vancs
Manufacturing Buyer: Therese Brauer
Cover Design: Philip Regan
Printing and Binding: Malloy, Inc.
Cover Printing: John Pow Co.

Printed in the United States of America
07 06 05 04 03   10 9 8 7 6 5 4 3 2 1

This book is dedicated to our parents, William and Marabelle Sultz and Jacob Jay and Marie Young. Guiding these warm, loving, and dignified people through the health care system during the last years of their lives taught us more about the feats, functions, and foibles of medical care than all the research conducted, literature read, and services administered.

About the Authors

Harry A. Sultz, DDS, MPH is Professor Emeritus of Social and Preventive Medicine at the University at Buffalo School of Medicine and Biomedical Sciences and Dean Emeritus of its School of Health Related Professions. Currently, he is an Adjunct Professor at the School of Law. He has also served as Adjunct Professor, Health Systems Management, School of Management and Clinical Assistant Professor, Department of Family Medicine.

Dr. Sultz has written five previous books, contributed chapters to several other books for professional audiences and published numerous articles for medical and allied health journals. An epidemiologist, health care services planner, and researcher, he established and, for 26 years, directed the Health Services Research Program of Buffalo's School of Medicine. His extensive research experience serves as background for the various editions of this book and for the courses that he teaches about health care and health policy. He also has long service as an expert consultant to several governmental and voluntary agencies and institutions.

Kristina M. Young, MS, is Clinical Assistant Professor of Social and Preventive Medicine at the School of Medicine and Biomedical Sciences at the State University at Buffalo. She is also an adjunct faculty member of the University's School of Law. Currently, she teaches graduate level courses in the organization of health care and in health policy. She also is president of Kristina M. Young and Associates, Inc., a management consultation and training group specializing in health care and human services organizations. Previously, she served as president of a corporate training and development organization; as executive vice president of a not-for-profit organization dedicated to advancing the joint interests of a major teaching hospital and a health maintenance organization; and as the vice president for research and development for a teaching hospital system and executive director of its health, education, and research foundation.

Contents

Foreword. vii

Acknowledgments. ix

Introduction. xi

Chapter 1   Overview of Health Care:
                  A Population Perspective 1

Chapter 2   Benchmark Developments in U.S. Health Care . . 33

Chapter 3   Hospitals: Origin, Organization,
                  and Performance. 63

Chapter 4   Ambulatory Care. 115

Chapter 5   Medical Education and the
                  Changing Practice of Medicine 143

Chapter 6   Health Care Personnel. 179

Chapter 7   Financing Health Care 221

Chapter 8   Managed Care 271

Chapter 9   Long-Term Care 297

Chapter 10 Mental Health Services 335

Chapter 11 Public Health and the Role of
                  Government in Health Care 367

Chapter 12 Research: How Health Care Advances. 395

Chapter 13 The Future of Health Care 419

Appendix A Abbreviations and Acronyms. 459

Appendix B Websites **469**

Index **471**

Foreword

The last few years have brought tremendous upheaval in the formerly tradition-bound and physician-dominated U.S. health care system. The widespread penetration of managed care, with its service management and cost control strategies, and the resulting open market competitions among health care providers have changed the face of the health care industry. In addition, medicine's most recent technological and pharmaceutical advances have altered the manner in which many diseases are treated and clinical services are delivered.

This volume, *Health Care USA*, has added significance in this period of enormous upheaval and turmoil affecting the health care professions and institutions. It offers a clear overview of the health care industry and the issues that confront it. It describes the changing roles of the components of the system as well as the technical, economic, political, and social forces responsible for those changes. Students of health care and related professions and neophyte practitioners need a broad understanding of the United States's new health care system. Critical insights into diverse health care topics and issues are necessary to function effectively and relate intelligently to the various segments of the health care sector.

This, the fourth edition of *Health Care USA*, brings the reader up-to-date on the significant developments that have occurred in health care during the past few years. The Balanced Budget Act of 1997 and related legislation are causing major changes in Medicare and other government-sponsored programs. Those changes and the recognized dominance of managed care have required major adjustments by the health care industry. In this edition, as in previous ones, the authors have meticulously screened a vast amount of new information and have included the most appropriate for updating this work. This text continues to retain its balanced, population perspective, which allows the reader to understand the forces that are driving these rapid changes in the organization and financing of health care as well as the changes themselves.

The breadth of this book is ambitious, as is necessary for any text in a course that attempts to analyze the complex structures, processes, and relationships of health care in the United States. The authors have crafted an exceptionally readable text by balancing and integrating the diverse subject matter and presenting it in appropriate depth for an introductory course on this topic. Because a "population" rather than an "individual" health care perspective is clearly the wave of the future, the authors' public health orientation makes this text particularly valuable. Their combined experience in the public health and medical care fields has allowed them to interpret health care developments with objectivity. It is an important feature in an introductory text that strives toward analysis, not advocacy, thereby allowing the formulation of one's own position.

Michel A. Ibrahim, MD, PhD
Dean and Professor of Epidemiology Emeritus
School of Public Health
University of North Carolina at Chapel Hill
Adjunct Professor of Epidemiology
Bloomberg School of Public Health / Johns Hopkins University

Acknowledgments

Because one of us has an academic base as a professor of social and preventive medicine and a former academic dean, and the other has served in a variety of executive positions in voluntary agencies, hospitals, a managed care organization, and now a professional training center, we bring different experiences to our interpretations of health care developments. When we teach together, as we often do, our students are at first amused, and then intrigued by the differences between academic and applied perspectives. They learn, by our willingness to debate the merits of different interpretations of the same information, to appreciate that health care is fraught with variance in understandings, dissonance in values, and contradictions in underlying assumptions.

We are grateful, therefore, to the students in the Schools of Medicine, Management, Law, and Millard Fillmore College who contributed to our knowledge and experience by presenting challenging viewpoints, engaging us in spirited discussions, and providing thoughtful course evaluations. Over the years, their enthusiasm for the subject stimulated us to enrich our coursework constantly in an effort to meet and exceed their expectations.

We acknowledge with our sincerest gratitude Susan V. McLeer, MD, Professor and Chair of the Department of Psychiatry, Drexel University College of Medicine, Philadelphia, Pennsylvania, who contributed the chapter on mental health services. A consummate clinician and academician, Dr. McLeer provided an exceptionally clear and insightful overview of the complex issues and service responses that characterize the field of mental health.

We also express our appreciation to those who helped turn teachers into authors by providing the necessary editing, literature searches, word processing, and other support services: Karen Buchinger, whose nursing, library, and information science expertise produced a most thorough and efficient publications search; Ebrahim Randeree, an outstanding doctoral student who helped us research current information for this edition's updates; Alice Stein, our loyal and diligent editor whose uncommon good sense and literary competence is reflected in the readability of this manuscript; and Sharon Palisano, our word processing specialist, who produced the many drafts of this manuscript with astute attention to the publisher's requirements and unparalleled attention to every detail.

We remain grateful to Michel Ibrahim, MD, Professor and former Dean of the School of Public Health of the University of North Carolina at Chapel

Hill, who initiated our working relationship with the publisher. We also recognize the important contributions of the publisher's staff who encouraged the effort, helped to shape the result, and motivated us to improve the book's utility for its users. To each of you, we offer our profound thanks.

Introduction

I n spite of its long history and common usage, the evolving U.S. health care system has been a growing puzzle to many Americans. The prevention, diagnosis, and treatment of disease and injury, and the rehabilitation and maintenance of individuals challenged by the residual effects of those conditions have generated an enormously complex, trillion-dollar industry. It includes thousands of independent medical practices and partnerships; managed care and provider organizations; public and nonprofit institutions such as hospitals, nursing homes, and other specialized care facilities; and major private corporations. In dollar volume, the U.S. health care industry is second only to the manufacturing sector. For personal consumption, Americans spend more only on food and housing than they do on medical care. Further, health care is by far the largest service industry in the country. In fact, the U.S. health care system is the world's eighth largest economy, second to that of France, and larger than the total economy of Italy.[1]

More intimidating than its size, however, is its complexity. Not only is health care labor-intensive at all levels, but also the types and functions of its numerous personnel change periodically to adjust to new technology, knowledge, and ways of delivering health care services.

As is frequently associated with progress, medical advances often create new problems while solving old ones. The explosion of medical knowledge that produced narrowly defined medical specialties has compounded a long-standing shortcoming of American medical care. The impressive capability to deliver sophisticated high-tech health care requires the support of an incredibly complex infrastructure that allows too many opportunities for patients to fall through the cracks between its finely tuned and narrowly defined services and specialists. In addition, our system has proven inept in securing even a modicum of universal coverage. Currently, over 44 million Americans are uninsured.

The increasing size, complexity, and technological sophistication of health care in the United States have further complicated its long-standing problems of limited consumer access, inconsistent quality of services, and uncontrolled costs. In addition, the development of the health care system has done little to address the unnecessary and wasteful duplication of certain services in some areas and the absence of essential services in others.

These problems have worried this country's political and medical leaders for decades and have motivated legislative proposals aimed at reform by seven successive U.S. presidents. One of the most highly publicized proposals was the National Health Security Act of 1993, developed by President Clinton.

In 1994 the American public witnessed an unusually candid and sometimes acrimonious congressional debate over President Clinton's proposal to significantly alter how health care would be financed and delivered in the United States. Vested interests advocating change and those defending the status quo both lobbied extensively to influence public and political opinion. In the end, the stakeholders in the traditional system convinced a public—apprehensive about more governmental control over personal health services—that the Clinton plan was too much, too liberal, and too costly, and it was therefore defeated. More recently, the Balanced Budget Act of 1997 contained the most sweeping Medicare reforms to date, as well as other reforms affecting many other health care industry sectors. In a "universal coverage" initiative, it included funding for a program to provide health insurance for the nation's 11 million uninsured children. Besieged by health care industry opposition to Medicare reimbursement reductions and new regulations, the act has already been materially amended by the Balanced Budget Refinement Act of 1999, and Congress has other amendments under review.

Nevertheless, health care is undergoing a revolution. As evidenced by the failure of the National Health Security Act and the ongoing responses to the Balanced Budget Act of 1997, Congress is failing to enact health care reform legislation that is equal in strength to the market forces already altering the health care environment. Health care reform is occurring as a market-driven, not a policy-driven, phenomenon.

In a world of accelerating consolidation to achieve ever higher standards of effectiveness, the medical care system is a promising candidate for change. The result of this new environment has been a surge of health care facility and service mergers and acquisitions, new programs, new names, and new roles that signal the onset of fundamental changes throughout the system. Hospitals are competing for patients. Clinics have sprung up in shopping plazas. Doctors have joined in networks, and the public has been inundated with a confusing alphabet soup of PPOs, HMOs, and DRGs.

The practice of medicine, long a cottage industry that valued individual entrepreneurship and physician control, has undergone dramatic change. Physicians have been most affected by recent health care system changes. They, who cherished the individual autonomy and privileged position afforded health care professionals, now face the vexing oversight of case and utilization management, practice guidelines, critical pathways, and clinical report cards. Unfortunately, the loss of professional control has also been accompanied by the loss of control over the allocation of health care dollars. The result has been a substantial decrease in annual physician incomes. Managed care organizations have controlled health costs by arbitrarily refusing reimbursement for certain medical procedures, reducing payments for others, and withholding a percentage of earned payments to physicians pending annual reviews of their practice performance.

Those physicians, hospitals, and other providers who resist the dramatic system alterations taking place are likely to be victims of their own unwillingness to adjust to the new reality. It is likely, therefore, that if legislated health care policy reform ever takes place, it will have little effect on the trends already in progress. Whatever the public, and even many health care professionals, thought they knew about health care and its delivery system is no longer true. Much has already changed, and more changes are on the way.

That is why this book has been written. It is intended to serve as a text for introductory courses on the organization of health care for students in schools of public health, medicine, nursing, dentistry, and pharmacy and in schools and colleges that prepare physical therapists, occupational therapists, respiratory therapists, medical technologists, health administrators, and a host of other allied health professionals. It provides an introduction to the U.S. health care system and an overview of the professional, political, social, and economic forces that have shaped it and will continue to do so.

To facilitate its use as a teaching text, this book has been organized in a succession of chapters that both stand alone as balanced discussions of discrete subjects and, when read in sequence, provide incremental additions of information to complete the reader's understanding of the entire health care system. Although decisions about what subjects and material were essential to the book's content were relatively easy, decisions about the topics and content to be left out were very difficult. The encyclopedic nature of the subject and the finite length of the final manuscript were in constant conflict.

Thus, the authors acknowledge in advance that nurses, dentists, pharmacists, physical and occupational therapists, and others may be disappointed that the text contains so little of the history and the political and professional struggles that characterize the evolution of their important professions. Given the centrality of those historical developments in students' educational preparation, it was assumed that appropriate attention to those subjects, using books written specifically for that purpose, would be included in courses in those professional curricula. To be consistent with that assumption, the authors tried to include only those elements in the history of public health, medicine, and hospitals that had a significant impact on how health care was delivered.

The authors had to make a similar set of difficult decisions regarding the depth of information to include about specific subjects in the text. Topics such as epidemiology, history of medicine, program planning and evaluation, quality of care, and the like each have their own libraries of in-depth texts and, in many schools, dedicated courses. Thus, it seemed appropriate in a text for an introductory course to provide only enough descriptive and interpretive detail about each topic to put it in the context of the overall subject of the book.

This book has been written from a public health or population perspective and reflects the viewpoint of its authors. Both authors have public health and preventive medicine backgrounds and long histories of research into various aspects of the health care system, have planned and evaluated innovative projects for improving the quality and accessibility of care in both the public and voluntary sectors, and have served in key executive positions in the health field.

The authors have used much of the material contained in *Health Care USA: Understanding Its Organization and Delivery* to provide students, consumers, and neophyte professionals with an understanding of the unique interplay of the technology, work force, research findings, financing, regulation, and personal and professional behaviors, values, and assumptions that determine what, how, why, where, and at what cost health care is delivered in the United States.

The first edition of this book was completed in 1996, and since then the magnitude of the changes taking place in health care, and the rapidity with which they have occurred, have been unprecedented. Although the forces reshaping the system are basically economic in nature, they impinge on every facet of health care from the education of the providers to the terminal care of the patients. Revered institutions, once thought immutable, have merged with others, completely altered their service missions, or just disappeared from the health care scene. Within incredibly brief periods of time, new organizations and corporations have become important influences in America's health care systems. Bending reluctantly to the cost-driven principles of expanding managed care, the practice of medicine has become significantly different from what it was only a few years ago. In this fourth edition, we have included important additions and updates to provide a current perspective on the health care industry's continuously evolving trends.

The authors hope that as this book's readers plan and expand their educational horizons and, later, their professional experiences, they will have the advantage of a more comprehensive understanding of the complex system in which they practice.

■ Note

1. U.S. Bureau of the Census, *Statistical Abstract of the United States, 1995*, 115th ed. (Washington, DC: United States Bureau of the Census, 1995).

Chapter 1

Overview of Health Care: A Population Perspective

This chapter provides a general overview of the U.S. health care industry, its policy makers, its values and priorities, and its various responses to health care diseases and problems. A template for understanding the natural histories of diseases and the levels of medical intervention is illustrated. Major influences in the continuing growth and change of the United States's health services system are briefly described in preparation for more extensive discussion in subsequent chapters. The conflicts of interest and ethical dilemmas resulting from medicine's technological advances and the advent of managed care are also noted.

In recent years, health care, especially its medical or curative aspect, has captured the interest of the public, political leaders, and an attentive media as never before. News of medical miracles, breakthroughs, disasters, deficiencies, and rising costs attracts a consistently high readership. For many, the fortunes and foibles of health care take on deeply serious meanings. There is a widespread sense of urgency among employers, insurers, consumer groups, and other policy makers about the seemingly unresolvable need to correct problems of access and cost without compromising quality of care. The last decade's major economic and social changes in the United States have altered the way Americans think about the role health care plays in their lives and about the strengths and deficiencies of the complex labyrinth of health care providers, facilities, programs, and services.

There is growing recognition that health care is a big business that consumes almost 13 percent of the United States's gross domestic product and now exceeds $1.3 trillion in costs. The corporatization of the health care industry is creating major opportunities for megamergers and for investors. Many health care providers and institutions have become commercial entrepreneurs beyond all expectations and to the concern of many. The commercialization of health care has created increasing conflicts between providers on one side and policy makers, managed care organizations, and other third-party payers on the other.

Physicians are seeking public support for their concern that managed care may constrain expenditures without adequate regard for the quality of care. Policy makers and care managers assert that physicians expressing concerns over quality is a way to resist scrutiny and accountability without regard for economic efficiency. Against this contentious background, health care policy debates will likely continue to be unproductive. Recriminations from both sides block attempts at constructive dialogue.

■ Problems of Health Care

Although there are philosophical and political differences that fuel the debates about health care policies and reforms, there is general agreement that the health care system in the United States, as in most other countries, is fraught with problems and dilemmas. In spite of its impressive accomplishments, the U.S. health care system exhibits inexplicable contradictions in objectives; unwarranted variations in performance, effectiveness, and efficiency; and long-standing difficulties in its relationships with the public and with governments.

The strategies for addressing the problems of cost, access, and quality over the last 30 years reflect the periodic changes in political philosophies. The government-sponsored programs of the 1960s were designed to improve access for older adults and low-income populations without regard for the inflationary effects on costs. These programs were followed by regulatory attempts to address first the availability and price of health services, then the organization and distribution of health care, and then its quality. In the 1990s, the ineffective patchwork of government-sponsored health system reforms was superseded by the emergence of market-oriented changes, competition, and privately organized managed care organizations.

The failure of government-initiated reforms created a vacuum that was filled quickly by the private sector. There is a difference, however, between recent governmental goals for health care reform and those of the market. Although the proposed government programs try to maintain some balance among costs, quality, and access, the primary goal of the market is to contain costs. As a result, there are serious concerns that market-driven reforms may not result in a health care system that equitably meets the needs of all Americans.

As Eli Ginzberg, writing in the *New England Journal of Medicine*, points out, as long as the dominant interest groups—government, employers, the public, and major provider groups—do not agree on how to change the system to accomplish widely desired reforms, the American people will continue temporizing. They are "unwilling to risk the strengths of our existing health care system in a radical effort to remedy admittedly serious deficiencies."[1]

■ Understanding Health Care

Health care policy usually reflects public opinion. Finding acceptable solutions to the perplexing problems of health care will depend on public understanding and acceptance of both the existing circumstances and the benefits and risks of proposed remedies. Many of the communication problems regarding health policy stem from the public's inadequate understanding of health care and its delivery system.

Early practitioners purposely fostered the mystique surrounding medical care as a means to set themselves apart from the patients they served. Endowing health care with a certain amount of mystery encouraged patients to maintain blind faith in the capability of their physicians, even when the state of the science did not justify it. When advances in the understanding of the causes, processes, and cures of specific diseases revealed that previous therapies and methods of patient management were based on erroneous premises, physicians were not held responsible. Although the world's most advanced and proficient health care system provides a great deal of excellent care, the lack of public knowledge has allowed much care to be delivered that was less than beneficial, and some that was inherently dangerous.

Now, however, the romantic naivete with which health care and its practitioners were viewed has eroded significantly. Since the revealing debates over President Clinton's health care reform proposal of 1993 and the public's increasing exposure to the concepts of managed care, attitudes toward health care and its practitioners have changed. Whether or not it was ever true, the long-held assumption by both health care providers and patients that their dictator–follower relationship was inviolate no longer exists.

Rather than a confidential contract between the provider and the consumer, the health care relationship now includes a voyeuristic collection of insurers, payers, managers, and quality assurers. Providers no longer have a monopoly on health care decisions and actions. Although the increasing scrutiny and accountability may be onerous and costly to physicians and other providers, it represents the concerns of those paying for health care—governments, insurers, employers, and patients—about the value received for their expenditures. That these questions have been raised reflects the prevailing opinion that those who now chafe under the scrutiny are, at least indirectly, responsible for generating the excesses in the system while at the same time neglecting the problems of limited access to health care for many.

Cynicism about the health care system has grown as increasing information about the problems of costs, quality, and access has become public. People who viewed medical care as a necessity provided by physicians who adhere to scientific standards based on tested and proven therapies have been disillusioned to learn that major knowledge gaps contribute to highly variable use rates for therapeutic and diagnostic procedures that have produced no measurable differences in outcomes. Nevertheless, recent attempts at systemwide reforms repeatedly have demonstrated the enormously complex issues that underlie the health industry's problems and the ineptitude of the system's leadership in addressing them. Writing in a 1996 issue of *Newsweek*, journalist Robert J. Samuelson stated, "We've had enough grand reforms which promise much and deliver little. They will never create our ideal health care system: one that provides all the care people want without huge costs or intrusive controls from either government or business. That system is impossible; too many of its goals collide."[2]

Many health care system employees also have become discouraged. Institutional and agency administrators who say they care about patients but must reflect overriding budget considerations in every action confuse and demoralize health care workers. Most individuals in health care chose a health occupation, not because of the income potential, but because they had a sense of caring and social justice. They made trade-offs and sacrifices for their values only to find that the reality is quite different. Nurses, the largest component of the health care workforce, are especially frustrated with their current role in hospitals. They feel overworked, unable to meet their own standards of quality care, and stressed to the point of leaving the profession. It is hoped that when the health care system again becomes stabilized in a more predictable economic environment, those contradictory messages from higher administrative levels will cease.

■ Why Patients and Providers Behave the Way They Do

In Chapter 3, the evolution of the U.S. system of hospitals makes clear the long tradition of physicians and other health care providers behaving in an authoritarian manner towards patients. Hospitalized patients, removed from their usual places in society, were expected to be compliant and grateful to be in the hands of someone far more learned than themselves. The fact that submissive patient behavior has characterized even otherwise domineering individuals when they become ill has interested a great many researchers. Because the health beliefs and actions of patients have much to do with their timely and appropriate use of the health care system and their disposition and motivation to cooperate in their treatment, physicians, nurses, and social scientists have studied patient behavior for decades to try to understand the "sick role."

In 1951 Talcott Parson suggested that ill individuals in Western-developed nations demonstrate predictable behaviors, and his theories are still recognized as contributing to the understanding of illness behavior. Frederick Wolinsky stated that Parson's description of the sick role was "an integral part of the sociocultural definition of health and illness." [3] Wolinsky reviewed the four major elements of Parson's assumptions. First, ill people believe they are not solely responsible for their condition and that it is not within their power to get well. Second, by virtue of their diminished function, ill people are exempt from normal personal and social obligations in proportion to the severity of their illness. Third, because illness is undesirable, sick people are expected to take appropriate action and enlist the aid of others in getting well. Fourth, sick people are obliged to obtain competent assistance, usually from a physician, to aid recovery and to comply with the treatment and advice received.

Parson's description of the sick role explains why patients often abdicate personal responsibility for their condition and recovery to a health care system more than willing to accept the authority to decide what is best for them. More recently, however, recognizing the benefits of more proactive roles for patients and the improved outcomes that result, both health care providers and consumers are encouraging significant patient participation in every health care decision.

■ Indexes of Health and Disease

Although health care providers, researchers, analysts, and others in the health services industry have created a detailed and comprehensive taxonomy of diseases and disabilities, definitions of what constitutes "health" are frustratingly ambiguous. The 1958 World Health Organization (WHO) definition, "a state of complete physical, mental and social well-being and not merely the absence of disease," is hardly measurable and rarely achievable—certainly not for any extended length of time. [4] Thus, much of "health" is so subjective that for all practical purposes, it is determined clinically by the converse—whether individual physical, physiological, and laboratory test values fall within or outside of "normal" parameters.

The body of statistical data about health and disease has grown enormously since the late 1960s, when the government began analyzing information obtained from Medicare and Medicaid claims, and computerized hospital and insurance data allowed the retrieval and exploration of huge files of clinical information. In addition, there have been continuing improvements in the collection, analysis, and reporting of vital statistics and communicable and malignant diseases by state and federal governments.

Data collected over time and international comparisons reveal common trends among developed countries. Birth rates have fallen, and life expectancies have lengthened so that older people make up an increasing proportion of total populations. The percentage of individuals who are disabled or dependent has grown as the health care professions have improved their capacity to rescue moribund individuals.

Infant mortality and maternal mortality, the international indicators of social and health care improvement, have continued to decline in the United States, but have not reached the more commendable levels of countries with more demographically homogeneous populations. In the United States the differences in infant mortality rates between inner city neighborhoods and suburban communities may be greater than those between developed and undeveloped countries. The continuing inability of the health care system to address those discrepancies effectively reflects the system's ambiguous priorities.

■ Natural Histories of Disease and the Levels of Prevention

For many years, epidemiologists and health services planners have used a matrix for placing everything known about a particular disease or condition in the sequence of its origin and progression when untreated; this schema is called the natural history of disease. Many diseases, especially chronic diseases that may last for decades, have an irregular evolution and extend through a sequence of stages. When the causes and stages of a particular disease or condition are defined in its natural history, they can be matched against the health care interventions intended to prevent the condition's occurrence or to arrest its progress after its onset. Because these health care interventions are designed to prevent the condition from advancing to the next, and usually more serious, level in its natural history, the interventions are classified as the "levels of prevention." Figures 1–1 through 1–3 illustrate the concept of the natural history of disease and levels of prevention.

The first level of prevention is the period during which the individual is "at risk" to the disease, but is not yet affected. Called the "prepathogenesis period," it identifies those behavioral, genetic, environmental, and other factors that increase the individual's likelihood of contracting the condition. Some risk factors, such as smoking, may be altered, whereas others, such as genetic factors, may not.

When such risk factors combine to produce a disease, the disease usually is not manifest until certain pathological changes occur. This stage is a period of clinically undetectable, presymptomatic disease. Medical science is working hard to improve its ability to diagnose disease earlier in this stage. Because many conditions evolve in irregular and subtle processes, it is often difficult to determine the point at which an individual may be designated "diseased" or "not diseased." Thus, each natural history has a "clinical horizon," defined as the point at which medical science becomes able to detect the presence of a particular condition. Because the pathological changes may become fixed and irreversible at each step in the disease progress, preventing

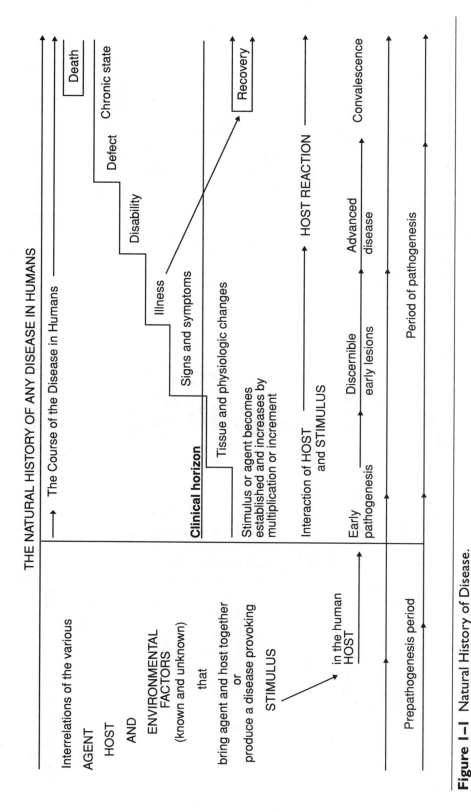

Figure 1–1 Natural History of Disease.

Source: Reprinted with permission from H.R. Leavell and E.G. Clark, *Preventative Medicine for the Doctor in His Community: An Epidemiologic Approach,* 3rd edition, p. 20, © 1965, the McGraw Hill Companies, Inc.

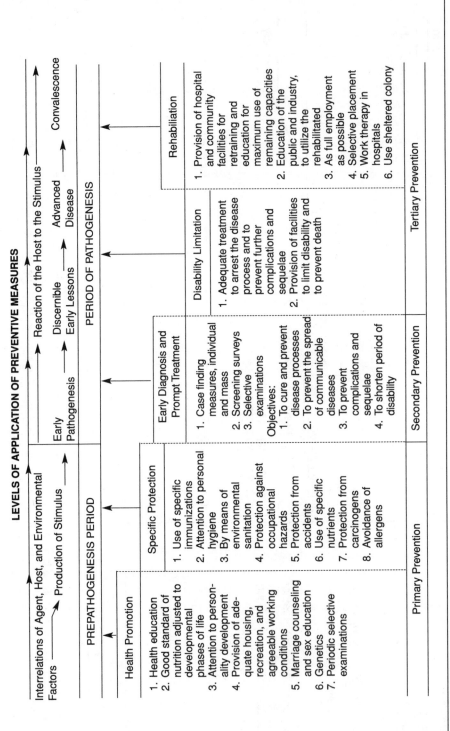

Figure I–2 Levels of Prevention.

Source: Reprinted with permission from H.R. Leavell and E.G. Clark, *Preventative Medicine for the Doctor in His Community: An Epidemiologic Approach,* 3rd edition, p. 21, © 1965, the McGraw Hill Companies, Inc.

each succeeding step of the disease is therapeutically important. This concept emphasizes the preventive aspect of clinical interventions.

Primary prevention, or the prevention of disease occurrence, refers to measures designed to promote health (e.g., health education to encourage good nutrition, exercise, and genetic counseling) and specific protections (e.g., immunization and the use of seat belts).

Secondary prevention involves early detection and prompt treatment to achieve an early cure, if possible, or to slow progression, prevent complications, and limit disability. Most of preventive health care currently is focused on this area.

Tertiary prevention consists of rehabilitation and maximizing remaining functional capacity when disease has occurred and left residual damage. This stage represents the most costly, labor-intensive aspect of medical care and depends heavily on effective teamwork by representatives of a number of health care disciplines.

Figure 1–4 illustrates the natural history and levels of prevention for the aging process. Although aging is not a disease, it is a condition often accompanied by medical, mental, and functional problems that should be addressed by a range of health care services at each level of prevention.

The natural history of diseases and the levels of prevention are presented to illustrate two very important aspects of the U.S. health care system. First, it quickly becomes apparent in studying the natural history and levels of prevention for almost any of the common causes of disease and disability that the focus of health care historically has been directed at the curative and rehabilitative side of the disease continuum. Serious attention has been paid to refocusing the system on the health promotion/disease prevention side of those disease schemas only after the costs of diagnostic and remedial care became an unacceptable burden, and the lack of adequate insurance coverage for over 40 million Americans became a public and political embarrassment.

The second important aspect of the natural history concept is its value in planning community services. The illustration on aging is a good example. That natural history and service levels blueprint provides the planning framework for a multidisciplinary health services planning group to identify and match the community's existing services with those proposed in the idealized levels of prevention. Within this framework, the group begins to plan and initiate the services necessary to fill the gaps.

■ **Major Stakeholders in the U.S. Health Care Industry**

It is important to come to an understanding of the health care industry and to recognize the number and variety of its stakeholders. The

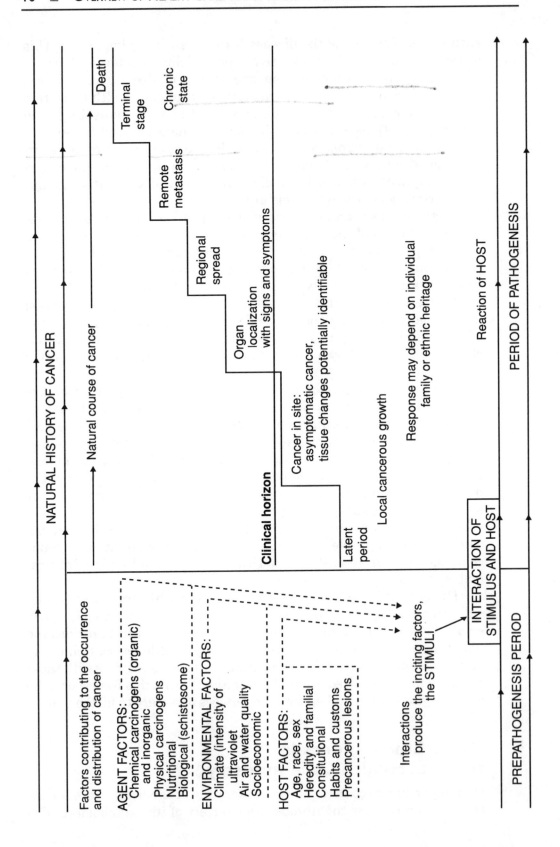

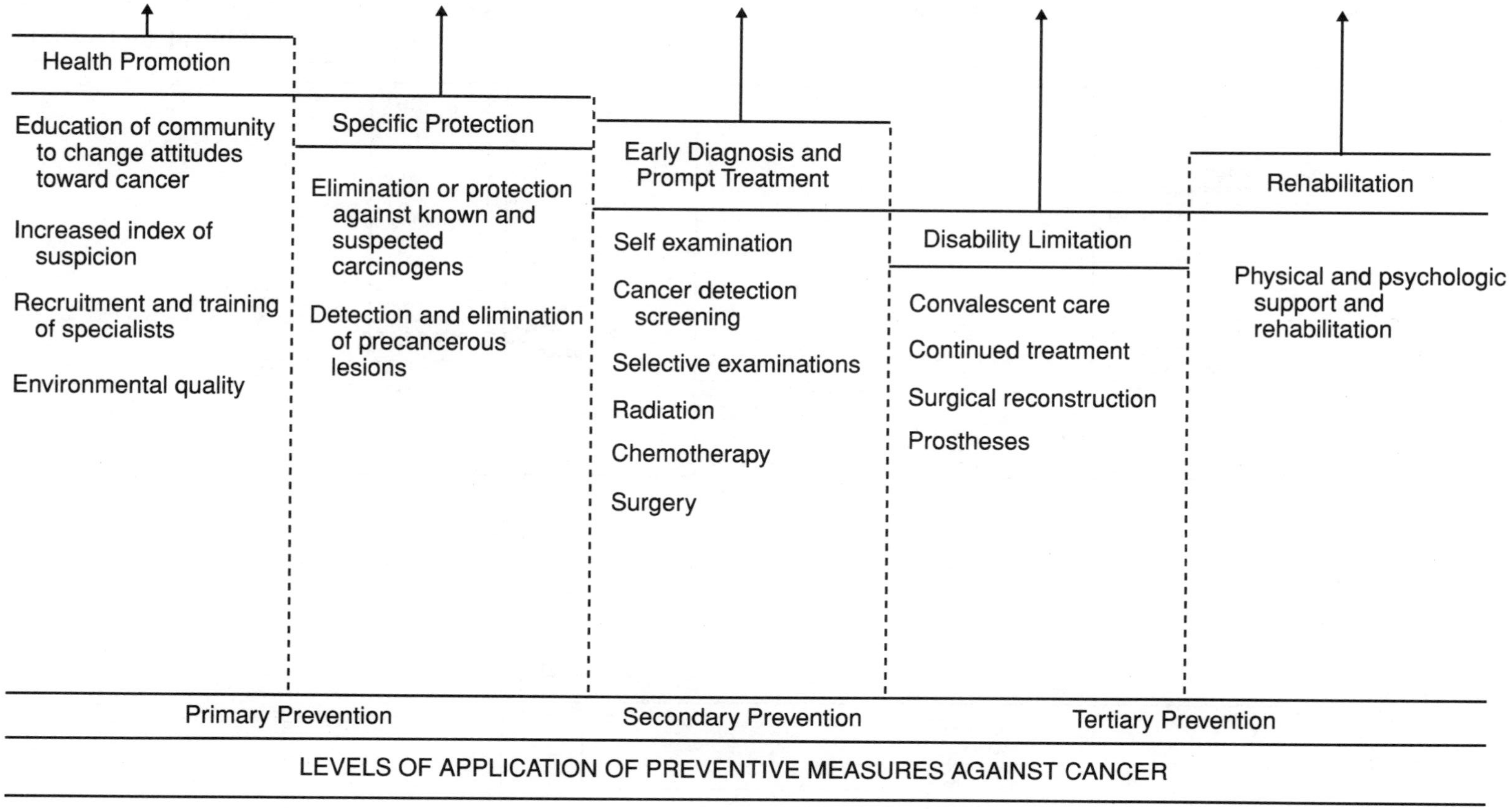

Figure 1–3 Natural History and Levels of Prevention of Cancer.

Source: Reprinted with permission from H.R. Leavell and E.G. Clark, *Preventative Medicine for the Doctor in His Community: An Epidemiologic Approach,* 3rd edition, p. 272–273, © 1965, the McGraw Hill Companies, Inc.

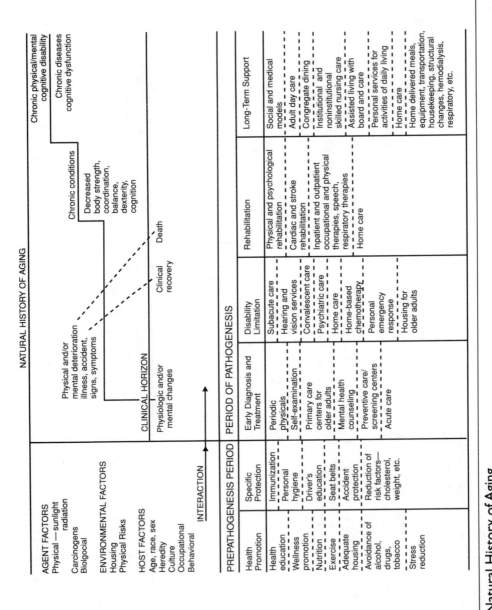

Figure 1-4 Natural History of Aging.

Source: Reprinted with permission from H.R. Leavell and E.G. Clark, *Preventative Medicine for the Doctor in His Community: An Epidemiologic Approach,* 3rd edition, p. 272–273, © 1965, the McGraw Hill Companies, Inc.

sometimes shared and often conflicting concerns, interests, and influences of these constituent groups cause them to periodically shift alliances to oppose or champion specific reform proposals.

The Public

First and foremost among health care stakeholders are the patients who consume the services. Although all are concerned with the issues of cost and quality, those who are uninsured or underinsured have an overriding uncertainty about access. It would be unrealistic to assume that the U.S. public will some day wish to treat health care like other inherent rights, such as education or police protection, but there is general agreement that some basic array of health care services should be available to all U.S. citizens. If and when the problem of universal access will be addressed politically in that or any other manner is open to conjecture. In the meantime, however, consumer organizations, such as the American Association of Retired Persons, and disease-specific groups, such as the American Cancer Society, the American Heart Association, and labor organizations, are politically active on behalf of various consumer constituencies.

Employers

Employers constitute an increasingly influential group of stakeholders in health care because they not only are paying for a high proportion of the costs, but also are taking more proactive roles in determining what those costs should be. Large private employers, coalitions of smaller private employers, and public employers now wield significant authority in managed care and other insurance plan negotiations. In addition, employer organizations representing small and large businesses wield considerable political power in the halls of Congress.

Providers

Health care professionals are the core of the industry and have the most to do with the actual process and outcomes of the service provided. Physicians, dentists, nurses, nurse practitioners, physician assistants, pharmacists, podiatrists, chiropractors, and a large array of allied health providers working as individuals or in group practices and staffing health care institutions are responsible for the quality and, to a large extent, the cost of the health care system.

Hospitals and Other Health Care Facilities

Much of the provider activity is shaped by the availability and nature of the health care institutions in which providers work. Hospitals of different types—general, specialty, teaching, rural, profit or not-for-profit, independent or multifacility systems—are central to the existing health care system. However, they are becoming but one component of more complex integrated delivery system networks that also include nursing homes and other levels of care, medical practices, and managed care organizations.

Governments

Since the advent of Medicare and Medicaid, federal and state governments, already major stakeholders in health care, have become the dominant authorities over the system. Governments serve not only as payers, but also as regulators and providers through public hospitals, state and local health departments, Veterans Affairs medical centers, and other facilities. In addition, of course, governments are the taxing authorities that generate the funds to support the system.

Alternative Therapies

Unconventional health therapies—those not usually taught in established medical and other health professional schools—contribute significantly to the amount, frequency, and cost of health care. In spite of the scientific logic and documented effectiveness of traditional, academically based health care, it is estimated that one in three adults uses alternative forms of health interventions each year and that more office visits are made to alternative care providers than to primary care physicians.

It is estimated that over $10 billion per year is spent on such alternative forms of health care as rolfing, yoga, spiritual healing, relaxation techniques, herbal remedies, energy healing, megavitamin therapy, the commonly recognized chiropractic, and a host of exotic mind–body healing techniques.[5]

That the public is willing to spend so much time and money on unconventional therapies suggests a substantial level of dissatisfaction with traditional scientific medicine. The popularity of alternative forms of therapy also indicates that its recipients confirm the effectiveness of the treatments by referring others to their practitioners. Whether or not these methods can be rationalized scientifically, if people feel better with their use and they do not deter individuals with treatable diseases from seeking conventional therapy, they serve a beneficial purpose. Insurance companies and managed care organizations are now considering alternative therapies as less expensive and probably equally effective options for keeping their beneficiaries feeling well.

In January 1995, the *Wall Street Journal* reported that several of the largest individual health insurance companies, including Mutual of Omaha and Prudential Insurance Company of America, would begin paying for selected unconventional therapies for heart disease and other chronic conditions.[6] In addition, the National Institutes of Health (NIH) has established an Office of Alternative Medicine to fund studies of the efficacy of such therapies. Thus, as a somewhat paradoxical development, some of the most ancient concepts of alternative health care are gaining broader recognition and acceptance in an era of the most innovative and advanced high-technology medicine.

More for monetary than therapeutic reasons, a number of hospitals are now offering their patients some form of alternative medicine. According to an American Hospital Association survey, over 15 percent of U.S. hospitals had opened alternative or complimentary medicine centers by the year 2000. With a market estimated to be over $27 billion and patients willing to pay cash for alternative medicine treatments, hospitals are willing to rationalize the provision of several "unproven" services.[7]

Managed Care Organizations and Other Insurers

The insurance industry has long been a major stakeholder in the health care industry and probably had more to do with defeating the Clinton health care reform plan than any other group. Although the traditional, indemnity-type plans such as Blue Cross and Blue Shield are being replaced rapidly by managed care plans, they still are very much in evidence. Managed care plans may be owned by insurance companies just as the indemnity plans are, or they may be owned by hospitals, physicians, or consumer cooperatives. Managed care organizations and the economic pressures they can apply through the negotiation of capitated fees have produced much of the change that has occurred in the regional systems of health care during the last few years.

Long-Term Care

The aging of the U.S. population will be a formidable challenge to the country's systems of acute and long-term care. Nursing homes, home care services, other adult care facilities, and rehabilitation facilities will become increasingly important components of the nation's health care system as they grow in number, size, and complexity. The creation of seamless systems of care that permit patients to move back and forth among ambulatory care offices, acute care hospitals, subacute care services, home care, and nursing homes within a single, integrated network of facilities and services will provide a continuum of services required for the more complex care of aging patients.

Mental Health

The mental health component of health care is often neglected in the debates on system reforms. Yet, psychiatric hospitals, community mental health facilities, and community-based ambulatory services serve large segments of the population and are critically important to the effectiveness of the health care system. Mental health and physical health are *contiguous* conditions and should, but do not, generate the same concern and unprejudiced funding.

Voluntary Facilities and Agencies

Voluntary not-for-profit facilities and agencies provide significant amounts of health counseling, care, and follow-up and research support, and should be considered major stakeholders in the health care system. It is interesting that, although the voluntary sector traditionally has not received the recognition it deserves for its contribution to the nation's health care, it is now suggested as the safety net to replace the services to be eliminated in cost-cutting proposals.

Health Professions Education and Training Institutions

Schools of public health, medicine, nursing, dentistry, pharmacy, optometry, allied health, and other health care professions have a significant impact on the nature, quality, and costs of health care. As they prepare generation after generation of competent health care providers, these schools also inculcate the values, attitudes, and ethics that will govern the practices and behaviors of those providers as they function in the health care system. The influences of these schools, particularly as they contribute to the leadership of academic health care centers, will be addressed in Chapter 5.

Professional Associations

National, state, and regional organizations representing health care professionals or institutions have considerable influence over legislative proposals, regulation, quality issues, and other political matters. The lobbying effectiveness of the American Medical Association (AMA), for example, is legendary. The national influence of the American Hospital Association and the regional power of its state and local affiliates are also impressive. Other organizations of health care professionals, such as the American Public Health Association, the Group Health Association of America, the American Nurses Association, and the American Dental Association, play significant roles in health policy decisions.

Other Health Industry Organizations

The size and complexity of the health care industry encourage the involvement of a great number of commercial entities. Several, such as the insurance and pharmaceutical enterprises, are major industries themselves and have significant organizational influence. The medical supplies and equipment business and the various consulting and information and management system suppliers are also important players.

Research Communities

It is difficult to separate much of health care research from the educational institutions that provide for its implementation. Nevertheless, the national research enterprise must be included in any enumeration of stakeholders in the health care industry. Government entities, such as NIH and the Agency for Healthcare Research and Quality, and not-for-profit foundations, such as the Robert Wood Johnson Foundation and the Pew Charitable Trusts, exert tremendous influence over health care research and practice by encouraging investigations that serve policy decision making and defining the kinds of research that will be supported.

■ Development of Managed Care

Managed care refers to arrangements that link health care financing and service delivery and allows payers to exercise significant economic control over how and what services are delivered. Common features in managed care arrangements are:

- *Provider panels.* Specific physicians and other providers are selected to care for plan members.
- *Limited choice.* Members must use the providers affiliated with the plan or pay an additional amount.
- *Gatekeeping.* Members must obtain a referral from a case manager for specialty or inpatient services.
- *Risk sharing.* Providers bear some of the health plan's financial risk through capitation and withholds.
- *Quality management and utilization review.* The plan monitors provider practice patterns and medical outcomes to identify deviations from quality and efficiency standards.

Health plans with these features are called managed care organizations (MCOs). The most common MCOs are health maintenance organizations (HMOs) and preferred provider organizations (PPOs). MCOs may directly employ medical staff, as in a staff model, or contract with independent providers or individual practice associations (IPAs), or any combination of arrangements in between. Whatever the arrangement, however, in managed care, the provider is always economically accountable to the payer.

Prepaid health plans, in which consumers pay a set fee in advance to cover a specified array of services in a particular time period, are not new. They were developed more than 150 years ago for miners and other isolated workers. Farmers also arranged for prepaid medical care through their rural health cooperatives. Among the early prepaid group practice plans were Group Health of Puget Sound, the Kaiser-Permanente Medical Care Program, and the Health Insurance Plan of New York. Nevertheless, the growth of prepaid plans was constrained by organized medicine, which opposed any reimbursement mechanism other than fee for service, until 1973, when the Nixon administration's Health Maintenance Organization Act was passed. The act encouraged and funded the development of HMOs as a strategy to contain the rising costs of health care. Using the prepayment concept, managed care expanded rapidly during the 1980s as increasing numbers of employers included HMOs among their employee health benefits options.

Enrollment of Medicaid and Medicare recipients in managed care organizations was originally considered a viable strategy for containing costs and improving the access and comprehensiveness of care for the medically disadvantaged and for older Americans. The Balanced Budget Act of 1997 created Medicare + Choice, which gave beneficiaries the option of switching from the original fee-for-service Medicare to membership in a health maintenance organization. The HMO option was attractive to older citizens because it included extra benefits such as prescription drug coverage. After a brief experience with Medicare, however, the large managed care organizations withdrew from the program, citing inadequate government compensation for serving Medicare beneficiaries.

State-authorized Medicaid programs also are unlikely to be successful. Medicaid populations have not been welcomed in many elements of the health care system. Large numbers of Medicaid recipients have used the system episodically and frequently through hospital emergency departments, often because they could see no viable alternative.

Managed care has been confusing and controversial to all segments of the population. The array of new organizations and the state and regional variations in how managed care organizations operate only add to the confusion. In addition, managed care models range from full capitation, in which all providers are paid a negotiated amount per patient regardless of the amount of service, to partial capitation, in which medical specialists still retain the fee-for-service reimbursement arrangement, to total fee-for-service arrangements with a penalty to providers who exceed expense targets. When reimbursement variations are combined with different provider arrangements, it is little wonder that many citizens have difficulty understanding their options. For those who enroll in managed care plans and experience limited provider access and utilization control for the first time, patient education and expeditious grievance procedures become particularly important.

■ Rural Health Networks

Rural health systems are often incomplete, with shortages of various services and duplications of others. Federal and state programs have addressed this situation by promoting the development of rural health networks. Although relatively new, most of these networks strive to provide local access to primary, acute, and emergency care and to provide efficient links to more distant regional specialists and tertiary care services. Ideally, rural health networks should assemble and coordinate a comprehensive array of services that include dental, mental health, long-term care, and other health and human services. Realistically, many of those services are lacking, and rural communities sometimes offer various incentives to attract or gain access to specific providers. When successful, however, rural health networks are a significant advantage to their communities. With sufficient structure and administrative capability, the networks can control the development of their service systems and negotiate effectively with managed care organizations.

With costs increasing and populations declining in many rural communities, it has been difficult for rural hospitals to continue their acute inpatient care services; yet, these hospitals are often critically important to their communities. Because a hospital is usually one of a few major employers in rural communities, its closure has economic and health care consequences. Communities lacking alternative sources of health care within reasonable travel distance not only lose payroll and related business, but also lose physicians, nurses, and other health personnel and suffer higher morbidity and mortality rates among those most vulnerable, such as infants and older adults.[8]

Some rural hospitals have remained viable by participating in some form of multi-institutional arrangement that permits them to benefit from the personnel, services, purchasing power, and financial stability of larger facilities. Many rural hospitals, however, have found it necessary to shift from inpatient to outpatient or ambulatory care. The development of ambulatory care services by rural and urban hospitals is a strong health care system trend, as is the increased use of less expensive ancillary personnel. In many rural communities, the survival of a hospital depends on how quickly and effectively it can replace its inpatient services with a productive constellation of ambulatory care, and sometimes long-term care, services.

These rural hospital initiatives have been supported by federal legislation since 1991. This legislation provided funding to promote the essential access community hospital (EACH) and the rural primary care hospital (RPCH). Both are limited service hospital models developed as alternatives for hospitals too small and geographically isolated to be full-service acute care facilities. Regulations regarding staffing and other service requirements are relaxed in keeping with the rural settings[9] and include allowing physician's assistants, nurse practitioners, and clinical nurse specialists to provide primary or inpatient care without a physician in the facility if medical consultation is available by phone.

The Balanced Budget Act of 1997 included a Rural Hospital Flexibility Program that replaced the EACH/RPCH model with a critical access hospital (CAH) model. Any state with at least one CAH may qualify for the program, which exempts CAHs from strict regulation and allows them the flexibility to meet small, rural community needs by developing criteria for establishing network relationships. While the new program maintains many of the same features and requirements as its predecessor, it adds more flexibility to limited service hospitals by increasing the number of allowed occupied inpatient beds from 6 to 15 and the maximum length of stay before required discharge or transfer from 72 to 96 hours. The new program also allows maintenance of up to 25 total beds, with a swing bed program that allows flexibility in their use. The goal of the CAH program is to enable small rural hospitals to maximize reimbursement and meet community needs with responsiveness and flexibility.

The Balanced Budget Act also serves rural hospitals by providing Medicare reimbursement for "telemedicine" and other video arrangements that link isolated facilities with clinical specialists at large hospitals. Advances in telemedicine technology make it possible for a specialist to be in direct visual and voice contact with a patient and provider at a remote location.

Rural health care organization networks have been formed in response to market changes. They may be formally organized as not-for-profit corporations or informally linked for a defined set of mutually beneficial purposes. Typically, they advocate at local and state levels on rural health care issues, cooperate in joint community outreach activities, and seek opportunities to negotiate with managed care organizations to provide services to enrolled populations.

■ Priorities of Health Care

Certainly, the priorities of health care—the emphasis on dramatic tertiary care, the costly and intensive efforts to fend off the death of terminal patients for a few more days or weeks, the heroic and often futile attempts to save extremely premature infants at huge expense while thousands of women go without the prenatal care that would decrease prematurity—contribute to the obvious mismatch between the rising costs of health care and the failure to improve the measures of health status in the United States. It is difficult to rationalize the goals of a system that invests in the most sophisticated and expensive neonatal services to save premature, high-risk infants while cutting back on the relatively inexpensive and effective prenatal services that would have prevented many of those poor birth outcomes in the first place.

Were health care to be governed by rational policies, the benefits to society of investing in early prenatal care that is unquestionably cost-effective would be compared with trying to salvage extremely low-weight, high-risk infants who often need prolonged care because they are inadequately developed, dysfunctional human beings. Clearly, current priorities favor heroic medicine over the more mundane, far less costly preventive care that results in measurable economic and human benefits.

The Tyranny of Technology

In many respects, the health care system has done and is doing a remarkable job. There have been important advances in medical science that have brought measurable improvements in the length and quality of life. The paradox is, however, that as our technology gets better and more expensive, more people are being deprived of its benefits. Health care providers can be so mesmerized by their own technological ingenuity that things assume greater value than persons. As one example, hospital administrations and medical staffs commonly dedicate their most competent practitioners and most sophisticated technology to the care of terminal patients, while allocating far fewer resources to primary and preventive services for ambulatory clinic patients and other community populations in need of basic medical services. Some community hospitals are recognizing this disparity by conducting outreach and education programs for the medically underserved. As long as reimbursement policies continue to favor illness intervention rather than prevention, however, most institutions will find it difficult to initiate and maintain prevention initiatives and allocate staff to the potentially more productive care of ambulatory clinic populations.

No better example of the pervasive influence of technology exists than that of the continuing advances in diagnostic imaging. Although clinicians still depend on the long-established and relatively simple radiograph technology, they now have at their disposal several new and highly sophisticated computer-assisted imaging techniques that vastly expand their capability to visualize body structures and functions. The total spent on new imaging procedures in the United States is in the billions of dollars and rising annually.

The recurring theme among health services researchers assessing the value of technological advances is a series of generally unanswered questions, such as the following:

- How does the new technology benefit the patient?
- Is it worth the cost?
- Are the new methods better than previous methods, and can they replace them?
- Is treatment planning enhanced?
- Is the outcome from disease better, or is the mortality rate improved?

Although many of the latest advances have gained great popularity and widespread acceptance, the rigorous assessments that address these basic questions have yet to be conducted.

Much of the philosophy underlying the values and priorities of the health care system today can be attributed to the unique culture of U.S. medicine. That philosophy owes much to the aggressive, "can do" spirit of the frontier. The United States's physicians want to do as much as possible. They order more diagnostic tests than their colleagues in other countries, prescribe drugs frequently and at relatively higher doses, and are more likely to resort to surgery whenever possible. Patients and their physicians regard the body as a machine, like a car, which helps explain their enthusiasm for annual checkups and devices like pacemakers and artificial hearts. Diseases are likened to enemies to be conquered. Physicians expect their patients to be aggressive, too. Those who undergo drastic treatments in order to "beat" cancer are held in higher regard than patients who resign themselves to the disease. Some physicians and nurses feel let down when dying patients indicate they do not want to be resuscitated or stipulate restrictions to palliative care only.

The treatment-oriented rather than prevention-oriented health care philosophy was encouraged by an insurance system that, before managed care, rarely paid for any disease prevention other than immunization. It is also understandable in an era of high-technology medicine that there is much more satisfaction and remuneration from saving the lives of the injured and diseased than in preventing those occurrences from happening in the first place.

The capitation concept and HMOs evolved from the expectation that health care could be improved if the financial incentives could be reversed. Rather than allowing providers to profit from treating sickness, managed care concepts reward providers for keeping patients well. However, the treatment orientation so pervades U.S. health care that even the widespread development and acceptance of HMOs has yet to result in a significant and effective national effort to accomplish health maintenance and disease prevention.

■ Social Choices of Health Care

The emphasis on cure also has disinclined the health care professions to address those situations over which they have had little control. Acquired dependence on cigarettes, alcohol, and drugs must be counted among the significant causes of impaired health in our population. The future effects on health and medical care associated with these addictions probably will exceed all expectations. Similarly, the acquired immune deficiency syndrome (AIDS) epidemic is as much a social and behavioral phenomenon as it is a biological one. Yet, outside of the public health disciplines, the considerable influence and prestige of the health care professions have been noticeably absent in steering public opinion and governmental action toward an emphasis on health. Similarly, by comparison with resources expended on treatment after illness occurs, relatively little attention is given to changing high-risk behaviors even when the consequences are virtually certain and nearly always extreme.

■ The Aging Population

The aging of the U.S. population is of major significance among the health care system's emerging issues. It will increasingly affect every aspect of health care. The rate of aging is five times that of overall population growth. By the year 2050, it is estimated that 30 percent of the U.S. population will be over age 65. The number of persons over 85 will double, but the under-35 population will decline by 10 percent.

The growth of the population 65 and older presents a serious challenge to health care providers and policymakers. Those 85 and older are the fastest growing segment of the aging population. Projections by the U.S. Census Bureau suggest that the population 85 and older will grow from about 4 million in 2000 to 19 million in 2050 (see Figure 1–5).[10] The size of this age group is especially demanding of the health care system because these individuals tend to be in poorer health and require more services than the younger elderly.

The sheer magnitude of the "baby boom" that followed World War II, coupled with the recent levels and composition of immigration to the United States, are important factors in the growth and diversity of the aging population. Seventy-five million babies were born in the United States between 1946 and 1964, which is 70 percent more than during the preceding two decades. The baby boom "bulge" in population is illustrated in Figure 1–6.[11]

Although the current population of older adults is predominately White, there will be more racial diversity and more persons of Hispanic origin within the United States's older population in the coming years. There were relatively large population gains among older adults of Asian and Hispanic origin between 1980 and 1990, and those gains will increase substantially in subsequent decades.[12]

The older Hispanic population is projected to more than double from 1990 to 2010 and to be 11 times greater by 2050. The Hispanic older population, which was less than half the size of the Black older

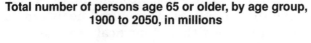

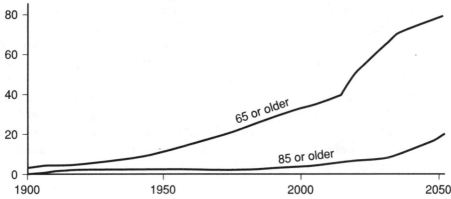

Figure 1–5 Total Number of Persons Age 65 or Older, By Age Group, 1900 to 2050, in Millions.
Note: Data for the years 2000 to 2050 are middle-series projections of the population.
Reference population: These data refer to the resident population.
Source: U.S. Census Bureau, decennial census data and population projections.

population in 1990, is growing much faster than the Black older population. By 2030, older Hispanic adults, projected to be 7.8 million, will outnumber the expected 6.8 million older Black adults.[13] A comparable surge in the number of older adults is projected for Asians and Pacific Islanders (see Figure 1–7).

Although the older adults of the future will stay more active after retiring and be better educated, the burden of incurable chronic diseases of later life will be an enormous challenge to the health care system. As medical advances find more ways to maintain life, the duration of chronic illness and the number of chronically ill patients will increase. Consequently, the need for personal support will increase even more. The intensity of care required by frail older adults has the potential of affecting worker productivity. It is common for women to leave the work force or work part-time in order to care for frail relatives at a time when they would like to build retirement benefits for their own old age.

The increased number of elderly with chronic physical ailments and long-term cognitive disorders raises significant questions about the capability of the U.S. health care system. Much has yet to be learned by practitioners serving the aged. Health care professionals are just beginning to recognize and gradually respond to the need to

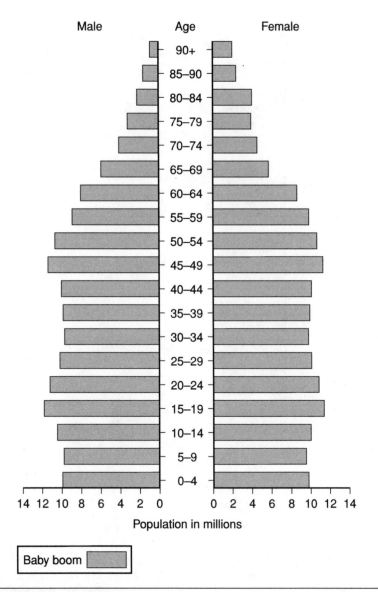

Male   Age   Female

Population in millions

Baby boom

Figure 1–6 Projected Population by Age and Sex.
Source: Reprinted from J.C. Day, U.S. Bureau of the Census, *Population Projections of the United States, by Age, Sex, Race and Hispanic Origin: 1993 to 2050*, Current Population Reports, pp. 25–1104, U.S. Government Printing Office, Washington, DC, 1993 (middle series projections).

focus health care for older adults away from medications or other quick-fix remedies. The system is slowly acknowledging that the traditional medical service model is inappropriate for the care of those with multiple chronic conditions. Chronically ill older patients need a multidisciplinary mix of services that must meet a broad spectrum of physical, medical, and psychosocial needs. This challenge will require

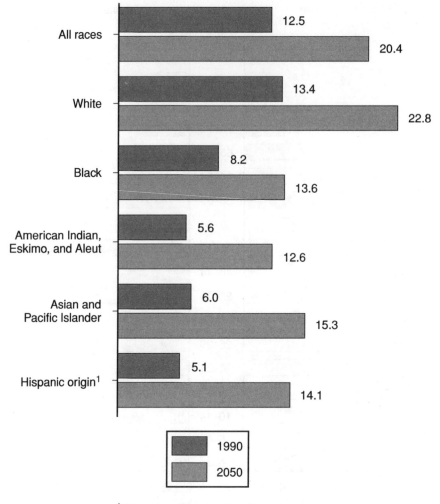

Figure 1–7 Percent Older Adults by Race and Hispanic Origin: 1990 and 2050.
Sources: Reprinted from U.S. Bureau of the Census, 1990 from *U.S. Population Estimates by Age, Sex, Race, and Hispanic Origin: 1980 to 1991*, Current Population Reports, pp. 25–1095, U.S. Government Printing Office, Washington, DC, 1993; 2050 from *Population Projections of the United States, by Age, Sex, Race and Hispanic Origin: 1993 to 2050*, Current Population Reports, pp. 25–1104, U.S. Government Printing Office, Washington, DC, 1993 (middle series projections).

a large increase in the number of health care providers trained in the special philosophies and skills of geriatric health care. The provisions of the Balanced Budget Act of 1997 that institutionalized the program of all-inclusive care for the elderly (PACE) in the revised Medicare reimbursement scheme symbolize growing acceptance of innovative ways to meet the needs of the older Americans.

The growing number of older adults faces serious gaps in financial coverage for long-term care needs. Unlike the broad Medicare program coverage for the acute health care problems of older Americans, the long-term care services that are needed to cope with the chronic disability and functional limitations of the aging are largely unaddressed by either Medicare or private insurance plans. With the exception of the relatively small number of individuals with personal long-term care insurance, the major costs of long-term care services are borne by the individual older adults and their caregivers.

As a last resort, the Medicaid program has become the major public source of financing for nursing home care. Medicaid eligibility, however, requires that persons of means "spend down" their personal resources to meet the means-test criteria. For those disabled older adults who seek care in the community outside of nursing homes, Medicaid offers limited assistance. Thus, the health policy issues associated with the multidisciplinary long-term care needs of older adults mount with every year's increase in the proportion of aged Americans and every upturn in the costs of health care.

■ Access to Health Care

Much attention has been paid to the economic problems of health care, and considerable investments of research funds have been made to address the issues of health care quality. The third major problem, however—that of limited access to health care among the estimated 40 million uninsured or underinsured Americans—continues to confound decision makers. The issue, of course, is more a moral than an economic one. Unlike most other developed nations, the United States has yet to decide on the ethical precepts that should underlie the distribution of health care. Although references frequently are made to those millions of citizens, including children, who are virtually locked out of the system, only a few professionals have had the courage to address this troublesome issue in open debate.

Polar positions have been taken by those who have addressed the question of whether society in general or governments in particular have an obligation to ensure that everyone has the right to health care and whether the health care system has a corresponding obligation to make such care available. Consider these opposing viewpoints by P.H. Elias and R.M. Sade, respectively.

> *Physicians who limit their office practice to insured and paying patients declare themselves openly to be merchants rather than professionals. The mercantile approach has several consequences. First, it demeans the individual physician and cheapens the profession. Second, it puts the third-party payer, as a service purchaser,*

in a position of greater importance than the patient. Third, it fosters the myth that physicians as a group are greedy and self-serving rather than dedicated and altruistic. And most important, it deprives a large segment of our fellow humans of care. Physicians who value their professionalism should treat office patients on the basis of need, not remuneration.[14]

The concept of medical care as the patient's right is immoral because it denies the most fundamental of all rights, that of a man to his own life and the freedom of action to support it. Medical care is neither a right nor a privilege: it is a service that is provided by doctors to others who wish to purchase it. It is the provision of this service that a doctor depends upon for his livelihood. . . . If the right to health care belongs to the patient, he starts out owning the services of a doctor without the necessity of either earning them or receiving them as a gift from the only man who has the right to give them; the doctor, himself.[15]

Although health care providers debate their individual and personal obligations to provide uncompensated care, the system itself finessed the problem for a long time by shifting the costs of care from the uninsured to the insured. This unofficial but practical approach to indigent care was ethically tolerable as long as the reimbursement system for paying patients was so open-ended that the cost of treating the uninsured could easily be passed on to paying patients. The cost shifting that worked under retrospective reimbursement, however, was not feasible under prospective payment and diagnostic reimbursement guidelines. Under the current price-competitive market pressures, health care providers are in the uncomfortable position of having to apply some kind of government intervention to address the problems of health care access.

Thus, the shifting winds of health care reform only underscore the confusion of the health policy of the United States. At the same time, U.S. health policy makers would like to assure the public that the health care system provides all citizens with comparable access to health care while maintaining the freedom of the providers from government interference in decisions about service production and delivery—and add for good measure that the system exercises budgetary and cost controls in the process.

It is obvious that these goals are contradictory and that attainment of any two leaves the third uncontrolled. Thus, policy makers have been forced to choose among pairs of these goals, or fail to achieve all three. In the 1990s, the government chose to let providers and insurers work out what care would be delivered and how, as long as they met government requirements for budgetary and cost controls. The third goal, equitable access, seems to have been deferred indefinitely. The achievement of some kind of universal coverage that ensures all Americans have access to a basic level of health care will not be resolved effectively until the system's stakeholders and the supporting public can formulate and reach consensus on the fundamental values underlying the problem.

■ Quality of Care

Another health care system problem area relates to variations in the quality and appropriateness of medical care. The uncertainty that pervades current clinical practice is far greater than most people realize. Problems in the quality and appropriateness of a great many diagnostic and therapeutic procedures impact heavily on costs.

Since the November 1999 report of the Institute of Medicine that estimated that medical errors take from 44,000 to 98,000 lives per year, Congress, the president, medical institutions, and the public have been stirred to respond to a problem that has existed for years. The increasing complexity of the health care system, the potency of its pharmaceuticals, the dangers inherent in invasive surgical procedures, and the potential for error in the many information transfers that occur during hospital care combine to put patients at serious risk. The strategies proposed to cope with these problems, as well as the physician report cards, clinical guidelines, and other mechanisms designed to address inexplicable variations in the provision of medical care, are discussed in subsequent chapters.

It is important, however, to recognize the seriousness of the medical error problem. Health care errors are the leading cause of preventable deaths in the United States. Deaths resulting from medical mishaps in acute care hospitals alone are between the 5th and 8th leading causes of all deaths in the United States. The overall burden on society is much greater when both fatal and nonfatal events are counted and when medical mishaps in medical offices, ambulatory centers, and long-term care facilities are considered.[16]

■ Conflicts of Interest

One of the greatest advantages of the high-technology health care systems that serve most metropolitan areas in the United States is the ability of physicians and patients to benefit from referrals to a broad range of highly specialized clinical, laboratory, rehabilitation, and other services. The array of comprehensive diagnostic and therapeutic resources available in most communities greatly enhances the clinical capability of health care providers and the care of their patients.

In recent years, however, more and more providers have begun to invest in laboratories, imaging centers, medical supply companies, and other health care businesses. In many cases, these are joint ventures with other institutions that conceal the identity of the investors. When health care providers refer patients for tests or other services to health care businesses that they own or in which they have a financial stake, there is a serious potential for conflicts of interest. In fact, for the last several years, this referral for profit has been a sensitive medical issue during congressional debates. Both federal and state governments and the AMA have conducted studies that confirm that physician-owned laboratories, for example, perform more tests per patient at higher charges than those in which physicians have no investments. These conflicts of interest undermine the traditional professional role of physicians and significantly increase health care expenditures. Government attempts to limit self-serving entrepreneurial activities of physicians are driven by economic concerns. The ethical implications should be of concern to the medical profession. A major contribution would be made to the code of conduct for health care providers if the AMA provided physicians with a few clear guidelines regarding the growing encroachment of commercialism on medical practice.[17]

■ Health Care's Ethical Dilemmas

Once almost an exclusive province of physicians and other health care providers, moral and ethical issues underlying provider/patient relationships and the difficult decisions resulting from the vast increase in treatment options are now in the domains of law, politics, journalism, health institution administrations, and the public. Since the 1970s, the list of ethical issues has expanded as discoveries in genetic identification and engineering, organ transplantation, a mounting armamentarium of highly specialized diagnostic and therapeutic interventions, and advances in technology have allowed the lives of otherwise terminal individuals to be prolonged. In addition, an energized health care consumer movement advocating more personal control over health care decisions, economic realities, and the issues of the most appropriate use of limited resources are but a few of the topics propelling values and ethics to the top of the health care agenda. There is a social dimension to health care that never existed before and that the health professions, their educational institutions, their organizations, and their philosophical leadership are just beginning to address.

Clearly, the rapid pace of change in health care and the resulting issues have outpaced U.S. society's ability to reform the thinking, values, and expectations that were more appropriate in a bygone era. Legislative initiatives are, correctly or not, filling the voids. The 1997 decision of the U.S. 9th Circuit Court of Appeals permitting physician-assisted suicide for competent, terminally ill adults in the state of

Oregon is an unprecedented example. New York State's 1990 passage of health care proxy legislation that allows competent adults to appoint agents to make health care decisions on their behalf if they become incapacitated is another. Living wills that provide advance directives regarding terminal care are now recognized in all 50 states.

Issue by issue, the country is trying to come to grips with the ethical dilemmas that modern medicine has created. The pluralistic nature of this society, however, and the Judeo-Christian concepts about caring for the sick and disabled that served so well for so long make sweeping reformation of the ethical precepts on which health care has been based very unlikely.

As Americans continue to live longer and new technologies vastly improve the treatment of disease, a new generation of health plans will evolve. The basic issues of cost, quality, and access, however, will undoubtedly persist, joined by a host of new concerns. How to improve Americans' health behaviors, how to involve consumers more effectively in health care decisions, and how to determine responsibility for medical management are among the challenges of this decade.

■ Notes

1. E. Ginzberg, "Health Care Reform—Why So Slow?" *New England Journal of Medicine* 322 (1990): 1464–1465.
2. R.J. Samuelson, "A Little More Piece of Mind," *Newsweek* 128, no. 17 (1996): 55.
3. F. Wolinsky, *The Sociology of Health Principles, Practitioners and Issues*, 2nd ed. (Belmont, CA: Wadsworth, Inc., 1988).
4. World Health Organization, *The World Health Organization: A Report on the First Ten Years* (Geneva, Switzerland: 1958).
5. D.I. Blumberg et al., "The Physician and Unconventional Medicine," *Alternative Therapies* 1, no. 3 (July 1995): 31–35.
6. B. Carton, "Health Insurers Embrace Eye-of-Newt Therapy," The *Wall Street Journal*, 30 January 1995, B1.
7. R. Abelson and P.L. Brown, "Alternative Medicine Is Finding Its Niche in Nation's Hospitals," The *New York Times*, 13 April 2002, B1, B3.
8. K. Fickenscher and M.L. Voorman, "An Overview of Rural Health Care," in *Improving Health Policy and Management: Nine Critical Research Issues for the 1990s*, ed. S.M. Shortell and U.E. Reinhardt (Ann Arbor, MI: Health Administration Press, 1992), 111–149.
9. Fickenscher and Voorman, "An Overview of Rural Health Care," 111–149.
10. Federal Interagency Forum, http://www.agingstats.gov/chartbook2000/population.html (8 September 2000). Accessed 15 September 2002.
11. J.C. Day, *U.S. Bureau of the Census, Population Projections of the United States by Age, Sex, Race and Hispanic Origin: 1993 to 2050, Current Population Reports (middle series projections),* (Washington, DC: Government Printing Office, 1993), 25–1104.

12. U.S. Bureau of the Census, *U.S. Population Estimates by Age, Sex, Race and Hispanic Origin: 1980–1991, Current Population Reports* (Washington, DC: Government Printing Office, 1993), 15-1095, table 1.

13. J.C. Day, *U.S. Bureau of the Census, Population Projections of the United States by Age, Sex, Race and Hispanic Origin: 1993 to 2050, Current Population Reports (middle series projections).*

14. P.H. Elias, (Letter to Editor), *New England Journal of Medicine* 314, no. 6 (1986): 391.

15. R.M. Sade, "Medical Care as a Right: A Refutation," *New England Journal of Medicine* 285 (1971): 1281, 1289.

16. K.W. Kizer, "Patient Safety: A Call to Action: A Consensus Statement from the National Quality Forum," *National Quality Forum for Health Care Measurement and Reporting*, www.qualityforum.org (21 March 2001). Accessed 16 September 2002.

17. A.S. Relman, "Self Referral: What's at Stake," *New England Journal of Medicine* 327 (1992): 1522–1524.

Chapter 2

Benchmark Developments in U.S. Health Care

This chapter describes the major developments in health care in the United States and the important legislative, political, economic, organizational, and professional influences that transformed health care from a relatively simple process to one professional service, and finally, to a huge, complex, corporation-dominated industry. The effects of medical education, scientific advances, rising costs, changing population demographics, and American values and assumptions regarding health care are noted.

From its earliest history, health care, or more accurately, medical care, was dominated by physicians and their hospitals. In the nineteenth and early twentieth centuries, participation in U.S. medicine was generally limited to two parties—patients and physicians. Diagnosis, treatment, and fees for services were considered confidential between patients and physicians. Medical practice was relatively simple and usually involved long-standing relationships with patients and, often, several generations of their families. Physicians collected their own bills, and set and usually adjusted their charges to their estimates of patients' ability to pay. This was the intimate physician–patient relationship the profession held sacred.

Free from outside scrutiny or interference, individual physicians had complete control over where, when, what, and how they practiced, and, not surprisingly, they preferred to do business that way. In 1934, the American Medical Association (AMA) published this statement: "No third party must be permitted to come between the patient and his physician in any medical matter."[1] The AMA was concerned about such issues as nonphysician-controlled voluntary health insurance, compulsory health insurance, and the few capitated contracts for medical services negotiated by remote lumber or mining companies and a few workers' guilds. For decades, organized medicine repeatedly battled against these and other outside influences that altered "the old relations of perfect freedom between physicians and patients, with separate compensation for each separate service."[2]

As early as the nineteenth century, some Americans carried insurance against sickness through an employer, fraternal order, guild, trade union, or commercial insurance company. Most of the plans, however, were simply designed to make up for lost income during sickness or injury by providing a fixed cash payment.[3] Sickness insurance, as it was originally called, was the beginning of social insurance programs against the risks of income interruption by accident, sickness, or disability. Initially, it was provided only to wage earners. Later, it was extended to workers' dependents and other people.[4]

The drive for compulsory health insurance began to build in the United States around 1915, after most European countries had initiated either compulsory programs or subsidies for voluntary programs. The underlying concern was to protect workers against loss of income resulting from industrial accidents common at the time. Families with only one breadwinner, often already at the edge of poverty, were devastated by loss of income due to sickness or injury, even without the additional costs of medical care.

At the time, life insurance companies sold "industrial" policies that provided lump sum payments at death, which amounted to $50 or $100. The money was used to pay for final medical expenses and funerals. Both Metropolitan Life and Prudential Insurance Company rose to the top of the insurance industry by successfully marketing industrial policies that required premium payments of 10 to 25 cents per week.[5]

In 1917, World War I interrupted the campaign for compulsory health insurance in the United States. In 1919, the AMA House of Delegates officially condemned compulsory health insurance with the following resolution:

> *The American Medical Association declares its opposition to the institution of any plan embodying the system of compulsory contributory insurance against illness or any other plan of compulsory insurance which provides for medical service to be rendered contributors or their dependents, provided, controlled, or regulated by any state or the federal government.[6]*

The majority of physician opposition to compulsory health insurance was attributed to an unfounded concern that insurance would decrease, rather than increase, physician incomes, and to their negative experience with accident insurance that paid physicians according to arbitrary fee schedules.[7]

■ The Great Depression and the Birth of Blue Cross

The Depression of 1929 shook the financial security of both physicians and hospitals. Physician incomes and hospital receipts and admission rates dropped precipitously. As the situation grew worse, hospitals began experimenting with insurance plans. The Baylor University Hospital plan was not the first, but it became the most influential of those insurance experiments. By enrolling 1,250 public school teachers at 50 cents a month for a guaranteed 21 days of hospital care, Baylor created the model for, and is credited with, the genesis of Blue Cross Hospital Insurance. Baylor started a trend that developed into multi-hospital plans that included all the hospitals in a given area. By 1937, there were 26 plans with more than 600,000 members, and the American Hospital Association (AHA) started approving the plans. Physicians were pleased with the increased availability of hospital care and the cooperative manner in which their bills were paid. The AMA, however, was characteristically hostile and called the plans "economically unsound, unethical, and inimical to the public interest."[8]

The AMA contended that urging people "to save for sickness" could solve the problem of financing health care.[9] Organized medicine's consistently antagonistic reaction to the concept of health insurance, whether compulsory or voluntary, is well illustrated by medicine's response to the 1932 report of the Committee on the Costs of Medical Care. The establishment of the committee represented a shift of concern from lost wages to medical costs. Chaired by a former president of the AMA and financed by several philanthropic organizations, a group of 45 to 50 prominent Americans from the medical, public health, and social science fields worked for five years to address the problem of financing medical care. After an exhaustive study, a moderate majority recommended adoption of group practice and voluntary health insurance as the best way of solving the nation's health care problems. But even this relatively modest recommendation was too much for some physicians on the panel. They prepared a minority report denouncing voluntary health insurance as more objectionable than compulsory insurance. Health insurance, predicting or having predicted the minority, would lead to "destructive competition among professional groups, inferior medical service, loss of personal relationship of patient and physician, and demoralization of the profession."[10]

The dissenting physicians, however, did favor government intervention to alleviate the financial burden on physicians resulting from their obligation to provide free care to low-income populations. The AMA's House of Delegates reiterated its long-standing opposition to health insurance of any kind by declaring in 1933 that the minority report represented "the collective opinion of the medical profession."[11]

From the 1930s to the present, there have been many efforts to enact various forms of compulsory health insurance. It was only when the proponents of government-sponsored insurance limited their efforts to older adults and the medically indigent, however, that they were able to succeed in passing Medicaid and Medicare legislation in 1965. Voluntary insurance against hospital care costs became the predominant health insurance in the United States during those decades.

Although the advocates of government-sponsored health insurance had little success in improving the access of patients to medical care, the Blue Cross plans effectively improved hospitals' access to patients.

Sensitive to the power of the health care industry to defeat health insurance proposals by raising the battle cry of "socialized medicine," almost all proposed plans emphasized accommodations to the interest of physicians and hospitals. Especially after World War II, when the federal government began to heavily subsidize hospital construction and medical research, the expansion of the health care industry, and particularly physician resources, became the overriding policy objective.

The government gave a huge boost to the private health insurance industry by excluding health insurance benefits from wage and price controls and by excluding workers' contributions to health insurance from taxable income. The effect was to encourage employees to take wage increases in the form of health insurance fringe benefits rather than cash.

Because insurance companies simply raised their own premium rates rather than trying to exert pressure on physicians and hospitals to contain costs, the post–World War II health insurance system pumped an ever increasing proportion of the national income into health care. Clearly, contributing to the inflationary spiral was preferable to incurring the wrath of physicians and hospitals by infringing on their prerogatives to set prices and control the costs of their work. Medicare and Medicaid followed the same pattern. In fact, the preamble to the original legislative proposals specifically prohibited any interpretation of the legislation that would change the way health care was practiced.

■ The Dominant Influence of Government

Although the health insurance industry contributed significantly to the spiraling costs of health care in the decades after World War II, it was only one of several influences. The federal government's coverage of health care for special populations played a prominent role. Over the years, the U.S. government developed, revised, and otherwise adjusted a host of categorical or disease-specific programs designed to address needs not otherwise met by state or local administrations or the private sector. Federally sponsored programs account for about 40 percent of this country's personal health care expenditures. Most physicians and other health professionals are trained at public expense, the government provides almost 6 percent of the funds available for research and development, and most not-for-profit hospitals have been built or expanded with government support. State and local governments also contribute, but in much smaller amounts.[12]

Although many of these programs are described in more detail in Chapter 7, it is important to recognize the health care policy implications of certain federal initiatives. Certainly, the Social Security Act of 1935 was the most significant social initiative passed by any Congress. The act established the principle of federal aid to the states for public health and welfare assistance, maternal and child health, and children with disabilities services. It was the legislative basis for a number of significant health and welfare programs, including the all-important Medicaid and Medicare titles.

The government increased its support of biomedical research through the National Institutes of Health, which was established in 1930, and the categorical programs that addressed heart disease, cancer, stroke, mental illness, mental retardation, maternal and infant care, and many other conditions. Programs such as direct aid to schools of medicine, dentistry, pharmacy, nursing, and other professions and their students; support of health planning; health care regulation; and consumer protections, which were incorporated in the various 1962 amendments to the 1938 Food, Drug, and Cosmetic Act, were all part of the Kennedy–Johnson presidential policy era called Creative Federalism. The aggregate annual investment in those programs made the United States government the major player and payer in the field of health care.

Grants-in-aid programs alone, excluding Social Security and Medicare, grew from $7 billion at the start of the Kennedy administration in 1961 to $24 billion in 1970. President Nixon expressed his intent to undo the categorical programs and shift revenues to the state and local governments. For broad general purposes, this direction was labeled New Federalism. In spite of his efforts, grants-in-aid programs grew to almost $83 billion in 1980. Congress had resisted block grants and allowed only limited revenue sharing to take place.[13]

In the meantime, federal and state governments were underwriting the skyrocketing costs of Medicare and Medicaid with no effective controls over expenditures. The planners of the Medicare legislation made several misjudgments. They underestimated the growing number of older adults in the United States, the scope and burgeoning costs of the technological revolution, and the public's rising expectations for the latest in every diagnostic and treatment modality.

The Medicare and Medicaid programs did provide access to many desperately needed health care services for older Americans, people with disabilities, and low-income populations. Because rising Medicare reimbursement rates set the standards for most insurance companies, however, its inflationary effect was momentous. In the mid-1960s, when Medicare was passed, the United States was spending about $42 billion on health care, or approximately 8.4% of the gross national product (GNP). The cost of U.S health care now exceeds a trillion dollars and consumes about 15 percent of the GNP.

The three major health care concerns—access, cost, and quality—are particularly problematic because attempts to control one or two of those problems exacerbates the one or two remaining. It is impossible to correct all three problems simultaneously. The government attempted to improve access through the Hill-Burton Act of 1946, which increased the number and size of health care facilities substantially. In addition, President Johnson's Medicare and Medicaid legislation ensured health care payment for older Americans and low-income populations and succeeded in bringing millions of patients into a now overbuilt system. These changes, however, were made at the cost of skyrocketing expenditures and questionable quality. The health care system's excess capacity and virtually unchecked funding improved access to competent and appropriate medical care for many, but also resulted in untold numbers of clinical tests, prescriptions, surgery, and other expensive procedures that were often of questionable necessity. Almost all of the federal health legislation since the passage of Medicare and Medicaid has been aimed at reducing the costs of health care but has focused little on the reciprocal effects of reducing both the availability and quality of health care.

■ Efforts at Planning and Quality Control

The federal government did not ignore the issues of cost and quality; the efforts to address those concerns were essentially doomed to be ineffectual by their very designs. To get legislation passed that might alter the existing constellation of health care services or that would scrutinize how well clinicians actually practiced, the powerful medical and hospital lobbies had to be accommodated. This meant the legislation had to be "provider friendly," allowing physicians, hospital administrators, and other health professionals to maintain control over how the legislation was interpreted and enforced.

Two legislative initiatives of the 1960s typify the circumstances surrounding federal efforts to address the problems of the health care delivery system. In 1965 the Public Health Service Act was amended to establish a nationwide network of regional medical programs to address the leading causes of death: heart disease, cancer, and stroke. Throughout the country, groups of physicians, most of whom were associated with academic medical centers, and a few nurses and other health professionals, met to discuss innovative ways to bring the latest in clinical services to the bedside of patients. As might have been predicted, representatives of each clinical specialty argued for funds to do more of what they were already doing. As a consequence, the regional medical programs improved the educational and clinical resources of their regions but did not dramatically improve the prevention or control of their target conditions.

A parallel program, the Comprehensive Health Planning Act, was passed in 1966 to promote comprehensive planning for more rational systems of health care personnel and facilities in each service region. The legislation required federal, state, and local partnerships. It also required that there be a majority of consumers on every decision-making body.[14]

Almost all the regional medical programs and Comprehensive Health Planning Act programs across the country soon were dominated by medical–hospital establishments in their regions. Although there were many productive outcomes from the money spent through the two programs, conflicts of interest regarding the allocation of research and development funds were common, and there was general agreement that the programs were ineffective in achieving their goals. The two programs were combined, therefore, by the National Health Planning and Resources Development Act of 1974.

Clearly, political rather than objective assessments led Congress to presume that combining two ineffective programs would result in one successful program. Nevertheless, the legislation called for a new organization, the Health Systems Agency (HSA), to have broad representation of health care providers and consumers on governing boards and committees.

After several years, nothing had changed. Data submitted to the U.S. Department of Health, Education, and Welfare by the HSA indicated that provider board members were not representative of the overall provider work force or the consumer population. The physician/hospital administrator establishment was overrepresented, and other provider groups were underrepresented. HSA board members were predominately white males, although nonwhites and females were heavily represented in the work force and consumer population. The HSA's function of recommending approvals of certificates of need for new or added facilities and equipment was compromised by the vested interests on the governing boards. The general ineffectiveness of HSA boards and committees in containing costs and preventing unnecessary duplication of services in their regions was recognized, and federal support ultimately was withdrawn.[15]

Several other programs besides Medicare and Medicaid were initiated during the Johnson administration to address the prevalence of mental illness and to support the education of health care professionals. The Health Professions Educational Assistance Act of 1963 provided direct federal aid to medical, dental, nursing, pharmacy, and other professional schools, as well as to their students. The Nurse Training Act supported special federal efforts for training professional nursing personnel and, during the same period, the Maternal and

Child Health and Mental Retardation Planning Amendments initiated comprehensive maternal and child health projects and centers to serve people with mental retardation. The Economic Opportunity Act supported the development of neighborhood health centers to serve low-income populations.[16]

The Johnson era programs, particularly Medicare and Medicaid, put the federal government deeply into the business of financing health care. President Johnson's ambitious activation of the concept of creative federalism enriched the country's health care system and improved the access of many impoverished citizens to continually improving medical care, but it also fueled the inflationary spiral of health care costs that has yet to be constrained. It is apparent that, during the last three decades, none of the attempts to correct the unnecessary duplications of facilities and services and their excessive or inappropriate use, or to contain their costs, have been successful.

■ Managed Care Organizations

In 1973 the Health Maintenance Organization Act supported the development of health maintenance organizations (HMOs) through grants for federal demonstration projects. An HMO is an organization responsible for the financing and delivery of comprehensive health services to an enrolled population for a prepaid, fixed fee. HMOs were expected to hold down costs by changing the profit incentive from fee for service to promoting health and preventing illness.

The concept was accepted widely, and between 1992 and 1999, HMOs and other types of managed care organizations experienced phenomenal growth, accounting for more than half of all privately insured persons.[17] (See Figure 2–1.) Subsequently, the fortunes of managed care organizations changed as both health care costs and consumer complaints increased.

Although the majority of Americans are now receiving their health care through some sort of prepaid managed care, the evidence that significant savings will be realized is fragmentary. Stiff increases in HMO premium rates suggest that the widespread application of HMO concepts will not provide the long-sought containment of runaway health care costs. In addition, both consumers and providers are suggesting that the HMO controls on costs are compromising the quality of care. Consumer concerns about restrictions on choice of providers, limits on availability of services, and quality of health care has evoked a managed care backlash and generated support for government regulation of managed care organizations.

In fact, the most recent available data from a large, nationally representative sample of privately insured persons under age 65 found little difference between HMOs and other types of insurance.[18] Hospital use, emergency room visits, and surgeries did not differ signifi-

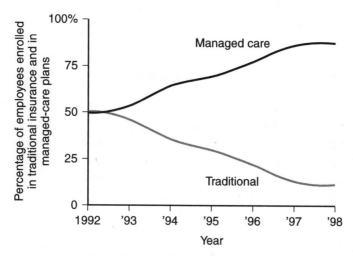

Figure 2–1 HMO Migration. *Source:* ASIAN WALL STREET JOURNAL [STAFF PRO-DUCED COPY ONLY] by LAURIE MCGINLEY. Copyright 1999 by DOW JONES & CO INC. Reproduced with permission of DOW JONES & CO INC in the format Textbook via Copyright Clearance Center.

cantly. In addition, reports of unmet need or delayed care, important indicators of access to care, differed little between HMO enrollees and people with other types of insurance. The study did find, as expected, that HMOs increase ambulatory and preventive care but reduce specialist care and raise administrative barriers to care.

The limits placed by the administrative barriers on how much health care HMO enrollees can use are considered by many patients to be an unwarranted intrusion on traditional physician/patient relationships. Public opinion polls suggest that many consumers do not trust HMOs to provide the care they need if they become sick. It is likely, therefore, that pressure by consumers for less restrictive forms of managed care will make future care management strategies and cost savings more difficult for HMOs.

■ The Reagan Administration

Beginning with the Reagan administration and continuing to this day are attempts, some successful, to undo or shrink the federally supported programs begun in the 1960s and 1970s. Unlike Nixon and Ford, Reagan succeeded in implementing New Federalism policies that were all but stymied in previous administrations. A significant reduction in government expenditures for social programs occurred.

Decentralization of program responsibility to the states was achieved primarily through block grants. Although his attempts at deregulation to stimulate competition had little success, Reagan's implementation of prospective payment to hospitals based on diagnosis-related groups, rather than retrospective payment based on hospital charges, signaled a new effort to contain health care costs.[19]

The conversion of categorical and disease-specific programs to block grants, the withdrawal of federal support for professional education, and the creation of a Medicare resource-based relative value scale to adjust and contain physicians' fees are but a few examples of presidential or congressional actions to reduce the federal government's financial commitment to health care.

■ Biomedical Advances: The Evolution of High-Technology Medicine

Health care in the United States dramatically improved during the twentieth century. In the first half of the century, the greatest advances led to the prevention or cure of many infectious diseases. The development of vaccines to prevent a wide range of communicable diseases, from yellow fever to measles, and the discovery of antibiotics saved vast numbers of Americans from early death or disability.

In the second half of the twentieth century, however, technological advances that characterize today's health care were developed. As so often happens with technological change, once the scientific concepts that underlie the initial breakthroughs are understood, the pace of technological development accelerates rapidly. Since the 1960s, the rate of technological advance has increased so quickly that the announcement of new discoveries or more sophisticated equipment has become commonplace.

A few of the seminal medical advances that took place during the 1960s were the following:

- The Sabin and Salk vaccines ended the annual epidemics of poliomyelitis.
- The mild tranquilizers Librium and Valium were introduced and widely prescribed, leading Americans to turn to medicine to cure their emotional as well as physical ills.
- The birth-control pill was first prescribed and became the most widely used and effective contraceptive method.
- The heart-lung machine and major improvements in the efficacy and safety of general anesthesia techniques made possible the first successful heart bypass operation in 1964. Three years later, the first human heart transplant took place.

In 1972 the computed tomography (CT) scan was invented. The CT scan, which, unlike X-rays, can distinguish one soft tissue from another, is installed widely in U.S. hospitals. This valuable and profitable diagnostic imaging device started an extravagant competition among hospitals to develop lucrative patient services by making major capital investments in high-technology equipment. Later, noting the convenience and profit associated with diagnostic devices such as CT scanners and magnetic resonance imaging, medical groups purchased the device and placed them in their own offices. This practice represents one example of how hospitals, physicians, and other health service providers have come to act as isolated economic entities, rather than as members of a community of health care resources established to serve population needs. The profit-driven competition and resulting redundant capacity continue to drive up utilization and costs for hospitals, insurers, and the public.[20]

New technology, new drugs, and new and creative surgical procedures have made possible a wide variety of life-enhancing and life-extending medical accomplishments. Operations that once were complex and hazardous, requiring hospitalization and intense follow-up care, have become relatively common ambulatory surgical procedures. For example, the use of intraocular lens implants after the removal of cataracts has become one of the most popular surgical procedures (see Chapter 4). Performed on over a half million Americans annually, the procedure takes less than an hour, has very high success rates, and complications are rare. Although the ambulatory procedure costs less than it would in an inpatient setting, the aggregate costs for eye surgery will grow as demand for the operation escalates among the increasing number of older Americans.

Almost every medical or technological advance seems to be accompanied by new and vexing financial and ethical dilemmas. The greater ability to extend life raises questions about the quality of life and the right to die. New capabilities to use costly and limited resources to improve the quality of life for some and not others create other ethical problems.

Whatever its benefits, the increased use of new technology has contributed to higher health care costs. However, there are those who believe that if the new technology were used properly and not overused for the sake of defensive medicine or to take advantage of its profit potential, it would actually lower health care costs.[21]

Both the AMA and the federal government have developed programs to explore these issues and provide needed information for decision makers. The AMA has three programs to assess the ramifications of medical advancements: the Diagnostic and Therapeutic Technology Assessment Program, the Council on Scientific Affairs, and AMA Drug Evaluations.[22]

In the Technology Assessment Act of 1972, Congress recognized that ". . . it is essential that, to the fullest extent possible, the consequences of technological applications be anticipated, understood, and considered in determination of public policy on existing and emerging national problems."[23] To address this goal, the Office of Technology Assessment (OTA), a nonpartisan support agency that works directly with and for congressional committees, was created. OTA relies on the technical and professional resources of the private sector, including universities, research organizations, industry, and public interest groups, to produce their assessments and provide congressional committees with analyses of highly technical issues. It was intended to help officials sort out the facts without advocating particular policies or actions.

The Agency for Health Care Policy and Research, created by Congress in 1989 and now called the Agency for Healthcare Policy and Quality, is intended to support research to better understand the outcomes of health care at both clinical and systems levels. It has a particularly challenging mission as technological and scientific advances make it ever more difficult to sort out the complexities of health care and determine what works, for whom, when, and at what cost.

■ Roles of Medical Education and Specialization

Medical schools and teaching hospitals in the United States are the essential components of all academic health centers and the principal architects of the medical care system. In addition to their research contributions to advancements in health care and their roles as major providers of health services, they are the principal places where physicians and other professional personnel are educated and trained. Year after year, professional schools graduate thousands of medical, nursing, and other professionals whose attitudes, values, and skills have been shaped by the educational and socialization process of their professional preparation. The annual infusion of new graduates of professional schools serves to continuously reinforce the values and policies of their teachers and role models.

During the last 25 years, medical education and policies regarding the size and nature of the physician work force have influenced the size, structure, and operation of the American health care industry. From post–World War II to the mid-1970s, there were numerous projections of an impending shortage of physicians. The response at federal and state levels was to double the capacity of medical schools and to encourage the entry of foreign-trained physicians.[24]

The explosion of scientific knowledge in medicine and the technological advances in diagnostic and treatment modalities encouraged specialization. In addition, the enhanced prestige and income of specialty practice attracted the majority of medical school graduates to specialty residencies. It soon became evident that specialists were being produced in numbers that would lead to an oversupply. Also, they needed to be close to their referring doctors and to associate with major hospitals, which caused graduates to concentrate in urban medical centers. At the same time, the shortage of nonspecialists among rural and inner city populations became more serious.

Medical schools and hospitals, however, were not willing to address these related problems by giving up their high-demand, productive, and well-regarded specialist training emphasis. Instead, they developed a more acceptable physician work force policy to maintain or increase their training capacities. Schools erroneously assumed that producing an oversupply of physicians would force more physicians into primary care in underserved rural and inner city areas. Unfortunately, this trickle-down work force policy did little to change these problems and only added to the swelling ranks of specialists. Most new physicians still chose specialties in which the supply was already adequate and elected to practice where the surplus of physicians was increasing.

Hospitals added to the problem by developing residencies that met their own service needs without regard for oversupply. Supplemental Medicare payments for teaching hospitals and indirect medical education adjustments for hospital-based residents were and still are strong incentives for hospitals to add residents.[25]

The failure of past physician work force policies is evident. In 1989, despite major increases in the physician supply, rural areas in the United States had fewer than 100 physicians per 100,000 persons, compared with up to six times that many in major cities. Further, increasing the number of medical graduates did not correct the imbalance between specialists and generalists.[26]

The rapid growth of managed care plans in the 1990s was expected to produce profound changes in the use of the physician work force. The emphasis on prevention and primary care and the employment of generalist physician "gatekeepers" to control inappropriate or unnecessary use of physician specialists was expected to cause a significant oversupply of specialists by the year 2000. To stave off the surplus, many medical schools and their teaching hospitals endeavored to produce equal numbers of primary care and specialist physicians instead of the one-third/two-thirds ratio that had existed for years.

As soon as the effort produced a sizable increase in the number of primary care physicians, new medical work force projections refuted the prior predictions and forecast a shortage, rather than a surplus, of specialists. Current evidence indicates that the demand for specialists is exceeding the supply. Quite appropriately, a majority of new medical school graduates are once again electing to prepare for practice in a medical specialty. Clearly, estimating a future physician shortage or surplus is a tenuous endeavor.

The forces of reform are exerting increasing pressures on schools of medicine and the other major health professions to change their curricula in keeping with the new emphasis on population-based thinking, prevention, and cost-effectiveness. The inflexibility of traditional departmental organization and the relatively narrow areas of expertise required of faculty, however, present formidable obstacles to needed educational reforms. Roger Bulger, president of the Association of Academic Health Centers, urges academic medical centers to "demonstrate a real commitment to multiprofessional, interdisciplinary team approaches to a patient centered system," and considers the "forces that separate various health professions" and the "devalued status of teaching within our institutions" as preventing adequate responses to the changing environment.[27]

■ Influence of Interest Groups

Many of the problems associated with U.S. health care result from a system shared among federal and state governments and the private health care industry. The development of fully or partially tax-funded health service proposals initiated waves of lobbying efforts by interest groups for or against the initiatives. Federal and state executives and legislators continue to receive intense pressure from supporters and opponents of health care system changes.[28] Lobbying efforts from special interest groups have become increasingly sophisticated and well financed. Since the 1970s, former congressional staffers appear on the payrolls of private interest groups and former lobbyists assume positions on Capitol Hill. This strong connection between politicians and lobbyists is evidenced by the record number of dollars spent to defeat the Clinton Health Security Act of 1993.

Five major groups have played a key role in the debate on tax-funded health services: providers, insurers, consumers, business, and labor. Historically, physicians, the group most directly affected by reforms, developed the most powerful lobbies. Although the physician lobby is still among the best financed and most effective, it is recognized as not representing the values of large numbers of physicians detached from the AMA. In fact, there are several different medical lobbies as a result of political differences among physicians.

The American Medical Association

The AMA, founded in 1847, is the largest medical lobby with a membership of 287,000 individuals, yet it represents less than half of U.S. medical professionals. The AMA was at the height of its power from the 1940s to the 1970s, opposing government-provided insurance plans by every president from Truman through Carter. Compromises gained in the final Medicare bill still affect today's program. In the 1980s, however, the AMA steadfastly opposed cuts in Medicare proposed by the Reagan–Bush administration. James S. Sammons, then AMA executive vice president, led the opposition and alienated several congressional members through the use of highly confrontational tactics. Since 1989, when James Todd replaced Sammons, the AMA has changed its relationship with Congress. Initially locked out of White House discussions on the Clinton plan, the AMA was later included and supported the idea of expanding health care access to all Americans. Nevertheless, cost containment, malpractice reform, and physician autonomy still remain as areas of contention.[29]

Other Physician Groups

The American College of Physicians (ACP), founded in 1915, has 77,000 members. The ACP strongly supported the Clinton plan. The American Academy of Family Physicians (AAFP), founded in 1947, has 73,000 members, mostly in primary care. Using its Washington connection of executive vice president Robert Graham, who was at the Department of Health and Human Services during the Carter and Reagan administrations, the AAFP was able to gain larger Medicare fee increases for primary care doctors. The American Society of Internal Medicine (ASIM), founded in 1956, is also interested in promoting primary care. Although its membership of 26,000 is much smaller than either the ACP or the AAFP, it is helped by its presence in Washington. ASIM was the strongest supporter of the Clinton plan, but did not fully endorse it because of concerns about excessive cost containment. In contrast to the groups protecting the interests of primary care physicians, the American College of Surgeons (ACS), founded in 1913, has 52,000 members and serves as an advocate for surgeons. The ACS was skeptical about the Clinton plan because of its emphasis on primary care.[30]

As in the case of physicians, the lobbying efforts of hospitals also have been weakened by a loss of unity. In the late 1970s, the powerful hospital lobby was able to defeat President Carter over the issue of increased cost containment. However, in 1983, President Reagan was able to successfully pass Medicare's prospective payment system, which benefited some providers but harmed others. Prospective payment set the more expensive hospitals against the less expensive ones, southern hospitals against northern ones, for-profit hospitals against not-for-profit ones, and urban hospitals against rural ones.[31]

The influence of the AHA has decreased as a result of the persistent competition in the hospital industry. Founded in 1898, the AHA is the largest hospital group, with a combined membership of approximately

42,000 facilities and individuals. Despite its large size, Reagan's Medicare victory caused disagreement within AHA's membership and lessened its leverage on the national scene. As differences have begun to subside, the power of the AHA has increased but never again has reached the level it attained in the late 1970s.

Other Hospital Groups

The Federation of American Health Systems (FAHS) has a membership of 1,400 hospitals and health systems and was founded in 1966 to represent the for-profit portion of the hospital population. When the AHA lost power in the mid-1980s, the FAHS was there to take over. The group staunchly opposes any government-imposed price controls. This stance decreased its influence after the first President Bush was defeated in 1992. Now that President George W. Bush has reclaimed the presidency for the Republican Party, the FAHS has regained some influence.

The Catholic Health Association of the United States, founded in 1915, represents the fewest members: 700 hospitals and 300 nursing homes. As such, it exercises little political power. [32] It should be noted, however, that in the current political environment, hospital associations, individually or collectively, have little influence on the legislative agenda. While addressing the complicated problems of the U.S. health care system was one of the hottest political issues before the terror attacks of 2001, health care has dropped in political priority well below the troubled national economy and homeland security.

The American Nurses Association

The American Nurses Association (ANA) is the only major nursing interest group and serves 200,000 members. The ANA was founded in 1896, however, nurses were not very politically active until about 1980. The organization now has an elaborate network of congressional district coordinators who develop effective campaign organizations for nurses within their districts. The ANA endorsed the Clinton plan in mid-September of 1993 and earned several concessions, including elimination of state restrictions of scope of practice, direct Medicare reimbursement, and a doubling of federal support for training.[33]

Insurance Companies

Even more than physicians, nurses, or hospitals, insurers' political efforts have been viewed as completely self-serving. The efforts of insurance companies to eliminate high-risk consumers from the insurance pools and their frequent premium rate hikes have contributed significantly to the focus on cost containment and the plight of the uninsured and underinsured in the debate on health care reform. Yet, the

Health Insurance Association of America, founded in 1956 and representing some 300 small companies, was responsible for that seemingly endless onslaught of television commercials featuring middle-class people worrying about limited choice of physicians and other potential dangers of cost containment in the Clinton plan.[34]

Other insurers groups include the Group Health Association of America (GHAA), founded in 1959, and the Blue Cross and Blue Shield Association, founded in 1946. The GHAA's 1,100 individual members welcomed the idea of numerous new cash-paying customers that would have been created by the Clinton plan. The 69 organizations encompassed by Blue Cross/Blue Shield often have served as insurers of last resort for Americans, resulting in a large proportion of high-risk people in its pool of nearly 70 million. The fact that enactment of reforms would change their demographic disadvantage made Blue Cross/Blue Shield an ally of Clinton and of reform in general.[35]

Consumer Groups

Although provider groups have been most effective in influencing health care legislation, the historically weak consumer movement has gained strength. Much of the impetus for health care reform on the national scene was linked to pressure on politicians from consumers concerned about rising costs and lack of security in health care coverage. Despite widespread disagreement among groups about the extent to which government involvement is needed, all are concerned about the questions of cost, access, and quality in the current health care system.

Better educated and more assertive citizens have become more cynical about the motives of leaders in both the political and health arenas, and much more effective in influencing legislative decisions. A prominent example is the American Association of Retired Persons (AARP). Founded in 1958, AARP is one of the most influential consumer groups in the health care reform movement. Because of its size and research capability, it wields considerable clout among legislators who are very aware that AARP's 33 million older citizens are among the most determined voters.

Although a single consumer group may have some influence in shaping a legislative proposal, consumer group coalitions that rally around specific issues are much more effective in generating political pressure. For example, a political battle over revamping the Food and Drug Administration (FDA) was initiated in 1995 when conservative think tanks and drug company officials urged a receptive Congress to make major changes in the agency's operations. These changes were intended to weaken the agency's investigative powers and reduce the time required for drug companies to introduce new drugs to the consumer market. The proposed changes would require the FDA to meet deadlines for investigating and approving new drugs and allow pharmaceutical companies to submit one, rather than two, well-controlled studies as proof of effectiveness.

Consumer groups entered the debate on both sides of the issue. The biggest and best organized was the Patients' Coalition, which is made up of more than 50 national nonprofit health groups. It includes such dissimilar organizations as the American Cancer Society, National Hemophilia Foundation, Arthritis Foundation, and several acquired immune deficiency syndrome (AIDS) organizations such as the AIDS Action Council and Gay Men's Health Crisis. The coalition rushed to the FDA's defense and urged Congress to reject the proposals that could hurt consumers. Other consumer groups support the positions of the Pharmaceutical Research and Manufacturers Association, the main industry trade group that claims that FDA reforms could be accomplished without risking safety and effectiveness.[36]

The battle continues, however, between those who think that keeping new drugs from the market while safety and effectiveness are carefully tested is denying help to those patients who might benefit from them, and those who presume that drug manufacturers would take advantage of less rigorous testing to foist unproven or dangerous drugs on the market for profit. While the two sides continue to debate, administrative changes have taken place that shortened the assessment time for cancer-treating drugs in an effort to prolong life for dying patients. In addition, the 2003 budget of the FDA was increased over that of the previous year by 21%. The additional support during a time of severe fiscal exigency reflects both strong governmental support for the FDA and the need to strengthen its ability to respond to possible biological terrorism attacks. [37]

Business and Labor

In the 1960s and 1970s business groups were among those that blocked health reform legislation. Today, such legislation is seen as inevitable, and employer mandates and insurance costs have become central concerns. Here, too, there is division. Small firms tend to oppose reform because they might not be able to afford to insure their workers. Large firms favor reform because their insurance coverage costs are likely to be reduced.

The National Federation of Independent Businesses, founded in 1943, has 570,000 individual members and is the largest representative of small firms. The National Association of Manufacturers (NAM) has a much smaller membership of 12,500 individuals. Founded in 1895, it represents the interests of large employers. The U.S. Chamber of Commerce was founded in 1912 and represents 200,000 individuals and businesses. The Chamber and NAM have similar views on reform; they both generally welcome the equalizing effect of an employer mandate but are wary of intense government regulation.[38]

Whenever business groups are involved in an issue, labor unions are sure to make their presence felt as well. The American Federation of Labor and Congress of Industrial Organizations (AFL-CIO), once over 14 million individuals strong, has had a tremendous influence on national health policy. Though job losses during the current economic downturn have reduced membership by over a million members, the influence of organized labor is significant. Intimately connected with the AFL-CIO is the Service Employees International Union (SEIU), founded in 1921. The SEIU is the largest union representing health care workers, with a membership of one million individuals, and its president, John J. Sweeney, also is chairman of the AFL-CIO's health care committee.

During the mid-1940s, labor unions began to demand health care benefits as an alternative to wage increases not possible during postwar wage and price controls.[39] The two major national unions, the AFL and the CIO consolidated their power by merging in 1955. During the late 1960s, they were able to address the issues of occupational safety and health and achieved passage of the Occupational Safety and Health Act of 1970. Today, occupational safety and health hold a prominent place on the national agenda, and efforts to weaken the 1970 legislation or reduce its enforcement are met with strong opposition from organized labor.

The Pharmaceutical Industry

Earlier editions of this text did not list the prescription drug industry as a major special-interest lobbying organization. In recent years, however, the profit-laden pharmaceutical industry increased its spending on lobbying tactics and campaign contributions to unprecedented levels. With prescription drug prices and pharmaceutical company profits at record highs, the industry correctly anticipated public and congressional pressure to legislate controls on drug prices and drug coverage for older adults on Medicare.

Between 1997 and 1999, the drug industry spent $235.7 million to lobby Congress and the executive branch. As lawmakers moved to add a prescription-drug benefit to Medicare that would include price controls, the drug industry hired 297 lobbyists—one for every two members of Congress.[40] Campaign contributions also rose to almost $14 million, a 147 percent increase over previous years. An industry that can spend that amount of money to block a comprehensive Medicare drug benefit that reins in sky-high drug costs is clearly costing the American public dearly. In fact, for the first time in the history of the U.S. health care system, insurers that cover prescription-drug costs report that pharmaceutical costs now exceed the costs of hospital care.

Public Health Focus on Prevention

Although the groups discussed in the previous section are primarily concerned with the diagnostic and treatment services that constitute over 95 percent of the U.S. health care system, there is an important public health lobby that speaks for health promotion and disease prevention. Often overlooked because of this country's historical emphasis on curative medicine, public health organizations have had to overcome several negative perceptions. Many health care providers, politicians, and others associate public health with governmental bureaucracy or link the care of low-income populations with welfarism. Nevertheless, the American Public Health Association (APHA), founded in 1872 and having an aggregate membership of 50,000, has substantial influence on the national scene. However, because the positions of public health advocates are considered liberal in nature, the influence of the APHA wanes when the Republicans are in power and rises during Democratic administrations.

The significant contributions of both governmental and voluntary organized public health agencies to the health of the American public and the political struggles that led to those accomplishments are described in Chapter 11.

■ Economic Influences: Rising Costs

The single most important impetus for health care reform throughout recent history has been rising costs. Since the introduction of Medicare and Medicaid in 1965, almost all federal health law has been aimed at cost containment, but without success. Overall health care costs rose from 5.3 percent of the U.S. gross domestic product (GDP) in 1960 to over 13.7 percent in 1998. Unless there are significant constraints on rising health care costs, economists are predicting growth to 18 percent of the U.S. GDP before 2004.[41]

Chapter 7 presents a comprehensive overview of the complex and interlocking systems of fiscal incentives and constraints that contribute to the rising costs of health care and the difficulties inherent in attempts to exercise control over those costs.

■ The Uninsured and Problems of Access to Medical Care

The problems of access to health care, exacerbated by rising costs and reductions in Medicaid coverage, are generally related to place of residence and employment status. The lack of easily accessible health care services in rural and inner city areas often presents serious problems for low-income and lower middle-income families. For the medically indigent outside of Medicaid programs, however, the absence of adequate health insurance constitutes an almost insurmountable barrier to obtaining other than emergency medical care. The risk of being uninsured or underinsured is greater for those who are unemployed, employed at low-level jobs that do not offer group health insurance, or are unable to work and are not covered by Medicaid.

The number of Americans without adequate or any health insurance was estimated at 37 million during the health care reform debates of 1994. In 1996, that number was estimated to have grown to 40 million. In 2002, estimates of the number of uninsured individuals were around 41 million. Of most importance when considering the magnitude of the problem is that the composition of that uninsured population is constantly changing. When those on Medicaid or other unemployed persons find jobs that provide group health insurance, those individuals leave the ranks of the uninsured. They are replaced, however, by those who become unemployed or lose Medicaid coverage.

The Health Insurance Reform Act, also called the Health Insurance Portability and Accountability Act (HIPAA), signed into law in 1996, was intended to address the problem of the growing number of uninsured. The legislation permits individuals to continue insurance coverage after a loss or change of employment by mandating the renewability of insurance coverage except for specific reasons, such as the nonpayment of premiums. The act also regulates the circumstances in which an insurance plan may limit benefits because of preexisting conditions. It also mandates special enrollment periods for individuals who have experienced certain changes in family composition or employment status.

The legislation ensures portability of preexisting insurance by prohibiting insurers from declining to offer individual coverage for reasons of health status, medical condition, or other factors, such as the loss of eligibility for group coverage.[42] The HIPAA legislation is discussed in more detail later in this chapter.

▪ The Aging of America

The elimination or control of many infectious diseases through immunization and antibiotics; the implementation of basic public health measures that contribute to the safety of food, water, and living and working conditions; a far more nutritious food supply; and constantly improving medical care—all have combined to extend the life expectancy of people in the United States. Although AIDS, accidents, and violence are causing an increasing number of deaths among young people, the vast majority of Americans live to advanced ages. In

1950 individuals over age 65 constituted only 8.1 percent of the total population of the United States. The population over 65 is projected to increase to 21.8 percent by 2030, and about half of those older people will be 75 years or older. The population over 85 years of age is increasing even faster. By 2050 it is expected that one in four of those over 65 will be 85 or older.[43]

The increased longevity of the population, particularly those with serious or disabling chronic illness, poses serious challenges to the U.S. health care system. The problems of financing and delivering an increasingly broad array of medical and other long-term care services are already serious and will become more critical as the proportion of dependent older adults grows in relation to the number still in the work force.

Although the medical model of curing illness, maximizing function, and preventing premature death has been beneficial to many older Americans, it offers little to the growing number of older citizens who are not acutely or morbidly ill, but who have irreversible physical or mental limitations that require diligent care by others. Although the number and kinds of institutionally and community-based long-term care services (described in Chapter 9) have increased, many are struggling to balance actual and perceived patient needs against their allowed benefits, rising costs, and limits imposed by third-party payers.

Of increasing importance is the need for mechanisms to support caregivers as elder care becomes the responsibility of more and more Americans. Changes in U.S. social structures have increased the stress on today's adults because they are required to provide financial, functional, or emotional support to aging family members. More women working outside the home, a high divorce rate, the geographic dispersion of family members, an increase in the number of adults simultaneously caring for both children and aging relatives, and the rise in the proportion of older adults taking care of even older relatives make respite services, adult day care, and other strategies to reduce stress and caregiver "burnout" mandatory.

■ Values and Assumptions That Guide Priorities

Under the leadership of the U.S. Department of Health and Human Services Public Health Service, a consortium of 300 organizations collaborated in a process that led to the design of a decade-long national plan for reducing preventable deaths, disabilities, and diseases. The 1990 plan was called *Healthy People 2000: An Overview of the National Health Promotion and Disease Prevention Objectives*. Most states have developed their own *Healthy People 2000* objectives tailored and targeted to their own populations.

Healthy People 2000 contains the following impressive statements:

The greatest opportunities for improvement and the greatest threats to the future health status of the people reside in certain subpopulations that have historically been disadvantaged economically, educationally, and politically. "Healthy People 2000" calls for special attention to reducing—and finally eliminating—disparities in death, disease, and disability rates experienced by these groups compared with the general population. . . . For the coming decade, perhaps no challenge is more compelling than that of equal opportunity for good health.[44]

Unfortunately, Americans seem to hold values that shape their responses to proposals for changes in health delivery or financing that put the goals of *Healthy People 2000* out of reach. There is a moral commitment to the uninsured population, but much of that concern is self-serving and results from the fear of unexpected unemployment. There is a genuine desire to achieve personal peace of mind, and empathy for those without it. However, there also is a lack of self-blame. As in other endeavors, there is an absence of personal accountability among both providers and consumers in the fields of health care.

Nothing illustrates the unrealistic posturing of the public health sector better than the latest set of 10-year targets for health improvement in the United States. Assembled by a consortium of over twice as many national, professional, and voluntary organizations as produced *Healthy People 2000, Healthy People 2010* essentially ignores the failure to meet 85 percent of the last decade's goals and establishes several hundred more equally unattainable objectives. Notably lacking in these monumental efforts to establish health improvement goals is either the organizational commitment or the strategies to make them happen.

It is indicative of a self-indulgent society that there is a limited willingness to take personal responsibility, to sacrifice for the benefit of others, and to judge each proposed change in the health service structure in terms of reasoned self-interest. The result is a basic incongruity in the U.S. system of health care. The system strives to improve an already superb ability to care for the individual patient, but it fails dismally to address the problems of the larger society.

In a country facing epidemics of teenage pregnancy, sexually transmitted diseases, drug addiction, drive-by shootings, and crack-addicted infants, there seems to be a striking capacity for ignoring the truth about matters of public health and public good. Warren Bennis, author of *Why Leaders Can't Lead*, attributes this disregard in large part to the United States's historical commitment to individual freedom. He explains why the decline in societal concern for the less fortunate that started in the 1980s was so well accepted.

The conflicts between individual rights and the common good are far older than the nation, but they have never been as sharp or as mean as they are today. In fact, as the upwardly mobile person has replaced the citizen, we have less and less that is good. The founding fathers based the constitution on the assumption that there was such a thing as public virtue. James Madison wrote, 'The public good . . . the real welfare of the great body of people . . . is the supreme object to be pursued.' At the moment, we not only cannot agree on what the public good is, we show no inclination to pursue it.[45]

Even the institutions in which health care providers work reflect similar values. Rosemary Stevens, author of *In Sickness and in Wealth*, writes:

By 1980 hospitals seemed obsessed with the language of management. Instead of an increased emphasis on chronic care and social services after the advent of Medicare and Medicaid—not an unreasonable expectation in programs dedicated to the older adult and low-income populations—hospital administrative training programs began to require courses in financial management. Administrators became managers, presidents, or CEOs; and the hospital journals rang with news of "product lines" (patient care), of capital financing, of diversification and innovation and of the "bottom line."[46]

Under pressure to adjust to rapidly changing economic circumstances, many hospitals are engaging with providers in joint investments that raise serious questions about conflicts of interest. Ventures into the construction of privately owned high-technology diagnostic facilities by providers who refer patients for those services proliferate in competition with hospital facilities, apparently without concern for the ethical issues involved.

■ Oregon Death with Dignity Act

November 8, 1994, was a pivotal date for U.S. social legislation. By a slim margin, Oregon voters approved Ballot Measure 16, the Oregon Death with Dignity Act, also known as the Oregon Physician-Assisted Suicide Act. The act legalized physician-assisted suicide by allowing "an adult resident of Oregon, who is terminally ill to voluntarily request a prescription for medication to take his or her life."[47] The person must have "an incurable and irreversible disease that will, within reasonable medical judgment, produce death within six months." The Death with Dignity Act was a response to the growing concern among medical professionals and the public about the extended, painful, and demeaning nature of terminal medical care for patients with certain conditions. An additional consideration for some voters was the worry that the extraordinary costs associated with lengthy and futile medical care would exhaust their estates and leave their families with substantial debts.

A survey of Oregon physicians showed that two-thirds of those responding believe that physician-assisted suicide is ethical in appropriate cases, and almost half of the responding physicians (46 percent) said that they might assist in a suicide if the patient met the criteria outlined in the act.[48]

The issue of euthanasia and physician-assisted suicide has been debated for years in other countries. Although among westernized countries only Northern Australia has legalized physician-assisted suicide, the Netherlands has a long history of allowing euthanasia within the medical community.[49] Although technically illegal, there are specifications guiding the practice, and doctors following the guidelines are not prosecuted.[50]

Provisions of the Oregon Death with Dignity Act

A physician must meet multiple requirements before he or she can write a prescription for a lethal combination of medications. After the initial request, the physician must ensure that the patient is fully informed about the diagnosis, the prognosis, the risks, and the likely result of the medications and the alternatives including comfort care, pain control, and hospice care. Then, a consulting physician must confirm that the patient's judgment is not impaired by a mental condition and that the decision is fully informed and voluntary. The patient will then be asked to notify next of kin. Family notification is not mandatory, however, and physician-assisted suicide will not be denied if the patient chooses not to notify his or her family. After a 15-day waiting period, the patient must again repeat the request. If the patient does so, the physician is then permitted to write the fatal prescription.[51]

The Fourth Annual Report on Oregon's Death with Dignity Act, issued by Oregon Public Health Services, Center for Health Statistics, covered the period from the program's inception in 1997 through 2001.[52] In 2001, a total of 44 prescriptions of lethal doses of medication were written by 33 physicians. Thirty-nine such prescriptions were written in 2000. Although the number of prescriptions written increased, the number of terminally ill patients who ingested lethal medication remained small. Just 19 of the 44 patients that received lethal prescriptions in 2001 actually ingested the legally prescribed medication.

Physicians reported that multiple end-of-life concerns contributed to the patients' requests for lethal medication. The most frequently reported concerns included losing autonomy (94 percent), decreasing ability to participate in activities that make life enjoyable (76 percent), and losing control of bodily functions (53 percent).

The Health Insurance Portability and Accountability Act (HIPAA)

Enacted in 1996, HIPAA is a complex law that has already begun to restructure health care. The effect of its Title 1 was to ensure the health insurance coverage of workers and their families when they change or lose their jobs. The law also prohibits cancellation of coverage because of pre-existing medical conditions.

More sweeping, however, is the part of the law called "Administrative Simplification," which required medical records to be computerized by October 2003. It is intended to reduce the costs and administrative burden of health care by standardizing the electronic transmission of many administrative and financial transactions. The standardization must also maintain the privacy of health information. As a result, the entire health care industry is involved in a costly high-tech upgrade of complex medical and financial documents to comply with the legislation.[53]

■ The Internet and Health Care

Data collection and information transfer are critical elements of the health care system, so it is not surprising that the Internet has become a major influence in U.S. health care. Ninety-eight million Americans are now using the Internet to find health care information.[54] Consumers now have access to vast resources of health and wellness information, have the ability to communicate with others sharing similar health problems, and are able to gain valuable data about medical institutions and providers that permit well-informed choices about services and procedures. The number of people who have successfully completed an Internet search for answers to health care questions has almost doubled since 1998.[55] Internet users are becoming more educated and participatory in clinical decision making. Physicians and other providers are now challenged by the need to deal with a more knowledgeable and involved patient population.

Health care consumers turn to the Internet, at least in part, because of dissatisfaction with the amount of information available from traditional sources. A host of Web sites offer everything from interactive health assessments to personalized diet and fitness programs. Internet use also provides the benefit of anonymity, convenience, and freedom from inhibitions. For those reasons, it is becoming a growing alternative to traditional in-office counseling, particularly in the field of mental health. The mental health field has initiated a variety of forms of on-line therapy for consumers who are more comfortable with the impersonal nature of Internet communication.

Providers also are entering the online world of health care communication. After a slow start, provider-sponsored Web sites are proliferating at a rapid pace. In addition to information for consumers about the provider's training, competencies, and experience, many providers encourage e-mail exchanges that invite queries and provide opportunities to respond to consumer informational needs.

A wide variety of other Web-based entrepreneurial ventures have also begun to take advantage of the huge and growing market of Internet surfers. Both dependable and questionable entrepreneurs are offering consumers opportunities to cyber-shop for pharmaceuticals, insurance plans, medical supplies and equipment, specific physician services, and other health-related commodities. The public is well advised to be cautious in making commitments on the Internet. A listing of some of the most reliable consumer-oriented Web sites may be found in Appendix B.

■ The Basic Issues

The basic issues underlying efforts to improve the U.S. health care system remain, as they have for decades, concerns for costs, access, and quality. Although knowledge, technology, and resources have developed so that superb and dramatic medical care can be provided to meet even the most formidable needs of this country's population, such care is provided at unacceptable cost, with unnecessary duplications of effort, and to the exclusion of the health maintenance and preventive activities that might have reduced the incidence of the medical conditions that required those curative efforts. It is, by every assessment, a health care system focused on providing excellent care for the individuals within it, while virtually ignoring the more basic health service needs of the larger populations outside of it.

Emeritus Professor of Public Health at Yale University School of Medicine George Silver described the current health care dilemma with these observations:

> *The pressures on Congress, professional groups such as the American Medical Association and the American Hospital Association, and the health care insurance companies are directed toward developing a legislative package that will ameliorate the suffering of the underserved, provide coverage for the uninsured, control costs, and satisfy doctors and hospitals without huge tax increases or intolerable additional wage assessments.*
>
> *Physicians are sullen and discontented under the burden of regulations and constraints that seriously impede their flexibility and ability to utilize professional judgment freely. Patients are angry with inflated costs, rising insurance premiums, and various impediments and obstacles to maintaining a comfortable, friendly*

relationship with doctors. Other patients are unable to obtain needed medical services to the extent required, or at all. Critics and reformers attack the medical profession as greedy, uncaring, and even incompetent. Malpractice accusations proliferate, and costs and judgments soar.[56]

■ Notes

1. R.L. Numbers, "The Third Party: Health Insurance in America," in *The Therapeutic Revolution: Essays in the Social History of American Medicine*, eds. M.J. Vogel and C.E. Rosenberg (Philadelphia: University of Pennsylvania Press, 1979).
2. Numbers, "The Third Party: Health Insurance in America."
3. Numbers, "The Third Party: Health Insurance in America."
4. P. Starr, "Transformation in Defeat: The Changing Objectives of National Health Insurance, 1915–1980," in *Understanding Universal Health Programs, Issues and Options*, eds. D.A. Kindig and R.B. Sullivan (Ann Arbor, MI: Health Administration Press, 1992).
5. Starr, "Transformation in Defeat."
6. "Minutes of the House of Delegates," *Journal of the American Medical Association* 74 (1920): 1317–1328.
7. Numbers, "The Third Party: Health Insurance in America."
8. R.G. Leland, "Prepayment Plans for Hospital Care," *Journal of the American Medical Association* 100 (1933): 113–117.
9. Starr, "Transformation in Defeat."
10. Committee on the Costs of Medical Care, *Medical Care for the American People: The Final Report of the Costs of Medical Care* (Chicago: University of Chicago Press, 1932).
11. "Minutes of the Eighty-Fourth Session, 12–16 June 1933," *Journal of the American Medical Association* 100 (1933): 44–53.
12. P.R. Lee and A.E. Benjamin, "Health Policy and the Politics of Health Care," in *The Nation's Health*, 4th ed., eds. P.R. Lee and C.L. Estes (Boston: Jones & Bartlett Publishers, 1994).
13. Lee and Benjamin, "Health Policy and the Politics of Health Care."
14. T.J. Litman and L.S. Robins, *Health Politics and Policy*, 2nd ed. (Albany, NY: Delmar Publishers, 1991).
15. B. Cheekoway et al., "Representation of Providers on Health Planning Boards," *International Journal of Health Services* 11, no. 4 (1981): 573–581.
16. Lee and Benjamin, "Health Policy and the Politics of Health Care."
17. L. McGinley, "HMO Fracas Moves to Who Makes Medical Decisions," *Wall Street Journal*, 18 February 1999, A24.
18. J.D. Reschovsky et al., "Do HMOs Make a Difference? Comparing Access, Service Use and Satisfaction Between Consumers in HMOs and non-HMOs," *Inquiry* 36, no. 4 (Winter 1999/2000): 419–425.
19. P.R. Lee and C.L. Estes, *The Nation's Health*, 4th ed. (Boston: Jones & Bartlett Publishers, 1994).

20. L.B. Ropes, *Health Care Crisis in America* (Santa Barbara, CA: ABC-CLIO, 1991).
21. G. Gallwas, "The Technological Explosion: Its Impact on Laboratory and Hospital Costs," *Pathologist* 31, no. 2 (1980): 86–91.
22. W.T. McGivney and W.R. Hendee, "Technology Assessment in Medicine: The Role of the American Medical Association," *Archives of Pathology and Laboratory Medicine* 112, no. 12 (1988): 1181–1185.
23. Office of Technology Assessment, *Assessing the Efficacy and Safety of Medical Technologies* (Washington, DC: Government Printing Office, 1978).
24. U.E. Reinhardt, "Reinhardt on Reform" (interview done by Donna Vavala), *Physician Executive* 21, no. 1 (1995): 10–12.
25. J.M. Eisenberg, "If Trickle-Down Physician Workforce Policy Failed, Is the Choice Now between the Market and Government Regulation?" *Inquiry* 31, no. 3 (1994): 241–249.
26. S.A. Schroeder, "Academic Medicine as a Public Trust," *Journal of the American Medical Association* 262 (1989): 803–812.
27. R.J. Bulger, "Generalism and the Need for Health Professional Educational Reform," *Academic Medicine* 70 (1995): 315–345.
28. J.P. Smith, "The Politics of American Health Care," *Journal of Advanced Nursing* 15 (1990): 187–197.
29. R.M. Sorian, *A New Deal for American Health Care: How Reform Will Reshape Health Care Delivery and Payment for a New Century* (New York: Faulkner and Gray, 1993).
30. Sorian, *A New Deal for American Health Care.*
31. Ibid.
32. Ibid.
33. Smith, "The Politics of American Health Care."
34. Sorian, *A New Deal for American Health Care.*
35. Ibid.
36. L. McGinley, "Patients' Groups Jump into Battle over Proposals to Restructure FDA," *Wall Street Journal*, 22 February 1996, B5.
37. U.S. Food and Drug Administration, http://www.fda.gov/bbs/topics/news/2003/NEW00873.htmy (7 March 2003). Accessed 10 March 2003
38. Sorian, *A New Deal for American Health Care.*
39. Sorian, *A New Deal for American Health Care.*
40. "Drug Firms' Political Outlays Skyrocket," *Wall Street Journal*, 7 July 2000, A14.
41. Reinhardt, "Reinhardt on Reform."
42. U.S. Government Internet Resources, Congressional Internet Services, The Thomas Home Page (http://thomas.loc.gov), 1996.
43. U.S. Senate Special Committee on Aging, *Aging in America* (Washington, DC: U.S. Department of Health and Human Services, 1988).
44. *Healthy People 2000: Midcourse Review and 1995 Revisions* (Washington, DC: Department of Health and Human Services, Public Health Service, 1995).
45. W. Bennis, *Why Leaders Can't Lead, The Unconscious Conspiracy Continues* (San Francisco: Jossey-Bass Publishers, 1989), 40.

46. R. Stevens, *In Sickness and in Wealth: American Hospitals in the Twentieth Century* (New York: Basic Books, 1989).
47. E.J. Emanuel and E. Daniels, "Oregon's Physician-Assisted Suicide Law: Provisions and Problems," *Archives of Internal Medicine* 156, no. 8 (1996): 46, 50.
48. M.A. Lee et al., "Legalizing Assisted Suicide: View of Physicians in Oregon," *New England Journal of Medicine* 334 (1996): 310–315.
49. E.J. Emanuel, "Euthanasia: Historical, Ethical, and Empiric Perspectives," *Archives of Internal Medicine* 154 (1994): 1890–1901.
50. M.A.M. De Wachter, "Active Euthanasia in the Netherlands," *Journal of the American Medical Association* 262 (1989): 3316–3319.
51. Emanuel and Daniels, "Oregon's Physician-Assisted Suicide Law: Provisions and Problems," 825–829.
52. *Fourth Annual Report on Oregon's Death with Dignity Act,* Center for Health Statistics, Oregon Public Health Services, http://www.ohd.hr.state.or.us/chs/pas/ar-smmry.cfm (20 August 2002). Accessed 4 September 2002.
53. Centers for Medicare and Medicaid Services, Health and Human Services, http://cms.hhs.gov/hipaa1/default.asp (17 July 2002). Accessed 12 September 2002.
54. Reuters Medical News, "Number of Americans Going Online to Find Health Data Continues to Increase," *Medscape,* http://www.medscape.com (11 August 2000).
55. Reuters Medical News, "Number of Americans Going Online to Find Health Data Continues to Increase."
56. G.A. Silver, "The Route to a National Health Policy Lies through the States," *The Yale Journal of Biology and Medicine* 64 (1991): 443–453.

Chapter 3

Hospitals: Origin, Organization, and Performance

This chapter's overview of the genesis of U.S. hospitals provides a basis for understanding their characteristics and organization. The major private and governmental insurance initiatives that contributed to the growth and centrality of hospitals in the health care system are defined. The chapter also discusses the diverse functions of hospitals, the staff who perform in them, and the management structures in which they work. Important aspects of the relationship between staff and patients are reviewed with particular emphasis on the rights and responsibilities of patients in that often intimidating environment. The chapter concludes with a discussion of the quality of care provided in hospitals, and an explanation of the forces of health care system reform that made managed care an ubiquitous influence on hospital economics, service patterns, and provider relationships.

O
f all the familiar institutions in U.S. society, the hospital is, at the same time, the most appreciated, most maligned, and least understood. Besides serving as a place for the treatment of the sick and injured, it may function as a research laboratory, an educational institution, and a major employer within the community.

Being a hospital patient is usually at best an unpleasant personal trial, at worst a serious, perhaps life-threatening event. Where else in the free world, outside of a prison, does an individual voluntarily submit to being confined to a room in scanty institutional garb, poked, prodded, jabbed with needles, questioned, fed, toileted, and alternately ignored and attended, seemingly at the whim of a legion of strangers?

■ Historical Perspective

The often strained relationship between patients and hospital personnel such as doctors, nurses, aides, technicians, and therapists dates back to the earliest history of health care in the United States. The indifference to patients' needs for information, comfort, and humane contact that is today a common complaint about hospital care is rooted not only in the overall history of medical care, but also—and especially—in the history of hospitals.

Hospitals in early America served quite different purposes from those of today. They were founded to shelter older adults, the dying, orphans, and vagrants, and to protect the inhabitants of a community from the contagiously sick and the dangerously insane.

During the eighteenth century, Boston was the largest city in the new democracy, with about 7,000 citizens. Philadelphia and New York each had about 4,000 people. Whatever passed for medical care in those days was provided in the home. It was necessary, however, in these and other seaport towns, to provide refuge for sailors and other shipboard victims of contagious diseases who often were unceremoniously left ashore when the ships departed. The town responded by organizing pesthouses, quarantine stations, or isolation hospitals to segregate the sick from the town inhabitants and prevent the spread of disease. Because these facilities were not intended to be used by the local citizenry, they usually were located well outside the city limits.

As populations grew, mental illness became an additional problem. Individuals whose behavior offended or frightened the townspeople came to the attention of the town board. It was common in those days for the town board to order relatives or friends to build a small stronghouse, or cell, on their property to contain a person with mental illness. If the individual had no relatives or friends, the town might lease him or her at an auction to the lowest bidder, who would take responsibility for confining that individual for one year, usually in exchange for his or her labor.

The existence of pesthouses, or isolation hospitals, also provided the towns with what seemed an ideal solution for dealing with other individuals whose presence posed a risk to or offended its inhabitants. Over time, people with mental illness or in poor health, the homeless, and the petty criminal joined the contagious ill that occupied those facilities.

Bellevue Hospital was originally the Poor House of New York City, established in 1736 to house the "poor, aged, insane, and disreputable." In 1789 the Public Hospital of Baltimore was established for low-income populations, people with mental or physical illness, and the seafaring of Maryland. One hundred years later, in 1889, it became the now prestigious Johns Hopkins Hospital.

Eventually, almost every city of any size in early America had a pesthouse to isolate patients during epidemics. Most cities also had an almshouse for low-income populations, sometimes with an added infirmary. Many of today's county or municipal hospitals were originally combinations of almshouses and infirmaries.

The largest county institution, Eloise Hospital in Wayne County, Michigan, was started in 1835 to serve the "old, young, deaf, dumb, blind, insane, and destitute." It grew to 6,000 beds to care for acute and chronic illness and mental diseases, and to provide domiciliary services to low-income populations. The Kings County Hospital in Brooklyn, Philadelphia General Hospital, and Cleveland City Hospital are similar examples.

Most hospitals in the United States in the nineteenth century were disgraceful, the antithesis of what their patients needed. They were dirty, unventilated, and contaminated with infections. They were overcrowded and offered little or no medical care. The only nurses available were former inmates or women who could get no other work. As a result, they only accelerated the spread of disease. The public, however, knew little of these conditions. Because visiting was restricted, patients were effectively cut off from the outside world. Persons with family or the means to obtain home medical or nursing care shunned hospitals.

Certain religious orders, however, saw the hospitals' clients as so helpless, so miserable with incurable disease, or so maimed by accident, that they presented an opportunity for spiritual outlet for those seeking salvation through good works. Thus began the close relationships of the Protestant and Catholic religions with hospitals and hospital nursing. Religious nursing groups played a major role in the evolution of hospital care. Catholic religious orders were the first groups responsible for kindly and humane nursing performed by fairly well educated, sincere, and devoted disciples. The American branch of St. Vincent de Paul Sisters of Charity, founded by Mother Elizabeth Seton in 1809, established hospitals that still stand in major cities across the United States.

The Protestant nursing movement began in Germany and was brought to Pennsylvania in 1850. It was based on the formal training of nurses in religion, nursing, and nursing education. The nurse teachers were called deaconesses. The Protestant church hospital, or deaconess movement, had an important influence on nursing.

Ironically, it was the Civil War of the 1860s that brought about public appreciation of the work of women in nursing. When sick or wounded soldiers were returned to their home towns attended by obviously dedicated and capable nurses, it was the first time that relatives of those soldiers encountered women as nurses outside their own homes. Nursing gained a much more positive image and came to be viewed as a respectable career option for women.

All of this early hospital care was focused on only the most unfortunate of the population with physical and mental illness. Although provided in the most deplorable conditions, hospital care reflected the early American concept of charity and public responsibility, which required that provision be made for low-income populations, people with

physical or mental illness, vagrants, and criminals. Institutions originally classified as almshouses provided refuge for all of them. Later,
physicians realized the efficacy of separating the sick population from
the rest of the needy and putting them in facilities more properly
called hospitals. The Pennsylvania Hospital in Philadelphia, the New
York Hospital in New York City, and the Massachusetts General Hospital in Boston were founded by physicians who obtained citizen funding for charitable hospitals. Their motives, however, were not alto-
gether in the interests of the patients. They wanted a place to practice
surgery and obstetrics, to obtain patients to serve for the instruction
of medical students, and to protect the well population from people
with physical or mental illness.

■ Sources That Shaped the Hospital Industry

Health Insurance

The transformation of hospitals from simple, charitable institutions
to complex, technical organizations was accompanied by a parallel
growth of private hospital insurance. The percentage of the United
States population with hospital insurance grew from 9 percent in
1940 to over 74 percent in 1986.[1]

By the 1960s, billions of dollars were flowing into hospitals from
insurance companies, such as Blue Cross/Blue Shield, medical society
plans, and other plans sponsored by unions, industry, physicians, and
cooperatives. The availability of hospital insurance removed an important cost constraint from hospital charges. The ability of insurers
to cope with ever rising hospital costs by distributing relatively small
premium increases over large numbers of subscribers opened the
floodgates to hospital admissions. Expanding hospital services and
relatively unrestrained reimbursement rates created an inflationary
spiral that was to persist for decades.

In addition, medical advances and medical specialization encouraged hospitalization, and the hospital industry expanded to meet the
demand. Following World War II, the American Hospital Association
(AHA) convinced Senators Lister Hill and Harold Burton to sponsor
legislation that provided federal monies to the states to survey hospitals and other health care facilities and to plan and assist construction of additional facilities. The Hill-Burton Hospital Construction
Act was signed as Public Law 79-75 in 1946 and became a major influence in the expansion of the hospital industry.[2] Over 4,600 projects
to expand existing facilities or construct new ones were initiated
within 20 years of its passage. Federal support of hospital construction was critically important to the location of hospitals in underserved rural areas.

Medicare and Medicaid

In 1966, the hospital industry was the recipient of another major legislative contribution to its fiscal well-being by the passage of Medicare, Title XVIII of the Social Security Act. The legislation provided the growing population of Americans over age 65 with significant hospital and medical benefits. In one decisive legislative action, the large population of older Americans, the group most likely to need hospitalization, was assured of hospital care, and the hospitals were assured that they would be reimbursed on the basis of "reasonable costs."

The companion program, Medicaid, Title XIX of the Social Security Act, was established at the same time to support medical and hospital care for persons classified as medically indigent. Unlike Medicare, Medicaid required the states to establish joint federal-state programs that covered persons receiving public assistance and, if they wished, others of low income. Because the states had broad discretion over eligibility, benefits, and reimbursement rates, the programs that developed differed widely among the 50 states.

Medicare, and to a lesser extent, Medicaid, had enormous impact on hospitalization rates in the United States. In a little over 10 years after the implementation of Medicare, persons over age 65 were spending well over twice as many days in the hospital as those age 45 to 64.[3] Because the rising Medicare rates became the standards for establishing hospital reimbursement rates in general, Medicare probably did more to fuel the rising costs of hospital care than any other factor.

The Medicare and Medicaid programs also had another effect. Because these programs provided government funding for the hospital care of the low-income population and older adults, they altered the long-standing nature or mission of hospitals by diminishing the traditional charitable or social role of those voluntary institutions. It wasn't long after the implementation of those programs that hospitals became increasingly focused on profit, maximizing the more lucrative activities, and closing or reducing services that operated at a loss. In the 1980s, hospitals, along with most of U.S. industry, became market-oriented and aggressively enterprising. The monetary incentives built into the Medicare system favored entrepreneurial, short-term financial interests.

Rosemary Stevens, author of *In Sickness and in Wealth: American Hospitals in the Twentieth Century*, writes: "One effect was to bring hospitals into prominence as enterprises motivated by organizational self-interest, by the excitement of the game, by greed."[4] She concludes:

Medicare and Medicaid, supposedly designed to promote egalitarianism, fostered sharp inequities in the health-care system while disarming criticism from low-paid American workers and the poverty population. The stage was set for today's struggles to rethink, once

again, the American health-care system—and to redefine the rela-
tive roles of voluntarism, government, and business for the last few
years of the twentieth century.[5]

■ Growth and Decline in Numbers of Hospitals

The number of hospitals in the United States increased from 178 in 1873 to 4,300 in 1909. In 1946, at the close of World War II, there were 6,000 American hospitals, with 3.2 beds available for every 1,000 persons. That year Congress passed the Hill-Burton Hospital Construction Act to fund expansion of the hospital system to achieve the goal of 4.5 beds per 1,000 persons.[6] The system grew thereafter to reach a high of approximately 7,200 acute care hospitals.

During the 1980s, however, medical advances and cost-containment measures caused many procedures that once required inpatient hospitalization to be performed on an outpatient basis. Outpatient hospital visits increased by 40 percent with a resultant decrease in hospital admissions. Fewer admissions and shortened lengths of stay for patients resulted in a significant reduction in the number of hospitals and hospital beds. Health care reform efforts and the acceptance of managed care as the major medical practice style of U.S. health care resulted in enough hospital closings and mergers to reduce the number of governmental and community-based hospitals in the United States to approximately 5,000.

Types of Hospitals

Acute care hospitals are distinguished from long-term care facilities such as nursing homes, rehabilitation centers, and psychiatric hospitals by the fact that the average stay of their patients is less than 30 days. Such hospitals have one of three basic sponsorships:

1. They may be operated as voluntary not-for-profit entities.
2. They may be owned and managed by profit-making corporations.
3. They may be public facilities, supported and managed by governmental jurisdictions.

proprietary →

Hospitals may also be divided into teaching and nonteaching hospitals. Teaching hospitals are affiliated with medical schools and provide clinical education for medical students and medical and dental residents. They, and many hospitals not affiliated with medical schools, also provide clinical education for nurses, allied health personnel, and a wide variety of technical specialists.

Only about one-fifth of hospitals are teaching facilities affiliated with one or more of the 130 medical schools in the United States. Most teaching hospitals are voluntary not-for-profit institutions, or government-sponsored public hospitals. Voluntary not-for-profit hospitals, sponsored by religious groups or other community-based organizations, constitute about two-thirds of all acute care hospitals. They include large numbers of small, community general hospitals and smaller numbers of large, tertiary care facilities. It is these large tertiary care facilities that are usually affiliated with medical schools. The presence of medical school faculty with strong research interests on their staffs and the availability of medical residents to assist in the collection of clinical data put teaching hospitals in the forefront of clinical research on medical conditions and treatments.

Investor-owned, for-profit hospitals grew from a few physician-owned facilities prior to the 1965 Medicare and Medicaid legislation to about 39 percent of all current hospitals.[7] Most for-profit hospitals belong to one of the large hospital management companies that dominate the for-profit hospital network.

Public hospitals include those operated by a city, county, the military, the U.S. Department of Veterans Affairs (VA), or the U.S. Public Health Service. Public hospitals are usually large and well staffed with full-time attending physicians and residents. Such hospitals are usually teaching hospitals, with a heavy preponderance of economically disadvantaged patients. Public hospitals in many localities deliver the fiscally problematic, but essential, community services that other hospitals are reluctant to provide. These high-cost, low-return services include sophisticated trauma centers, psychiatric emergency services, alcohol detoxification services, other substance abuse treatment, and burn treatment.

See Table 3–1 for a complete distribution of U.S. hospitals by type of ownership.

Table 3–1 U.S. Registered Hospitals by Ownership Status, 2000*

OWNERSHIP STATUS	NUMBER OF HOSPITALS
Not-for-profit	3,003
Investor-owned (for-profit)	749
State and local government	1,163
Total community hospitals	4,915
Federal government	245
Total all U.S. hospitals	5,810

Source: Hospital Statistics,™ *2002 edition, Health Forum LLC, an American Hospital Association Company, copyright 2002.

The number of beds in not-for-profit, state and local government, and federal hospitals has decreased significantly in the last decade while the much smaller number of beds in for-profit facilities has increased slightly. Overall, there are approximately 825,000 staffed beds among the hospitals in the United States.[8] Because declining occupancy rates have caused hospitals to take beds out of active service, this figure is significantly fewer than the actual number of licensed beds in U.S. hospitals.[9] Since 1983, a 33.4 percent decline in hospital inpatient days has produced an 18 percent decline in the number of staffed hospital beds.[10]

■ Financial Condition of Hospitals

The fierce competition among hospitals to survive potentially catastrophic economic challenges caused many to rethink their attitudes toward their patients. Hospitals now face the almost impossible task of making their facilities and services more user-friendly while implementing organizational changes and staffing reductions designed to keep them economically viable in a highly aggressive marketplace.

At least one-third of U.S. hospitals are failing financially and another third are in precarious condition. Caught between rising costs and falling revenues, hospitals have been desperately seeking ways to cope with deteriorating market conditions.

Beginning in the mid-1990s, thousands of hospitals were involved in mergers, acquisitions, and other multihospital deals in an effort to capture and solidify market shares and gain economies of scale. In 1996 alone, 235 deals involved 768 hospitals.[11] Although the service and financial outcomes of the mergers and other deals vary from location to location, there is little evidence that the multihospital strategies are meeting expectations. In fact, some of the mergers that combined facilities with differing administrative and clinical cultures have only added to their economic problems.

Those economic problems result from a combination of factors over which the hospitals have little control. The Balanced Budget Act of 1997, which reduced payments for Medicare patients below the costs of treating them, wreaked havoc on U.S. hospitals. At the same time, hospital charges were held in check by hard-bargaining managed-care organizations.

In contrast to the restraints on revenues, costs were rising at an unprecedented pace. Costly new technology, pharmaceuticals, and services, as well as significant inflationary increases combined with declining occupancy to significantly reduce operating margins.

The federal government, realizing the Balanced Budget Act cuts to hospital revenues were too deep, passed a Balanced Budget Relief Act to restore a small portion of those cuts. The financial damage, however, is significant, and additional cuts in Medicare payments to providers proposed in the 2003 Medicare budget have the potential to push hospitals already teetering on the edge of insolvency into bankruptcy.

■ Academic Health Centers, Medical Education, and Specialization

Medical, dental, nursing, pharmacy, and allied health schools and their teaching hospitals are the principal sources of education and training for most health care providers. Major universities with several or all of those different schools join them in organizational entities called academic medical centers or academic health centers. Much of the basic and clinical research in medicine and other health care disciplines is conducted in these health centers and their related hospitals. The teaching hospitals usually provide the most technologically advanced care in their communities and also offer inpatient and ambulatory care for economically disadvantaged populations. Thus, the three objectives of academic health centers—education, research, and service—are fulfilled most adequately by teaching hospitals.

The influence of these medical centers on health care during the last few decades has been extraordinary. The advances that occurred in the medical sciences and technology that resulted in the introduction of life-saving drugs, anesthetics, surgical procedures, and other therapies, and the development and use of sophisticated computerized diagnostic techniques increased both the use and the costs of hospital services. Physicians could intervene more successfully in the course of an ever-increasing array of conditions of disease and injury, and they enthusiastically exercised those capabilities. This increased intervention resulted in increases in both the life expectancy of most Americans and the proportion of the gross national product devoted to health care. However, these advances also significantly expanded the knowledge base and performance skills required of physicians to practice up-to-date clinical medicine.

Medical education and training, led by the academic medical centers, responded by increasing the number of physicians with in-depth expertise in increasingly narrow fields of clinical practice. Specialization and subspecialization grew, subdivided, and grew more. More and more physicians limited their activities to narrower and narrower fields of practice. In doing so, they greatly increased the overall technological sophistication of hospital practice along with the number of costly consultations that take place among specialist hospital physicians; the amount of expensive equipment, supplies, and space maintained by hospitals to serve specialist needs; and, in general, the complexity of patient care. The contributions of highly specialized clinical practice to the quality of hospital care have been both extraordinarily beneficial and regrettably negative. Although the super-specialists of U.S. medicine have given the profession its justified reputation for heroic medical and surgical achievements, specialization also has fragmented and depersonalized patient care and produced a plethora of often questionable tests, procedures, and clinical interventions.

Although academic medical centers have contributed admirably to the advancement of medicine, and especially hospital-delivered medical and surgical care, they have not brought their impressive expertise to bear effectively on solving the delivery system problems that have plagued their industry. Rather, the commitments of academic medicine to high-technology research and patient care and its adherence to traditional organizational structures and professional roles have prevented it from taking the lead in correcting health care system problems. As a result, medical education and medical organizations in general are reacting to, rather than guiding, the changes taking place.

The Balanced Budget Act and Academic Medical Centers

The financial pressures on almost all U.S. hospitals are particularly damaging to the teaching hospitals of academic medical centers. A number of major teaching hospitals are reporting huge losses because of the rising costs of new drugs, medical devices, information technology, and staffing, combined with falling revenues. Meanwhile, those teaching hospitals in crisis are absorbing the added costs of treating more patients without health insurance.

Among the teaching hospitals losing large sums of money are some of America's most prestigious hospitals: Massachusetts General Hospital, Stanford University Hospital, UCLA Medical Center, Georgetown University Medical Center, University of Connecticut Health Center, Henry Ford Health Center, and the University of Pennsylvania Health System. While the University of Connecticut Health Center showed a $16 million deficit in 1999, the University of Pennsylvania Health System lost $16 million a month or over a half million dollars a day. In both cases, as in other medical centers, substantial numbers of jobs as well as programs are being cut in an attempt to achieve financial stability through restructuring.[12]

■ The Hospital System of the Department of Veterans Affairs

The tax-supported, centrally directed Veterans Health Administration of the VA is the country's largest health care system and a significant component of America's medical education system. In 1997, the VA owned and operated 173 hospitals, 133 of which were affiliated with 102 medical schools. The VA also operates 133 nursing homes, 40 domiciliaries, and about 100 clinics. With its large number of hospitals and other facilities, 12,241 full-time, salaried physicians, 990 dentists, and 33,898 nurses, the medical care program of the VA would be expected to be a prime target for the congressional cost-cutters of large and expensive federal programs. It would be reasonable to expect that, with the excess hospital bed capacity that exists in the United States, and the well-recognized and costly inefficiencies of the VA medical care system, the VA hospitals would be included in the general effort to reduce the federal government's role in the provision of health care. However, quite the opposite has been true. The VA has regularly escaped the competitive pressures of the rest of the system. Instead, with broad bipartisan political support, the VA has received an annual congressional appropriation consistently higher each year than requested in the president's budget. Apparently, the strong political advocacy for veterans in the United States restrains any congressional initiative to give up VA hospitals in favor of subsidizing the care of veterans in the private sector.[13]

Like the rest of the hospital industry, the VA is reorganizing its facilities to lower costs, improve the quality of its care, and better integrate its patients throughout the system. Its major change has been the creation of 22 networks called Veterans Integrated Service Networks (VISNs). Each VISN functions as a vertically integrated delivery system.[14]

An important part of the VA's organizational transition is its Health Services Research and Development Service (HSR&D). It works to improve the quality of health care for veterans by examining the impact of the organization, financing, and management of health services on their quality, cost, access, and outcomes. HSR&D programs span the continuum of health care research and delivery, from clinical research to dissemination of research results, to the application of the findings to clinical, managerial, and policy decisions. The latter activities are especially important because the VA is facing rising costs and an aging and sicker patient population.

■ Structure and Organization of Hospitals

The organizational structure of today's hospital is a complex maze of committees, departments, personnel, and services. In addition to being a caring, people-oriented institution, it is at the same time a many-faceted, high-tech business. It operates just like any other large business, with a hierarchy of personnel, channels of authority and responsibility, and constant concern about its bottom line. Likewise, the people who work in hospitals exhibit the same range of human characteristics as their counterparts in other businesses. Patients and their families trying to obtain the best possible results from the services of a hospital, therefore, should base their approach on the same principles that they use in dealing with other service entities. They need to determine who is in charge, what services to expect from whom and when, with what results, and at what cost to them.

The following general description of hospital structure and organization uses the voluntary not-for-profit community hospital as the example, because this type of institution has historically provided the model for hospital organization. The direction, control, and governance of the hospital are divided among three influential entities: the medical staff, the administration, and the board of directors or trustees. The major operating divisions of a hospital represent areas of the hospital's functions. Though they may use different names, the usual units are medical, nursing, patient therapy, diagnosis, fiscal, human resources, hotel services, and community relations.

Medical Division

The medical staff is a formally organized unit within the larger hospital organization. The president or chief of staff is the liaison between the hospital administration and members of the medical staff. Typically, the medical staff consists primarily of medical physicians, but it also may include other doctoral-level professionals, such as dentists and psychologists.

A major role of the medical staff organization is to recommend to the hospital board of directors the appointment of physicians to the medical staff. The board of directors approves and grants various levels of hospital privileges to physicians. Such privileges commonly include the right to admit patients to the hospital, to perform surgery, and to provide consultation to other physicians on the hospital staff. Another medical staff function is to provide oversight and peer review of the quality of medical care in the hospital. It performs this function through a number of medical staff committees, which coordinate their efforts closely with the hospital's administration and committees of the hospital's board of directors.

Members of the medical staff who have completed their training and are in practice are referred to as attending physicians. In addition, the hospital usually has a house staff of physicians who are engaged in postmedical school training programs under the supervision of attending staff members. These members of the house staff are referred to as residents. They rotate shifts to provide 24-hour coverage for the attending medical staff's patients in the specialty departments to which they are assigned.

There is no universal rule as to how a hospital's medical departments or divisions are organized. Most often, the types of practice of the hospital's medical staff determine the specialty components within the medical division. Medicine, surgery, obstetrics and gynecology, and pediatrics usually are major departments. In larger hospitals and in most teaching hospitals, the subspecialty areas of medical practice are represented by departments as well. In the internal medicine specialty, subspecialty departments might include cardiology or cardiac care, ophthalmology, urology, oncology, gastroenterology, pulmonary medicine, endocrinology, otolaryngology, and a variety of others. In the surgical area, subspecialties might include orthopaedics, thoracic, neurosurgery, cardiac surgery, and plastic and reconstructive surgery. Each medical department or division in a hospital is headed by a physician department head or chairman, who is charged with overseeing the practice and quality of medical services delivered in the department. In a teaching hospital, either the department head or other designated attending physician is responsible for coordinating the required educational experiences of medical students and residents.

Nursing Division

The nursing division in any hospital usually comprises the single largest component of the hospital's organization. It is subdivided by the type of patient care delivered in the various medical specialties. These nursing units are composed of a number of patient beds grouped within a certain area to allow centralization of the special facilities, supplies, equipment, and personnel pertinent to the needs of patients with particular conditions. For example, the kinds of equipment and skills and the level of patient care needs vary considerably between an orthopaedic unit and a medical intensive care unit.

A head nurse, often carrying the title of "nurse manager," has overall responsibility for all nursing care in his or her unit. Such care includes carrying out the attending physician's and house staff physician's orders for medications, diet, and various types of therapy. In addition, the nurse manager supervises the unit's staff, which may include nurses' aides and orderlies. The nurse manager is also responsible for coordinating all aspects of patient care, which may include services provided by other hospital units, such as the dietary department, physical therapy department, pharmacy, and laboratories. The nurse manager also has the responsibility for coordinating the services of departments such as social work, discharge planning, and pastoral care for the patients in the unit.

Because nursing services are required in the hospital at all times, staff is usually employed in three eight-hour shifts. Normally, the nurse manager of a unit will work during the day shift and two other members of the nursing staff will assume what is referred to as charge duty on the other two shifts of the day. Charge nurses report to the nurse manager.

A nursing supervisor may have management responsibility for a number of nursing units. These nursing supervisors in turn report to a member of the hospital's administration, who is usually a vice president for nursing or an assistant administrator.

It is also common to find an individual with the title of ward clerk or unit secretary on each nursing unit. The ward clerk assists the head nurse with paperwork and helps coordinate the other hospital services related to patient care.

Allied Health Professionals

Not as well known as the physicians and nurses who are central to the care and treatment of patients in hospitals is the wide array of personnel who provide other hospital services that support the work of the physicians and nurses, and the others who operate behind the scenes to make the facility run smoothly.

Staff members in an increasingly diverse array of health care disciplines are now classified as allied health personnel, and their roles in the complex health care system often are not recognized or well understood by the public. Allied health personnel support, complement, or supplement the functions of physicians, dentists, nurses, and other professionals in delivering health care to patients. They contribute to environmental management, health promotion, and disease prevention.

There are now well over 200 allied health occupations and specialties, and advancing medical technology is likely to create the need for even more personnel with highly specialized training and relatively unique skills. Those who are responsible for highly specialized or technical services that have a significant impact on health care are prepared for practice through a wide variety of educational programs offered at the college level.

The range of allied health professions may be best understood by classifying them by the functions they serve in the delivery of health care. Some disciplines may serve more than one of these functions:

- *Laboratory technologists and technicians* play a major role in the diagnosis of disease, the monitoring of physiologic function, and the effectiveness of medical interventions. Medical technologists, nuclear medical technologists, radiologic technologists, and cytotechnologists are but a few of the specialists upon whom hospitals depend.
- *Allied health practitioners of the therapeutic sciences* are essential to the treatment and rehabilitation of patients with a wide variety of injuries and medical conditions. Examples include physical, occupational, and speech therapists and physician assistants.

- *Behavioral scientists* are crucial to the social, psychological, and patient education activities related to health maintenance, disease prevention, and accommodation to disability. Professionals in this category include social workers, health educators, and rehabilitation counselors in mental health, alcoholism, and drug abuse.
- *Specialist support service personnel* include those who perform administrative and management functions and others with special expertise who often work closely with the actual providers of patient care. Health information administrators, formerly called medical record administrators, food service administrators, dietitians, and nutritionists are examples of personnel in this category.

The following descriptions of some of the key hospital services reflect the close functional relationships among the various kinds of highly specialized individuals required to staff hospital services.

Diagnostic Services

Every hospital either maintains or contracts with laboratories to perform a wide array of tests to help physicians diagnose illness or injury and monitor the progress of treatment. One such laboratory is the pathology laboratory, which examines and analyzes specimens of body tissues, fluids, and excretions to aid in diagnosis and treatment. These laboratories usually are supervised by the hospital's pathologist, who is a physician specialist.

The radiology department, which is directed by a physician specialist called a radiologist, provides radiographs for a variety of diagnostic purposes and also may provide radiation therapy for the treatment of certain disorders. In the last few years, a wide array of more sophisticated imaging equipment has been developed that incorporates computer technology. This includes computed tomography (CT), magnetic resonance imaging (MRI), and positron emission tomography (PET). Unlike radiograph technology, which is limited to providing images of the body's anatomical structures, these imaging advances have unique abilities to visualize structures in several planes, and with PET, even quantify complex physiological processes occurring in the human body. Thus, they add immeasurably to the understanding and treatment of major ailments including heart disease, stroke, cancer, epilepsy, and Alzheimer's disease.

A variety of other diagnostic services also may be available through specific medical specialty or subspecialty departments, such as cardiology and neurology. For example, a noninvasive cardiac laboratory administers cardiac stress testing to assess a patient's heart function during exercise. Obstetricians commonly use an imaging capability called ultrasonography to visualize the unborn fetus.

Rehabilitation Services

Rehabilitation or patient support departments provide specialized care to assist patients in achieving optimal physical, mental, and social functioning following resolution of an illness or injury. One such department is physical medicine, where diagnosis and treatment of patients with physical injuries or disabilities is conducted. This department is headed by a specialist physician called a physiatrist, who usually works with a team of physical therapists, occupational therapists, and speech therapists. Other health-related specialists, such as social workers, may provide additional services to support the rehabilitation of patients with complex problems.

Other Patient Support Services

The hospital pharmacy purchases and dispenses all drugs used to treat hospitalized patients. The department is headed by a licensed pharmacist, who is also responsible for others who work under his or her supervision.

Among other functions, the social services department helps patients about to be discharged to arrange financial support and coordinate needed community-based services. Generally, the social services department helps patients and their families achieve the best possible social and domestic environment for the patients' care and recovery. Such services are available to all hospital patients and their families.

Discharge planning services (discussed in more detail later in this chapter) may or may not be a part of the social services department. Frequently, staffing includes both nurses and social workers who are responsible for planning posthospital patient care in conjunction with the patients and their families. The discharge planning department becomes involved when the patient requires referral for one or more community services or placement in a special care facility after discharge.

Nutritional Services

The nutritional services department includes food preparation facilities and personnel for the provision of inpatient meals, food storage, and purchasing and catering for hospital events. It may also operate a cafeteria for employees and, in larger hospitals, may sponsor educational programs for student dietitians. An important function of this department's staff is educating patients on dietary needs and restrictions. This department usually is headed by a chief dietitian with a degree in nutritional science and may be staffed by any number of other dietitians and clinical nutrition specialists with specific expertise in dietary assessment and food preparation.

Administrative Departments

Hospitals contain other professional units that provide a wide variety of nonmedical services essential to the management of the hospital's physical plant and business services. Patients are certainly aware of two of them: the admissions department, through which a hospital stay is initiated, and the business office, through which a hospital stay is terminated. These units are two of the many components of the hospital's complex management structure.

The general administrative services of the hospital are headed by a chief executive officer or president who has the day-to-day responsibility for managing all hospital business. He or she is the highest ranking administrative officer and oversees an array of administrative departments concerned with financial operations, public relations, and personnel. Most larger hospitals have a chief operating officer, who oversees the operation of specific departments, and a chief financial officer, who directs the many and varied fiscal activities of the hospital. Those key administrative officers are commonly positioned as corporate vice presidents. The large number of employees and the wide array of individual skills required to competently staff a hospital calls for a personnel or human resources department with highly specialized labor expertise. That department also is usually headed by a vice president for human resources. Because nursing is such a large component of the hospital's service operations, larger facilities also maintain a chief nursing executive at the vice president level.

During the past 20 years, as the information needs of hospitals have increased in volume and complexity, new departments, often referred to as management information systems, have evolved. These departments usually are directed by computer science professionals and are responsible for managing hospitals' extensive computer systems. Those systems extend from office word processing to medical record transcription, to transmittal of clinical laboratory findings, to financial data processing. Increasingly, hospitals' management information systems departments are engaged in the computer management of patient care data necessary to evaluate the quality and cost-effectiveness of hospital services.

Hotel Services

Hotel services are so called because they are generally associated with the hospitality functions common to hotels. They include building maintenance, security, laundry, television, and telephone services.

■ Complexity of the System

Unlike the nonhospital health services, over half of which employ fewer than five persons, almost two-thirds of hospital employees work in facilities with more than 1,000 workers.[15] Major hospital systems may have thousands of employees, significant turnover of personnel requiring training and indoctrination of new employees to the complicated procedures of the organization, and a maze of information transmission requirements with high potential for miscommunication. The newer diagnostic and therapeutic methods that are increasingly effective are also increasingly complex.

Thus, even this very limited description of the hospital's complex structure and organization should make it clear that, with so many different kinds of employees and so many interrelated systems and functions, it is a small wonder that hospitals work at all, much less as well as they do. With the multitude of tasks that are performed every day by the hundreds of employees in a busy hospital, misunderstandings and information breakdowns in patient care are inevitable. In acknowledgment of the fact that their organizations are too complex and their employees too compartmentalized in their responsibilities to solve system problems, the majority of this country's hospitals have patient representatives, sometimes called patient advocates, to serve as ombudsmen for the patients. They are prepared to intervene on behalf of the patients in a wide variety of situations. The phone numbers of those patient representatives are usually provided to patients in the material given them during the admission process or left conspicuously in their rooms.

■ Types and Roles of Patients

Nowhere in the early development of hospitals was the patient considered as anything other than an unavoidable burden to society. In its mercy, society provided the hospital as a refuge—and incidentally, a workplace for the physician and his disciple, the medical student. Patients receiving this charity were expected to be grateful for the shelter and nursing care and even for the opportunity to lend their bodies and illnesses for medical practice. On the other hand, patients who could afford to pay for their medical and nursing care continued to receive it in the comfort and dignity of their homes.

By 1900 proper training in nursing, effective anesthetic agents, modern methods of antisepsis and sterilization, and other medical advances had revolutionized hospital practices. Hospitals changed from merely supplying food, shelter, and meager medical care to the unfortunate needy and contagious to providing skilled medical, surgical, and nursing care to everyone. However, the belief persisted that patients in the hospital, removed from their usual social environment, were in a dependent relationship with charitable authorities. Remnants of the idea that these professionals have the knowledge and authority to decide what is best for grateful and uncomplaining patients persist to this day, regardless of the expense to the patient or the merit of the services.

Unfortunately, the behavior of many patients and their families has been conditioned to reinforce this philosophy. In the hospital, otherwise assertive, independent individuals tend to assume a passive and dependent "sick role." Numerous sociological studies of patient behavior have concluded that the patients who behave in the traditional submissive sick role help to preserve the authoritarian attitude of health care providers that most consumers now consider patronizing and inappropriate.[16]

Rights and Responsibilities of Hospitalized Patients

Patients in hospitals have individual rights, many of which are protected by state statutes and regulations. The constitution of the United States and, in particular, its Bill of Rights, is not suspended when a citizen enters a hospital. In fact, since 1972 the AHA has published a "Statement on a Patient's Bill of Rights," which is displayed prominently in every hospital in the country. In addition, hospitals are required by their accrediting body to make this information known to every patient admitted. Very importantly, the statement recognizes that the hospital, in addition to the physician, has a responsibility for the patient's welfare. In fact, the ultimate responsibility for everything that happens within the hospital, including the medical care provided, lies with the hospital institution and its board of directors.

Many hospitals, other institutions, and government agencies have modified the language of the original AHA Statement on a Patient's Bill of Rights to more accurately represent their individual interpretations of their responsibilities or to better communicate with special populations. In addition to posting these statements on the walls of the facility, hospitals also distribute their modified versions under their own organization title with the admission documents handed to patients.

The following description of major patients' rights is a synthesis of the statements posted by several hospitals. Patients have the right to:

1. Receive respectful and considerate treatment, including respect for their personal privacy during examinations, tests, and all forms of interaction with their physicians, staff members, and others involved in their care.
2. Know the names and titles of all individuals providing their care, and the name of the physician responsible.
3. Complete and understandable explanations of their diagnosis, treatment, and prognosis. They also have the right to designate another individual to receive such explanations in their behalf.

4. Receive from the physician all information necessary to give informed consent prior to any procedure or treatment. Such information should include a description of the procedure or treatment, the estimated period of convalescence, the risks involved, the risk of not accepting the treatment or procedure, and any alternative options.

5. Request and receive consultation on their diagnosis and treatment or obtain a second opinion.

6. Set limits on the scope of treatment they will permit or refuse treatment and be informed of the consequences of such refusal.

7. Leave the hospital, unless unlawful, even against the advice of their physicians, and receive an explanation of their responsibilities in exercising that right.

8. Request and receive information and assistance in discharging financial obligations to the hospital and review a complete bill, regardless of the source of payment.

9. Discuss or review the contents of their medical records, obtain copies if lawful in their state, and have the information contained therein treated as confidential.

10. Receive assistance in planning and obtaining necessary support services following their discharge.

Those endowed with individual rights are always expected to assume certain reciprocal individual responsibilities. Patients are obligated to act responsibly toward physicians and hospitals by cooperating with all reasonable requests for personal and family information. It is to their own benefit that patients inform medical or hospital personnel if they do not understand or do not wish to follow instructions. If a patient would like a family member or other advocate to be involved in treatment decisions, that individual should be identified to the physician and the hospital and contact information should be provided.

It is also incumbent upon patients to recognize that hospitals are highly stressful institutional settings and that other patients, as well as the hospital personnel, deserve consideration and respect. Courtesy to others in the close confines of hospital quarters is most appreciated.

There is no other institutional setting in which individual rights are at greater risk of being compromised than in a hospital. However, it is important to recognize that the risks do not arise from a purposeful disregard for patients by physicians or the hospital staff or from their individual or collective determination to subject patients to treatment against their will. The personal integrity of patients may be unintentionally violated as a result of certain institutional circumstances and factors unique to the hospital setting. These institutional circumstances arise from the fact that the hospital, like most large complex organizations, has a life of its own, which pulses with an infinite array of daily scheduled events that pervade every aspect of its functioning. There are schedules for bed changing, patient bathing, serving meals, administering medications, obtaining specimens, providing therapy, checking vital signs, performing surgery, housekeeping, admitting, discharging, doing rounds, receiving visitors, performing examinations, and finally, preparing patients for the night.

The vast number of tasks that evolve from the care needs of up to several hundred ill people each day requires the planning and scheduling of every activity if they are all to be accomplished within a 24-hour period. However, the hospitalized individual who has never seen the light of day before 7:00 A.M., gets ill at the sight of food before 11:00 A.M., or needs a morning shower prior to appearing before another human being soon learns that the hospital schedule not only will not adjust to personal habit but can, if allowed, produce some decidedly uncomfortable and perhaps harmful situations.

The pressure of the daily schedule makes it difficult for hospital personnel to pay attention to the special needs of individual patients. Even though a patient's particular schedule of tests, procedures, treatments, and examinations is uniquely related to his or her condition and the physician's orders, it also is influenced by the needs of fellow patients and the schedules of the physicians, technicians, technologists, nurses, nurses' aides, therapists, students, and numerous others involved directly or indirectly in the patient's care.

A patient's treatment also may be modified by the schedule of those daily institutional events, which, though unrelated to his or her treatment, can have an impact on what happens or does not happen on any given day. Such institutional events include inspections, grand rounds, nursing inservices, unplanned staffing shortages, and an array of technical problems with any of the hundreds of pieces of medical equipment used to perform the daily functions of a sophisticated hospital.

As it becomes clearer that the schedule, rather than the patients' needs, drives the caregivers, the second major reason why patient rights may be in jeopardy in the hospital setting emerges. Physicians may not be aware of the many aspects of daily care in the hospital that determine whether patients will be comfortable and reasonably satisfied during their hospital stay. Physicians are likely to spend only a few minutes a day with each patient. That means that, almost all the time, patients depend on the nursing staff and other support personnel for the medical and personal care they should receive. Very importantly, nurses are supposed to be continuously monitoring each patient's condition and alerting the physician to any change in a patient's status. However, the number of patients for whom a nurse is responsible and the number of tasks that the nurse is required to perform during the course of a single work shift makes it extremely difficult, or sometimes impossible, to fulfill that obligation. In addition, the increasing number of caregivers involved with each patient provides additional opportunities for failures of communication and subsequent mistakes in the treatment programs for individual patients. Although hospitals do their best to develop fail-safe systems to protect patients against the possibility of human error in the delivery of their care, mistakes can happen. One patient can receive a medication intended for another. The report of a laboratory test can get lost and require the repeat of an uncomfortable procedure. A physician's instructions can be overlooked, and the patient may be deprived of something he or she was supposed to receive. Or, the patient may continue receiving something that was supposed to be stopped. A nurse's note alerting the physician to a change in the patient's condition may be missed, and the patient may fail to receive something that he or she requires.

Progressive hospital systems encourage patients to recognize their vulnerability during hospitalization and urge them or their family members to function as active participants in, rather than passive recipients or observers of, hospital care. In addition, state health departments, which certify hospitals to operate, ensure the right of patients to press complaints about hospital care and services. Hospitals are required by law to investigate patient complaints and respond to them. In fact, a hospital must provide a written response if a patient so requests.

Important Decisions, Informed Consent, and Second Opinions

No description of the structure and processes of hospitals would be complete without mention of the very important personal decisions regarding medical care that patients are asked to make, often, unfortunately, under circumstances that are stressful if not intimidating. A cornerstone of the personal rights of hospitalized patients is the right to know:

- What is being done to them and why
- What the procedure entails
- How the procedure can be expected to benefit them
- What risks or consequences are associated with a procedure
- What is the probability of risks and consequences occurring

In short, in almost all cases, the doctrine of informed consent ensures patients have ultimate control over their own bodies. This doctrine, first recognized legally in 1914, has been reaffirmed repeatedly over the years and is now generally recognized to encompass not only all of the above elements, but also the right to receive information about alternative forms of treatment to the one being recommended.

A physician has no legal right to substitute his or her judgment for the patient's in matters of consent. This principle means that, even though a physician may believe a certain intervention is in the patient's best interest, the patient has the absolute right to reject that recommendation. The right of patients to refuse a certain procedure or treatment until they are satisfied that it is in their best interest allows them to stay in control of their health care.

That is why it is considered appropriate for patients to obtain second opinions to satisfy concerns about the necessity for various tests and other procedures. Because there is evidence that seeking the opinion of a second physician regarding the need for surgical and other invasive procedures often results in a decision to reject the original advice, many insurers now require a confirming second opinion before agreeing to pay for surgical procedures.

In many medical situations the wisest course of action is uncertain or debatable. The need for certain surgical procedures is one good example. Few people realize that the medical needs for some common operations have never been clearly defined by scientific studies. When such studies have been performed, many procedures, even those that surgeons once favored, have turned out to offer no real benefit or improvement over alternative treatments. Unlike the introduction of new drugs, which must be extensively tested to document safety and benefits before they can be marketed, new operations have been introduced and become popular based on clinical impressions, rather than the systematically collected information necessary to determine in what circumstances the benefits justify the risks. Because the best estimates are that only 20 percent of the more than 20 million operations performed in the United States each year involve critical, life-threatening emergencies in which the physician must operate immediately, patients usually have time to deliberate carefully over the need for surgery and its potential risks and benefits.

■ Diagnosis-Related Group Hospital Reimbursement System

Only a decade ago, a patient stayed in the hospital until the physician decided that he or she was well enough to leave. If the patient was going to a nursing home or some other institution, sometimes that patient had to remain in the hospital until a bed became available in the other institution. In most cases, however, physicians had a considerable amount of leeway in making decisions about the length of a patient's stay in the hospital, and they usually tried to balance the best interests of the patients with those of the hospital.

For this and other reasons, the length of time patients stayed in the hospital varied, even among those being treated for the same condition. In fact, the patterns of medical care varied considerably from one geographic location to another. For many years, physicians on the West Coast of the United States have discharged patients from hospitals two or more days earlier than their counterparts in the Northeast for patients with the same conditions. Apparently, differing regional medical practice patterns guide physician behaviors.

In any case, each hospital monitored its own situation. Each had a utilization review committee made up of physicians and administrators who were required to review the lengths of stay of hospitalized patients and ensure that neither the quality of care nor the efficiency of the hospital was being compromised by physicians' decisions.

During the 1970s and early 1980s, however, the cost of hospital care rose so fast and so far that health insurance companies and big corporations that paid huge insurance premiums to cover the hospitalization costs of their workers dramatically increased the pressure on federal agencies to find a way to stem the rising tide of hospital expenses.

Two factors made change imperative. Hospitals were paid a set amount for each day a patient stayed in the facility. That amount was determined retrospectively by determining what it cost per day per bed to operate the hospital the year before. Under that arrangement the hospital had no incentive to keep costs down. In fact, if it did, it would receive a smaller daily reimbursement rate the next year than if it spent freely. Further, it became clear to the government and the insurance companies that they were paying not only for uncontrolled costs per hospital day, but also for hospital days that weren't necessary. On a national scale, hundreds of thousands of hospital days that didn't benefit the patients, at a cost of several hundred dollars per day, amounted to a huge and valueless financial burden. Hospital costs were forcing the federal Medicare program, which served older Americans, to exceed all financial projections.

There was another worry as well. Not only are unnecessarily long hospital stays expensive, but they also can be dangerous to the patients' health. Older patients are especially vulnerable. Patients are exposed to infections and diseases in hospitals that they would not face at home. In addition, many older patients lose the ability to do some of the basic activities of daily living like dress, feed, or toilet themselves during a long stay in a hospital. Those patients come out of the hospital less able to function than when they went in. Shortened stays in hospitals, especially for older patients, can often be beneficial as well as less expensive.

In 1983, the federal government initiated a new program that addressed those two problems. The new arrangement radically changed the way hospitals would be reimbursed for costs of treating Medicare patients. The new payment system is referred to as diagnosis-related groups (DRGs) and is designed to provide hospitals with a financial incentive to discharge patients as soon as possible. It is a prospective payment system, which means that the patient's diagnosis determines how much the hospital will be paid, and the hospital knows that amount in advance. The payment is a set amount based on the average cost of treating that particular illness or condition. If the patient requires less care or fewer days in the hospital than the DRG average, the hospital is paid the average cost regardless, and the hospital makes money. If the patient requires a longer stay or more care than the DRG average, the hospital loses money.

This carrot and stick system was adopted quickly by almost all states and hospital insurance companies and now affects all hospital patients, not just Medicare patients. It quickly changed hospital behavior. The built-in system of financial rewards and punishments caused hospitals to discharge patients more quickly and sometimes before they were completely recovered, a practice that has increased the need for home-delivered health care services. In addition, medical staff is much more conservative about ordering tests and procedures that are of marginal value in diagnosis and treatment. Now hospitals do everything they can to ensure that their average cost in a particular DRG category stays within the reimbursement limit. In most cases, the incentive to discharge patients as soon as possible does not cause problems. In some cases, however, it does, and patients have to be readmitted for further treatment. A more detailed discussion of the impact of this reimbursement method on the financial viability of hospitals is provided in Chapter 7, which deals with the financing of health care.

■ Discharge Planning

The hospital is responsible for employing discharge planners to help patients arrange for safe and appropriate accommodations after a hospital stay. Using information provided by the patient or the patient's family, a discharge planner must see to it that the patient who needs follow-up services, such as home care, will obtain them. The planner must then help make the specific arrangements that are necessary. If the patient requires a transfer to another level of institutional care, such as a nursing home, it is the responsibility of the discharge planner to arrange that transfer before the patient can be discharged from the hospital.

The hospital's financial incentive to discharge patients as soon as possible should never cause patients to be discharged before they are medically ready to leave and arrangements have been made to ensure that they will receive the necessary posthospital care. Patients who feel that either of these two conditions will not have been met by their anticipated discharge date have the right to appeal that date. If they cannot persuade their physician or discharge planner to reconsider the discharge decision, they can ask the hospital for a written notice of discharge. For those receiving Medicare, the written notice will allow two free Medicare-covered days in the hospital, whether or not they decide to appeal.

The hospital's discharge notice must include instructions on how the patient can have the hospital's decision reviewed by the peer review organization (PRO). The PRO is an organization under contract with the federal government to ensure that hospitals and physicians follow Medicare rules. Every geographic area in the United States is covered by a federally designated PRO. Patients have three calendar days after receiving written notice to ask the hospital to refer their case to the PRO. The PRO then has three working days to return its decision.

The PRO will reverse the decision to discharge and require Medicare to cover the costs of the additional days if it is convinced that the patient is in need of continuing hospital care. If the PRO does not reverse the decision, the hospital can bill the patient directly for any stay after two days following its written notice to the patient. There is also a mechanism to appeal the PRO's decision and a further process for a Medicare appeal.

■ Subacute Care

It was inevitable under recent economic pressures that hospitals would find ways to increase utilization, fill empty beds, and increase revenues. Subacute care, a level of care that falls between inpatient hospitalization and long-term or nursing home care, provided one such opportunity.

Subacute care is a mix of rehabilitation and convalescent services that requires 10 to 100 days of care. It is a level and duration of care inappropriate to either acute care hospitals or most skilled nursing facilities. Yet, both hospitals and nursing homes have created special units within their facilities to provide for subacute care. Because that care level falls between well-established reimbursement formulas, setting up subacute care facilities has allowed hospitals and nursing homes to find different ways to capture the highest reimbursement rates.

Some hospitals have licensed their subacute care facilities separately from the rest of the hospital to exempt them from the prospective payment system. Others have converted a hospital-based skilled nursing facility to subacute care. Still others have transformed an entire acute care facility to a long-term care facility. Unlike acute care facilities, these long-term care hospitals receive higher cost-based reimbursement from Medicare.[17]

In any case, subacute care, viewed as a new financial opportunity for health care institutions, has become one of the fastest growing developments in the hospital and nursing home industries. Managed care providers welcome the opportunity to direct patients to subacute care facilities that can treat them effectively for a fraction of the cost of traditional hospital care.

The rapid development of subacute care and the accompanying switch from prospective payment to cost-based reimbursement, however, has prompted the federal government's Health Care Financing Administration and agencies in several states to take steps to halt the spread of subacute care units within both hospitals and nursing homes until the value of subacute care can be determined. Questions about whether hospitals or nursing homes are more suitable to administer subacute care have been raised. In addition, because the focus of subacute care is more on new forms of reimbursement than on a new type of service, studies are underway to determine the cost-effectiveness and usefulness to patients of this type of care. Clearly, it is a high-stakes development in the hospital industry.

■ Market-Driven Reforms Affecting Hospitals

Although the American public and Congress resisted the health care system reforms proposed by President Clinton in the failed Health Security Act of 1993, market forces continued to alter the health care environment with remarkable rapidity. With consumers, employers, government, and commercial payers intensifying their demands for lower costs, higher quality, better access, and more information about outcomes, most hospitals undertook a series of competitive efforts to retain and, if possible, improve their market positions. Many engaged in mergers and consolidations intended to affect economies of scale and place them in a better position to negotiate with managed care organizations and other payers. Others, in communities with excess hospital capacity, either closed or converted to other uses, such as ambulatory or long-term care facilities.

Since 1980, approximately 2,000 hospitals have closed in the United States, and hospital inpatient days have declined by one-third. Further, with an increasing number of medical services occurring in ambulatory settings, hospitals are facing the need to reduce inpatient capacity and refocus their service efforts on intensive care and other inpatient essentials.[18]

The major reformation of the hospital industry has been a formidable challenge to traditionally conservative hospital executives, boards of trustees, and medical staffs steeped in their long-standing institutional cultures. Many find it difficult to comprehend the inevitability of health care system shifts and the magnitude of the organizational changes that will be required for institutional survival.

Market-driven health care reforms were particularly problematic to the voluntary, not-for-profit hospital sector. Unlike aggressive for-profit organizations, hospitals are coalitions of multiple cultures that define employee performance and service quality on broadly varying parameters. Diffuse purposes and services in voluntary hospitals had long accommodated excess capacity and variability of skills and performance among providers and support staff. Such conditions would not have been tolerated in profit-driven organizations with more precisely focused missions. Decades of financial support subsidized by retrospective reimbursement of essentially unlimited expenditures discouraged frugality and efficiency. The prevailing philosophy was that no cost was too great when it came to health care, and the reimbursement system supported that view.

Managed Care

The growth of managed health care in communities across the United States continues to have a profound impact on the hospital industry. Managed care organizations, striving to provide cost-effective care to increasingly large populations of enrollees, exert significant influence over both the utilization and the cost of hospital services. Additionally, managed care organizations obtain and pay serious attention to measures of performance among hospitals so that they can ensure that their enrollees have timely access to high quality care. Negotiating with managed care organizations and competing with other hospitals in an open market on the basis of documented performance and cost-effectiveness have been new and formidable challenges to most hospitals.

Controlling costs without decreasing the quality of the product, the essential principle of successful commercial ventures, presents a dilemma to much of the voluntary hospital sector. In many instances, voluntary hospitals remained financially viable for reasons unrelated to the efficiency and quality of their performance. Now, however, with health care purchasers increasingly relying on revealing measures of service cost and quality, their continued viability will depend on accountability for every aspect of performance with zero tolerance for waste of effort and resources. Those hospitals that cannot compete successfully for the major patient populations under the control and oversight of managed care organizations are unlikely to survive the reformation of the hospital industry.

Reengineering

With the marketplace redefining the core business of hospitals rather than simply requiring them to be more cost-efficient, eliminating or replacing redundant or inefficient services may not be an adequate response. Rather, hospital executives are being urged to engage in more radical organizational changes to hold their market share and prosper.[19] It is increasingly clear that hospitals, once the hub of the health care system, will be reduced in importance to just one, albeit critical, component of multilevel health service networks. Reflecting the revolutionary changes that have occurred in other industries, hospitals must now discontinue their traditional structures and processes and literally rebuild them from scratch in new forms.

In 1993, Michael Hammer and James Champy wrote an important book called *Reengineering the Corporation: A Manifesto for Business Revolution*. They define reengineering as "the fundamental rethinking and radical redesign of business processes to achieve dramatic improvements in critical, contemporary measures of performance, such as cost, quality, service and speed."[20]

Unlike the incremental quality improvement strategies of continuous quality improvement (CQI) or total quality management (TQM), which depend on input from the employees near the points of service, real restructuring or reengineering comes from the top of an organization. Reengineering recognizes that the expertise of employees at the points of service is largely confined to their individual functions and departments and that they lack the broad perspective demanded by corporate restructuring. In addition, frontline managers embrace incrementalism more readily than reengineering because they can act incrementally without exceeding the range of their vision.

Patient-Focused Care

One of the consequences of the rise of high-technology hospital care was the industrialization of patient care activities. The corporate thinking that swept the hospital industry in the 1970s and 1980s brought production-line concepts to what formerly had been very personal, high-touch, rather than high-tech, relationships between patients and caregivers, primarily nurses.

Rather than patient-oriented, the care became task-oriented with every chore identified and delegated to the person at the lowest skill level who was capable of carrying it out. Thus, a nurse might be assigned the task of going from patient to patient just taking vital signs, temperatures, blood pressures, and pulses. Another individual, not necessarily a nurse, might be only bathing those same patients, another drawing blood, another handing out medications, and so forth. The end result for patients was a succession of relatively anonymous caregivers, none of whom had a knowledgeable relationship with the objects of their attention. Responsibility and accountability for the total care of patients became increasingly diffuse, opportunities for patients to fall into the cracks between the host of caregivers increased, and more midlevel managers were necessary to oversee operations. Any questionable gains in efficiency were achieved at the costs of patient satisfaction, communication, and personal care.

The production-line technique designed by Henry Ford to permit the production of automobiles by uneducated and unskilled workers responsible only for the repetitive performance of a single task seems hardly appropriate for the highly skilled professional personnel dealing with the complex problems of hospital patients. Nevertheless, the model persisted until recently among hospitals, as it did in the automobile industry. The concept of "quality circles" demonstrated so well by the Japanese finally convinced even rigid U.S. automakers and their unions that production lines have limited application in the world of high technology.

In the meantime, patient satisfaction studies have reflected an increasing crescendo of patient complaints about the loss of identity, dignity, and respect for them as individuals that characterize their hospital stay. Particularly frustrating to many hospital patients and their families is the difficulty they experience in obtaining information or even identifying someone capable of answering questions. In the experience of these authors, the lack of communication between hospital staff, including physicians, and the patients and their families is the most aggravating aspect of their hospital experience.

After an extensive survey of over 6,000 hospital patients and 2,000 individuals who accompanied patients during their hospital stays, as well as research drawn from field visits and focus groups, the Picker/Commonwealth Program for Patient-Centered Care, established in 1987, was able to identify a series of patient care failings common among hospitals. Unquestionably, the diffusion of clinical responsibility that complicates communication among caregivers and the flow of information between caregivers and patients affect the quality of clinical care. In addition to making patient experiences unpleasant and stressful, communication and coordination breakdowns make for needless duplications of effort and the delay or omission of important procedures and tasks. One devastating finding was that as many as 20 percent of patients concluded that no one was in charge of their hospital care.

It is significant in the Picker/Commonwealth findings that the most technologically sophisticated teaching hospitals with the most specialized medical staffs also are viewed as the least sensitive to the personal and cultural values, concerns, and perceptions of their patient populations. Conversely, the cultural homogeneity of staff and patients and the relative simplicity of small community hospitals are viewed as more conducive to patient-sensitive care. Clearly, the advances in medical care and the industrialization of many, if not most, hospitals has caused the medical system to lose touch with its essential constituency—its patients—and its essential mission to serve their needs.[21]

Of course, some very large and sophisticated hospitals did not follow the crowd, and they stand out as highly mission-oriented, innovative, and sensitive to patient needs and wants. They reshaped their patient care systems on the strengths of their highly skilled nursing personnel to be extremely responsive to patient concerns and to measure precisely how patients experience the process and outcomes of the care they receive.

Beth Israel Hospital in Boston and Cedars-Sinai Medical Center in Los Angeles are two excellent examples of patient-focused hospital care. The quality of nursing care is deemed as important to the safety and well-being of patients in those hospitals as it is to the progress of their medical care. Excellent hospitals give nurses a meaningful role in the care and treatment of patients, and Beth Israel Hospital has been cited many times as the model for other hospitals. Its primary care nursing program, developed in 1974, has one of the most successful histories of patient-centered care. Each patient is assigned a registered nurse who is responsible for designing a coordinated individual plan of care. The primary care nurse assumes 24-hour responsibility for maintaining continuity of care from admission to discharge and coordinates all other caregivers in the process.[22]

Similarly, Cedars-Sinai Medical Center pioneered the concept of patient-focused care with organizational redesigns, clinical practice guidelines, and firm accountability for the quality of patient care. The dedication and effectiveness of the nursing staff is reflected in its reputation as one of the world's most diversified and sophisticated medical centers and its repeated 95 percent patient satisfaction ratings.[23]

Clearly the trend is moving away from the industrial model of hospital care that eroded public trust and confidence and toward small team responsibility for the quality of patient services. A recent survey of hospital chief executive officers (CEOs) indicated that nearly half of all hospitals were contemplating or had implemented patient-focused care programs.[24]

Integrated Health Systems

The forces of cost containment, the rise of purchaser influence, declining trends in inpatient utilization, and demands of emerging managed care organizations for higher levels of service organization and accountability converged in the 1980s to compel hospitals to rethink their strategic market positioning. In contrast to the two previous decades, which were marked by service expansion and diversification and competition with neighboring institutions for market share, conditions in the health care business environment of the 1980s suggested that future viability would depend on removing excess capacity through consolidation and improved coordination of services.

Earlier government efforts at controlling costs and overexpansion, such as the certificate-of-need legislation and other cost-control designs affecting Medicare that had been passed in the 1970s, were now viewed as largely ineffective. Instead, the federal government was turning to direct control of reimbursement through the new DRG system. During the same period, the emerging health maintenance organization (HMO) movement, begun with the passage of the Health Maintenance Organization Act of 1973, was gaining influence in health care markets across the country. The impact of managed care became the preeminent factor in reshaping the strategic positioning of hospitals and, with them, many related health care services.

Managed care organizations, with their population perspective, required hospitals to shift from a strategy of serving more individual patients with ever larger numbers of services, to devising systems that emphasized efficient, effective, coordinated care for insured population groups. In communities throughout the country, managed care organizations became increasingly successful in acquiring employer group contracts, and, with them, the power to control the health care utilization behavior of major portions of community populations. For hospitals and for physicians, the purchaser of services was shifting from individual patients to managed care companies, which purchased services on behalf of large segments of communities.

The demands of managed care organizations for efficiency, cost controls, coordination of services, and accountability for service outcomes necessitated radical shifts in hospital strategic planning. McManus et al. characterize the impacts of these changes, "Providers will not just treat episodes of illness or injury, but will focus on wellness, prevention and primary care, and truly manage the total health and well-being of patients. Success will no longer be measured by census, admissions and profits, but by the health and well being of communities served."[25]

The ability of hospitals to compete successfully for patients would now be determined by their adeptness at creating systems that could address the multiple health care needs of population groups while meeting their insurers' parameters for cost control and quality. In addition, as managed care organizations achieved higher levels of penetration within communities, their negotiating position with service providers began including requirements to share economic risk through payment arrangements, such as withholding fees and capitation.

As major players in the health care delivery system, hospitals were forced to respond to the new imperatives of managed care by leading efforts at reorganizing and reconfiguring service delivery components within their communities. Both horizontal and vertical system integration strategies began to emerge as hospitals sought to make their organizations attractive to the managed care industry.

Horizontal Integration

Under the general business definition, horizontally integrated organizations are aggregations that produce the same goods or services. They may be separately or jointly owned and governed, operated as subsidiary corporations of a parent organization, or exist in a variety of other legal or quasi-legal relationships. According to Roger Kropf:

> *In the hospital industry, horizontal integration was viewed as potentially advantageous because a chain of hospitals might be able to purchase supplies and services at a volume discount, would be able to hire specialized staff at the corporate level to increase expertise, would be able to raise capital less expensively on the securities markets, and would be able to market hospital services under a single brand name in a number of communities.*[26]

Both for-profit and not-for-profit hospitals engaged in horizontal integration in an effort to meet the economic imperatives of the changing industry climate. The horizontal integration strategy spawned large numbers of hospital mergers and acquisitions and significant growth in the number of multihospital systems during the 1980s. As the trend in inpatient utilization and lengths of stay continued their declines throughout the 1980s, managed care organizations and other large purchasers of health care were increasing demands for the availability of comprehensive, continuous care housed within discrete, accountable systems. For this and other reasons, horizontal integration as a primary strategic initiative declined in favor.

Mergers and acquisitions have continued to the present, but often for reasons different from the advantages initially identified. Now, in communities across the United States, with managed care saturating markets more than penetrating them, consolidation of facilities, staff, and other resources of previously separate organizations has become critical to the survival of a rational health care delivery system.

Vertical Integration

Vertically integrated organizations are ones that operate a variety of business entities, each of which is related to the other. In health care, a vertically integrated system includes several service components, each of which addresses some dimension of a population's health care needs. The system may be fully comprehensive, with a complete continuum of services ranging from prenatal to terminal care. Other systems may contain some, but not all, of the services required by a population. A fully comprehensive vertically integrated system in its ideal form would include all facilities, personnel, and technological resources to render the complete continuum of care, which comprises (1) all outpatient primary care and specialty diagnostic and therapeutic services, (2) inpatient medical and surgical services, (3) short- and long-term rehabilitative services, (4) long-term chronic institutional and in-home care, and (5) terminal care. Such a system also would include all required support services such as social work and health education. In theory, vertically integrated systems offer attractive benefits to their sponsoring organizations, patients, physicians, and other providers, as well as payers.

Sponsors of vertically integrated organizations gain the advantage of an increased market share across a mixture of high-profit, loss-generating, and break-even revenue sources. They benefit from an increased likelihood of retaining patients for many or all of their service needs. In addition, they are advantageously positioned to negotiate with managed care organizations by ensuring the availability of comprehensive, continuous care for an insured population, at competitive prices. For patients, the most obvious benefit is continuity of care throughout the various system components and improved case management. Physicians and other providers benefit both from greater certainty about the flow of patients to their practices and improved ease of referrals. Managed care organizations and other large purchasers view integrated organizations favorably because of the relative ease of negotiating pricing with one organization instead of several. In addition, quality monitoring, patient case management, and physician and other provider activity can be managed and monitored more efficiently when they are all part of the same organization.

Role of Physicians

Although hospitals have been the designers of integrated systems, physicians, and particularly primary care physicians, form their foundations. The core architecture of any integrated health care organization is a cadre of committed primary care physicians. They are the indispensable actors in an effectively organized geographic distribution strategy, and in managed care networks. Eventually, the result of managed care growth will be the shifting of economic power in most medical communities to primary care physicians.[27]

Involving physicians from the outset in decisions concerning the organization of the integrated system, with due consideration of their roles and economic status, is critical to a system's success. Because physicians are decision makers about what types, how much, and how often care is needed for the system's population, they are critically important to all decisions that impact system organization, patient flow, and referral. In addition, they are the predominant route of entry for all patients who will use a system's services.

Over the years, as the number of vertically integrated systems has grown, a variety of clinical and economic physician-to-system organizations and arrangements also has evolved. As managed care organizations have gained influence in shaping integrated structures and have introduced risk sharing through capitation or other payment models, physicians have seen the benefits of economic alignment with the integrated systems' sponsoring institution.

In the process of creating integrated systems, hospitals have used a variety of mechanisms to attract, retain, and economically align both primary and specialty physicians. Purchasing physician practices, orchestrating the merger of two or more practices, and hiring physicians or groups of physicians as employees have been popular tactics. In addition, hospitals and health systems have created a variety of organizational schemes to recruit otherwise independent practitioners into structures that participate with the hospital in contracting with managed care plans and other group purchasers.

Integrated Care Arrangements

The types and hybrids of hospital/physician/payer arrangements evolving within integrated systems are numerous and diverse. The following three models are provided as illustrations:

1. The management services organization (MSO) model utilizes a separate corporation to provide administrative services to physician groups, negotiate and administer managed care payment arrangements, operate information systems, and carry out the utilization review, quality management, and case management requirements of managed care contracts. The MSO may be owned by a hospital, managed care organization, or private individuals.
2. In the physician-hospital organization (PHO) model, the physicians affiliated with a particular hospital or health care system establish a corporate entity in joint ownership with the hospital. The physicians and hospital are then positioned to negotiate with managed care and other purchasers in a manner reflecting their mutual interests.
3. A hospital or health care system may employ sizeable groups of primary care and specialty physicians. In this model, the hospital is positioned to negotiate with managed care organizations for services and reimbursement on behalf of their physician employees for predetermined arrays of service.

Market Responses to Managed Care

The evolution of health care market responses to the entry of managed care is a subject of significant interest to researchers, payers, consumers, and providers. The economic imperatives and requirements for accountability on both economic and clinical parameters have caused radical shifts in the position of hospitals, physicians, patients, and payers. As managed care plans increase their penetration into markets, the behaviors of market constituents change along some predictable parameters.

In the earliest stage, when managed care is an insignificant influence, services are fragmented, discontinuous, owned and operated by discrete entities, and competitive with like services throughout the marketplace. Fee-for-service payment predominates, and the system tolerates significant overcapacity relative to population needs, along with numerous duplications of facilities and services. Physicians and other providers maintain an insular focus on individual patient and individual service.

In the next stage, brought about by the entry of managed care organizations into the market, some consolidation of services takes place, with some horizontal integration of hospitals and merger of support services in an effort to achieve incremental economies in operations.

The third stage occurs when managed care organizations have succeeded in capturing a material portion of the population. Impetus is generated for vertical integration to facilitate negotiations for insured population groups.

The fourth stage occurs when managed care becomes the predominant form of health insurance in a community. At this point, economic risk sharing arrangements are often introduced as requirements for managed care contracts. Vertically integrated systems continue expansion into more fully comprehensive continuums of care, and further refinements of their relationships with physicians are recasting them as negotiating bodies.

As health care systems evolved in market areas across the United States, forms of arrangement among hospitals, integrated systems, and managed care organizations diversified into new hybrids. The key factor in these developments was that each component of the health care delivery system became accountable for its costs and outcomes of care. All of the developments in response to the emerging dominance of managed care in the U.S. health care delivery system involved wrenching change in the behavior and practices of physicians, consumers, hospitals, managed care plans, traditional insurers, and other purchasers of health care services. System integration mandates also required changes in the processes of care delivery, decisions about capital investment, redesign of information and management systems, and renewed emphasis on health promotion and health maintenance.

Despite its other criticisms, the emergence of managed care has benefited consumers by enhancing continuity and coordination of services and increasing emphasis on health promotion. More efficient use of limited resources also is a positive outcome of systems integration. Regardless of their form, vertically integrated systems of care appear to represent a more rational and continuous approach to delivering health services than the prior fragmented arrangements characterized by the fee-for-service environment.

The emergence of the new system of health care delivery dominated by managed care organizations and the power of other large purchasers does have trade-offs, however. "At the individual level, the clinical choices of consumers may be constrained. Domination of a market by a few networks may foreclose some legitimate clinical alternatives."[28] Anecdotal reports of inappropriate care because of the apparent economic influences on physicians and hospitals continue to surface regularly in the popular media. Medical journals report frequently on alleged compromises in patient care quality as a result of payment constraints imposed by managed care contracts.

Unfortunately, the evolving system of health care delivery presents more questions than it answers. Significant among these questions are:

- How has access to necessary health services for people who are medically indigent been affected by the rise of managed care?
- How have vertically integrated health systems affected the costs, availability, and access to state-of-the-art technology for the populations they serve? In markets highly saturated with managed care, has the cost of health care services declined and/or have the outcomes of care improved?

The implementation of integrated systems will unquestionably continue, driven largely by economic imperatives. Continuing study, observation, and research will be required to determine the long-range effects of these health care reforms on consumers and providers of health care services.

■ The Quality of Hospital Care

It has always been easier to evaluate the quality of the medical care provided in hospitals than that provided in medical offices or other delivery sites because of the availability of comprehensive medical records and other sources of clinical information, systematically collected and stored for later recovery. The definition of quality, however, derives both from various operational factors and from the measures or indicators of quality selected and the value judgments attached to them. For many years, quality was defined as "the degree of conformity with preset standards," and encompassed all of the elements, procedures, and consequences of individual patient–provider encounters. Most often, however, the standards against which care was judged were implicit rather than explicit and existed only in the minds of peer evaluators.

The peer review technique had both benefits and failings. A common peer review quality assurance process used in hospitals until the 1970s was the chart audit. Periodically, an audit committee made up of several providers appointed by the hospital medical staff would review a small sample of patient records and make judgments as to the quality of care provided.

Such audits were ineffective for several reasons. First, the evaluators used internalized or implicit standards to make qualitative judgments. Second, there was no rational basis for chart selection that would permit the evaluators to extrapolate the sample findings to the broader patient population. Third, even if deficiencies were identified, the auditors were reluctant to take corrective action because their deficient colleagues might be on the next audit committee reviewing their patient care.

Avedis Donabedian of the University of Michigan made an important contribution to quality of care studies by defining the three basic components of medical care—structure, process, and outcome. Structural components are the qualifications of the providers, the physical facility, equipment, and other resources, and the characteristics of the organization and its financing.[29] Until the 1960s the contribution of structure to quality was the primary, if not the only, quality assurance mechanism in health care. Traditionally, the health care system relied on credentialing mechanisms, such as licensure, registration, and certification by professional societies and specialty boards, to ensure the quality of clinical care.

Hospital reviews for accreditation by the then Joint Commission on Accreditation of Hospitals were also based almost exclusively on structural criteria. Judgments were made about physical facilities, the equipment, the ratios of professional staff to patients, and the qualifications of the various personnel. The underlying assumption of structural quality reviews was that the better the facilities and the qualifications of the providers, the better the quality of the care rendered.

The past focus on structural criteria assumed quite erroneously that enough was known about the relationship of the structural aspects of care to its processes and outcomes to identify the critical or appropriate structural indicators. It was much later that hospital accreditation involved process criteria, and more recently, outcomes.

The process components are what occur during the encounters between patients and providers. Process judgments include what was done, how appropriate it was, and how well performed, as well as what was omitted that should have been done. The assumption underlying the use of process criteria is that the quality of the actions taken during patient encounters determines or influences the outcomes.

The outcomes of care are all the things that do or do not happen as a result of the medical intervention. Only recently has quality assurance in the hospital field focused on the relationships among structure, process, and outcomes. In the past it had always been argued by providers that so many different variables influence the outcomes of medical care that it is inappropriate and unfair to providers to attribute patient outcomes solely to medical interventions. That argument was dismissed, however, with the introduction of computerized information systems and sophisticated analytical techniques that permit the collection and analysis of data on most or all of the potential intervening influences and allow the findings to be adjusted for patient differences. Now, quality of care data are routinely standardized to account for age, sex, severity of illness, accompanying conditions, and other variables that might influence outcomes.

Landmark Studies of Quality of Hospital Care

In the early 1960s the Columbia University School of Public Health and Administrative Medicine, with M.A. Morehead as director, conducted a study of the quality of hospital care provided to members of the Teamsters Union in New York City. The union was investing about $20 million per year in hospital services for their members and their families. It was a huge sum at that time, and the union wanted to determine whether the quality of those services justified that large expenditure. Teams of medical experts in a variety of specialties were asked to review large samples of patient records and decide whether the care was justified, appropriate, and acceptably provided. The standards of care on which the decisions were based were not explicit and agreed upon beforehand but left to personal judgments of the medical experts reviewing the records.[30]

As might be expected from academically based board-certified specialists using internalized standards for judging the quality of care, they found that medical care provided by physicians, most like themselves, those who were fellows of specialty boards, was more likely to be optimal. They also concluded, after assembling the findings for all of the individual medical and surgical specialties, that the care provided in hospitals closely affiliated with medical schools was better than that provided in other hospitals.

In spite of the bias introduced into the study by the use of implicit standards that reflected the evaluators' personal values, beliefs, and practice styles, the report, for the first time, documented incontrovertibly the proportion of hospital admissions that were deemed unnecessary or questionable; the amount of care that was considered inappropriate, poor, or questionable; and a finding, that the public has yet to fully appreciate, that there are significant differences among hospitals and medical staffs in the quality of care they provide.

It is important to note that the Teamsters study was followed by a host of parallel studies that were more rigorously designed and that used consensually derived explicit performance criteria that reached essentially the same conclusions. This research repeatedly finds that the quality of hospital care is highly variable and is related to the influence of medical school affiliations and to the specialty training of the medical staff.

Variations in Medical Care

In 1973, two researchers, John Wennberg and Alan Gittlesohn, published what would be the first of a series of papers documenting the variations in the amounts and types of medical care provided to patients with the same diagnoses living in different geographic areas.[31]

Those publications emphasized that the amount and cost of hospital treatment in a community had more to do with the number, specialties, and individual preferences of the physicians than the medical conditions of the patients.

At the same time, concerns about the variability of hospital care and the conclusions from studies on its quality prompted federal action. The Social Security Act was amended to create a national network of local professional standards review organizations (PSROs). PSROs were charged with ensuring that health care services purchased in whole or in part by the Medicare, Medicaid, or maternal and child health programs conform to appropriate professional standards and are delivered effectively and efficiently.

The structure and operations of PSROs reflected two long-standing societal assumptions about quality of health care reviews: (1) that providers are the most appropriate evaluators of the quality of the work of other providers, and (2) that, because of regional variation in practice patterns, the review process must be local to be most effective. Both assumptions subsequently were found to be faulty. What was clear, however, when the legislation was passed, was the expectation that physicians would take this opportunity to demonstrate that they could assume responsibility and accountability for monitoring the quality of medical care in their geographical regions.

PSROs engaged in concurrent reviews of the medical necessity of admissions to hospitals and retrospective reviews of some of the medical care provided under Medicaid and Medicare. In fact, they still exist in somewhat different form as professional review organizations. However, rather than having any broad impact on the quality of medical care in their regions, their effectiveness has been limited to judgments about individual cases.

Given the magnitude of the resources devoted to quality assurance and the central role that peer review plays in these efforts, it is of interest to note the work of Ronald Goldman of the Quality Management Office, Department of Veterans Affairs, published in the *Journal of the American Medical Association* in 1992. Using computerized searches of the medical literature, he identified 12 studies that reported data on inter-reviewer agreement of implicit evaluations of patient care episodes based on reviews of medical records. After careful analysis of the findings, he concluded that, "Most of these studies found agreement corrected for chance to be in the range regarded as poor, indicating that physician agreement regarding quality of care is only slightly better than the level expected by chance."[32]

Hazards of Hospitalization

Medical errors have been a serious problem in hospitals for years, but improving patient safety did not become a serious national concern until recently. Although those in the health professions and more knowledgeable members of the public have long been aware of the error-prone nature of hospital care, it was not until the November 1999 release of a report prepared by the prestigious National Academy of Science's Institute of Medicine (IOM) on medical mistakes that the magnitude of the risks to patients receiving hospital care became common public knowledge.

By extrapolating the findings of several well-conducted studies of adverse events occurring in hospitals to the 33.5 million hospital admissions in the United States during 1997, the IOM report concluded that as few as 44,000 and as many as 98,000 deaths occur annually because of medical errors.[33] The report put the magnitude of the problem in the context of other comparable concerns by noting that more people die from medical errors in a year than motor vehicle accidents or breast cancer and that medication errors alone kill more people than workplace injuries.

Errors are defined as "the failure to complete a planned action as intended or the use of a wrong to achieve an aim."[34] Specific types of errors are defined in Exhibit 3–1.

There is general agreement that system deficiencies are the most important factor in the problem, and not incompetent or negligent physicians and other caregivers. Modern medicine with its highly effective but extremely complex diagnostic and therapeutic methods can be formidably risky. Extensive surgical procedures are error-prone as

---

Exhibit 3–1 Types of Errors

DIAGNOSTIC

Error or delay in diagnosis
Failure to employ indicated tests
Use of outmoded tests or therapy
Failure to act on results of monitoring or testing

TREATMENT

Error in the performance of an operation, procedure, or test
Error in administering the treatment
Error in the dose or method of using a drug
Avoidable delay in treatment or in responding to an abnormal test
Inappropriate (not indicated) care

PREVENTIVE

Failure to provide prophylactic treatment
Inadequate monitoring or follow-up of treatment

OTHER

Failure of communication
Equipment failure
Other system failure

Source: Copyright L. Leape, A.G. Lawthers et al., "Preventing Medical Injury," *Quality Review Bulletin,* 19(5) 1993: 144–149.

are increasingly powerful therapeutic drugs. Miscommunication among overstressed employees is common in busy hospitals. With so many steps and so many people involved in the care of hospital patients, the potential for error grows with every patient day, and small lapses develop into large tragedies.

The IOM report presents a series of recommendations to improve the quality of care during the next 10 years. The report lays out a comprehensive strategy for reducing medical errors through a combination of technological, policy, regulatory, and financial strategies intended to make health care safer. Better use of information technology such as bedside computers, avoidance of similar-sounding and look-alike names and packages of medications, and standardization of treatment policies and protocols would help to avoid confusion and reliance on memory and handwritten communications. The most controversial of the recommendations, however, is the call for a nationwide mandatory reporting system that would require states to report all "adverse events that result in death or serious harm."[35]

The health care system and its practicing physicians will have to make radical changes in cultural attitudes and individual prerogatives, however, before the necessary system changes and reporting requirements can be institutionalized. The IOM report, which moved awareness of the magnitude of medical errors from the anonymity of the hospitals to the nation's media and subsequently to the halls of Congress, has already produced vociferous debate over issues of mandatory or voluntary reporting. Questions of liability, confidentiality, and avoidance of punishment must be settled before any reporting legislation can be passed. In the meantime, other recommendations for more focus on patient safety by professional groups, medical societies, health care licensing organizations, and hospital administrations could be followed with more immediate benefits.

Shortage of Nurses Creating Staffing Crisis

Three factors have combined to drive a hospital nursing shortage to crisis proportions. First, increasing dissatisfaction with staffing reductions, overwork, and too little time to maintain the quality of patient care is driving nurses out of hospitals into early retirement or into home or ambulatory care. Second, with the deteriorating reputation of nursing as a career and many other more attractive options, fewer young people are entering that clinical field. Last, aging of the current nurse workforce will accelerate staffing losses. With one-third of the currently employed nurses over 50 years of age and a diminishing pool of new nurses entering the pipeline, hospital nursing in the United States is at a critical juncture.[36]

The consequences are serious. There is increasing evidence that nurse staffing is related to patient outcomes in both medical and surgical cases. Studies indicate a direct link between the number of registered nurses and the time they spend with patients and the number of serious complications and patient deaths. Low nurse staffing increases the likelihood that some patients will suffer pneumonia, shock and cardiac arrest, and gastrointestinal bleeding, and some patients will die as a result.[37]

The shortage of nurses and its consequences have drawn the attention of Congress. During July 2002, Congress passed and the president signed the Nurse Reinvestment Act, which authorizes financial aid programs to attract students into nursing. Clearly, however, many changes need to be made in the hospital work environment to undo the damage that has been done to the reputation of hospital nursing before it will again be an attractive career alternative. One option being debated is state mandates of minimum nurse to patient ratios in acute care hospitals. Whether minimum ratios will induce nurses to return to the hospitals and produce better patient outcomes or create more problems than they would solve is still being debated.

Current Research Efforts in Quality Improvement

After the Joint Commission for the Accreditation of Hospitals recognized the development of multi-institutional hospital networks and changed its name to the Joint Commission on the Accreditation of Healthcare Organizations, it produced a new and quantitatively measurable definition of quality with a results focus. The new definition characterizes the quality of a provider's care as the degree to which the care delivered increases the likelihood of desired patient outcomes and reduces the likelihood of undesired outcomes, given the current state of medical knowledge.

This objective and quantitative definition of quality contrasted sharply with the previous subjective and qualitative definition that required estimates of adherence to somewhat nebulous performance standards. It also left room for nonclinical outcomes, such as accessibility (the ease with which patients can avail themselves of services) and acceptability (the degree to which health care satisfies patients).

Hospitals now conduct regular patient satisfaction studies to obtain patients' views about the services they receive. Such studies encompass several aspects of care, including access, convenience, information received, financial coverage, and perceived quality. It is particularly important for hospital executives to monitor how well their patients' comfort and communication needs were met. Patient satisfaction studies add a new dimension to the definition of quality. "Quality" becomes what the patient receives as judged by the patient, rather than what the facility provides as judged by the providers.

During the decade of the 1980s, when the focus on health care costs caused insurance companies, businesses, and government regulators to become more interested in what was going on in health care, the appropriateness of care became an increasingly important issue. Closely related to the cost and quality dilemma associated with high technology was the problem that some patients received too many procedures, tests, and/or medications that were inappropriate, useless, or even harmful. Although some of the tests and procedures were probably performed to protect the physician or hospital from potential malpractice litigation, some reflected unexplainable regional variations in medical practice, and some were clearly driven by the reimbursement system at the time that rewarded physicians for doing more, not less.

A large number of studies have examined the appropriateness of the use of various medical tests and procedures. Using similar methodologies, researchers compared medical records against well-established criteria for performing specific medical procedures. Those procedures were then rated as performed for "appropriate," "inappropriate," or "equivocal" reasons. The RAND Corporation summarized the findings of a number of RAND-supported research studies, as shown in Figure 3–1.[38]

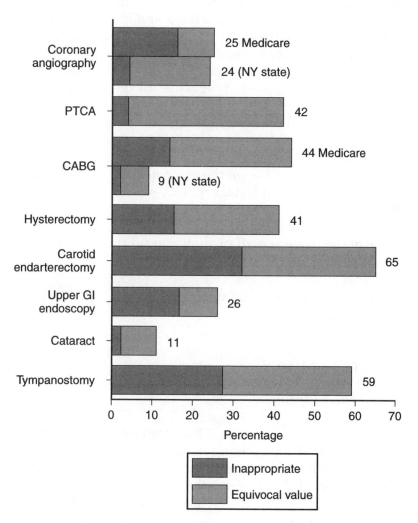

Notes: PTCA, percutaneous transluminal coronary angioplasty; CABG, coronary artery bypass grafting.

Figure 3–1 *Proportion of Procedures Judged Either "Clinically Inappropriate" or "Of Equivocal Value": Summary of Selected Studies.*
Source: Reprinted with permission from RAND Health Research Highlights, Assessing the Appropriateness of Care: How Much Is Too Much? RB-4522, © RAND.

Overall, it appears that a significant proportion of medical procedures are performed for inappropriate reasons. The proportion of all procedures judged to be questionable or equivocal also shows wide-ranging variation. "On average, it appears that one-third or more of all procedures performed in the United States are of questionable benefit."[39]

Responsibility of Governing Boards for Quality of Care

Although the medical staffs and other professional providers of patient care in hospitals make the decisions and carry out the procedures that lead to the patient care outcomes, it is the governing boards of hospitals that are ultimately responsible for the quality of the care provided. The board is responsible for the hospital's quality assurance and risk management programs, all the quality improvement programs, and the oversight of the medical staff. The latter responsibility is discharged primarily through its oversight of and final decisions regarding appointments and privilege delineations of medical staff members. Otherwise, oversight of the medical staff is delegated to the various committees of the medical staff organization.

The board oversees the hospital's quality assurance programs and related functions by monitoring specific information regarding program effectiveness in the identification and resolution of patient care problems and of the medical staff in quality assurance. Some of the indicators that hospital boards regularly review are:

- Mortality rates by department or service
- Hospital-acquired infections
- Patient complaints
- Patient falls
- Adverse drug reactions
- Unplanned returns to surgery
- Hospital-incurred traumas

Needless to say, only the most diligent and dedicated lay board members are capable of interpreting these data and then formulating clear and understandable explanations for their occurrence. Health care reforms are intended to address these problems specifically.

Incremental Quality Improvement

Many hospital executives faced with growing resistance to the cost of redundant services and to inexplicable performance variability have turned to prevailing management strategies to improve the efficiency and quality of their service operations. With impetus created by a mandate from the Joint Commission, hospital administrators have engaged their employees in programs of continuous quality improvement or total quality management (CQI/TQM). These programs are predicated on the theory that empowering staff who are closest to the points of service delivery and trained in the techniques of incremental improvement will most effectively identify and solve operational problems and improve the quality and efficiency of patient care. The programs depend heavily, however, on the willingness of those in the upper levels of the management hierarchy to grant, and employees in the lower level to accept, the authority to make decisions and control resources commensurate with their scope of responsibility.

Although there is ample evidence that CQI/TQM often works well to improve the operations of individual units within hospitals, there are a number of obstacles to achieving broad institutional change through strategies of incremental improvement. Evaluative research suggests that employees accustomed to working in the authoritarian management hierarchy common to most hospitals are apprehensive about assuming the power to make more decisions and the accompanying accountability for the consequences of those decisions.[40] What many employees want instead is a way to communicate their expertise to management without assuming more responsibility in an environment in which it is all too easy to make well-intended errors.

It may also be too little and too late for hospitals under severe competitive pressures to engage in cautious process improvement efforts. J.P. Lathrop, author of *Restructuring Health Care*, considers the use of quality improvement initiatives to achieve significant institution-wide change a proven failure. He points out that, after three decades of trying to influence operating performance by implementing incremental changes, all the hospital industry has to show for it are unacceptable annual increases in the hospital-medical care portion of the consumer price index.[41]

▪ Forces of Reform: Cost, Quality, and Access

The performance benchmarks of cost, quality, and access that, with few exceptions, hospitals addressed for decades with moderate enthusiasm and little, if any, effect, have now become the survival criteria for the future. Since the scientific breakthroughs and technology advancements that made hospitals the complex institutions they have become, hospital care has been both admired for its diagnostic and therapeutic accomplishments and criticized for its costly inefficiencies, duplications, and inequities in access and quality. Ironically, the same high technology that contributed so much to hospitals' medical achievements also has been used to reveal their performance shortcomings in uncompromising detail. The sophisticated computerized clinical information systems that supported the research that focused on the cost-effectiveness or outcomes of expensive medical interventions has increasingly documented and given public recognition to system deficiencies. Studies like that of the IOM,[42] which took two years of reviewing scientific papers, conducting hearings, and making site visits at health care institutions, came to the conclusion that the poor quality of health care is a major problem in the United States. Citing widespread overuse of expensive technologies, underuse of inexpensive "caring" services, and error-prone application of health care services, these studies concluded that the system deficiencies not only wasted money, but also actually harmed patients.[43] The IOM report from 1999 revealed the magnitude of those errors by estimating the number of lives lost annually through medical mistakes.

The media attention to these operational deficiencies and organizational breakdowns, combined with the changing values and expectations of a better-educated consumer public, has had a significant impact on public and professional perceptions of health care systems. Public confidence in the leaders of medical institutions and professions has fallen dramatically from 73 percent in the mid-1960s to 35 percent in 1988.[44]

A recent study by Princeton Survey Research Associates, however, reflects the public's changing opinions about who to blame for the problems that arise in obtaining health care.[45] About half (51 percent) of those with some form of health coverage said their family has had at least one negative experience with a health insurance plan in the last year. About a third had problems getting their insurer's approval for a particular form of treatment. Others (20 percent) had difficulty obtaining an appointment with a physician, and 14 percent of those studied were forced to change physicians or lose their coverage. Under these frustrating circumstances, Americans are attributing most of their problems to their insurers rather than their physicians. Thus, the latest ratings of the health care industry put managed care plans at the bottom of the public esteem scale, just below the pharmaceutical companies responsible for the high costs of prescription drugs. In this latest survey, nurses were ranked as the most esteemed component of the health care industry, followed by physicians.

Certainly, the continuing public debate over the escalating costs of health care and the increasing number of major employer/employee disputes over sharing the costs of insurance premiums have raised the level of health cost awareness of most Americans. In addition, the disruptions in long-standing relationships between specialist physicians and patients in managed care arrangements and the position promulgated by managed care organizations that some medical care is wasteful and unproductive have focused patients' attention on the possibility that in some cases there may be inverse relationships between costs and quality.

Whatever the final form of U.S. health care after the industrywide reformation takes place, there is general agreement that hospitals will no longer be the axis on which the rest of the system turns. Reduced in both capacity and importance, hospitals will simply be essential components of community-based and integrated systems of primary, tertiary, long-term, and home health care with significant public health and disease prevention functions.

Stephen Shortell of Northwestern University has encapsulated in seven steps the changes that hospitals will have to make to reposition themselves to function effectively in the future. Those steps are:

1. Becoming part of an integrated health system
2. Developing new management structures
3. Building capacity for population-based needs assessment
4. Forging new relationships with physicians
5. Reengineering clinical processes
6. Implementing total quality management
7. Focusing on outcomes

It is important to note that there will be great variation in the capability of America's thousands of hospitals to adjust to what they will interpret as radical reversals of form and function. In the new hospital market economy, however, it appears likely that the Darwinian law of nature, survival of the fittest, will determine which hospitals will remain to serve the American public in the twenty-first century.

■ Notes

1. R. Stevens, *In Sickness and in Wealth: American Hospitals in the Twentieth Century* (New York: Basic Books, Inc., 1989).
2. Stevens, *In Sickness and in Wealth*, 399.
3. Stevens, *In Sickness and in Wealth*, 293.
4. Stevens, *In Sickness and in Wealth*, 319.
5. Stevens, *In Sickness and in Wealth*, 320.
6. E.D. Teisberg et al., *The Hospital Sector in 1992* (Boston: Harvard Business School, 1991).
7. J. Greene and S. Lutz, "Hospital Chairs," *Modern Healthcare* 1, no. 21 (1995): 43–49.

8. M.L. Seifert et al., "Hospital, Employment, and Price Indicators for the Health Care Industry: First Quarter 1999," *Health Care Financing Review* 21, no. 1 (Fall 1999): 79–121.

9. American Hospital Association. Resource Center Fact Sheet: Fast Facts on U.S. Hospitals from *Hospital Statistics*. www.hospitalconnect.com/aha/resource_center/fastfacts/fast_facts_US_hospitals.html (14 August 2000).

10. Siefert, "Hospital, Employment, and Price Indicators for the Health Care Industry," 79–121.

11. D. Bellandi, "Spinoffs, Big Deals Dominate in '99," *Modern Healthcare* 30, no. 2 (Jan. 10, 2000): 36.

12. "Money Crunch: One-Third of U.S. Hospitals Face Financial Ruin." *American Hospital Association News*. www.hospitalconnect.com/jsp/article.jsp?dcrpath=AHA/NewsStory_Article/data/AHANEWS2A1484domain=AHA NEWS (11 July 2000). Accessed 13 August 2000.

13. J.K. Iglehart, "Health Policy Report: The American Health Care System," *The New England Journal of Medicine* 326, no. 14 (1992): 962–967.

14. R.R. Gillies et al., "Best Practices in Managed Organized Delivery Systems," *Hospitals and Health Services Administration*. Vol. 42, no. 3, Fall 1997, 299–321.

15. U.S. Department of Commerce, *County Business Patterns*, Government Printing Office, 1997, 34–36.

16. A.C. Bachmeyr, *Hospital Care in the United States: A Study by the Commission on Hospital Care* (Cambridge, MA: Harvard University Press by Commonwealth Fund, 1947).

17. G. Anders, "Hospitals Rush to Remodel to Offer Subacute Care—And Get Paid Twice," *Wall Street Journal*, 3 October 1996, A1, A8.

18. S.M. Shortell, *The Future of Hospitals and Health Care Management* (Washington, DC: VA Office of Research and Development, n.d.).

19. R.J. Bulger, "The Role of Academic Health Centers in a Reformed Health Care System," *The Journal of American Health Policy* 2, no. 6 (1992): 33–38.

20. M. Hammer and J. Champy, *Reengineering the Corporation: A Manifesto for Business Revolution* (New York: HarperCollins Publishers, Inc., 1993).

21. M. Gerteis et al., *Through the Patient's Eyes: Understanding and Promoting Patient-Centered Care* (San Francisco: Jossey-Bass, Publishers, 1993).

22. L. Sunshine and J.W. Wright, *The Best Hospitals in America* (New York: Henry Holt and Company, 1987).

23. Sunshine and Wright, *The Best Hospitals in America*.

24. C.E. Aydin et al., *Patient-Focused Care in the Hospital: Restructuring and Redesign Methods to Achieve Better Outcomes*, vol. 4 (New York: Faulkner & Gray, 1995).

25. G.L. McManus et al., "The Integrator of Care: A Coordinated Health Care System," *Health Care Strategic Management* 10, no. 2 (1993): 1, 17–19.

26. R. Kropf, Chapter 13, "Planning for Health Services" in *Health Care Delivery in the United States*, ed. A.R. Kovner (New York: Springer Publishing Co., Inc., 1995), 353.

27. J.C. Goldsmith, "Driving the Nitroglycerin Truck," *Healthcare Forum Journal* (March/April 1993): 40.

28. D. Schactman and S.H. Altman, "Market Consolidation, Antitrust, and Public Policy in the Health Care Industry: Agenda for Future Research," *Health Tracking Report* (Princeton, NJ: The Robert Wood Johnson Foundation, 1995), 14.

29. A. Donabedian, "Evaluating the Quality of Medical Care," *Millbank Memorial Fund Quarterly* 44, no. 2 (1966): 166–206.

30. Columbia University, *A Study of the Quality of Hospital Care Secured by a Sample of Teamster Family Members in New York City* (New York: Columbia University School of Public Health and Administrative Medicine, 1964).

31. J.E. Wennberg and A. Gittlesohn, "Small Area Variation in Health Care Delivery," *Science* 182 (14 December 1973): 1102–1108.

32. R.L. Goldman, "The Reliability of Peer Assessments of Quality of Care," *Journal of the American Medical Association* 267 (1992): 958–960.

33. L.T. Kohn et al., *To Err Is Human: Building a Safer Health System* (Washington, DC: Institute of Medicine, 1999), 1–4.

34. L.T. Kohn et al., *To Err Is Human: Building a Safer Health System*, 3.

35. L.T. Kohn et al., *To Err Is Human: Building a Safer Health System*, 75.

36. R.W. Dworkin, "Where Have All the Nurses Gone?," *The Public Interest* (Summer 2002): 23–36.

37. J. Needleman et al., "Nurse Staffing Levels and the Quality of Care in Hospitals," *New England Journal of Medicine* 346, no. 22 (May 2002), 1715–1722.

38. RAND Health Research Highlights, *Assessing the Appropriateness of Care: How Much Is Too Much?*, RB-4522 (Santa Monica, CA: RAND Corporation, 1998).

39. RAND Health Research Highlights, *Assessing the Appropriateness of Care: How Much Is Too Much?*

40. M.A. Counte et al., "Total Quality Management in Healthcare Organizations: How Are Employees Affected?" *Hospital and Health Services Administration* 37, no. 4 (1992): 503–518.

41. J.P. Lathrop, *Restructuring Health Care: The Patient-Focused Paradigm* (San Francisco: Jossey-Bass, Publishers, 1993).

42. K.N. Lohr, *Medicare: A Strategy for Quality Assurance*, vol. I (Washington, D.C.: National Academy Press, 1990).

43. R.H. Palmer and M.E. Adams, "Quality Improvement/Quality Assurance Taxonomy: A Framework," in *Putting Research to Work in Quality Improvement and Quality Assurance*, eds. M.L. Grady, J. Bernstein, and S. Robinson (Washington, D.C.: U.S. Department of Health and Human Services, 1993), 13–37.

44. R.J. Blendon, "The Public's View of the Future of Health Care," *Journal of the American Medical Association* 259 (1988): 3587–3593.

45. Princeton Survey Research Associates, "Health Care and the 2000 Election," http://www.pbs.org/criticalcondition/information/surveyHSP.pdf (16 October 2000). Accessed 24 October 2000.

Chapter 4

Ambulatory Care

This chapter reviews the major elements of ambulatory (outpatient) care. Ambulatory care encompasses a diverse and growing sector of the health care delivery system. Physician services are the chief component. However, hospital outpatient and emergency departments, community health centers, departments of health, and voluntary agencies also contribute important services, particularly for the uninsured and vulnerable populations. Ambulatory surgery is a continuously expanding component of ambulatory care, as new technology enables more procedures to be performed safely and economically outside the hospital.

■ Overview and Trends

Ambulatory care comprises health care services that do not require overnight hospitalization. Ambulatory care is the predominant mode of health care delivery in the United States. Once largely consisting of visits to private physicians' offices and hospital outpatient clinics and emergency departments, ambulatory care today encompasses a broad and expanding array of services.

New medical and diagnostic procedures and technological advancements have allowed procedures previously requiring hospitalization to be performed on an outpatient basis. As early as a decade ago, most surgical procedures commonly warranted a few, and often several, days' stay in the hospital. Now, the majority of all surgical procedures are performed on an ambulatory basis.

In addition to the numerous new diagnostic and treatment tools available in the outpatient setting and the advanced technology that makes outpatient treatment safe and effective, financial mandates also have played a major role in moving services to the ambulatory arena. Beginning in the 1980s, prospective hospital reimbursement replaced retrospective payment on a national scale through Medicare's initiation of the diagnosis-related group (DRG) payment system. The new payment system provided financial incentives to decrease the duration of inpatient stays and to increase efficiency in service delivery. Hospitals responded to the new payment system by shifting procedures and services amenable to outpatient delivery from the more expensive inpatient environment to less expensive and more efficient ambulatory delivery systems.

Both DRGs and increasing pressures from health care purchasers to control costs contributed to the rapid expansion of health maintenance organizations (HMOs) and other forms of managed care. With an emphasis on providing services in the least expensive, most effective manner possible, managed care organizations exerted a powerful influence that compelled a shift toward the appropriate use of ambulatory services to replace more expensive, but, ostensibly, no more effective inpatient care.

Ambulatory care capacity has expanded in both the hospital-based and nonhospital-based, or "free-standing," settings. Historically, virtually all ambulatory or outpatient clinics were operated within the hospital's main facilities or in contiguous facilities on the hospital campuses. Most larger hospitals still operate clinic services on site, and many have retained ambulatory surgical services within the main facility in response to community need, physician demand, and teaching activity. In many cases, the conversion of underutilized inpatient units has also provided a cost-effective means of accommodating the shift to ambulatory surgical services and other ambulatory procedures within the hospital.

The past decade has also seen a growing trend in the expansion of hospital service networks to include geographically distributed free-standing facilities throughout their service areas, both for routine diagnosis and treatment and for ambulatory surgical services. In addition to cost considerations, two other factors have influenced this trend for hospitals. First, the 1980s and 1990s saw a rising consumer demand for facilities and services that are conveniently located and easily accessible, two factors frequently lacking on hospital campuses and the large building complexes associated with them. This is particularly true for large teaching hospitals, which are often located in congested urban centers and perceived as inconvenient to increasing numbers of suburban dwellers. Second, with the growing concerns of inner city hospitals about competition with other institutions for market share of profitable outpatient services and referrals for inpatient care, hospitals recognized the need to expand their service distribution network to larger segments of the community by establishing conveniently located facilities. Also, hospitals have recognized that some ambulatory services, such as surgery, can be operated most efficiently off site, removed from the scheduling complexities and other requirements of a system that must accommodate a vast array of provider and patient needs.

Independent of hospital organizations, for-profit corporations' free-standing facilities providing ambulatory, primary, specialty, and surgical services have proliferated. In addition to profitability and cost-control features attractive to insurers, responsiveness to consumer preferences also has been a primary driver in these developments.

The decade of the 1990s saw a continuing upward trend in the total number of ambulatory care facilities owned and operated by hospitals and independent chains. Services provided by these facilities are diverse and represent a response to population demographics in their respective service areas as well as reimbursement opportunities. A partial listing of the array of ambulatory care facilities includes adult day care, cancer treatment, diagnostic imaging, kidney dialysis, pain management, physical therapy, cardiac rehabilitation, outpatient surgery, occupational health, women's health, and wound care. The number of visits to hospital-sponsored outpatient facilities of all these types continued to increase throughout the 1990s.[1]

A significant corollary to developments in ambulatory care delivery for hospital-operated and independent organizations has been the entry of physicians into the business of outpatient diagnostic, treatment, and surgical services previously available to their practices only in the hospital setting. The same factors operative in the larger industry—technological advances making the purchase, maintenance, and operation of the required equipment feasible and cost-effective in free-standing facilities; consumer demand for convenient, user-friendly environments; and profitability—have compelled this development.

Physician involvement in this arena has paralleled that of hospitals in practice areas, such as ophthalmological surgery for lens replacement and laser therapy, certain types of gynecological surgery, fiber-optic gastrointestinal diagnosis, chemotherapy, renal dialysis, computed tomography (CT) scanning, magnetic resonance imaging (MRI), and more. The implications of this trend for hospitals' business volume and revenue have been significant as physicians and hospitals emerge as competitors engaged in the same lines of business.

Although ambulatory care is discussed in the context of its major organizational models, it is important to bear in mind that the ambulatory care delivery system is changing and growing rapidly. Its management in various organizational models is evolving and includes new efforts to measure its quality relative to cost. Its service constellation also is growing rapidly and becoming more diverse. As the reimbursement system continues to evolve and new treatment modalities are developed, the role of ambulatory service providers is undergoing continuous refinement. Although we cannot expect to address every extant hybrid of the evolving ambulatory care delivery system, this chapter provides a framework for understanding the origins, development, and future direction of this increasingly important sector of our health care delivery system.

■ Private Medical Office Practice

When discussing ambulatory care, it is common to think of services organized and delivered under some institutional aegis, such as a hospital or the community-based clinics of public health departments. However, private physician office practices constitute the predominant mode of ambulatory care in the United States. In 2000, the National Center for Health Statistics estimated that 823.5 million visits were made to physician offices.[2] The way physicians organize and operate their private practices has evolved because of a variety of factors. The single most significant development has been a continuing increase in the number of group practice arrangements and their size. An increasing number of physicians are partners or salaried employees of group practices.[3]

The origins of group practice can be traced to the Mayo Clinic in the late nineteenth century. The Mayo Clinic group practice generated considerable controversy among physicians. A 1932 report by The Committee on the Costs of Medical Care endorsed organized group practices and the use of insurance payments. The American Medical Association (AMA) condemned the report, declaring that group and salaried physicians were unethical. The controversy erupted into a legal battle when Group Health Insurance (GHI) was organized in Washington, D.C., in 1937. The AMA informed physicians that the plan was unethical and expelled all GHI-salaried physicians. Hospitals received lists of "reputable physicians." "The Washington, D.C., Medical Society and the AMA were subsequently indicted, found guilty, and fined for having conspired to monopolize medical practice."[4] Around the country, local medical societies lost attempts to obstruct the formation of group practices. For the next few decades, nasty confrontations occurred as physician participation in developing group health plans was sought. Participating physicians were socially ostracized and denied hospital privileges. By the 1950s, because of effective legal challenges against organized medicine and a physician shortage, opposition to group practice subsided.

Before 1950, most physicians had solo practices. Since then, rising specialization, changing economics, and the desire for more control over their lifestyles have caused physicians to group together, either in single fields, such as primary care, or into multispecialty groups. Group practice involves several physicians practicing together in some type of coordinated arrangement. In contrast to an individual physician, fee-for-service payment basis, most groups pay their members a salary augmented with a percentage of the net profits.

The old solo-practice model made the physician solely responsible for his or her entire patient caseload 24 hours a day, 7 days a week, every day of the year. Before the proliferation of specialties, these physicians normally provided all the medical care required by their patients, with the exception of surgery or occasional consultation. The demands on the time and stamina of these practitioners were enormous. Aside from occasional informal coverage arrangements with a colleague to allow for time off, their schedules were relentless and unpredictable.

Beginning in the 1960s, several factors influenced a major shift from the solo mode of private practice to group practice development. Social movements in the United States produced a heightened awareness of lifestyle adaptations that allowed healthy accommodation for personal growth and balance between professional and work responsibilities. In the same period, medical specialization burgeoned as the pace of the acquisition of new knowledge and technological advances increased exponentially. Rapidly advancing knowledge in every field of medicine and the resulting specialization created new challenges, both for the solo generalist and the specialist. Most obvious were increasing demands on physicians to maintain a command of a body of knowledge that was continuously yielding new diagnostic and therapeutic breakthroughs in virtually every field of practice.

With the introduction of Medicare reimbursement in 1966, the private medical office and its financial, billing, and reimbursement processes were inextricably altered. Prior to government's entry into the private practice financing arena, physicians were reimbursed largely from two sources: personal patient payments and third-party private insurance. The latter was made mostly under plans offered by Blue Cross/Blue Shield and a relatively small number of other private indemnity carriers. Billing and collection were relatively simple. When Medicare began providing primary coverage for everyone over age 65, private physicians' offices found themselves dealing with not only a new carrier but also a vast array of new government regulations and fee schedules. In addition, supplemental private insurance contracts became available for Medicare recipients to reimburse the balance Medicare did not cover. For the private physician's office, regulation, record maintenance, and billing requirements burgeoned overnight in complexity and volume. Solo-practice office administration, once the province of the physicians themselves, with possibly a receptionist and a part-time bookkeeper, began to require an increased level of sophistication and a great deal more time.

Other factors also influenced the shift to group practice. Malpractice insurance costs began to rise dramatically in the 1970s. Inflation fueled rising office lease and rental expenses. The need for more sophisticated administrative support services increased with advancing technology and more complex billing and recordkeeping requirements. And as technology advanced and diagnostic equipment such as electrocardiography became available for in-office use, groups benefited by sharing purchase costs and ensuring the volume necessary to justify ongoing staffing and maintenance. Physicians recognized that group practice could provide major economies of scale in office operations by providing opportunities to share the administrative overhead for office operations.

Group practice evolved in two forms. One consisted of groups of physicians in the same discipline, usually primary care, surgery, obstetrics, or pediatrics. The other form was multidisciplinary specialty practices, usually including primary care physicians in collaboration with several major specialties or subspecialties. There were important features that both generalist and specialist physicians found more attractive in group practice than solo practice. First, although typically each physician carried his or her own caseload of patients, physicians could arrange a routine, preplanned schedule of after-hours call and weekend and vacation coverage among group members. This enabled members to preplan and schedule time off with certainty of coverage. Another attractive dimension of group practice was that it provided a professionally supportive environment.

With the continuing growth of medical information and knowledge required to maintain state-of-the-art competencies and an ever-expanding range of diagnostic and therapeutic alternatives available to them, physicians were able to easily access each other's knowledge and experience in an informal consultative environment provided by the group. Also, this interchange of information not only provided professional support to physicians but also introduced an informal system of peer review to each physician's practice, which, at least in theory, could contribute to patient care quality. Group practice also enabled patients to be oriented to alternative coverage arrangements, so their expectation of seeing or contacting another physician in the absence of their own could be established in advance.

Multispecialty group practices evolved for many of the same reasons as single-specialty groups. For specialists, a major benefit was that membership in a group meant that reliance on patient referrals from other community physicians was reduced because economic incentives made keeping the business inside the group beneficial to all group members. Patients also benefited by having diagnosis, treatment, and consultation services brought together at one convenient location. The arrangement also facilitated communication and coordination of results and findings and speeded the turnaround of information.

Surgical group practices evolved similarly to those in the general and other specialty medical fields for similar reasons. However, surgeons have tended to avoid multispecialty grouping. Instead, most are either general surgeons or specialists in such areas as gastrointestinal, cardiothoracic, vascular, or orthopaedic surgery. Economies of scale afford the same advantages in these practices as those in general medical and multispecialty practices with respect to sharing operating costs.

Growth in managed care caused changes in the characteristics of physician practices. Between 1990 and 1996, the percentage of physicians contracted with managed care organizations increased from 61 percent to 88 percent.[5] A 2001 report from The Center for Studying Health System Change found that 90 percent of physicians contract with managed care organizations.[6] Also, during the last decade, practices grew in size. In 1990, the average group practice size was 10.6 physicians; in 1996 it was 14.5 physicians. In the same period, the proportion of physicians working as sole practitioners or self-employed in group practices declined, while the proportion of physician employees grew from 32 percent to 42 percent.[7] Larger practice size enabled physician groups to compete more aggressively for contracts in the managed care marketplace, helped to control costs through greater administrative efficiency, and facilitated spreading the financial risks associated with managed care contracts. Recent reports suggest that physician group size may be decreasing, as managed care organizations loosen contracting restrictions.[8]

■ Other Ambulatory Care Practitioners

In addition to physicians, there are a number of other licensed health care professionals who conduct practices independently in ambulatory settings. Among the most common are dentists, podiatrists, social workers, psychologists, physical therapists, and optometrists. Like physicians, they may practice singly or in single-specialty or multispecialty groups. For example, there are general solo-practice dentists and multispecialty dental groups who provide general preventive and curative services, as well as services in specialties such as periodontics and orthodontics. Likewise, psychologists in a group may include both generalists and specialists in forensic, child, and other types of psychological interventions. Chapter 6 discusses physicians, nurses, and other health professions in detail.

■ Ambulatory Care Services of Hospitals: History and Trends

Acute care voluntary hospitals have operated outpatient clinics since the nineteenth century. The early ones were located predominantly in urban centers whose indigent populations lacked access to private medical care. At that time, the provision of outpatient services was largely a function of government-sponsored public hospitals. With the proliferation of the voluntary not-for-profit hospitals beginning in the early twentieth century, outpatient clinics provided a means for those hospitals to fulfill part of their charitable mission by serving low-income populations who had little, if any, access to private physicians. Hospital outpatient clinics also provided a teaching setting for university-affiliated hospitals, which trained physicians as part of their community mission.

Historically, hospital outpatient clinics were viewed as a low-status component of the constellation of hospital care. J.H. Knowles, who was then director of the Massachusetts General Hospital, wrote in 1965, "Turning to the outpatient department of the urban hospital, we find the stepchild of the institution. Traditionally, this has been the least popular area in which to work, and as a result, few advances in medical care and teaching have been harvested here for the benefit of the community."[9]

Because they cared for a population that was largely people with low incomes, hospital outpatient clinics addressed complex medical and social problems, poor compliance with treatment regimens, and discontinuity in care. The outpatient clinics were not generally well supported by the hospital with equipment and staff. They were most often staffed by medical students, who were mandated to serve there, and by the hospital-affiliated physicians of lowest tenure or rank, who agreed to see clinic patients in return for admitting privileges.

Although it remains true that hospital outpatient clinics, particularly those in urban centers, still function as the community's safety net for people who are medically indigent, the status of those services within the hospital and the roles and positions of physicians working in them have changed radically. The change has been most dramatic since the early 1980s, when an array of factors converged to increase both the volume and the scope of available hospital outpatient services. Far from the stepchild image characterized by Knowles, outpatient clinical services are now viewed by hospitals as the primary areas of profitable development, helping to ensure a source of inpatient admissions and generating revenue from the use of hospital ancillary services.

In many significant ways, the hospital outpatient clinics of today are light years apart from those of only 20 years ago. No longer the repository for reluctant physicians and students obligated to work there, they are increasingly organized along the lines of private physician group practices, and are aesthetically pleasant, well equipped, and customer oriented. With respect to the hospitals' financial picture, the direction is clear. In 1980 outpatient services revenue constituted only 13 percent of total voluntary hospital revenues in the United States.[10] The figure rose dramatically throughout the 1980s and 1990s and continues to increase. By 1998 the outpatient share of total revenue had risen to 32.8 percent, and by 2001 represented 35.8 percent (see Figure 4–1).[11]

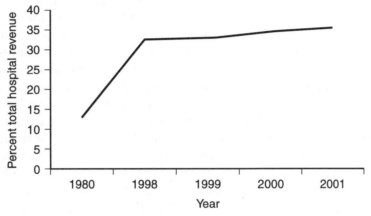

Figure 4–1 Outpatient Revenue as a Share of Total Voluntary Hospital Revenue. *Source:* I. Fraser et al., "Ambulatory Care: A Decade of Change In Health Care Delivery," *Journal of Ambulatory Care Management* 16, no. 4; Center for Medicare and Medicaid Services, "Health Indicators, Table 1: Selected Community Hospital Statistics, 1998–2001.

Because clinic services traditionally were organized both for the social goal of caring for the needy and for providing teaching and research opportunities, they have tended to be organized by human organ systems and the specific diseases that afflict them. For example, medical clinics, in addition to general medicine, might include clinics for dermatology (skin), cardiology (heart), gastroenterology (digestive tract), rheumatology (bone and connective tissue), and other specialties. In addition to general surgery, surgical clinics might include such specialties as orthopaedics (bone), vascular (circulatory system), and others. This type of organization was attractive to attending specialists, researchers, and educators because it allowed narrowly focused concentration on particular patient complaints and illnesses. Beyond this benefit, however, the complex interactions among physicians and patients inherent in this anatomic organization of services have a broad range of both positive and negative implications for both.

For the patient, specialty clinics provide a sophisticated approach to diagnosis and treatment by physicians with special interests and training in their conditions. Also, the teaching functions of clinics often result in extremely thorough and exhaustive examination and case review for the students' benefit that might not otherwise occur in a nonteaching setting.

Treatment in hospital specialty clinics also has drawbacks for patients. Often, specialty clinics treat patients only on certain days each week or on two or three days per month, depending on demand for the service. Patients with multiple conditions may have to visit several specialty clinics, necessitating numerous return visits at which different physicians see them. Because communication among physicians in different specialty clinics can be uncertain, patients may receive conflicting advice or instruction, may be medicated inappropriately with drugs prescribed by several different specialists, and may "fall through the cracks" when a complaint arises that does not seem to fit the specialty area of one of their providers. Similarly, for the physician, this type of categorical treatment environment requires a high degree of initiative to maintain accurate, current information on a patient being treated by multiple specialists. Beginning in the 1950s, as medical specialization increased, additional subdivision of the teaching hospitals' outpatient clinic services was required to support medical training needs, further exacerbating these problems of continuity and coordination of care. The training requirements of medical students and residents, who could be required to rotate through different specialty clinics as often as monthly, created still more rifts in continuity for patients who, in the course of one illness, might be seen by several different practitioners in the same clinic.

Beginning in the early 1980s, several influences began to have an impact on how hospital outpatient clinic services were organized and delivered. One major influence was the adoption of the DRG hospital reimbursement methodology, which emphasized decreased lengths of stay to achieve cost savings. For hospitals, an anticipated result would be declining inpatient revenues. Another major factor was the growing importance of managed care organizations and their emphasis on the role of primary medical care. These issues also brought a heightened realism to several years of growing concern on the part of medical educators. The uncontrolled proliferation of specialists at the expense of maintaining a balanced supply of general physicians would have to be reversed to respond to payer and rising consumer demands for more cost-effective, efficient, and coordinated care.

Facing declining inpatient revenue, increasing influences of managed care, and shifting medical education emphasis to primary medicine, hospitals initiated reorganization and expansion plans for outpatient clinic services that focused heavily on primary care areas. Teaching hospitals planned jointly with their affiliated medical schools, and nonteaching facilities followed suit to pursue expansion of both the volume and the array of outpatient services with primary care as the core. Teaching hospitals also undertook outpatient clinic reorganizations, creating primary care centers under the direction of paid, full-time "geographic" faculty department heads with administrative, clinical, and teaching oversight responsibility.

Hospitals hired full-time and part-time physicians as employees who, with medical school faculty appointments, undertook ongoing responsibility for day-to-day patient care, teaching, and supervision of students and residents. Primary care physician employees were organized into practice group models along the lines of private group practices. This primary care model provided a rational structure for the general medical care of clinic patients and helped ensure appropriate referrals and coordination of patient care within and among the outpatient clinic specialty units.

The group model of outpatient primary care also more adequately supported the hospitals' teaching mission by alleviating reliance upon voluntary physician staffing of clinic sessions and student supervision responsibilities. Medical students and residents were provided a more supportive and consistent learning environment by interacting with members of the practice group continuously instead of with different mentors over the course of their rotation. Patients benefited from improved coordination of their care and the opportunity to develop a relationship with an individual provider, who functioned as their private attending physician. Although the distribution and organization of most specialty clinic services has not changed appreciably in teaching hospitals, developments in the organization of primary care in hospital-based clinics have made a major contribution to the coordination and appropriate delivery of services to hospital-based outpatient clinic consumers.

Outpatient business continued to expand, and while hospital admissions and lengths of stay decreased, similar reorganizations also were undertaken in certain consumer-sensitive service areas. As one example, during the 1980s, the upscale, childbearing-age female population began spinning off into a major consumer group. Hospitals saw an opportunity to attract new business by reorganizing obstetrics and gynecology services. The old, hospital-based clinics were relabeled with attractive titles such as "Women's Center," and facilities were renovated, decorated, and equipped to mimic state-of-the-art private medical offices. The purely clinical services were augmented by free or low-cost health information and education services, with emphasis on prevention, wellness, and personal service. Hospitals undertook extensive public relations and media campaigns to attract the privately insured and self-paying population. Many other similar initiatives were undertaken by hospitals in other outpatient clinical areas that appeared to hold promise for new business and enhanced revenue streams.

Although major changes have occurred in the organization and delivery of hospital outpatient clinics over the past 20 years, fiscal and operational challenges remain for the urban-based teaching hospitals' outpatient clinics. Some have enjoyed considerable success in attracting new patients with private insurance and self-pay capability and have succeeded in achieving a healthier balance in their previously predominant caseload of Medicaid or charity care patients. However, as long as our health care system leaves millions of individuals with inadequate or no insurance concentrated heavily in urban areas, it can be expected that the caseloads of hospital-based outpatient clinics will remain heavily dominated by the medically indigent population.

■ Hospital Emergency Services

Over 90 percent of all U.S. community hospitals provide emergency services.[12] In 2000, there were an estimated 108 million visits to hospital emergency departments, a 14 percent increase since 1997.[13] The increase in emergency department visits is attributed to overall population growth and increases in the numbers of older Americans. Individuals 75 years of age and older use emergency departments 66 percent more often than the general population.[14] Today, emergency departments in most hospitals are highly sophisticated facilities equipped with advanced technology and specialty staff, available 24 hours a day, 365 days a year. Although they are designed to care for life-threatening illness or injury, the public increasingly looks to them for medical care that ranges from the unnecessary to the routine. A high proportion of emergency department visits are deemed to be nonurgent (see Figure 4–2).

One contributing factor to inappropriate emergency department use is that patients' self-interpretation of symptoms may cause them to believe erroneously that they have a serious or life-threatening condition that warrants emergency care. Also, when a private physician receives after-hours calls or a call regarding a complaint that could be serious, and it is neither practical nor seems appropriate for the patient to be seen in the physician's office, the physician may direct the patient to the emergency department for immediate care. Physicians may also use the emergency departments of their affiliated hospitals to perform certain tests or examinations requiring equipment not available in their offices. Finally, the single most important source of emergency services' inappropriate use is by individuals who perceive that they have no alternative for care when they are ill. Because state and federal regulations generally require that hospitals turn no one away, patients know that the emergency department is a guaranteed resource regardless of their ability to pay or the nature of their complaint.

Because they are organized to treat discrete episodes of serious illness and injury immediately, emergency departments are a poor consumer choice for routine care. First, the care is much more expensive

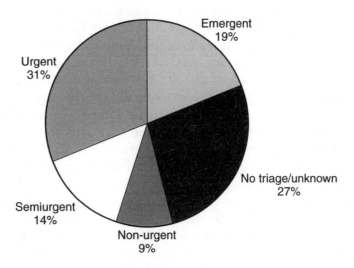

Notes: "No triage" was checked when the hospital did not determine immediacy rating upon arrival at emergency department. Emergent is less than 15 minutes. Urgent is 15–30 minutes. Semiurgent is 1–2 hours. Nonurgent is 2–24 hours.

Figure 4–2 Percent Distribution of Emergency Department Visits by Immediacy with Which the Patient Should Be Seen, 1998.
Source: Reprinted from Advance Data, No. 313, May 5, 2002; National Center for Health Statistics.

than in an appropriate ambulatory setting because it consumes the time of specialist personnel for conditions in which that level of personnel is unnecessary. Second, waiting times are often extremely long because true life-threatening cases appropriately have priority. Third, the emergency department, by its nature, is not organized or staffed to provide follow-up care for routine illnesses. To promote appropriate care for patients who inappropriately present at the emergency department, staff will refer them, when possible, to ambulatory primary care services within the hospital for treatment. Managed care organizations have attempted to curb inappropriate emergency department use by their members by requiring patients to obtain telephone preauthorization before going to the emergency department and by imposing financial disincentives through copays of emergency department fees when the visit does not result in hospitalization. However, the consumer backlash against such subscriber restrictions on emergency department use has resulted in several states passing "prudent layperson" legislation, which requires insurance companies to reimburse costs based upon care that a reasonable person would consider necessary.[15]

Despite the recognition that inappropriate emergency department use drives up costs and results in inadequate continuity of care, many individuals who lack resources to pay for care or are unaware of or otherwise unaccepting of other sources of care find the emergency department to be the only alternative available. Until the health care system successfully reduces financial barriers to care and achieves a universal, basic level of access to routine medical care, a large volume of inappropriate emergency department use can be expected to persist.

In the past, like other teaching hospital outpatient clinics, the emergency department was a place of indenture for medical interns or residents who were required to provide coverage as a component of their training. Often, to earn extra income, residents would contract to "moonlight" extra hours for their assigned hospital or for other hospital emergency departments. Nonteaching hospitals also often hired residents on a contracted basis to cover the emergency department or required attending staff to provide rotating coverage.

From both the physicians' and patients' perspective, this staffing configuration was less than ideal. Physicians working in emergency departments under these arrangements often had little training or experience with the illnesses and injuries encountered there. Over the past 20 years, the greatly expanded knowledge, techniques, and equipment available for the care of critically ill and injured patients and concerns about liability resulting from deploying physicians without specific training and experience in emergency care have resulted in dramatic changes in how emergency departments are staffed and organized and services are delivered.

Since 1979, emergency medicine has been recognized as a medical specialty with accompanying requirements for extended specialty training and experience to attain board-certified status, as in the other medical specialty fields. Now, physicians qualified by training and experience in this specialty staff most hospital emergency departments. Several corporations employ groups of board-qualified or board-certified emergency medicine physicians and contract their services to hospitals. Medical schools with accredited training programs in emergency medicine may staff their affiliated hospitals' emergency departments as a faculty practice group and provide clinical training there for department residents, similar to the organization of other outpatient clinics.

In addition to physicians, emergency departments are staffed by nurses who often have advanced education and training in the triage and care of critically ill or injured patients. Emergency departments also employ an array of other personnel who provide clerical support, medical, and nursing assistance. Depending on the needs of the population served by the hospital, emergency department staff may also include mental health professionals and social workers. Typically, other needs of patients presenting at the emergency department are met by on-call arrangements with staff members of other hospital departments.

■ Free-Standing Services

Nonhospital-based, or free-standing, ambulatory care facilities may be owned and operated by hospitals, hospital systems, or physician groups or by independent, for-profit or not-for-profit single entities or chains. Many hospital systems, independent entities, and chains operate multiple ambulatory care facilities that provide a wide and rapidly expanding array of services, including ambulatory surgery, occupational health services, physical rehabilitation, substance abuse treatment, renal dialysis, cancer treatment, diagnostic imaging, cardiovascular diagnosis, sports medicine, and urgent/emergent care. With technological advances making treatment outside the hospital feasible, the drive to reduce costs and consumer demand for convenient, free-standing services has become a major component of the health care delivery system. Estimates place the number of free-standing outpatient care facilities at over 7,000.[16]

The diversity of services available in free-standing facilities prevents a comprehensive discussion of their organizational features in this text. However, the following services illustrate major characteristics of free-standing facilities that have had a significant impact on the rapid evolution of ambulatory care services.

Primary Care Centers

As an outgrowth of many of the same factors that fueled the reorganization, expansion, and enhancement of hospital-based clinic services, free-standing primary care centers have proliferated rapidly since the 1980s. For hospitals, the desire to capture new market share, ensure the flow of inpatient admissions, bring new volume to ancillary departments such as laboratory and radiology, enhance revenues, and improve service delivery efficiency to meet the demands of managed care all have contributed to the move toward off-site facility development. For teaching hospitals, these facilities, like hospital-based clinics, continue to play important roles in providing a teaching environment for students and residents in internal medicine, family medicine, obstetrics and gynecology, and pediatrics. Depending on state licensure requirements, they may be operated as extension clinics of the hospital or as hospital-affiliated corporate entities.

Typically, free-standing primary care facilities approximate the appearance and organization of a private physician's office. Staff physicians may themselves be the owners, or they may be employees of the owner entity. In hospital-operated facilities, staff physicians are commonly employees of the owner hospital, or, in the case of a teaching facility, physicians may be jointly compensated through a medical school–affiliated faculty practice group and the hospital.

In addition to primary care physicians, staff may include registered nurses, nurse practitioners, physician assistants, medical office assistants, laboratory personnel, receptionists, clerical help, medical record personnel, social workers, and case management staff. In many ambulatory care facilities, nurse practitioners and physician assistants, under physician supervision, are the mainstays of the day-to-day operation, providing a broad range of services, including physical assessments, diagnosis, patient histories, education, and counseling. Nurse practitioners, often with specialized training in specific areas such as pediatrics, women's health, geriatrics, and adult medicine, are generally acknowledged to be highly effective in carrying out their responsibilities and are well accepted by patients. Among numerous other studies yielding consistent findings, S.A. Brown and D.E. Grimes,[17] who analyzed nurses in primary care roles, reported that nurse practitioners spend more time with patients than physicians do and score higher on patient compliance and satisfaction measures than physicians. They also cited the lower average cost per visit of the nurse practitioner. Registered nurses, nurse practitioners, and physician assistants also triage patients and counsel and educate patients through phone contact.

Urgent/Emergent Care Centers

The first urgent/emergent care center was established in 1973. There are now estimated to be more than 2,000 such facilities in the United States. Ownership is diverse, including for-profit corporate chains, single entities, private physician groups, and HMOs. These facilities are designed to fill consumer needs for convenient care of nonlife-threatening illness. They operate for extended hours, including evenings, weekends, and holidays, and, in addition to maintaining an appointment schedule, most will accept patients on a walk-in basis. Physician staff members are usually specialists in internal, family, or emergency medicine. The center may employ registered nurses, nurse practitioners, physician assistants, and reception or other support staff, and may provide radiology and basic laboratory services. Acceptable payment usually includes all forms of insurance and credit cards.

From the consumer standpoint, urgent/emergent care centers fill gaps in the delivery system created by the rigidity of private physician appointment scheduling and unavailability during nonbusiness hours. The centers also can provide a much more convenient and user-friendly alternative to a hospital emergency department during hours when private physicians are not available. In addition, for individuals who may be new to a community and have not had the opportunity to establish a relationship with a physician, these centers can meet immediate needs in a convenient, economical manner without incurring the long waits and expense of the hospital emergency department. Typically located in highly visible facilities, such as storefronts in commercial areas, they offer valued convenience and ease of accessibility to their consumers. Because they are a less expensive alternative to the hospital emergency department, managed care organizations usually will reimburse fully their members' use of urgent/emergent care facilities when their physicians are not available.

In contrast to free-standing primary care centers, urgent/emergent care centers make clear to prospective patients that they do not provide ongoing routine care. If patients do not have a routine source of care, center staff usually will encourage them to obtain one and may provide information about area physicians or primary care centers that are accepting new patients as a means to encourage continuity. To maintain positive relationships with area physicians whose patients they have treated, the centers will routinely forward records of treatment to the patients' physicians. Because the majority of urgent/emergent care centers are established as profit-making opportunities, and Medicaid reimbursement rates have been low for non-hospital-administered outpatient care, they are typically located in areas most likely to attract patients who self-pay in full or are privately insured.

Hospitals have expressed concern that these centers may succeed in culling significant numbers of paying patients, leaving to their emergency departments a disproportionate share of the most ill and expensive-to-treat charity patients. In areas where the centers have proliferated, the private physician community also has voiced concerns about the availability of such facilities affecting patients' motivation to develop a relationship with a primary physician. Nonetheless, the growth in numbers of urgent/emergent care centers is a clear indication that they are perceived by consumers as a positive alternative to the hospital emergency department.

Ambulatory Surgery Centers

Ambulatory or outpatient surgery now accounts for over 50 percent of all surgeries performed.[18] The National Center for Health Statistics defines ambulatory surgery as "surgical and non-surgical procedures performed on an ambulatory (outpatient) basis in a hospital or free-standing center's general operating rooms, dedicated ambulatory surgery rooms, and other specialized rooms such as endoscopy units and cardiac catheterization labs."[19] Outpatient surgery volume continues to be a major contributor to the overall growth trend in ambulatory care. Nationwide, in 1997 ambulatory surgery industry revenues totaled $5 billion.[20]

From 1982 to 1992, outpatient surgeries in community hospitals increased over 200 percent, while inpatient procedures declined by more than 32 percent.[21] In the decade between 1983 and 1993, the number of free-standing ambulatory surgery centers grew from 239 to more than 1,800. The National Center for Health Statistics reported 20.8 million ambulatory surgery visits in 1996, with an estimated 17.5 million visits (84 percent) occurring in hospitals and 3.3 million visits (16 percent) occurring in free-standing centers.[22] (See Figure 4–3.) The 20.8 million visits comprised approximately one-half of the combined total of 40.1 million ambulatory surgery visits and inpatient discharges with surgical and nonsurgical procedures.[23] (See Figure 4–4.) Figure 4–5 compares the numbers of four procedures that are most frequently performed on an ambulatory basis with the numbers of these procedures performed on inpatients.

Beginning in the 1970s, several factors promoted the increase in ambulatory surgical procedures as alternatives to inpatient surgery. One of the most significant factors was the development of general anesthetics that resolved safely and quickly, enabling patients to return to normal functioning within a few hours. Advancements in surgical equipment, techniques, and materials reduced or eliminated the invasive nature of many procedures and their complications and risks. With these and other technological advances making outpatient surgery increasingly feasible and safe, mounting financial pressures have resulted in Medicare, insurance companies, and managed care organizations requiring that certain procedures be performed in the less costly ambulatory setting unless physicians are able to demonstrate undue medical risks to the patient. In 1991, Medicare covered 1,200 ambulatory surgical procedures; in 1998, it covered 2,200.[24]

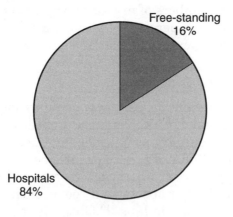

Figure 4–3 Percent Distribution of Ambulatory Surgery Visits by Type of Facility, 1996. *Source:* Reprinted from *Advance Data*, No. 300, August 12, 1998; National Center for Health Statistics.

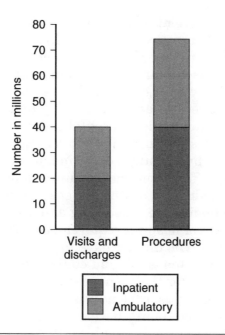

Figure 4–4 Utilization Measures for Ambulatory Surgery Visits and Discharges of Hospital Inpatients with Procedures, 1996.
Source: Reprinted from *Advance Data*, No. 300, August 12, 1998; National Center for Health Statistics.

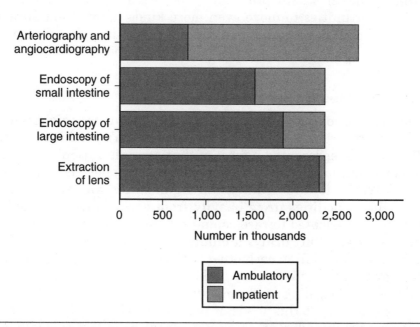

Figure 4–5 Number of Leading Ambulatory and Inpatient Procedures Combines, 1996.
Source: Reprinted from National Center for Health Statistics Report Series 13, No. 139, 1998; M.F. Owens and L.J. Kozak, *Ambulatory and Inpatient Procedures in the United States*, 1996.

This shift from inpatient to ambulatory surgery provided opportunities for hospitals to convert space into efficient, cost-effective care delivery areas, encouraging the development of separate surgical management systems for ambulatory and complicated cases. Although initially this conversion entailed capital expenditures and staffing additions, it became apparent quickly that well-managed ambulatory surgical centers could be profitable enterprises.

In the 1980s, free-standing ambulatory surgical facilities, owned and operated either by hospitals or by independent entities, began proliferating. They offered several advantages over the in-hospital services, including enhanced aesthetics, ease of accessibility, and the opportunity to customize the scheduling and organization of service delivery independent of hospital requirements. They were embraced rapidly by physicians who did not have to contend with the rigors of operating room scheduling, staff, and equipment availability typical in the hospital setting. For their part, patients viewed the free-standing facilities as far more user friendly and responsive to their needs than their hospital-based counterparts.

The quality of patient care has benefited significantly from improved technology and advanced, less traumatic surgical techniques applied in the ambulatory setting. Patients experience fewer complications, much faster recovery, and less disruption to normal activity from ambulatory than from hospital inpatient surgery. Continuing advances in surgical and anesthetic procedures and technology are expected to provide opportunities to move even more kinds of inpatient surgery into the ambulatory setting. Recent developments include growing applications for laser surgery, laparoscopic surgery, and endoscopy.

Community Health Centers

Community-based ambulatory care services known as "neighborhood health centers" originated during Lyndon Johnson's presidency in the mid-1960s and represented a facet of that administration's social reform movement labeled the "war on poverty." Supported by the U.S. Office of Economic Opportunity, the organization and staffing patterns of these facilities drew heavily from earlier models of public health services oriented toward community need. Centers were established in cities and in rural communities across the country, and although they differed from each other with respect to their size and the scope of available services, they had certain common characteristics rooted in federal funding requirements.

Designed to meet the needs of people in urban and rural areas who are medically indigent, community health centers typically are staffed by multidisciplinary teams that might include physicians, nurses, social workers, dietitians, and support personnel. This staffing pattern attempts to create a comprehensive service approach to address the multidimensional nature of the health and health-related needs of low socioeconomic populations. Target patients are minorities, childbearing-age women, infants, persons with HIV infection, substance abusers, and individuals and families who are homeless. In addition to primary care and preventive services, community health centers help patients to link with other supportive programs and services such as welfare, Medicaid, the Women, Infant and Children supplemental nutrition program (WIC), and the Child Health Insurance Program. Many community health centers also offer on-site laboratory testing, pharmacy services, and radiology services and may provide transportation, translation, and health education services. To facilitate access to services, community health centers may also employ outreach workers drawn from the centers' service areas. These workers receive training in health and social service needs assessment and advocacy for early intervention and continuity of care.

Today, community health centers receive funding under the Public Health Service Act, with grants administered by the Bureau of Primary Care, Health Resources and Services Administration of the Department of Health and Human Services. The program has grown substantially over the years from 104 centers in the early 1970s to over 1,000 in 1998. In addition to centers in medically underserved urban and rural communities, the program currently includes targeted health centers for public housing residents, individuals and families who are homeless, Native Americans, and migrant workers. Community health centers are recognized as an important "safety net" for the nation's low-income populations as well as uninsured populations who have no, or limited, access to services from other sources. Of the 11 million people served by the centers, over 40 percent are uninsured and almost two-thirds live below the federal poverty level (see Table 4–1).[25]

The community health center program currently serves 11 million people annually through a federal appropriation of approximately $1 billion. Federal funding is allocated to needy communities through grants. Community health centers may be organized under the aegis of local health departments, as part of larger human service organizations, or as stand-alone, not-for-profit corporations. Other revenue sources include state and local governments, Medicare and Medicaid, private insurance, and patient fees. Medicaid reimbursement provides the largest share of the centers' revenue.[26] In 1989, health centers received a financial boost when the Federally Qualified Health Center Program was enacted to provide reimbursement for "reasonable costs" through the Medicaid and Medicare programs, regardless of whether these services are reimbursable when supplied by other providers. However, the Balanced

Table 4–1 Characteristics of Community Health Centers' Service Recipients

CHARACTERISTIC	PERCENTAGE
Ethnicity	
White	35%
Hispanic	31%
African American	27%
Asian/Other	7%
Ages/Gender	
Children	42%
Women of Childbearing Ages	32%
Other	26%
Economic Status	
Below poverty	65%
100%–200% poverty	20%
> 200% poverty	15%
Payer Source	
Uninsured	41%
Medicaid	33%
Private	14%
Medicare	4%
Other public	4%

Source: Reprinted with permission from K. Davis, K.S. Collins, and A. Hall, Community Health Centers in a Changing U.S. Health Care System, *Policy Brief*, © 1999, The Commonwealth Fund.

Budget Act of 1997 required cost-based reimbursement to be phased out by 2003. As a result, beginning in 2003, states will pay federally qualified health centers the difference between the amount received from managed care organizations and the amount they are owed under reasonable cost principles.[27]

Community health centers are facing major challenges from changes in the health care marketplace. Medicaid managed care enrollment is causing a loss of patient base, and discounted managed care fees are eroding revenue. Also, increasing numbers of uninsured patients are causing the level of uncompensated care to rise. Community health centers are responding to the challenges through measures such as forming contractual relationships with managed care organizations, creating networks and coalitions with other providers to improve their negotiating position, and updating facilities and services to attract more patients.[28] In light of their "safety net" functions, the Bush administration announced $11.7 million in grant availability in 2002 "to double the number of patients served by our health centers."[29]

■ Public Health Services

The delivery of ambulatory health services by state or municipally supported sources has its roots in the early American ethic of community responsibility for care of needy members. Since the colonial period, altruistic citizens sought the charity of the community to provide for the less fortunate by supporting the development of almshouses or "poor houses" to care for needy and orphaned children. Many of these institutions became the precursors of community hospitals.

With the evolution of state and local governments' roles in providing welfare services and the development of the public health discipline in the late nineteenth and early twentieth centuries, tax-supported state and local departments of health began providing ambulatory services. As the provision of personal health services evolved under health department auspices, so did the opposition of organized medicine, based on the contention that government was competing with private practice medicine for patients. The influence of organized medicine's opposition was largely successful in limiting the health departments' personal health services to providing care for patients only in the lowest income population groups and to offering other types of care in which private physicians had little interest.

Services that became the domain of health departments included administration of preventive public health measures, such as disease screening, immunization programs, and communicable disease case finding and treatment. Also, for population groups lacking the means to pay or with only Medicaid coverage, health department services often filled gaps for family planning, obstetrical care, well-baby care, and pediatric and adult medicine. All levels of government carry out public health activities and services, but "the most visible activity occurs in the 3,000 county, city and other municipal health departments throughout the country."[30]

Today, the scope of services available from local health departments varies widely. These services can range from purely prevention-oriented programs, such as immunizations and well-baby care, to complete personal health services offered through free-standing ambulatory care centers. Many health departments also provide home care services, usually through a public health nursing division. Home care services may include communicable disease case finding, infant and child health assessments, and follow-up visits for ambulatory care patients to ensure compliance. Some health departments operate certified home health agencies under the auspices of Medicare to provide home-based services for older adults. In many municipalities, the local health department has responsibility for providing school-based, preventive services, such as vision screening and other types of screening services, general physical examinations, and immunizations. Historically, support for such services has included combinations of city, county, and state funding, plus federal or state disease-specific or block grant funds.

Public health ambulatory services staff may include physicians, nurses, aides, social workers, and clerical and administrative staff, who function under the overall administrative direction of a local health officer. This health officer may or may not be a physician, depending on the population size of the jurisdiction and individual state or municipal requirements. Depending on the area, the governmental aegis may be state, county, or city.

Beginning with the Reagan era in the 1980s and its philosophy of advocating private enterprise over government sponsorship as a means to promote more efficient and effective public service, there has been a decided movement of local health departments to privatize personal health services. Federal and state subsidies for public health services have declined, accompanied by decreased grant funding for disease-specific programs. During the same period, community penetration of hospital and other organization-sponsored ambulatory care programs increased markedly. With the enactment of the State Child Health Insurance Program through the Balanced Budget Act of 1997, every state and many local health departments have been activated in a massive outreach effort to identify and enroll uninsured children. Programs vary widely among the states; however, in many instances, departments of health are actively involved at the state and local levels in planning and implementing the activities of this initiative.

More recently, in the effort to control health care costs, the federal and some state governments have begun vigorously advocating mandated enrollment of Medicaid clients into managed care programs. In general, the politically oriented, cumbersome bureaucratic organization of health departments position them poorly as providers to compete for managed care contracts, as compared to their more agile, business-oriented private sector counterparts.

The September 11 attacks and threats of bioterrorism have brought a renewed focus to the role of federal, state, and local public health organizations in providing public protection and supporting national security. With acknowledgement that "over the past two decades, the infrastructure has greatly deteriorated," the Centers for Disease Control and Prevention has been awarded new grants to focus on interventions that will respond to community public health threats.[31]

■ Voluntary Agencies

Not-for-profit agencies operate a variety of ambulatory health care services throughout the United States. Services have evolved from a variety of sources, often cause related, to address the needs of population groups afflicted by specific diseases or types of conditions. Asthma, diabetes, multiple sclerosis, and cerebral palsy are but a few of the conditions addressed. As not-for-profit organizations, many are chartered by states as charitable organizations and maintain tax-exempt status with the Internal Revenue Service. These designations allow them to collect charitable contributions for which their donors may receive tax deductions. Governed by boards of directors who receive no compensation for their services, these organizations may be operated by a totally volunteer staff or employ numerous paid professionals and have annual operating budgets of several million dollars.

Characteristically, voluntary ambulatory health care agencies were established through the advocacy of special interest groups that desired to address the health care or health-related needs of a population group whose needs were not being adequately met by existing community services. Some operate as single entities, others as independent affiliated agencies of national organizations. Planned Parenthood Federation of America is an example of one such organization. Its clinics provide preventive care, education, and direct services for gynecological care and contraception in numerous locations throughout the United States. Another example is the United Cerebral Palsy Association, which provides or arranges for specialized medical, social service, rehabilitative, and other services for individuals with cerebral palsy and their families. Frequently, legislative advocacy related to the organization's interests at the federal, state, and local levels is a major component of not-for-profit organization activity.

Financial support for voluntary ambulatory health care agencies is diverse. Sources may include charitable contributions, private payment, third-party insurance reimbursement (including Medicare and Medicaid), and federal, state, or local government grants. Since the 1980s, federal and state grant support for categorical services of the type offered by these agencies generally has declined, forcing increased reliance on other sources of support. In many agencies, large proportions of their client populations are uninsured or underinsured and lack personal resources. With the loss of grant subsidies, agencies have had to increase private fund-raising and curtail services to remain viable. Managed care has threatened voluntary agencies that serve populations with special needs. Managed care organizations tend to group populations and circumscribe their coverage without regard for the service gaps filled by the agencies providing specialized services. The result is to effectively preclude individuals from using voluntary agency services by denying reimbursement. Voluntary agencies are responding to these challenges in several ways. To better position their organizations for managed care contracting, they are forming coalitions and networks to capture larger segments of the service population, instituting new quality and efficiency monitoring systems to aid in contract negotiations, and working through their professional advocacy groups to ensure that the interests of their patients and clients are protected.

Although voluntary agencies provide only a small fraction of the total ambulatory care service, as compared to hospitals and other ambulatory care organizations in the United States, they are important as repositories of community values, as symbols of community charity and volunteerism, and as advocates for populations with special needs.

■ Continued Future Expansion

The focus of the U.S. health care delivery system has shifted from the hospital to expanding use of ambulatory care services. Cost reduction initiatives by government payers, private insurers, and managed care organizations have been major driving forces in this shift. Advances in medical technology and diagnostic and treatment modalities that allow services to be provided safely and effectively in the outpatient setting also have strongly influenced this change, as have consumer demands for more convenient, accessible services. Hospitals have accommodated these trends by expanding the scope and volume of their outpatient services through staffing reorganization, the development of free-standing facilities, and a higher level of sensitivity to consumer preferences. Numerous independent providers of ambulatory care also have successfully entered the market and, in many areas, now command major proportions of market share, often in competition with hospitals. As cost reduction and quality improvement initiatives continue to be fueled by market conditions, and technological advances allow more procedures to be moved to the outpatient setting, the continued expansion of ambulatory care in the delivery system can be expected.

■ Notes

1. K. Levit, et al., "Trends in U.S. Health Care Spending, 2001," *Health Affairs 22*, no.1 (2003): 159.
2. National Center for Health Statistics, "Physician Visits Reach 824 Million in 2001," News Release 5 June 2002, http://www.cdc.gov/nchs/releases/02news/physician.htm. Accessed 21 December 2002.
3. U.S. Department of Labor, Bureau of Labor Statistics, "Physicians and Surgeons," *Occupational Outlook Handbook: 2002–2003 Edition*, Bulletin 2540, http://stats.bls.gov/oco/ocos074.htm. Accessed 20 December 2002.

4. M.W. Raffel and N.K. Raffel, *The U.S. Health System: Origins and Functions*, 4th ed. (Albany, NY: Delmar Publishers, 1994), 36–44.

5. K. Levit et al., "National Health Expenditures, 1996," *Health Care Financing Review* 19, no. 1 (Fall 1997): 169.

6. American Medical Association, "Managed Care Brings More Income, Less from Capitation," http://www.ama-assn.org/sci-pubs/amnews/pick_02/bisb1202.htm (December 2, 2002). Accessed 21 December 2002.

7. Levit et al., "National Health Expenditures, 1996," 170.

8. American Medical Association, "Practice Size Trend: Small to Big, Then Small Once Again," http://www.ama-assn.org/sci-pubs/amnews/pick_02/bil21104.htm (4 November 2002). Accessed 21 December 2002.

9. J.H. Knowles, "The Role of the Hospital: The Ambulatory Clinic," *Bulletin of the New York Academy of Medicine* 41 (1965): 68–70.

10. I. Fraser et al., "Ambulatory Care: A Decade of Change in Health Care Delivery," *Journal of Ambulatory Care Management* 16, no. 4 (1993): 1–8.

11. Centers for Medicare & Medicaid Services, U.S. Department of Health and Human Services, "Health Indicators, Table 1: Selected Community Hospital Statistics: 1998–2002," http://www.cms.hhs.gov/statistics/health-indicators/t1.asp (Last modified 22 November 2002). Accessed 20 December 2002.

12. American Hospital Association, *Hospital Statistics* (Chicago: American Hospital Publishing, 1993–94), xiii.

13. National Center for Health Statistics, "National Hospital Ambulatory Care Medical Care Survey: 2000, Emergency Department Summary," *Advance Data,* No. 326 (April 22, 2002), http://www.cdc.gov/nchs/data/ad/ad326.pdf. Accessed 23 December 2002.

14. National Center for Health Statistics, "National Hospital Ambulatory Care Medical Care Survey: 2000, Emergency Department Summary."

15. National Center for Health Statistics, "National Hospital Ambulatory Care Medical Care Survey: 2000, Emergency Department Summary."

16. B. Japsen, "Another Year of Major Growth in Outpatient Care," *Modern Healthcare* (25 May 1998): 58.

17. S.A. Brown and D.E. Grimes, *Nurse Practitioners and Certified Midwives: A Meta-Analysis of Nurses in Primary Care Roles* (Washington, DC: American Nurses Association, 1993).

18. National Center for Health Statistics, "Ambulatory and Inpatient Procedures in the United States, 1996," http://www.cdc.gov/nchs/products/pubs/pubd/series/sr13/140-131/sr13_139.htm. (Last reviewed 31 August 2002.) Accessed 21 December 2002.

19. M.J. Hall and L. Lawrence, "Ambulatory Surgery in the United States, 1996," *National Center for Health Statistics Advance Data*, No. 300 (12 August 1998): 3.

20. Japsen, "Another Year of Major Growth in Outpatient Care," 62.

21. American Hospital Association, *Hospital Statistics*, 4.

22. L.J. Kozak et al., "Ambulatory Surgery in the United States," *National Center for Health Statistics,* no. 283 (14 March 1997): 4.

23. Kozak et al., "Ambulatory Surgery in the United States," 1.

24. Japsen, "Another Year of Major Growth in Outpatient Care," 62.

25. K. Davis et al., "Community Health Centers in a Changing U.S. Health Care System," *The Commonwealth Fund Policy Brief* (May 1999),

http://www.cmwf.org/programs/minority/davis_ushealthcenters_300.asp. Accessed 28 July 2000.

26. M.K. Gusmano et al., "Exploring the Limits of the Safety Net: Community Health Centers and Care for the Uninsured," *Health Affairs* 21, no. 6 (2002): 190.

27. K. Davis, et al., "Community Health Centers in a Changing U.S. Health Care System," 1.

28. K. Davis, et al., "Community Health Centers in a Changing U.S. Health Care System," 5.

29. M.K. Gusmano et al., "Exploring the Limits of the Safety Net: Community Health Centers and Care for the Uninsured," *Health Affairs* 21, no. 6 (2002): 188.

30. S. Wall, "Transformation in Public Health Systems," 65.

31. B. Frist, "Public Health and National Security: The Critical Role of Increased Federal Support," *Health Affairs* 21, no. 6 (2002): 119.

Chapter 5

Medical Education and the Changing Practice of Medicine

This chapter provides an overview of the growth and change in medical education from the colonial apprentice system to today's high technology, specialty-oriented instruction in the basic sciences and clinical fields. The evolution of specialty and subspecialty practice is discussed, as is the funding of graduate medical education. The changes in the practice of medicine and physician relationships with hospitals and insurers following the introduction of managed care are also reviewed. More recent developments such as clinical practice guidelines, physician report cards, Internet usage, and new ethical issues are defined. The chapter concludes with a discussion of the future of medical practice.

There were no medical schools in colonial America. Women treated the sick at home with the help of medicinal herbs, the advice of friends, and some self-help publications of questionable credibility. There were a few university-trained physicians in Europe, but not many came to the colonies. Those European physicians trained other physicians in an apprentice relationship. Because there was no formal method of testing or licensing new physicians after they concluded their apprenticeship, they were free to practice with no outside control.

The first medical school in America was established in 1756 at the College of Philadelphia (later the University of Pennsylvania). Shortly after that, a second one was founded at King's College (later Columbia University) in 1768. Both schools remained very small, graduating only a handful of students each year.

Training under a single physician remained the most common method of physician education until the founding of hospitals in the mid-eighteenth century. Physicians not only brought their own apprentices to the hospital, but they also encouraged other students to observe patient treatment. This practice became so popular that the Philadelphia Hospital began to charge students who were not apprenticed to physicians on the staff. By 1773, the hospital decided to regulate this system so that an aspiring physician could pay a fee to the hospital and be formally apprenticed to the institution for five years.[1] Physicians were granted a certificate on the completion of their apprenticeship.

By 1800, there were still only four medical schools in the United States. In addition to the ones in Pennsylvania and New York, Harvard University had opened one in 1783 and Dartmouth College in 1797. The schools were small, with three or four faculty members teaching all the courses. At the time, there were still very few restrictions on who could practice medicine. Regulatory procedures were almost nonexistent. The first law concerning medicine in the colonies was enacted in Virginia in 1639 to control physician fees.[2] Various states attempted to enact medical licensing legislation during the eighteenth and early nineteenth centuries, but, "by the time of the Civil War, not a single state had a medical licensure act in effect."[3] Moreover, as the number of medical schools grew, their diplomas came to be viewed as licenses to practice.

In 1821, Georgia became the first state to restrict medical licenses to graduates of medical schools.[4] Opposition was strong, especially from the apprentice-trained physicians. However, as physicians from medical schools began to outnumber those from the apprentice system, the MD degree became the standard of competence. The endorsement of formal medical education over apprenticeship training encouraged an increase in the number of medical schools.

Many of the new medical schools had weak programs and no hospital affiliations. In 1892, Harvard became the first medical school to require four years of training. In 1893, Johns Hopkins initiated a four-year curriculum as part of a pioneering effort to improve medical education. The Johns Hopkins model became the standard for subsequent reform of all medical education.[5]

Many medical schools during this period operated without strict admission requirements, a well-trained faculty, or a place for clinical observation and practice. As a consequence, the quality of the medical degree varied greatly from school to school. Medical societies were organized largely to improve the quality of education and practice. The first such society was the Medical Society of Boston, organized in 1736.[6]

By the turn of the nineteenth century, most states had medical societies. In 1847, most of those state societies affiliated with the newly formed American Medical Association (AMA). "Though the goal of the AMA at the time was to improve medical education, its early attempts to reform or close some of the weaker medical schools were ineffective."[7] Many of the AMA members opposed closing the weaker schools because they were associated with them and had a vested interest in keeping them open. As a result, attempts to establish a national standard for medical teaching floundered for a few decades.

The Association of American Medical Colleges (AAMC), founded in 1876 by 22 medical schools, also addressed the issue of national standards. The AAMC supported a four-year curriculum such as the one introduced by the medical schools of Harvard and Johns Hopkins, but it lacked the influence to accomplish the desired reforms.

■ The Flexner Report and Medical School Reforms

At the beginning of the twentieth century, the AMA restructured and became capable of exerting significant pressure for the reform of medical education. In 1904, the organization created a new Council on Medical Education, and, at the same time, began the *Journal of the American Medical Association* (JAMA). The AMA used the journal to publish medical school failure statistics on state board licensing examinations and to group schools by their failure rates.

Strong leadership in the AMA and the AAMC demanded that poor schools improve or leave the association. The most important educational reform accomplishment of the AMA, however, began in 1905, when it obtained the help of the Carnegie Foundation for the Advancement of Teaching to investigate and rate medical schools. Abraham Flexner of the Carnegie Foundation headed a study of the medical schools in the United States and Canada. Flexner proposed to examine the entrance requirements at each institution, the size and training of the faculty, endowment fees, the quality of laboratories, and the relations between the medical schools and hospitals.

In 1909, Flexner started his educational survey of all 155 medical schools in the United States and Canada. He visited each school, interviewing the dean and a few faculty members and inspecting labs and equipment. After each visit he summarized the facts observed during his visit and mailed the summary to the dean for verification. The deans and faculty of each school cooperated happily with Flexner in the mistaken belief that Carnegie was contemplating a contribution to their school.

Flexner's full report, *Medical Education in the United States and Canada,* was published by the Carnegie Foundation in 1910. The report was an accurate and searing description of abuses in the medical schools. Schools were referred to as a "disgrace" and a "plague spot." The assets and liabilities of each school were described in detail, and corrective measures were offered. In the aftermath of this criticism, some schools closed and others consolidated. Flexner had recommended that the number of schools be reduced from 155 to 31, but, a decade later, the number was down only to 85.[8]

Not all observations in Flexner's report were negative. Dartmouth, Yale, and Columbia were able to make alterations that improved the quality of their programs. Schools that received praise for excellent performance included Harvard, Western Reserve, McGill,

Toronto, and especially Johns Hopkins, which was described as a "model for medical education."[9]

Coming from an independent body, the Flexner report gave increased leverage to medical reformers. Licensing legislation was pursued more vigorously, and new requirements for the length of medical training and for the quality of laboratories and other facilities were established. The AMA and the AAMC accelerated efforts at reform and, in 1942, established the Liaison Committee on Medical Education to serve as the official accrediting body of medical schools.

One of the most important outcomes of Flexner's report was that it stimulated support for medical education from foundations and wealthy individuals. Flexner subsequently joined one of the Rockefeller charities, the General Education Board, which then donated enormous sums to medical education. Schools that received the most favorable ratings from Flexner shared most of the money. Because most were associated with universities, the university-affiliated medical schools gained significant influence over the direction of medical education.[10]

▪ Academic Medical Centers

Federal research grants of the 1950s and 1960s encouraged the research-oriented medical schools and their teaching hospitals to become the country's centers of scientific and technological advances in health care. Most of the large tertiary care hospitals affiliated with the approximately 80 medical schools were attracting patients with complicated medical conditions and getting better results than their smaller unaffiliated counterparts.

Because university medical complexes were increasingly recognized as leading the way toward a more sophisticated and effective health care system, the federal government assisted in extending that expertise through the regional medical program legislation of 1965. One of many federal grant programs of that decade, it funded the development of regional medical programs across the United States to upgrade medical knowledge about the leading causes of death: heart disease, cancer, and stroke. The regional medical programs supported research, continuing professional education, service innovation, regional networking among hospitals and other health care facilities, and dissemination of medical center knowledge and skills among networks of other health care professionals and facilities within designated geographic regions.

University medical complexes, which were the centers of research, teaching, and service innovations, gained the most from the legislation. By 1974, however, the university-based regional medical programs had lost their political support and were included in the health systems agency legislation instead of being separately refunded. Without designated funding, they soon disappeared.

By then, however, the university medical centers were well established as the proponents of cutting-edge advances in research and clinical medicine. Each center was regarded as a regional hub in the overall infrastructure of the health care system. By the early 1980s, federal support had increased the number of medical schools to 127.

Academic medical centers broadened into academic health centers by adding to their complexes such professional schools as nursing, pharmacy, dentistry, and allied health. Together with their large teaching hospitals and other clinical facilities, these academic medical centers became a powerful force in the health care arena.

Academic health centers have become the principal places of education and training for physicians and other health care personnel, the sites for most basic research in medicine, and the clinical settings in which many of the advances in diagnosis and treatment are tested and perfected. The teaching hospitals of academic health centers also are the major providers of the more sophisticated patient care required by trauma centers, burn centers, neonatal intensive care centers, and the technologically advanced treatment of cancer, heart disease, and neurological and other conditions. In addition to their complex tertiary care services, teaching hospitals in most cities provide much of the primary care for economically disadvantaged populations.

Although academic health centers may include schools of nursing, dentistry, pharmacy, or allied health, medical schools, and their affiliated teaching facilities dominate the centers' education, research, and clinical service activities. The highly specialized, high-technology nature of their clinical teaching, research, and service to uninsured, economically disadvantaged patients makes them the most expensive type of health care facility in America's health care system. In addition, care at teaching hospitals is, of necessity, less efficient. Because student physicians order more diagnostic tests and procedures and often have to consult with senior doctors regarding diagnoses and treatment procedures, lengths of stay are longer and, therefore, more costly. Available data suggest that hospitals affiliated with academic health centers are 20 to 30 percent more expensive than other hospitals.[11] However, because health care has shifted from an era of abundant resources to one of stringent economic constraints, academic medical centers are under increasing pressure to cut back on high-cost activities or face ballooning deficits and possible extinction.[12]

Much of the problem stems from the fact that some of the costs of education, research, and care of low income populations in the 125 academic health centers have been covered by charging fees up to 30 percent higher than those of competing clinical facilities. As a result, cost-conscious managed care companies are diverting patients to less costly facilities.[13] The problem was compounded by significant reductions in federal payments for hospitalizations under the Medicare and Medicaid programs.

Medical schools have depended on a variety of sources for revenue. A major source for most schools has been the clinical practice of faculty. In the mid-1990s, about one-third of the total income of most medical schools came from their faculty practice plans. Research grants and contracts contributed about 18 percent. Medical schools receive relatively small proportions of their total revenue from state and local government appropriations and from tuition and fees. Endowment revenue varies widely from school to school.[14]

The diverse funding of medical schools means that there is no single source on which they can depend to maintain their fiscal viability. Unlike graduate medical education, which is funded through direct and indirect education payments from Medicare, medical schools rely on their ability to successfully compile the necessary revenues from multiple sources.

The federal government has subsidized graduate medical education (GME)—the training of resident physicians—through the Medicare program in amounts that reached almost $7 billion annually from 1992. Serious decreases in Medicare's subsidies to teaching hospitals contained in the Balanced Budget Act of 1997 had significant implications for GME. Because over half of the total patient revenues of academic health center hospitals came from Medicare and Medicaid, reductions in the support from those programs affected academic health centers in two ways.[15] By scaling back subsidies for GME and by encouraging beneficiaries to enroll in managed care plans, these programs reduced both annual revenues and the number of patients receiving care at academic health centers. The result has been severe decreases in the revenue of academic medical centers and significant decreases in the number of patients available for clinical training and research.[16]

The health care industry's response to the Balanced Budget Act of 1997 was vigorous. Lobbyists for hospital associations, academic health centers, pharmaceutical firms, and other professional organizations convinced Congress that cutting $105 billion from provider support over a period of five years was too much too soon. The loss of federal support, they predicted, would have catastrophic effects on both medical education and hospital care. Today's residents are tomorrow's fully-trained physicians, so subsidies for training residents have important implications for access to medical care and the cost-effectiveness of that care. Congress responded by passing the Balanced Budget Refinement Act of 1999, which restored $17.2 billion in provider support and stretched the implementation of some of the reductions to a period of 10 years.[17]

The financial impacts on academic health centers of the loss of federal dollars combined with the economic pressures of managed care are extremely serious. Many of the major centers are reporting significant dollar deficits, even after major staffing reductions. Yet, the complex missions of the 125 academic health centers leave them few options for maintaining financial viability. Federal and state budget reductions and the economic pressures from new competitive health care markets are forcing them to consider unprecedented initiatives. Already, there is evidence that medical schools in areas of high managed care penetration have difficulty in competing for National Institutes of Health research grants.[18] The finding suggests that the research base of medical schools is diminished when teaching hospitals and faculty practice plans negotiate discounted fees with managed care plans. In addition, when faculty are pressed to bring in more clinical revenue, they have less time for research.

To avoid continuing losses, some medical centers have or are considering the drastic step of selling their teaching hospitals, often to for-profit chains. Others have reduced their costs by implementing major reductions in staff, including the elimination of specialty residency positions. A number of academic health centers merged with other facilities to combine resources and achieve economies of scale in high-cost specialty care, such as transplants, brain surgery, and spinal surgery. The most creative solution seems to be in the formation of large networks of hospitals and physicians that can improve efficiency by offering patients all kinds of needed care at a variety of sites through one organization. Duke University Medical Center not only set up formal relationships with the physicians in its area, but also joined with an insurance company to form its own health maintenance organization.[19]

The long-range effects of these various cost-savings arrangements on the traditional mission of academic health centers have yet to be determined. It is probable, however, that as academic health centers become more competitive, they may also lessen their commitment to traditional academic, research, and indigent care missions.

■ Graduate Medical Education Consortia

There are two types of physicians: the MD (Doctor of Medicine) and the DO (Doctor of Osteopathic Medicine). MDs are also known as allopathic physicians. In 1998, there were 125 schools of medicine and 19 schools of osteopathy.[20] Although both MDs and DOs may use all accepted methods of treatment including drugs and surgery, DOs place special emphasis on the body's musculoskeletal system.

No national agency grants licenses to practice medicine. Instead, after completing a residency, a physician must obtain a license from the medical board of the state where he or she plans to practice. Each state is independent in determining who may practice within the state and may have special requirements or restrictions for licensure.

To provide direct patient care, physicians are required to complete a three- to seven-year graduate medical program accredited by the Accreditation Council for Graduate Medical Education (ACGME) in one of the recognized medical specialties.[21]

Among approximately 1,500 health care organizations, there are nearly 7,000 residency programs, which are loosely held together by accreditation and certification processes, medical schools, program directors, and hospital executives. Given the large number of programs and their loose-knit organization, questions about the quality of the programs and their pertinence to issues of personnel supply and specialty distribution inevitably have been raised. U.S. residency programs were described at the 1992 Macy Foundation conference, "Taking Charge of Graduate Medical Education: To Meet the Nation's Needs in the 21st Century," as "responsive principally to the service needs of hospitals, the interests of the medical specialty societies, the objectives of the residency program directors, and the career preferences of the medical students."[22]

The situation has been addressed with varying success by a number of GME consortia. These consortia are formal associations of medical schools, teaching hospitals, and other organizations involved in the training of residents. The consortia have central coordination and direction that encourages the members to function collectively. The major aims of GME consortia are to improve the structure and governance of residency programs, to increase the ambulatory care training experiences, to address imbalances in physician specialty and location, and to use their collective resources and influence to accomplish those aims.[23] Although GME consortia have existed for more than 25 years, they were only recently endorsed by the AAMC, the National Council on Graduate Medical Education, the New York State Council on Graduate Medical Education, the Macy Foundation, and others. A 1993 survey conducted by the AAMC and the Maine Medical Center identified 36 GME consortia, most of which were formed around academic medical centers.[24]

Whether or not these and other newly formed consortia succeed in improving the organizational structure and governance of GME and addressing the imbalances in medical specialty production to make the medical work force more accountable to society's needs, or whether medicine's historical reluctance to take decisive actions that alter the status quo will bring government intervention, is an open question. As in so many other aspects of health care, it is likely that market forces, rather than policy decisions, will determine the outcomes.

■ Delineation and Growth of Medical Specialties

As far back as 1866, the issue of medical specialization was debated within the AMA. The questions raised were similar to the concerns expressed today. There was general resistance to the development of medical specialties, prompted both by concern for the quality of patient care and by costs. Questions were raised about whether specialists would fragment care by not treating the whole patient and whether surgeons, trained to operate, would disregard noninvasive alternative medical treatments.

The AMA's slow response to specialty interests prompted specialists to form their own societies and associations. In the last half of the nineteenth century, organizations arose for physicians interested in ophthalmology, otology, gynecology, obstetrics, and pediatrics. After World War I, with specialization increasing among physicians, specialty hospitals were founded in some cities, and general practitioners found themselves eased out of hospitals by specialists. In response, the American Academy of General Practice was formed in 1947 to advocate for general practice departments in hospitals. It was not until 1969, however, that general practice, now called family medicine, became a recognized specialty.

Despite the growth in the number of specialists, at the time of the Flexner Report there was no standard for adequate specialty training. The length of specialty training required by various medical schools and hospitals ranged from just a few weeks to three years, and the quality of graduating specialists varied from excellent to incompetent. A physician with almost any amount of training could practice as a specialist.

In 1917, the United States Army, in need of physicians, examined the qualifications of those physicians who wished to be classified as specialists. Even though many had practiced for years as specialists, the results were shocking. Very high percentages of physician specialists were rejected by the service as unfit to practice as specialists and some were deemed unfit to practice any branch of medicine at all.

The army's finding of highly variable competence among specialists did not surprise leaders in medical education. As improved technology and the development of safer and more effective anesthesia and antiseptic techniques made surgery a more acceptable medical option, the demand grew, and the numbers of surgeons and hospitals increased in response. The American College of Surgeons (ACS), established in 1912, set up standards and a board in 1917 for certifying specialists. At the same time, the AMA started inspecting internship sites and produced a listing of approved internship hospitals.

Although both the AMA and the ACS began to rate the quality of postgraduate training, they quickly realized that they could not make their findings public. "Conditions were so bad the results were suppressed."[25] In 1924, the Council on Medicine Education began to approve hospitals for residency specialty training programs. For the next 40 years, residency programs were initiated in all kinds of hospitals with little regard for the quality of the training experience. Often poorly planned and supervised, residents' educational experiences were secondary to their obligations as house staff to serve whatever patient load they were assigned. Additionally, because residencies were the responsibility of single-specialty departments, the opportunities for developing expert clinical knowledge and skills depended on how much interest a few attending physicians had in teaching and the type of patient admitted to that specialty service.

Problems in the quality of training resulting from the lack of standards abounded. Reform was needed, and, a half century after the Flexner Report, the AMA again requested an outside examination of the medical education process. The AMA commissioned a Citizens Committee on Graduate Medical Education, chaired by John S. Mills, who issued his report in 1966. Key recommendations of the report included the elimination of independent internships and giving the accreditation of residency training programs to institutions rather than to individual medical departments. In 1970, the AMA endorsed the inclusion of the first year of graduate medical education in a program approved by an appropriate residency review committee. The term "internship" was dropped, and, by 1980, the AMA had issued recommendations for broad training in the first postdoctoral year.

The current curriculum requirements for becoming a specialist are well defined and standardized. The physician must graduate from medical school, serve in a residency program in an approved setting, and pass a qualifying examination. The appropriate specialty board then certifies the physician. The boards are sponsored by the major specialty society in the area of study and the appropriate specialty section of the AMA.

■ Specialty Boards and Residency Performance

Boards were formed for each specialty to ensure a proper instructional program and training period followed by an examination and certification to practice. The American Board of Ophthalmology, established in 1933, was the first specialty board. In the same year an advisory board for medical specialties was organized. Shortly thereafter, the American Board of Medical Specialties achieved official recognition of specialty boards in medicine. By 1991, there were 24 member boards.

Within the 24 medical specialties, there are now over 90 subspecialty areas. The number of subspecialties in medicine has increased significantly as different kinds of specialists train in similar subspecialties. For instance, the specialties of Emergency Medicine, Family Medicine, Internal Medicine, and Pediatrics all have subspecialties in Sports Medicine. The specialty and subspecialty areas of medicine are listed in Table 5–1.[26]

Table 5-1

AMERICAN SPECIALTY BOARD	SUBSPECIALTY CERTIFICATIONS
Allergy and Immunology	Diagnostic Laboratory Immunology
Anesthesiology	Critical Care Medicine
	Pain Medicine
Colon and Rectal Surgery	
Dermatology	Dermatopathology
	Clinical and Laboratory Dermatological Immunology
	Pediatric Dermatology
Emergency Medicine	Medical Toxicology
	Pediatric Emergency Medicine
	Sports Medicine
	Undersea and Hyperbaric Medicine
Family Practice	Adolescent Medicine
	Geriatric Medicine
	Sports Medicine
Internal Medicine	Allergy and Immunology
	Adolescent Medicine
	Cardiovascular Disease
	Critical Care Medicine
	Critical Cardiac Electrophysiology
	Clinical and Laboratory Immunology
	Endocrinology, Diabetes, and Metabolism
	Gastroenterology
	Geriatric Medicine
	Hematology
	Infectious Disease
	Interventional Cardiology
	Medical Oncology
	Nephrology
	Pulmonary Disease
	Rheumatology
	Sports Medicine

continued

Table 5-1 (continued)

AMERICAN SPECIALTY BOARD	SUBSPECIALTY CERTIFICATIONS
Medical Genetics	Molecular Genetic Pathology
Neurological Surgery	
Nuclear Medicine	Cooperates with American Board of Pathology and American Board of Radiology in Radioisotopic Pathology and Nuclear Radiology
Obstetrics and Gynecology	Critical Care Medicine Gynecologic Oncology Maternal and Fetal Medicine Reproductive Endocrinology
Ophthalmology	
Orthopaedic Surgery	Hand Surgery
Otolaryngology	Otology Neurology Pediatric Otolaryngology Plastic Surgery Within the Head and Neck
Pathology	Blood Banking/Transfusion Medicine Chemical Pathology Cytopathology Dermatopathology Forensic Pathology Hematology Immunopathology Medical Microbiology Molecular Genetic Pathology Neuropathology Pediatric Pathology
Pediatrics	Allergy and Immunology Adolescent Medicine Critical Laboratory Immunology Developmental Behavioral Pediatrics Medical Toxicology Neonatal-Perinatal Medicine Neurodevelopmental Disabilities Pediatric Cardiology Pediatric Critical Care Medicine Pediatric Emergency Medicine Pediatric Endocrinology Pediatric Gastroendocrinology

Table 5-1 (continued)

AMERICAN SPECIALTY BOARD	SUBSPECIALTY CERTIFICATIONS
Pediatrics *(continued)*	Pediatric Hematology-Oncology
	Pediatric Infectious Diseases
	Pediatric Nephrology
	Pediatric Pulmonology
	Pediatric Rheumatology
	Sports Medicine
Physical Medicine and Rehabilitation	Spinal Cord Injury Medicine
	Pain Medicine
	Pediatric Rehabilitation Medicine
Plastic Surgery	Hand Surgery
	Plastic Surgery Within the Head and Neck
Preventive Medicine	Aerospace Medicine
	Occupational Medicine
	Medical Toxicology
	Public Health and General Preventive Medicine
	Undersea and Hyperbaric Medicine
Psychiatry and Neurology	Addiction Psychiatry
	Child and Adolescent Psychiatry
	Clinical Neurophysiology
	Forensic Psychiatry
	Geriatric Psychiatry
	Neurodevelopmental Disabilities
	Pain Medicine
Radiology	Neuroradiology
	Nuclear Radiology
	Pediatric Radiology
	Vascular and Interventional Radiology
Surgery	Vascular Surgery
	Pediatric Surgery
	Surgery of the Hand
	Surgical Critical Care
Thoracic Surgery	
Urology	

Source: Reprinted with permission from *Approved ABMS Specialty Boards and Certificate Categories,* pp. 111–114, © 2002, ABMS (This is not a complete list of specialties and subspecialties.)

The usual procedure for subspecialization is for specialists to complete their residency training and become board certified. Then they take another period of training, called a "fellowship," which prepares them to subspecialize or conduct research in a specific area.

Each specialty board has a residency review committee (RRC) charged with the responsibility of preserving the quality of GME. In 1928, the AMA published the guidelines for approved residencies and fellowships that set educational standards for residencies. The Accreditation Council for Graduate Medical Education (ACGME), formed in 1972 by the American Board of Medical Specialties, the American Hospital Association, the AMA, AAMC, and the Council of Medical Specialty Societies, extends authority to RRCs to determine the standards for its residencies.

The ACGME supervises and receives reports from each RRC. Thus, "the RRC and all specialties establish guidelines for acceptable standards for graduate medical education . . . The RRC also controls the number of residents allowed in each program and in general oversees the conduct of the residencies."[27]

In addition to the controls of the ACGME and its five parent organizations, numerous influences affect different aspects of residency content and training. These include 24 specialty boards and residency review committees, hospital directors, medical school deans, program directors, training directors, faculty, house staff, and specialty societies. The problems inherent in this disjointed system of control will intensify as health care reforms force consideration of changes to accommodate specialty imbalance, physician supply, reductions in funding, managed care, shifts from inpatient to ambulatory care, and the general reconfiguration taking place in the health care industry.

Medical schools and their teaching hospitals are now challenged to figure out how to compete in managed care environments, maintain the quality of educational programs, and support increased teaching in ambulatory settings when hospital and faculty practice revenues decrease. Additionally, medical schools and affiliated hospitals will have to demonstrate more responsiveness to societal needs in the context of their teaching and service missions. For the many medical schools that have emphasized the specialty and high-technology sciences and paid little attention to the goals and methods of preventive or social medicine, it will be a serious challenge to show that the outcomes of medical education are consistent with the needs of society.[28]

■ Funding of Graduate Medical Education

Before about 1950, the cost of GME was negligible because faculty volunteered time for the supervision of residents, and residents received very small stipends. Today, residents are earning living wages with fringe benefits, faculty are paid for the time they spend teaching house staff, and compensation may be provided for overhead expenses, such as food service, laundry, teaching space, and administration. There also are numerous indirect costs associated with the extra time and resources required for teaching residents.

Until about 1975, hospitals incorporated the costs of GME into patient charges, and third-party payers accepted those costs as an appropriate method of support for medical residency training. Medicare, as the largest payer of hospital bills, was estimated to cover about one-third of the total cost of GME. After 1975, and continuing through the 1983 Medicare prospective payment system, the direct costs of medical education became a "pass-through," which meant it was reimbursable outside the daily hospital rate.

Teaching hospitals, however, continued to have costs that exceeded their reimbursement rates, and Medicare chose to compensate them by paying an additional, indirect medical adjustment rate based on resident-to-bed ratios. That adjustment became an incentive for hospitals to keep their resident-to-bed ratios as high as possible.

■ The Physician Workforce and U.S. Medical Schools

In the mid-1960s, the federal government expected a national shortage of physicians in the United States. New policies and programs were established to increase the number of physicians. The number of U.S. medical schools increased by 50 percent and the number of medical students doubled. The number of physicians in the United States increased from less than 300,000 in 1965 to 702,000 in 1996.[29] Although the number of physicians more than doubled, the population increased by only 45 percent during the same period. The number of physicians per 100,000 population in the United States jumped from 137 in 1973 to 264 in 1996.[30]

Although there were 800,000 active physicians by the year 2000, and the number of physicians per 100,000 population had reached 276, there was, and still remains, wide geographic variation in physician capacity. Physicians per 100,000 population ranged from 448 in Massachusetts to a low of 177 in Idaho.[31]

It is important to note that as far back as 1981, the Graduate Medical Education National Advisory Committee predicted an oversupply of physicians. Medical schools, however, did not respond to the warning. Not only did they not reduce their physician output, but they also increased the number of their graduates. Between 1990 and 1997, the number of MD graduates increased by 3.6 percent, and the much smaller number of DO graduates increased by 32 percent.

During the same period, the total number of residents in accredited residency programs increased even more. The number of medical residents rose from 82,902 in the 1990–1991 year to 98,143 in the 1997–1998 year.[32] Much of that increase was due to the influx of international medical graduates. Nearly one quarter of the physicians practicing in the United States graduated from medical schools in other countries. Most of those graduates gained entry to the U.S. health care system by completing an accredited medical residency. For more than a decade, the total number of residency positions has continued to increase, with graduates of foreign medical schools making up a large percentage of the total number.[33]

Between 1990 and 2000, more than 45,000 international medical school graduates (IMGs) entered practice in the United States after serving residencies in U.S. hospitals.[34] In fact, most of the hospitals in the United States depend on IMGs to fill their residency positions. About one-fourth of all hospital residencies are filled by IMGs and, consequently, they represent approximately one-fourth of the physician workforce in the United States.[35]

In 1998, in response to complaints about the lack of basic clinical and communication skills among some IMGs, a requirement was initiated that they must pass a clinical skill assessment before entering a residency. Although there was a surge of IMG entrants immediately before the requirement went into effect, there has been a significant drop in IMG entrants since the requirement was initiated. As a result, the quality of the applicants has improved while still providing enough IMGs to fill the residency positions not taken by U.S. medical graduates.[36]

Ratios of Generalist to Specialist Physicians and the Changing Demand

Primary care or generalist physicians are widely defined as those who practice family medicine, general internal medicine, and general pediatrics. Physicians practicing obstetrics and gynecology also are sometimes included as primary care practitioners. For years, the numbers of generalist physicians have been considered too low to meet the basic health care needs of large segments of the general population. Additionally, the emphasis on medical diagnosis and treatment by combinations of specialist and subspecialist physicians has been criticized as contributing significantly to the complexity and rising costs of medical care.[37]

In the early 1990s, the growth of managed care raised concerns that the long-standing 60:40 ratio of medical specialists to primary care physicians would leave the United States with an inadequate number of primary care physicians and an oversupply of specialists.

Those forecasts led to a number of federal and state policies that encouraged the training of more primary care practitioners. There followed a significant increase in the number of physicians practicing in the primary care fields of family medicine and pediatrics.

Contrary to the early predictions, however, the marketplace demand for medical specialists did not decrease, and the increased supply of primary care physicians appears adequate to meet population needs. In fact, rather than the predicted national oversupply of specialist physicians, many areas of the country are experiencing an inadequate supply of specialists to meet community needs.[38]

The preponderance of medical specialists among all practicing physicians in the United States was not brought about by design. There never has been a master plan to create a more ideal, or even specific, distribution of specialties within the physician workforce. The number, types, and preparation of physicians have been left to the often independent actions of medical schools, their teaching hospitals, the American Board of Medical Specialties, and the ACGME.

The current ratio of generalist physicians to specialists, about 40:60,[39] is the result of individual career choices made by medical students before graduation. Thus, one of the most important influences of academic health centers is the socialization process that shapes the skills, values, and attitudes of generation after generation of physicians and other health care professionals. It is the educational and training exposures to the different specialty practices and to the practitioners of those specialties that influence a student's personal career objectives and subsequent practice pattern. It is significant in considering the origins of the specialist/generalist imbalance that, until very recently, almost every aspect of most medical school and teaching hospital experiences favored the practice of specialty medicine. Many medical students who had every intention of becoming generalist physicians were induced by exposure to the medical education environment to change their minds.

There are several reasons for the dominant choice of residencies. The hierarchy of respect in the cultures of most academic medical centers tends to denigrate primary care as less intellectually demanding, less prestigious, and requiring less skill than the subspecialties. Although untrue, specialists in medical schools convey the message indirectly—and sometimes directly—to patients, medical students, and other physicians, that generalists are not competent to handle the wide range of problems they face. Although generalists cannot have the same expertise in every field that a specialist has in one field, generalists develop a very high level of knowledge in all aspects of primary care and are capable of making appropriate and judicious use of the expertise of specialists when the need arises.

The primary care experience in most medical schools also is skewed when medical students and residents see most patients in tertiary care hospitals, and work in clinics that are considered of low priority and managed inefficiently, and rarely find a preeminent primary care faculty person to serve as a role model. In addition, the differences in working hours, being on-call, income, and public recognition that favor specialists cause many medical students and residents to rethink initial interests in primary care medicine.[40]

Nevertheless, most medical schools encourage medical graduates to accept residencies in one of the primary care fields. Admission committees give preference to candidates for admission that evidence interest in primary care medicine. Family practice departments cultivate promising students and most medical schools have moved some of their clinical training sites from tertiary care hospitals to ambulatory service settings and private group practice offices to give students more primary care experience.

Among the most persuasive influences on the practice specialty decisions of graduating medical students are the market conditions that determine the need for and success of potential various medical specialists. Medical students are very much aware of the demand and supply for specialists and subspecialists in urban communities and the opportunities for generalists in managed care environments. They also know that they will have the option to seek further training in a subspecialty at a later date if they aspire to more specialized practice.

■ Primary Care Physicians— Gatekeepers of the System

Managed care has given primary care physicians a new and important role as gatekeepers in the current health care system. Gatekeepers are primary care physicians who serve as the point of first contact for patients seeking medical care. Gatekeepers have the responsibility to provide primary care to patients enrolled in managed care plans and to refer them to specialists when the need arises. Gatekeepers are expected to coordinate all of the health services needed by their patients.

The term "gatekeeper" has been applied to these primary care physicians because the managed care plans require the primary care physician's approval before they will pay for a visit to a specialist or emergency room. The gatekeeper role has been a controversial one, however, because the gatekeeper's own reimbursement is often linked to the number of referrals made to specialists. It is common among managed care plans to reduce the income of gatekeepers who cost the plan more for medical specialty care than the plan expects. By pressuring the primary care gatekeepers to limit the number of referrals to more expensive specialist physicians, managed care plans put gatekeepers in uncomfortable, if not unethical, dilemmas. Primary care gatekeepers must choose to delay or deny patients the benefit of specialist consultation or treatment or to provide those services themselves that are more appropriately delivered by specialists. Neither choice is in the best interests of patients. Widespread criticism and a number of lawsuits claiming injury from delay or denial of care have prompted some managed care organizations to remove the financial penalties to gatekeepers for inordinate numbers of referrals to specialists.

■ Preventive Medicine

The Pew Charitable Trusts created the Pew Health Professions Commission with the "goal of helping health professional schools respond to the changes in the health care system and in the health care needs of Americans."[41] The group published a report in 1991 that outlined what will drive future health care. They concluded that a health-oriented approach that stresses disease prevention will characterize future health care systems. Concerns will be addressed at a community level. This increased emphasis on community health will necessitate changes in medical schools and teaching hospitals and require that learning in a community environment be part of physician training. Physicians will need to be well versed in social and environmental health determinants. The focus on preventive care and treatment techniques that use technology to the patient's advantage are the challenges facing the new physician.

Medicine and medical education, however, have a history of being incredibly inept in establishing health promotion and disease prevention as a high priority in the U.S. health care system. "Although practicing preventive medicine is a cost saving mechanism, nationwide we spend most health care dollars treating preventable disease."[42] Parameters for prevention are clearly established in many areas, but studies show that only a small percentage of physicians actually adhere to the guidelines. For example, a study of 1,000 California physicians found as few as 10 percent asked their patients about their risk of exposure to HIV.[43] Similar statistics regarding mammography, adult immunization, and other areas indicate that health promotion and preventive medicine are underused.

There is a need for change in all areas of medical education. Not only is the use of preventive medicine cost-effective, but lack of its use has become a focus of malpractice suits. Residents need to be instructed in preventive medicine concepts as they apply to the specific population they serve.

Most family medicine residency training programs across the country include preventive medicine education, but actual implementation in medical practice varies considerably.[44] The major reasons family physicians do not "incorporate screening tests into routine medical care are cost, inconvenience to the patient, lack of facilities or equipment and . . . little behavioral change through counseling."[45]

■ Changing Physician/Hospital Relationships

Until recently, physicians and hospitals maintained unique, commensal relationships that brought both of them profits from a single source—patient admissions. The independence and autonomy of physicians were respected, and their relationship to the hospital in the care of patients was disregarded by paying the physician separately on a fee-for-service basis and the hospital on the basis of costs incurred. Because hospitals were dependent on physicians to admit patients and make use of the hospitals' resources, hospitals courted physicians by providing them with time, equipment, staff, and other perquisites with little regard for the effects on hospital costs. Additionally, hospitals were challenged to keep their physical facilities attractive, their hotel services efficient, their support services responsive, and their medical staffs as reputable as possible to attract patients and encourage physicians to select their facilities.

In turn, physicians had responsibilities to the institution itself and to the patients they admitted to the hospital. As a component of a hospital's tripartite governance structure, the medical staff organization was responsible to the board of trustees and the administration for a host of organizational activities that required medical expertise. Through the medical staff organization and its committees, physicians have been obligated to provide the knowledge and authority to establish clinical policies and procedures, perform utilization review, ensure quality, and determine the credentialing standards for admission to the hospital's medical staff.[46]

The roles and responsibilities of physicians, however, are changing from when they were the sole determinants of hospital admissions, diagnostic tests and therapeutic procedures, the length of hospital stays, the use of hospital-owned services and other resources, and referrals. Although physicians still admit patients to hospitals, they do so under a broad range of constraints that have markedly affected their independence and autonomy. The spiraling costs of unchecked and mutually beneficial financial and practice relationships of physicians and hospitals have incurred demands from government, employer groups, third-party payers, and managed care plans that have radically altered the business of hospitals and their physician connections. In an environment of constrained resources and competing demands, the relationships between physicians and hospitals are now different and often far more stressful.

Under the prospective payment system, hospitals are at financial risk if the lengths of patient stays or the costs of resource use exceed that allowed for specific patient diagnoses. As a result, hospitals are constantly monitoring and sometimes questioning physician decisions in providing patient care. Albeit indirectly, the administration of the hospital now has a role in clinical decision making, and it is an interaction in which neither party engages enthusiastically.

There are other reasons why physicians can no longer ignore the financial consequences of their clinical decisions. Managed care plans that contract with hospitals to provide services to their members select those hospitals that demonstrate operating efficiency and cost-effectiveness.

Physicians who are not sensitive to the impact of their practice patterns on the financial burden of their hospitals and do not cooperate in keeping them competitive will find themselves increasingly unwelcome on the hospitals' medical staffs.

In addition to these stresses on the internal relationships of hospitals and physicians, there are external conflicts. The new economic environment is causing hospitals and physicians to strain their traditional, long, and fruitful relationship by going into competition with each other. Group practice growth, as well as new diagnostic and therapeutic technologies that permit many procedures to be performed on an ambulatory basis, but that formerly required inpatient hospitalization, have given physicians the financial resources and patient volume to acquire and use those technologies. These entrepreneurial activities have placed physicians in direct competition with hospitals.

In an analogous move, as their inpatient admissions decreased, hospitals have shifted a great many of their activities to community-based ambulatory settings that competed, in some instances, with their own medical staff. Clearly, the competition for patients in the reformed environment has changed traditional hospital–physician relationships.[47]

One significant change has been the introduction of new hospital-based subspecialty physicians called "hospitalists." In the United States, the hospitalist movement and the term *hospitalist* were introduced in the mid-1990s. In Europe and Canada, the role of a hospital-based specialist who only managed inpatients has been well established for years.

Unlike hospital-based emergency or critical care specialists, hospitalists may manage patients in any of the inpatient units. Primary care physicians "hand off" their hospitalized patients to hospitalists who serve as physicians of record while those patients are in the hospital. Hospitalists then return the patients to their primary care physicians at the time of hospital discharge.

There are several benefits attributed to the use of hospitalists. Hospitalists spend a great deal of time in the hospital, so they are familiar with the hospital systems and can expedite care. They can provide more continuous observation of patients and respond more rapidly to crises and changes in patient condition. Hospitalists also become more expert in recognizing and caring for common inpatient disorders.

As with any major changes in clinical practice, the hospitalist concept is not without controversy. Some primary care physicians fear the loss of authority and income and worry that they could ultimately lose hospital privileges. Nevertheless, the hospitalist movement is growing, and hospitalists can choose from a wide selection of employment opportunities.[48]

■ Cost Containment and the Restructuring of Medical Practice

Historically, physicians were self-employed, engaged in solo practice or with a small number of associates, and received payment on a fee-for-service basis. With the exception of litigated circumstances of alleged malpractice, there was little or no outside accountability for the medical decisions and procedures that occurred during the diagnosis and treatment of patients. It was not until acute concern over the rising cost of health care resulted in cost containment initiatives that the method of reimbursement for medical services was significantly altered, and physicians were subjected to practice parameters and evaluations. Insurance companies, which for decades had simply increased premiums to compensate for escalating charges, began to employ various strategies to hold down costs and stabilize premiums by monitoring physician services rendered.

The introduction of combined, capitated, or other risk-sharing financing and delivery had a dramatic impact on the health care system. The health maintenance organization (HMO) arrangement, in which health care providers are reimbursed a set amount per patient and are required to provide a comprehensive set of health care services, has become the major type of payment mechanism. The old fee-for-service system has yielded to capitation payments that provide a base income and may include bonuses or other financial incentives.

In addition to affecting income and methods of payment, managed care also has subjected physicians to utilization reviews. Testing, treatment, and surgery decisions are monitored and evaluated. Physicians have rallied against the loss of authority and income, and some have countered by forming their own preferred provider organizations (PPOs) and independent practitioner organizations (IPOs). Physicians in PPOs have applied some of the principles of managed care, including utilization review and management. However, according to Peter Kongstvedt, most PPOs use straight fee-for-service payments, whereas IPOs tend to compensate primary care physicians by capitation but pay the majority of specialists on a fee-for-service basis.[49] IPOs usually do not assume financial risk for patient services. Their primary function is to aggregate and analyze data about the community's HMOs and PPOs and advise their members about the requirements for participation.[50]

More recently, marketplace competition, consumer backlash, and contentious physician relationships have prompted managed care organizations to shift business strategies. Insurers are doing away with gatekeeper restrictions and offering less restrictive managed care products to meet consumer demands for more flexibility. They have done little, however, to improve their relationships with physicians. There has been as shift away from prepayment capitation arrangements in favor of the more traditional fee-for-service payments to providers. The payments to providers for fee-for-service claims are so drastically discounted by the insurers, however, that physicians continue to feel mistreated.

Faced with the need to provide quality and price incentives, many managed care organizations using capitation strategies are conducting practice pattern evaluations to determine physician salaries. Atlanta consultant Kay Freeman predicts that in the next 10 years, groups with a deepening stake in capitation will base 80 percent of compensation on physician performance evaluation.[51] Physician practice evaluations based on resource use and patient outcomes will become more widespread as a way of adapting to limited resources. Managed care organizations already set goals for a target number of patient visits per year. How well the physician meets or exceeds patient visit and resource use objectives may determine his or her compensation.

The move to link their salaries to practice performance prompted physicians to exert pressure on the AMA to deal with the possibility of loss of income and autonomy. The AMA, however, sidestepped the issue, leaving the methods by which physicians will deal with changes wrought by capitation an open question.

■ Hold Harmless Clauses

Managed care organizations have affected both the liability risks of their network physicians and their reimbursements through "hold harmless" clauses in their contracts. A common type of hold harmless clause limits physician reimbursement to the fee paid by the managed care organization for covered services. Physicians are prevented from balance billing patients for charges that exceed the insurer's fee scale. "In Tennessee only those HMOs who require physicians to accept this hold harmless clause may obtain a license."[52] Even in the case of an HMO bankruptcy, a physician may be prohibited from balance billing a patient. Other types of hold harmless clauses attempt to shift liability for damages arising from adverse outcomes of medical decisions from the insurer to the physicians. Physicians assume full responsibility, even if the plan was partly at fault because of an error in utilization review.

There is also a hold harmless clause that gives the managed care organization the right to do a background check on the physician. The information obtained from this check may be released without liability to the plans owned, managed, or administered by the managed care organization.

As might be expected, the number and extent of these hold harmless clauses in managed care organization contracts have presented numerous legal problems for participating physicians.

■ Clinical Practice Guidelines

Just as managed care has impinged on physician practice autonomy, so has the development of practice guidelines. Their growing acceptance as the means to more cost-effective and efficient health care has raised concerns about further intrusions by outside forces into the process of clinical decision making. Practice guidelines are defined as "systematically developed statements to assist practitioner and patient decisions about appropriate health care for specific clinical circumstances."[53]

Clinical practice guidelines evolved in the late 1970s and early 1980s after publication of data showing wide variations in the applications of medical procedures in regions in the United States and increased use of questionable, inappropriate, and unnecessary services that added significantly to the spiraling costs of health care. These studies are discussed in detail in Chapter 12, but it is important to note here that the variations in the level of health care interventions were so great as to suggest that physicians were unaware of the relative effectiveness of various procedures, and that patients were not benefiting from much of the care they received.

Health care researchers conjectured that assessments of the outcomes or relative effectiveness of various medical procedures would lead to practice guidelines and eliminate ineffective, unnecessary, or inappropriate procedures and their related costs. To this end, Congress created the Agency for Health Care Policy and Research in 1989. The agency was directed to fund outcomes research and start developing practice guidelines. After a slow start, the agency started releasing practice guidelines for specific conditions. Although fewer than two dozen guidelines had been released by 1995, the agency's efforts sparked a great deal of guideline development by other institutions and agencies.[54] The RAND Corporation, medical specialty societies, HMOs, insurers, and others have now produced over 1,600 practice parameters.[55]

Although a number of specialty societies have developed and promoted practice guidelines as a service to their members, many physicians feel that practice guidelines threaten their autonomy. After years of making clinical decisions without outside scrutiny or interference, practice guidelines appear to be yet another means for

third-party payers and policy makers to make physicians document
their performance and demonstrate their cost-effectiveness.

Acceptance of practice guidelines seems to be dependent on who
developed them and how they are presented. The guidelines that are
trusted the most have been developed by the physicians' own organizations, such as the AMA or a specialty society. Guidelines developed
by insurers or pharmaceutical firms are trusted the least.

The type of practice in which physicians are engaged is also a factor in guideline acceptance. Physicians most deeply involved in managed care, such as those in staff or group model HMOs, are most likely
to believe that guidelines will improve the quality of patient care.[56]

The widespread application of clinical practice guidelines is expected to have a significant effect on medical practice. The nature of
that effect is difficult to predict, however. Guidelines are considered
by some to be the means to prevent unnecessary and negligent events
and to clarify when negligence has occurred. Others think that employers, insurers, providers, and others who base treatment and payment decisions on practice guidelines are likely to face complicated legal questions if harm results. In any case, with government agencies,
health systems, third-party payers, specialty societies, and managed
care organizations promoting the use of guidelines, it is certain that
they will become an integral part of medical practice.

■ Physician Report Cards

As recently as the mid-1970s, the code of ethics of the AMA explicitly
prohibited "information that would point out differences between doctors." Thirty-two states had passed laws supporting the AMA's position. The laws were intended to prevent misleading or competitive ad-
vertising of office hours, charges, or services. The position of organized
medicine, however, reflected a long history of protecting physician
performance from public scrutiny.[57]

Subsequently, the state laws supporting the AMA's position
were determined to be violations of the First Amendment. Passage
of freedom of information acts that prohibited governments from
hiding information from the public removed the barriers that prevented the public from comparing the performance of physicians. In
1986, when the Health Care Financing Administration released
hospital-specific mortality rates for Medicare patients, the dam was
broken. In December 1991, *Newsday* published the first information
regarding physician performance ever made public. Never again
would the public be denied access to government data about the
quality of medical care. The *Newsday* publication was based on New
York State's pioneering effort to compare and publish hospital-specific, severity-adjusted heart surgery mortality rates. Although New
York State had intended to publish only the names of the hospitals

involved, a *Newsday* freedom of information request, supported by the State Supreme Court, forced release of the rankings of the heart surgeons involved.[58]

Within less than a decade, the contentious matter of exposing the comparative performance of physicians on a wide spectrum of variables has been resolved in favor of the consumers of medical care. Although physicians have protested and lobbied against each additional revelation as inaccurate, unfair, and misleading, consumer groups are winning out. A dozen states have passed legislation that gives the public access to physician information including disciplinary records, malpractice actions, and whether a physician has lost privileges at a hospital. Florida has gone so far as to release the exact amount of every malpractice payment going back to the 1980s and allows the public to request a summary of each case that includes the patient's allegations.[59]

Medical societies in general support physician-profiling programs that report a physician's education, training, licensure, and membership in professional societies, state disciplinary actions, and serious misdemeanor convictions. They object strongly to medical malpractice and hospital disciplinary information as not true indicators of the quality of care.

Information technology has made it possible to assemble and adjust performance data so service entities, be they physicians, hospitals, or managed care plans, can be compared on a wide variety of parameters of importance to consumers. Concise and relevant information on the quality of services provided can be invaluable to patients reviewing their options. Report cards allow the public to see information regarding the comparative performance of physicians and hospitals. It is also important to recognize that report cards have introduced incentives that encourage providers to improve their performance. Physicians want good report cards, and their behavior changes rapidly when they realize their colleagues are doing better than they are.

Internet sites have greatly facilitated access to report card information. Health Grades, Inc. provides a consumer website, www.healthgrades.com, that provides quality ratings and profiles for over 5000 hospitals, 620,000 physicians, and 16,000 nursing homes. In addition, information is available on other health care providers such as home health agencies, chiropractors, fertility clinics, and assisted living residences.[60]

■ The Escalating Costs of Malpractice Insurance

The steeply rising costs of medical liability insurance are a growing concern for practicing physicians, medical schools, and teaching hospitals. In the last decade, schools of medicine and hospitals have seen their liability premium costs increase from six to ten times—from thousands to millions. In some states, physicians, and especially specialists, have seen their premiums triple or quadruple in just a few years.

Rising liability insurance costs reflect steep increases in the amount of malpractice jury awards. Also, during an economic downturn, insurance companies that depended on investment income are forced to raise premiums to keep their businesses viable.

In any case, the effect has been demoralizing to many physicians. Physicians are leaving high premium states, choosing to retire early, or reducing high-risk aspects of their practice to lower their insurance costs. Many communities are deprived of certain medical services, such as obstetrics, as a result. It appears that legislative limits placed on jury awards will be required to resolve the problem.

■ Growing Concern About Ethical Issues

Two developments have focused attention on a number of issues of medical ethics. Rather than concerns about unethical or unprofessional conduct, these ethical issues reflect the practice dilemmas faced by physicians working in the rapidly changing health care environment. The first set of ethical concerns relates to the various policies promoted by managed care organizations. Efforts of such organizations to manage the financing, costs, accessibility, or quality of the care delivered cause them to subject physicians to a range of guidelines, treatment parameters, peer reviews, and financial incentives and penalties. Cost avoidance policies that require preauthorization for the more expensive procedures, substitution of less expensive tests, and restraint of hospitalization in favor of alternative ambulatory services raise questions about increased risks to patients.

Interestingly, an opposite set of ethical concerns could be raised about the risk to patients subjected to the practices of fee-for-service traditional medicine, which the managed care policies try to avoid—unnecessary hospitalizations, needless or inappropriate tests and procedures, ineffective treatments, and uncoordinated care by multiple providers. There is no question, however, that particular control strategies of managed care present related ethical issues. Increasingly, physicians admit that they exaggerate the severity of an illness to help patients get necessary care. Systems that encourage deceitful practices, be they fee-for-service or managed care, diminish the professional standards of medicine.

The second development that is creating vexing ethical issues is the remarkable advance in technological capability that has occurred in the last few years. Medicine's ability to save more severely brain-injured patients, increasingly premature infants, terminally ill or brain-dead patients, and others with no promise of functional survival has increased the need for ethical guidelines. At present, individual physicians can decide how they will advise families of such patients. If the family and the physician cannot agree about treatment, there is no set procedure for deciding what to do. These and other ethical dilemmas brought about by the technological advances in medicine present formidable challenges to the ethics committees of hospitals and professional organizations.

Among the most critical of future ethical issues are those related to advances in the field of molecular biology and gene manipulation and therapy. International research efforts, such as the Human Genome Project and the discovery and characterization of molecular correlates of human health and disease, with all their potential use and abuse ramifications, present a mind-boggling ethical challenge. The future use of individual genetic blueprints for diagnosis and treatment as well as for predicting future medical events has scientists, policy makers, and ethicists concerned about potential runaway applications of the technology. Amidst all the potential benefits of this amazing scientific advance are fears of the unethical application of the technology.

■ Physicians and the Internet

Patients are not the only ones using the Internet to obtain online health information. Recent studies found that after a slow start, 70 percent of U.S. physicians are now using the Internet to access the sites of peer-reviewed research, medical publishers, medical societies, and health care provider organizations.[61] The number of new medical Web sites has been growing at the rate of 10 percent per month, listing information about everything from medical meetings around the world to disease-specific displays of pharmaceutical companies to quality information provided by national medical organizations. In addition, physicians themselves have developed personal Web sites to establish their credentials, explain their practice specialties, and attract patients and referrals.

In addition to information on professional meetings and seminars and the latest developments in clinical practice, physicians can obtain the latest data from more than 4,000 clinical trials. The U.S. National Institutes of Health Web site, ClinicalTrials.gov, allows physicians as well as the public to learn about federal, university, and private medical studies at more than 47,000 locations nationwide. Information is provided about the research locations, designs, purpose, criteria for participation, and diseases or treatments under study.

The Internet release of that information long before it can be evaluated as suitable for publication through established methods and published in one of the traditional peer-reviewed medical journals has set off a heated debate between the leading figures in academic medicine and advocates of open access.

■ Provider Network Contracting

The important and extensive development of medical group practices is discussed in Chapter 4. Another, more recent departure from the traditional mode of solo physician practice is the establishment of physician networks.

Integrated Provider Networks

The dramatically altered relationships between hospitals and physicians brought about by health care reforms have fostered the development of integrated provider networks (IPNs). Physicians and hospitals have united in IPNs to serve their mutual interests in market development and to ensure patient flow. The successful network "brings together the interests of primary care physicians, specialists and the hospital in a coordinated system of access points and referral practices."[62]

"The clinic without walls model of health care delivery allows individual physicians to effectively merge their practice into a single practice organization while still maintaining their own individual medical locations."[63] Member physicians are permitted a great deal of autonomy in this arrangement. The model is characterized by a separate legal entity with individual physicians owning interests. Although the hospitals where physicians have admitting privileges may help these groups with start-up costs, the hospitals and physicians are not directly linked. Fees for services are retained by the group with a consequent high level of economic and operational integration and risk sharing.

Management Services Organizations

Management services organizations (MSOs) are practice support organizations that provide management and administrative services to physicians, hospitals, and other providers.[64] MSOs provide resources and specialized services in administrative and management areas and collective purchasing opportunities. Key business decisions regarding accounting systems and utilization review are undertaken by the MSO. MSOs may be owned by a provider or jointly by hospitals and physicians. The economic integration of MSOs is not usually sufficient to permit collective contract negotiations with third-party payers.

Because member physicians maintain complete responsibility for the operation of their own practices, MSOs provide a high degree of individual physician autonomy. There are no divisions of patient fees or distribution of profits. Services provided by contractual relationships between the MSO and individual providers are paid for at the market rate.

Physician-Hospital Organizations

"Physician-hospital organizations (PHOs) directly integrate physicians and hospitals by means of a separate entity in which both provider types have ownership interests."[65] PHOs are more flexible and encompass a broader scope of functions than MSOs. Physicians and hospitals participate in ownership and management of the PHO jointly. It is a separate legal entity that permits collective contract negotiations with third-party payers. There may be opportunities to engage in risk sharing through capitation and other methods of reimbursement. The PHO can demonstrate a competitive advantage for managed care contracting because of the inclusive health care product offered to third-party payers. Physicians are able to maintain existing practice sites and preserve autonomy.

Medical Foundations

A medical foundation is a Section 501(c)(3) tax-exempt foundation that delivers medical care.[66] The foundation is a separate legal entity that purchases practice assets of individual participating physicians. Physicians deliver medical services in accordance with their contractual relationships. Physician providers are reimbursed for their services by the foundation, which owns all the accounts and revenues received from patient care. Although foundations do provide a successful integration of providers into one delivery system, this arrangement involves a loss of autonomy for the physician. Because the foundation has a tax-exempt status, it must engage in charitable activities and accept restrictions on the use and distribution of its assets.

Customizing the Models

The integrated provider network models just described may be modified or combined to meet the various needs of different communities. They represent a number of options that providers may consider to enhance their involvement and control in the evolving health care delivery system.

■ The Future of Medical Practice

It is ironic that, just at the time when scientific and technologic advances have prepared the U.S. health care system to make its greatest contributions to the prevention and treatment of disease, the financing and delivery problems of the system are in frustrating disorder. Unfortunately, until those problems are solved, health care never will be able to achieve the full potential of its scientific and technical capacity. In the midst of all the changes that are taking place, one circumstance seems abundantly clear: Physicians and their professional organizations are incapable of resolving the problems they now face.

Physicians can work closely with the hospitals to serve their mutual needs. They can contract with managed care organizations to continue to serve the enrollees who were previously their fee-for-service patients. They can join the various provider networks to retain some negotiating power among the shifting market forces. But they can't solve the problems that affect them the most because those are the problems of the larger society. Even if all the participants in the system, the providers, consumers, payers, insurers, and managed care organizations, try to solve the health system problems, they can't do it. This situation is occurring at a crucial time in the evolution of medical care: The components of the system are struggling for long-term viability, if not survival, in an environment that is changing rapidly.

The imbalance among the access, cost, and quality of health care that provoked the market-driven reforms evolved from an entrepreneurial system that tried constantly to improve an already superb ability to diagnose and treat the ills of individual patients while failing dismally to address the needs of the larger society. The more sophisticated the medical care technology became, the more indifferent providers seemed to become toward meeting the health needs of populations rather than individuals.

Now, the health care system's problems of cost, access, and quality have demonstrated, at great expense, that it is not enough for physicians and other health professionals to serve the individuals they choose, one patient at a time. The education and socialization of health professionals has failed when many, if not most, feel no obligation to address the health needs of groups of people in ways that benefit public health and decrease the need for costly medical interventions.

Most physicians and other health care professionals in clinical practice have not been adequately prepared to exercise their potential to prevent disease, address the problems of unequal access to competent care, and assume accountability for the effectiveness of their therapies. The high level of autonomy physicians enjoyed for decades is rapidly disappearing because they failed to bring their salient knowledge and skills to bear on relevant societal problems. The power to direct the course of health care in the United States has rapidly shifted from the providers to the insurers and purchasers.

Instead of fighting to retain the status quo in battles already lost, physicians and other health care professionals should be making it clear to the larger society that the dynamics driving the health care revolution cannot be dealt with separately by vested interests. Medicine isn't solely responsible for inventing more health care than people want to pay for. Medicine responded to the public desire to have the best and the most of medical services. But medicine now has a responsibility to make the public understand that the problem is beyond those within the system. As politically onerous as it might be, U.S. citizens and their representatives have to assume the responsibility for carefully and deliberately creating a new form of health care organization that will ensure a coherent, efficient, and effective health care delivery system. Until that happens, physicians will continue to lose the authority, autonomy, and status that formerly characterized the practice of medicine.

■ Notes

1. M.W. Raffel and N.K. Raffel, *The U.S. Health System: Origins and Functions,* 4th ed. (Albany, NY: Delmar Publishers, Inc., 1994).
2. R.S. Jones, "Organized Medicine in the United States," *Annals of Surgery* 217, no. 5 (1993): 423.
3. Jones, "Organized Medicine in the United States," 424.
4. Raffel and Raffel, *The U.S. Health System: Origins and Functions,* 5.
5. Raffel and Raffel, *The U.S. Health System: Origins and Functions,* 6.
6. Jones, "Organized Medicine in the United States," 424.
7. Raffel and Raffel, *The U.S. Health System: Origins and Functions,* 6.
8. Raffel and Raffel, *The U.S. Health System: Origins and Functions,* 11.
9. Raffel and Raffel, *The U.S. Health System: Origins and Functions,* 11.
10. Raffel and Raffel, *The U.S. Health System: Origins and Functions,* 12.
11. G.F. Anderson et al., "Academic Health Centers: Exploring a Financial Paradox," *Health Affairs* 18, no.2, 163.
12. S. Their and N. Keohane, "How Can We Assure the Survival of Academic Health Centers," *Chronicle of Higher Education* (13 March 1998).
13. R.F. Jones, S.C. Sanderson, "Clinical Revenues Used to Support the Academic Mission of Medical Schools, 1992–93," *Academic Medicine* 71 (1996): 299–307.
14. AMA-CME Report, 10-A-98, http://www.ama-assn.org/meetings/public/annual 98/reports/cme.rpt10.htm (June 1998). Accessed 14 August 2000.
15. Academic Health Centers Summary, "Task Force on Academic Health Centers." http://www.cmwt.org/progsumm/ahcs_summ.asp (16 July 2000). Accessed 14 August 2000.
16. Their and Keohane, "How Can We Assure the Survival of Academic Health Centers."
17. The Medicare, Medicaid and SCHIP Refinement Act of 1999, Conference Agreement. http://www.himanet.com/publicdocs/agreement.html (17 November 1999). Accessed 4 August 2000.
18. E. Moy et al., "Relationship between National Institutes of Health Research Awards to U.S. Medical Schools and Managed Care Penetration," *Journal of the American Medical Association* 278, no. 3 (1997): 217–25.

19. Their and Keohane, "How Can We Assure the Survival of Academic Health Centers."

20. Occupational Outlook Handbook, Professional and Technical Occupations, Physicians and Surgeons, Nature of the Work. http://stats.bls.gov/oco/ocos074.htm (14 July 2000). Accessed 9 August 2000.

21. National Resident Matching Program, "About Residency." http://www.eraspo5.aamc.org/nmrp.index.htm (3 May 2000). Accessed 7 August 2000.

22. T.Q. Morris and C.M. Sirica, "Taking Charge of Graduate Medical Education: To Meet the Nation's Needs in the 21st Century" (Proceedings of a conference sponsored by the Josiah Macy, Jr. Foundation, New York, June 1992.)

23. J.V. Kelly et al., "Graduate Medical Education Consortia: Expectations and Experiences," *Academic Medicine* 69, no. 12 (1994): 931–943.

24. Kelly et al., "Graduate Medical Education Consortia," 931–943.

25. Raffel and Raffel, *The U.S. Health System: Origins and Functions,* 16.

26. American Board of Medical Specialties, *Annual Report and Reference Handbook—2002* (Evanston, IL: 2002), 111–14.

27. Jones, "Organized Medicine in the United States," 427.

28. H.S. Jonas et al., "Educational Programs in U.S. Medical Schools, 1993–1994," *Journal of the American Medical Association* 272, no. 9 (1994): 694.

29. National Center for Health Statistics, Bureau of Health Professions, "Table 104, Primary Care Doctors of Medicine According to Specialty: United States and Outlying U.S. Areas, Selected Years 1949–97." http://www.cdc.gov/nchs/products/pubs/pubd/hus/tables/99hus104.pdf (20 September 1999). Accessed 4 August 2000.

30. National Center for Health Statistics, Bureau of Health Professions, "Table 105, Active Health Personnel According to Occupation and Geographic Region: United States, 1980, 1990, and 1996." http://www.cdc.gov/nchs/products/pubs/pubd/hus/tables/99hus105.pdf (20 September 1999). Accessed 4 August 2000.

31. "Non-Federal Physicians per 100,000 Population by State, 2000, Physician Characteristics and Distribution in US, 2002–2003," *American Medical Association* (2002): 48.

32. R.M. Daugherty, Jr., "Adjusting the Size of the Education Pipeline," American Medical Association—Medical Schools Section: Council of Medical Education CME Report 6-1-98. http://www.ama-assn.org/annual99/reports/cmerpts/rtf/cmerep10.rtf. Accessed 6 August 2000.

33. National Center for Health Statistics, Bureau of Health Professions, "Table 107, First-Year Enrollment and Graduates of Health Professions Schools and Number of Schools According to Profession: United States, Selected Years 1980–98." http://www.cdc.gov/nchs/products/pubs/pubd/hus/tables/99hus107.pdf (20 September 1999). Accessed 14 August 2000.

34. R.D. Lamm, "The Coming Dislocation in the Health Professions," *Healthcare Forum* 39, no. 1 (January/February 1996): 58–62.

35. G.P. Whelan et al., "The Changing Pool of International Medical Graduates Seeking Certification Training in US Graduate Medical Education Programs," *Journal of the American Medical Association* 288, no. 9 (2002): 1079–1084.

36. Whelan et al., "The Changing Pool of International Medical Graduates Seeking Certification Training in US Graduate Medical Education Programs," 1079–1084.

37. R.A. Cooper, "Seeking a Balanced Physician Work Force for the 21st Century," *Journal of the American Medical Association* 272, no. 9 (1994): 680–687.

38. E.S. Salsberg and G.J. Forte, "Trends in the Physicians Workforce, 1980-2000," *Health Affairs* 21, no. 5: 165–173.

39. U.S. Department of Labor, Bureau of Labor Statistics, "Occupation Outlook Handbook, 2000–2001 ed." http://www.stats.bls.gov/ocd/ocds078.htm. Accessed 6 August 2000.

40. E. Steiner and J.M. Stoken, "Overcoming Barriers to Generalism in Medicine: The Residents' Perspective," *Academic Medicine* 70, no. 1 (1995): 589–594.

41. E.H. O'Neil, "Education as Part of the Health Care Solution," *Journal of the American Medical Association* 268, no. 9 (1992): 1146.

42. S.A. Inwald and F.D. Winters, "Emphasizing a Preventive Medicine Orientation During Primary Care/Family Practice Residency Training," *Journal of the American Osteopathic Association* 95, no. 4 (1995): 267.

43. Inwald and Winters, "Emphasizing a Preventive Medicine Orientation," 268.

44. S.E. Radecki and S.A. Brunton, "Health Promotion/Disease Prevention in Family Practice Residency Training: Results of a National Survey," *Family Medicine* 24, no. 7 (1992): 536.

45. C.P. Thomas, "The Cluster Committee: Setting the Stage for Community-Responsive Care," *American Journal of Preventive Medicine* 11, no. 1 (1995): 9–18.

46. C. Harris et al., "Physician-Hospital Networking: Avoiding a Shotgun Wedding," *Health Care Management Review* 17, no. 4 (1992): 17–28.

47. Harris et al., "Physician-Hospital Networking."

48. R.C. Coile, Jr., "Hospitalists Redefine the Future of Inpatient Medicine," *CQOnline*, http://www.cost-quality.com/restpast/vbi4a2html (December 2000). Accessed 28 August 2002.

49. P. Kongstvedt, *The Managed Health Care Handbook* (Gaithersburg, MD: Aspen Publishers, Inc., 1989).

50. Kongstvedt, *The Managed Health Care Handbook.* A-64.

51. R.L. Lowes, "Groups Get Serious about Judging Their Doctors," *Medical Economics* 72, no. 9 (1995): 59.

52. M.E. Overlook, "Managed Care and the Infamous Hold Harmless Clause," *Journal of the Tennessee Medical Association* 86, no. 10 (1993): 454.

53. Institute of Medicine, "United States Committee on Clinical Practice Guidelines," in *Guidelines for Clinical Practice: From Development to Use,* eds. M.J. Field and K.N. Lohr (Washington, D.C.: National Academy Press, 1992), 63.

54. Agency for Health Care Policy and Research, "AHCPR Clinical Practice Guideline Topics," *Agency for Health Care Policy and Research News Report* (Silver Spring, MD: AHCPR Publications Clearing House, March 1994).

55. M.C. Toepp and N. Kuznets, *Directory of Practice Parameters: Titles, Sources, and Updates* (Chicago: American Medical Association Office of Quality Assurance and Medical Review, 1994), vi.
56. Louis Harris and Associates, *Health Care Outlook/Hospital Strategic Outlook, Physician Survey,* 1992.
57. M.L. Millenson, *Demanding Medical Excellence* (Chicago: University of Chicago Press, 1997): 173.
58. Millenson, *Demanding Medical Excellence,*193.
59. "Special Report, Docs Fight to Hide Lawsuits," *New York Daily News, Sports Final* (April 17, 2000), 12.
60. Health Grades, Inc. www.healthgrades.com. Accessed 12 March 2003.
61. "Physician Use of Internet Explodes," *Health Management Technology* 20, no. 2 (March 1999): 8–9.
62. R.J. Blendon and M. Brodie, *Transforming the System: Building a New Structure for a New Century* (Washington, D.C.: Faulkner and Gray Healthcare Information Center, 1994), 81–94.
63. G.A. Niederman and B.A. Johnson, "Integrated Provider Networks, A Primer," *Medical Group Management Journal* 41, no. 6 (1994): 62–68.
64. Niederman and Johnson, "Integrated Provider Networks, A Primer." 62–68.
65. Niederman and Johnson, "Integrated Provider Networks, A Primer." 62–68.
66. Niederman and Johnson, "Integrated Provider Networks, A Primer." 62–68.

Chapter 6

Health Care Personnel

This chapter defines the major health care professions with particular emphasis on their educational preparation, credentials, numbers, and roles in the health service system. The factors that influence demand for the various health care providers and the workforce issues that divide them are also reviewed. The chapter concludes with a discussion of the development of health workforce policy and some expectations for the future.

A s one of the nation's largest and most important industries, health care is also one of the largest employment sectors. The explosion of technology and other medical advances that fueled health care system expansion between 1960 and 1984 was accompanied by an incredible 292 percent increase in health industry employment. During that period, health care employment rose from slightly over 1.5 million to over 6 million.[1] The health sector's wage and salary share of the total U.S. private economy more than doubled, increasing from 3.1 to 7.4 percent.

The Department of Labor estimates that over 11 million people, or approximately 10 percent of the U.S. workforce, are employed in the health care industry (see Figure 6–1).

Public policies, such as Medicare and Medicaid, tax policy for employer health insurance, public support for capital financing of hospitals and nursing homes, medical research, and education of physicians spurred the growth of the health sector. More recent policies, designed to contain growth and costs, have slowed the rate of increase in employment and shifted the employment sites from hospitals to other service delivery settings. Although hospitals are still a major employer, recent employment growth has been among health maintenance organizations (HMOs), ambulatory clinics and services, home health providers, and offices of health practitioners.

◼ Health Professions

There are more than 200 occupations and professions among the over 11 million workers in the health care field. As the system continues to change, making use of new technology, expanding in some sectors and contracting in others, additional vocations will appear. As the health care industry and its

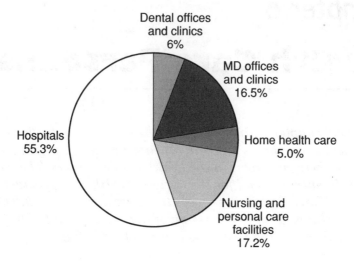

Dental offices
and clinics
6%

MD offices
and clinics
16.5%

Hospitals
55.3%

Home health care
5.0%

Nursing and
personal care
facilities
17.2%

Figure 6–1 Distribution of Health Care Employment by Settings.
Source: Reprinted from *U.S. Industrial Outlook,* Health and Medical Services, U.S. Department of Commerce.

workforce continue to grow, the personnel employed will be required to possess more specialized knowledge and more sophisticated skills.

The increasing sophistication of health care services fosters specialization to attain higher levels of technical competence, but it also reduces the flexibility of providers to develop more efficient staffing patterns. Specialization among the workforce increases personnel costs as additional employees are required to perform specific tasks. Smaller service facilities, especially in rural areas, are burdened most by the need for infrequently used specialists.

As a result, there is growing acceptance of multiskilled health practitioners. Hospitals, in particular, are employing individuals trained in more than one skill. A large number of combinations are feasible: occupational therapy assistants also are serving as physical therapy assistants; radiologic technologists are performing ultrasound; and a variety of nonclinical personnel are performing phlebotomy.

■ Health Care Personnel and Health Care Reforms

Predicting future demand and deploying health care personnel with any confidence is difficult while the health care system is in such an extraordinary state of transition. It is certain, however, that the manner in which health care personnel are employed is the single factor most amenable to change because of government or industry actions and workplace innovations. Yet, as the health care system struggles to adapt to changing market conditions, new technology, and calls for greater accountability in matters of costs, quality, and access, little attention has been paid to the potential effects of those changes on the health care workforce.

Other than the concerns expressed about the intrusion of managed care policies into traditional physician–patient relationships and the imbalance between medical generalists and specialists, the future of the large and diverse body of other health professionals has not been the subject of health care policy debates. Yet, the people who make up the vast majority of the health care workforce—nurses, pharmacists, therapists, technicians, technologists, and other allied health professionals—will be affected directly by health care system changes and will contribute significantly to the success or failure of the forthcoming health care reforms.

One development is certain. The aging of the American population will spur a boom in health care employment. The Bureau of Labor Statistics predicts that half of the next decade's 10 fastest growing occupations will be in the health care fields. The two occupations that head the list are personal care aides and home health aides. In 1996, the agency expected that by 2005, 640,000 new jobs would be created in these two categories.[2]

Three circumstances are contributing to the home health care job growth. Technological advances now permit sophisticated medical procedures to be performed in home settings; cost constraints force people to forego or shorten hospital stays; and the larger number and increased longevity of aging Americans will increase the need for the home care services of nurses, therapists, and aides. The Bureau of Labor Statistics projects tens of thousands of new jobs, outside of hospital workers, for physical and occupational therapists and aides, medical record technicians, speech pathologists, radiologic technologists, and psychiatric aides. In addition to home care, those new employment opportunities will occur in primary care clinics, health maintenance organizations, ambulatory surgical centers, and physicians' offices.[3]

■ Credentialing and Regulating Health Professionals

Government regulation of the health professions is considered necessary to protect the public from incompetent and unethical practitioners. Because each state assumes and exercises most of that responsibility for itself, how health care occupations are regulated and the manner in which regulation is carried out varies from state to state. About 50 health occupations are regulated throughout the United States.

Regulatory restrictions limit health care service agencies in how they may use personnel and limit their ability to explore innovative ways to provide patient care. Similarly, regulatory restrictions influence educational programs to focus curricula on what has been prescribed by regulatory boards and their related accrediting bodies, even when those practice patterns have been replaced by more advanced procedures. Many states have taken steps to revise their credentialing systems to provide greater flexibility and responsiveness to fast-changing health care technology.[4]

The health care occupations have been regulated by one of three procedures: state licensure, state or national certification, or state or national registration. In licensure, the state law defines the scope of practice to be regulated and the educational and testing requirements that must be met to engage in that practice. Licensure, the most restrictive of the three types of regulation, is intended to restrict entry or practice in certain occupations and to prevent the use of professional titles by those without predetermined qualifications. For example, it is illegal for individuals to perform procedures defined in the statutes as medicine or dentistry or call themselves physicians or dentists without the appropriate license.

Most licensure boards are composed primarily of practitioners whose concern is for setting standards and assessing competence for initial entrance into the field. Except by requiring attendance at continuing education courses, licensure boards have done very little about ensuring continuing competence, dealing with impaired practitioners, or disciplining wayward members of their professions. However, they do have the power to censure, warn members, or even revoke licenses.

Certification is the regulating process under which a state or voluntary professional organization, such as a national board, attests to the educational achievements and performance abilities of persons in a health care field of practice. It is a much less restrictive regulation than licensing and means that the individual has obtained advanced or specialized training in that area of practice. When applied to such fields as psychology and social work, certification does not make it illegal for unqualified individuals to engage in activities within the scope of practice in those fields as long as they do not claim or use the titles of certified psychologist or social worker. Certification allows the public, employers, and third-party payers to determine which practitioners are appropriately qualified in their specialty or occupation.

Certification generally has no provision for regulating impaired or misbehaving practitioners other than putting them on probation or dropping them from certification. Unlike licensure, certification has no legal basis for preventing an impaired or professionally delinquent individual from practicing. It is a weakness of certification that it is left to third-party payers or employers to insist on only certified practitioners.

Registration began as a mechanism to facilitate contacts and relationships among members of a profession and potential employers or the public. It is the least rigorous of regulatory processes, ranging from simple listings or registries of persons offering a service, such as private duty nurses, to national registration programs of professional or occupational groups that require educational and testing qualifications. Because most registration programs are voluntary, they have little to do with continuing competence or disciplinary actions.[5]

■ Health Care Occupations

Although space does not allow for the description of all or even most of the occupations in health care, several major health care vocations are outlined here. Chapter 5 is devoted to the evolution of the various modes of medical practice, the influence of medical education and academic medical centers, and the issues impacting on physician autonomy, so the information regarding physicians in this chapter is purposely limited.

Physicians

There are 126 schools in the United States that award the Doctor of Medicine (MD) degree. Their enrollment has been stable for several years and they consistently graduate about 15,700 students per year. There are 19 accredited colleges that confer the Doctor of Osteopathy degree (DO). In the last two decades their enrollment has nearly doubled and they now graduate about 2,300 students per year. The combined growth in the number of physicians graduated was about 12 percent. Doctors of medicine and doctors of osteopathy share the same privileges in most U.S. hospitals.

The number of women enrolled in U.S. medical schools has more than doubled in the last 20 years. In 2001, the entering class was 48 percent female. The number of minority students enrolled in medical schools nearly tripled during the same period. In 2001, minority students represented 34.6 percent of the entering class.[6]

Although medical education in the United States begins in undergraduate medical school, it continues intensively for as many as eight years of graduate medical training. Most states require one year of graduate medical education before a physician may be licensed. That year, which used to be called an internship, is now considered the first of three years of residency training regarded by the medical profession as the minimum needed to practice medicine.

Residency training prepares a physician to practice a medical specialty. In a period of three to eight years, depending on the specialty, residency qualifies a physician for certification by 1 of 24 medical specialty boards. Further residency training, often called a fellowship, can lead to a certificate in 1 of over 90 subspecialties. A listing of these medical specialties and subspecialties may be found in Chapter 5.

Since U.S. medical schools consistently graduate about 5,000 fewer new physicians per year than are employed as first-year residents, the gap is filled by physicians trained in medical schools outside of the United States. The annual number of foreign nationals who graduate from medical schools outside the United States and then enter this country to practice each year increased rapidly until a hands-on clinical skills assessment was required in 1998. The responsibility for evaluating the credentials of International Medical Graduates (IMGs) entering the United States to enter residency programs lies with the Educational Commission for Foreign Medical Graduates (ECFMG), a private non-profit organization sponsored by major U.S. medical organizations including the American Association of Medical Colleges.

Though the more stringent certification process and the heightened security concerns following the tragic events of September 11 may have deterred some IMGs from pursuing the opportunity to train in the United States, the number entering this country, over 6,000 IMGs in 2002, is more than adequate to meet the annual shortfall of U.S. medical school graduates.[7]

The impetus for this influx is the demand for resident house officers in both teaching and nonteaching hospitals. All but the most prestigious hospitals, particularly those in rural or inner city areas, depend heavily on foreign medical graduates to staff their clinical services. Future planning for the physician work force in the context of the projected shortage of physicians will have to be sensitive to the future role of foreign medical graduates, particularly in underserved areas.[8]

After finishing their residency training, most of these international medical school graduates (IMGs) remain in the United States to practice. As a result, IMGs now constitute about one-quarter of the active U.S. physician workforce. There is also a relatively stable group of about 1,350 U.S. citizens who attend medical schools outside the country and return to practice each year.

About 40 percent of the almost 800,000 practicing physicians in the United States are in primary care. In 2000, about 22 percent of active primary care physicians were in general pediatrics, 30 percent in general or family practice, and 47 percent in general internal medicine practice.[9]

The number and size of managed care organizations that depended on primary care physicians to minimize patient referrals to specialists and subspecialists temporarily altered the usual ratio of specialists to generalist physicians. Since managed care organizations relaxed those restrictions in response to intense public and physician disapproval, however, medical specialists are again in demand. In fact, there are serious shortages in certain medical specialties that affect the efficiency and quality of medical care in various geographic areas. Depending on the region of the country, radiologists, obstetricians, anesthesiologists, gastroenterologists, gerontologists, cardiologists, urologists, pulmonologists, orthopedic and general surgeons, hematologists, oncologists, and a variety of intensive care physicians may be in short supply.[10]

The projected shortage of physicians may accelerate an existing trend towards substituting nurse practitioners, physician assistants, and various types of technicians and technologists for physicians in the provision of certain medical services. In addition, chiropractors and other alternative medical providers are experiencing increased popularity. By 2015, there are expected to be as many as 275,000 nurse practitioners, physician assistants, and nurse midwives, 150,000 chiropractors and acupuncturists, and 100,000 other physician substitutes providing services that overlap those provided by physicians. Their combined effort will be equivalent to the services of 65 physicians per 100,000 population.[11]

Nursing

Nursing often became an employment position for women during the nineteenth century through association with a religious or benevolent group. A physician, Ann Preston, organized the first training program for nurses in the United States in 1861, at Philadelphia's Woman's Hospital. Training was open to all women "who wished greater proficiency in their domestic responsibilities."[12]

At the turn of the century, hundreds of new hospitals were built under the aegis of religious orders, ethnic groups, industrialists, and elite groups of civic-minded individuals. Because student nurses were a constantly renewable source of low-cost workers to staff the wards, even some of the smallest hospitals maintained nursing schools.[13] Hospital nursing school programs, therefore, were primarily sequences of on-the-job training rather than academic courses. As the programs evolved, stronger academic components were introduced, eventually leading to baccalaureate degrees instead of hospital diplomas.

World War I had a profound effect on the nursing profession. Before the war, nursing was divided into three domains—public health, private duty, and hospital. Public health nursing was the elite pursuit and was recognized as instrumental in the campaign against tuberculosis and promoting infant welfare. Only a few nurses worked for hospitals. In 1920, over 70 percent of nurses worked in private duty, about half in patients' homes and half for private patients in hospitals.

The war emphasized the drama and effectiveness of hospitals, and it soon became the center of nursing education in the increasingly specialized acute care medical environment. The social medicine and public health aspects of nursing were subjugated to the image of nursing as a symbol of patriotism, national sacrifice, and efficiency. The war experience established nurses as dedicated associates in hospital science. Nursing leaders promoted the idea of upgrading nursing through high-quality hospital nursing schools, preferably associated with universities. The choice to idealize the role of the nurse as dedicated and deferential to the physician specialist in the hospital marginalized the independent role of the nurse in social medicine and public health.[14]

World War II brought increased funding for the educational preparation of nurses. Later, the Nurse Training Act of 1964, the Health Manpower Act of 1968, and the Nurse Training Act of 1971 added substantially to the federal support of nursing education.[15] Nevertheless, state funding provides the largest support for nursing schools, some 80 percent of which are in colleges and universities. A recent survey by the American Association of Colleges of Nursing found that 72 percent of responding nursing schools that receive state dollars are fully funded by their states.[16]

Different levels of nursing education were developed at a variety of educational institutions. A registered nurse (RN) may be trained in a two-year associate degree program at a community college or a junior college, a two- to three-year diploma program offered through a hospital, or a four- to five-year bachelor of science degree program at a university or college.

The increasing complexity in health care forced specialization in nursing as it did in medicine. Nurses with a bachelor's degree may undertake advanced studies in several clinical areas to develop the needed competence for teaching, supervision, or advanced practice. Clinical nurse specialists in hospitals play important liaison roles between the medical practitioners in narrow and highly technical subspecialties, the patients, and supportive nursing services. By the 1960s, master's degree and doctoral programs were developed for nurses who wished to specialize.

The number of registered nurses increased by more than 1 million between 1980 and 2000. The number of employed nurses in 2000 reached over 2,200,000.The last four years of that period, however, showed the slowest growth in the RN population of those two decades.[17]

More than 80 percent of all registered nurses are employed. Few of the remainder are seeking employment. Over 60 percent of employed nurses have been working in hospitals. The following table illustrates the distribution of nurses in the United States by field of employment. The data were obtained during the last national sample survey of registered nurses conducted in 2000. (See Table 6–1.)[18]

One of the major changes occurring in nursing is in the type of program that nurses enter to obtain their basic education. Almost 90

Table 6–1 Employment of Registered Nurses by Setting, Year 2000

	PERCENT DISTRIBUTION
Hospital	62.1
Nursing home	8.4
Ambulatory care setting	8.1
Home health	6.5
Community/Public health	4.8
Student health service	2.9
Nursing education	2.3
Occupational health	1.0
Other	3.9
Total	100.0

Source: Data from U.S. Department of Health and Human Services, Health Resources and Services Administration, Bureau of Health Professions, National Center for Health Workforce Analysis, 2000 National Sample Survey of Registered Nurses.

percent of nurses now receive their basic education in an institution of higher education, compared with 20 percent in 1960. Although nurses with baccalaureate degrees or higher education are still in the minority, representing approximately one-third of nurses, the numerical count is more impressive. More than 900,000 nurses have baccalaureate or higher degrees, and 1 in every 10 nurses is working on an advanced degree.[19]

Nurses began to specialize during the 1950s. After World War II, nurses were in short supply and hospitals began to group the least physiologically stable patients in one nursing unit for intensive care. The more competent nurses cared for the sickest patients. But instead of lowering the need for nurses, the critical care nurse (CCN) specialty began, and the need for staff nurses continued to grow.

There are now more than 50 U.S. schools that have at least one of the three types of doctoral programs in nursing. The doctor of nursing (ND) is the first professional doctoral degree building on liberal arts or scientific education and preparing the student to take the state licensing exam to practice as an RN. The doctor of nursing science (DNS and DNSc) degrees are professional doctorates that prepare the nurse for advanced clinical practice. The nursing PhD is an academic degree with requirements similar to the PhD in other fields—extensive preparation in a narrow field and a dissertation.[20]

During the 1980s, the importance of nursing research was recognized by the addition of the National Center for Nursing Research within the National Institutes of Health.

Men comprise a very small percentage of the nurse population, although their numbers are increasing. In 2000, only about 5.4 percent of registered nurses were men, but that was double the proportion of male RNs in 1980. Rapid increases are also occurring in the numbers of RNs identifying themselves as members of a minority group. The percentage of minority RNs has tripled since 1980.

The trend that is a matter of concern, however, is the continued aging of the employed RN population. In 1980, over 52 percent of registered nurses were under 40 years of age. In 2000, less than a third, 31.7 percent, were under 40 years of age. There are two primary reasons for the worrisome change. Within the four years between 1996 and 2000, the departure of RNs from the licensed pool increased six to seven times to almost 175,000 nurses. With the slowing of new entrants into the field, current projections foresee the number of losses approaching and then exceeding the number of new nurses each year.[21]

Although the nurse-to-population ratio in the United States continues to be the highest in the world, with one nurse for every 145 Americans, that ratio will recede rapidly as the population increases and total nursing school enrollment decreases.

If current trends continue and contributing problems are not addressed, the demand for nurses will exceed the supply. The current shortage of nurses, which is estimated to be about 6 percent of jobs unfilled, is projected to grow to 15 percent in 2015 and 29 percent in 2020. (See Figure 6–2.)

Hospital consolidations in response to market pressures and the widespread acceptance of managed care are affecting nursing employ-

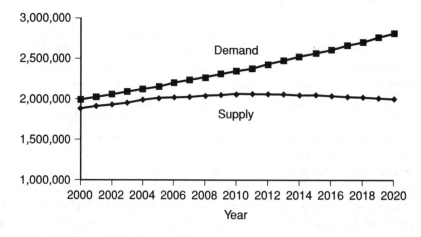

Figure 6–2 National supply and demand projections for FTE registered nurses: 2000 to 2020.

Source: Bureau of Health Professions, RN Supply and Demand Projections.

ment in several ways. Hospital workforces have been reorganized to adjust to fiscal restraints, reductions in the number of admissions, and shortened lengths of stay. At the same time, increases in the intensity of nursing care required by the more complicated illnesses of the patients who are admitted to hospitals suggest the need for higher nurse-patient ratios. Thus, although many hospitals employ fewer nurses for inpatient care, those retained are expected to maintain clinically sophisticated nursing skills, monitor lesser trained persons employed to provide direct patient care, and manage nursing units filled with seriously ill patients.

Fewer nurses taking care of more severely ill patients during even shorter hospital stays combined with the need to supervise nonprofessional and unlicensed personnel performing nursing tasks has increased nursing workloads, lowered morale, and raised serious concerns about the declining quality of care.

Not surprisingly, concerns for the quality of care, frustration with unresponsive hospital managers, and burn-out from working in understaffed facilities has made hospital nursing a less attractive career. As a result, many competent nurses have retired or sought employment in non-inpatient settings. Nurses formerly employed in serving hospitals have been absorbed in ambulatory service facilities such as surgery centers and group practices. Others have chosen to reorient themselves to the quite different job requirements of nurses in home care organizations and long-term care facilities.

Unfortunately, young men and women who might have chosen nursing as a career have been warned off by the experience of those in the field. This, coupled with the aging of the existing nurse workforce, portends a severe and growing shortage of clinical nurses that will seriously affect nurse recruitment among hospitals.

Licensed Practical Nurses (LPNs)

A licensed practical nurse (LPN) works under the direct supervision of an RN or physician. One-year LPN training is offered at technical or vocational schools or community or junior colleges. Both RNs and LPNs must pass a national licensing examination after attending an accredited nursing school. In addition to hospitals, RNs and LPNs are employed in nursing homes, rehabilitation centers, private physician offices, home health care, HMOs, and industrial or educational positions.

LPNs held 700,000 jobs in 2000. Although 28 percent worked in hospitals that year, their employment within hospitals is decreasing. The reduction in inpatient days and the substitution of unlicensed personnel has decreased the number of LPNs in hospitals by almost 10,000 per year over the last several years. The demand for LPNs in the other work settings, however, is increasing. Nursing homes employ 29 percent of the LPNs, and another 14 percent are employed in physician offices and clinics. The remainder work in home health care, residential care facilities, schools, and government agencies.[22]

Nurse Practitioners

Nurse practitioners are RNs with advanced education and clinical experience. Most nurse practitioners specialize. Neonatal nurse practitioners work with newborns. Pediatric nurse practitioners treat children from infancy through adolescence. School nurse practitioners serve students in elementary and secondary schools, colleges, and universities. Adult and family nurse practitioners are generalists who serve adults and families. Occupational health nurse practitioners work in industry providing on-the-job care. Psychiatric nurse practitioners serve people with mental or emotional problems. Geriatric nurse practitioners care for older adults.[23]

The earliest nurse practitioners were nurse midwives and nurse anesthetists. Nurse midwives examine women throughout pregnancy, educate them about labor and birth, assist them in managing labor, deliver the infant, and care for the newborn and mother. A nurse midwife usually is an RN who completes a one-year or two-year master's degree program in nurse midwifery. They are licensed by the state and also may be required to be certified by the American College of Nurse Midwives. Currently, almost all of the midwife-assisted births take place in a hospital or birthing clinic.

The need for nurse midwives has grown as birthing centers have attracted women who prefer a more "home-like" birthing experience.

> *Research shows that a woman who experiences a healthy pregnancy, labor, and delivery is as safe in the hands of a nurse midwife as she would be in the hands of a physician. A report by the Institute of Medicine (1982) emphasized that nurse midwives are particularly effective in managing the care of pregnant women, and that such care results in fewer premature and underweight babies, indicating a significant level of professional recognition on the part of the physicians.[24]*

The roots for the nursing specialty of nurse anesthetist go back over a century, when nurses administered anesthesia in Catholic hospitals. Early training was provided in hospitals, but in 1945, the American Association of Nurse Anesthetists established a certification program. Nurse anesthetists are now required to have a master's degree from an accredited school and must pass the national certification examination. Most nurse anesthetists work with physician anesthesiologists in hospitals, ambulatory surgery centers, and urgent care centers providing comprehensive care to patients who need anesthesia. Approximately 20 percent of anesthesia being administered to patients is by nurse anesthetists working alone.[25]

The current nurse practitioner movement began in the 1960s because of the shortage of physicians. The goal was to have specially prepared nurses augment the supply of physicians by working as primary care providers in pediatrics, adult health, geriatrics, and obstetrics. Nurse practitioners had to overcome some resistance from organized medicine and legal difficulties caused by restrictions in most state nurse practice acts, which included a prohibition against nurses diagnosing and treating patients. Nurse practitioners sought state-by-state changes in nurse practice acts, and, by 1975, most states had started certifying or accepting the national certification of nurse practitioners, nurse midwives, and nurse anesthetists.[26]

Two-thirds of the first 131 nurse practitioner programs were certificate programs and one-third were master's programs. The certificate programs ranged from 3 to 24 months, with an average of about 8 months. The master's programs, which ranged from 10 to 21 months, averaged 15 months. The programs specialized primarily in training for practice in pediatrics, midwifery, maternity, family medicine, adult health, or psychiatry. As in most ventures into uncharted territory, several approaches to nurse practitioner preparation were tested. Eventually, it was accepted that a nurse practitioner should be an RN with a master's degree. National certification and recertification are necessary.[27]

Efforts at health care cost containment have increased the demand for cost-effective nurse practitioners. Managed care organizations have been particularly successful in using nurse practitioners and physician assistants to bolster their complement of staff physicians. Rural hospitals, with limited reserves of physicians, make substantial use of nurse practitioners and physician assistants. Rural hospital executives consider the use of nurse practitioners and physician assistants to be a cost-effective means to provide an expanded scope of services and improve access to primary care.[28]

Nurse practitioners and physician assistants also are heavily involved in emergency department care. They manage a wide range of conditions in about 4 percent of all emergency department visits in the United States.[29]

A nationwide survey of public attitudes toward health care provided by nurses conducted in the late 1980s showed that nurses were highly regarded by the public and that most people were willing to receive more of their health care from nurses.[30]

Clinical Nurse Specialist

A different, but related, type of advanced nursing practice is the clinical nurse specialist. Just as the role of nurse practitioners evolved over several decades to meet demands for increased access to primary health care, so too did the role of the clinical nurse specialist, which was developed in response to the specialized nursing care needs of increasingly complex patients.[31] Like specialist physicians, clinical nurse specialists develop in-depth knowledge and skills that make them valuable adjunct practitioners in specialized clinical settings.

Medicare Revisions

The Balanced Budget Act of 1997 contains several provisions that affect nurses and other nonphysician providers. The new law treats nurse practitioners, clinical nurse specialists, and physician assistants as Medicare-covered providers in all settings. It also sets their reimbursement rate at 85 percent of the physician fee schedule. Intended to improve access in medically underserved areas, the new service demand created by the policy change is projected by the Congressional Budget Office to increase spending by about $500 million over the next five years.[32]

Dentistry

Dentistry in early America was primitive. Tooth extraction was performed by either an itinerant tooth-drawer, the neighborhood doctor or barber, or in many cases, the local blacksmith. Because there were no regulations, anyone could practice dentistry, and skilled craftsmen and artisans turned their talents to dental practice.

During the nineteenth century, most people turned to their local physicians, some of whom practiced dentistry as their principal occupation, for dental care. Until about 1850, almost all prominent dentists were medical doctors who had chosen dentistry rather than general medicine as their vocation.[33] It was also in the nineteenth century that dentistry began its emergence from a trade to a profession. Dental schools were established to replace preceptorships, and dental practitioners participated in developing laws to regulate the profession.[34]

In 1840, the State of Maryland chartered the first dental school, the Baltimore College of Dental Surgery. The course of study lasted two years, the same as that required for a medical degree. By 1884, 28 dental colleges existed. Although a few were affiliated with universities, most were privately owned. New York took the lead in regulating the profession by licensure. The state's dental society was empowered in 1868 to establish a board of censors to examine candidates. In time, it became the State Board of Dental Examiners. By the end of the century, most other states also had passed licensure laws.

The mix of university-affiliated and independent dental schools resulted in significant variations in the quality of dental education. In 1922, 12 years after the Carnegie Foundation for the Advancement of Teaching had issued the Flexner report evaluating U.S. medical education, the foundation created a commission to examine dental education. The commission's report appeared in 1926 and resulted in a complete reorganization of dental education in the United States.[35]

World War II brought about profound changes in Americans' attitudes toward dentistry. Citizens were shocked to learn that the dental health of the nation's young men was deplorable. Among the first 2 million draftees summoned by the Selective Service System, one out of five lacked even the minimum standard of 12 functioning teeth. The Selective Service had to eliminate all dental standards to avoid mass disqualification of selectees. As a consequence, after the war, the United States made a vigorous effort to improve the dental health of the country's population.

Before World War II, dentists were not involved in public health, and few dental schools taught anything on the subject. A decade after the first graduate course of study in dental public health was established in the 1940s by the University of Michigan, the new field of public health dentistry emerged in the United States. Today, a number of schools have established courses leading to advanced degrees in the field, and there is an American Board of Dental Public Health to certify them as specialists.

The U.S. Public Health Service established the National Institute of Dental Research (NIDR) in 1948. Ultimately incorporated into the NIH, the NIDR played a major role in furthering basic and applied dental research.

Also beneficial to dentistry during the postwar years was the increase in insurance group plans that provide payment for routine dental care, plus, in certain instances, more extensive dentistry at an additional premium. By 1980, almost 100 million Americans were covered, to some degree, by a dental insurance plan, and today it is a common employee benefit.

The overall number of dentists per U.S. citizen reached its highest point in 1987, but will continue to decrease in the coming decades. There have been major decreases in the annual number of dental graduates, while the general population continues to increase.

Nine practice specialties have developed in dentistry:

1. Dental Public Health
2. Endodontics
3. Oral and Maxillofacial Pathology
4. Oral and Maxillofacial Radiology
5. Oral and Maxillofacial Surgery
6. Orthodontics and Dentofacial Orthopedics
7. Pediatric Dentistry
8. Periodontics
9. Prosthodontics

Unlike in medicine, however, more than three-fourths of the approximately 155,000 practicing dentists in the United States are general practitioners.[36] In 1998, there were 55 U.S. dental schools, a decrease of five since 1980. These dental schools graduate approximately 4,000 dentists per year, a drop of over 1,500 graduates per year in the last two decades.

The demographic composition of America's dental profession is also changing. From a low of 13 percent in 1980, minorities now constitute one-third of the annual enrollment in dental schools. Women are also more prominent in dental school enrollment. Female dental students, once a rarity in dental schools, now comprise approximately 40 percent of first-year enrollments.[37]

Overall, dentists are working fewer hours for increased earnings. Dentistry has successfully resisted managed care and capitated payments and remained a "cottage industry." With most dentists in solo practice choosing to serve only those with dental insurance or the fiscal means to pay prevailing fees, many of the population groups with the greatest need for dental services will continue to be underserved. Neither dental education nor the current practice model places high priority on the creation of a dental safety net for underserved populations.[38]

Pharmacy

Pharmaceutical practice dates back to ancient Egypt, Rome, and Greece. The first apothecaries appeared in Europe during the twelfth century, and by 1546 the Senate of the city of Nuremberg, Germany, recognized the value of standardizing drugs to ensure uniformity in filling prescriptions.[39]

Hospital pharmacists were apprentice physicians in early America. In 1765, John Morgan proposed that medicine and pharmacy be separate, and by 1811 the New York Hospital had a full-time pharmaceutical practitioner.[40] The American Pharmaceutical Association was organized on October 7, 1852. Professional training programs were developed for pharmacists, and by 1864 there were eight colleges of pharmacy in the United States.[41]

There are now 79 colleges of pharmacy in the United States, each with its own application restrictions. Some colleges even take students right out of high school. It takes at least five years to earn a bachelor of science degree in pharmacy. A doctor of pharmacy degree (PharmD) normally requires at least six years. Each pharmacist is licensed by graduating from an accredited college of pharmacy, passing a state examination, and completing an internship with a licensed pharmacist.[42] Schools of pharmacy graduate about 8,000 students annually. The number of active pharmacists in the United States is now over 185,000, an increase of 43,000 since 1980.[43]

In 1976, the American Pharmaceutical Association created the Board of Pharmaceutical Specialties. It has approved nuclear pharmacy, clinical pharmacy, nutritional support pharmacy, and pharmacotherapy as specialties in which pharmacists may be certified.[44]

Sixty percent of pharmacists work in community pharmacies, many of which are owned by large commercial chains. There, they may supervise other employees, manage overall business needs, computerize patients' records, and advise physicians and patients about drug dosage, side effects, and interaction with other medications. Twenty-five percent of pharmacists work in hospitals, and the balance are employed by clinics, nursing homes, HMOs, and the federal government.[45]

In 1999, in response to a concern for a possible shortage of licensed pharmacists, Congress directed the Department of Health and Human Services to conduct a study of the pharmacist workforce in the United States. Released in December 2000, the study concluded that declines in pharmacy school applications combined with a sharp increase in demand for pharmacy services will result in a significant shortage of pharmacists.

Unless there are fundamental changes in pharmacy education and practice, the study predicted that the emerging shortage will result in less time for working pharmacists to counsel patients, greater potential for overworked pharmacists to make medication errors, and fewer pharmacists to join pharmacy school faculties.[46]

Podiatric Medicine

Podiatric medicine is specifically concerned with the diagnosis and treatment of diseases and injuries of the lower leg and foot. Podiatrists can prescribe drugs; order radiographs, laboratory tests, and physical therapy; set fractures; and perform surgery. They also fit corrective inserts called orthotics, design plaster casts and strappings to correct deformities, and design custom-made shoes. There are seven accredited schools in the United States where students can apply, generally after they have completed a bachelor's degree. The four years of professional training is similar to that for physicians. A residency is not required, but most podiatrists spend approximately one year completing a residency in a hospital after they graduate. All doctors of podiatric medicine must be licensed by the state in which they practice.[47] It is probably in the care of older adults, enabling people to live at home and function independently for as long as possible, that podiatric medicine makes its greatest public health contribution.[48]

In recent years, the seven colleges of podiatric medicine graduated approximately 600 students annually. Since 1975, the number of active podiatrists in the United States almost doubled, increasing from 6,400 to 12,242.[49]

Podiatric care is more dependent on disposable income than other medical services. Medicare and most private health insurance programs cover acute medical and surgical foot services, as well as diagnostic radiographs and leg braces. However, routine foot care ordinarily is not covered.[50]

Chiropractors

Chiropractors treat the whole body without the use of drugs or surgery. Special care is given to the spine, as chiropractors believe that misalignment or irritations of spinal nerves interfere with normal body functions. Daniel David Palmer of Iowa was a "magnetic healer" in the late nineteenth century who believed that disease and maladies are the result of nerve interference caused by misaligned vertebrae. He and his son, B.J. Palmer, created the first chiropractic school to teach their philosophies of health. Today there are 18 private chiropractic colleges. Students need at least an associate degree before applying to one of the accredited chiropractic colleges. After completion of the Doctor of Chiropractic (DC) degree, all states require chiropractors to be licensed to practice.[51] About 2,500 graduates of chiropractic colleges enter the growing profession each year. In the last 20 years, the number of active chiropractors rose 25,600 to approximately 50,000.[52]

Chiropractors follow a holistic approach that recognizes exercise, diet, rest, environment, and heredity as factors affecting each patient. Chiropractors use radiographs to examine a patient's spine and compare it to "ideal" posture. Manipulations, typically with hand thrusts or with a chiropractic tool called an activator, are given to patients. Some recent studies have shown that, although chiropractic treatment generally costs more than medical treatment by a primary care physician, patients still see the chiropractor more often and for a longer period of time.[53]

Physicians have long questioned chiropractic practice because of the lack of scientific data that suggest the efficacy of chiropractic treatments. "Spinal manipulation for nonmusculoskeletal conditions is contrary to current scientific evidence and is not supported by available quality studies."[54] Nevertheless, patients are generally satisfied with chiropractic care and, for specific conditions causing back pain, chiropractors achieve outcomes comparable to those of physicians.[55]

Chiropractic practice has strong public support and chiropractors have used that patronage to make significant gains in legal and legislative areas. Regardless of medicine's questions about chiropractic's lack of scientifically proven effectiveness, chiropractors achieved Medicare coverage, participate in most managed care, and many other insurance policies contain some form of chiropractic coverage.

Optometry

A Doctor of Optometry (OD) is a health care provider who examines patients' eyes to diagnose vision problems and eye disease, prescribes drugs for treatment, and prescribes and fits eyeglasses and contact lenses. An optometrist should not be confused with an ophthalmologist (once called an oculist) or an optician. An ophthalmologist is a physician who specializes in the treatment of eye diseases and injuries and uses drugs, surgery, or the prescription of corrective lenses to correct vision deficiencies. An optician is a licensed health professional who fits eyeglasses or contact lenses to individual patients as prescribed by ophthalmologists.

Optometrists must graduate from 1 of the 17 accredited four-year colleges of optometry and pass both written and clinical state board examinations to obtain a license to practice.[56] More than 1,200 students graduate each year to swell the current number of active optometrists to over 30,000.[57]

Most students apply to an optometry program after completing a bachelor's degree. Some students are accepted before graduation and complete their undergraduate requirements while taking the professional optometry courses, thus reducing their professional preparation from eight to seven years.[58] One-year residency programs are available for optometrists who wish to specialize in family practice optometry, pediatric optometry, geriatric optometry, occupational vision care, low vision rehabilitation, vision therapy, contact lenses, hospital-based optometry, or sports vision.

Optometrists usually work in private practice, but many are now forming small group practices. Optometrists can hire opticians and optometric assistants to help them increase their productivity and thus care for more patients. "Persons over 45 visit optometrists and ophthalmologists more frequently because of the onset of vision problems in middle age and the increased likelihood of cataracts, glaucoma, diabetes and hypertension in old age."[59] Because more than half of the people in the United States wear glasses or contact lenses, and there is a constant need for eye care by the majority of the aging population, growth in the field of optometry is expected to remain consistent.[60]

Health Care Administrators

Health care administrators are managers who plan, organize, direct, control, or coordinate medicine and health services in hospitals, clinics, nursing care facilities, and physicians' offices. As hospitals have grown in size and number, there has been a parallel increase in the need for health service managers. By the mid-1930s, college degrees were being offered in hospital and health administration.

There are now approximately 29 colleges granting bachelor's degrees and 64 graduate programs in health services administration. "Currently, the annual demand estimated by the Bureau of Labor Statistics for health administrators exceeds the supply of graduates from ACEHSA [Accrediting Commission on Education for Health Services Administration] accredited programs."[61] There also are short certificate or diploma programs, usually lasting less than one year, in health services administration or in medical office management. Health service managers include both generalists and specialists. A generalist is a top administrator managing an entire facility, whereas a specialist is in charge of a specific clinical department or a service within the larger organization. A bachelor's degree usually is preferred for an entry-level position. Higher-level executive officers usually hold graduate degrees.[62]

Many administrative positions have been filled with individuals who have training in business, public health, public administration, and other fields. The majority of health care administrators are employed in hospital settings, but others work in clinics or physicians' offices, and for HMOs. Administrative duties involve the planning, organizing, financing, controlling, and coordinating of health care services. A recent study lists skills with which administrators are primarily concerned, such as:

- Cost/finance
- Leadership
- Interaction with professional staff
- Health care delivery

Serious questions emerged from the study as to whether the master of health administration (MHA) degree should be replaced by the functionally specialized and analytically rigorous master of business administration (MBA) degree as the more suitable preparation for health care executives.[63]

Fellows of the American College of Healthcare Executives participated in a study that ranked the issues that would be most critical for health care organizations in the twenty-first century. The domains that were considered the most important are, in descending order of priority:

1. Cost/finance
2. Leadership skills
3. Professional staff interactions
4. Health care delivery concepts
5. Accessibility to care
6. Ethics
7. Quality and risk management
8. Technology
9. Marketing[64]

Allied Health Personnel

Unlike professionals in medicine, dentistry, nursing, and pharmacy, allied health personnel represent a varied and complex array of health care disciplines. Their roles in providing health care are not generally recognized or well understood by the public. Allied health personnel support, complement, or supplement the professional functions of physicians, dentists, or other health professionals in delivering health care to patients, and they assist in environmental health control, health promotion, and disease prevention. A number of more recent categories of health care specialists were created to implement the new procedures, equipment, and diagnostic, surgical, and therapeutic techniques that proliferated during the last three decades. There are now well over 200 allied health occupations and specialties.[65]

The range of allied health professions may be understood best by classifying them according to the functions they serve. They may be grouped into the following four categories:

1. Laboratory technologists and technicians
2. Therapeutic science practitioners
3. Behavioral scientists
4. Support services

It should be recognized, however, that some allied health disciplines should be included in more than one of these functional classifications.[66]

Laboratory Technologists and Technicians

Laboratory technologists and technicians have a critically important role in the diagnosis of disease, monitoring of physiological function and effectiveness of intervention, and application of highly technical procedures. This category includes radiologic technologists and nuclear medicine technologists (described below), as well as medical technologists, cytotechnologists, and others.

Radiologic Technology. A radiologic technologist works under the supervision of a radiologist, a physician who specializes in the use and interpretation of radiographs. The radiologic technologist will use radiographs, fluoroscopic equipment, and high-tech imaging machines such as ultrasonography, computed tomography, magnetic resonance imaging, and positron emission tomography units to produce films that allow physicians to study the internal organs and bones of their patients. These technologists are graduates of a two-year or four-year program that trains them for working with patients, choosing the appropriate equipment and adjusting it, preparing films, and keeping an accurate record of all treatments. Radiologic technologists need to be certified by the American Registry of Radiologic Technologists and licensed by the state in which they work.[67]

> *The vacancy rate for radiologic technologists is the highest in any health care profession. The U.S. Department of Labor predicts that, by the year 2010, the country will need 75,000 more radiologic technologists than it did in 2000. This demand comes in addition to the more than 31,000 specialized technologists needed within the field as well. Rapid technological advances are making it difficult for technologists to keep up with the changes.[68]*

Nuclear Medicine Technology. Nuclear medicine technologists use diagnostic imaging techniques to detect and map radioactive drugs in the human body. They administer radioactive pharmaceuticals to patients, then monitor the characteristics and functions of tissues or organs in which they localize. Abnormal areas show higher or lower concentrations of radioactivity than normal ones do.

Nuclear medicine technologists are prepared in one-year certificate programs offered by hospitals to those who are already radiologic technologists, medical technologists, or RNs, or who are in two-year to four-year programs offered in university schools of allied health. Nuclear medicine technologists must meet the minimum federal standards on the administration of radioactive drugs and the operation of radiation detection equipment. In addition, about half of all states require technologists to be licensed. Technologists also may obtain voluntary professional certification or registration.[69]

Therapeutic Science Practitioners

Practitioners of the therapeutic sciences are essential to the treatment and rehabilitation of patients with diseases and injuries of all kinds. Physical therapists, occupational therapists, speech pathology and audiology therapists, physician assistants, radiation therapists, respiratory therapists, dietitians, and dental hygienists are only some of the allied health disciplines in this category.

Physical Therapy. Physical therapists treat and assist in rehabilitation for patients with injuries and disabilities. Physicians often refer patients to physical therapists for treatment that can relieve pain, restore strength, increase mobility, and improve the condition of the muscles and skin.

Employment opportunities have grown rapidly in the physical therapy field, and the demand now exceeds the supply. All states require that a physical therapist graduate from an accredited college, fulfill a clinical internship, and pass the state examination to obtain a license to practice.[70] The Board of Certification of Advanced Clinical Competence within the American Physical Therapy Association (APTA) has developed the following six areas of specialization for physical therapists:[71]

1. Cardiopulmonary physical therapy
2. Clinical electron physiologic physical therapy
3. Neurologic physical therapy
4. Orthopaedic physical therapy
5. Pediatric physical therapy
6. Sports physical therapy

A master's degree is required for physical therapists interested in teaching or doing research.

Most physical therapists are employed outside a hospital in rehabilitation centers, nursing homes, schools for the handicapped, home health agencies, physician offices, or solo practice. Some self-employed physical therapists join with others to create group practices.[72]

Physical therapists supervise physical therapy assistants to aid them with meeting the needs of an increasing number of patients. A physical therapy assistant graduates with an associate degree prepared.to take the national certification examination.[73]

In 1998, there were 134 physical therapy programs in the United States graduating slightly under 5,000 new practitioners per year.

The number of active physical therapists is now well over 100,000, more than tripling the number of practitioners over three decades. Similarly, the increase in the number of physical therapy assistants reflects the burgeoning demand for the services. An estimated 3,400 graduates each year from 148 physical therapy assistant programs have yet to fill all the jobs available. The U.S. Department of Labor projects a 34.5 percent increase in the employment of physical therapists and a 44.7 percent increase in physical therapy assistants and aides between 1998 and 2008.[74]

Occupational Therapy. Occupational therapists assist patients in recovering from accidents, injuries, or diseases to maintain daily living skills and work abilities. A wide range of patients work with occupational therapists, from those with irreversible physical disabilities resulting from head injuries or muscular dystrophy to those with mental disabilities or disorders. Occupational therapists develop a rehabilitation plan and arrange appropriate educational, vocational, and recreational activities suitable to each patient.[75]

A bachelor's degree in occupational therapy is the minimum requirement for entry into this field. In addition, 36 states and the District of Columbia require a license to practice occupational therapy. Graduates from an accredited program are prepared to take the registry examination administered by the American Occupational Therapy Association and any state examinations necessary for licensing.

Most occupational therapists are employed by hospitals, but many also work in offices, nursing homes, community mental health centers, adult day care programs, rehabilitation centers, and residential care facilities. Private practice is currently the fastest growing sector of this profession. As the population ages and patients with critical problems survive more frequently, the demand for occupational therapists will continue to increase.[76]

There are 96 occupational therapy programs graduating approximately 4,300 new practitioners each year. There were about 49,000 active occupational therapists in 1998. The U.S. Department of Labor projects a 30.3 percent increase in the employment of occupational therapists by 2008.[77]

Occupational therapy assistants are prepared in 114 programs graduating 2,800 practitioners per year. Their numbers are also expected to increase rapidly to keep pace with the growing demand for occupational therapy services.[78]

Speech Language Pathology. Speech language pathologists evaluate and treat patients with speech problems in hospitals, schools, clinics, and private practice. About one-half of all speech pathologists are employed in the education system—from preschools to universities.[79]

A master's degree in speech language pathology or audiology is generally required for clinical employment; however, some states only require a bachelor's degree in speech language pathology for people working in schools with students who have communication problems. Because speech and audiology are so closely related, expertise in one field requires a complete knowledge of the other.[80]

Forty-three states regulate speech language pathologists. The American Speech-Language-Hearing Association offers a Certificate of Clinical Competence to those with a master's degree who have had 375 hours of supervised clinical experience, completed a nine-month postgraduate internship, and passed a national written examination.

The current number of active speech pathologists and audiologists, 97,000, is expected to increase by 37 percent by 2008, a 37.3 percent increase in the number of active practitioners.[81]

Physician Assistant. The emergence of physician assistants (PAs) closely parallels the creation of nurse practitioners. In the 1960s there was a shortage of health care providers. Duke University initiated the first physician assistant program in 1961. It was a new provider model designed to benefit from the experience and expertise of the many hospital corpsmen and medics that were discharged from the armed forces. As the flow of returning corpsmen and medics tapered off, individuals without prior health care training were accepted into physician assistant programs. The Medex program, which began at the University of Washington and was later adopted at a number of other universities, is well known. It was designed to train general assistants to family medicine physicians and internists. Today there are over 50 accredited programs, with more in development. In 1971, the American Medical Association (AMA) adopted the "Essentials of an Approved Educational Program for the Assistant to the Primary Physician." This established a minimum standard of quality to which all accredited programs are to be held. Under these specifications, PAs are "academically and clinically prepared to provide health care services with the direction and responsible supervision of a doctor of medicine or osteopathy."[82]

PAs are certified in primary care, surgery, or both. National certification requires graduation from an AMA-accredited program and testing by the National Commission on Certification of Physician Assistants. Unless they are recent graduates, PAs in almost all states are required to be certified before applying for state licensure.[83] PAs may evaluate, monitor, diagnose, perform routine therapeutic procedures, counsel, and refer patients to other appropriate services when necessary. Thirty-five states grant prescription-writing privileges to PAs. They also may take postgraduate courses to specialize in such fields as neonatology, pediatrics, emergency medicine, occupational medicine, and surgery.[84]

PAs, like nurse practitioners, were accepted slowly, but are now in high demand. Their cost-effectiveness makes them very attractive. Even though the performance of these midlevel practitioners always has been judged to be excellent, their salaries are lower than physicians, and they can be educated and trained at approximately one-third of the costs of preparing a physician.[85]

Most PAs are employed in the primary care aspects of family medicine, general practice, internal medicine, or pediatrics. Many educational institutions with PA programs involve students in delivering health care to geographically underserved areas. Most PA programs have developed specific curriculum content to address the health and medical problems of disadvantaged populations and have linkages with area health education centers, community education centers, rural health clinics, community/migrant health centers, and other primary health care agencies and settings.[86]

Physician assistant/physician teams have demonstrated very high efficiency and effectiveness. "In ambulatory managed care settings, PAs have been shown to be capable of handling approximately 80 percent of the health care services required to manage patient problems at physician-equivalent levels of patient satisfaction and quality of care."[87]

There are 95 PA programs in the United States, double the number that existed only 15 years ago. They graduate approximately 2,700 new practitioners each year. The U.S. Department of Labor projects a 50 percent increase in the number of PAs employed by 2008.[88]

Behavioral Scientists

Behavioral scientists are crucial in the social, psychological, and community and patient educational activities related to health maintenance, prevention of disease, and accommodation of patients to disability. They include professionals in social work, health education, community mental health, alcoholism and drug abuse services, and other health and human service areas.[89]

Social Work. Almost one-third of all social workers are employed in hospitals and health-related facilities. Social workers counsel patients and families and assist them in addressing the personal, economic, and social problems associated with illness and disability. They arrange for community-based services as necessary to meet patient needs after discharge from a health facility. A bachelor's degree is required from an accredited college program. However, a master's degree from an accredited graduate school of social work is preferred and may be a requirement for employment.

Rehabilitation Counselor. A rehabilitation counselor gives personalized counseling, emotional support, and rehabilitation therapy to patients limited by physical or emotional disabilities. Patients may be recovering from illness or injury, have psychiatric problems, or have intellectual deficits. Once an injury or illness is stabilized, the rehabilitation counselor will test the patient's motor ability, skill level, interests, and psychological makeup and develop an appropriate training or retraining plan. The goal is to maximize the patient's ability to function in society.

There are 73 accredited rehabilitation counseling programs. Many rehabilitation counselors have earned a master's degree, although a bachelor's degree is the typical entry-level requirement. The Commission on Rehabilitation Counselor Certification (CRCC) offers voluntary certification.

Support Services

Support services are necessary for the highly complex and sophisticated system of health care to function. Specialists who provide services frequently work behind the scenes, performing administrative and management duties and often working closely with the actual providers of health care services. Health information administrators, dental laboratory technologists, electroencephalographic technologists, food service administrators, surgical technologists, and environmental health technologists are some of the allied health professionals in this category, and they serve to illustrate the diverse nature of the required support disciplines in allied health.

Health information administrators are responsible for the activities and functions of the medical record department in a hospital or other health care facility. They are accountable for planning and maintaining an information system that permits patient data to be received, recorded, stored, and retrieved easily to assist in diagnosis and treatment. These data also may be used to track disease patterns, provide information for medical research, assist staff in evaluating the quality of patient care, and verify insurance claims. Health information administrators supervise the staff in the medical records department and are responsible for the confidentiality of all the information within their departments.

A bachelor's degree in health information administration is the entry-level credential. The Council of Certification of the American Health Information Management Association gives a national accreditation examination for Registered Records Administrator (RRA).[90]

Currently, there are over 50 programs preparing health information administrators and over 150 programs training medical records and health information technologists/technicians. Each year, the programs graduate over 800 and 2,000 practitioners, respectively. In the year 2000, there were over 25,000 health information administrators and approximately 136,000 health information technologists/technicians employed in the health system. The U.S. Department of Labor estimates a 49 percent increase in the employment of these health information personnel by 2010.[91]

Table 6-2 provides a more inclusive list of the number of educational programs that prepare allied health professionals, the number of students enrolled, and the number of graduates in 1997.

Table 6–2 Number of Selected Allied Health Programs (Calendar Year 1997), and Students and Graduates (Academic Year 1996–97)

OCCUPATION	PROGRAMS	ENROLLMENTS	GRADUATES
Anesthesiologist's Assistant	2	105	27
Art Therapist	26	1,201	398
Athletic Trainer	61	2,709	678
Cardiovascular Technologist	16	516	213
Clinical Laboratory Scientist	333	6,615	2,996
Clinical Laboratory Technician— Associate Degree	224	6,313	2,047
Clinical Laboratory Technician— Certificate	39	921	508
Cytotechnologist	65	421	335
Dental Assistant	228	7,211	4,343
Dental Hygienist	216	11,207	4,771
Dental Laboratory Technician	34	1,141	383
Diagnostic Medical Sonographer	75	1,500	744
Dietetic Technician	72	2,981	714
Dietitian/Nutritionist	534	15,724	6,455
Electroneurodiagnostic Technologist	10	156	36
Emergency Medical Technician— Paramedic	97	5,781	3,035
Genetic Counselor	22	317	151
Health Information Administrator	55	2,599	816
Health Information Technologist	153	7,208	2,144
Histologic Technician— Associate Degree	10	168	59
Histologic Technician—Certificate	22	89	65
Histotechnologist	4	12	9
Medical Assistant	271	24,333	9,665
Medical Illustrator	5	81	42

Table 6–2 (continued)

OCCUPATION	PROGRAMS	ENROLLMENTS	GRADUATES
Music Therapist	49	2,388	331
Nuclear Medicine Technologist	110	1,330	661
Occupational Therapist	96	13,882	4,223
Occupational Therapy Assistant	114	7,038	2,790
Ophthalmic Dispensing Optician	15	792	284
Ophthalmic Laboratory Technician	1	14	4
Ophthalmic Medical Technician/Technologist	10	128	51
Orthotist/Prosthetist	2	69	65
Pathologists' Assistant	2	32	7
Perfusionist	27	301	122
Physician Assistant	2	32	7
Physical Therapists	134	16,573	4,746
Physical Therapy Assistant	148	7,084	3,361
Radiation Therapist	98	849	422
Radiographer	639	20,200	8,009
Rehabilitation Counselor	68	3,748	1,360
Respiratory Therapist	293	11,796	4,202
Respiratory Therapy Technician	160	5,385	2,501
Specialist in Blood Bank Technology	22	66	35
Surgical Technologist	142	3,794	2,055
Therapeutic Recreation Specialist	28	3,359	1,052
Total	4,827	205,861	79,589

Source: Reprinted with permission from *Health Professions Education Directory, 26th Edition,* 1998–1999, © 1998, American Medical Association.

Career Advancement in Allied Health

It should be noted that the entry-level degree for practice in the allied health fields ranges from the certificate or associate degree in some disciplines to the bachelor's degree in others and the master's degree in still others. Two-year programs that offer associate degrees or certificates produce allied health personnel who, for the most part, perform under the supervision of those with more advanced training. Because the allied health fields offer so diverse an array of programs, the opportunity for career advancement through educational "laddering" is probably without equal.

It is commonplace for graduates of allied health programs to practice for a period of time and then advance their careers by entering higher-level programs and achieving more advanced degrees. For example, it is not unusual for occupational therapists or physical therapists with bachelor's degrees to pursue master's degrees and doctorates in related fields and then become researchers, university faculty, and more advanced clinical practitioners. Allied health practitioners are uniquely positioned to achieve career goals at the highest level of their competence.[92]

Alternative Therapists

Rather than diminishing the public's interest in alternative forms of health care, the increasing sophistication of scientific medicine seems to have fostered a more receptive climate for implausible and inexplicable forms of therapy. Across the country, and notably on the West Coast and in the Midwest, there is widespread interest in alternative medicine. David Eisenberg of Boston's Beth Israel Hospital reported in the *New England Journal of Medicine* that 34 percent of Americans spent $10.3 billion out of pocket on some form of alternative medicine in 1990.[93]

In 1992, with one-third of Americans resorting to alternative medical therapies, the National Institutes of Health created an Office of Alternative Medicine (OAM) to examine whether alternative therapies work. The more perplexing question of how they work was to be investigated later. Interest is so strong that OAM's budget was increased from $2 million in 1992 to $5.4 million in 1995. In 1998, when more than 40 percent of Americans reported use of alternative or complementary therapies, the OAM was elevated to the National Center for Complementary and Alternative Medicine (NCCAM), and its mandate expanded. Its funding also expanded, reaching $68.7 million in fiscal year 2000.

The center recently announced a five-year plan that includes the first international study of traditional medicines, including ancient Chinese and American Indian methods. The plan proposes the first NIH study of botanicals that will sort through 1,500 medicinal herbs for evaluation. Unusual therapies, such as telepathic healing, that are on the far fringes of medical practice will also be investigated.[94]

Because estimates of alternative treatment use by cancer patients range from a low of 9 percent to as high as 50 percent, the American Cancer Society has a Committee on Unproven Methods of Cancer Treatment that maintains a list of 23 questionable cancer treatment modalities. The use of alternative therapies by cancer patients is usually with family and physician knowledge. About 50 percent of the patients using unproven therapies continue following conventional treatment as well.[95]

Many alternative therapies involve lifestyle programs, such as macrobiotics, natural food diets, yoga, and other stress-reducing techniques. Others focus on mind-body techniques including biofeedback, visualization, music therapy, and prayer. Still others are traditional practices of other cultures—acupuncture, homeopathy, and microdose pharmacology.

Along with alternative techniques comes a new class of alternative practitioners. To name a few, there are certified trager practitioners (CTPs), who rock and cradle the patient's body for relaxation and mental clarity; doctors of naturopathy (NDs), who use natural healing methods that include diet, herbal medicine, and homeopathy; advanced certified rolfers (ACRs), who use deep massage to restore the body's natural alignment; and registered polarity practitioners (RPPs), who use touch and advice on diet, self-awareness, and exercise to balance energy flow.

Naturopathic doctors, in particular, have made great strides in the last few years. Although they do not have medical degrees and may be trained in schools that are loosely monitored, many states now allow naturopaths to prescribe conventional drugs, deliver babies, and perform minor surgery. Twelve states already license naturopaths and seven more are contemplating licensing legislation.[96]

The gains of naturopaths and other alternative practitioners reflect the public's frustration with much of conventional medicine, high drug prices, and media reports of disproved treatments. The interest of insurance companies in alternative forms of medicine is also important. Insurers say that when traditional medicine is ineffective and an alternative form of therapy, such as acupuncture, for a condition like chronic pain costs less and satisfies the patient, they will pay for it. As a result, several states now require insurance companies to cover naturopathic procedures and others, such as acupuncture.[97]

■ Factors That Influence Demand for Health Personnel

Without attempting to include all of the interrelated factors that influence demand for various types of health personnel, it is important to recognize some major determinants of the size and nature of the health care employment sector. Regardless of the potential for legislatively mandated reforms of the health care system, the number and skill requirements of each discipline within the health care workforce will depend on the interdependence of these factors.

Changing Nature of Disease, Disability, and Treatment

The aging of the population and advances in the treatment of acute and life-threatening conditions will result in an increasing survival of people with chronic illness or disabilities. The growing number of patients with deteriorating mental capacities, cardiac conditions, cancer, stroke, head and spinal cord injuries, neonatal deficits, and congenital disorders will significantly increase the demand for workers who provide and support prolonged medical treatment, rehabilitation, and nursing home or custodial care.

Physician Supply

Although many categories of health personnel perform independently of physicians, most of the decisions regarding the use of health care resources, acceptance of other therapeutic modalities, and treatment provided by nonphysicians are made by physicians. It is important to recognize, therefore, that the anticipated changes in the numbers and types of physicians will have a direct impact on the demand for many other types of health care personnel.

Technology

Medical and nonmedical technology used in the provision of health care has important implications for the number and skill requirements of the health care workforce. Advances in computerization, information systems, miniaturization, radiologic imaging, and laser technology have the potential to both increase and decrease the demand for various kinds of personnel. Some technologies, such as transluminal coronary angioplasty, have led to the elimination of more laborious medical interventions. Others, such as sophisticated patient monitoring systems, have facilitated the shifts to new service settings, such as ambulatory surgical centers. Also, automation of clinical laboratory testing has reduced the need for laboratory personnel. Thus, the mix of skills and numbers of personnel ebb and flow with the discovery and application of new service modalities.

Financing Health Services

Methods of payment for health services have always had some effect on the kind and amount of services provided and thus on the demand for health care personnel. The availability of private and governmental health insurance coverage under fee-for-service circumstances resulted in financial incentives for providers to make use of all the resources and procedures appropriate, and sometimes those of questionable appropriateness, to the patient's condition. A significant amount of the increase in health care costs has been attributed to those financial inducements. The imposition of the diagnosis-related group prospective payment system for hospital services that rewards hospitals for containing resource use and the development of HMOs that operate on capitated rather than fee-for-service payments were attempts to reverse the financial incentives. In each case, the provider benefits from achieving the desired results with the least amount of resource consumption. The effects of these and other reimbursement schemes yet to be applied will have profound effects on hospitals, medical specialists, and others who provide health care services, and consequently, on the demand for health care personnel.

Influence of Managed Care

It was anticipated that expansion of managed care would alter the size and nature of the health care workforce in the United States. Managed care's emphasis on health promotion, preventive medicine, early primary care interventions, and the discouragement of patient-initiated visits to medical specialists was expected to significantly affect the organization and use of health services.

Had managed care organizations exercised a serious and energetic population perspective as forecast, there would have been a significant increase in the demand for midlevel health practitioners, health educators, social workers, case managers, and others competent to influence individuals towards preventive health measures and away from high-risk behaviors. Those workforce changes did not occur. The two primary influences on health workforce composition during the last 10 years were technical advances in diagnostic and clinical medicine requiring new types of operating and support personnel, and the significant increase in ambulatory surgery that prompted transfer of nurses and others from hospitals to group practices and ambulatory care facilities.

Expansion of Home Care

Health care reforms are likely to continue the shift in health service delivery sites from acute care hospitals to ambulatory, home care, and long-term care settings. With the emphasis on cost containment and an array of high-tech devices that contribute to more efficient techniques for providing nursing care and occupational, physical, and respiratory therapy in the home, the home care component of the health care industry is expected to expand significantly in the next decade. In addition, there is a growing body of evidence that therapy provided in the home helps patients recover faster and reduces hospital readmissions. It is anticipated that the growing number of managed care organizations that emphasize offering the most appropriate services in the most appropriate settings will encourage home-delivered services to take advantage of the economies and benefits of that service option.

As the hospital employment market for nurses and other allied health professionals declines, there is likely to be a corresponding expansion of opportunities for health care providers to be employed in home care and long-term care industries. It should be noted, however, that the expansion of home care will be accompanied by new professional challenges. As hospitals discharge patients earlier in their recovery and as physicians grow more comfortable in depending on home care for patients they might otherwise have hospitalized, more specialized knowledge and skills will be required of home care service providers, and the quality, as well as the economy, of care will become of increasing concern.

Corporatization of Health Care

It appears that the solo practice of medicine, dentistry, podiatry, and other health professions is fast becoming a practice pattern of the past. The increase in group practices; the development of several forms of provider organizations; the evolution of hospital networks; the assembly of vertically integrated systems that link hospitals, nursing homes, home care, and other services; and the diversification of health providers into various health-related corporate ventures—all reflect the corporatization of health care.

The effect already has been pronounced. In the last two decades, employment in physicians' offices far outpaced the growth of the health care industry as a whole. In addition, the introduction of the corporate approach to health care is likely to increase the need for business managers, fiscal staff, planners, data analysts, and other types of personnel more commonly found in large business organizations than in health care facilities.[98]

■ Health Care Workforce Issues

Policy makers at every level of government, insurers, educators, providers, and consumers have a vested interest in the issues that pertain to the health care workforce. Those issues have been clearly defined in a publication of the Association of Academic Health Centers as follows:

- The adequacy of supply of various health professionals, such as nurses, allied health professionals, primary care physicians, and geriatricians
- The geographic distribution of health professionals, especially their shortage in rural and underserved urban areas
- The underrepresentation of minorities in all health professions, in both primary and specialty care, as well as in the health professions educational programs
- The potential oversupply and poor distribution of specialty physicians

- The questions about the appropriate scope of practice for various health professionals and concern about legal restrictions on scope of practice for nonphysician practitioners
- The concern about the quality and relevance of the health professions educational programs; whether educational institutions are producing the health professionals needed for an effective and productive workforce in the twenty-first century
- The costs associated with educating health professionals and the impact that changes in the health care delivery system may have on the financing of health professions' education
- The competency testing of health care professionals
- The redefinition of health professions as technology and the delivery system change, and various professions reconsider the credentials needed to practice within the profession
- The concern about the supply of faculty to train health professionals[99]

■ The Health Workforce in a Chaotic System

During the twenty-first century, the aging of the population, the shifting nature of diseases, health care reforms, new technology, managed care, and economic factors will significantly change the demand for services provided by different types of practitioners. The market for services will expand in some disciplines and contract in others. It will be necessary to modify the roles and scope of practice of many of the health care professions to adapt to changing service patterns. Yet, the lack of any single body in the United States being responsible for making data-based demand/supply projections and policy decisions leaves these important issues to be addressed piecemeal by a number of interested bodies.

Federal and state governments, educational institutions, professional organizations, insurers, and provider institutions have separate and often conflicting interests in health work force education and training, regulation, financing, entry-level preparation, and scope of practice. The various levels at which policy decisions are made and the disparate interests that influence those decisions present major obstacles to ensuring a coherent, efficient, and rational health workforce in the United States.

Nevertheless, those policies supported the production of an enormous number of health professionals to serve the health care system of the late twentieth century. Daniel M. Fox, in "Political History of Health Workforce Policy," compared the magnitude and success of past health workforce policies in the United States to the positive influence on labor policy of the GI Bill of Rights.

Until the 1990s, the assumptions that guided health workforce policy—like those of foreign and defense policy—seemed self-evident to the people who made policy for spending and taxation. Debates about public financing for health profession education were almost always about when, rather than whether, it is desirable to increase public spending. Educators of health professionals and their allies had considerably warmer relationships with budget officials and senior legislators than, for example, enthusiasts for public health, services for the mentally ill, or more spending for the poor.[100]

In the 1990s, the assumption that it was in the public interest for the country to continually invest in more biomedical research and increase the number of health professionals while at the same time encourage consumer demand was viewed with increasing skepticism. The advent of managed care and its significant effect on health personnel practices, the diagnostic and therapeutic technologies that moved many of the medical care procedures from hospitals to ambulatory settings, and the market forces that encourage primary care while shrinking the tertiary health care system have made all previous assumptions about health work force policies obsolete. Economic considerations rather than health, access to care, or professional opportunity are driving new and contentious workforce policies. Without unifying and persuasive leadership, the dissonance among the stakeholder institutions and agencies that prepare, employ, and regulate health care professionals will continue to be an obstacle to remediating the health workforce dilemma.

In the absence of a concerted and broad-based effort that spans everything from the size of professional school classes to the enhancement of reimbursement for provider disciplines in short supply, the production of a health care workforce of market-relevant size and distribution will be left to the fluctuating and often ineffective influences of supply and demand. Unfortunately, the policies and decisions of the various stakeholders impact differently on the demand and supply of the various health professions. In addition, there are deep-seated distrust and jurisdictional issues among the health professions, the different policy-making bodies, and the state and federal authorities. The obstacles to the development of an integrated policy-making framework that will lead to coherent workforce policies are monumental.

With health workforce policies influenced independently by federal and state governments, educational institutions, insurers, the professions, and the competitive healthcare marketplace, the next few years are certain to be increasingly chaotic. Driven by an ever more cost-conscious health care market, rapid changes will continue in the organization and financing of health care. As occurred in the case of hospital nursing, those unpredictable changes may force health services personnel to make unwelcome adaptations to different work settings and service responsibilities.

Nevertheless, an aging population and technological advances will have a significant effect on the health care industry over the next decade. Already one of the largest industries in the United States, health care's 11 million jobs will grow by 3.1 million new positions by 2006. In fact, about 13 percent of all wage and salary jobs created between 2000 and 2010 will be concentrated in the health care industry. Projected rates of employment growth will be slowest in the large hospital sector, 8 percent, compared to 80 percent in the smaller home health care services.[101]

■ Notes

1. A. Kahl and D. Clark, "Employment in Health Services: Long-Term Trends and Projections," *Monthly Labor Review* (August 1986): 17–36.
2. S. Chartrand, "Aging Baby Boomers Will Mean a Surge in Health Care Jobs," The *New York Times,* 7 July 1996: D1.
3. Chartrand, "Aging Baby Boomers Will Mean a Surge in Health Care Jobs."
4. S.N. Collier, "Report of the State Issues Task Force," *Pew Health Professions Commission State Issues Task Force* (November 1991): 1–9.
5. Collier, "Report of the States Issues Task Force," 7.
6. B. Barzansk and S.I. Etzel, "Educational Programs in U.S. Medical Schools, 2001–2002," *Journal of the American Medical Association* 288, no. 9 (2002): 1067–1072.
7. J.A. Hallock, "ECFMG and the Challenges Facing International Medical Graduates", Association of American Medical Colleges, *Reporter* http://www.aamc.org/newsroom/reporter/may02/viewpoint.htm. Accessed 26 March 2003.
8. R.A. Cooper, et al., "Economic and Demographic Trends Signal an Impending Physician Shortage," *Health Affairs* 21, no. 1 (2002): 140–154.
9. E.S. Salsberg and G.J. Forte, "Trends in the Physicians Workforce, 1980–2000," *Health Affairs* 21, no. 5 (2002): 165–173.
10. J. Greene, "Report Details Reasons for Arizona Physician Shortage," http://www.Ama-assn.org/sci-pubs/amnews/pick_01/prsb1210.htm (10 December 2001). Accessed 4 October, 2002.
11. S.S. Mick, "Foreign Medical Graduates and U.S. Physician Supply: Old Issues and New Questions," *Health Policy* 24, no. 3 (1993): 213–225.
12. P. O'Brien, "All a Woman's Life Can Bring: The Domestic Roots of Nursing in Philadelphia, 1830–1885," *Nursing Research* 36 (1987): 12–17.
13. Stevens, *In Sickness and in Wealth,* 96–98.
14. C. Kovner, "Nursing," In *Health Care Delivery in the United States,* ed. A.R. Kovner (New York: Springer Publishing Co., 1995), 101–121.
15. R.D. Lamm, "The Coming Dislocation in the Health Professions," *Healthcare Forum* 39, no. 1 (1996): 558–562.
16. L.H. Aiken and C.M. Fagin, *Charting Nursing's Future* (Philadelphia: J.B. Lippincott Co., 1992), 9.

17. K. Green, "Nurse Practitioners," *Occupational Health Quarterly* 40, no. 3 (Fall 1996): 36–41.
18. "The Registered Nurse Population: Findings from the National Sample Survey of Registered Nurses," Chapter II, "The Registered Nurse Population, 1980–2000," Bureau of Health Professions, Health Resources and Services Administration, U.S. Dept. of Health and Human Services, http://ftp.hrsa.gov/healthworkforce/rnsurvey2000/rnsurvey00-1.pdf (22 February 2002). Accessed 5 October 2002.
19. "Projected Supply, Demand, and Shortages of Registered Nurses: 2000–2020," National Center for Health Workforce Analysis, Bureau of Health Professions, Health Resources and Services Administration, U.S. Dept. of Health and Human Services, http://ftp.hrsa.gov/bhpr/national-center/rnproject.pdf (22 February 2002). Accessed 5 October 2002.
20. U.S. Department of Health and Human Services, Health Resources and Services Administration, Bureau of Health Professions, *United States Health Workforce Personnel Factbook* (1999), 73, 74.
21. B. Bullough and V. Bullough, *Nursing Issues for the Nineties and Beyond* (New York: Springer Publishing Co., 1994), 90.
22. Bullough and Bullough, *Nursing Issues for the Nineties and Beyond,* 16–17.
23. 2000 National Occupation and Employment and Wage Estimates, Bureau of Labor Statistics, http://www.bls.gov/oco (20 July 2000). Accessed 7 October 2002.
24. Bullough and Bullough, *Nursing Issues for the Nineties and Beyond,* 16–17.
25. Bullough and Bullough, *Nursing Issues for the Nineties and Beyond,* 15.
26. H.A. Sultz, et al., *Nurse Practitioners,* USA (Lexington, MA: Lexington Books, 1979), 215–229.
27. S.L. Krein, "The Employment and Use of Nurse Practitioners and Physician Assistants by Rural Hospitals," *Journal of Rural Health* 13, no. 1 (Winter 1997): 45–58.
28. R.S. Hooker and L. McKaig, "Emergency Department Uses of Physician Assistants and Nurse Practitioners: A National Survey," *American Journal of Emergency Medicine* 14, no. 3 (May 1996): 245–249.
29. Aiken and Fagin, *Charting Nursing's Future,* 4.
30. I. Dunn, "A Literature Review of Advanced Clinical Nursing in the United States of America," *Journal of Advanced Nursing* 25, no. 4 (April 1997): 814–819.
31. C. Snow, "Home-Care Firms Fill Chronic-Care Niche," *Modern Healthcare* 26, no. 44 (1996): 50.
32. Bullough and Bullough, *Nursing Issues for the Nineties and Beyond,* 16–17.
33. M. Ring, Dentistry: *An Illustrated History* (New York: Harry N. Abrams, 1985), 203.
34. H.T. Loevy and A.A. Kowitz, "Dental Development in the Midwest of America," *International Dental Journal* 12, no. 3 (1992): 157–164.
35. Ring, *Dentistry,* 283–284.

36. U.S. Department of Health and Human Services, Health Resources and Services Administration, Bureau of Health Professions, *United States Health Workforce Personnel Factbook* (1999), 55.

37. U.S. Department of Health and Human Services, *United States Health Workforce Personnel Factbook*, 63.

38. E. Mertz and E. O' Nell, "The Growing Challenge of Providing Oral Health Care Services to All Americans," *Health Affairs* 21, no. 5 (2002): 65–77.

39. F.B. Gable, *Opportunities in Pharmacy Careers* (Lincolnwood, IL: NTC Publishing Group, 1993), 10–14.

40. G.J. Higby, "American Hospital Pharmacy from the Colonial Period to the 1930s," *American Journal of Hospital Pharmacy* 51, no. 22 (1994): 2817–2823.

41. F.B. Gable, *Opportunities in Pharmacy Careers,* pp. 15–17.

42. U.S. Department of Labor, Bureau of Labor Statistics, *Occupational Outlook Handbook* (April 1994), 169–171.

43. U.S. Department of Health and Human Services, *United States Health Workforce Personnel Factbook*, 77, 78.

44. R.R. Maddox, "Specialization and Pharmacy's Future," *The Annals of Pharmacotherapy* (June 1990): 637–639.

45. U.S. Department of Labor, Bureau of Labor Statistics, *Occupational Outlook Handbook,* 169.

46. "The Pharmacist Workforce: A Study of the Supply and Demand for Pharmacists," Bureau of Health Professions, Health Resources and Services Administration, Department of Health and Human Services, http://bhpr.hrsa.gov/healthworkforce/pharmacist.html (20 December 2000). Accessed 4 September 2002.

47. U.S. Department of Labor, Bureau of Labor Statistics, *Occupational Outlook Handbook,* 163–165.

48. J.F. Jekel, "A Public Health Perspective on Podiatric Medicine," *Journal of the American Podiatric Medical Association* 80, no. 3 (1990): 158–160.

49. U.S. Department of Health and Human Services, *United States Health Workforce Personnel Factbook*, 77, 78.

50. U.S. Department of Labor, Bureau of Labor Statistics, *Occupational Outlook Handbook,* 164.

51. Healthcare Careers Center of Western New York, Inc., *Healthcare Careers: Job Descriptions* (Buffalo, NY: State University of New York at Buffalo, 1996).

52. U.S. Department of Health and Human Services, *United States Health Workforce Personnel Factbook*, 81.

53. J.G. Carey and A. Jackman, "The Outcomes and Costs of Care for Acute Low Back Pain among Patients Seen by Primary Care Practitioners, Chiropractors, and Orthopedic Surgeons," *New England Journal of Medicine* 333 (October 5, 1995): 913–917.

54. P. Brown, "Chiropractic: A Medical Perspective," *Minnesota Medicine* 77 (February 1994): 21–25.

55. M.M. Shekelle and L. Rachel, "An Epidemiologic Study of Episodes of Back Pain Care," *Spine* 20, no. 15 (1995): 168.

56. U.S. Department of Labor, Bureau of Labor Statistics, *Occupational Outlook Handbook,* 161–163.
57. U.S. Department of Health and Human Services, *United States Health Workforce Personnel Factbook,* 75.
58. Healthcare Careers Center of Western New York, Inc., *Healthcare Careers.*
59. U.S. Department of Labor, Bureau of Labor Statistics, *Occupational Outlook Handbook,* 161.
60. U.S. Department of Labor, Bureau of Labor Statistics, *Occupational Outlook Handbook,* 161.
61. P. Hillsenrath, "Health Services Management Manpower and Education: Outlook for the Future," *Journal of Health Administration Education* 11, no. 3 (1993): 412.
62. U.S. Department of Labor, Bureau of Labor Statistics, *Occupational Outlook Handbook,* 44–46.
63. R. Hudak, et al., "Health Care Administration in the Year 2000: Practitioners' Views of Future Issues and Job Requirements," *Hospital and Health Services Administration* 38, no. 2 (1993): 183.
64. R. Hudak, et al., "Health Care Administration in the Year 2000," 181–195.
65. New York State Department of Health, *Final Report of the New York State Labor: Health Industry Task Force on Health Personnel* (Albany, NY: New York State Department of Health, 1989), 1–71.
66. H.A. Sultz, *Allied Health Personnel* (Consultant Report to the Labor-Health Industry Task Force on Health Personnel, New York State Department of Health, 1987).
67. Healthcare Careers Center of Western New York, Inc., *Healthcare Careers.*
68. C. Broadwater, "Shortage of Radiologic Technologists Greater Than in Any Health-Care Field," *The Charleston Gazette,* Gazette Online.
69. U.S. Department of Labor, Bureau of Labor Statistics, *Occupational Outlook Handbook,* 213–216.
70. U.S. Department of Labor, Bureau of Labor Statistics, *Occupational Outlook Handbook,* 171–172.
71. Sultz, *Allied Health Personnel.*
72. U.S. Department of Labor, Bureau of Labor Statistics, *Occupational Outlook Handbook,* 171–172.
73. Healthcare Careers Center of Western New York, Inc., *Healthcare Careers.*
74. U.S. Department of Labor, Bureau of Labor Statistics, Career Guide to Industries, Health Services, "Table 2, Employment of Wage and Salary Workers in Health Services by Occupation, 1998, and Projected Change, 1998–2008." http://stat.bls.gov./oco/cg/cgs035.htm (19 April 2000). Accessed 18 August 2000.
75. Healthcare Careers Center of Western New York, Inc., *Healthcare Careers.*
76. U.S. Department of Labor, Bureau of Labor Statistics, *Occupational Outlook Handbook,* 168–169.
77. U.S. Department of Labor, Bureau of Labor Statistics, Career Guide to Industries, Health Services, "Table 2, Employment of Wage and Salary Workers in Health Services by Occupation, 1998, and Projected Change, 1998–2008." http://stat.bls.gov./oco/cg/cgs035.htm (19 April 2000). Accessed 18 August 2000.

78. U.S. Department of Labor, Bureau of Labor Statistics, Career Guide to Industries, Health Services, "Table 2, Employment of Wage and Salary Workers in Health Services by Occupation, 1998, and Projected Change, 1998–2008." http://stat.bls.gov./oco/cg/cgs035.htm (19 April 2000). Accessed 18 August 2000.

79. U.S. Department of Labor, Bureau of Labor Statistics, *Occupational Outlook Handbook,* 180.

80. Healthcare Careers Center of Western New York, Inc., *Healthcare Careers.*

81. U.S. Department of Labor, Bureau of Labor Statistics, Career Guide to Industries, Health Services, "Table 2, Employment of Wage and Salary Workers in Health Services by Occupation, 1998, and Projected Change, 1998–2008." http://stat.bls.gov./oco/cg/cgs035.htm (19 April 2000). Accessed 18 August 2000.

82. P.E. Jones and J.F. Cawley, "Physician Assistants and Health System Reform," *Journal of the American Medical Association* 271, no. 16 (1994): 1266–1272.

83. R. Atwater, "Filling in the Primary Care Gaps," *Medical Interface* (October 1994): 84–118.

84. Jones and Cawley, "Physician Assistants and Health System Reform," 1271.

85. Atwater, "Filling in the Primary Care Gaps," 118.

86. Jones and Cawley, "Physician Assistants and Health System Reform," 1267.

87. Jones and Cawley, "Physician Assistants and Health System Reform," 1269.

88. U.S. Department of Labor, Bureau of Labor Statistics, Career Guide to Industries, Series, Health Services, "Table 2, Employment of Wage and Salary Workers in Health Services by Occupation, 1998, and Projected Change, 1998–2008." http://stat.bls.gov./oco/cg/cgs035.htm (19 April 2000). Accessed 18 August 2000.

89. Sultz, *Allied Health Personnel.*

90. Healthcare Careers Center of Western New York, Inc., *Healthcare Careers.*

91. U.S. Department of Labor, Bureau of Labor Statistics, 2001 National Occupational Employment and Wage Estimates, Health Care Practitioners and Technical Occupations, http://stat.bis.gov./OES http://stat.bis.gov./OES 23 December 2002, Accessed 27 March 2003.

92. Sultz, *Allied Health Personnel.*

93. D.M. Eisenberg, et al., "Unconventional Medicine in the United States: Prevalence, Costs, and Patterns of Use," *New England Journal of Medicine* 328, no. 4 (1993): 246–256.

94. U.S. National Institutes of Health, National Center for Complementary and Alternative Medicine, Annual Report. http://nccam.nih.gov (10 March 2000). Accessed 21 April 2000.

95. L.S. McGinnis, "Alternative Therapies, 1990: An Overview," *Cancer* 67, no. 6 (1991): 1788–1792.

96. A. Petersen, "States Grant Herb Doctors New Powers," *Wall Street Journal,* 22 August 2002, D1.

97. B. Carton, "Health Insurers Embrace Eye-of-Newt Therapy," *Wall Street Journal,* 30 January 1995, B1.

98. United States Department of Labor, *The American Workforce: 1992–2005* (Washington, DC: Bureau of Labor Statistics, 1994), 96–119.

99. C.J. McLaughlin, "Health Work Force Issues and Policy-Making Roles," in *Health Work Force Issues for the 21st Century,* eds. P.F. Larson, M. Osterweis, and E.R. Rubin (Washington, DC: Association of Academic Health Centers, 1994), 1–3.

100. D.M. Fox, "The Political History of Health Workforce Policy," in *The U.S. Health Workforce: Power, Politics, and Policy,* eds. M. Osterweis, C.J. McLaughlin, H.R. Manasse et al. (Washington, DC: Association of Academic Health Centers, 1996), 31–46.

101. "Career Guide to Industries 2002–2003," Health Services, Bureau of Labor Statistics, U.S. Department of Labor, http://stats.bls.gov/oco/cg/cgs035.htm (16 October 2001). Accessed 8 October 2002.

Chapter 7

Financing Health Care

This chapter reviews the most currently available data on national health care expenditures and sources of payment and provides an historical overview of the developments that played major roles in creating the national health care reimbursement infrastructure. Major factors that impact health care costs are identified and discussed. Significant trends in health care spending are reviewed, along with underlying reasons for evolving changes. The roles of government as a payer and provider of services are presented with an overview of the costs associated with government administration of payments and services.

The financing of the U.S. health care system has evolved from a variety of influences, including provider, employer, purchaser, consumer, and political factors. These influences continue to produce major tensions in ongoing debates about the role and responsibility of the government as payer, consumer financial responsibility, the relationships of costs to quality, the impact of payment systems on quality, and the overall effects managed care has on the health care delivery system. A focal point of the debates is the question of whether market-driven or government-driven strategies should be used to control health care expenditures.[1] Two core issues include controlling rising costs and the estimated 41 million Americans who remain uninsured or underinsured for health care.

The discussion of health care finance necessarily includes managed care, which, as a system of financing linking both the delivery of and payment for services, impacts consumers, purchasers, and providers. Managed care continues to reshape how health care services are delivered and paid for in the United States, and is discussed in depth in Chapter 8.

■ Health Care Expenditures in Perspective

National health care expenditures in 2000 totaled $1.3 trillion, or 13.2 percent of the gross domestic product (GDP).[2] The rate of growth in health care spending has closely paralleled the growth rate in the GDP since 1994.[3] The share of GDP devoted to health care has remained relatively stable since 1992.[4] (See Figure 7–1)[5]

Expenditures in the U.S. on health care have increased 87% since 1990, and are more than five times the amount spent in 1980. The $1.3 trillion in national health expenditures (NHE) in 2000 represents 13.2% of the Gross Domestic Product (GDP), more than 8 percentile points higher than the industry's share in 1960. More than half of this increase occurred from 1980 to 1992, when the share rose from just under 9% to 13.1%. Since 1993, the health care share of the GDP has remained remarkably constant with a modest decline in 1997, and a small increase in 2000.

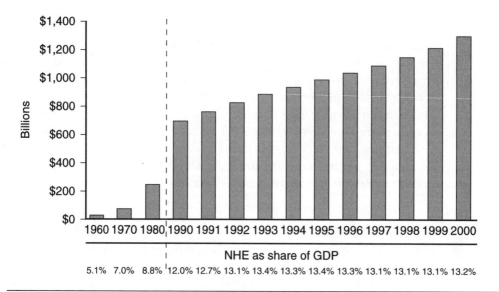

Figure 7–1 National Health Expenditures and Their Share of Gross Domestic Product, 1960–2000

Sources: Centers for Medicaid and Medicare Services (CMS), Office of the Actuary, National Health Statistics Group. CMS Web site, 2000 National Health Care Expenditures Data Files for Downloading, nhegdpoo.csv, at www.hcfa.gov/stats/nhe-oact/.

During the years 1992–1996, growth in expenditure rates was successively slower than at any time since tracking of national health expenditures (NHE) began in 1960.[6] In contrast, between 1980 and 1990, average annual growth rates exceeded 10 percent and were major stimuli for numerous cost-containment efforts, ultimately creating the momentum for health care reform.[7]

Fundamental changes in the nation's health care delivery resulting from the impact of a dramatically evolving health care industry marketplace accounted for slowing average growth rates. The impact of managed care, through its focus on controlling utilization, was a major factor in slower spending growth. Throughout the decade of the 1990s, market factors that enabled large purchasers of health insurance to negotiate arrangements aggressively with providers contributed significantly to the impact of expenditure-cutting managed care initiatives. Beginning in the 1980s, and continuing through the 1990s, restrictions imposed on hospital and physician practices through prospective payment and restrictive fee schedules also contributed to the decline in health expenditure growth. Between 1988 and 1997, government's contribution to national health care expenditures rose from 40.4 percent to 46.2 percent.[8] The initial impact of the Balanced Budget Act of 1997 (BBA) on Medicare spending and savings from the curtailment of fraud and abuse resulted in a decrease in government health care expenditures.[9] For the first time in 10 years, in 1998 the component of national health care expenditures funded from government sources deviated from its pattern of steady increases and declined to 45.5 percent.[10] In 2000, two major pieces of legislation added to Medicare funding: the Balanced Budget Refinement Act and the Medicare, Medicaid, and State Child Health Insurance Program Benefits Improvement and Protection Act.[11] However, increased growth in private sector health care spending due to rising premiums among employer-sponsored health plans offset growth in government expenditures. As a result, government's share of total spending in 2000 remained at 45 percent of national health care expenditures.[12]

Growth in health care expenditures results from a complex array of factors, in addition to the general rise of inflation that affects all sectors of the economy and the rate of excess inflation associated with medical care costs. Historically, major factors that have resulted in increased costs include:

■ Applications of more advanced and more types of technology
■ Growth in the population of older adults
■ Emphasis upon specialty medicine
■ The uninsured and underinsured
■ Labor intensity
■ Reimbursement system incentives

An overview of each factor follows.

New Diagnostic and Treatment Technology

The array of medical interventions and diagnostic modalities has increased exponentially in the past 30 years, including a vast expansion of pharmaceuticals to treat acute conditions and manage chronic ones. In part, costs have risen because of the increase in absolute availability of treatments and diagnostic techniques that did not exist previously. The development of angioplasty as a routine treatment for blocked coronary blood vessels is one example. The capacity of diagnostic modalities such as magnetic resonance imaging is being continuously upgraded and enhanced through new, computerized technology that is significantly expanding its applications. Many other diagnostic, therapeutic, and surgical techniques are undergoing revolutionary changes resulting from the availability of new equipment and computer-aided technologies. Minimally invasive laparoscopic procedures are just one example of these new techniques. The continued development of innovations can be expected.[13] Advances of these types have, and will continue to, come at a significant price. Information and computer-aided technologies require expensive software and hardware, new patient care equipment, and highly trained personnel. The large capital investments required understandably create economic and professional imperatives for their use. Historically, the health care reimbursement system required neither documentation of the necessity for the use of technological interventions nor estimates of their benefit. The tendency to favor broad, rather than discretionary, use grew with the number of interventions available. Managed care organizations, which require preapprovals, procedure authorizations, and physician economic incentives, continue the effort to dampen the overuse of technology and avoid unnecessary interventions.

The continuing vast expansion in the number of new pharmaceutical agents to treat acute and chronic conditions, increased managed care enrollment providing more access to drug coverage at lower out-of-pocket costs, and "direct to consumer" marketing of prescription drugs via television, radio, and print media are combining to make the rise in spending on drugs a focal point of national attention.[14] Spending for prescription drugs has grown faster than any other category of personal health expenditure in the past four years, totaling $121.8 billion in 2000, or 10.8 percent of total health expenditures.[15]

Growth in the number of older adults is another major factor in rising health care expenditures. The U.S. Administration on Aging reports that in the last century, the number of individuals 65 years of age and over increased by a factor of 11, from 3.1 million in 1900 to 33.2 million in 1994[16] (see Figure 7–2). The age group of 85 and older is projected to be the fastest growing segment of the older population throughout the rest of the century.[17]

Although the length of hospital stays has decreased, the use of in-home services is increasing.[18] Persons over the age of 65 are the major consumers of inpatient hospital care. These individuals account for more than one-third of all hospital stays and one-half of all days of care in hospitals.[19] In addition, the aging of the baby-boom population born between 1946 and 1964 is expected to have a profound effect on health care services consumption beginning with the second decade of the twenty-first century. The first wave of the baby-boom population will reach 65 years of age by 2011. From 2011 to 2021, significant growth also will occur within the age bracket of 45 to 64 years, an age group that uses more medical services than do adults in the immediately younger age bracket.[20] These demographic developments embody major implications for future health care spending.

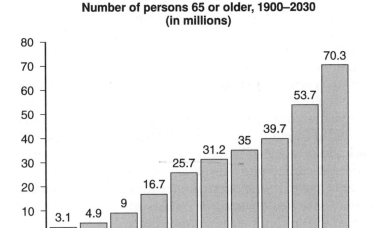

Number of persons 65 or older, 1900–2030 (in millions)

Year (as of July 1)

Note: Increments in years are uneven. Based on data from the U.S. Bureau of the Census

Figure 7–2 Number of Persons 65 or Older, 1900–2030
Sources: "Projections of the Total Resident Population by 5 Year Age Groups, Race, and Hispanic Origin with Special Age Categories: Middle Series, 1999 to 2000," U.S. Census Internet Release Date: January 13, 2000 with "Population Projections of the United States by Age, Sex, Race and Hispanic Origin: 1995–2050," Current Population Reports, P25–1130. Data for 2000 are from the 2000 Census.

The Growth of Specialized Medicine

Growth in specialized medicine has occurred in parallel with advancements in medicine's science and technology. Growth in the numbers and types of specialists has been accompanied by Americans' high utilization of specialty care, at least in part driven by specialists' availability. Unlike other industrialized nations, where physician specialists represent half or fewer of physicians in general practice, approximately 65 percent of practicing physicians in the United States are specialists.[21] In addition to this unbalanced proportion of specialty practitioners, the high value that Americans place on advanced technology has made specialty care synonymous with high-quality care. This perception may be accurate when the most appropriate treatment choice for an illness requires a specialist's services, but because specialists' services are generally more costly, their inappropriate use generates unnecessary expenses. Use of more costly specialists for primary care needs also tends to cause higher use of both diagnostic and therapeutic services than may be necessary for appropriate treatment. Historically, the health insurance models prevalent in the United

States carried no prohibitions against self-referrals to specialty care. Patients freely referred themselves to specialists based on their own interpretations of symptoms.

This use of specialists for first-line diagnosis and treatment has been a common and costly practice. Restraining costs associated with inappropriate specialty care continues to challenge managed care organizations, which seek to have patients treated at the lowest cost and most appropriate level of care. The efforts to restrain costs in this manner have raised much public outcry by both physicians and patients concerning the practice of "gatekeeping." Numerous legislative initiatives at the state and federal levels pertaining to patients' rights to obtain insurance payment for specialty treatment and physician prerogatives to refer for specialty care without insurance company interference are discussed in the chapter on managed care (see Chapter 8).

The Uninsured and Underinsured

Among all developed countries of the world, the United States has the highest proportion of population with no health insurance coverage.[22] In 2002, the U.S. Bureau of the Census estimated that 41.2 million Americans, or 14.6 percent of the population, had no health insurance, an increase of approximately 1.4 million uninsured persons since 2000.[23] Seventy-two percent of uninsured individuals are in families where at least one person is working full time, and only 17 percent are in families with no attachment to the work force.[24] Nearly two-thirds of the uninsured have incomes less than 200 percent of the Federal poverty level (FPL) or are from families with low incomes.[25] Figure 7-3 provides a snapshot of family income level for the uninsured. In addition, many individuals with health insurance coverage are considered to be underinsured because the extent of their insurance coverage is insufficient to protect them in the event of a major illness or injury.

The lack of health insurance or insufficient coverage carries major consequences by affecting the ability of individuals to receive timely and needed care for prevention, as well as for acute and chronic conditions. The resulting financial consequences can be significant. Lack of insurance coverage drives individuals to seek care in hospital emergency departments at costs higher than care provided at the physician's office or other ambulatory settings. The National Center for Health Statistics reports that nonurgent cases account for more than half of all visits to hospital emergency departments.[26] Further, uninsured or underinsured individuals tend to be low users of preventive services and are known to delay seeking care, even for acute conditions. These behaviors often result in increased illness severity and more complications, factors that add to diagnostic and treatment

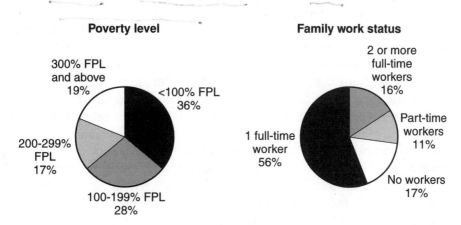

**The nonelderly uninsured
by poverty level and work status, 2000**

Total = 38 million uninsured

Figure 7–3 The Nonelderly Uninsured By Poverty Level and Work Status, 2000
Source: This publication was reprinted with permission of the Henry J. Kaiser Foundation of Menlo Park, California. The Kaiser Foundation is an independent health care philanthropy and is not associated with Kaiser Permanente or Kaiser Industries.

costs. Uninsured Americans have been found to be up to four times as likely as insured patients to require avoidable hospitalizations.[27] Increased costs are absorbed by providers as free care, passed on to the insured in the form of higher health insurance premiums, or paid by taxpayers in increased taxes levied to support public hospitals or public insurance programs.[28]

A Labor-Intensive Industry

Health care is a labor-intensive industry, with many industry segments operating on a 24 hours a day, 7 days a week basis. It is one of the largest industries in the United States, employing approximately 10.3 million workers, many of whom represent some of the most highly educated, trained, and compensated individuals in the workforce. The U.S. Department of Labor reports that approximately 13 percent of all wage and salary jobs created by 2010 will be in health services, and that 9 of the 20 occupations expected to grow the fastest will be in health services.[29]

Among the most important factors that continue to produce high employment demands are technological advances in care, which increase the array of services available to patients, and continued growth in the aging population with more intense and diverse health care service needs.

Economic Incentives That Fuel Rising Costs

Finally, both private and government health care financing mechanisms are recognized as major contributors to rising costs. Until the widespread introduction of prospective payment and the philosophy and financing mechanisms of managed care began in the 1980s, both government and private third-party payers reimbursed largely on a piecework, fee-for-service, retrospective basis. This system created economic incentives favoring high utilization. Simply, the more procedures or interventions applied, the greater the reimbursement. This economic incentive operated similarly for both physicians and hospitals. In combination with the other factors fueling increased consumption of health care resources, these economic incentives created by the health care financing system are acknowledged to have played a major role in rising expenditures. The history of failed attempts to change the health care financing system is reviewed later in this chapter, providing a foundation for the discussion of managed care and its emergence as the predominant form of health care financing and delivery in the United States.

■ Components of Health Care Expenditures

Figure 7–4 depicts the expenditure distribution of the national health care dollar. Of the total $1.3 trillion in 2000 health care expenditures, the largest portion, $412.1 billion or 32.8 percent, was spent on hospital care. The next largest component of expenditures was physician services, totaling $286.4 billion, or 22.8 percent of the health care dollar. Prescription drugs consumed a total of $121.8 billion or 9.7 percent. Nursing home care provided in free-standing, nonhospital-based facilities, at $92.2 billion, represented 7.3 percent of expenditures. Administration and net costs of private health insurance were $80.9 billion, or 6.4 percent.[30]

■ Sources of Health Care Payment

Figure 7–5 depicts the distribution of national health care expenditures by payment source.[31] Table 7–1 provides an overview of the history of national health care expenditures by sources of funds and amounts.

Private health insurance currently funds more than one-third of total expenditures. In 2000, private health insurance spending totaled $443.9 billion, a significant increase of 8.4 percent over the prior year, making this source of payment one of the fastest growing payer sectors.[32] Reasons for the acceleration in private health insurance spending include rising benefit costs (especially for prescription drugs) and a shift of managed care plan types to higher-cost options.[33] With benefit

Where the health care dollar went, 2000

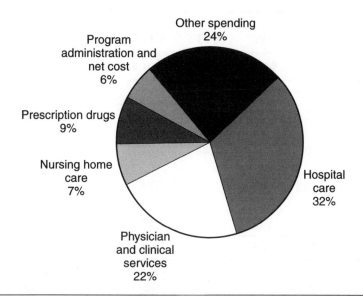

Figure 7–4 Where the Health Care Dollar Went, 2000
Source: Reprinted from Office of the Actuary, Center for Medicare and Medicaid Services, National Health Statistics Group.

Where the health care dollar came from, 2000

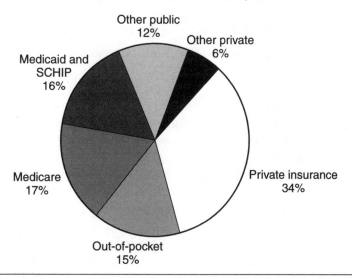

Figure 7–5 Where the Health Care Dollar Came From, 2000
Source: Reprinted from Office of the Actuary, Center for Medicare and Medicaid Services, National Health Statistics Group.

Table 7–1 National Health Expenditures by Source of Funds and Amounts, Selected Calendar Years, 1980–2000

SOURCE OF FUNDS	1980	1988	1993	1997	1998	1999	2000
NHE, billions	$245.8	$558.1	$888.1	$1,091.2	$1,149.8	$1,215.6	$1,299.5
Private funds	140.9	331.7	497.7	588.8	628.8	666.5	712.3
Consumer payments	126.4	293.8	445.0	521.8	557.7	593.8	638.4
Out-of-pocket payments	58.2	118.9	146.9	162.3	174.5	184.4	194.5
Private health insurance	68.2	174.9	298.1	359.4	383.2	409.4	443.9
Other private funds	14.5	37.9	52.7	67.0	71.1	72.7	73.8
Public funds	104.8	226.4	390.4	502.4	520.9	549.0	587.2
Federal	71.3	154.1	274.4	358.8	367.7	384.8	411.5
Medicare	37.4	89.0	148.3	208.2	209.5	212.6	224.4
Medicaid[b]	14.5	31.0	76.8	94.9	99.6	108.4	118.4
Other federal[c]	19.4	34.1	49.3	55.8	58.6	63.8	68.7
State and local Medicaid[b]	11.5	24.1	44.8	64.8	71.8	78.3	84.3
Other state and local[c]	22.0	48.2	71.1	78.8	81.5	85.9	91.4

[b] includes State Children's Health Insurance Program expansion, Title XIX.
[c] includes State Children's Health Insurance Program, Title XXI.

Source: Office of the Actuary, Center for Medicare and Medicaid Services, National Health Statistics Group.

costs rising faster than premiums in recent years, insurers have increased their rates to offset higher costs and improve corporate financial performance. Recent increases in premium growth may signal the end of managed care's impact on slowing the growth in spending.[34]

Public funds contributed a total of 45.2 percent, or $587.2 billion, to national health care expenditures in 2000. Medicare and Medicaid, the federal government's two largest health care payment sources, together accounted for 83.3 percent of all federal funds expended for health care and 26.4 percent of total national health care expenditures. Medicare financed $224.4 billion of spending for the health care of 39.2 million older Americans and Americans with disabilities, or 17 percent of the nation's total health care spending.[35]

In 2000, public sources of funds, primarily Medicare and Medicaid, accounted for 59 percent of all hospital payments. In contrast with funding sources for hospital care, private insurance remains the predominant form of payment for physician services, accounting for 47.8 percent of total payments.[36]

Although Medicaid constitutes only 16.9 percent of payments for hospital care and 6.6 percent of physician payments, it is the predominant form of payment for nursing home care. In 2000, federal and state Medicaid sources together provided 48.2 percent, or $44.4 billion, of nursing home payments. Consumers paid $24.9 billion, 27 percent of the total payments to nursing homes, as out-of-pocket expenditures in 2000.[37] Not that long ago, the costs of long-term care, including nursing home expenses, were not privately insurable. Long-term care insurance has been widely available for approximately 15 years. However, premium costs are significant and, as with most insurance products, increase with age. Since 1993, the percentage of nursing home costs covered by private insurance has increased little, from 5.1 percent to 8.0 percent in 2000.[38] State Medicaid programs providing medical assistance to the economically needy continue as a major payment source for individuals who either initially qualified for assistance based on income or subsequently become eligible through depletion of personal assets in paying for long-term institutional care.

■ Evolution of Health Insurance: Third-Party Payment

Health insurance is the primary source of payment for health care costs in the United States. The role of insurance is of major importance to understanding both the structure and function of the U.S. health care delivery system. As a financing mechanism that helps protect individuals from personal monetary devastation when expensive care is required, insurance helps decrease risks of costly delays in seeking treatment for conditions that might otherwise escalate to more serious and more costly states. The impact of inadequate or no insurance for over 40 million Americans is repeatedly highlighted in the national debates over the need for health care reform that will provide universal coverage.

The U.S. system of health insurance currently includes numerous private entities that provide either indemnity coverage (reimbursement to those insured) or coverage on a prepaid, managed care basis. Government-sponsored and government-administered programs such as Medicare and Medicaid do not provide care directly, but rather contract with providers such as physicians and other health professionals, hospitals, and health maintenance organizations (HMOs) to deliver services to their beneficiaries. This section reviews the definition of insurance as it applies to health care and discusses the development and importance of private and government-sponsored health insurance.

The historic definition of insurance by which it is still commonly understood is a mechanism through which individuals pay an advance sum to a pool in which payments from numerous individuals offset the cost of a possible future costly event. Central to this definition is that events insured against are rare or unlikely to befall a particular individual, but can be predicted with a fair level of accuracy in a group. This latter understanding is the basis for payment or premium setting that helps to keep the costs of coverage reasonable for individual participants by pooling risks.

As early as the middle of the nineteenth century, a movement was started to insure workers against loss of wages resulting from injuries. Later, insurance to cover lost wages resulting from catastrophic illness was added to accident policies. It was not until the 1930s, however, that health insurance as it is known today—that is, insurance that pays all or part of the costs of medical treatment to the provider (as opposed to offsetting lost wages due to illness or injury through direct cash payment)—was inaugurated. Throughout the 1930s and early 1940s, the voluntary hospital sector and local employers, in part in response to hospitals' difficulty in collecting payment from individuals who lacked financial resources, organized group hospital prepayment plans. This response reflected hospitals' dependence on private payments. In 1935, over 70 percent of hospital income was derived from private individuals.[39]

In 1930, a group of teachers enacted a contract with Baylor Hospital in Dallas, Texas, to provide coverage for certain hospital expenses.[40] This initial event created a model for the development of what was to become Blue Cross, a private, not-for-profit insurance empire that grew over the succeeding four decades into the dominant form of health insurance in the United States. The Blue Shield plans to provide physician payments began shortly after Blue Cross emerged, and by the early 1940s, numerous Blue Shield plans were operating across the country. In 1946, the American Medical Association (AMA) financed the Association Medical Care Plans, which later became the National Association of Blue Shield Plans.

These developments, through which health insurance was transformed from a mechanism to reimburse individuals for lost wages resulting from injury or illness to one that reimburses providers for the costs of medical care, carried gigantic implications. The first is antithetical to the central concept of insurance. Whereas insurance originally was designed to guard against the low risk of a rare occurrence, such as premature death, and for unpredictable events such as accidents, today's medical care insurance provides coverage of predictable, routine use of the health care system as well as unforeseen and unpredictable illnesses or injuries. Coverage for routine use of health care services added a new dimension to the concept of insurance. Perhaps the term "assurance" more appropriately describes the health care payment system that evolved. In Great Britain, "assurance" is used to denote coverage for contingencies that must eventually happen (e.g., life assurance), whereas "insurance" is reserved for coverage of those contingencies (like fire and theft) that may never occur.[41]

The establishment and subsequent proliferation of the "Blues" signaled a new era in U.S. health care delivery and financing. They played a significant role in establishing hospitals as the centers of medical care proliferation and technology, and, by providing reimbursement for expensive services, they put hospitals within the reach of middle-class working Americans for the first time. The insulation from costs of care provided by the Blues had a major impact on utilization. By the late 1930s, annual hospital admission rates for Blue Cross enrollees were 50 percent higher on average than for the nation as a whole, and more than 80 percent of beneficiaries occupied private or semiprivate rooms (as opposed to wards).[42] In addition to contributing to increased utilization of hospital services by removing financial barriers, the Blue Cross movement had other major, lasting impacts on national policy making. Rosemary Stevens notes, "In the United States, the brave new world of medicine was specialized, interventionist, mechanistic and expensive—at least as interpreted, through pre-payment, for workers in major organizations."[43] By 1940, the Blue Cross movement represented a major financing alternative, countering forces that had long lobbied politically for a form of national health insurance, a concept opposed vehemently by private medicine. The plans also stimulated the American Hospital Association (AHA) and local hospitals to consider providing similar forms of reimbursement for low-income populations, modeled after the Blue Cross divisions of benefits recognizing private, semiprivate, and ward care. This latter movement, which continued for the next 20 years, focused attention on government as a potential source of insurance that was designed for low-income populations, the unemployed, or sporadic seasonal workers and that was modeled along Blue Cross lines.[44]

By 1938, uniform features of all Blue Cross plans were firmly established. These features included not-for-profit status, supervision by state insurance departments, direct payments through contract arrangements with providers, and the use of community rating, in which single premiums were charged to all individuals in a defined group without regard to age, sex, occupation, and health status. Community rating helped ensure nondiscrimination against groups with varying risk characteristics in order to provide coverage at reasonable rates for the community as a whole. However, as commercial insurers entered the health care insurance marketplace, they used "experience rating," basing premiums on historically documented patterns of utilization, Blue Cross plans, to remain competitive, began offering a variety of benefit packages. Ultimately, the Blue Cross plans were compelled to switch to experience-rating schemes to avoid attracting a disproportionate share of high-risk individuals, for whom commercial insurance was prohibitively expensive.

Before World War II, commercial insurance companies had little significant involvement with, or interest in, insuring individuals for health care costs. Their portfolios had been limited largely to indemnity payments, considered a much less risky enterprise than insuring for use of the health care delivery system. However, post–World War II saw new fringe benefits added to labor contract benefit packages to offset the impact of federal wage and price controls. The financial incentives of these new developments fueled commercial insurers' entry into the health care insurance marketplace. In 1997, there were 944 U.S. health and medical insurance firms that reported a total of over $203.2 billion in revenue. Fifty of the largest firms accounted for over 75 percent ($152.8 billion) of the total revenue from the health and medical insurance sector.[45]

■ Self-Funded Insurance Programs

Since the late 1970s, self-funding (full or partial) and self-insurance of employee health benefits have become increasingly common, particularly among large employers. Through the self-funded mechanism, the employer (or other group, such as a union or trade association) collects premiums itself and pools these into a fund or account from which it pays claims against medical benefits instead of using a commercial carrier. Self-insured plans normally use the services of an actuarial firm to set premium rates and a third-party administrator (TPA) to administer benefits, pay claims, and collect data on utilization. Many TPAs also are now providing case management services for potentially extraordinarily expensive cases to help coordinate care and control employer risk of catastrophic expenses.

Self-insurance offers significant advantages to employers. Employers can avoid certain additional administrative and other charges made by commercial carriers, such as fees for writing and activating policies. By self-funding benefits, employers also can avoid premium taxes and accrue interest on the cash reserves held in the benefit account. With administrative services-only arrangements, an employer will self-fund its benefit plan, retain the cash reserve, and use the commercial carrier to process claims and handle related administrative tasks for its group. In another model, the minimum premium plan, the employer shares risk through a contractual agreement with an insurer that assumes liability for certain payments that exceed a predetermined level.[46] A major stimulus to the development of self-insurance programs has been their exemption from the Employee Retirement and Income Security Act of 1974 (ERISA), which mandates minimum benefits under state law. This exemption has allowed employers much greater flexibility in designing benefit packages and provided one mechanism to control benefit costs. In the period 2001–2002, premiums for employer-sponsored health plans increased by 12.7 percent, the highest increase since 1990. In past years, increases in costs for plans in which the employer purchases coverage from an insurer were almost double those for self-insured employers.[47] Now, however, significant increases in medical claims expenses and the rise in premium costs is closing the gap between self-insured plans and ones in which the employer purchases coverage from an outside insurer. In 2002, premium increases varied only one-half percent between the two different insurance arrangements.[48]

Major controversies continue to arise from the ERISA exemption of self-insured employer plans. One controversy is based in states' interpretations of their responsibilities for consumer protection through regulation of the types and scope of required coverage in employer-provided plans. ERISA has historically preempted such regulation. Another major area of dispute centers on the states' losses of premium revenue taxes as they struggle with growing financial burdens of uncompensated care and caring for uninsured populations. An additional area of major national controversy and legal actions surrounding ERISA is its prohibition against employees suing employer-provided health plans. Under ERISA, organizations that administer employer-based health benefit plans maintain a degree of legal immunity from litigation and liability for withholding coverage or failing to provide necessary care. Other challenges to ERISA involving employee rights to sue health plans continue to be heard in state and federal courts.

■ Government as a Source of Payment

The combined federal, state, and local governments' role in financing health care services has evolved from a relatively minor one to one of major importance for health care services in the United States. Originally focused on specific population groups—most notably providing health care for those in government service, their dependents, and particular population groups, such as American Indians—a combination of public programs, chief among them Medicare and Medicaid, now constitute over 43.3 percent of total personal health care expenditures.[49]

Government payment for health services includes federal support of U.S. Public Health Service hospitals, the Indian Health Service, state and local inpatient psychiatric and other long-term care facilities, services of the Veterans Affairs hospitals and health services, services provided by the Department of Defense to military personnel and their dependents, workers' compensation, public health activities, and other government-sponsored service grants and initiatives.

In the absence of a comprehensive national health and social services policy, government's role in financing health care services can be described as a system only in the loosest interpretation of that term. It may be more accurate to describe government's various roles in health care financing as a mosaic of individual programs of reimbursement, direct payments to vendors, grants, matching funds, and subsidies. Some financing programs are interrelated or interdependent, representing tiers, first-pocket, or second-pocket approaches; others are totally independent of each other. Many are overlapping in their intent; some, like the Medicaid program, are conglomerates of federal and state source funds with policy making subject to federal, state, and local administrative and legislative influences.

As a framework for discussion of the role of government as a source of health care service payments, bear in mind that this system of financing operates primarily in a vendor/purchaser relationship, with government contracting with health care services providers rather than providing services itself. An obvious example is the Medicare program, in which the federal government purchases hospital, home health, nursing home, physician, and other medical services under contract with suppliers. The Medicaid system operates similarly. This vendor/purchaser arrangement stands in contrast to other industrialized nations, such as Great Britain, with comprehensive programs of national health insurance in which the government is both the payer and the operator of the system. America's history of fierce resistance from the private sector—both organized medicine and, to a lesser degree, the voluntary medicine and hospital system—has served to work against the enactment of a comprehensive national health care system. The activity of the private sector lobby can be traced from early attempts to provide some form of national health insurance, beginning in the first decade of the twentieth century and continuing through the defeat of the Clinton administration's National Health Security Act.

Medicare and Medicaid, the two largest government-funded programs, are discussed in the following sections. Attempts at cost containment are discussed relative to each program. Other government-financed programs are discussed in Chapter 11.

Medicare

Were it not for the successful opposition of the private sector, most notably the AMA, the Social Security Administration would have included a form of national health insurance in 1935. It was not to be for another 30 years, during which time numerous presidential and congressional acts for national health insurance were proposed and defeated, that Title XVIII of the Social Security Administration, Medicare, was enacted by Congress to take effect in July 1966. Medicare became the second mandated health insurance program in the United States, after workers' compensation.

The enactment of Medicare legislation was a historical benchmark for several reasons. First, it gave every American 65 years of age or older covered by the Social Security system entitlement to a range of medical benefits, which signaled a giant step for government's entry into the personal care financing arena. On the federal level, the Medicare program was established under the aegis of the Social Security Administration, and hospital payment was contracted to local intermediaries chosen by hospitals. Over 90 percent of hospitals chose their local Blue Cross association as the intermediary. As an alternative to government certification required for participation in the Medicare Program, the Social Security Administration agreed that accreditation by the then Joint Commission on Accreditation of Hospitals would suffice.[50] The sponsors and advocates of this legislation could not have foreseen its impact on the costs of the delivery system or on the growth of the hospital and health care complexes of the United States. Describing the enactment of Medicare as a "watershed," Rosemary Stevens states:

> *Thus with the stroke of a pen, the elderly acquired hospital benefits, the hospitals acquired cost reimbursement for these benefits, the Blue Cross Association was precipitated into prominence as a major national organization (since the national contract was to be with the association, with subcontracting to local plans), and the Joint Commission was given formal government recognition.*[51]

The act establishing Medicare specifically stated that there should be "prohibition against any federal interference" with the practice of medicine or the way in which medical services were provided.[52] However, as could have been predicted, the government's implicit acceptance of responsibility for the care of older adults through the allocation of dollars generated a flood of regulation in the attempt to address both control of expenditures and quality of the medical services and products for which it was now a major payer.

As originally implemented, the Medicare program consisted of two parts, which differed in sources of funding and benefits. Part A provided benefits for care provided in the hospital, outpatient diagnostic services, extended care facilities, and short-term care at home required by an illness for which the patient is hospitalized. This portion of coverage was mandatory and was funded by Social Security payroll taxes. Part B was structured as a voluntary program covering physician services and services ordered by physicians, such as certain diagnostic tests, medical equipment and supplies, and home health services. This portion was funded from beneficiary premium payments, matched by general federal revenues.

Medicare was by no means fully comprehensive in its coverage. Beneficiaries were required to share costs through a system of deductibles and coinsurance. A deductible required the beneficiary to reach a set amount in personal outlays each 12-month period before Medicare payment was activated. Coinsurance required that 20 percent of costs for hospitalization be covered by the patient. The program also set limits on the total days of hospital care that would be paid based on a lifetime pool of days limit. Medicare payments for posthospital stays in extended care facilities were limited to 100 days. These limitations gave rise to a proliferation of supplemental, or "Medi-gap," policies, designed particularly to cover coinsurance requirements for hospital care. Both Blue Cross and commercial insurers wrote these policies. Sweeping changes in the Medicare program currently are underway as a result of the BBA. Highlights of those changes are addressed later in this chapter.

Almost from its inception, Medicare spending surpassed projections. In the year of enactment, 1965, hospital insurance costs under Medicare were projected at $3.1 billion; in 1970, the figure was revised upward to $5.8 billion.[53] Although hospital costs for the growing older adult population increased more rapidly than expected in those five years, the rise over projected Medicare expenses could not be explained in major part by that phenomenon. Rosemary Stevens cites a 1976 study by the U.S. Human Resources Administration to help explain the burgeoning Medicare hospital expenses.[54] This study attributed less than 10 percent of increases to growing utilization and the increasing older adult population. Twenty-three percent of the increase over projected hospital costs was attributed to general inflation and the remaining 66 percent to huge growth in hospital payroll and nonpayroll expenses, including profits.

The reimbursement mechanism for Medicare payment to hospitals mirrored that of the Blue Cross intermediaries. Payment was cost based and retrospective on a per-day-of-stay basis. While facilitating the rapid incorporation of a huge, almost 20 million people strong, pool of beneficiaries into the new benefit system, this system also served to fuel utilization in an era of rapidly advancing medical technology and its introduction of more sophisticated and equally more expensive treatments. Coronary artery bypass grafting and orthopaedic prosthetics are just two examples of procedures that were not available on a widespread basis only 10 years earlier, but that rapidly became treatments of choice, replacing more conservative and far less costly interventions. Paid on a retrospective basis for costs incurred in the care of the Medicare beneficiaries during a prior period, hospitals had a strong incentive toward utilization of services and production of charges with no incentives for efficiency.

The 1960s also was a period in which aging hospital facilities, many initially constructed or expanded with Hill-Burton funds in the late 1940s and 1950s, were in need of major renovations or modernizations to keep pace with new, sophisticated care and diagnostic technology. This was an era in which medical and surgical intensive care services that required specially designed and equipped units evolved, incurring demand for major capital investments. New technology and treatment advances were rendering hospitals out of date. A 1967 federal conference on medical costs estimated that $10 billion would be needed for modernization of the nation's hospitals.[55] The Medicare reimbursement formula, which included a component that enabled hospitals to pass a portion of capital costs back to the third-party payer, provided a new opportunity for hospitals to generate additional capital by accumulating operating reserves for capital expansion. This reimbursement feature further promoted maximum utilization and spending. In the period 1966–1978, numerous amendments to the Social Security Act made significant changes to both the Medicare and Medicaid programs.

In general, amendments in the first five years following passage were largely directed toward increasing the types of covered services and expanding the population of eligible members. During the later period, amendments addressed a rising tide of concerns about the costs and the quality of the programs. Some significant changes to the Medicare program resulting from amendments, and the years they were enacted, include the following:

1967

- The requirement for physician certification of medical necessity for general hospital admissions and coverage of outpatient hospital services was dropped.
- Full payment of reasonable charges of pathologists and radiologists for inpatient services was authorized, eliminating the deductible and coinsurance requirements.
- Coverage was added for:
  - Nonroutine podiatric care under Part B
  - Diagnostic radiographs taken at a patient's home or in a nursing home
  - Durable medical equipment for home use
  - Outpatient physical therapy services under Part B
- A lifetime reserve of 60 days of inpatient coverage for hospital care was added.

1972

- Medicare eligibility was extended to people with disabilities who had received cash benefits under Social Security's disability insurance provisions for at least 24 months.

■ Part B premiums were capped at the most recent percentage increase in Social Security cash benefits.
■ Coverage was added for:
  – Speech-language pathology outpatient services
  – Social Security insureds and their dependents with end-stage renal disease requiring hemodialysis or transplantation
■ Requirements were added for:
  – Approval of hospital capital expenditures by state or local planning agencies
  – Public disclosures of survey findings in health care institutions and agencies with respect to compliance conditions for Medicare participation
  – Professional care review and placement in intermediate care facilities
■ Requirements were rescinded for:
  – Coinsurance payments for home health care services under Part B
  – Medical social services in skilled nursing facilities
■ Authorization was granted for:
  – Single annual per capita payments to HMOs, provided certain enrollment and other provisions were met, and partial return of cost savings to the HMOs
  – Validation of Joint Commission on the Accreditation of Hospitals survey results through sampling by state Medicare certifying agencies
  – Establishment of advance approval of skilled nursing facility and home health care benefits and minimum periods of eligibility for posthospitalization services
  – Grant and contract funds for experimental and demonstration studies of prospective reimbursement, the three-day hospital stay requirement for skilled nursing facility admission, ambulatory surgery centers, intermediate care facilities, home health and day care services, and reimbursement of nurse practitioner and physician assistant services and the services of clinical psychologists
  – Limited reimbursement for chiropractic services to a specific diagnosis
  – Established professional standards review organizations (PSROs, discussed later in this chapter)

1977

■ Added:
  – Numerous provisions directed toward control of fraud and abuse
  – Reimbursement for nurse practitioners and physician assistants working in designated rural and urban medically under-

served areas, subject to conditions for medical supervision and other criteria

1978

■ Added incentives to the end-stage renal disease program to promote use of less costly home dialysis and renal transplantation, promote studies of end-stage renal disease, and establish renal disease coordinating activities for program planning and evaluation

The Omnibus Budget Reconciliation Acts of 1980 and 1981 added another plethora of amendments to the Medicare legislation with a strong, continuing cost-containment focus. Many initiatives were directed toward reducing hospitalization and lengths of hospital stay. Representative amendments explicitly advocated the use of home health services as an alternative to hospital care. These included elimination of the limit on the annual number of reimbursable home health care visits, elimination of the three-day hospitalization requirement for home health visit coverage eligibility, and elimination of the need for occupational therapy as a requirement for initial entitlement to home health care services. The prior exclusion from Medicare participation of proprietary home health care agencies in states that did not require agency licensure also was lifted. Other amendments ended coverage for alcohol detoxification facilities and brought the PSROs under increasing cost and effectiveness scrutiny.

The efforts at cost containment and quality control represented by the amendments of the 1970s and 1980s were followed by an array of initiatives that addressed growing concerns about the value and effectiveness of services being delivered by the rapidly growing outlay of Medicare dollars. Since inception, Medicare legislation required hospitals to conduct utilization review as a safeguard against unnecessary or poor quality. Compliance was poor, however, because hospitals, unaccustomed to external accountability, did not fully exercise their new obligation to report to outside authorities. This attitude stemmed from strongly held values for autonomy and self-evaluation among hospitals and their medical staff and, in part, from the altruism inherent in the operation of heretofore privately supported institutions. At the same time, the Medicare legislation, seemingly reflecting these altruistic motives, contained no "teeth" to enforce utilization or quality standards or to balance the incentives for service expansion built into the retrospective payment system.

In addition to the expansion of services and facilities occurring in the voluntary hospital sector, investor-owned for-profit hospitals saw the opportunity for expansion offered by Medicare's guarantee of full-cost reimbursement. By 1970, there were 29 investor-owned for-profit hospital chains. Both not-for-profit and for-profit hospital enterprises proliferated without the controlling impact of market competition inherent in providing goods or services directly to consumers. By 1980, more than 92 percent of hospital expenditures were flowing through organized third parties: government, Blue Cross, or commercial insurers.

From the mid-1960s through the 1980s, federal initiatives attempted to brake spiraling hospital costs and address quality concerns. Virtually all of these initiatives were unsuccessful. In response to concerns over duplication of services and duplication of major capital expenditures for facility expansion, the Comprehensive Health Planning (CHP) Act was passed in 1966 to provide funds to states to organize local health-planning bodies with the intent of achieving adequate facilities and services on a regionwide basis without unnecessary duplication. Competition for patients and parochial interests of institutions, however, served to work against effectiveness in achieving rational regional plans. New York was the first state to adopt certificate-of-need legislation, requiring state permission for significant capital expenditures, with permission in part based on appropriateness to a defined regional or areawide plan. Other states followed rapidly. Again, the intent was to preclude spending for duplicative or unnecessary capital expansion for buildings and technology.

Because interested parties from hospital and other health care institutions conducted the initial reviews of applications, the processes became relatively meaningless. Similarly, federal legislation was passed in 1974 to form local health systems agencies (HSAs) to replace CHP agencies, with the intent to develop plans for local health resources based on quantified population needs. Although the governance structure required participation by consumers, interested parties from the provider groups dominated discussions. HSAs were fundamentally unsuccessful in materially influencing decisions about service or technology expansion. Their decisions became undeniably political, and attempts to achieve consensus based on real service needs were counterbalanced by community interests in economic and employment expansions. Concurrent with attempts to slow cost increases through a planning approach, a number of other legislative initiatives took shape that were directly related to concerns over Medicare costs and service quality.

The establishment of PSROs in 1972 signaled the first federal attempt to review care provided under Medicare (and Medicaid and certain other federally funded health care programs) and to eliminate unnecessary hospital days for federally supported patient care. This program, structured to attenuate backlash from the private medical care community, asserted that structured physician review of hospital cases in each locality was the most appropriate means to evaluate the quality and necessity of care. Each local PSRO was a not-for-profit organization composed of a representative group of local physicians. Determinations of the quality and necessity of care were made and passed to the local Medicare intermediary for implementation of payment decisions.

Plagued by questionable effectiveness and high administrative costs, PSROs were replaced by peer review organizations (PROs) through a provision of the Tax Equity and Fiscal Responsibility Act of 1982 (TEFRA). Hospitals were required to contract with a PRO by 1984. The PRO attempted to achieve greater effectiveness in cost control and quality by providing more specific and measurable goals in both areas. Eventually, the PRO's role was extended to include outpatient care, home health care, and care for the military and their dependents. In 1993, the program's mission was changed again because of high administrative costs and questionable effectiveness. The focus changed from detecting poor clinical quality and overuse to achieving care improvements through measurement and reporting of variation in care quality. Based on standards and outcomes, it was hoped that results shared with hospitals and physicians would provide a basis for working toward quality improvement. This change in purpose reflected the quality improvement initiatives that took hold in U.S. industry in the early 1990s.

TEFRA, aimed at providing financial incentives to hospitals to contain costs, was followed in 1983 by enactment of a case payment system that radically changed hospital reimbursement under Medicare. In the new scheme, reimbursement for inpatient operating costs shifted from the retrospective to prospective mode. The new reimbursement system was based on preset payments for services rendered to patients with similar diagnoses, rather than on costs incurred. The diagnosis-related group (DRG) payment system based hospital payments on established fees for services required to treat a specific diagnosis rather than discreet units of services. The components of each DRG include numerous major diagnostic categories (MDCs) defined by the body's major organ systems. MDCs are further subdivided into DRGs based on the patient's diagnosis, demographic characteristics, and relevant clinical data. The payment an individual hospital receives under this system is ultimately calculated using input from a host of other data known to impact costs, such as teaching status and wage data for its geographic area.

It is most important to recognize the impact of such a system in reversing incentives for hospitals to consume rather than conserve resources. Instead of financially rewarding hospitals for high use of services, as was the case under retrospective reimbursement, the DRG system provided incentives for the hospital to spend only what was needed to achieve an optimal patient care outcome. If that outcome could be achieved at a resource cost lower than the preset payment, the hospital realized an excess payment for the case. If the hospital spent more to treat a particular ailment than allowed, it had to absorb the excess costs. The overall objective was to induce hospitals to seek greater efficiency by "rewarding" those with the profits generated by cases whose treatment costs fell below the DRG price and "punishing" those whose treatment costs exceeded the DRG price by requiring them to subsidize the difference. The DRG system also made financial provisions for cases classified as "outlier" due to extraordinary complications outside the hospital's reasonable control. The DRG system did not build in allowances to the payment rate for direct medical education expenses for teaching hospitals, hospital outpatient expenses, or capital expenditures. These continued to be reimbursed on a cost basis. The principle of case-based prospective payment has been adopted in varying forms by numerous states as a basis for their hospital reimbursement systems, and private third-party payers also have adopted the concept.

When the prospective payment system was implemented, numerous concerns were raised by hospitals, health care providers, and consumers about its possible effects on the course of health care spending, hospital financial viability, physician practice autonomy, and the quality of patient care. The roots of these concerns included questions about:

■ The new system's effectiveness in controlling cost escalation
■ The ability of hospitals to streamline inpatient care delivery sufficiently and quickly enough to avoid major financial losses
■ The effects on physician practice patterns of hospitals' pressure to minimize inpatient services and lengths of stay
■ The competency and capacity of the home health care industry to accommodate service needs of patients discharged in less advanced stages of recovery
■ The overall impact on the quality of inpatient outcomes

"Quicker and sicker" was the slogan popularized by the media during the first years of the prospective payment system to characterize the drive to discharge patients as rapidly as possible due to pressure to decrease inpatient lengths of stay. The media also popularized the term "patient dumping." It referred to documented cases of hospitals' inappropriately transferring low-income or uninsured patients at high risk of long, expensive, and potentially unprofitable service needs to other hospitals.

In general, research on the impact of the prospective payment system demonstrated that many early concerns were unfounded and that the system did have a measurable impact on the overall growth of Medicare spending. Also, continuing advancements in medical care, technology, and health care delivery systems were occurring during the early 1980s. These advancements significantly increased the resources available to treat Medicare patients. For example, until 1983, growth rates in Medicare expenditures for inpatient and outpatient services had increased at comparable rates. Since 1983, the volume of Medicare outpatient services covered under Part B (hospital outpatient services and physician services not included in the prospective payment system) increased dramatically, in part counterbalancing the impact of prospective payment on total Medicare spending.[56] Medical advancements and changing physician practice patterns also affected costs in the inpatient setting.[57] The impact of the prospective payment system on the quality of patient care, as demonstrated by comparisons of selected quality indicators before and after the system's implementation, was the subject of research efforts. The federal Prospective Payment Assessment Commission (ProPAC), established to monitor the effects of the prospective system, and empirical studies reviewed hospital readmission rates as one quality indicator.

On balance, the studies revealed few, if any, effects upon Medicare patient readmission rates attributable to the new method of hospital payment.[58] The RAND Corporation also conducted several studies of another indicator of patient care quality, in-hospital mortality rates. The studies reviewed almost 17,000 records of Medicare patients admitted to hospitals for five common conditions. Findings included a drop of 24 percent in the average length of hospital stay for these conditions and an overall improvement in mortality rates among the five conditions studied.[59]

Evidence supports that the prospective payment system slowed hospital cost growth during the early years following implementation, largely through reductions in lengths of stay, hospital personnel, and new medical technologies. However, total Medicare cost growth later re-accelerated, in part because of increased volume in outpatient spending and other factors whose impact have not been clearly determined.[60] Concerns about the capacity of the home health care industry to meet anticipated increases in demand from patients experiencing more rapid hospital discharges dissipated quickly. Both the not-for-profit and proprietary sectors of the industry responded vigorously. In addition, many hospitals undertook initiatives to create new or expand existing home health care services as components of integrated systems. Between 1990 and 1998, spending for home health care services experienced almost a fivefold increase, from $1.6 billion to $7.8 billion.[61]

Concerns about patient dumping were formally addressed in 1985 by the Consolidated Omnibus Budget Reconciliation Act (COBRA), which included provisions requiring hospitals to provide care to everyone who presented in their emergency departments, regardless of ability to pay. Stiff financial penalties, as well as risk of the loss of

Medicare reimbursement eligibility by hospitals inappropriately transferring patients, accompanied the COBRA provisions.

At least in the early years of the prospective payment system, hospitals did not suffer the negative financial impact predicted by some; they actually posted substantial profits.[62] In fact, the federal government in part justified later reductions in prospective payment on the basis that early payments were too high relative to costs.[63] It has even been suggested that the large surpluses generated by not-for-profit hospitals in the early years of prospective payment fueled hospital costs by making new surpluses available for investment.[64]

From the outset, the prospective payment system's potential cost-containment effectiveness was circumscribed by its limitation to inpatient hospital care only for Medicare recipients. Aggressive shifting of Medicare-covered services to the outpatient setting, as well as shifting hospital costs onto private pay patients, were two major reactions that attenuated the prospective payment system's cost-containment results.

Before the implementation of Medicare DRGs, several states experimented with methods to control rising hospital costs by implementing uniquely designed rate-setting programs known as "all payer" rate systems. These programs enabled states to bring Medicare payments, along with other payers' reimbursement, into a prospective mode. The movement began in Maryland in 1977, when the state succeeded in obtaining a Medicare waiver that allowed it to implement its own Medicare payment rules.[65] New York, New Jersey, and Massachusetts followed. The experience of these states was positive in reducing total hospital cost growth, and they succeeded in limiting the difference between private charges and actual costs by capping the differential through statutory limit. This differential previously had been shifted by hospitals to unregulated commercial payers to absorb the amount hospitals were prohibited from charging Medicaid and Blue Cross plans. The differential had provided one method for hospitals to cover costs of uncompensated care. The growth of the uncompensated care volume in the 1980s, along with protests by commercial insurers who felt they were absorbing an unfair portion of that burden through shifting of the differential, led states to implement "charity care" pools to more equitably distribute costs of care for the uninsured and population groups lacking the means to pay. This was another positive byproduct of the all-payer rate system experiments. Ultimately, however, the payment under the new DRG system proved to be more lucrative than under the waivered status of their own systems, and experimenting states dropped their all-payer rate systems; by 1989, all had joined the DRG system.

New, drastic changes in the Medicare program, targeting cost reductions and quality improvements, have been the escalating focal points of national policy debates since 1994. These debates have oc-

curred against the backdrop of the nation's health
delivery system reforms brought about by contin
aged care and the surge of competitive forces tha
of the Clinton Plan.

From the inception of Medicare, physician reimbursement
Medicare Part B was provided on a fee-for-service basis with reimbursement based on prevailing fees for specific services within a specified geographic area. Coupled with a cost-of-living factor designed to
provide a payment ceiling specific to a geographic area, a "prevailing
fee" was defined as an amount not to exceed the 75th percentile of
charges for a particular service by all physicians within a community.
Although physician payments constituted a relatively small portion of
total national expenditures, their rate of increase throughout the
1970s and 1980s in the Medicare program (an average of 18 percent
annually between 1975 and 1987) was sounding an alarm.[66]

Medicare enacted a price freeze for physician services that lasted
15 months and was later extended an additional 7 months for physicians who did not accept fee assignments in the Medicare program.[67]
Assessments of the effects of the price freeze suggested that the lower
fees were offset by an increase in the volume of services.[68] Several explanations were offered for this phenomenon. One was sheer increases
in volume of high-growth services during the 1980s, such as cataract
surgery, and the availability of new diagnostic tests. Another was that
reductions in out-of-pocket expenses by Medicare recipients drove up
the demand for services.[69] In any event, the results of the price freeze
highlighted questions about how physicians respond to economic pressures, in particular whether those pressures increase motivation to
use more services in order to compensate for lower reimbursement.
The concerns over absolute cost increases, undergirded by rising concerns about overuse of costly specialty care, prompted congressional
cost-containment action, this time aimed at physician payments.

The Omnibus Budget Reconciliation Act of 1989 (OBRA) established a new method of Medicare physician reimbursement that became effective in 1992. This new method used a resource-based relative value scale (RBRVS) to replace the fee-for-service reimbursement
system based on prevailing fees. It addressed both price and volume issues. Under the old system, payments for services were made at the
lower of the physician's usual charge, the actual billed charge, or an
average of similar physician charges in a geographic area. Payment increases were capped by the annual amounts of increase in an inflationary factor, the Medicare Economic Index. The RBRVS system was an
attempt to contain costs by instituting the same payments for the
same services, whether performed by a generalist or a specialist physician. The RBRVS system was structured to include three components
in the fee: a measure of total work performed, an allowance for medical

practice costs, and an allowance for malpractice insurance expense. The system assigned each service a specified number of relative value units, which are multiplied by a national conversion factor to arrive at the fee. In addition, the relative value units are adjusted for geographic area variations in costs. The hoped-for results were cost containment, through reductions in the numbers of expensive procedures, and attenuation of the incentive for physicians to specialize.

The OBRA also introduced a 1992 cap of 20 percent above the Medicare-approved amount that could be paid for a specific procedure. The cap was reduced to 15 percent in subsequent years. OBRA also created what are known as Medicare Volume Performance standards, which are another method to cap payment increases on an annual basis, in addition to the Medicare Economic Index already in use.

Altman and Wallack summarize the shortcomings of the RBRVS system:

> *The fundamental criticism of the RBRVS system is that, while it controls total Medicare spending for physician services in the aggregate, it does so by arbitrarily lowering the prices for all physician services provided under the program and for all physicians. It does not however, provide much of an incentive for the individual physician to question the provision of a given service. On the contrary, by lowering the prices each physician receives per service, the system may be encouraging physicians to offer more services to compensate for lost revenues.*"[70]

The Balanced Budget Act of 1997

Medicare system reforms enacted by the prospective payment system and through the PSROs, provider-sponsored organization plans (PSOs), and related regulatory efforts of the 1980s, were radical approaches in their times. Indeed, the new fiscal mandates and their accompanying requirements for quality and accountability coupled with the rising influences of managed care, market competition, technology advances, and consumerism produced heretofore unprecedented changes in physician practice patterns, hospitals' affinities for technological acquisitions, and consumer expectations of hospital care. The Medicare prospective payment system even succeeded in demonstrating that in medical care "more is not necessarily better," as lengths of stay and service intensity were reduced to accommodate the DRG framework, with no demonstrable negative impact on the overall quality of patient care outcomes.

The first half of the 1990s witnessed one of the most publicly and vigorously debated issues of the century: President Clinton's National Health Security Act. Although the act never reached a congressional vote, many months of debate served to thrust national concerns about health care into the public limelight. Concerns included increased Medicare spending, lack of access to services, costs to beneficiaries, and provider choice. Popular and political sensitivities to these issues continued to rise against the backdrop of an escalating national dialogue about predictions of the impending insolvency of the Hospital Insurance Trust Fund.[71]

Several trends supported the need for radical changes in the Medicare system. First, the Congressional Budget Office was projecting that Medicare costs would grow at approximately 9 percent per year while the economy would expand at approximately 5 percent.[72] This projection suggested that if costs were not addressed, funding the Medicare program would soon require cuts in other government programs, major increases in taxes, or larger budget deficits, all unsatisfactory alternatives.

Second, the structure of the Medicare program was becoming rapidly outmoded as compared with national trends in the health insurance industry. Medicare remained a largely fee-for-service indemnity program, whereas employer-sponsored plans, Medicaid, and private insurance plans were rapidly embracing managed care principles, including capitated payment systems and case management techniques to control costs and monitor quality. Recognition was growing that a program with the national scope and impact of Medicare could ill afford resistance to current trends in health care financing and consumer sensitivity. With Medicare payments accounting for 31 percent of hospital spending and 21 percent of spending on physician services, the program has significant impact on the overall health care financing system.[73]

Third, Medicare coverage, even as compared with basic plans offered by employer-sponsored insurance programs, public programs, and individual private policies, was inadequate in its present form. To fill gaps, Medicare beneficiaries purchase "Medi-gap" policies. Medicare recipients with no access to these policies because of medical history or financial distress are left to shoulder copays and large coinsurance expenses. Some Medicare beneficiaries are eligible for Medicaid subsidies of these expenses. However, these Medicaid subsidies only serve to create additional state financial burdens to compensate for inadequacies of a federal program at a time when the states are struggling to meet the needs of the uninsured and the costs of uncompensated care.

Following acknowledgment of the president's and Congress's discord on a national health reform program, in 1995 congressional attention was sharply focused on stemming the tide of Medicare cost growth (with federal deficit reduction as a backdrop) and how to achieve broader choices for Medicare beneficiaries, primarily through managed care plans, which were providing models of cost containment and consumer satisfaction.[74] After two decades of experimentation and experience with cost-containment and quality improvement measures, a new mandate for reform emerged. Ensuring that the Medicare system could meet the needs of the incoming baby-boom generation with the same benefits afforded to their predecessors formed the summary challenge.[75]

During the presidential and congressional campaigns of 1996, public knowledge of the health care issues were brought to light during debate on the National Health Security Act, and emerging consumer concerns about managed care coalesced into the rapid formulation and passage of the Health Insurance Portability and Accountability Act of 1996 (HIPAA), also called the Kasselbaum-Kennedy Bill in reference to its bipartisan sponsors. Important features of the act include prohibiting insurance companies from denying coverage because of preexisting medical conditions or denying the sale of personal insurance policies to individuals who were previously covered in group plans.

The act requires insurance companies to offer group plans to all employers (regardless of size) in markets where they already sell group plans. Further, it prohibits the exclusion of employees or their dependents from group plan participation based on health status. The act ensures that individuals who change jobs will be eligible for coverage immediately, without regard to preexisting medical conditions. It also established a pilot program to enable workers to save tax-free dollars for future medical expenses through medical savings accounts (MSAs). Another important provision increased the available tax deduction for health insurance premiums of self-employed individuals to 100 percent by 2003.[76] Although the act accomplished some ostensibly beneficial outcomes relative to decreasing the numbers of uninsured, it by no means addressed the serious, underlying problems of the health care system in general or the Medicare and Medicaid programs in particular.

The 1998 federal budget process reflected pressures to produce a balanced budget and to respond meaningfully to national health care issues from both consumer and cost-containment perspectives, with particular attention on initiating steps to address the impending insolvency of Medicare Part A and deal with consumer concerns about choice and quality in health plans. The resulting Balanced Budget Act (BBA) created a major new policy direction for Medicare and Medicaid reforms and took important incremental steps toward universal coverage through an initiative to extend coverage to uninsured children with a $23 billion allocation for new State Children's Health Insurance Programs (SCHIPs).[77]

The act was characterized as containing "some of the most sweeping and significant changes to Medicare and Medicaid since their inception in 1965."[78] Overall, the BBA proposed to reduce growth in Medicare and Medicaid spending by a total of $125.2 billion between federal fiscal years 1998 and 2002 (see Figure 7–6). Actual Medicare spending for the period 1998–2002 demonstrates the impact of the

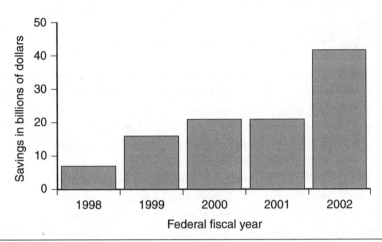

Figure 7–6 Balanced Budget Act of 1997 Projected Savings, 1998–2002
Source: Reprinted from Congressional Budget Office.

BBA. After growing at an average annual rate of 11.1 percent for the fifteen years prior to 1997, the average annual rate of spending growth between 1998 and 2000 dropped to 1.7 percent, resulting in approximately $68 billion in savings.[79]

Among the most significant policy shifts intended to result from the BBA was the departure from the largely fee-for-service model that opened the Medicare program to private insurers through its Medicare + Choice Program. This shift was to allow, for the first time, sharing of financial risk for the Medicare program with the private sector. The participation of private insurers was intended to increase both the impact of competitive market forces on the program and consumer awareness of alternatives to the fee-for-service system.

In addition to its payment changes, numerous structural and regulatory changes also were contained in the BBA. The Secretary of Health and Human Services was authorized to carry out a host of initiatives related to the implementation of changes. Federal commissions were constituted to carry out monitoring and recommendation functions during the BBA implementation. These included an independent National Bipartisan Commission on the Future of Medicare whose functions entailed:

■ Reviewing and analyzing of the financial condition of the Medicare program over time
■ Formulating recommendations on:
  – Ways to ensure the future financial viability of the Hospital Insurance Trust Fund
  – The scope and types of coverage to be included under the Medicare umbrella of approved services

    – The level of premium contribution by beneficiaries
    – Age eligibility
    – Contributions to medical education

The ProPAC and the Physician Payment Review Commission would be replaced by a Medicare Payment Advisory Commission.

The following discussion summarizes additional changes in the Medicare program intended by the BBA. Highlights of the BBA as it was intended to affect the Medicaid program are reviewed in a separate section of this chapter.

The $115.1 billion in Medicare savings to be attained by 2002 were to be derived from payment changes to hospitals, physicians, ambulatory care services, postacute care services (skilled nursing facilities, home health care agencies, certain rehabilitation hospitals, hospices, providers of durable medical equipment), and managed care organizations. The balance of targeted savings would result from regulatory changes, decreases in reimbursement of hospitals for medical education expenses, and other changes to both Part A and Part B provisions.

The share of each service's contributions to the total is shown in Figure 7–7. Hospitals, the largest Medicare spender, were to contribute more than one-third of the total savings.

In summary, the BBA's major provisions included:

1. Establishing a New Medicare Part C
Beginning in January 1999, Medicare participants were given the choice of remaining in the Medicare fee-for-service program (Parts A and B of the "old" system) or enrolling in new Medicare + Choice

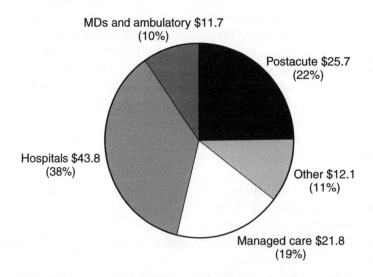

Figure 7–7 Where the Health Care Dollar Came From, 2000
Source: Reprinted from Congressional Budget Office.

plans. The Medicare + Choice plans offered a much broader set of options than previously available under the Medicare risk plans of HMOs. Options included HMO plans; point-of-service plans, in which participants have the freedom of choosing providers on approval of their primary physicians; preferred provider organization plans (PPOs), in which participants may choose a network of providers they believe best suits their needs; PSOs; and other insurance plans that may be operated in conjunction with MSAs.

2. Changing Provider Payment Methods and Amounts

Both direct reductions in the amount of Medicare payments and reductions in the previous system of planned increases in payments affected hospitals' inpatient and outpatient services, home health agencies, skilled nursing facilities, physicians, ambulatory surgery centers, clinical laboratories, and durable medical equipment providers.

Premiums for Part B Medicare beneficiaries also increased. New prospective payment systems were required for hospital outpatient services, skilled nursing facilities, home health agencies, and rehabilitation hospital services. The BBA also introduced reductions in the allowances for indirect medical education expenses of teaching hospitals and provided financial incentives to hospitals for voluntarily reducing the numbers of medical residents.

3. Conducting Demonstration Projects

The BBA required demonstration projects encompassing the Medicare + Choice programs and special HMO programs for older adults and military retirees. Seven demonstration projects were planned to assess the impact of pricing competition in the Medicare + Choice program in selected urban and rural areas. Other demonstrations authorized the continuation of capitated prepayment to "social health maintenance organizations," which provide the full spectrum of community-based and long-term care services. Another project provided Medicare reimbursement to the Department of Defense for services provided to Medicare-eligible military retirees. The BBA also changed programs for all-inclusive care for the elderly (PACE) from demonstration program status to a standard benefit.

4. Developing Prevention Initiatives

Benefits that promote early disease detection and prevention were added and expanded for services such as mammography, Pap smears, prostate and colorectal cancer screening, diabetes management, and osteoporosis screening. Programs providing Medicare coverage for pneumococcal and influenza vaccination were extended through 2002.

5. Providing Rural Hospital Initiatives

The BBA provided additional payments to rural hospitals that meet certain criteria and provided enhanced flexibility that enables rural hospitals to maximize Medicare revenue. Changes reflecting added flexibility included relaxation in requirements for obtaining higher "disproportionate share" allowances based on characteristics of the hospitals' service populations, and approval of Medicare payment for "distance medicine," which provides specialty consultations via telephone and video transmission.

6. Providing Anti-Fraud and Abuse Provisions

New provisions provided specific sanctions that included permanent exclusion from participation in the Medicare program of individuals or entities convicted of three health care–related crimes, refusal or termination of Medicare provider agreements with providers convicted of a felony, and civil monetary penalties for accepting kickbacks ($50,000 for each kickback violation) or contracting or arranging services with excluded providers. Provisions also enabled Medicare to refuse or terminate participation agreements with entities that purposely transfer ownership or control from an immediate family member in anticipation of a conviction, punitive assessment, or exclusion from a federal health care program.

7. Establishing Program Integrity Provisions

These provisions addressed nonphysician-provided services and supplies, such as durable medical equipment, nutrition supplies, and home dialysis supplies, and the relationship between the organization or individual ordering and the one providing those services or supplies. Statewide or areawide fee schedules replace the previous "reasonable charge" methodology. Provisions require durable medical equipment suppliers, home health agencies, and comprehensive outpatient rehabilitation facilities to fully disclose information on the identity of each person with a controlling or ownership interest in the enterprise and to post a minimum surety bond of $50,000.

Physicians and others who order laboratory procedures or durable medical supplies are required to provide diagnostic information to support such orders.

Medicare beneficiaries may request itemized billings and the "explanation of benefits" included with Medicare statements must contain a toll-free number for beneficiaries to obtain further information.

The implementation of the Medicare BBA provisions has not escaped delays, widespread controversy, and material revisions. Significant changes to the Medicare program structure, and the payment methods and amounts for hospitals, skilled nursing facilities, rehabilitation services, home health agencies, and managed care plans, all drew fire from their respective industries' advocacy groups, professional organizations, and consumers.

In the words of the U.S. Comptroller General in testimony before the U.S. Senate Special Committee on Aging in early 1999, "The outcry from providers to undo BBA reforms aimed at savings and efficiency was intense. In response, Congress made refinements."[80] In November of 1999, just prior to the date when several of the BBA's provisions were to take effect, President Clinton signed the Consolidated Appropriations Act for Fiscal Year 2000 (CAA). The CAA provided $17 billion in additional allocations for health care providers negatively impacted by the BBA and outlined new, later implementation schedules for many of the BBA's original mandates. Examples of some of the CAA's significant provisions are as follows:

- Delay in the implementation of the prospective payment system for hospital outpatient services
- Increases in payments for the care of severely ill skilled nursing facility patients
- Restoration of funding to teaching hospitals
- A moratorium on the imposition of payment limits for certain rehabilitation services
- Adjustments in the prospective payment system for inpatient rehabilitation hospitals
- Postponement of payment rate reductions to home health care agencies
- Special payment structure considerations for teaching hospitals and hospitals serving rural communities

The initial impact of BBA reimbursement reductions along with other factors occurring in 1998 appeared to slow the actual rate of Medicare spending growth further than anticipated by the BBA alone (see Figure 7–8 and Table 7–2). Other factors impacting the rate of

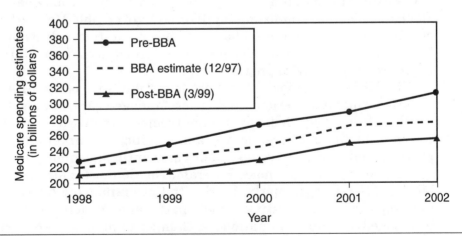

Figure 7–8 Medicare Spending $88.5 Billion Less than Projected (FYs 1998–2002). *Source:* Reprinted from CBO, An Analysis of the President's Budgetary Implications of the BBA of 1997, December 1997, U.S. Congressional Budget Office.

Table 7–2 Medicare Spending Projections Pre- and Post-BBA (in Billions)

	FY1998	FY1999	FY2000	FY2001	FY2002	FIVE-YEAR DIFFERENCE
Pre-BBA spending	$227.0	$248.2	$273.0	$285.6	$313.7	—
Estimated spending reductions under BBA (12/97)	(6.9)	(15.5)	(27.6)	(17.1)	(35.9)	($103.0)
Estimated spending under BBA (12/97)	220.1	232.7	245.4	268.5	277.8	—
Revised estimated spending under BBA (3/99)	211.0	214.0	229.0	246.0	256.0	—
Additional spending reductions per revised estimate	(9.1)	(18.7)	(16.4)	(22.5)	(21.8)	(88.5)

Source: Reprinted from CBO, An Analysis of the President's Budgetary Proposals for FY 2000: A Preliminary Report, March 3, 1999 and CBO, Budgetary Implications of the BBA of 1997, December 1997, U.S. Congressional Budget Office.

Medicare spending growth in 1999 were widespread publication of federal efforts to curtail Medicare fraud and abuse and a dramatic rise in the average time for processing claims as a result of more stringent criteria for claims review.[81] However, BBA provisions were predicted to hold down Medicare growth in the near term.[82]

Medicare + Choice managed care enrollments following enactment of the BBA totaled approximately 6.5 million by the second quarter of 1999, representing approximately 16 percent of eligible Medicare beneficiaries. During the initial phases of implementation, approximately 33 million Medicare beneficiaries chose to remain in the traditional Medicare fee-for-service program.[83]

The Medicare managed care enrollment initiative of the BBA continues to experience serious challenges. Managed care organizations, faced with lowered Medicare reimbursement, the costs of working through the federal bureaucracy, and significant market shifts impacting profitability, have lost their early enthusiasm for participation in the Medicare + Choice Program. The Center for Medicare and Medicaid Services (formerly the Health Care Financing Administration) reported that an estimated one-half million beneficiaries would be affected by plan terminations or changes in plan service areas in 2002. Overall, about 2.2 million beneficiaries have been affected by plan withdrawals over the past four years.[84] In an effort to stimulate and maintain managed care organization participation in Medicare +

Choice, Congress enacted the Balanced Budget Refinement Act of 1999 (BBRA) to slow planned payment reductions, provide bonuses for establishing plans in new geographic areas, and provide exemptions from quality assurance requirements for preferred provider organizations. In addition, the Benefits Protection and Improvement Act of 2000 enacted provisions to increase managed care organization and provider payments.[85]

Several demonstration projects mandated by the BBA are underway. Examples include rural health care institutions' payment demonstrations, incorporating health status adjustments into Medicare + Choice payments, and telemedicine projects for urban and rural hospitals. It is anticipated that information gleaned from these demonstration projects will provide valuable input into future decisions about reimbursement methodologies and program standards.

Aggressive efforts at curtailment of Medicare fraud and abuse were bolstered by the BBA, coupled with provisions of the HIPAA. As mandated by the BBA, efforts are focused on Medicare program compliance in billing criteria, regulations, and program standards. The BBA's new methods of reimbursement and compliance, with the attendant new rules, are a particular focus in monitoring and reviewing recipients of Medicare payments. The BBA dubbed this effort the "Comprehensive Plan for Program Integrity," which includes promoting provider integrity and targeting vulnerabilities with known risks: inpatient hospital stays, congregate care, managed care, community mental health centers, and nursing homes.[86] The HIPAA created a stable source of funding for fraud control and dedicated resources for program integrity activities under the Medicare Integrity Program. Annually, the Office of the U.S. Inspector General (OIG) audits the Medicare program's fee-for-service payments. In 2002, the OIG reported that 6.3 percent of 2001 claims totaling $12.1 billion should not have been paid due to errors or outright fraud.[87] Since 1996, the Health Care Financing Administration reports that aggressive efforts at curtailing fraud and abuse have recovered nearly $1.9 billion, and that other efforts to prevent wasteful and improper spending have saved an estimated $60 billion.[88]

The professional, political, economic, and popular dynamics entailed by the breadth and aggressiveness of the cost-containment measures contained in the BBA teach important lessons about enacting significant health care reform measures. The stakes in maintaining a financially viable system of publicly funded benefits are enormously high for a diverse constituency of providers, payers, and consumers that wield material political influence. As evidenced by reaction to the BBA and resulting Congressional and presidential actions, Medicare system financing reform will continue to be a complex and evolving process.

Medicaid

Enacted into law in 1965, Medicaid legislation was passed as Title XIX of the Social Security Act and is administered by the U.S. Health Care Financing Administration. It is a mandatory joint federal and state program in which federal and state support are shared based on the state's per capita income. Its intent is to provide basic medical care services to the economically indigent population who qualify by reason of low income or who qualify for welfare or public assistance benefits in the state of their residence. An important distinction must be made between the entitlement program of benefits, such as those provided by Medicare, and Medicaid, which represents a type of transfer payment to low-income populations. Medicare, funded from contributions of a tax on an individual's payroll matched by the employer, is an entitlement because the individual has contributed to his or her cost of coverage. On the other hand, Medicaid, which is funded by personal income and corporate and excise taxes, is a transfer payment representing funds transferred from more economically affluent individuals to those in need.[89]

The design, benefit coverage, and joint federal and state reimbursement structure of Medicaid reflect two decades of lobbying influence by the hospital industry, state governments, and social welfare reformers to ensure a minimum level of benefits for the economically needy. The Kerr-Mills Act of 1960, an amendment to Title I of the Social Security Act, provided federal aid to states for the voluntary establishment of programs to pay for the medical care of economically needy persons over the age of 65. State participation was optional and included specific requirements for the range of medical services covered. The Kerr-Mills program, which was implemented by 25 states, is considered the forerunner of Medicaid.[90]

Medicaid federal guidelines initially established a mandated core of basic medical services that must be available in each state program. Included are inpatient and outpatient hospital services, physician services, diagnostic services, and nursing home care for adults. Amendments to Title XIX have expanded mandated benefits to include home health care, preventive health screening services, family planning services, and assistance to recipients of Supplemental Security Income (SSI). State Medicaid programs currently also must extend benefits to all pregnant women who meet federal income level guidelines and children whose family incomes fall below specified federal income guidelines. Individual states have broad discretion to include additional services in their Medicaid programs, and many have elected extended benefits well beyond the core of mandated benefits. In doing so, they also may set limitations on the extent of utilization covered for nonmandated benefits. Medicaid also reimburses certain qualified ambulatory care services operated under federal guidelines, notably those serving high-need, underserved population groups, typically in urban centers and rural areas.

Unlike Medicare, which reimburses providers through intermediaries such as Blue Cross, Medicaid reimburses service providers directly. Rate-setting formulas, procedures, and policies vary widely among states. Because of the broad variations in benefits and reimbursement policies, Medicaid has been described as "50 different programs."[91]

Along with the rising demand for nursing home care required by older Americans, Medicaid has assumed an increasing share of this costly service burden. The increasing numbers of older adults in the general population, coupled with the catastrophic level of expense entailed in long-term institutional and home-based care, have created a rapidly expanding pool of new people who are eligible for Medicaid coverage. Individuals with modest savings and income rapidly deplete personal resources in paying for nursing home or extensive nursing care in the home. Expenses for nursing home care reach over $40,000 per year. At this rate of personal resource use, middle-class individuals can be rendered economically needy in a short period of time and thus quickly meet state eligibility guidelines for Medicaid. The Medicaid program currently funds approximately half of annual expenditures for nursing home care, approximately $40 billion per year. With Medicare coverage limited to approximately three months of nursing home services and little availability of private insurance coverage, private out-of-pocket payments continue to provide almost all of the remaining half of nursing home payments.[92]

In 1996 Congress passed the Personal Responsibility and Work Opportunity Reconciliation Act, which has become commonly known as the "welfare reform bill." This legislation carried important implications for the Medicaid program. By placing new restrictions on eligibility for participation in the SSI program, the bill decreased the number of individuals who would otherwise be eligible for Medicaid due to their SSI status.

For example, it barred legal resident aliens who entered the United States on or after a specified date in 1996, and whose coverage is not mandatory, from Medicaid participation for five years. With the exception of emergency services, states have the option of providing Medicaid for aliens entering the United States before the specified 1996 date, and of instituting coverage after the five-year ban.

Like Medicare, Medicaid spending grew at a rapid pace during the period 1980–1995. Major reasons for the growth in spending include:

■ Growth in the size of covered populations and expanded coverage and use of services

■ Increases in provider payment rates, as compared to general inflation

- The disproportionate share hospital program, which facilitated program expansion and increased federal matching funds
- Growth in the populations of older adults and people with disabilities requiring intensive acute or long-term care and related services
- Advances in medical technology that prolong the lives of extremely low birth weight babies and other severely compromised individuals who require extensive, and often long-term, expensive services

From 1980 to 1990, growth in Medicaid expenditures of almost 300 percent[93] led to numerous initiatives on the state and federal levels to control spending. States tested various prepaid, managed care approaches and, like the Medicare program, some also implemented utilization review requirements and prospective payment systems modeled on DRG reimbursement. In response to the growth in costs, many states obtained waivers from the federal government to mandate Medicaid client enrollment in managed care plans. Several states experimented with voluntary Medicaid managed care enrollment, contracting with HMOs on a fully or partially capitated basis to provide some or all of their Medicaid benefits under federally approved demonstration projects.

Since 1993, when federal waivers and demonstration project opportunities were made available to the states, Medicaid managed care enrollment accelerated substantially. Between 1993 and 1996, enrollments increased by over 170 percent.[94] Growth in Medicaid managed care enrollment has continued since 1996, but at a considerably slower pace (see Figure 7–9). In 2001, Medicaid provided health and long-term care coverage for almost 44 million individuals. Fifty-six percent of beneficiaries are enrolled in a form of managed care.[95] Combined state and federal Medicaid expenditures totaled $202.7 billion in 2000, an increase of 8.3 percent over 1999.[96]

The Balanced Budget Act of 1997

Provisions of the BBA were intended to reduce the growth of federal Medicaid outlays by $10.1 billion by 2002. Savings were expected to result primarily from reductions of disproportionate share payments made to the states, which would be held at 1995 levels for some states and reduced in others. Reductions were expected to have the greatest impact on urban, inner city hospitals. It was also expected that new state prerogatives to establish their own provider reimbursement rates would result in savings. In 2002, the Center for Medicare and Medicaid Services reported that intended reductions in Medicaid spending growth were attenuated by the Benefits Improvement and Protection Act which increased limits on states' federal matching funds for disproportionate share payments and by increases in Medic-

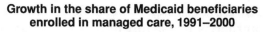

**Growth in the share of Medicaid beneficiaries
enrolled in managed care, 1991–2000**

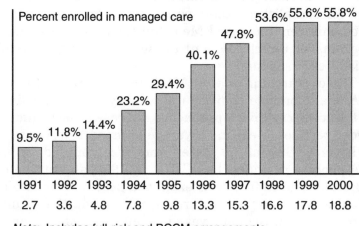

	1991	1992	1993	1994	1995	1996	1997	1998	1999	2000
Millions of people:	2.7	3.6	4.8	7.8	9.8	13.3	15.3	16.6	17.8	18.8

Note: Includes full-risk and PCCM arrangements.

Figure 7–9
Source: CMS, 2001.

aid enrollment that resulted in sharp increases in the rate of Medicaid spending.[97]

The BBA eliminated the requirement for states to obtain federal waivers to mandate Medicaid managed care enrollment. It also lifted the requirement for managed care organizations to limit their Medicare and Medicaid enrollment to less than 75 percent of their total enrollment. Also, with the introduction of new PSOs into the managed care marketplace, the BBA potentially initiated significant new competition for enrollment.

Additional savings were anticipated from allowing states to reduce their federal cost-sharing requirements for individuals entitled to both Medicare and Medicaid benefits. The BBA also contained new quality improvement standards, beneficiary grievance and resolution processes, and fraud and abuse protections. The issuance of the final rules concerning consumer protection provisions of the BBA was long delayed. First issued by the Clinton Administration in January of 2001, the Bush Administration delayed their approval three times, ultimately discarding them and issuing its own proposal in August of 2001. Final adoption occurred in June 2002.[98]

Consumer protections include requirements that enrollees be given the choice of at least two managed care plans, access to adequate provider networks, reasonable access to emergency services, and access to an internal appeals process.[99]

The BBA's child health initiative targeted 10 million children who are eligible for Medicaid but not enrolled or whose family income is too high to qualify for Medicaid but too low to afford private insurance coverage. The BBA granted states federal block grant funds and gave states the authority to use any of three vehicles, singly or in combination, for establishing their programs to provide coverage for uninsured children: increased Medicaid funding, state health insurance programs, or direct payment for services using up to 15 percent of their block grant funds.

The overarching goal of Medicaid reforms enacted through the BBA was to provide additional flexibility to state Medicaid programs that allows creative approaches to reach more individuals with needed services or expand coverage for needed services.

By late 1999, all 50 states were receiving federal support from BBA allocations under the SCHIP. By 1999, almost 2 million children had been enrolled in new or expanded health insurance programs."[100] A goal was established to enroll 1 million additional uninsured children in each subsequent year into either Medicaid or SCHIP.[101] In early 2003, the Center for Medicare and Medicaid Services reported that 5.3 million children were covered under the SCHIP during fiscal year 2002, representing a 15 percent increase from the prior year.[102] Currently, Medicaid covers approximately one in five children. Low-income children are more likely to be enrolled in Medicaid or to be uninsured and less likely to have private coverage than children with higher incomes (see Figure 7–10).[103]

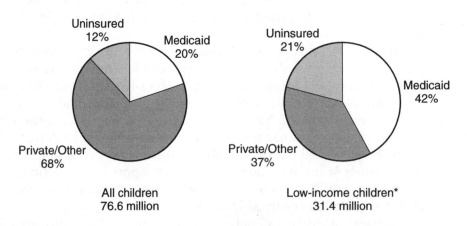

Health insurance coverage of children, by income, 2000

Uninsured 12%
Medicaid 20%
Private/Other 68%
All children 76.6 million

Uninsured 21%
Medicaid 42%
Private/Other 37%
Low-income children*
31.4 million

*Below 200% of the federal poverty level, or $27,476 for a family of three in 2000.

Figure 7–10

Source: This publication was reprinted with permission of the Henry J. Kaiser Foundation of Menlo Park, California. The Kaiser Foundation is an independent health care philanthropy and is not associated with Kaiser Permanente or Kaiser Industries.

Experience from the first years of Medicaid managed care enrollment demonstrates some evidence of improved access to a regular provider, but more difficulties in obtaining care and greater dissatisfaction with care as compared with traditional Medicaid plan enrollees.[104] In theory, the economic incentives of managed care organizations using full or partial prepaid arrangements with service providers should promote their efforts to ensure timely, appropriate access to preventive services and care. However, with most states paying relatively low provider rates as compared with Medicare and the complex health and social needs of many Medicaid patients, the future success of Medicaid managed care programs to accomplish the goals of improved access and lower costs remains in question.

Other Services Funded by Government

Federal, state, and local governments participate in a broad array of health care and health-related programs and services. At the federal level, the Department of Health and Human Services, in addition to encompassing the Centers for Medicare and Medicaid Services, also maintains the other Public Health Service divisions concerned with public health and safety, research, disease prevention, and health promotion. The Veterans Health Administration includes a vast system of hospitals, nursing homes, and outpatient services that serve former members of the armed forces. Administered through the Department of Defense, the Military Health Service program provides health care services to all members of the armed forces and their dependents, worldwide.

All states bear material responsibility for their Medicaid programs. States also may support medical schools, mental institutions, and departments of health that license and oversee the operation of hospitals and nursing homes. Many states also provide direct care services or support such services at the local level and engage in health education and promotion initiatives.

At the local level, many city and county governments support public hospitals and departments of health. City and county departments of health often provide direct care services for children and adults, monitor and investigate infectious disease cases and implement control measures, and participate in health promotion and education initiatives.

■ The Future: Continuing Change

The allocation of finite resources in a manner acceptable to the political, professional, economic, and consumer constituencies defines the challenge of health care financing for the twenty-first century. Concerns about the resources expended are only one facet of the challenge; patient care results in terms of improved functionality and perceived quality of life also must be considered.

Concerns about health care costs in relation to the quality of care continue to be at the center of national discussion and debate. The large numbers of uninsured and underinsured individuals, rising health insurance premiums, managed care companies' withdrawals from the Medicare + Choice program, and dramatically rising prescription drug costs are high on consumer, provider, and political agendas. Impacts of the BBA are signaling new trends in health care spending linked to its major effects on hospitals, nursing homes, the home health care industry, and numerous other suppliers of health services. The future integrity of the Medicare program remains a looming concern amid predictions that benefits spending again will exceed revenue.

The control of health care services delivery has undergone a shift from the care providers to managed care organizations. With this shift also has come increasingly negative consumer reactions to restrictive managed care reimbursement requirements. New reimbursement arrangements between providers and payers are developing continuously as the system adjusts and evolves. It is clear that market forces in the health care delivery industry will continue exerting fast-paced, pervasive, and high-impact effects that will force actions by both public and private payers.

The U.S. health care delivery system has become the most sophisticated and expensive in the world; however, at the same time it has been unable to adequately address the issue of universal coverage. Richmond and Fein rationalize this paradox with the thesis that, over the years since World War II, "legislative and regulatory interventions" reflected a "deficit model" in which the expansion of knowledge, services, technology, providers, and facilities was assumed to be able to compensate for any system inadequacies. They suggest that this "expansion ethos" drove system growth and costs with little attention to balancing the allocation of resources to ensure service access for low-income populations and an equitable distribution of services and resources between urban and rural settings.[105] As pointedly illustrated by the failure of the National Health Security Act, institutional, professional, economic, statutory, and political barriers continue to impede the formulation of a national consensus on appropriate resource allocations and cost controls.

Market forces are reforming health care financing and delivery. In the next decade, managed care principles, responding to market forces, will govern the major portion of all U.S. health care expenditures, including Medicare and Medicaid. Whether arising from default or initiative, what ultimately emerges as the system of financing and delivery of health care services in the United States will be radically different for the payers, consumers, and providers of care from the systems that were its predecessors.

■ Notes

1. T.P. Weil, "Let's Merge Competitive and Regulatory Strategies to Achieve Cost Containment," *Journal of Health Care Finance* 25, no. 3 (Spring 1999): 65.
2. K. Levit et al., "Inflation Spurs Health Spending in 2000," *Health Affairs* 21, no. 1 (Jan./Feb. 2002): 172.
3. Health Care Financing Administration, Office of the Actuary: National Health Statistics Group, "National Health Expenditures Aggregate and Per Capita Amounts, Percent Distribution, and Average Annual Percent Growth, by Source of Funds: Selected Calendar Years, 1980–2000," http://cms.hhs.gov/statistics/nhe/historical/#as (14 June 2002). Accessed 15 September 2002.
4. Health Care Financing Administration, Office of the Actuary: National Health Statistics Group, "National Health Expenditures Aggregate and Per Capita Amounts, Percent Distribution, and Average Annual Percent Growth, by Source of Funds: Selected Calendar Years, 1980–2000."
5. Department of Health and Human Services, Center for Medicare & Medicaid, Office of the Actuary, National Health Statistics Group, "National Health Expenditures and Their Share of Gross Domestic Product, 1960–2000," http://cms.gov/charts/series/sec1.pdf (June 2002). Accessed 12 April 2003.
6. K. Levit, et al., "Inflation Spurs Health Spending in 2000," 172.
7. K. Levit, et al., "National Health Expenditures, 1996," *Health Care Financing Review* 19, no. 1 (1997): 162.
8. K. Levit, et al., "Health Spending in 1998: Signals of Change," *Health Affairs* 19, no. 1, (2000): 124.
9. K. Levit, et al., "Health Spending in 1998: Signals of Change," 124.
10. K. Levit, et al., "Health Spending in 1998: Signals of Change," 124.
11. K. Levit, et al., "Inflation Spurs Health Spending in 2000," 172.
12. K. Levit, et al., "Inflation Spurs Health Spending in 2000," 172.
13. R.C. Coile Jr., B.E. Trusko, "Healthcare 2020: Challenges of the Millennium," *Health Care Management Technology* 20, no. 7 (August 1999): 37.
14. K. Levit, et al., "Health Spending in 1998: Signals of Change," 129.
15. K. Levit, et al., "Inflation Spurs Health Spending in 2000," 177.
16. U.S. Department of Health and Human Services, Administration on the Aging, "Profile of Older Americans: 1999." http://www.aoa.dhhs.gov/aoa/stats/profile/profile99.html (2002). Accessed 12 July 2000.
17. F.S. Hobbs, B.L. Damon, "65+ in the United States," *P23190 Current Population Reports: Special Studies*, http://www.census.gov/prod/1/pop/p23-190/p23-190.html (13 April 1999). Accessed 15 June 2000.
18. R.C. Coile Jr., et al., "Healthcare 2020: Challenges of the Millennium," p. 37.
19. R.C. Coile Jr., et al., "Healthcare 2020: Challenges of the Millennium," p. 37.
20. S. Smith, et al., "The Next Decade of Health Care Spending: A New Outlook," *Health Affairs* 18, no. 4 (July/August 1999): 89–90.
21. U.S. Department of Labor, Bureau of Labor Statistics, *Occupational Outlook Handbook 2001–02 Edition*. http://stats.bls.gov/oco/ocos074.htm (19 April 2000). Accessed 22 July 2000.
22. F.A. Sloan et al., "State Strategies to Reduce the Growing Numbers of People Without Health Insurance," *Regulation* 22, no. 3 (1999): 24.

23. U.S. Department of Commerce, U.S. Census Bureau, "Numbers of Americans With and Without Health Insurance Rise, Census Bureau Reports," September 30, 2002. http://www.census.gov/Press-Release/www/2002/cb02-127.html. Accessed 12 October 2002.

24. Kaiser Commission on Medicaid and Uninsured, "The Uninsured: A Primer" http://www.kff.org/content/2002/4050 (March 2002). Accessed 12 August 2002.

25. American College of Physicians-American Society of Internal Medicine, "No Health Insurance: It's Enough to Make You Sick." http://www.acponline.org/uninsured (30 November 1999). Accessed 22 July 2000.

26. The Kaiser Commission on Medicaid and Uninsured, "The Uninsured: A Primer."

27. The Kaiser Commission on Medicaid and Uninsured, "The Uninsured: A Primer."

28. American College of Physicians-American Society of Internal Medicine, "No Health Insurance: It's Enough to Make You Sick."

29. U.S. Department of Labor, Bureau of Labor Statistics, *Career Guide to Industries,* 2002–2003. http://www.bls.gov/oco/cg (26 June 2002). Accessed 10 September 2002.

30. Centers for Health Care Financing Administration, Office of the Actuary, National Health Statistics Group, "The Nation's Health Care Dollar: 2000, Where the Health Care Dollar Went," http://www.hcfa.gov/stats/nhe-oact/tables/chart.htm (17 July 2002). Accessed 7 September 2002.

31. Centers for Health Care Financing Administration, Office of the Actuary, National Health Statistics Group, "The Nation's Health Care Dollar: 2000, Where the Health Care Dollar Went."

32. Department of Health and Human Services, Center for Medicare & Medicaid Services, Office of the Actuary, National Health Statistics Group, "Personal Health Care Expenditures by Type of Expenditure and Source of Funds: Calendar Years 1993–2000." http://cms.hhs.gov/statistics/nhe/historical/t9.asp. Accessed 13 October 2002.

33. K. Levit et al., "Inflation Spurs Health Spending in 2000," 178.

34. K. Levit et al., "Inflation Spurs Health Spending in 2000," 176.

35. Department of Health and Human Services, Office of the Actuary, National Health Statistics Group, "National Health Expenditures Aggregate and per Capita Amounts, Percent Distribution, and Average Annual Percent Growth, by Source of Funds: Selected Calendar Years 1980–2000."

36. Department of Health and Human Services, Center for Medicare & Medicaid Services, Office of the Actuary, National Health Statistics Group, "Personal Health Care Expenditures by Type of Expenditure and Source of Funds: Calendar Years 1993–2000."

37. Department of Health and Human Services, Center for Medicare & Medicaid Services, Office of the Actuary, National Health Statistics Group, "Personal Health Care Expenditures by Type of Expenditure and Source of Funds: Calendar Years 1993–2000."

38. Department of Health and Human Services, Center for Medicare & Medicaid Services, Office of the Actuary, National Health Statistics Group, "Personal Health Care Expenditures by Type of Expenditure and Source of Funds: Calendar Years 1993–2000."

39. R. Stevens, *In Sickness and in Wealth: American Hospitals in the Twentieth Century* (New York: Basic Books, 1989), 183.

40. F. Wilson and D. Neuhauser, *Health Services in the United States*, 2nd ed. (Cambridge, MA: Ballinger Publishing Co., 1982).

41. A. Kovner, *Jonas' Health Care Delivery in the United States*, 5th ed. (New York: Springer Publishing Co., 1995), 275.

42. Stevens, *In Sickness and in Wealth*, 188.

43. Stevens, *In Sickness and in Wealth*, 190.

44. Stevens, *In Sickness and in Wealth*, 193.

45. U.S Department of Commerce, U.S. Census Bureau, "Summary 1997 Economic Census, Finance & Insurance Subject Series." http://www.census.gov/prod/ec97/97f52-sm.pdf (March 2001). Accessed 12 April 2003.

46. K.E. Thorpe, "Health Care Cost Containment: Results and Lessons from the Past 20 Years," in *Improving Health Policy and Management*, ed. S.M. Shortell and U.E. Reinhardt (Ann Arbor, MI: Health Administration Press, 1992), 266.

47. J. Gabel et al., "Job-Based Health Benefits in 2002: Some Important Trends," *Health Affairs* 21, no. 5 (2002): 144.

48. J. Gabel et al., "Job-Based Health Benefits in 2002: Some Important Trends." 145.

49. Department of Health and Human Services, Center for Medicare & Medicaid Services, Office of the Actuary, National Health Statistics Group, "Personal Health Care Expenditures by Type of Expenditure and Source of Funds: Calendar Years 1993–2000."

50. Stevens, *In Sickness and in Wealth*, 281.

51. Stevens, *In Sickness and in Wealth*, 281.

52. Stevens, *In Sickness and in Wealth*, 286.

53. *Medicare and Medicaid: Problems, Issues and Alternatives* (Washington, DC: U.S. Senate, Commission of Finance, February 1970).

54. Stevens, *In Sickness and in Wealth*, 286–287.

55. R.M. Ball, "Problems of Cost—As Experienced in Medicare," in *Report of the National Conference on Medical Costs* (Washington, DC: U.S. Department of Health, Education and Welfare, Government Printing Office, 1967), 65.

56. Thorpe, "Health Care Cost Containment: Results and Lessons from the Past 20 Years," 241.

57. Thorpe, "Health Care Cost Containment: Results and Lessons from the Past 20 Years," 246.

58. Thorpe, "Health Care Cost Containment: Results and Lessons from the Past 20 Years," 246.

59. Thorpe, "Health Care Cost Containment: Results and Lessons from the Past 20 Years," 246.

60. Thorpe, "Health Care Cost Containment: Results and Lessons from the Past 20 Years," 246.

61. Levit et al., "National Health Expenditures, 1996," 169.

62. Thorpe, "Health Care Cost Containment: Results and Lessons from the Past 20 Years," 240.

63. Thorpe, "Health Care Cost Containment: Results and Lessons from the Past 20 Years," 244.

64. Thorpe, "Health Care Cost Containment: Results and Lessons from the Past 20 Years," 244.

65. Kovner, *Jonas' Health Care Delivery in the United States*, 312.

66. Kovner, *Jonas' Health Care Delivery in the United States*, 316.

67. Thorpe, "Health Care Cost Containment: Results and Lessons from the Past 20 Years," 249.

68. Thorpe, "Health Care Cost Containment: Results and Lessons from the Past 20 Years," 249.

69. Thorpe, "Health Care Cost Containment: Results and Lessons from the Past 20 Years," 249.

70. S.H. Altman and S.S. Wallack, "Health Care Spending: Can the United States Control It?" in *Strategic Choices for a Changing Health Care System*, ed. S.H. Altman and U.E. Reinhardt (Chicago: Health Administration Press, 1996): 18.

71. Board of Trustees, Federal Hospital Insurance Trust Fund, *1995 Annual Report of the Board of Trustees of the Hospital Insurance Trust Fund* (Washington, DC: U.S. Government Printing Office, 1995).

72. R.D. Reischauer, "Medicare: Beyond 2002, Preparing for the Baby-Boomers," *The Brookings Review* 15, no. 3 (1997): 24.

73. Department of Health and Human Services, Center for Medicare & Medicaid Services, Office of the Actuary, National Health Statistics Group, "Personal Health Care Expenditures by Type of Expenditure and Source of Funds: Calendar Years 1993–2000."

74. Reischauer, "Medicare: Beyond 2002, Preparing for the Baby-Boomers," 318.

75. Reischauer, "Medicare: Beyond 2002, Preparing for the Baby-Boomers," 24.

76. Department of the Treasury, Internal Revenue Service, "Publication 535, Business Expenses for Use in Preparing 2002 Returns." http://www.irs.gov/pub/irs-pdf/p535.pdf (2001).Accessed 12 April 2003.

77. *The Balanced Budget Act of 1997, Public Law 105-33, Medicare and Medicaid Changes* (Washington, DC: Deloitte & Touche LLP and Deloitte & Touche Consulting Group LLC, 1997): 1.

78. *The Balanced Budget Act of 1997, Public Law 105-33, Medicare and Medicaid Changes*, 1.

79. Medicare Payment Advisory Commission, "Report to the Congress: Medicare Payment Policy (March 2003), Chapter 1, Context for Medicare Spending." http://www.medpac.gov/publications/congressional_reports/Mar03_ch1.pdf Accessed 16 April 2003.

80. U.S. Senate Special Committee on Aging, "Medicare: Program Reform and Modernization Are Needed but Entail Considerable Challenges," 106th Cong., 1st sess., February 8, 2000, 13.

81. U.S. Congressional Budget Office, U.S. Senate Committee on Finance, "The Impact of the Balanced Budget Act on the Medicare Fee-for-Service Program," June 10, 1999, by Paul N. Van de Water, Assistant Director for Budget Analysis, 2.

82. U.S. General Accounting Office, "Medicare: New Spending Estimates Underscore the Need for Reform," Testimony Before the Committee on the Budget of the House of Representatives, 25 July 2001. http://www.d-n-i.net/fcs/pdf/gao_medicare_testimony.pdf. Accessed 3 September 2002.

83. Health Care Financing Administration, "First Medicare + Choice Private Fee-for-Service Plan Approved," *Medicare News.* http://cms.hhs.gov (5 August 2000). Accessed 13 July 2000.

84. R.A. Berenson, "Medicare + Choice: Doubling or Disappearing?" *Health Affairs Web Exclusives 2001*, W66. http://www.healthaffairs.org/readeragent.php?ID=/usr/local/apache/sites/healthaffairs.org/htdocs/library/v21n1/s2.pdf (28 November 2001). Accessed 12 April 2003.

85. M.N. Ross, "Improving the Medicare + Choice Program: Recommendations of the Medicare Payment Advisory Commission," Statement before the Committee on Finance, U.S. Senate. http://www.medpac.gov/publications/congressional_testimony/tst040301finance_M%20c.pdf. Accessed 12 April 2003.

86. Health Care Financing Administration, "Fact Sheet: Fighting Fraud, Waste and Abuse in Medicare and Medicaid," http://www.cms.gov/media/press/release.asp?counter=375 (1 April 2000) 1–4. Accessed 12 April 2003.

87. National Health Care Anti-Fraud Association, "Health Care Fraud: A Serious and Costly Reality for All Americans." http://www.nhcaa.org (September 2002). Accessed 3 September 2002.

88. Health Care Financing Administration, "Fact Sheet: Fighting Fraud, Waste and Abuse in Medicare and Medicaid."

89. A.L. Koch, "Financing Healthcare Services," in *Introduction to Health Services,* 4th ed., ed. S.J. Williams and P.K. Torrens (Albany, NY: Delmar Publishers, Inc., 1993), 309.

90. F. Wilson and D. Neuhauser, *Health Services in the United States,* 2nd ed. (Cambridge, MA: Ballinger Publishing Co., 1982), 170.

91. C. Brecher, "The Government's Role in Health Care," in *Jonas' Health Care Delivery in the United States,* 5th ed., ed. A. Kovner (New York: Springer Publishing Co., 1995), 327.

92. Koch, "Financing Healthcare Services," 312–315.

93. Levit et al., "Health Spending in 1998: Signals of Change," 131.

94. Health Care Financing Administration, "Managed Care in Medicare and Medicaid," *Fact Sheet*, 28 January, 1997, 2.

95. Kaiser Commission on Medicaid and the Uninsured, *Medicaid and Managed Care.* http://www.kff.org. (December 2001). Accessed 18 September 2002.

96. K. Levit et al., "Inflation Spurs Health Spending in 2000," *Health Affairs* 21, no. 1, (Jan./Feb. 2002): 174.

97. S. Heffler et.al., "Health   Spending Projections for 2001–2011: The Latest Outlook," *Health Affairs* 21, no. 2 (March/April 2002): 211.

98. Families USA, "Medicaid Managed Care Final Regulations Issued." http://www.familiesusa.org/mmcsept2002.pdf (September 2002). Accessed 12 April 2003.

99. Families USA, "Medicaid Managed Care Final Regulations Issued."

100. Department of Health and Human Services, Center for Medicare and Medicaid Services, "State Children's Health Insurance Program Aggregate Enrollment Statistics for the 50 States and District of Columbia for Federal Fiscal Years 2000 and 1999." http://cms.gov/schip/fy99-00.pdf. Accessed 12 April 2003.

101. Department of Health and Human Services, Center for Medicare and Medicaid, "The State Children's Health Insurance Program, Annual Enrollment Report, October 1, 1998–September 20, 1999." http://cms.hhs.gov/schip/enroll99.pdf. December 1999. Accessed 12 April 2003.

102. Department of Health and Human Services, Center for Medicare & Medicaid Services, "SCHIP Covers 4.6 Million Children in 2001." http://www.cms.hhs.gov/schip/schip02.pdf (30 January 2003). Accessed 18 April 2003.

101. The Henry J. Kaiser Family Foundation, "Health Coverage for Low-Income Children," *Key Facts on Medicaid and the Uninsured* (Washington, DC: The Henry J. Kaiser Family Foundation, May 2002), 1.

103. Kaiser Commission on Medicaid and the Uninsured, "Medicaid and Managed Care."

104. J.B. Richmond and R. Fein, "The Health Care Mess: A Bit of History," *Journal of the American Medical Association* 273, no. 1 (1995): 69–71.

Chapter 8

Managed Care

Managed care has emerged as the predominant mode of health care administration and financing in the United States. This chapter provides an historical perspective on the development of managed care and an overview of managed care organization, fundamentals, and practices. It addresses current developments in the managed care industry and reviews their impacts on providers and consumers of health care services in light of recent legislative initiatives in Medicare, Medicaid, and the private industry. Future trends in managed care are presented and discussed in the context of current developments and analysts' predictions.

To gain a perspective on the national movement to reform the way U.S. health care is financed and delivered, it is useful to reflect briefly on the health care financing and delivery system that had emerged by the 1970s. Since 1900, when the primary source of payment for care was personal, out-of-pocket resources, the U.S. system had spawned both government and private insurers of health care. Having "stuck its toe in the water" by providing and insuring medical care in relatively minor ways in earlier years (e.g., workers' compensation benefits, welfare programs of the Social Security Administration), the federal government committed to a role as a major payer with the passage of Medicare and Medicaid amendments to the Social Security Act in 1965.

Beginning in the 1950s, technology exploded and continued to advance almost continuously during every succeeding year. Hospitals became high-technology centers, consuming spiraling volumes of resources in care delivery and billions of dollars in capital to expand, renovate, and update facilities. Physician expenditures also spiraled upward, and costly specialty care burgeoned. By 1970, the U.S. health care delivery system had emerged as the world's undisputed leader in high-technology and sophisticated medicine, but not without high costs. In 1960, national hospital care expenditures totaled $9.3 billion; in 1970, $28.0 billion; and in 1980, $102.7 billion. In the decade 1980–1990, national hospital expenditures more than doubled again to $256.4 billion.[1] Physician service expenditures saw parallel growth. In 1960, they totaled $5.3 billion; in 1970 they reached $13.6 billion; and by

1980 they had more than tripled, totaling $45.2 billion. Between 1980 and 1990, physician service expenditures more than tripled again to a total of $146.3 billion.[2] In 2000, physician service expenditures stood at $286.4 billion.[3] These increases could not be explained by national economic factors, because the rate of growth vastly outstripped inflation and growth in the gross domestic product. (See Figure 8–1.) In the decade of the 1990s, the rate of expenditure growth slowed markedly in response to managed care, market forces, the new reform efforts of the Balanced Budget Act of 1997, and other factors.

Distanced from the sting of rising health care costs by 30 years of employer-funded indemnity health insurance, working Americans used the delivery system without restrictions and very little, if any, cost consciousness. They grew to expect and demand what was perceived as the "best" care. For most, affordability or costs did not enter into the decision-making equation. Similarly, many physicians were untethered in their treatment decisions by economic considerations among their well-insured patients. The length of hospital stay and use of consultant specialists and tests were at the physicians' sole medical and economic discretion, without financial implications for the patient.

In the period following Medicare and Medicaid enactment, the hospital industry flourished. Between 1965 and 1969, net voluntary hospital income increased from $227 million to $400 million.[4] The total

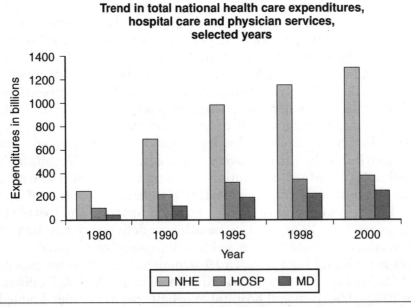

Figure 8–1 Trend in National Health Care Expenditures, Hospital Care and Physician Services, Selected Years

Source: Centers for Medicare and Medicaid Services, Office of the Actuary, National Health Statistics Group.

assets of not-for-profit voluntary hospitals rose from $16.4 billion to $26.7 billion in the same five-year period.[5] Concerns about rising costs and quality of services began only one year after Medicare and Medicaid were enacted and have risen steadily in volume and pitch for over 30 years. Congress and state governments tried with marginal success to reduce or slow the growth of absolute costs. It seemed, however, that no matter how cleverly structured or exquisitely sensitive the control effort, the system was equal to the challenge. To counterbalance efforts to cut or control reimbursement, the system responded with cost shifting, utilization volume increases, and justification for added technology and personnel. Added to these counterweights were environmental factors not within the system's control, such as growing poverty, the acquired immune deficiency syndrome (AIDS) epidemic, inflation, and increasing societal ills, such as substance abuse and violence, all of which carry high health care costs.

Despite over 60 years of failed political attempts to address the need for national health insurance, it was the growing perception that the United States was losing its competitive base in world manufacturing markets due to escalating costs, in part attributable to employer health insurance expenditures, that brought the need for broad reform to the forefront of the U.S. political scene. As Rosemary Stevens stated, "the driving force was cash."[6] In 1982, Chrysler found it was paying more than $300 million a year for health care, but "didn't know what it was buying or from whom."[7] Lee Iacocca, then chairman of the Chrysler Corporation, went on record as saying that the cost of the company's health insurance premiums was adding an incremental cost to the price of their cars that, if unabated, soon would render the company unable to compete in the marketplace. This statement epitomized the by-then ubiquitous signs that serious, major reform measures were necessary.

At the federal level, the Reagan and Bush administrations made reform attempts through legislation introducing Medicare prospective payments, the resource-based relative value scale, and other incremental measures. However, none of these efforts could be characterized as anything other than specific cost-control measures, far from the sweeping reforms clearly needed—reforms that would not only control costs, but also provide universal access to care for the growing numbers of medically uninsured or underinsured Americans. In 1992, President Bush proposed a type of reform based on a voucher system that would address access for the low-income working population by providing a tax credit to qualifying families. However, it was widely criticized and rapidly defeated as creating another federal financial burden and being ineffective in ensuring the universal access sought by more liberal forces.

The election of President Clinton in 1992 began the first earnest effort to move comprehensive health care reform to the front of the political agenda; it became the subject of one of this nation's most widely publicized social reform movements in history. With universal access, a minimum level of benefits to every U.S. citizen, nationwide applications of cost-control strategies based in a competitive marketplace model, and mandated employer participation, Clinton's National Health Security Act attempted to address the concerns about the costs, quality, and access of the U.S. health care system of the past 50 years. By the fall of 1994, opposition precluded the bill from reaching the congressional floor. The momentum it created, however, by raising public and corporate awareness has continued to fuel a reshaping of the U.S. system of health care financing and delivery that began in the mid-1970s. The influence of managed care, the rise of health care consumerism, and the impact of market forces are joining to create a new health care marketplace.

■ Managed Care Fundamentals

Managed care embodies a direct relationship and interdependence between the provision of and payment for health care. Central to understanding managed care is the population orientation and the organization of care-providing groups or networks who take responsibility and usually share financial risk with the insurer for a population's medical care and health maintenance. The population basis enables the insurer to determine, from actuarial data, projected use of services related to age, gender, and other factors. Levels of service utilization are estimated as a basis for expected costs over a defined time period. These estimates enable the insurer to establish premiums or charges for benefit coverage. Miller and Luft describe the other characteristic of managed care plans—the provider network—as "the single most important feature distinguishing a managed care from an indemnity (fee-for-service) plan."[8] That feature is key to enabling the insurer to exert influence over the delivery, use, and costs of services.

By linking the insurance of and delivery of services, managed care, in effect, reverses the financial incentives of providers that are prevalent in the fee-for-service model. Fee for service is essentially a piecework, pay-as-you-go system in which the care provider is financially rewarded for high use. The more services provided, the greater the reimbursement. Managed care, however, uses the concept of prepayment, in which care providers are paid in advance a preset amount for all the services their insured population is projected to need in a given time period. Capitation, a method by which providers are paid for services on a per-member-per-month basis, is a common form of prepayment. The provider receives payment whether or not services are used. For example, if a physician exceeds the predetermined payment level, he or she may suffer a financial loss. Similarly, if the physician uses fewer resources than predicted, the excess may be retained as profit.

Fee-for-service payments that withhold a portion of the customary fee (usually 15 to 20 percent) are another form of payment that seeks to provide positive financial incentives for efficient resource management. In the withhold scheme, physicians are provided a target amount of resources, usually on an annual basis, to provide a preestablished array of services to a defined population. If the target is met, the withheld amount is returned to the physician. If targets are exceeded, a financial penalty in the form of retention of all or a percentage of the withheld fees is incurred. The intent of these methods is to reverse the provider's financial incentives. Financial benefit derives from controlling, rather than promoting, utilization. Capitation and fee-for-service payments with withholding can be used with all types of individual and institutional providers.

Many other forms of physician payment in managed care systems exist that address the direction of financial incentives relative to achieving more efficient use of resources. The key element of all such physician prepayment arrangements is to encourage cost-conscious, efficient, and effective care.

The concept of prepayment has been used for decades among certain employer groups that contracted with physician groups and hospitals to serve their employees on a prepaid basis. It was not until the 1970s, however, when increasing concerns over the rising costs of employee health benefits to businesses prompted passage of the Health Maintenance Organization (HMO) Act of 1973, that managed care and the concept of prepayment were thrust into the national forefront.

It is important to distinguish the definition of HMO from the broader definition of managed care. HMOs are organizations or legally organized entities that share the common characteristic of responsibility for both financing and delivering comprehensive health care services to a defined group of beneficiaries or members for a prepaid, fixed fee. The HMO's responsibility both for financing and providing health care services distinguishes it from the fee-for-service system, in which insurance companies are responsible for reimbursing either the provider or member for the costs of care but carry no responsibility for providing care or arranging it.

Managed care, although the term implies organization of care, does not in itself refer to any particular type of organizational entity. Managed care rather refers to a body of principles and concepts that govern a variety of insurer and provider relationships. Implicit in the body of principles and concepts is that provision of services and payment are interdependently linked. Also implicit in the definition of managed care is a requirement of oversight of the enrolled population's use of medical resources as a function of providers' behaviors.

The principles and concepts of managed care operate on the assumption that the linkages of service provision and its reimbursement are based on a defined population group for whose insurance a set premium is charged and for whom service costs are reimbursed on a prepaid basis. From its earliest roots, which can be traced back more than 60 years to prepaid health plans, the goal of managed care has been to control costs by controlling health care utilization.

With this definition in mind, it becomes clear that HMOs represent a form of managed care, but that a virtually infinite number of other provider/insurer relationships are possible using managed care principles. Although managed care and HMOs are not technically synonymous, all HMOs use the concepts and principles of managed care with the goal of controlling costs by controlling utilization. The achievement of this goal is largely based on the transfer of some measure of financial risk from the insurer to the care providers. To a lesser extent, use and, therefore, cost control is also attempted by some managed care plans that transfer some financial risk from the insurer to the managed care member. Transfers of financial risk most commonly take the form of copayments and deductibles. Copayments require that the member pay a set fee each time a covered service is received, such as a copayment for each physician office visit. A deductible requires the member to meet a predetermined, out-of-pocket expenditure level before the managed care organization assumes payment responsibility for the balance of charges. Typically, deductible requirements are set for a specific time period and do not carry forward into succeeding periods.

■ HMO Act of 1973

The HMO Act of 1973 provided both loans and grants for the planning, development, and implementation of combined insurance and health care delivery organizations and required that a minimum prescribed array of services be included in the HMO arrangement. These mandated services included:

- Physician care
- Outpatient services
- Short-term mental health services
- Specified substance abuse treatment
- Laboratory and radiology services
- Home health care
- Family planning services
- Specified social services
- Immunizations and other preventive health services
- Health education

- Emergency care arrangements
- Arrangements for out-of-area coverage

This legislation also mandated that employers with 25 or more employees offer an HMO option if one was available in their area. The legislation required that employers contribute to employees' HMO premiums in an amount equal to what they contributed to an indemnity plan premium. Initially, this employer mandate helped stimulate growth of HMO membership in regions where federally funded and qualified plans were first established.

As authorized by the 1973 legislation, HMOs were organizations that combined providers and insurers into one organizational entity. As originally established, members of HMOs usually were required to obtain all their medical care within the organization.

Initially, there were two major types of HMOs. The first was a group, or staff, model and was the type most commonly established from the initial HMO legislation. It employed groups of physicians to provide the majority of ambulatory care needs of its members. Some specialty services often were provided within the HMO and by community physicians under a contracted arrangement with the HMO. In the staff model, the HMO also operated the facilities in which its physicians practiced, providing on-site ancillary support services, such as radiology, laboratory, and pharmacy services. The HMO usually purchased hospital care and other services for its members through fee-for-service or prepaid contracted arrangements. Established in 1938, the Kaiser-Permanente Health Care System, an early forerunner of the HMO movement, became among the best known staff model HMOs. Staff model HMOs were referred to as "closed panel" because they employed the physicians who provided the majority of their members' care, and those physicians did not provide services outside the HMO membership. Similarly, community-based physicians could not participate in HMO member care without prearrangement or authorization by the HMO.

The second type of HMO stimulated by the 1973 legislation was the individual practice association (IPA). IPAs are physician organizations composed of community-based independent physicians, in solo or group practices, who provide services to HMO members. An IPA HMO, therefore, does not operate facilities in which members receive care, but rather provides its members services through private physician office practices. Like the staff model HMO, hospital care and specialty services not available through IPA-participating physicians can be purchased by the HMO from other area providers, either on a prepaid or fee-for-service basis. IPA physicians are allowed to have a nonexclusive relationship with their HMO that permits them to treat nonmembers as well as members. However, HMO relationships with an IPA also can be established on an exclusive basis. In this scenario, an HMO takes the initiative in recruiting and organizing community physicians into an IPA for the purpose of serving its members. Because the HMO was the organizing force in such an arrangement, it is common for the HMO to require exclusivity by the IPA, limiting its services only to that HMO's membership.[9]

The staff model and IPA-type organizations illustrate two major types of HMOs, but each type has spawned several hybrids since the 1973 HMO Act. Other major forms of managed care organizations emerged throughout the 1980s in response to national cost and quality concerns, notably on the part of the federal government and industry as the major health insurance purchasers. Peter Kongstvedt identifies three additional HMO models as the most common: group practice, network, and direct contract.[10] In a group practice model, an HMO typically contracts with a multispecialty group practice to provide all the physician services required by the HMO's enrollees. The physicians remain independent—employed by their group rather than the HMO. Such an arrangement may or may not be exclusive. Depending on the terms of their HMO contract, these physicians may be allowed to see patients insured by other entities or restricted in their practice to see only members of a particular HMO. In the network model HMO, the HMO contracts with more than one group practice and may maintain contracts with several physician groups representing both primary care and specialty practices. The direct contract model HMOs maintain contractual relationships with individual physicians, in contrast to the physician groups as in the IPA and network models. The direct contract approach, although more cumbersome to administer than the other models, gives the HMO the advantages of maintaining a higher level of control over fee arrangements by reducing physician negotiating power to an individual basis and avoiding the risk of lost services to its members by contractual termination of a large group of providers.

■ The Evolution of Managed Care

By 2000, national managed care enrollment stood at 80.1 million, more than double the enrollment of 1992.[11] (See Figure 8–2.) As enrollment accelerated, concerns emerged about managed care organization (MCO) restrictions on consumer choice of providers and services. In response, the MCOs spawned what have become known as point-of-service (POS) plans that allow members to use providers outside the MCOs' approved provider networks. To exercise this choice, POS members are charged copayments and deductibles higher than those charged for in-network services. As managed care enrollment

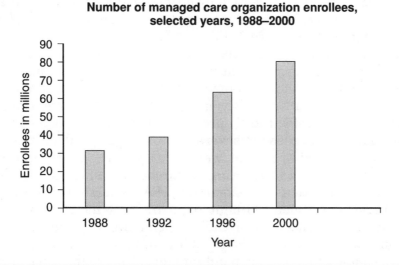

Figure 8–2 Number of Managed Care Enrollees, Selected Years, 1988–2000
Source: Adapted from Henry J. Kaiser Family Foundation, "Trends and Indicators in the Changing Health Care Marketplace," *2002 Chartbook.*

increased and the market became increasingly competitive, MCOs developed more flexible plan offerings that, although more costly to consumers, allowed for more choice in providers. In 2002, POS plans represented 18 percent of total managed care enrollment.[12]

Concurrent with the growth of the HMO and managed care movement throughout the 1980s, another organizational entity arose, not technically defined as an HMO, but encompassing important managed care characteristics. Preferred provider organizations (PPOs) were formed by physicians and hospitals to serve the needs of private, third-party payer, and self-insured firms. Through these arrangements, PPOs guarantee a certain volume of business to hospitals and physicians in return for a negotiated discount in fees. PPOs offer attractive features to both physicians and hospitals. Physicians are not required to share in any financial risk as a condition of participation, and PPOs reimburse physicians on the fee-for-service basis to which they are accustomed. By providing predictable admission volume, PPOs helped hospitals to shore up declining occupancy rates and attenuate the competition for admissions with other hospitals. To control costs, PPOs used negotiated discount fees, requirements that members receive care exclusively from contracted providers (or incur financial penalty), requirements for preauthorization of hospital admission, and second opinions for major procedures, such as surgery. PPOs maintain systems of utilization review and review of hospital lengths of stay as both a prospective and retrospective means to control costs and advocate for more efficient service utilization by hospitals and physicians. In 2002, PPOs were the most popular managed care plans, with a 52 percent market share.[13] (See Figure 8–3.)

As MCOs continued growing in size and numbers, their organizational forms became significantly more diversified to respond to marketplace demands and to manage operational costs and maximize profits. In 1988, staff models constituted about 42 percent of MCO membership. By 1999, they represented less than 1 percent.[14] This change occurred because of several factors. Staff model MCOs, confronted by the need to expand, were faced with the large capital outlay requirements of constructing or purchasing additional facilities. Increased competition from expanding IPA models, often in the position to offer enrollment without requiring new members to switch physicians for themselves or their dependents, was another factor. Staff model MCOs needed the flexibility of their IPA counterparts to remain competitive in an expanding marketplace. In response, both staff model and group MCOs have increasingly transformed into mixed models that operate both the traditional staff model and an IPA model through contracts with community physicians and practice groups. In 1990, approximately one-third of staff models were mixed

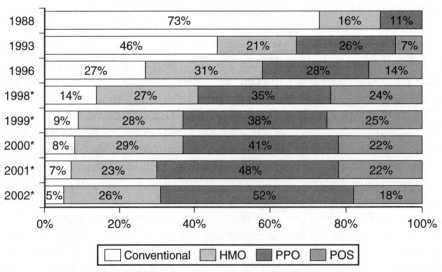

Health plan enrollments for covered workers by plan type, 1988–2002

Year	Conventional	HMO	PPO	POS
1988	73%	16%	11%	
1993	46%	21%	26%	7%
1996	27%	31%	28%	14%
1998*	14%	27%	35%	24%
1999*	9%	28%	38%	25%
2000*	8%	29%	41%	22%
2001*	7%	23%	48%	22%
2002*	5%	26%	52%	18%

*Distribution is statistically different from the previous year shown: 1996–1998, 1998–1999, 1999–2000, 2000–2001, 2001–2002.

Figure 8–3 Health Plan Enrollments for Covered Workers by Plan Type, 1988–2002
Source: This publication was reprinted with permission of the Henry J. Kaiser Foundation of Menlo Park, California. The Kaiser Foundation is an independent health care philanthropy and is not associated with Kaiser Permanente or Kaiser Industries.

models. By 1994, 57 percent of staff models were operating as mixed-model MCOs.[15]

MCOs continue offering increasingly diversified products and services to maintain the highest appeal to employer purchasers seeking the cost savings that result from employees' transfer from indemnity plans to MCOs. The ability of an MCO to offer what has become known as the "triple option," which includes HMO, PPO, and POS plans, is believed to increase purchaser appeal and competitiveness.

Other trends that emerged in MCOs included increased shifting of financial risk from MCOs to physicians, primarily through increased use of capitation. MCOs also increased patient cost-sharing requirements in the form of copayments and deductibles as an effort to hold down premiums. Increased patient cost sharing also has been shown to decrease the use of services. Researchers at Group Health Cooperative of Puget Sound found that adding a $5 copayment resulted in an 11 percent reduction in primary care visits, a 3 percent reduction in specialist visits, and a 14 percent decrease in physical examinations.[16] Another trend has been MCOs' increased use of clinical practice guidelines that provide scientifically based, uniform protocols for the treatment of specified medical conditions (see Chapter 12). Guidelines are embraced by MCOs as one means to promote consistency in clinical practice and thereby reduce costs. Guidelines are assumed by many to promote the quality of clinical outcomes by helping to decrease variability in provider practices. However, because of inadequate data and tracking systems, the process of medical care and its outcomes in MCOs continue to pose important questions about guidelines and their contributions to controlling costs or improving quality.[17]

Whatever the form of organization providing managed care, the inherent operating principles of these organizations recognize that the cost drivers are the forms of payment to providers and incentives implicit to it. There is a massive body of literature spanning 40 years of research suggesting that higher health care expenditures do not in all cases contribute to, and in fact, may detract from, the quality of care rendered through medical interventions. More recent research data also suggest that major cost savings could be realized by a higher level of scrutiny of the appropriateness of the interventions used.[18] Both directly (by changing reimbursement incentives) and indirectly (by instituting quality control measures that seek to standardize care practices and decrease variation in resource use for the treatment of common illnesses), managed care principles resulted in major shifts in the patient, provider, and payer relationships.

The effects of physician prepayment and the accompanying share of financial risk have a direct impact on the health care delivery system far beyond the impact on individual practitioners. Physicians are the predominant influence over the use of virtually all patient care resources. They largely control all hospital admissions, prescription pharmaceuticals consumption, and laboratory, imaging, and other diagnostic service use. They also control the extent of use of specialty services, surgical services, home health care, and rehabilitation care. Because of the central role of physicians in controlling health care resource consumption, managed care organizations of all types continue to place heavy emphasis on the physician behavior aspect of their systems.

One additional feature common to physician performance in managed care is the emphasis placed on the role of the primary care physician. In recognition of and response to rising concerns about the overuse of specialists and its attendant costs, primary care physicians have been assigned the major role in managed care systems. Dubbed "gatekeepers," they are viewed as the most influential resource in ensuring appropriate, timely, and coordinated patient care. By requiring passage through the primary care gate, managed care organizations seek to avoid unnecessary use of high-cost services for complaints that can be treated effectively at the primary level. Authorization of specialty referrals by the primary physician are used to help ensure coordination and avoid duplication of these services.

■ Emerging Developments in Managed Care

Today, over 175 million Americans, more than 90 percent of all privately insured individuals, receive their health insurance through their employer.[19] In 2002, 95 percent of all workers covered by employer health benefits were enrolled in some type of managed care plan; only 5 percent were enrolled in conventional type plans.[20] The surge in employee enrollment in managed care throughout the 1990s, with accompanying decreases in premium costs, is acknowledged as a significant contributor to the decline witnessed in the average annual growth of national health care expenditures throughout this period.[21]

After four years of declining costs, health insurance premiums began increasing again in 1998. In that year, premiums rose 8.2 percent, more than double the increase of the three prior years.[22] Many reasons were offered for the rise in premiums, including the insurance "underwriting cycle," in which insurers underprice during periods of market growth, then increase premiums later to restore profitability. Managed care plans realized high profitability in the early 1990s, when large-scale migration occurred from traditional health insurance to managed care plans. Following this period of major growth, in 1996 and 1997 nearly two-thirds of managed care plans and health insurers suffered losses.[23] Other reasons cited for increasing premiums included investor pressure on insurers to increase profits, rapidly escalating prescription drug costs and utilization, consumer demands for more choice and access to services, and increasingly difficult negotiations with providers seeking higher reimbursement.[24]

Premiums continue their six-year trend of increases. Between 2001 and 2002, they rose 12.7 percent, the largest increase in health insurance costs since 1990. Double-digit increases occurred across both managed care and conventional plans. (See Figure 8–4.) Unlike earlier increases attributed to the insurance underwriting cycle, current increases indicate a rise in claims expense, including prescription drug costs.[25]

The rise in premiums carries significant implications. Increased premium costs, coupled with requirements for larger employee contributions, cause workers to drop coverage. This effect increases in severity as the annual earnings of employees decrease, meaning that lower wage workers who can least afford the risk of high health care costs are the most likely to become uninsured. Increased premiums cause employers to pass along higher shares of premium expenses to workers, result in significant increases in copayment and deductibles, and introduce financial risk-sharing for prescription drug costs. Some experts estimate that for every 1 percent increase in premiums, 300,000 individuals lose their health insurance coverage.[26] Experts

**Increases in health insurance premiums
compared to other indicators, 1988–2002**

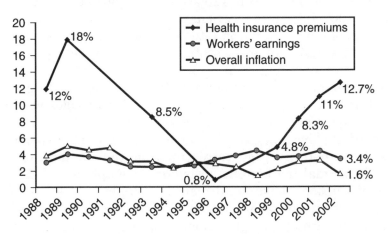

Note: Data on premium increases reflect the cost of health insurance premiums for a family of four.

Figure 8–4 Increases in Health Insurance Premiums Compared to Other Indicators, 1988–2002

Source: This publication was reprinted with permission of the Henry J. Kaiser Foundation of Menlo Park, California. The Kaiser Foundation is an independent health care philanthropy and is not associated with Kaiser Permanente or Kaiser Industries.

predict significant continuing premium increases in the future, so the number of uninsured Americans is likely to grow.

In what is termed the managed care "backlash" that began in 1998, over 1,000 bills aimed at addressing a wide range of consumer issues with their health plans were introduced into almost every state legislature and to Congress. A presidential commission was established to review the need for guidelines in the managed care industry.[27] In 1998, the president imposed patient protection requirements on private insurance companies providing health coverage to federal workers.[28] Public dissatisfaction with constraints over the right to receive care deemed necessary and the freedom of physicians to refer patients to specialists received wide publicity. Public concerns driving sentiments toward more government regulation of the managed care industry include the belief that managed care is hurting the quality of patient care and that the managed care industry is not doing as good a job for patients as other sectors of the health care industry. Compiled results from a series of public opinion polls shed light upon Americans' sentiments about managed care, other health care institutions, and the services of other industries. Results demonstrate that in terms of service to consumers, other industries rate well above managed care organizations. Between 1997 and 2000, the proportion of people who say that managed care companies are doing a good job for consumers declined by 22 percentage points.[29] (See Table 8–1.) First introduced in 1998, a federal "Patient Bill of Rights" failed to attain passage. The most recent proposal, the Bipartisan Patient Protection Act of 2001, introduced by Senators Kennedy and McCain, passed both houses of Congress, but in late 2002 remained stalled in partisan debate.[30] More than half of the states now have passed patient protection legislation covering such issues as patients' rights to standing specialty referrals, disclosure of restrictive prescription drug formularies, and women's direct access to obstetricians/gynecologists.[31]

In another response to the managed care "backlash," increasing numbers of employers began allowing employees to make personal decisions about their coverage, retreating from the standard practice of the employer making benefit decisions on employees' behalf. This movement, dubbed "consumer-driven" health plans, attempts to make patients more knowledgeable about their health care choices and associated costs through the provision of comparative information, both in Web-based and traditional formats. Three types of plans are being offered. The first uses an account against which the employee may draw to purchase care. When the account is exhausted, employees pay out-of-pocket until an annual deductible is satisfied, after which a major medical plan is activated. The second type allows employees to design their own provider networks and benefits, based on anticipated needs and costs. The third uses Web-based information to enable em-

Table 8–1 The Public's Assessment of the Job Various Industries Are Doing Serving Their Consumers, 1997–2000

PERCENT SAYING "A GOOD JOB"	1997	1998	1999	2000
Computer software companies[a]	80%	77%	80%	78%
Banks	75	72	68	73
Hospitals	77	73	71	72
Car manufacturers	70	69	70	67
Airlines	–	78	71	66
Telephone companies	80	76	67	64
Life Insurance companies	64	63	61	62
Drug companies	79	73	66	59
Oil companies	59	64	55	39
Health insurance companies	55	48	41	39
Managed care companies	51	45	34	29
Tobacco companies	34	32	31	28

[a]In 1997 these were called "computer companies."

Source: HEALTH AFFAIRS by BLENDON ET AL. Copyright 1998 by PROJECT HOPE. Reproduced with permission of PROJECT HOPE in the format Textbook via Copyright Clearance Center.

ployees to choose from established groupings of provider networks and benefits to "customize" coverage. It is estimated that about 1 percent of the employer coverage market, or 1.5 million employees, are enrolled in consumer-driven plans.[32] Predictions vary widely regarding the future of such arrangements in the health insurance marketplace. Experts are calling for additional research on the impacts of such plans on care quality, consumer satisfaction, access, and costs.[33] Since 1994, managed care organizations have undergone many changes in their operating policies, mergers, and consolidations. More recently, the most prominent changes have come as responses to consumer demands reflected by state patient protection legislation, a loosening of early restrictions on patient choice of provider, provider specialty referrals, and patient access to information about operating policies, especially regarding denials of payment. A literature analysis of managed care organization performance between 1997 and 2001 indicates that overall, managed care organizations have not accomplished their early promises to change clinical practice and improve quality while lowering costs. Analysis findings suggest that a systematic revamping of information systems, coupled with appropriate incentives and revised clinical processes, will be required to produce the desired changes.[34]

■ Medicare and Medicaid Managed Care

The creation of the Medicare + Choice program through the Balanced Budget Act of 1997 (BBA) signaled a new effort to reform the Medicare program. The BBA intended to expand Medicare managed enrollments by offering a large number of new plan options that include HMOs, preferred provider plans, provider-sponsored organizations, and other insurance plans operated with medical savings accounts. The BBA eliminated and replaced previous Medicare managed care plan models. The major existing models include Medicare risk plans and cost plans. In risk plans, Medicare pays a per-member premium, established on a county-of-residence basis. Risk plans initially required members to receive all of their services within the plan's provider service networks, but were later modified to allow out-of-network options. Typically, risk plans provide coverage for all Medicare-required services and offer additional coverage for added benefits such as pharmacy and vision care. Medicare cost plans reimburse HMOs a predetermined monthly amount per beneficiary based on a total projected budget. Adjustments for variations are made at year-end. Unlike in the risk plans, cost plan members were free to obtain services outside the managed care provider network. Medicare would pay its standard reimbursement, with the member responsible for coinsurance and deductibles.

In 2002, Medicare managed care enrollment stood at 5 million, representing 12 percent of total Medicare beneficiaries, and a decline of 1.3 million managed care participants since 2000.[35] The Medicare payment reductions, complex administration, market competition, and other factors are continuing to take a toll on the Medicare + Choice program. Following rapid growth in the number of Medicare HMOs available during the 1990s, participation has continued declining since 1999 (see Figure 8–5). By 1998, there were 346 Medicare HMOs available; by 2003, there were only 155.[36] The Center for Medicare & Medicaid Services has responded with certain administrative changes, and the Benefits Improvement and Protection Act of 2000 increased payments to health plans. However, studies continue to cite inadequate payment adjustments for the health status of enrollees as a major reason for health plans' discontinuation of participation.[37] A 2000 report of the U.S. General Accounting Office revealed that because of risk selection, Medicare actually paid more to Medicare + Choice health plans than it would have spent for participants in traditional Medicare.[38] In 2000, Medicare began phasing in a new risk-adjustment system based on hospital stays. A more compre-

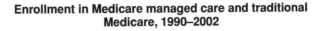

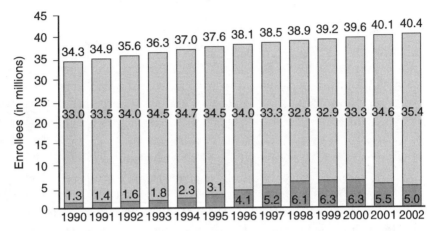

Figure 8–5 Enrollment in Medicare Managed Care and Traditional Medicare, 1990–2002
Source: This publication was reprinted with permission of the Henry J. Kaiser Foundation of Menlo Park, California. The Kaiser Foundation is an independent health care philanthropy and is not associated with Kaiser Permanente or Kaiser Industries.

hensive risk adjustment that includes ambulatory care is expected to be in place by 2007.[39]

The Center for Medicare & Medicaid Services reviewed emerging trends in premium and benefit structures reported by health plans participating in Medicare + Choice. Among these are premium increases for extra benefits; increases in enrollees' out-of-pocket expenses, particularly for brand name prescription drugs; and increased copays.[40] These trends are consistent across the managed care industry, requiring participants to share more financial risk.

Medicaid managed care enrollment reached 20.8 million by 2001—57 percent of total national Medicaid enrollment (see Figure 8–6).[41] All 50 states currently offer some type of Medicaid managed care plans. Managed care for Medicaid recipients is expected to improve access through the establishment of contracted provider networks and promote greater accountability for quality and costs. Enrollment can be either voluntary or mandatory, depending on a particular state's decision. Prior to the BBA, states wishing to enact mandatory enrollment were required to obtain a federal waiver. Provisions of the BBA lifted this requirement. Where managed care

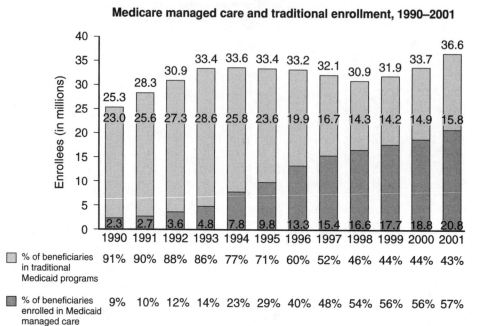

Figure 8–6 Medicaid Managed Care and Traditional Enrollment, 1990–2002

Source: This publication was reprinted with permission of the Henry J. Kaiser Foundation of Menlo Park, California. The Kaiser Foundation is an independent health care philanthropy and is not associated with Kaiser Permanente or Kaiser Industries.

enrollment is mandatory, states are required to offer a choice of managed care plans and make efforts to inform beneficiaries about their choices and how to access enrollment sites.

In general, Medicaid managed care plans use three plan models: primary care case management, full-risk HMOs, and prepaid health plans.[42] Historically, states had difficulty obtaining arrangements with commercial HMOs for Medicaid clients. As a result, several states created Medicaid-only plans. However, now that more states are mandating HMO enrollment, and private sector competition for payments is increasing, plans are more amenable to enrolling Medicaid clients.

"Carve-outs" is a term frequently associated with Medicaid managed care plans. A carve-out refers to one or more services for which a managed care plan is not obligated to provide coverage under its contract with Medicaid. Coverage for services is carved out because a managed care plan is either unable (because of unavailability of services) or unwilling (because of potentially high costs, questionable medical necessity, or both) to include selected services in its Medicaid managed care contract.[43] Mental health and substance abuse treatment services are those most commonly carved out. By retaining the risk for carved-out services, states have been able to increase the involvement of more commercial HMOs in the care of Medicaid recipients.

■ Managed Care Organizations and Quality

As managed care became the predominant mode of health care financing, concerns about the quality of care and the criteria and processes used to monitor and report it received increased scrutiny by physicians, other health professionals, the professional literature, the popular media, purchasers, and consumers. Also, with the growth of Medicare and Medicaid managed care enrollment, government and public policy makers have become increasingly involved in quality issues. The intensity of scrutiny is increasing in part because of concerns that as managed care organizations become more competitive, they will reduce services or more tightly restrict their use in the effort to hold down premiums.

Nationally, the most influential managed care organization quality assurance body is the National Committee on Quality Assurance (NCQA). The NCQA was formed in 1979 in a joint effort of two managed care trade organizations, the American Managed Care and Review Association and Group Health Association of America. The two organizations first merged to become the American Association of Health Plans, and then created the NCQA when it appeared that the federal government was considering establishing an entity to monitor health plans. In 1990, the NCQA became an independent, not-for-profit organization, with its primary source of revenue generated from fees for accreditation services.[44]

Managed care plan organization accreditation by a nationally recognized, independent organization rose in significance among employers, other purchasers, the professional community, and the public. This trend has resulted in increased demands for the NCQA's accreditation services, and a doubling of its operations budget since 1993.[45] The NCQA provides accreditation services on a voluntary request basis, with an average charge of $40,000 per health plan. The accreditation process includes advance collection and review of organizational information, and a three- or four-day visit by an NCQA team of physicians (often medical directors of other plans) and support staff. The review focuses on six major areas: management, physician credentials, member rights and responsibilities, preventive health services, utilization, and medical records. Samples of actual medical records are reviewed for diagnostic accuracy, appropriateness of care, diagnosis follow-through, and the use of preventive services. Managed care organizations may be granted accreditation for three years, one year, or on a provisional basis. Beginning in 1999, the NCQA began including outcomes of care and measures of clinical processes in its accreditation reviews, increasing the likelihood that accreditation status will accurately reflect the quality of care delivered.[46]

The Health Plan Employer Data and Information Set (HEDIS) evolved from a partnership among health plans, employers, and the NCQA in 1989.[47] It provides a standardized methodology for managed care organizations to collect, calculate, and report information about their performance to allow employers, other purchasers, and consumers to compare different plans. HEDIS has evolved through several stages of development and refinements and continues to do so, particularly as it is adapted for use in the Medicare and Medicaid managed care programs. A general version contains 71 measures of managed care organization performance, divided into the following 8 categories:

1. *Effectiveness of care*—members' receipt of services within specific time frames and the use of preventive services
2. *Accessibility and availability of care*—timeliness of care, without undue inconvenience
3. *Satisfaction with care*—summaries of member opinions about the managed care organization and its services
4. *Costs of care*—premiums, deductibles, and coinsurance
5. *Health plan stability*—status of the provider network, membership and enrollment trends, organizational structure, and financial status
6. *Informed choices*—patient education and other efforts to involve members in decisions about their health care
7. *Utilization*—the rates at which members use services and procedures
8. *Descriptive information*—factors that define and characterize the managed care organization and quality improvement activities [48]

Each category also contains its own specific performance measures.

The HEDIS reports are published by the NCQA and often are referred to as managed care organization "report cards." They are available to purchasers and to the public on a Web site.[49]

A special adaptation of HEDIS was released to the states in 1996 for use in monitoring the performance of contractors providing Medicaid managed care services. The reports are intended to assist managed care organizations with quality improvement efforts, support states in informing Medicaid recipients about managed care organization performance, and promote standardization of managed care reporting across the public and private sectors.[50] Beginning in 1997, managed care organizations with Medicare risk contracts were required to provide the Health Care Financing Administration with reports on certain HEDIS measures for their Medicare members.

HEDIS has several significant limitations, which include:

■ The accuracy of the data is not independently verified.
■ Compliance with NCQA reporting guidelines is not independently verified.
■ Aggregation precludes analytic flexibility.
■ The absence of risk adjustment can produce misleading conclusions.

There is also an overriding concern that "report card" indicators may be incorporated without adequate scientific proof that they are related to the quality of care.[51]

Although the HEDIS reporting systems represent important steps forward in promoting the accountability of managed care organizations to purchasers and consumers, the validity and reliability of report cards have not yet been subjected to the operational and scientific rigor appropriate to the importance of the decisions that the report cards influence. Arnold Epstein, professor of medicine and health care policy at Harvard University School of Medicine, has proposed the following "Desirable Characteristics of Quality Indicators or Groups of Quality Indicators for Use in Report Cards":*

■ Reliable
■ Valid, based on scientific evidence of effectiveness
■ Data collection reasonably straightforward
■ Risk adjustment appropriate
■ Measures of outcome related to care under control of providers
■ Reflective of aspects of care with an important impact on mortality, morbidity, and/or cost
■ Sensitive to changes induced by conservation of resources
■ Variation in performance among the entities rated
■ Representative of the services delivered by health care organizations
■ Reflective of population-based measures for health plans when feasible
■ Modifiable over time
■ Updated to reflect changing medical knowledge
■ Core measures retained to reflect temporal trends
■ New quality measures developed to prevent gaming

Managed care organizations also apply numerous internal techniques to manage quality, many of which directly or indirectly relate to physician performance. Much attention also is focused on the quality of the institutional providers, especially on the hospitals with which they contract for services. Database systems are used to track use of services

---

Source: Used with permission from *The Role of Quality Management in a Competitive Workplace*, by A.M. Epstein (Chicago: Health Administration Press, 1996), 227.

on both a prospective and retrospective basis to control resource use and monitor quality. Some managed care organizations employ nurses or other clinically trained professionals to follow potentially expensive cases to ensure care coordination and avoid misuse or duplication of services. The methods being used by managed care organizations to maintain control of costs and promote quality are numerous, diverse, and growing in volume and sophistication with increased experience.

■ The Future of Managed Care

Managed care organizations were at the forefront of major changes in the health care industry. A slowing growth rate of national health care expenditures was attributed in significant measure to the growth in managed care organization enrollment.[52] However, analysts' earlier predictions that managed care premiums would rise materially in 1998 and beyond have proven true. Regulations created in response to the managed care "backlash," coupled with rising prescription drug costs and other factors, have resulted in higher operating costs for HMOs. Regulation, in addition to a trend that has seen the costs of benefits rising faster than premiums, is resulting in increased costs to employers as well as to consumers through premium increases.

New arrangements among subscribers, insurers, and providers are occurring continuously as the system evolves. One observation likely to hold true for the foreseeable future is that the market forces in the health care delivery industry will continue to exert a more fast-paced, pervasive, and high-impact series of effects than any initiative forthcoming from state or federal legislative origins. It is likely that states will continue efforts to regulate managed care plans in response to consumer and provider pressures and that interest groups will advocate for an increasing array of mandated benefits and protections. Consolidations and mergers among managed care organizations are predicted to continue as the market evolves.

■ Notes

1. Health Care Financing Administration, Office of the Actuary: National Health Statistics Group, "Hospital Care Expenditures Aggregate and Per Capita Amounts and Percent Distribution, by Source of Funds, Selected Calendar Years, 1960–1998." http://cms.hhs.gov/statistics/nhe/historical/t5.asp (10 January 2000). Accessed 10 June 2000.
2. Health Care Financing Administration, Office of the Actuary: National Health Statistics Group, "Physician Service Expenditures, Aggregate and Per Capita Amounts and Percent Distribution by Source of Funds, Selected Calendar Years, 1960–1998."

3. Department of Health and Human Services, Center for Medicare & Medicaid Services, Office of the Actuary: National Health Statistics Group, "National Health Expenditures Aggregate Amounts and Average Annual Percent Change, by Type of Expenditure: Selected Calendar Years 1980–2000." http://cms.hhs.gov./statistics/nhe/historical/t2.asp. (Modified 17 July 2002). Accessed 29 November 2002.

4. R. Stevens, *In Sickness and in Wealth: American Hospitals in the Twentieth Century* (New York: Basic Books, 1989), 291.

5. Stevens, *In Sickness and in Wealth*, 287.

6. Stevens, *In Sickness and in Wealth*, 287.

7. Stevens, *In Sickness and in Wealth*, 309.

8. R. Miller and H. Luft, "Managed Care Plans: Characteristics, Growth and Premium Performance," *Annual Review of Public Health* 15 (1994): 439.

9. P.R. Kongstvedt, *The Managed Health Care Handbook* (Gaithersburg, MD: Aspen Publishers, 1989), 17.

10. P.R. Kongstvedt, *The Managed Health Care Handbook*, 12.

11. The Henry J. Kaiser Family Foundation, "Trends and Indicators in the Changing Health Care Marketplace, 2002 Chartbook." www.kff.org/content/2002/3161/marketplace2002_finalc.pdf. (May 2002). Accessed 9 September 2002.

12. Kaiser Family Foundation and Health Research and Educational Trust, "2002 Employer Health Benefits Survey, Chart 7." http://www.kff.org/content/2002/20020905a. (Fall 2002). Accessed 10 September 2002.

13. Kaiser Family Foundation and Health Research and Educational Trust, "2002 Employer Health Benefits Survey, Chart 11." http://www.kff.org/content/2002/20020905a. (Fall 2002). Accessed 10 September 2002.

14. Interstudy Publications, *"Total HMO Enrollment Continues to Increase, Though Growth Rates Slow Significantly. "* http://www.hmodata.com/pdf/ir91pr.pdf. (10 December 1999). Accessed 11 September 2002.

15. J. Gabel, "Ten Ways HMOs Have Changed During the 1990s," *Health Affairs* 16, no. 3 (1997), 136.

16. D. Cherkin et al., "The Effect of Office Visit Co-Payments on Utilization in a Health Maintenance Organization," *Medical Care* (July 1989), 669–678.

17. Gabel, "Ten Ways HMOs Have Changed During the 1990s," 143.

18. A. Kovner, *Jonas' Health Care Delivery in the United States*, 5th ed. (New York: Springer Publishing Co., 1995), 318.

19. J. Gabel, "Job-Based Health Benefits in 2002: Some Important Trends," *Health Affairs* 21, no. 5 (2002), 143.

20. Kaiser Family Foundation and Health Research and Educational Trust, *"2002 Employer Health Benefits Survey, Chart 11."*

21. U.S. Congressional Budget Office, "Projections of National Health Expenditures: 1997–2008, The Economic and Budget Outlook: Fiscal Years 1999–2008." http://www.cbo.gov/showdoc.cfm?index=316&sequence=13 (January 1998). Accessed 18 June 2000.

22. K. Levit et al., "Health Spending in 1998: Signals of Change," *Health Affairs* 19, no. 1 (2000), 131.

23. National Coalition on Health Care, "Deja Vu All Over Again: The Soaring Cost of Private Health Insurance and Its Impact on Consumers and Em-

ployers," http://www.nchc.org/releases/press050500.html (May 2000). Accessed 5 April 2003.

24. National Coalition on Health Care, "Deja Vu All Over Again: The Soaring Cost of Private Health Insurance and Its Impact on Consumers and Employers."

25. J. Gabel, "Job-Based Health Benefits in 2002: Some Important Trends," 144.

26. National Coalition on Health Care, "Deja Vu All Over Again: The Soaring Cost of Private Health Insurance and Its Impact on Consumers and Employers," 7.

27. R.J. Blendon et al., "Understanding the Managed Care Backlash," *Health Affairs* 17, no. 4 (1998): 80.

28. J. Havemann, "Citing Success, White House Plans to Widen Patient Rights Initiative," *The Washington Post* (9 April 1999), A18, http://www.washingtonpost.com. Accessed 4 June 2000.

29. R.J. Blendon and J.M. Benson, "Americans' Views on Health Policy: A Fifty-Year Historical Perspective," *Health Affairs* 20, no. 2 (2001): 40.

30. U.S. Office of Management and Budget, Executive Office of the President, "S. 1052–Bipartisan Patient Protection Act, Sens. McCain (R) AZ, Kennedy (D) MA, Edwards (D) NC," http://www.whitehouse.gov/omb/legislative/sap/107-1/text/S1052-s.html (6 June 2001). Accessed 5 November 2002.

31. National Conference of State Legislatures, "State Legislators on Patients' Bill of Rights: Do No Harm," http://www.ncsl.org/programs/press/2001/pr010621.htm. (21 June 2001). Accessed 12 September 2002.

32. J. Gabel et al., "Consumer-Driven Health Plans: Are They More Than Talk Now?" *Health Affairs*, Web Exclusive. http://www.healthaffairs.org/WebExclusives/Gabel_Web_Excl_112002.htm. (November 20, 2002). Accessed 24 November 2002.

33. J. Gabel, et al., "Consumer-Driven Health Plans: Are They More Than Talk Now?"

34. R.H. Miller and H.S. Luft, "HMO Plan Performance Update: Analysis of The Literature, 1997–2001," *Health Affairs* 21, no. 4 (2002): 81.

35. The Henry J. Kaiser Family Foundation, "Trends and Indicators in the Changing Health Care Marketplace, 2002 Chartbook," 24.

36. The Henry J. Kaiser Family Foundation, "The Medicare Program: Medicare+Choice." http://www.kff.org/content/2003/2052-05/2052-05.pdf (February 2003). Accessed 4 April 2003.

37. The Henry J. Kaiser Family Foundation, "The Medicare Program: Medicare+Choice."

38. The Henry J. Kaiser Family Foundation, "The Medicare Program: Medicare+Choice."

39. The Henry J. Kaiser Family Foundation, "The Medicare Program: Medicare+Choice."

40. U.S. Department of Health and Human Services, Center for Medicare and Medicaid Services, "Private Health Plan Access, Premiums, Benefits and Cost Sharing as of February 2003," http://cms.hhs.gov/healthplans/trends/allupdate2-26-2003rev.pdf (26 February 2003). Accessed 4 April 2003.

41. The Henry J. Kaiser Family Foundation, "Trends and Indicators in the Changing Health Care Marketplace, 2002 Chartbook."
42. J. Holahan et al., "Medicaid Managed Care in Thirteen States," *Health Affairs* 17, no. 13 (1998): 51.
43. Holahan et al., "Medicaid Managed Care in Thirteen States," 50.
44. J.K. Iglehart, "The National Committee for Quality Assurance," *New England Journal of Medicine* 335, no. 13 (1996): 995.
45. Iglehart, "The National Committee for Quality Assurance," 996.
46. L.G. Pawlson and M.E. O'Kane, "Professionalism, Regulation, and the Market: Impact on Accountability for Quality of Care," *Health Affairs* 21, no. 3 (2002): 202.
47. S.H. Altman et al., *Strategic Choices for a Changing Health Care System* (Chicago: Health Administration Press, 1996), 217.
48. P.L. Grimaldi, "HEDIS is Bigger and Better," *Nursing Management* 28, no. 1 (January 1997):18.
49. Pawlson and O'Kane, "Professionalism, Regulation, and the Market: Impact on Accountability for Quality of Care," 202.
50. Grimaldi, "HEDIS is Bigger and Better," 22.
51. Altman et al., *Strategic Choices for a Changing Health Care System*, 224.
52. K.R. Levit et al., "National Health Spending Trends in 1996," *Health Affairs* 17, no. 1 (Jan/Feb 1998): 35.

Chapter 9

Long Term Care

The number of Americans requiring long-term care services is increasing. Advances in medical care have made a longer life span not only possible but more probable, even in the presence of ongoing chronic disease and disability. This chapter provides an overview of some of the diverse array of long-term care services presently provided in institutional, community, and home-based settings. Particular attention is given to the long-term care needs of older adults because they are the fastest growing proportion of the population in the United States today and are the major consumers of long-term care services.

Each individual life span, from birth to death, can be seen as a connected flow of events—a continuum. The unrelenting progression of time is the one constant within which the diverse range of life's possibilities is expressed. An infant may be born with a birth defect, a young adult may suffer a head injury from an automobile accident, or an older adult may have a stroke. Such unanticipated events as these have a profound long-term impact on an individual's capacity to develop or to maintain abilities for self-care and independence. These individuals may require very different kinds and intensities of personal care assistance, health care services, and/or psychosocial and housing services over an extended segment of their life span.

The age, diagnosis, and ability to perform personal self-care, and where care is delivered, can vary widely for recipients of long-term care. Thus, long-term care requires diversified, yet coordinated, services and flexibility within the service system to respond to each recipient's changing needs over time.

The ideal health care delivery system provides participants with comprehensive personal, social, and medical care services. This ideal delivery system requires mechanisms that continually guide and track individual clients over time through the array of services at all levels and intensity of care that they require.[1] Because it generates a continuous flow of high costs over an extended period, long-term care has a particular need to use what the American Hospital Association calls a seamless continuum of care[2] that will promote the highest quality of life but still respond to growing public concerns about cost-effectiveness.[3] The particular package of services provided to each person should, at its best, be tailored to meet his or her needs for particular services. Service needs vary from assistance with personal care and basic needs for food and safe shelter to rehabilitation when possible and socialization opportunities. Additionally, the type and extent of physical disability and the intensity of services required determine the location where the long-term care is provided. For example, an older individual who is paralyzed following a stroke may be able to remain at home with services that dovetail with family caregivers in the home. Another with a similar disability might be institutionalized in a nursing home because that care environment best meets the particular requirements of the situation. Configuring a package of services that will promote independence and maintain the lifestyle quality as far as is possible within personal, community, and national resources makes the variety of long-term care services complex and sometimes confusing. Concern about cost-effectiveness and the desire to accommodate personal and family desires, finances, and reimbursement eligibility result in the need for both the availability of an array of services and coordination of those services to meet individual needs in the most effective way.

Within the last 50 years, extensive changes in demographics and the types and availability of health care services have occurred in the United States. The economic ramifications of a rapidly increasing population of older Americans, advances in medicine that have made many heretofore unknown life-sustaining measures available to health care professionals, and an emphasis on preventive care and healthy lifestyle all have had an impact on the continued growth of the population, who presently require or potentially will require long-term care services. Older adults represent the largest population group requiring long-term care services. Current estimates place the population 65 years of age and older at 35 million, or about one of every eight Americans, and the number of persons aged 65+ is expected to comprise 20 percent of the population by 2030.[4, 5] The population 85 years of age and older is expected to grow to 18.9 million by 2050, making this group the fastest growing population segment over the next four decades (see Figures 9–1 and 9–2).[6] Many will grow old alone due to the trend toward having smaller families and the increased rate of divorce. The increasing economic need for family members to delay retirement and work outside the home also reduces the availability of family caregivers to participate in the informal family caregiving system.

■ Development of Long-Term Care Services

The colonists who emigrated from Europe to the New World brought with them many of the social values and institutional models of their native countries. One of these, the almshouse, was a place where peo-

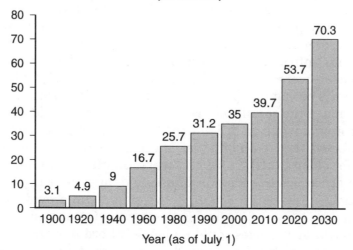

Number of persons 65 or older, 1900–2030 (in millions)

Year (as of July 1)

Note: Increments in years are uneven. Based on data from the U.S. Bureau of the Census

Figure 9–1 Number of Persons 65+, 1900–2030 (numbers in millions)
Source: "Projections of the Total Resident Population by 5 Year Age Groups, Race, and Hispanic Origin with Special Age Categories: Middle Series, 1999 to 2000," U.S. Census Internet Release Date: January 13, 2000 with "Population Projections of the United States by Age, Sex, Race and Hispanic Origin: 1995–2050," Current Population Reports, P25–1130. Data for 2000 are from the 2000 Census.

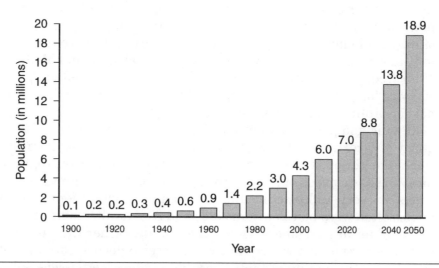

Figure 9–2 Population 85 Years and Over: 1900 to 2050
Source: Reprinted from U.S. Census Bureau Facts, Profiles of an Aging Nation, U.S. Department of Commerce.

ple who were sick or had disabilities, or older adults who were without adequate family or financial support, could be cared for in a communal setting. Almshouses were organized by charitable community members who purchased private homes and converted them into communal residences. Municipal and county governments also created homes and "infirmaries" to care for impoverished older adults. These early models were the basis for "homes for the elderly," which existed up until the economic upheavals of the Great Depression and the restructuring of the social welfare system following World War II.

The economic devastation experienced during the Great Depression affected the availability of long-term care services, especially homes for older adults, in several ways. Small private nursing homes became attractive to people in financial danger of losing their homes to mortgage foreclosure. Taking in outsiders and providing care generated a new source of income. Following the Great Depression, many local charitable agencies could no longer afford to provide care based on the almshouse tradition, and the federal government became more involved in developing, overseeing, and paying for long-term care services as part of the social welfare reforms, such as the 1935 Social Security Act.[7] The Social Security Act provided financial assistance for particular categories of older Americans and people with disabilities. Additionally, the Social Security Act established a form of old age and survivors insurance that allowed workers and their employers to contribute to a fund that could be used on retirement to supplement income. This form of income security reduced the extent of indigence frequently found in the older population and increased the amount of secure income that older Americans could spend on services and care in later years. Government lending programs available to not-for-profit organizations beginning in the 1950s spurred the development of nursing homes in this sector; major growth in the proprietary sector did not occur until after the passage of Medicare and Medicaid in 1965. Today, two-thirds of nursing homes are operated on a proprietary or for-profit basis, and slightly more than one-fourth operate as not-for-profit organizations (see Figure 9–3).

Public and private homes for older adults often varied in the adequacy of care and the kinds of services provided. Nursing homes often were thought of as homes where minimal custodial care required to meet the basic needs of food, clothing, and shelter was provided, sometimes in very unhygienic and inhumane environments. Nursing homes often were places where older and frail adults, some of society's most vulnerable members, were taken to die, rather than being seen as a residence option where they could receive needed care to prolong or enhance the quality of their lives. Physical care often was substandard, and emotional, spiritual, and social needs were ignored. Because many frail, older people suffer from perceptual and cognitive disabili-

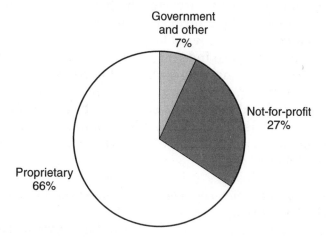

Percent distribution of nursing home facilities by ownership

Government and other
7%

Not-for-profit
27%

Proprietary
66%

Figure 9–3 Percent Distribution of Nursing Home Facilities by Ownership.
Source: "The National Nursing Home Survey, 1999." National Center for Health Statistics, Vital and Health Statistics, Series 13, no. 152, June 2002.

ties in addition to physical disabilities, their behavior in a group setting often was considered by nursing home staff to be a problem, and sometimes it led to the overuse of physical and chemical restraints such as sedatives and mood-altering drugs.

The provision of home nursing care also has a long tradition in the United States as an alternative to institutional care provided in hospitals and nursing homes. Family members traditionally have provided home care to their own relatives. An interest in providing formal professional home care services began in the late nineteenth century as a social response to the unhealthy living conditions of immigrants residing in urban tenements. Such crowded and unsanitary conditions became a public health concern because they were frequently implicated in the spread of contagious diseases, such as tuberculosis, typhoid, and smallpox. Agencies such as the Visiting Nurses Association were established to provide trained nurses to tend to the sick in their homes. Their role quickly expanded to include preventive education regarding hygiene, nutrition, and coordination of social welfare intervention, especially in caring for society's most vulnerable populations of people with illnesses, low incomes, or disabilities.[8]

The passage of Medicare and Medicaid legislation in 1965 provided more stable sources of reimbursement than were previously available through private pay and charitable funding, and also promoted expansion of the long-term care industry. Medicare and Medicaid have affected the long-term care industry in several overt ways. They established minimal standards of care and services required for recipients to qualify for reimbursement, as well as funding sources for older Americans, people with disabilities, and those lacking the means to pay. This funding simultaneously attracted both the scrupulous and the unscrupulous into the long-term care industry, as it quickly became apparent that being a provider of long-term care could be very profitable.

The long-term care industry came under increasing scrutiny in the early 1970s during congressional hearings on the nursing home industry, following several hundred exposés published in newspapers and additional publications such as the *Nader Report* and Mary Adelaide Mendelson's book, *Tender Loving Greed*.[9] The litany of nursing home corruption and abuses that were exposed during that period includes:[10, 11]

- Care that did not recognize the right to human dignity
- Lack of activities for residents
- Untrained and inadequate staff, including untrained administrators
- Unsanitary conditions
- Theft of residents' belongings
- Inadequate safety precautions (especially fire protection)
- Unauthorized and unnecessary use of restraints
- Both overmedication and undermedication of patients
- Failure to act in a timely manner on complaints and reprisals against those who complained
- Discrimination against patients who were members of minority groups
- Lack of dental and psychiatric care
- Negligence leading to injury and death
- Ineffective inspections and nonenforcement of laws that were meant to regulate the nursing home industry
- Reimbursement fraud

These congressional hearings and simultaneous public outcry resulted in more strict enforcement of Medicare and Medicaid guidelines and credentialing, increased establishment and enforcement of nursing home and home care licensure, more active accreditation procedures by the Joint Commission on Accreditation of Healthcare Organizations, laws related to elder abuse reporting, federal guidelines regulating the use of physical restraints, and the establishment of ombudsman programs. All these measures have led to a much more regulated and responsive long-term care industry. More vocal and astute consumers also have provided economic and social mandates for high-quality standards of care—which had previously not been adhered to in any meaningful, organized quality assurance process—to be maintained in the long-term care industry overall. The Omnibus Budget Reconciliation Act of 1997 (OBRA) legislated new guidelines and restrictions on the use of physical and chemical restraints, established a nursing home resident bill of rights, mandated quality assurance standards, established a standard survey process, and mandated training and educational requirements.[12]

■ Modes of Long-Term Care Service Delivery

Long-term care programs are categorized by the site where care is delivered. Institution-based services are those long-term care services provided within an institution such as a nursing home, hospital with inpatient extended care or rehabilitation facility, or inpatient hospice. Community-based services coordinate, manage, and deliver long-term care services such as adult day care programs or care in the recipient's home.

Nursing home facilities and residential care facilities are two examples of institutional-based long-term care settings. Both provide a place of extended residence and, as such, care recipients are called residents, not patients. This terminology is formally mandated by legislation.[13] The major difference between skilled nursing facilities (SNFs) and residential care facilities lies in the intensity of care provided. A SNF that is Medicare and Medicaid certified is defined as "a facility, or distinct part of one, primarily engaged in providing skilled nursing care and related services for people requiring medical or nursing care, or rehabilitation services."[14] Skilled nursing care is provided by or under the direct supervision of licensed nursing personnel, such as registered nurses and licensed practical nurses, and emphasis is on the provision of 24-hour nursing care and the availability of other types of services.

OBRA eliminated the distinction between skilled and intermediate care.[15] In discussing the nursing home industry, the terms "nursing home" and "skilled nursing home" often are used interchangeably. Residential care facilities such as adult homes primarily provide domiciliary care, which is the "provision of room and board, ordinarily without medical care, for persons incapable of independent living."[16] Another source defines residential care facilities as part of a more generic term of "personal home care also known as a custodial, residential, domiciliary, and board and care homes, [that] provide shelter and meals to persons who do not need nursing care or therapy."[17]

Skilled Nursing Care

Current estimates are that 1.6 million Americans reside in 18,000 skilled nursing facilities.[18]Average total annual costs per resident are estimated at $53,300.[19] Of the $92.2 billion in nursing home expenditures in 2000, the largest proportion, 60.6 percent, was paid by a combination of federal and state funds, and 27 percent was funded by personal, out-of-pocket resources (see Figure 9–4).[20] Through the Medicaid program, combined federal and state funds contribute over 47 percent, or $44 billion, of free-standing nursing home expenditures, making this one of the largest components of state health care expenditures.[21] The nursing home industry remains the dominant sector of the long-term care industry, far outstripping the expenditures for home care (see Figure 9–5).[22] Projections of the future need for nursing home care vary widely. However, one recent study projects that nursing home residents will total 5.3 million by 2030, representing more than a three-fold increase over current estimates of the nursing home population.[23]

Despite the burgeoning numbers of older Americans, national trends in nursing home occupancy rates are declining. Between 1987 and 1996, rates of occupancy declined from 92.3 percent to 88.8 percent.[24] More recent reports indicate that occupancy is continuing to fall.[25] Several factors are believed to be contributing to the decline. Today's older adults are healthier than before, delaying the need for skilled nursing services. National Long-term Care Survey data indicate that the prevalence of disability fell by an average of 1.1 percent between 1982 and 1989 and by 1.5 percent between 1989 and 1994.[26] The vastly increased availability of assisted living facilities and the availability of other community-based assistance through day care and home care are also playing roles in delaying the need for skilled, institutional care. Demographers predict that this trend is likely to con-

Sources of nursing home payments

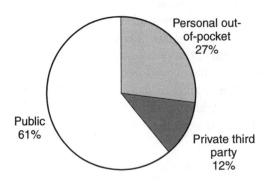

Figure 9–4 Sources of Nursing Home Payments
Source: Centers for Medicaid and Medicare Services (CMS).

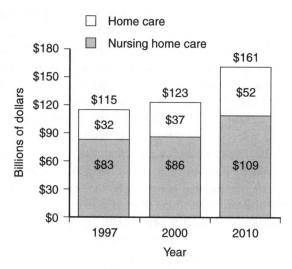

Figure 9–5 Projected Long-Term Care Expenditures for Older Adults
Source: Reprinted with permission from K. Davis and S. Raetzman, Meeting Future Health and Long-Term Care Need of an Aging Population, Issue Brief, p. 4. © 1999, *The Commonwealth Fund.*

tinue for the next two decades.[27] Declining occupancy as well as new financial constraints resulting from Medicare reimbursement reductions contained in the Balanced Budget Act of 1997 (BBA) took their toll on the industry. In 2000, approximately 1600 of the nation's 17,000 nursing homes were operating under bankruptcy protection.[28] Others implemented customized services for dementia and Alzheimer's disease residents in the effort to attract more business.[29]

Nursing home residents can be of any age, although most are adults in their later years. As age increases, admission to a nursing home becomes more likely and, according to one estimate, an older person faces more than a 40 percent risk of nursing home placement.[30] The typical nursing home resident is an older female with cognitive impairment who was living alone on a very limited income prior to nursing home placement. The decreased ability to physically function independently and a lack of family caregivers are additional factors associated with an increased risk of nursing home admission.

Typical staffing in SNFs includes a physician medical director, a nursing home administrator, a director of nursing, at least one registered nurse on the day and evening shifts, and either a registered nurse or a licensed practical nurse on the night shift. Additional registered nurses and licensed practical nurses are employed as needed to distribute medications and carry out medical treatments. Nursing assistants provide direct custodial care under the supervision of licensed nursing personnel. Ancillary professional staff include physical therapists, occupational therapists, pharmacists, nutritionists, recreational therapists, and social workers. Support staff, including kitchen, laundry, housekeeping, and maintenance workers, complete the employee complement. The exact number and staffing pattern also are based on the level of skilled nursing care required by the residents of any particular nursing home. The licensed nursing home administrator along with the owner/operator is responsible for carrying out the regulatory mandates regarding the mix and ratio of licensed and unlicensed personnel and the availability of licensed nursing personnel on an around-the-clock basis to provide skilled care and supervision.

Nursing homes are highly regulated by both state licensure and federal certification. OBRA increased government involvement in nursing home industry regulation by:[31]

- Mandating regularly scheduled comprehensive assessments of the functional capacity of residents in nursing homes
- Establishing training standards for nursing home aides
- Placing restrictions on the use of physical restraints and psychoactive drugs
- Establishing a nursing home resident bill of rights
- Setting guidelines for the role of the medical director, including continuing education, involvement, and responsibility

The licensure of nursing home administrators is carried out by each state. Criteria for licensure are set by individual states in relation to minimum age, educational requirements, passing examination scores, and continuing education requirements. Presently, 49 states and the District of Columbia use a standardized national licensure examination in determining licensure status; Texas has its own licensure examination.[32] Lack of compliance with state and federal mandates can lead to penalties such as direct fines, exclusion from Medicare and Medicaid certification, and withdrawal of licensure. Accreditation through the Joint Commission provides an additional quality check. Although highly desirable, Joint Commission accreditation remains voluntary.

Assisted Living Facilities

Assisted living facilities are directed toward long-term care for individuals who do not require skilled nursing services and whose needs lie more in the custodial and supportive realm. The Assisted Living Federation of America (ALFA) defines an assisted living residence as "a special combination of housing, personalized supportive services and health care designed to meet needs—both scheduled and unscheduled—of those who need help with activities of daily living."[33] Current estimates place the number of assisted living facilities at 28,000, housing over 1 million people.[34] The assisted living population is expected to grow to over 2 million individuals by 2025 (see Figure 9–6). Assisted living facilities vary significantly in size, ranging from just a few residents to several hundred. They may take the form of small to large homes with just a few residents, or large multi-unit apartment complexes with several hundred residents. Available services also vary, but generally include, in addition to housing, congregate meals, 24-hour monitoring for emergencies, medication supervision, and assistance with one or more activities of daily living such as bathing, dressing, and personal grooming. Assisted living facilities also typically provide scheduled activities including communal recreation and group transportation for medical appointments and for social and cultural events. Over 60 percent of assisted living facilities contract with home health agencies to provide skilled nursing care and with hospice service providers.[35] Oversight and regulation of assisted living facilities is carried out at the state level and varies from state to state. These variations in laws and regulations create a diverse operating environment, as well as a wide range of terminology and available services for consumers.[36] The quality of facilities, care, and services, therefore, may be an exclusive function of the policies of the owner organization or a combination of owner and organization policies coupled with state regulatory oversight. Costs of assisted living are borne largely from private resources, though in certain circumstances, Supplemental Security Income (SSI), private health insurance, long-term care insurance, or special government rent

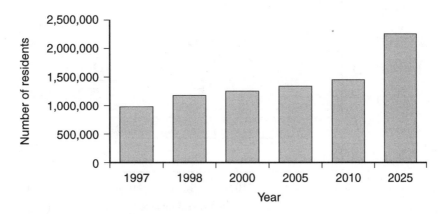

Figure 9–6 Actual and Projected Numbers of Residents of Assisted Living Facilities, Selected Years

Source: Reprinted with permission from www.ncal.org. Actual and Projected Numbers of Residents of Assisted Living Facilities, Selected Years, © American Health Care Association.

subsidies for low-income older adults may apply. The average monthly cost is estimated at $1,800, but costs can range across a broad continuum, depending on the level of amenities desired in a facility and the ranges and types of services required[37] (see Figure 9–7).

Residential institutions such as adult homes, board and care homes, and centers for people with mental or developmental disabilities also represent assisted living arrangements. Care provided in adult homes has been available only to people who are for the most part healthy but limited in their ability to do their own housekeeping, household maintenance, and cooking. The adult home, often in the past called a "rest home," provides a "supervised, supportive, protective environment with support services as required for residents having difficulty in caring for themselves."[38] Residents are expected to be able, for the most part, to meet unassisted their own personal care needs for dressing, eating, bathing, toileting, and ambulation. Oversight of residents is allowed and may include services such as supervision of medications to the extent of reminding residents to take their medication, or providing some assistance with bathing, grooming, transportation, laundry, and simple housekeeping. If provided at all, direct nursing care can be provided only in the case of minor illness of a temporary nature. Staffing levels in adult homes are state-defined. In adult homes of fewer than 20 beds, staffing typically is required only during residents' waking hours.

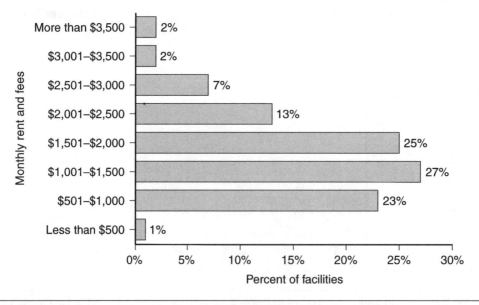

Figure 9–7 Average Monthly Rent and Fees in Assisted Living Facilities
Source: Reprinted with permission from Survey of Assisted Living Facilities, 1996, http://www.AHCA.org © American Health Care Association.

Home Care

Most simply defined, home care is community-based care provided to patients, more often referred to as "clients," in their own residences. Home care is usually thought of as a service only for older adults; however, more than one-fourth of all home care services is provided to individuals 64 years of age or younger (see Figure 9–8). Home care can be either a long-term provision of supportive care and services to chronically ill clients to avoid institutionalization, or short-term inter-mittent care of clients following acute illness and hospitalization un-til the clients are able to return to an independent level of functioning. Home care can be provided through either the formal system of paid professional home care providers, such as registered nurses, li-censed practical nurses, home health aides, and homemakers; specialty care providers, such as physical therapists and social workers who make home visits; or the informal system of caregivers consisting of family, neighbors, and friends of people in need of health care support services. Very often, a combination of both formal and informal systems is used to deliver care most expeditiously, although in other instances only one or the other may be used exclusively.

Professional home care services originated in social welfare initiatives in the early twentieth century in public response to the horrific living conditions of immigrants in U.S. industrialized cities. Public health concerns also were given impetus at that time as the germ theory of disease became accepted, and the control of contagious disease using preventive measures of hygiene and sanitation became a

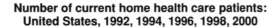

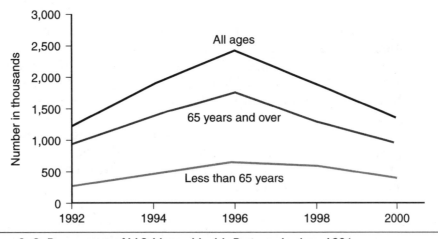

Figure 9–8 Percentage of U.S. Home Health Patients by Age, 1996
Source: Reprinted from B. Haupt, An Overview of Home Health and Hospice Care Patients: 1996 National Home and Hospice Care Survey, 1998, NCHS.

public health concern and mandate of local, state, and national health departments and agencies.

Formal home health care is playing an increasing role in the provision of care to those requiring long-term care services. The number of agencies increased by 26 percent between 1989 and 1994.[39] By 1996, the number of agencies serving Medicare beneficiaries had swelled to over 10,000.[40] Since 1996, the number of agencies serving Medicare beneficiaries has declined 28 percent to 7,152 in 2000, an impact attributed to changes in Medicare reimbursement enacted by the BBA.[41] Medicare is the largest single payer for home health care services, and in 2000 accounted for approximately 28 percent of total estimated home care expenditures (see Table 9–1). Total national expenditures for home health care were $41 billion in 1997 and declined to $32.4 billion in 2000 as a result of Medicare cost and utilization controls imposed by the BBA.[42] As a result, total home care spending showed a wide swing in annual growth through the 1990s, ranging from a high in 1990 of 28.2 percent to 0.8 percent in 2000.[43, 44]

The home care industry expanded its scope of services in response to demographic, economic, and legislative changes that include:

■ An increase in the number of older persons and their expressed desire to remain in their own homes for care whenever possible
■ Decreased numbers of informal caregivers who are available to provide in-home care to their relatives
■ Increased innovations in high-technology home care that have redefined and expanded the categories of diseases and chronic conditions that can be cared for efficaciously in the home care setting
■ Medicare and Medicaid reimbursement that allowed expanded coverage

Home care's material cost-effectiveness, when compared with institutional care, is pronounced[45] (see Table 9–2).

The initial growth spurt in the home care industry dates from the enactment of Medicare and Medicaid in the 1960s, which ensured a stable source of income available to certified agencies. The Medicare program made home health care much more accessible to older adults. Medicare Part A benefits cover skilled nursing care; physical, occupational, and speech therapies; and medical social services delivered in the home care setting. Eligibility criteria are strict and include four basic mandatory features.[46]

1. Home care must include the provision of skilled nursing care; physical, occupational, and speech therapies; and medical social services as warranted by the patient's condition.
2. The person must be confined to the home (homebound).

Table 9–1 Sources of Payment for Home Care in 2000

SOURCE OF PAYMENT	AMOUNT (IN BILLIONS)	PERCENT
Total	**32.4**	**100.0**[a]
Medicare	9.2	28.4
Medicaid	6.0	18.5[b]
Private (including private insurance)	9.1	28.0
Out-of-pocket	6.4	19.8
Other	1.7	5.2

[a] amounts may not add to totals due to rounding
[b] subset of all federal, state and local funds

Source: Center for Medicare and Medicaid Services, Department of Health and Human Services, "Personal Health Care Expenditures, by Type of Expenditure and Source of Funds, Calendar Years 1993–2000."

Table 9–2 Comparison of Hospital, Skilled Nursing Facility and Home Health Care Medicare Charges Per Day, 1998–2000

CHARGES	1998	1999	2000*
Hospital	2370	2533	2753
Skilled Nursing Facility	498	425	421
Home Health Care	93	93	100

* preliminary

Sources: National Association for Home Care; hospital and skilled nursing facility data: *Annual Statistical Supplement, 2000,* to the Social Security Bulletin, Social Security Administration, October 2001; Home care data: Health Care Financing Administration, Office of Information Services.

3. A physician must order that home care services are required.
4. The home care agency must meet the minimum quality standards as outlined by Medicare and be formally Medicare certified.

Beginning in 1982, growth in the number of private proprietary agencies was stimulated when Medicare reimbursement was opened up to the for-profit sector. The growth over the succeeding 25 years was pronounced in the proprietary sector, going from no Medicare-certified agencies in 1967 to 1,943 in 1985 and 2,863 in 2000[47] (see Figure 9–9). Today free-standing proprietary home health agencies comprise 40 percent of all Medicare-certified agencies.[48]

Thirty-eight states and the District of Columbia have licensure laws that mandate that any home health care agency operating in that state must meet state guidelines in order to be issued a license to operate.[49] Most states issue a license for one year and require that an application be resubmitted and an annual state reinspection be performed by a survey team. The state licensing agency has the right to investigate complaints and to conduct periodic reviews of all licensure requirements. Licensure laws can vary from state to state. In some instances, a state license is required only if the agency intends to participate in Medicare or Medicaid reimbursement as a home health care agency. Those few agencies that treat only private pay or private insurance patients may not require a license. However, most home health care agencies want to participate in Medicare and Medicaid reimbursement and actively seek to meet the guidelines established by Medicare and Medicaid for certification. The voluntary process of accreditation indicates that home care agencies have a commitment to continuous improvement in quality and accomplishment. Organizations that are actively engaged in the accreditation process for home health care agencies include the Community Health Accreditation Program, an independent, consumer-based subsidiary of the National League for Nursing; the Joint Commission; and the Association for Home Care and Hospice.

Professional caregivers are trained health care workers, such as registered nurses; licensed practical nurses; personal care aides; nursing assistants; homemakers; licensed occupational, physical, and res-

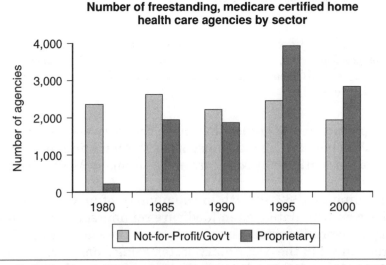

Figure 9–9 Number of Freestanding, Medicare Certified Home Health Care Agencies by Sector

Source: Center for Medicare and Medicaid Services, Center for Information Systems, Health Standards and Quality Bureau, February 2001.

piratory therapists; or social workers, who provide necessary health care services within their areas of expertise to clients in their homes. All care is provided under the direction of the client's physician. Most home care workers provide care under the auspices of proprietary (for-profit) home care agencies or through programs provided by not-for-profit agencies, and are employees of that agency or organization. A considerably smaller number are self-employed health care workers who contract privately with clients.

Until the proliferation of social programs in the 1960s and 1970s, those requiring long-term health care were almost always handled within the family, at the family home, and by family members or friends. This informal care system provided a valuable social service at little or no cost to the general public. This arrangement is still the most used system of long-term care—about 75 to 80 percent of older adults needing some level of assistance are cared for by family members. The informal care system offers a significant savings to the general public. However, the potential for caregivers to suffer physical and emotional burnout and the growing inability of family caregivers to handle care completely without partial or total outside assistance have begun to diminish these savings.

Recent estimates place the number of family caregivers at over 54 million, of whom 56 percent are women.[50] Because women are an integral part of the workforce along with men, the available pool of caregivers for family members needing care at home is significantly reduced from the past. Now, family caregivers are frequently required to make significant compromises in their finances, lifestyles, and personal freedom in order to care for another. The costs can be high. Stresses experienced by the caregiver can lead to exhaustion, illness, and depression. In addition, with greater longevity of the population, middle-aged individuals often find themselves caring for children and aged parents simultaneously. Dubbed the "sandwich generation," these caregivers suffer even more stress from this dual role. Employers also experience losses due to the demands of caregiving on their employees. One study conservatively estimates the annual costs of lost productivity for U.S. businesses due to caregiving at $11.4 billion. Employer costs are associated with worker replacement, absenteeism, workday interruptions, elder care crises, and supervisory time.[51] Some employers are responding with flexible scheduling and other considerations to help accommodate their employees' caregiving responsibilities.[52]

Recent estimates place the market value of long-term care delivered by unpaid family members and friends at over $250 billion per year, more than double the annual national health care expenditures for nursing home care[53] (see Figure 9–10). It is clear that both the economic and personal contributions of the informal caregiving system form the "bedrock" of the nation's chronic care system and require more policy-level attention and support.[54] Federal support has been slow to materialize, whereas states have assumed a more responsive role by developing programs to assist caregivers and expanding existing services. Twenty-five states have enacted legislation or regulations to support family caregivers. In 2002, California enacted legislation to provide state disability benefits to employees who use family medical leave to care for a seriously ill family member or to bond with a new child.[55]

Throughout the 1990s, dramatic increases in service use and spending in home health care were accompanied by mounting concerns about service quality and the fiscal integrity of Medicare-supported home health care services, and prompted responses from the Clinton administration and Congress.[56] In 1995, the Clinton administration initiated a pilot project, Operation Restore Trust (ORT), that investigated selected home health agencies in the five states with the highest rates of Medicare-covered home health care utilization. In 1997, ORT was expanded to selected home health care agencies in 12 states and included training for agency surveyors in identifying care improperly billed to Medicare.[57]

The BBA contained several provisions to enable the Health Care Financing Administration to more effectively control costs and address service quality issues in Medicare-funded home health agency services (see Chapter 7). The provisions included separating Medicare home health services funding into two streams, one to support

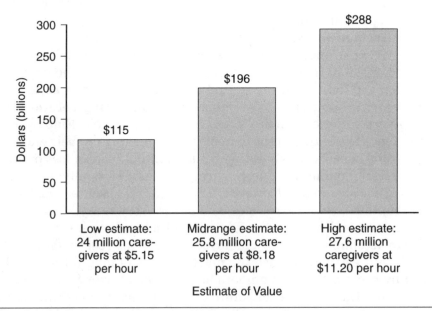

Figure 9–10 Economic Value of Informal Caregiving, 1997
Source: HEALTH AFFAIRS by /IGLEHART, JOHN K. Copyright 1999 by PROJECT HOPE. Reproduced with permission of PROJECT HOPE in the format Textbook via Copyright Clearance Center.

posthospital care and another to support services for chronic health problems. This change was targeted at reducing unnecessary and inappropriate services. Other provisions of the BBA changed Medicare reimbursement from a retrospective to a prospective basis, and several measures are being introduced to thwart fraudulent practices by home health clients and agencies.[58] The Clinton administration also proposed revisions in the federal standards that home health care agencies must meet to continue participation in the Medicare program. Revisions include:

- Requiring that home health agencies conduct criminal background checks of home health aides as a condition of employment
- Expanding the current home health aide qualifications to include nurse aides who have completed appropriate nurse aide training or competency evaluation requirements
- Requiring home health agencies to provide their staffs with continuous feedback on qualifications and performance as part of their continuous improvement programs
- Requiring home health agencies to discuss with patients the expected outcomes of care so that patients can be more involved in planning their own care
- Requiring home health agencies to coordinate all care prescribed by physicians for their patients, allowing several agencies to serve one patient without the coordination that is needed to assure quality[59]

Additional regulations were proposed by the Department of Health and Human Services in 1997 to require home health agencies to implement a standardized reporting system, the Outcomes and Assessment Information Set (OASIS), which is designed to monitor patients' conditions and satisfaction with services. It also requires the completion of standardized assessments of new patients within 48 hours of admission to a home health care agency and continuous updates of the admitting information, which includes documentation of changes in condition and patient and family satisfaction. The new Medicare prospective payment system for home health care services will be linked to OASIS data.[60]

Home health care services are an integral component of the health care delivery system's continuum, which can provide an effective, safe, and humane alternative to institutional care for the medical treatment and personal care of individuals of all ages. Unfortunately, home care also is an industry sector plagued by service quality and fiscal abuses that have prompted the need for far-reaching reforms. It has been proposed that "a guiding principle in any lasting reform of the Medicare postacute care benefits should be to make the system of services beneficiary-centered."[61] It is hoped that lessons learned from government support of home health services and responses to the industry prompted by the knowledge gained will allow a system to emerge that safeguards both payers and recipients from fraud and abuse while ensuring adherence to appropriate standards of quality care.

Hospice Care

Hospice is a philosophy supporting a coordinated program of care available to the terminally ill. The most common criterion for admission into hospice is that the applicant must have a diagnosis of a terminal illness with a limited life expectancy, usually anticipated to be of six months' duration or less. Aggressive medical treatment of the patient's disease may no longer be medically feasible or personally desirable. The disease may have progressed despite available medical treatments, making continuance of curative treatment futile or intolerable, or the patient may elect to discontinue such treatment for a variety of personal reasons, such as continued deterioration of quality of life relating to side effects of the treatment.

The term "palliative care" is often used synonymously with hospice care. Palliative care is care or treatment given to relieve the symptoms of a disease rather than attempting to cure the disease itself. Pain, nausea, malaise, and emotional distress caused by feelings of fear and isolation are only some of the difficulties that can be encountered by a patient during the final stages of a terminal illness. Hospice treatment is directed toward maintaining the comfort of the patient and enhancing the patient's quality of life and sense of independence for however long that life may last.

Hospice has its historical roots in medieval Europe. Hospices were originally way stations where travelers on religious pilgrimages were provided food and rest. Over time, the concept evolved into sanctuaries where care was given to impoverished people, or those who were sick or dying. The word "hospice" is derived from the same Latin root that forms the words "hospital" and "hospitality."

English physician Dame Cicely Saunders established St. Christopher's, a hospice located in a London suburb, in 1967, and it became a model for the modern hospice. Here, terminally ill patients were provided intensive symptom management, modern techniques of pain control, and psychological and emotional support. She brought the founding concepts of modern hospice to the United States in a lecture tour in the late 1960s, during which she emphasized that dying patients were also on a kind of pilgrimage and needed a more responsive environment than could be provided in high-technology, impersonal, cure-oriented hospitals.

The U.S. hospice movement began as a consumer-based grassroots movement supported by volunteer and professional members of the community who shared the belief that the hospice concept was a more humanized alternative to the care of the dying than was being provided in hospitals, which focused most intently on medical cure. Choosing to discontinue aggressive medical treatment, based on the recognition that the treatment is not altering the course of the disease, is considered failure by the medical system, and terminally ill patients can feel depersonalized and isolated inside a traditional hospital setting, where so much value is placed on a cure. Ideally, the physician, the patient, and the patient's family jointly recognize the need to refer the patient to hospice when the decision is made to stop aggressive curative treatment.

The first U.S. hospice was established in New Haven, Connecticut, in 1974. The number of hospices in this country has increased steadily since then, with over 2,200 Medicare-certified hospices in 44 states, and approximately 200 voluntary hospice organizations serving over one-half million individuals each year.[62] Growth in the availability of hospice care occurred following the enactment of 1982 legislation that extended Medicare coverage to hospice services, allowing the movement to escape its prior dependency on grant support and philanthropy. A 73-fold increase in the number of hospice providers occurred between 1984 and 1998. A dramatic increase followed passage of a 1989 Congressional mandate to increase Medicare rates by 20 percent.[63] The BBA divided the Medicare hospice benefit into three periods of an initial 90-day period, a subsequent 90-day period, and an unlimited number of subsequent 60-day benefit periods, so long as the individual continues to meet eligibility requirements. Consistent with the hospice philosophy, Medicare-covered services include those provided by a multidisciplinary team of nurses, social workers, counselors, physicians, and therapists. Drug therapies and medical appliances and supplies are also covered. Bereavement service for surviving family members is covered for 13 months following death of the patient.[64]

Hospice care may be provided in a variety of different settings, including in the home, in hospitals, in skilled nursing facilities, in assisted living facilities, or in hospice-operated facilities. Hospices may own their own facilities or lease beds from hospitals or other institutional providers and provide staffing and care plan supervision.[65] The most important unifying concept about hospice is that no matter where the care is delivered, a specialized interdisciplinary team of health care professionals works together to manage the patient's care. This interdisciplinary team is directed by a physician and coordinated by a nurse. The team members can include physicians, nurses, respiratory and physical therapists, pharmacists, pastoral care providers, social workers, psychologists, home health aides, and homemakers. Each team member contributes his or her particular skills and expertise to assist in managing pain, alleviating emotional distress, promoting comfort, and maintaining the independence of the hospice patient. Hospice care also includes the patient's family, so counseling (including bereavement counseling), spiritual support, and respite care are other important services that can be provided.

Volunteerism is emphasized in the hospice philosophy. Volunteers from the community are actively encouraged to participate in a wide range of hospice activities, from fund-raising to direct patient contact and family caregiver support. For example, volunteers may provide brief periods of respite care so that the regular family caregivers can attend to personal needs. Volunteerism is such an important concept in hospice that in some reimbursement mechanisms it is mandatory that community volunteers provide a specified percentage of the services provided by the hospice.

Hospice care has been demonstrated to be a cost-saving approach to the care of the terminally ill. The unique blend of care provided by a specialized team, use of volunteers, and frequent use of family members as primary caregivers in the home all decrease the expense involved. The focus on palliative care rather than on more high-technology, cure-oriented care also decreases the cost. The amount of savings involved in the use of hospice has been examined in a number of different research studies, but definitive figures remain in dispute. Hospice care continues to represent only about 1 percent of total Medicare spending, or about $2.8 billion per year.[66] Hospice is an optional Medicaid-covered service available in 44 states. Similar to Medicare, Medicaid expenditures of $325 million per year for hospice care represent only a small fraction of total expenditures.[67]

Managed care organizations and traditional health insurers have recognized both the humane and economic benefits of hospice care and typically include hospice in their benefit packages. Insurers may have their own team of hospice-type providers within their respective networks or may contract with community hospice organizations to provide the care. Medicare-eligible subscribers of Medicare-participating managed care organizations are automatically eligible for hospice care, and services must be provided through a Medicare-certified hospice organization. The patient is not required to obtain a referral from their managed care organization and is not required to disenroll from their managed care contract in order to receive hospice care.

A basic tenet of the hospice philosophy is that hospice care is provided based on a need for care, rather than on the patient's ability to pay. In instances where the patient does not have health insurance and cannot qualify for Medicare or Medicaid, hospice services may still be available. A sliding payment scale may be offered to the patient, with the hospice drawing on internal funds garnered through its fund-raising activities or bequests to supplement the scale.

Ongoing quality assurance to monitor the quality of care is an inherent concept in the provision of hospice care. Three standards used most frequently are licensure, certification, and accreditation. Licensure is based on state-imposed statutes as part of the consumer protection code of a state. Not all states have such licensing statutes. States that do have licensing statutes require that all hospices operating within their jurisdiction meet the standards set forth in the law. Certification means that hospices have been examined on the federal level and have been found to at least minimally meet mandated requirements for Medicare and Medicaid reimbursement. Certification status is important for patients, particularly those patients whose hospice care reimbursement source is Medicare or Medicaid. A hospice program that is not certified may still operate legally, but is ineligible to bill Medicare or Medicaid for its services.

Accreditation indicates that hospices meet voluntary standards of quality established by nongovernmental, independent monitoring organizations. Until recently, the Joint Commission offered a program of hospice accreditation. Another organization that continues to offer accreditation is a subsidiary of the National League of Nurses Community Health Accreditation Program. Many hospices have elected not to participate in voluntary accreditation programs because such programs often have stringent requirements, and many hospices may not have the resources necessary to meet them.

Respite Care

The informal caregiving system of family members and friends has traditionally provided the majority of in-home, long-term care services to people in the community who are frail, have chronic disabilities, or are in their later years. Family caregivers have been a key factor in keeping many long-term care recipients in their communities rather than using institutions. Providing care up to 24 hours a day can place enormous physical and emotional stress on family caregivers.

Respite care is temporary surrogate care given to a patient when that patient's primary caregiver must be absent. This often occurs with patients who require full-time supervision at home. In the 1970s, formal respite care programs originated to meet the increasing need for assistance following the rapid deinstitutionalization of individuals who had developmental disabilities or mental impairment. Since then, the respite care model has expanded to include any family-managed care program that helps to avoid or forestall the placement of the patient in a full-time institutionalized environment by providing planned, intermittent caregiver relief. Respite care offers an organized, reliable system in which both patient and primary caregiver are the beneficiaries.

Respite care can be offered in a variety of settings: the home, a day care situation, or at an institution with overnight care, such as hospitals or nursing homes. Respite care can occur under various auspices, including private, public, and voluntary not-for-profit agencies. The length of respite care varies, but it is intended to be short term and intermittent.

Respite care services are highly differentiated. Some are very structured and self-contained; others are highly flexible and exist in a more casual support capacity. A number of services are oriented to treating only patients with a particular ailment, but for many, the only criterion the patient must meet for admission is that he or she requires supervised medical treatment and nursing care that is provided by family or friends as principal caregivers. Models of respite care include:

- Alzheimer's disease care on an inpatient basis with admissions lasting for several weeks
- Community-based, adult day care centers that offer nursing, therapeutic, and social services
- In-home aides, where care is supplied by visiting aides
- Temporary patient furloughs to a hospital or nursing home at regular intervals

Hospital admissions for the express purpose of respite are much less likely to be allowed in a managed care environment than they were in the past.

Staffing of respite care programs varies widely in terms of use of professionals or nonprofessionals. For example, respite care could be as informal as having a member from the caregiver's church come into the home for a few hours while the caregiver goes out, or as professional as a specialized dementia day care program where nurses, aides, and recreational and physical therapists are specifically educated to care for dementia patients in a structured, caregiving environment. In instances where respite care is provided in an overnight institutional setting, like a nursing home or hospital, the staff providing care will be the same staff employed by the institution to provide care to their regular patients in the institution.

Formal respite programs in the United States remain sparse. One of the greatest barriers limiting the expanded use of respite care is cost. Family caregivers accustomed to operating on a limited budget may have trouble finding the funds to pay a compensatory hourly rate to a health care professional who supplies respite care. Although some respite care services offer care on a sliding scale, there are cases where almost any standardized fee is too high to be met by the family caregiver. In these situations, a number of not-for-profit voluntary organizations may be contacted for assistance. These organizations may supply home aides for respite care at a tolerable cost to patients who fall within certain financial or medical parameters.

At present very few provisions in the federal Medicare and Medicaid programs support formal respite care. Medicare contains no allowances for respite. Medicaid has stringent requirements regarding the specific type and length of care provided, as well as financial eligibility for services. In some states, there has been an attempt to provide some kind of subsidy for respite in the cases of citizens over age 60 with extremely low incomes. The cost of nursing home admission procedures makes respite admissions of less than two weeks financially ill-advised for the institution.

The available respite programs offered by voluntary agencies as the result of federal grants often provide service only for specific medical conditions, such as Alzheimer's disease. Some specialized dementia respite care programs currently are being developed and marketed to private pay customers, but such programs often are beyond the financial capability of many families.

One of the major barriers to responsive changes in the reimbursement mechanism to cover respite care is that funding mechanisms choose to look at respite care as meeting a social need but not an acute medical care need. In addition, community systems of respite care are difficult to organize because the level of need is intermittent and unpredictable. Family caregivers often are viewed as the most direct beneficiaries of respite care, rather than the patients who actually receive the health care. Despite the inescapable conclusion that respite care programs offer society value and cost savings through postponement or avoidance of costly institutionalization, reimbursement for respite services has yet to be acknowledged in any way that begins to recognize the inherent economic value of the informal family-provided care system.

Adult Day Care

An adult day care center provides a supervised program of either social activities and custodial care (social model), medical and rehabilitative care through skilled nursing (medical model), or a combination of both. An adult day care center operates during the day in a protective group setting outside the home, and participants must be transported to and from the site. The primary intent of adult day care is to prevent the premature and inappropriate institutionalization of older adults by providing socialization, health care, or both. Older adults maintain their mental and physical well-being longer and at a higher level when they continue to reside in their homes and communities. Furthermore, for those who depend on the services of a regular family caregiver, an adult day care center can provide respite for the caregiver and therapeutic social contacts for the care recipient.[68]

The concept of adult day care grew out of social concern for the quality of life and care of older adults and was based on the work of Lionel Cousins, who, in the 1960s, established the first adult day care center in the United States to "prepare patients for discharge by teaching and promoting independent living skills."[69] Originally, development and growth in such programs was slow because there was no national policy to support the idea, nor a permanent funding base, because the prototype Medicare and Medicaid programs supported and encouraged institutionalization. However, as the cost of institutionalization, the inhumanity of many nursing homes, and the burden placed on family caregivers have been recognized, the focus of long-term care has been redirected toward support of community-based care as a preferred alternative to institutionalization whenever possible. Since then, growth in the number of adult day care programs has been rapid. The first adult day care center in this country was opened in 1947, but by 1981 only 15 were active.[70] By 1984 there were more than 900 such programs. Today it is estimated that there are over 4,000 licensed and unlicensed centers in operation, with many more needed to meet demand. Most are operated by not-for-profit organizations.[71]

The services that adult day care centers offer are similar, but the emphasis varies with the model they follow. Most adult day care centers offer a variety of medical, psychiatric, and nursing assessments; counseling; physical exercises; social services; crafts; and rehabilitation in activities of daily living skills. Special-purpose adult day care centers have been created to serve particular populations of clients, such as veterans, older persons with mental health problems, the blind, people with Alzheimer's disease, or people with cerebral palsy.

Staffing patterns of adult day care programs vary from program to program and are directly related to the type of program and specific services being offered. The ratio of staff to patients also is diverse, but in the range of 1 staff member to every 3 to 12 clients. The mix of unskilled to skilled employees also is dependent on the kinds of services being offered. For example, in programs based on the medical model, it is more likely that more registered nurses, occupational therapists, and physical therapists will be employed to provide skilled assessment, direct care, and rehabilitative therapies than in a social model, where aides may perform most of the custodial care and a recreational therapist may be employed to plan and deliver recreational and socialization activities. The number of clients enrolled in a day care program varies according to the staffing pattern and facility size. The cost of care may vary widely depending on the range and scope of services provided. Medicare generally does not provide reimbursement for day care services. Medicaid may provide reimbursement for services in a medical model day care program, but this practice varies from state to state. Most services are paid for through private fees or through programs supported by grant funds or by charitable or religious organizations.

A substantial proportion of adult day care centers is regulated by state licensure laws, although licensing is not mandatory in all states. Most also are certified by the particular community agency that is funding the day care center. Licensure and credentialing ensure that the day care center meets minimum standards and guidelines set by the overseeing funding agency in order for the community agency to meet criteria for obtaining underlying federal government grants. In 1999, the Commission on Accreditation of Rehabilitation Facilities, along with the National Adult Day Services Association published adult day care standards, which include organizational measurement and quality, and information systems and outcomes quality. The new standards are expected to provide an enhanced level of quality guidance to adult day care management, as well as focus more recognition on the value of adult day care services in the overall continuum of long-term care.[72]

■ ## Innovations in Long-Term Care

Notable efforts have been made to provide innovative long-term care services that will meet the diverse medical needs, personal desires, and lifestyle choices of older Americans. The continuum of care model recognizes the complex configuration of individual needs and encourages the implementation of programs and services of adequate variety, intensity, and scope to provide the best configuration of care to any individual. Concepts such as aging-in-place, life care communities, and high-technology home care are some of the changes that offer enriched alternatives to long-term care recipients.

Aging-in-Place

Being moved to a nursing home or dependent care facility is seen by many as a change in lifestyle to be steadfastly avoided for as long as possible. Most people would prefer to remain actively engaged in their own support and care to the full extent of their ability in their own residence and within the context of their own family. Research indicates that longevity and quality of life are enhanced when older adults are able to remain in their own residences. The term "aging-in-place," when used in the context of people who are older and frail, refers to at least partial fulfillment of this desire. An aging-in-place health care system allows older adults to maintain their health while living as independently as possible in their own housing, without needing a costly, and in many cases traumatic, move to an institutional setting. The proportion of older people in our society is increasing, and government resources to assist them have come under increasing scrutiny in an effort to control escalating long-term care costs. The well-documented cost-effectiveness of health care programs that encourage the aging-in-place concept and the concurrent maintenance of independent living are being seen in a very favorable light.

A number of aging-in-place programs have been developed that guarantee participants a lifetime health care plan and support services. Institutionalization occurs only if it becomes medically imperative because necessary care cannot be delivered in the home setting. Services that participants receive may vary slightly, but most frequently include:

- Nursing services provided by registered and licensed nurses
- Home care aide
- Homemaker services to assist with meals and housekeeping
- 24-hour emergency response system
- Home-delivered groceries and/or meals
- Adult day care

Participants continue to have the full financial responsibility of home maintenance and upkeep because direct assistance with these tasks is limited to a list of names of prequalified tradesmen and mechanics.

In 1972, a model of aging-in-place service delivery called On Lok Senior Health Services was established as a demonstration project to provide health services to a selected population of frail older people in San Francisco. The term "On Lok" is taken from the Chinese language and means "peaceful and happy abode."[73] Participants in the On Lok program live in their own residences. An interdisciplinary team of health care professionals manages health care. If and when institutional care is required (either in a nursing home or hospital), or ancillary diagnostic or specialty physician services are needed, they are provided through contractual arrangements with outside providers. The prototype program was so successful that Congress mandated replication of this model by establishment of demonstration programs, called Program for All-Inclusive Care for the Elderly (PACE), in other parts of the country. The early success of PACE was evidenced by the fact that, although all its clients were certified eligible for nursing home placement, only 6 percent were placed in nursing homes; the rest were able to remain in their homes.[74] Also impressive was the low hospitalization rate of participants when compared with typical Medicare beneficiaries with similar health status. Cost savings to Medicare and Medicaid have been estimated conservatively at

5 to 15 percent. Through provisions of the BBA, PACE has been granted permanent status as a Medicare-approved benefit.[75] The BBA legislation authorized the establishment of up to 28 new not-for-profit operated programs and up to 10 proprietary programs. Twenty-five programs are currently in operation, all under the auspices of not-for-profit organizations.[76]

Continuing Care Retirement and Life Care Communities

Continuing care retirement communities (CCRCs) are available for those Americans who do not want to stay in their own homes as they get older, yet are essentially well enough to avoid institutionalization. The total number of CCRCs rose by 38 percent in 1997, from 478 to 662.[77] By 1999, the number was estimated at 900.[78] In CCRCs, participants are provided with residences on a retirement campus. CCRCs are apartment complexes designed for functional older adults, but, unlike ordinary retirement communities that offer only specialized housing, CCRCs offer a comprehensive program of social services, meals, and access to contractual medical services in addition to housing. Most CCRCs are sponsored by religious or not-for-profit organizations. Membership in one of these communities requires monthly payments but is reserved for an extended period of time, usually one full year or more.

A life care community is a type of CCRC, but the health care services are prepaid and can be guaranteed for life. Cost varies widely, and such programs are expensive. However, as advocates for this lifestyle point out, many Americans approaching their retirement years have sufficient equity in their homes that can be used to pay the entrance and monthly maintenance fees for a life care community.

Life care communities achieve financial viability by using an insurance-based model and, as such, are regulated by state insurance departments, as well as other regulatory agencies to which their services may be subject in their respective states. The program administrators establish eligibility criteria for participants using actuarial data from the insurance industry. The future lifetime medical costs of participants are anticipated, and rates and charges are set accordingly. Prospective continuing life care community (CLCC) residents are provided a contract outlining what the CLCC will provide in terms of home accommodations, social activities, services and amenities, and access to on-site levels of health care. Most CLCCs require a one-time entrance fee and a monthly fee. There are many variations to the types of contracts offered.[79] In general, services may include:

■ Meals
■ Scheduled transportation
■ Housekeeping services

- Housing unit maintenance
- Linen and personal laundry
- Health monitoring
- Wellness programs
- Some utilities
- Social activities
- Home health care
- Skilled nursing care

A life care community offers more comprehensive benefits and support systems for the older persons than any other option available today in the United States. Less than 1 percent of older citizens have taken advantage of this option, in great part due to the expense and need for an extended commitment.

High-Technology Home Care: Hospitals without Walls

Traditionally, home health care has focused on providing supportive care to persons with long-term disability and chronic disease. Recent changes in reimbursement mechanisms to a prospective payment system based on diagnosis-related groups have led to the more rapid discharge of all patients from hospitals following episodes of hospitalization for acute illness, exacerbation of chronic disease, progression of disability, or surgery. Patients frequently are discharged home while they still require advanced intensive therapeutic treatments and rely on complex, high-technology services such as ventilators, kidney dialysis, intravenous therapy for the administration of antibiotics, parenteral nutrition, and cancer chemotherapy.

The delivery of high-technology home care is not only more cost-effective than hospitalization or institutionalization in a nursing home, but also allows the client to move from the more dependent patient role to the more autonomous role as client in his own residence. Home health care agencies have accommodated this trend toward provision of advanced high-technology therapy in the home setting through innovations in the type and organization of the specialty services they provide. Improvements and innovations have taken place in the portability, mobility, reliability, and cost of medical devices such as IV therapy pumps, long-term venous access devices, continuous ambulatory peritoneal dialysis equipment, and ventilators. Innovative teams of home health care providers who are skilled practitioners in specialized areas such as intravenous therapy and kidney dialysis, and the concurrent development of innovative support teams of agency-employed pharmacists and specialty technicians who prepare and deliver necessary intravenous solutions, parenteral nutrition, and dialysis solutions and medications have made the home setting an appropriate environment for the delivery of high-technology therapies.

■ Long-Term Care Insurance

Long-term care insurance (LTCI) is a relatively new financing option for long-term care made available to the public in the past 10 years. In 1986, there were only 30 companies that offered this type of coverage,[80] but the number of companies has increased manyfold since then. Private long-term care insurance is the fastest growing type of health insurance sold in recent years.[81] The Health Insurance Association of America (HIAA) reports that sales of LTCI grew an average of 22 percent per year between 1987 and 1996.[82] By mid-1998, a total of 5.8 million policies had been sold.[83] The majority of policies have been purchased by individuals, but an increasing number of employers are now offering coverage through group purchase plans. However, most employers make no contributions toward the coverage, but rather offer access to coverage at group rates.[84]

The benefits of LTCI policies vary across a broad spectrum. The most desirable policies cover services across the continuum of potential long-term care needs, with maximum subscriber flexibility. Buyers are counseled by specialists to be wary of limitations relative to inflationary factors in the costs of coverage, renewability clauses, limits on payments for various modes of long-term care, requirements for prior hospitalization for eligibility for home care, cancellation features of policies, and lifetime benefit limits. As with life insurance, the premium cost reflects age at purchase of the policy. LTCI companies also utilize underwriting criteria and may reject applicants or increase premiums for individuals with preexisting conditions that render them at high risk for future long-term care services.

Insurance industry advocates and other analysts contend that individuals and society will benefit in the future from the proliferation of LTCI. In their view, public dependency, especially upon Medicaid to fund long-term care needs, would decrease, and individuals would have the ability to access the highest quality long-term care services without risk of impoverishment.[85]

The decision to invest in a long-term care insurance product is very personal and depends on many factors, primarily on the level of assets the individual has, or expects to have, at risk if long-term care is required. Other alternatives to LTCI, such as transferring assets to children to become financially eligible for Medicaid, using the equity in a home, selecting special living arrangements, and using personal savings, are not universally applicable. All these options need to be carefully assessed against the cost of LTCI in order to make viable and appropriate future plans.

■ The Future of Long-Term Care

We know that diverse long-term care programs will be needed in the future and in greater numbers to serve increasing needs, especially of older adults. Some of the causes underlying the intensifying need for diverse long-term care service options are:

- Changes in the demographics of the U.S. population
- Social and economic changes in families
- Increasingly sophisticated medical technology
- Greater consumer sophistication
- Increasing scrutiny of federal and state government financial involvement in support of long-term health care

The final configuration of the long-term care service delivery system is difficult to predict with certainty, although some conjectures about the future can be predicated on an analysis of the current trends in long-term care.

Long-term care services have become increasingly diversified and specialized, which allows programs and providers to focus on becoming experts in meeting specific needs for care in specialized populations such as people with Alzheimer's disease or AIDS. One danger to be avoided is allowing specialization to lead to fragmentation, duplication of services, and pressure to categorize participants into narrow service niches. New service areas, such as the development of subacute care facilities and the provision of transitional health care after acute care hospitalization and for medically complex long-term care patients, are being developed as the drive to discharge patients from hospitals more quickly results in a greater need for more intense supportive care environments beyond hospital walls. Service delivery systems that function within the managed care environment are becoming increasingly common, and the bundling of posthospitalization care with hospitalization into one episode of care provided through one integrated service provider is occurring more frequently. Whether such trends will contribute to a seamless continuity of care will remain under scrutiny.

The increased demand for home health care services is expected to continue because of the demonstrated cost-effectiveness and expressed client preferences for community-based services such as home care. Because both Medicare and Medicaid traditionally have favored reimbursement for institutional care over community-based care, additional legislative change in reimbursement emphasis is needed.[86] Effects of the new prospective payment system, reductions in Medicare reimbursement, and additional oversight entailed in the BBA have yet to see their true impact. Some industry specialists are already contending that the impact is having devastating results on provider viability and care quality that extend far beyond the intent of Congress to reduce costs.

Long-term caregivers traditionally have been paid less and given less status than those workers in the acute care health services. The long-term care industry is enduring an employment crisis with an inadequate number and quality of applicants to fill vacancies in the direct caregiver positions across all industry sectors. Factors contributing to the long-term care employment crisis include:

- The growing need for services
- Competition among employers
- Workload and working conditions
- Employee turnover
- Wages and benefits constrained by reimbursement policies
- Lack of social supports for workers, including child care and transportation
- Lack of opportunities for education and career mobility[87]

Staffing shortages directly and seriously impact the quality of long-term care services. The industry's ability to develop innovative approaches to attracting and retaining staff will have serious implications well into the future.

The needs of the informal caregiver system have been virtually ignored. Significant legislative action that recognizes these needs in terms of employer allowances and other programmatic and economic considerations at the federal and state levels are sorely needed if this critical system of long-term care is to remain intact as the older adult population expands rapidly over the next three decades.

An undercurrent of concern runs beneath all aspects of long-term health care delivery, especially with regard to the development of responsive, patient-centered, quality-driven, accessible, affordable, and cost-effective health care services for all citizens—including society's most vulnerable, people with chronic disabilities and frail older adults. Many concerns related to how long-term care will be financed in the future currently remain open-ended, and the part that long-term care services will play within the restructuring of the U.S. health care system is as yet undetermined, although it undoubtedly will be of major concern to the increasingly large portion of older adults in our society. The ensuing years will be a period of experimentation, innovation, and change in the long-term health care system.

■ Notes

1. C.J. Evashwick, "Strategic Management of a Continuum of Care," *Journal of Long-Term Care Administration* 21, no. 3 (1993): 13–24.
2. S.M. Shortell, *Transforming Health Care Delivery: Seamless Continuum of Care* (Chicago: American Hospital Publishing, 1994), 1–7.

3. C.M. Jack and D.L. Paone, *Toward Creating a Seamless Continuum of Care: Addressing Chronic Care Needs* (Chicago: Section for Aging and Long-Term Care Services of the American Hospital Association, 1994), 3–5.

4. U.S. Department of Health and Human Services Administration on Aging, "Profile of Older Americans, 2002." http://www.aoa.dhhs.gov/aoa/stats/profile/2002/1.html last modified 30 December 2002, Accessed 8 April 2003.

5. U.S. Department of Health and Human Services Administration on Aging, "Profile of Older Americans, 2002." http://www.aoa.dhhs.gov/aoa/stats/profile/2002/1.html last modified 30 December 2002, Accessed 8 April 2003.

6. U.S. Department of Health and Human Services Administration on Aging, "Older Population by Age: 1900–2050." http://www.aoa.dhhs.gov/aoa/stats/agepop2050.html last modified 20 February 2003, Accessed 8 April 2003.

7. H.H. Shore, "History of Long-Term Care," in *Essentials of Long-Term Care Administration*, ed. S.B. Goldsmith (Gaithersburg, MD: Aspen Publishers, 1994), 5–6.

8. J.M. Pavri, "Overview: One Hundred Years of Public Health Nursing: Visions of a Better World," *Imprint* 41, no. 4 (1994): 43–48.

9. R.M. Glasscote et al., *Old Folks at Homes: A Field Study of Nursing and Board-and-Care Homes* (Washington, DC: American Psychiatric Association, 1976), 3.

10. F.E. Moss and V.J. Halamandaris, *Too Old, Too Sick, Too Bad* (Gaithersburg, MD: Aspen Publishers, 1977), 15–37.

11. Glasscote et al., Old Folks at Homes, 1.

12. J.M. Evans et al., "Medical Care of Nursing Home Residents," *Mayo Clinic Proceedings* 70, no. 7 (1995): 694.

13. A.R. Somers and W.S. Livengood, "Long-Term Care for the Elderly: Major Developments of the Last Ten Years," *Pride Institute Journal of Long Term Home Health Care* 11, no. 1 (1992): 12.

14. Long Term Care Education.com, "Definition of the Skilled Nursing Facility," http://www.longtermcareeducation.com/A1/e.asp. 1, Accessed 6 April 2003.

15. M.E. Toso, "Strategic Planning in Long-Term Care," in *Essentials of Long-Term Care Administration*, ed. S.B. Goldsmith (Gaithersburg, MD: Aspen Publishers, 1994), 326.

16. L. Hyde, *The McGraw-Hill Essential Dictionary of Health Care, A Practical Reference for Health Managers* (New York: McGraw-Hill, 1998), 199.

17. L.R. Elgin, "Long-Term Care Insurance: Issues and Opportunities," *Nursing Economics* 11, no. 6 (1993): 359.

18. U.S. Department of Health and Human Services, National Center for Health Statistics, "Nursing Home Care," http://www.cdc.gov/nchs/fastats/nursingh.htm (2002). Accessed 19 September 2002.

19. U.S. Department of Health and Human Services, National Center for Health Statistics, "The National Nursing Home Survey: 1999 Summary." http://www.cdc.gov/nchs/products/pubs/pubd/series/sr13/160-151/sr13_152.htm (17 June 2002). Accessed 19 September 2002.

20. Center for Medicare and Medicaid Services, "Nursing Home Care Expenditures Aggregate and Per Capita Amounts and Percent Distribution, by Source of Funds: Selected Calendar Years 1980-2000." 1. http://cms.hhs.gov/statistics/nhe/historical/t.7.asp (17 July 2002) Accessed 6 September 2002.

21. Center for Medicare and Medicaid Services, "Nursing Home Care Expenditures Aggregate and Per Capita Amounts and Percent Distribution, by Source of Funds: Selected Calendar Years 1980–2000." http://cms.hhs.gov/statistics/nhe/historical/t7.asp (17 July 2002). Accessed 6 September 2002.

22. K. Davis and S. Raetzman, "Meeting Future Health and Long-Term Care Needs of an Aging Population," *Issue Brief* (New York, NY: The Commonwealth Fund, December 1999), 4.

23. J.M. Mulvey and B. Stucki, *Who Will Pay for the Baby-Boomers' Long-Term Care Needs: Expanding the Role of Long-Term Care Insurance* (Washington: American Council of Life Insurance, 1998), cited in M. Merlis, *Financing Long-Term Care in the Twenty-First Century: The Public and Private Roles* (Commonwealth Fund Publication 343, Institute for Health Policy Solutions, September 1999), 12.

24. J.A. Rhoades and N.A. Knauss, "Nursing Home Trends, 1987 and 1996," *MEPS Chartbook 3, AHCPR Pub. No. 99-0032* (Rockville, MD: Agency for Health Care Policy and Research), http://www.nchc.org/releases/press050500.html (1999) Accessed 5 April 2003.

25. J.C. Conklin, "Nursing Homes Add 'Special Care,'" *The Wall Street Journal*, 7 August 2000, B-1.

26. U.S. Congressional Budget Office, "Projections of Expenditures for Long-Term Care Services for the Elderly." http://www.cbo.gov/showdoc.cfm?index=1123&sequence=0&from=1 (March 1999). Accessed 7 August 2000.

27. Conklin, "Nursing Homes Add 'Special Care,'" B-1.

28. U.S. Department of Health and Human Services Assistant Secretary for Legislation, "Testimony on Nursing Home Bankruptcies Before the Senate Special Committee on Aging, September 5, 2000." http://www.hhs.gov/asl/testify/t00905a.html last revised 9 April 2003 Accessed 9 April 2003.

29. Rhoades and Knauss, "Nursing Home Trends, 1987 and 1996."

30. R.H. Moos and S. Lemke, *Group Residences for Older Adults: Physical Features, Policies, and Social Climate* (New York: Oxford University Press, 1994), 3.

31. Evans et al., "Medical Care of Nursing Home Residents," 697.

32. A. Cary, "Professional Standards and Credentialing," in *Handbook of Home Health Care Administration*, ed. M.D. Harris (Gaithersburg, MD: Aspen Publishers, 1994), 90–98.

33. Assisted Living Federation of America, "What is Assisted Living?" http://www.alfa.org (1997). Accessed 5 August 2000.

34. The National Center for Assisted Living, "Vital Assisted Living Stats," http://www.ncal.org/about/vital.htm 1, accessed 14 December 2002.

35. The National Center for Assisted Living, "About Assisted Living, Vital Assisted Living Stats," *1998 Facts and Trends: The Assisted Living*

Sourcebook 1998. http://www.ncal.org/about/vital.htm (1999). Accessed 27 November 2002.

36. The National Center for Assisted Living, *Assisted Living State Regulatory Review,* http://www.ncal.org/about/2001-reg-review.pdf (2001). Accessed 2 November 2002.

37. The National Center for Assisted Living, "About Assisted Living, Vital Assisted Living Stats."

38. A.K. Harrington, "Assisted Living in Alternative Residential Environments," in *Essentials of Long-Term Care Administration,* ed. S.B. Goldsmith (Gaithersburg, MD: Aspen Publishers, 1994), 297.

39. K. Millea, "Home Health Care Update," *Nursing95* (July 1995): 57–58.

40. National Association for Home Care, "Basic Statistics about Home Care." http://www.nahc.org/consumer/hcstats.html (Updated March 2000). Accessed 5 August 2000.

41. U.S. Department of Health and Human Services, Center for Medicare and Medicaid Services, "Private Health Plan Access, Premiums, Benefits and Cost Sharing as of February 2003," http://cms.hhs.gov/healthplans/trends/allupdate2-26-2003rev.pdf. 26 February 2003, Accessed 4 April 2003.

42. National Association for Home Care, "Basic Statistics about Home Care."

43. K. Levit et al., "Inflation Spurs Health Spending in 2000," *Health Affairs* 21, no. 1 (January/February 2002), 175.

44. K. Levit et al., "Inflation Spurs Health Spending in 2000," 176.

45. National Association for Home Care, "Basic Statistics About Home Care," Table 18.

46. S.E. Hardwick et al., *Across the States: Profiles of Long-Term Care Systems* (Washington, DC: American Association of Retired Persons, 1994), 6.

47. National Association for Home Care, "Basic Statistics About Home Care," Table 1.

48. National Association for Home Care, "Basic Statistics About Home Care," Table 1.

49. M.D. Harris, *Handbook of Home Health Care Administration* (Gaithersburg, MD: Aspen Publishers, 1994), 85.

50. National Family Caregivers Association, "54 Million Americans Involved in Family Caregiving Last Year Doubles the Previously Reported Figure," http://www.nfcacares.org/PRSurvey2000.html (October 13, 2002). Accessed 12 November 2002.

51. Metropolitan Life Insurance Co., "The MetLife Study of Employed Caregivers: Does Long Term Care Insurance Make a Difference?" (March 2001) http://www.caregiving.org/LTC%20study%20final.pdf. Accessed 11 November 2002.

52. P. Braus, "When Mom Needs Help," *American Demographics* 16, no. 3 (1994): 38–46.

53. National Family Caregivers Association, "Family Caregiving Statistics, 2001." http://www.nfcacares.org/nfc2002_stats.html (2002), 2002. Accessed 19 November 2002.

54. I. Peter et al., "The Economic Value of Informal Caregiving," *Health Affairs* 18, no. 2 (March/April 1999), 184.

55. Foley/Lardner, Attorneys at Law, "California Enacts Legislation to Provide Disability Benefits to Employees Who Take Family Care Leave," Vol. 02-33. http://www.foleylardner.com/files/tbl_s31publications/fileupload/137/1080/law%20watch%20vol%2002-33.pdf (30 September 2002). Accessed 14 November 2002.

56. Health Care Financing Review, *1996 Statistical Supplement*, 76.

57. Health Care Financing Administration, "Improving Quality, Tightening Standards," *Fact Sheet* (8 August 1997): 1.

58. Health Care Financing Administration, "Improving Quality, Tightening Standards," 1.

59. Health Care Financing Administration, "Improving Quality, Tightening Standards," 1–2.

60. U.S. Department of Health and Human Services, Center for Medicare and Medicaid Services, "OASIS Overview." http://cms.hhs.gov/oasis/hhoview.asp last modified 28 June 2002 Accessed 9 April 2003.

61. B.C. Vladeck, "Statement on Reforming Medicare Home Health Benefit before the House Commerce Committee, Subcommittee on Health and Environment, March 5, 1997," http://www.house.gov/commerce/health/hearings/030597/vladeck.pdf (5 March 1997). Accessed 9 April 1998.

62. National Association for Home Care, "Basic Statistics About Hospice," *2001 Hospice Stats,* http://www.nahc.org/consumers.hpcstats.html (Updated July 2001). Accessed 28 November 2002.

63. National Association for Home Care, "Basic Statistics About Hospice."

64. National Association for Home Care, "Basic Statistics About Hospice."

65. National Association for Home Care, "Basic Statistics About Hospice."

66. National Association for Home Care, "Basic Statistics About Hospice."

67. National Association for Home Care, "Basic Statistics About Hospice."

68. C.A. Cefalu and M. Heuser, "Adult Day Care for the Demented Elderly," *American Family Physician* 47, no. 4 (1993): 723–724.

69. R.S. Lamden et al., "Adult Day Care," in *Essentials of Long-Term Care Administration*, ed. S.B. Goldsmith (Gaithersburg, MD: Aspen Publishers, 1994), 285.

70. P.M. Kirwin, *Adult Day Care: The Relationship of Formal and Informal Systems of Care* (New York: Garland Publishing, 1991), 48.

71. National Respite Network & Resource Center, "Adult Day Care, One Form of Respite for Older Adults." http://www.chtop.com/ARCH/archfs54.htm#Funding. April 2002 Accessed 9 April 2003.

72. C. MacDonnell, "CARF Accredits Adult Day Care," *Nursing Homes* 48, no. 3 (1999): 53.

73. J.A. Miller, *Community-Based Long-Term Care* (New York: Sage Publications, 1991), 203.

74. Miller, *Community-Based Long-Term Care*, 213.

75. Deloitte & Touche, LLP, and Deloitte & Touche Consulting Group, LLC, *The Balanced Budget Act of 1997, Public Law 105-33 Medicare and Medicaid Changes* (Washington, DC: Deloitte & Touche, LLP, 1997): 4.

76. S. Parkin, "Providers Find Interim PACE Final Rule Too 'Inflexible,'" *Long-Term Care Provider.Com News & Analysis* http://www.longtermcareprovider.com (16 February 2000). Accessed 3 August 2000.

77. B. Japsen, "Another Year of Major Growth in Outpatient Care," *Modern Healthcare* (25 May 1998): 66.

78. J. Pynoos, "The Future of Housing and Residential Care for Older Persons," *Annals of Long Term Care* 7, no. 2 http://www.mmhc.com/nhm/articles/NHM9904/pynos.html (April 1999). Accessed 9 August 2000.

79. Senior Resource for Continuing Care Retirement Communities, "Continuing Care Retirement Communities (CCRCs) and Lifecare." http://www.seniorresource.com/hccrc.htm (2000). Accessed 11 August 2000.

80. O.J. Snowe, *Long-Term Care Improvement Act,* Congressional Record: 1472 (Washington, DC: U.S. Congress, 1994).

81. Somers and Livengood, "Long-Term Care for the Elderly: Major Developments of the Last Ten Years," 6–18.

82. House Committee on Government Reform, Subcommittee on Civil Services, *HIAA Statement: The Role of Private Long-Term Care Insurance in Financing Long-Term Care and the Importance of Offering Long-Term Care Insurance to All Federal Employees*, 105th Cong., 1st sess., 18 March 1999, 4.

83. Long Term Care Group, Inc., "The Long Term Care Industry," http://www.ltcg.com/ltcindustry.asp (2001). Accessed 10 November 2001.

84. M. Merlis, "Financing Long Term Care in the Twenty-First Century: The Public and Private Roles," *Institute for Health Policy Solutions* (New York, NY: The Commonwealth Fund, September 1999), 20.

85. M. Merlis, "Financing Long Term Care in the Twenty-First Century: The Public and Private Roles," 24.

86. S.E. Hardwick et al., *Across the States: Profiles of Long-Term Care Systems* (Washington, DC: American Association of Retired Persons, 1994), 6.

87. New York State Association of Homes and Services for the Aging, "The Staffing Crisis in New York's Continuing Care System, A Comprehensive Analysis and Recommendations." *Executive Summary* (March 2000): 1.

Chapter 10

Mental Health Services

Susan V. McLeer, MD

This chapter describes the clinical characteristics of people who receive mental health services. Historic trends and forces affecting the distribution and kinds of care are examined and compared with epidemiological data regarding the prevalence of psychiatric disorders to hypothesize whether national needs for mental health care are being met. Evolution in the science and technology available for the treatment of psychiatric disorders is reviewed briefly. Opportunities for improvement and evidence of the impact of managed care on effective mental health service delivery are examined.

In the early years of our nation, the mentally ill were confined at home, in jails, or in almshouses where they suffered severely. It was not until the early nineteenth century that sensitivity to the special needs of the mentally ill emerged through the Quaker emphasis on mental illness as being treatable. This approach, established earlier in Europe and known as "moral treatment," was tried in a few mental hospitals where patients received kind, but firm, treatment while participating in work, educational activities, and recreation.[1] Effective biological treatments were nonexistent, and the majority of patients did not have access to moral treatment; rather, they were confined under the most adverse circumstances. Hospitals became overcrowded custodial facilities, not only for the mentally ill, but also for criminals, alcoholics, and low-income, homeless people.

Awareness of the needs of the mentally ill became more focused following World War I with the return of thousands of men with disabilities and suffering from "war neurosis," also known as "shell shock," a condition synonymous with current criteria for posttraumatic stress disorder. In the 1930s, the first effective biological treatments emerged in the forms of insulin coma, drug-induced convulsions, and electroconvulsive therapy. Psychosurgery emerged briefly as an area of potential benefit to psychiatric patients. With the advent of World War II, the federal government became active in the mental health field, passing the National Mental Health Act in 1946, which resulted in the establishment of the National Institute of Mental Health (NIMH). Federal, state, and county dollars were allocated for training, research, and service in mental health. The Department of

Veterans Affairs recognized the need for increased mental health services and established psychiatric hospitals and ambulatory clinics.

Psychiatric care still remained focused on inpatient services, with the number of people placed in inpatient facilities expanding to a new maximum by the mid-1950s, when over half a million patients were hospitalized in state or county mental hospitals. Fortuitously, this corresponded with the development of the first psychoactive medications specifically targeted for treating psychiatric disorders. These agents included chlorpromazine (Thorazine) and reserpine, used for the treatment of schizophrenia and other psychotic disorders. These advances profoundly changed patterns of care, reducing the need for convulsive therapies and psychosurgery and providing patients with effective interventions that allowed them to live outside of a mental hospital. Ambulatory services were intensified with the addition of partial hospitalization programs, intensive after-care programs, and the development of nonhospital transitional residential facilities, or halfway houses, for the mentally ill.

By 1955, the U.S. Congress established the Joint Commission on Mental Illness and Health. The commission attacked the quality of care and patient access to care in the large state and county mental hospitals. This was the first time a federal body had considered the allocation of resources for the mentally ill. The commission's report began a substantial shift in sites for the provision of mental health services from the inpatient state and county mental hospitals to outpatient facilities. The commission's recommendations fell on fertile ground and were reiterated by President Kennedy in his first message to Congress.

By the early 1960s, the winds of change had been whipped up not only by the commission, but also by the development of new, efficacious psychotropic medications and psychosocial treatments that could provide effective intervention for many disorders outside the hospital. Congress passed the Mental Retardation Facilities and Community Mental Health Centers Construction Act, resulting in considerable federal support for community-based services. Large entitlement programs became accessible to the mentally ill, mainly Medicaid, Medicare, Supplemental Security Income (SSI), Social Security and Disability Insurance, and housing subsidies, among others.

Throughout the 1960s and 1970s, the federal government became more involved in financing mental health care. Community mental health centers developed and expanded, and more health professionals entered the mental health field. Federal and state money, originally targeted for severely mentally ill patients, were shunted through the community mental health systems to provide services for those with less severe illness.[2, 3] This shift in service was based on two untested assumptions that provided the underpinnings for changes in program planning in community mental health centers. These assumptions were: (1) mental disorders lie on a quantitative continuum, with severe mental illness not differing qualitatively from lesser forms of mental distress; and (2) early intervention can prevent the development of major psychiatric disorders. Neither assumption has been demonstrated to be valid. Nonetheless, based on these assumptions, much money was invested and services provided to people with mild to moderate dysfunction and "problems in living," with the hope that the incidence of severe mental illness would be reduced through primary prevention.[4]

Treatment of less severe problems was handled through psychosocial interventions without proven efficacy and without systematic and standardized evaluations of outcome. In addition, payment for mental health services with public dollars was allocated on the basis of units of service provided. Therefore, there was no incentive for limiting the duration of treatment, and patients were provided nonspecific, psychosocial interventions for years. From 1955 to 1980 the number of patient care episodes provided in organized mental health settings increased four-fold, from 1.7 million to 7 million.[5] Few of these patients were severely mentally ill.[6]

Simultaneously with the institution of these programmatic changes in community mental health centers, many severely mentally ill patients who formerly had been warehoused in large state or county mental hospitals were discharged to community boarding houses and nursing homes. The deinstitutionalization movement was presented as being important to the rehabilitation of those with severe mental illness. Emphasis was placed on the necessity of providing services in community settings. In actuality, the states, through Medicaid, were receiving major financial incentives to move patients from inpatient mental hospitals to nursing homes. This transfer, coupled with the changes in the staffing and programs at community mental health centers, resulted in many severely mentally ill patients finding limited access to care because the treatments provided at the mental health centers were no longer predominantly being targeted for this vulnerable group of people with severe disabilities. Advocacy groups such as the National Alliance for the Mentally Ill (NAMI) emerged, directing their efforts to have public dollars reallocated to support services, including the funding of biomedical research that targeted severe and persistent psychiatric disorders. Advocates maintained that the pivotal issue was the treatment of psychiatric illness, not the maintenance of mental health. Through their efforts and those of NIMH and clinical researchers across the United States, the assumptions fueling the staffing and programming of mental health centers during the 1970s and early 1980s were proved erroneous. Psychiatric disorders are not on a quantitative continuum, but are discontinuities in development. They are now believed to be biologically based illnesses that require specific, targeted treatments.

By the late 1970s, health care costs had soared, and the federal government became concerned with identifying mechanisms for restraining health-related spending. President Carter, recognizing that new research findings presented opportunities for improving care to the mentally ill, appointed a Presidential Commission on Mental Health. Because of fiscal constraints and political infighting in Washington and within the field of psychiatry itself, the majority of the commission's findings and recommendations were not put into operation. However, the commission's work quietly filtered down to the Department of Health and Human Services, resulting in substantial changes of great importance to those with severe mental illness. Psychosocial rehabilitation programs were expanded under Medicaid. Medicaid payment for outpatient mental health care was expanded, and copayment requirements for case management services were reduced. Patients with severe and persistent mental illness became eligible for SSI funding. These changes meant a substantial shift in quality-of-life issues for this population. However, by the mid-1980s, programs became sharply curtailed again, with cutbacks in housing subsidies and social services, and increased exclusion of people with mental illness from SSI benefits.

By 1990, although much controversy still raged regarding what services should be delivered to whom, the locus of mental health care in the United States had shifted significantly from inpatient to outpatient settings. Of the 1.7 million episodes of mental health services delivered in 1955, 77 percent were in inpatient settings and 23 percent in outpatient programs. However, by 1990, of the 8.6 million episodes of mental health services delivered, 67 percent were provided in outpatient programs, 7 percent in partial hospitalization settings (not 24-hour facilities), and 21 percent in inpatient services.[7] This trend is expected to continue as managed care programs become more firmly established and widespread.

Over the past 5 to 10 years, because of constant and rigorous pressure placed on Congress and legislative bodies by advocacy groups such as NAMI and psychiatric researchers, the focus on severe mental illness has returned. Through block grants, state departments of mental health have refocused their energies and reallocated resources to ensure the provision of services to the most vulnerable population—those afflicted with severe and persistent mental illness. Federal money has been reallocated for research and training, with efforts focused on treatment, not prevention. The results of these shifts have been considerable. Now, in the twenty-first century, the chances of people with severe mental illness receiving significant benefit through effective treatments have never been better. Yet few people access these treatments.

■ Recipients of Mental Health Services

The recipients of mental health services in the United States constitute a small subpopulation of those individuals afflicted with a mental illness. Access to mental health services is and has been controlled by a variety of factors, including, but not limited to, persistent myths regarding the nature and treatability of mental illness, nonparity in insurance coverage for mental illness, and political decisions regarding the distribution of resources in our communities.

Mental illness is enormously painful and debilitating, both for those directly afflicted and for their families. Well-designed epidemiological studies, conducted by the Epidemiologic Catchment Area (ECA) Program and the National Co-Morbidity Study, have reported that as much as 20 to 29 percent of the U.S. population will have a mental disorder during a one-year period.[8] However, many of these disorders are temporary and have minimal effects on individual function. Less than 7 percent of adults in the United States have mental disorders that persist for one year or more,[9] and approximately 9 percent of the population have reported significant disability associated with a mental disorder.[10] Individuals who most need mental health services are in these last two groups. A total of about 15 percent of the adult U.S. population uses mental health services in any given year (see Table 10–1).[11] However, over the course of a year, less than one-third of adults with diagnosable mental disorders receive treatment.[12] Factors recognized as contributing to barriers to care access include financial limitations, social stigmatization, misunderstandings about the treatability of conditions, personal and provider attitudes, cultural issues, and insensitive delivery system organization.[13]

Contrary to widely held assumptions, mental disorders can now be diagnosed and treated as effectively as physical disorders. They are classified according to criteria that provide predictability regarding the natural history of the illness and its responsiveness to specific, disorder-targeted treatments. Seventeen diagnostic categories (see

Table 10–1 Proportion of Adult Population Using Mental/ Addictive Disorder Services in One Year

TYPE OF SERVICE	PERCENTAGE OF POPULATION
Total health sector services	11%*
Specialty mental health	6%
General medical	6%
Human services professionals	5%
Voluntary support network	3%
Any of above services	15%

*Subtotals do not add to total due to overlap

Source: Reprinted from U.S. Department of Health and Human Services Publication No. SMA-96-3098.

the following) are described in the American Psychiatric Association's *Diagnostic and Statistical Manual of Mental Disorders*, and within these categories, the specific diagnostic criteria for over 450 conditions are delineated.[14] The criteria for specific diagnoses in each of these categories have been subjected to extensive field testing for diagnostic reliability and validity. Although even a superficial review of the criteria for all of the diagnoses exceeds the scope of this chapter, a brief review is provided for the 17 general diagnostic categories:*

1. *Disorders usually first diagnosed in infancy, childhood, or adolescence.* The disorders in this category cause dysfunction in the behavioral, cognitive, and/or affective domains and include, but are not restricted to, three diagnoses relating to mental retardation, and three specific and four pervasive developmental disorders, including autism, disruptive behavioral, and attention disorders. Selected anxiety disorders, such as separation anxiety disorder, also are included. Although these almost always appear first during childhood or adolescence, it should not be assumed that the psychiatric disorders found in this age group are restricted to those delineated here. Children and adolescents can develop other disorders that more usually have their onset in adulthood, e.g., bipolar disorders and major depression.

2. *Delirium, dementia, amnestic, and other cognitive disorders.* These are disorders in which the predominant disturbance is a significant deficit in cognition or memory, a deficit that represents a significant change from previous levels of functioning. These disorders formerly were referred to as organic mental disorders because the etiological agents were medical illnesses and/or toxins. However, the implication of calling these organic mental disorders was that other psychiatric disorders were not biologically based. Research has demonstrated clearly that this is not the case, with most serious psychiatric disorders having a strong, if not predominant, neurobiological substrate. Therefore, the disorders in this category have been reclassified simply to disorders of cognition or memory.

3. *Mental disorders due to a general medical condition not elsewhere classified.* This grouping of mental disorders is self-explanatory and refers to disorders of behavior or mood that have resulted from a nonpsychiatric medical disorder. Examples of disorders in this category are catatonia caused by a brain tumor or severe depression secondary to hypothyroidism.

4. *Substance-related disorders.* These disturbances of behavior, cognition, and/or mood are caused by the taking and/or abuse

Source: Reprinted with permission from the *Diagnostic and Statistical Manual of Mental Disorders,* Fourth Edition, Copyright 1994 American Psychiatric Association.

of a drug, alcohol, or tobacco; the side effects of medication; or exposure to toxins.

5. *Schizophrenia and other psychotic disorders.* These disorders are among the more prevalent in the population of patients with serious and persistent mental illness. They are classified primarily on the basis of the presence of psychotic symptoms, including hallucinations and delusions, but also can refer to patients with some of the other features of schizophrenia—mainly disorganized speech and/or grossly disorganized or catatonic behavior.

6. *Mood disorders.* These disorders have a disturbance in moods as the predominant feature and include depressive disorders, bipolar disorders (manic-depressive disorders), and mood disorders due to a general medical condition or ingestion of a substance such as alcohol. These conditions are further distinguished on the basis of a severity index that includes mild, moderate, severe without psychotic features, and severe with psychotic features. Both depressive and bipolar disorders can have associated hallucinations and delusions.

7. *Anxiety disorders.* As the name implies, the disorders in this section have anxiety as a common feature. However, 13 different anxiety disorders are delineated in this category, including panic attack, agoraphobia, social and specific phobias, general anxiety disorder, and obsessive-compulsive disorder. Also included in this section are those disorders caused by external stressors, including posttraumatic stress disorder and acute stress disorder. Some of these conditions are extremely debilitating.

8. *Somatoform disorders.* The central features of these disorders are symptoms that suggest a general medical condition but cannot be explained by the patient's medical status or any drugs or substances being ingested. The symptoms also cannot be explained by the presence of another psychiatric disorder.

9. *Factitious disorders.* These disorders are characterized by physical or psychological symptoms that are intentionally produced or feigned in order to assume a sick role. These must be distinguished from malingering, a condition in which a person produces or reports symptoms intentionally for secondary gain (e.g., court settlements resulting in substantial gains of money). In factitious disorders, the "gain" is limited to being recognized as ill.

10. *Dissociative disorders.* Five separate disorders are included in this category. All include a disruption in the integrative functions of consciousness, memory, identity, or environmental perception. Not infrequently there is a history of severe stress, particularly some form of interpersonal violence or abuse.

11. *Sexual and gender identity disorders.* This category includes sexual dysfunction (disturbances in sexual desire and arousal, orgasmic disorders, and sexual pain disorders); the paraphilias

characterized by recurrent, intense sexual urges, fantasies, or behaviors that involve unusual objects, activities, or situations that cause significant distress and/or impairment in function; and the gender identity disorders.

12. *Eating disorders*. These disorders are characterized by severe disturbances in eating behavior and include anorexia and bulimia. Both disorders can be severe and even life threatening based on extreme weight loss and/or suicidal behaviors.

13. *Sleep disorders*. These disorders are subdivided into two categories: (1) dyssomnias, characterized by abnormalities in the amount, quality, or timing of sleep; and (2) parasomnias, characterized by abnormal behavioral or physiological events occurring in association with sleep, with specific sleep stages, or sleep-wake transitions.

14. *Impulse control disorders not elsewhere classified*. This category includes intermittent explosive disorder, kleptomania (recurrent failure to resist impulses to steal objects not needed), pyromania (patterns of fire setting for pleasure, gratification, or relief of tension), pathological gambling, and trichotillomania (recurrent pulling out of one's hair).

15. *Adjustments disorders*. These disorders relate to the development of clinically significant behavioral or emotional symptoms in response to identifiable psychosocial stressors. These disorders are of less severity and/or duration than posttraumatic stress disorder or acute stress reactions.

16. *Personality disorders*. The disorders in this category are characterized by enduring patterns of inner experience and behavior that deviate markedly from those expected within the context of one's culture. To be considered a personality disorder, these patterns must be inflexible and pervasive, stable over time, and lead to distress or impairment. The personality disorders include paranoid, schizoid, schizotypal, antisocial, borderline, histrionic, narcissistic, avoidant, dependent, and obsessive-compulsive disorders.

17. *Other conditions that may be a focus of clinical attention*. This category includes a collection of disorders that are unrelated to each other, including medication-induced movement disorders, relational problems, problems related to abuse or neglect, noncompliance with treatment, malingering, bereavement, academic, and occupational problems.

Although these diagnostic categories are useful for obtaining precise diagnoses and prescribing specific treatment plans for mentally ill patients, they have not been used extensively by those who set policy and distribute resources nationally. Rather, the concept of "severe mental illness" has evolved, and those with mental disorders that fall into this broad category have been targeted to receive services. This group represents approximately 3 percent of the U.S. population (see Figure 10–1).[15, 16]

According to the National Advisory Mental Health Council,[17] severe mental illness encompasses a group of discrete mental disorders that differ in cause, course, and treatment. This population encompasses people afflicted with schizophrenia, schizoaffective disorders, autism, affective disorders (bipolar, formerly called manic-depressive disorder and severe depression), other psychotic disorders, as well as some of the anxiety disorders (severe panic disorders and obsessive-compulsive disorders). In addition to carrying a primary psychiatric diagnosis, people with severe mental illness are highly likely to have additional problems with substance abuse, as well as developmental disorders that are neurologically based (e.g., mental retardation or specific learning disabilities). These conditions further compromise patients' abilities to function.

The coexistence of two diagnoses is called "comorbidity" in the health field. According to the ECA Study, in one year, people with substance use disorders made 56.3 million visits to ambulatory mental health/addiction services. Of these, 62 percent were visits made by those with comorbid substance use and mental disorders.[18] In further

Figure 10–1 Percentages of the U.S. Adult Population with Mental Disorders and Severe Mental Disorders, Including Users of Mental Health Services, in One Year
Source: American Journal of Psychiatry, Vol. 150, p. 1449, 1993. Copyright 1993, the American Psychiatric Association; <http://AJP.psychiatryonline.org>. Reprinted by permission.

ECA studies, in both clinical and nonclinical settings, the prevalence of substance abuse comorbidity has been determined for specific psychiatric disordered patients. These findings indicated a range in prevalence of 23 to 80 percent, depending on diagnosis.[19] Specific rates are found in Table 10–2.

Substantial comorbidity also has been documented among people with mental retardation. In studies of clinical populations of people with mental retardation, 30 to 67 percent have been found to have comorbid psychiatric disorders.[20] The importance of these epidemiologic studies cannot be overemphasized because research on service provision to subpopulations with substantial comorbidity has demonstrated that comorbidity adds significantly to the complexity of providing adequate and effective treatments. The implications to resource allocation are considerable.

Only a little over half of the people who are most vulnerable and have severe mental illness use mental health services. It should be noted, however, that use of services does not imply adequate access or use of efficacious services. Although some of these individuals have severe disabilities, are treatment resistant, and hence, require life-long supervision of living arrangements, the vast majority are people who,

Table 10–2 Prevalence Rates for Comorbidity in the Psychiatric Setting Compared with the General Population

DIAGNOSIS COMORBIDITY	PREVALENCE RATE: CLINICAL SETTING*	PREVALENCE RATE: NONCLINICAL— MALE[a]	PREVALENCE RATE NONCLINICAL— FEMALE[b]	RATIO: CLINICAL TO NONCLINICAL[c]
Depressive disorders	30	8	23.4	3.8/1.3
Bipolar disorders	50	0.8	3.1	62.5/16.1
Schizophrenia	50	2.4	7.2	20.8/6.9
Antisocial personality disorders	80	14.6	10.1	5.5/7.9
Anxiety disorders	30	2.1[d]	7.9[d]	14.3/3.8
Phobic disorders	23	13.5	33.1	1.7/0.7

* Percent of patients diagnosed with comorbid addictive disorder.
[a] Percent of male population with comorbid psychiatric and addictive disorders.
[b] Percent of female population with comorbid psychiatric and addictive disorders.
[c] Ratio of clinical to nonclinical male; ratio of clinical to nonclinical female.
[d] Panic disorder.

Source: Reprinted with permission from N.S. Miller and J. Fine, "Current Epidemiology of Comorbidity of Psychiatric and Addictive Disorders," *Psychiatric Clinics of North America,* Vol. 16, p. 4, © 1993, Elsevier

with accurate diagnosis and access to efficacious treatment and rehabilitative services, can lead productive and fulfilling lives in the community. Yet many of these individuals go undiagnosed or untreated.

Children and Adolescents

Data on service use by children and adolescents with diagnoses of mental disorder and at least minimal impairment only recently have become
available from a National Institute of Mental Health survey of children
and adolescents between 9 and 17 years of age.[21] Almost 21 percent of
children and adolescents had some evidence of distress or impairment
associated with a specific diagnosis and also had at least a minimal level
of impairment on a global assessment measure. Approximately 9 percent of the entire child/adolescent sample (less than one-half of those affected) received some mental health services in the general medical and
specialty mental health delivery sectors, although the largest provider
of services to this population group was the school system.[22]

Clinical research targeted toward determining effective treatments
for children and adolescents suffering from mental illness has lagged
considerably behind that for adults. Although diagnostic techniques
have been highly refined through standardized diagnostic interviews
and symptom rating scales that facilitate the accurate identification of
those in need of service, research funding for treatment of mental illness in childhood and adolescence is decreasing. The effects of a mental
disorder on the developmental process of children are only beginning to
be appreciated, but they clearly interfere with emotional, social, and
cognitive growth and development. The need for early intervention that
provides treatment and rehabilitation is urgent. Yet few practitioners
have access to research findings regarding treatment efficacy, and few
well-trained child and adolescent psychiatrists are available to the population at risk. Some progress has been made in both psychopharmacological interventions and the development of specific, diagnosis-tar-
geted, psychosocial treatments of proven efficacy. If the needs of
children with mental illness are to be met, much more research is ur-
gently needed. The results of newer research on effective treatments of
specific disorders need widespread dissemination, with improved training and skills of those providing services for children and adolescents.

Older Adults

Although considerable advances have been made in the treatment of
mental disorders, a crisis looms in providing mental health services to
the older population. By the year 2020, the "baby boomers" will reach
age 65, with the result that almost 55 million Americans will be classified as "elderly."[23] In addition to sheer volume, epidemiologic studies
have indicated that baby-boomer cohorts have high prevalence rates

for depression, suicide, anxiety, and alcohol and drug abuse.[24, 25] The implications for resource allocation in light of these findings are enormous, particularly at a time when Medicare funding is being curtailed and the costs of pharmaceuticals are skyrocketing.

Older adults suffer from many of the same mental disorders suffered by their younger counterparts. However, assessment and diagnosis may be more difficult and complicated because of accompanying medical conditions that mimic or mask mental disorders and patients' reluctance to accurately report symptoms. Patients may tend to emphasize physical complaints and minimize complaints about their mental status. In addition, stereotypes about aging, leading older adults to believe that mental changes are to be expected, can make assessment and diagnosis particularly challenging.[26]

Primary care providers carry much of the burden of diagnosing mental disorders in older adults, and the rates at which they recognize and properly identify disorders often are low. In addition, primary care providers may be reluctant to communicate a diagnosis of mental disorder to their patients and have strikingly low confidence rates in diagnosing and prescribing treatments for these disorders.[27] Researchers estimate that as much as 63 percent of older adults with mental disorders may not be receiving treatment.[28]

Research is sorely needed on the treatment of some of the anxiety disorders and substance use disorders in older adults. Coordination of health care with monitoring of medications and their interactions is critical because older patients are frequently on many prescribed drugs that may affect behavior, mood, and cognition. The treatment of psychiatric disorders in older adults differs from that for other age groups because it must take into account anticipated drug interactions and age-related changes in metabolism and physiological function that affect drug levels and drug elimination. Progressive social isolation and financial losses also clearly affect symptom formation and may have substantial effects on treatment responsiveness and outcome.

The Organization and Financing of Mental Health Services

Mental health problems and disorders are treated by an array of providers representing several disciplines working in a diverse array of public and private settings. The loose coordination of facilities and services has resulted in the mental health delivery system being referred to as a "de facto mental health service system."[29] The system is usually described as having four major components:[30]

1. *The specialty mental health sector* with mental health professionals such as psychiatrists, psychologists, psychiatric nurses, and psychiatric social workers provides the majority of care in outpatient settings, private office practices, or private or public clinics. Most acute hospital care is provided in psychiatric units

of general hospitals or beds located throughout the hospitals.[31] Intensive treatment for adults and children is provided in private psychiatric hospitals or residential treatment centers for children and adolescents. Public sector facilities include state and county mental hospitals and multiservice facilities that provide or coordinate a wide range of outpatient, intensive case management, partial hospitalization, or inpatient services.

2. *The general medical / primary care sector* consists of health care professionals such as internists, pediatricians, and nurse practitioners in private office-based practices, clinics, hospitals, and nursing homes. This sector often is the initial point of contact and may be the only source of mental health services for a large proportion of mental health patients.

3. *The human services sector* is composed of social service agencies, school-based counseling services, residential rehabilitation services, vocational rehabilitation services, criminal justice/prison-based services, and religious professional counselors.

4. *The voluntary support network sector* consists of self-help groups and is a rapidly growing component of the mental health system.

Figure 10–2 illustrates the diversity of service types and settings that characterize acute and long-term care mental health services delivered under both public and private sponsorship.

The provision of mental health services has been funded in many ways, including private health insurance, Medicaid, Medicare, state

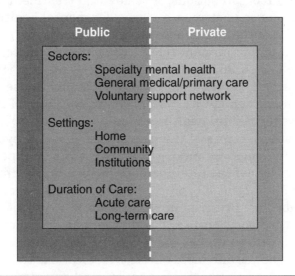

Figure 10–2 The Mental Health Service System
Source: Reprinted from *Mental Health: A Report of the Surgeon General,* 1999, Department of Health and Human Services.

and local services provided directly or through contracts with local agencies, Veterans Affairs hospitals and clinics, and other programs for specialized populations. Because many U.S. citizens lack basic health insurance coverage, and benefits provided by third-party payers for the treatment of mental disorders are more limited than benefits for the treatment of other health problems, people with severe mental illness are often in a position that necessitates dependency on the welfare system for services and supports for basic living.[32–36]

In his review on the establishment of mental health priorities, D. Mechanic writes that:

> . . . mental health policy has evolved in a disjointed and nonlinear fashion, reflecting the multiplicity of decision points, prevailing ideologies, emerging technologies, and financial, and other incentives as they interact with the local political, economic, and organizational frameworks of care.[37]

Mental disorders impose an enormous personal and financial burden on ill individuals, their families, and society as a whole. Their national toll is taken in reduced and lost productivity and the use of medical and other resources for diagnosis, treatment, and rehabilitation. The total cost of U.S. mental health services is estimated at $148 billion. In terms of lost productivity, additional indirect costs of all mental illness resulted in a nearly $79 billion loss to the U.S. economy.[38] The direct costs of mental illness include diagnostic and treatment services provided by various mental health practitioners and hospitals, mental health organizations, or residential treatment facilities for adolescents. Because insurance coverage for mental health services is typically less than that for general health care, various government agencies play a more prominent role in financing of services to the seriously mentally ill. In 1996, the United States spent over $99 billion for the direct treatment of mental disorders, substance abuse, Alzheimer's disease, and other dementias.[39] More than two-thirds of this amount, $69 billion, was for mental health services (see Figure 10–3).[40]

As in other sectors of the health care delivery system, outpatient prescription drugs are among the fastest rising expenses for mental health services. Of the total increase in spending for mental health between 1987 and 1996, 82 percent resulted from the increased use of psychotropic drugs.[41] Prescription drugs account for about 9 percent of total direct mental health costs and reflect, in part, the increasing availability of drugs with improved efficacy in treating mental disorders. Additionally, the newer and more effective medications that have been developed for treating psychosis, depression, and anxiety disorders are more costly than previously developed agents, reflecting both the needs of the pharmaceutical industry to recover research and development expenditures and the industry's drive to maximize profit margins.

Between 1986 and 1996, spending for mental health treatment declined as a percentage of total health spending, and public payers increased their contributions to total mental health spending. Some of the decline in spending for mental health relative to total health care may have been due to reductions in unnecessary or inappropriate hospitalizations and other improvements in efficiency. It may also have reflected increasing reliance on other, nonmental health, public human services and increased barriers to service access.[42]

■ Health Insurance Coverage and Managed Behavioral Health Care

The history of health insurance coverage for mental health services has been sullied by some of the private treatment providers being driven by financial considerations rather than by clinical need, resulting in an exaggeration of the severity of clinical diagnoses in order to maximize payments. Additionally, because coverage has been so limited for ambulatory services, hospitalization was overprescribed.[43] Mary Jane England, president of the American Psychiatric Association from 1995 to 1996, stated that costs had been increased "through sophisticated marketing campaigns targeting adolescents and substance abusers, resulting in many unjustified and even harmful hospitalizations as well as sharply increased costs."[44] On the other end of the continuum, those with severe and persistent psychiatric disorders—those who truly needed intensive services—found

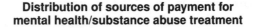

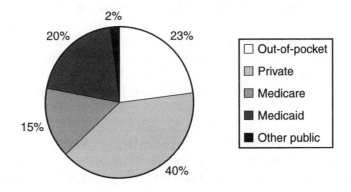

Figure 10–3 Distribution of Sources of Payment for Mental Health/Substance Abuse Treatment
Source: Created from: S.H. Zuvekas, "Trends in Mental Health Spending, 1987–1996," *Health Affairs,* Vol. 20, no. 2, p. 218.

that inpatient benefits would be used up before stabilization was gained. Less costly forms of intensive treatment, such as partial hospitalization and day hospitalization programs, frequently were not covered by insurance plans, resulting in the ill patient being transferred from the private into the public sector the moment insurance coverage was depleted. This transfer resulted in interrupted treatment, changes in providers, loss of continuity, substantial financial hardship, and impoverishment.

In the public sector, insurance programs, including those of federal, state, and local government, provided payment for services based on units of service delivered, called "the deliverables." Limits were placed on the duration of inpatient treatment, particularly through Medicare, but not substantially on the duration of day treatment, partial hospitalization, or outpatient treatments. Financial incentives were solidly in place for providing increased units of service. As long as need could be documented, there were few checks and balances on the use of ambulatory services or on evaluation of treatment efficacy, as long as payment would be forthcoming.[45] Mental health professionals, particularly in ambulatory settings, were frequently psychodynamically trained and provided patients with generic outpatient care, not targeted treatments of proven efficacy for specific psychiatric disorders. Bringing new research findings to clinicians in the trenches and retraining and reengineering service delivery are costly. Consequently, for as long as financial incentives for change were lacking, minimal effort went into ensuring that clinicians were providing state-of-the-art interventions. Incentives ensured that practitioners overused ambulatory services. Also, the private sector increased its use of inpatient services, and both sectors escalated their indicators of diagnostic severity. This not only resulted in an increase in the costs of caring for people with mental illness, but also provided support for assumptions held by third-party payers that:[46]

- Costs of psychiatric treatment are uncontrollable and unpredictable.
- Coverage encourages unnecessary and excessive use.
- Mental health care is not cost-effective.
- Psychiatric treatment is not accountable to insurance carriers

In fact, it appears that inadequate health insurance coverage for mental health services has paradoxically provided financial incentives for some private practitioners to abuse the system, resulting in increased use and costs without ensuring access to quality and efficacious care. Saul Feldman, chairman of the board at U.S. Behavioral Health and former director of the staff college at the National Institute of Mental Health, has summarized the financial incentives of the 1980s and 1990s by stating that without a structure for ensuring utilization review, the problem becomes one of "people getting too much of the wrong care, in the wrong place."[47]

In the mid-1990s, expenditures for health care hit new highs in the United States. Dramatic cost increases for mental health care paralleled those of the rest of medicine. Between 1986 and 1990, employer spending for meeting the mental health component of health care costs increased by 50 percent, with the most generous plans reflecting the greatest increases.[48] Feldman noted the following in his analysis of the role of the market in shaping new directions for mental health care:

> *But the greatest contributors to the development of managed mental health, a development they now bemoan, have been the service providers themselves, practitioners and facilities. By not paying sufficient attention to or not caring about costs and length of treatments, they killed or at least seriously wounded the goose that laid the golden egg, a goose that for them is not likely ever to be as prolific. It is ironic that those who are most unhappy about the advent of managed mental health have done the most to bring it about![49]*

As a consequence of these escalating costs, mechanisms for financing mental health services have been restructured radically. Managed care has been developed to manage costs through the provision of financial incentives that reward outcome, not service utilization. In fact, with managed care systems for people with mental illness, utilization is tightly controlled, and heavy users of mental health services are closely monitored.

Today, over 175 million Americans, more than 90 percent of all privately insured individuals, receive their health coverage through their employer. In 2002, 95 percent of all workers covered by employer benefits were enrolled in some type of managed care plan.[50] Under managed care contracts, mental health benefits are more limited than in other contracts. Packages typically cover a maximum of 20 outpatient visits and 30 days of hospitalization per year, far too little for those with severe and persistent mental illness. Managed care firms have frequently handled concerns about the costs associated with chronic mental illness by not incorporating coverage for these disorders in their basic contracts.[51] Insurers have additionally protected themselves from "catastrophic" costs by setting annual or lifetime limits upon benefit amounts that would be paid for mental illnesses. Nonetheless, even with these exaggerated concerns regarding costs, the growth of managed care has spawned an enormous managed behavioral health care industry with $4.4 billion in annual revenues, covering 176.8 million Americans. Concerns that the "worried well" would consume a disproportionate amount of service have resulted in insurers and health maintenance organizations (HMOs) instituting strict criteria for accessing reimbursement for mental health services. Utilization review mechanisms have been developed that require preapproval before referral for service.[52] Concerns regarding the potential costs of caring for those with severe and persistent mental illness have resulted in the majority of insurers and HMOs seeking mechanisms for offsetting financial risk through contracting with external vendors rather than providing or overseeing the provision of psychiatric care themselves.[53] Such patterns of delegation of both responsibility and financial risk to external vendors are referred to as "carve-outs."

There appear to be three stages in the evolution of behavioral health care carve-outs nationally.[54] The first is one in which the insurer, self-insured employer, or HMO contracts with a managed behavioral health care company (MBHCC) to offer services to all those with psychiatric or addictive disorders at a capitated rate (a designated amount per insured person per month). The MBHCC, in turn, contracts with local providers at a discounted fee for service. The MBHCC seeks to contain costs by maximizing the fee-for-service discount and terminating providers who are heavy users of costly services. In areas with a surplus of providers, this strategy has been effective in achieving heavily discounted fees for service, with providers experiencing considerable reduction in income. Partly in response to such financial pressure, many providers have organized into behavioral health networks. Such networks insist on group contracts, and provider membership is often contingent on providers agreeing to refuse individual contracts with insurers. Such structure provides a mechanism for limiting the discounting of fees for service. Behavioral health networks offer a broad continuum of services and usually utilize less expensive providers for time-intensive services such as psychosocial interventions. However, some insurers will not reimburse some of the low-cost providers (e.g., master's degree–level psychologists), thus setting the stage for further evolution of behavioral health carve-outs.

Carve-outs evolve into their second stage of development through increased "downstreaming" of financial risk. The insurer or HMO capitates with the MBHCC, which in turn capitates with the behavioral health network of providers. The unfortunate effect of this arrangement is that the provision of health care starts to resemble the selling of goods from third-world countries. Mainly the provider of the desired product receives only a small percentage of the money designated for the provision of the product because money is siphoned off by "middle men." The insurer, the HMO, and the MBHCC all take a slice of the capitated amount for service. The actual provider network may receive as little as $0.50 to $0.75 per member per month to cover total costs of providing behavioral health care to a designated population. The consequence of this cascading effect is that less money is available to support actual services to those in greatest need.

The third stage in managing behavioral health carve-outs is reached when provider groups or networks assume full risk and contract directly with corporations or government for the provision of behavioral health services to a defined population. Whether provider networks can (1) organize and position themselves to determine need, (2) control access to costly services based on need, (3) manage care through the behavioral health care continuum of service, (4) monitor quality as related to outcome, and (5) ensure that providers offer only cost-effective, state-of-the-art services is yet to be determined. Theoretically, by contracting directly to provide care to designated populations for a specific amount of money per covered life, provider networks could eliminate the costs of the insurer, the HMO, and the MBHCC, resulting in more resources to those in need of service. However, a potential conflict of interest is clearly present in such a system, because if patients are limited in their consumption of services, then more money is left for distribution to the providers. The risk of denying access to care in order to increase "profits" or bonuses to providers is ever present.

Recently, some insurers have stopped carving out behavioral health care and have capitated with health care networks to provide all the health care needs of a designated population. Such a practice passes the risk of chronic illness on to the health care provider network. Provider networks have, in turn, carved out behavioral health care either through discounted fees for service or capitated arrangements. Experience with such practice patterns is still limited. Outcome and financial data have yet to be analyzed.

As in managed care generally, the growing preoccupation with cost containment and tight oversight of service patterns has produced increasingly strict management of service utilization. Oversight is usually provided by a qualified person, usually remote from the site of service, who monitors rendered or proposed care using predetermined, protocol-driven criteria. Communication between the reviewer and provider is usually by telephone. Both positive and negative effects can be realized by such oversight. Positively, clinicians who have the skill to treat patients with concentrated, brief, but efficient treatments that limit hospitalization are rewarded. Standardization of care through the use of protocols with demonstrated efficacy is encouraged, thus potentially reducing much of the individual provider variations from medical care. Unmonitored provision of services with dubious levels of efficacy can be reduced as can the excessive use of hospitalization. On the other hand, service authorization by remote utilization managers, who are working from protocols that may not fit individual patients and who may not know the providers' credentials, expertise, and competence, may not be in the best interest of quality patient care.

Public sector initiatives recently have paralleled private sector efforts to control mental health services costs. Throughout the 1990s, state governments experiencing dramatic increases in Medicaid spending sought ways to control costs of mental health services for public beneficiaries. States, such as Massachusetts and Iowa, began contracting with MBHCCs in the anticipation that they would experience savings similar to private sector employers who were seeing reductions in psychiatric hospitalizations and lengths of stay.[55] For the most part, these programs provide payment for mental health services on a per capita basis. Such an approach builds on the cost savings incentives of managed care firms, relying heavily on closely monitored use of costly services and increased reliance on measuring outcome versus the number of units of service provided. In such systems, less is better, assuming an acceptable outcome level. Only the most preliminary data are available assessing the cost-effectiveness and outcome with managed care approaches in this publicly supported population with special needs. These data, however, are promising and suggest there are no significant differences in outcome, and that cost savings are considerable.[56–59] For example, in Massachusetts, mental health care costs declined 30–40 percent between 1991 and 1995 following the introduction of managed behavioral health care. No decrease in access or quality of care was documented.[60–61] States continue to turn to the managed behavioral health care industry to serve Medicaid and other populations receiving publicly financed mental health benefits. By 2000, over 85 percent of the managed behavioral health market was controlled by 11 managed behavioral health organizations.[62] Managed behavioral health has emerged as a major player in the public sector. Combined federal and state Medicaid spending on mental health and substance abuse was estimated at $21 billion in 1999, with between 25 and 40 percent of those funds being funneled through MBHCCs.[63]

Advocacy to achieve parity in mental health insurance benefits as compared with general health insurance benefits is a continuing issue dating back to the 1950s.[64] "Parity" refers to requirements that insurers cover mental health care at the same level as medical care. The 1990s saw much legislative activity on parity at both the state and federal levels as discrepancies between mental health and medical care coverage grew with claims that private employers and MBHCCs cut both care and costs too drastically.[65] Medical plans typically do not limit the number of covered outpatient visits or inpatient days of care. However, a typical employer-sponsored mental health plan in 1996 carried several limits, often including outpatient-visit or hospital-day limits in addition to annual or lifetime dollar limits in coverage. Discrepancies also occurred in deductibles, copayments, and coinsurance rates.[66] The impact of parity legislation in terms of both costs and quality of care is controversial. Some argue that such mandates would be costly and would have the impact of causing employers to reduce contributions to employee benefits. However, recent empirical studies show that employers switching to managed care see dramatic drops in mental health costs even when benefits are expanded.[67] In 1996, the Mental Health Parity Act of 1997 was introduced into Congress and was passed in 1997 after receiving overwhelming bipartisan support. Effected in 1998, this legislation equates aggregated lifetime limits and annual limits for mental health services with aggregate lifetime and annual limits for medical care. However, the law does allow many cost-shifting mechanisms, such as adjusting limits on mental illness inpatient days, prescription drugs, and outpatient visits; raising coinsurance and deductibles; and modifying the definition of medical necessity.[68] The act unfortunately does not require employers to offer mental health coverage, nor does it impose any limits on coinsurance, deductibles, days, or visits. Furthermore, coverage is not required for people suffering from substance use and abuse disorders, a problem of substantial public health significance.

By the middle of 1999, 24 states had passed mental health parity laws. In 2001, the Mental Health Equitable Treatment Act, which would have expanded coverage to an additional 15 million Americans, was introduced into Congress; however, by the close of 2002, Congress had abandoned the proposed legislation.[69] The states, on the other hand, had taken up the cause of parity with 20 additional states considering some form of mental health parity legislation. It should be noted that although parity legislation focuses on the removal of caps on benefits, which is an important, positive development, there still exist significant mechanisms that create financial barriers to accessing services necessary for people with severe and persistent mental illness. Both employers and insurers have a broad range of alternatives in responding to state and federal parity laws, including totally dropping mental health benefits or imposing other constraints.[70] Recent data from national employer surveys are disconcerting and indicate that mental health benefit coverage has declined considerably. In 1991, 36 percent of employees in all large firms had unlimited mental health outpatient visit benefits; by 1998, only 21 percent of employees had such benefits.[71] In 2002, the figure fell to 12 percent,[72] possibly due, in part, to employer concerns over significantly increasing health insurance premiums.

It is clear that people with severe and persistent mental illness should receive the services and support necessary for them to live relatively stable and high-quality lives within their communities. This population has been subjected to episodic rather than continuous care, in spite of professional community awareness that these people can be treated effectively through medication, support, and structure. Long-term impairments and disabilities require the coordination of enormous resources that cross funding streams and agency interests.

In a national survey conducted by the NAMI, members of families with mentally ill members indicated that:

- 59.3 percent needed help with illness management
- 67.9 percent needed help with crisis management
- 23.1 percent needed help with activities of daily living, including bathing, dressing, and personal hygiene
- 74.3 percent needed help with community living skills, including shopping and managing money
- 64.7 percent needed help with establishing and maintaining friendships
- 72.8 percent needed help with gaining and maintaining productive activities[73]

These issues must be addressed if individuals suffering from mental illness are to live lives not characterized by chaos, poverty, homelessness, and social ostracism.[74] According to extensive studies by the NAMHC, for an additional annual cost of about $6.5 billion, the nation could provide coverage for adults and children with severe mental disorders commensurate with coverage for other types of illness.[75] The NAMHC has presented compelling data that this investment would result in a 10 percent decrease in the use and costs of nonpsychiatric medical services and that this decrease, combined with reductions in indirect costs, would result in a savings of $8.7 billion—an estimated net economic benefit to the nation of $2.2 billion per year. The United States has the scientific, technical, and financial resources necessary to serve this special population suffering severe disabilities. Barriers need to be removed, services reengineered, and access to efficacious treatments ensured.

■ Barriers to Accessing Services

If so many people require mental health services but do not seek them out or receive them, what is preventing them from gaining access to necessary services?

In its introduction to the Special Report on Health Care Reform for Americans with Severe Mental Illnesses in 1993, the NAMHC states:

> *Many myths and misunderstandings contribute to the stigmatization of persons with mental illness and to their often limited access to needed services. For example, millions of Americans and many policy makers are unaware that the efficacy of an extensive array of treatments for specific mental disorders has been systematically tested in controlled clinical trials; these studies demonstrate that mental disorders can now be diagnosed and treated as precisely and effectively as are other disorders in medicine.[76]*

The mentally ill still suffer from stigmatization. A person is much more likely in casual conversation to mention that he or she is going to an appointment with the family doctor or gynecologist than mention an appointment with a psychiatrist. A poignant reminder of the stigmatization of the mentally ill is that in one of the New England states, mental health services were bureaucratically placed in the State Department of Corrections, an action that might be interpreted as mental illness being perceived as a criminal problem. In spite of the past 10 years being the "Decade of the Brain," with enormous advances in delineating the neurobiological basis and treatment of many psychiatric disorders, many people still feel that having a psychiatric disorder is shameful and in some way reflective of personal failure.[77]

Consumer and advocacy groups working with professional societies have done much to dispel the myths fueling these societal misunderstandings. Nonetheless, they continue to exist and provide both direct and indirect barriers to service. Directly, an undetermined number of people may not seek needed care because of personal and familial shame and embarrassment. The indirect consequences are even more significant. Those determining public policy and establishing guidelines for health insurance traditionally have viewed mental illness as being poorly defined, with diagnostic uncertainty and ineffective treatments. A major consequence of this misinformation is that health insurance coverage for psychiatric disorders continues to lag considerably behind coverage for other medical conditions.[78–82] The 1999 surgeon general's report on mental health emphasizes that dispelling the myths that contribute to stigmatization must be made a major national priority.[83]

■ Priorities for Mental Health Services

The NIMH National Plan delineates five essential areas that should be addressed in developing a comprehensive national plan for mental health services. These include:[84, 85]

1. *Epidemiology*. Accurate and current epidemiologic databases are available and need to be used to delineate the characteristics of those seeking mental health services, their demographics, risk factors, and cultural and family issues. Services need to be designed in accord with actual need and geographic distribution of need. Services need to be provided by mental health professionals who have the appropriate training in treatments of proven efficacy and the commitment to provide care with sensitivity and respect for factors associated with cultural and familial diversity.

2. *Assessment*. Assessment techniques used throughout various programs providing services for citizens with mental disorders vary tremendously in comprehensiveness, usability, sensitivity, and

selectivity. Accurate, standardized assessment tools have been developed. The best need wide dispersion, and mental health professionals need training to achieve complete, accurate assessment.

3. *Treatment.* The gap between empirical research findings on the efficacy of specific pharmacological and psychosocial treatments and the use of these treatments in clinical settings is enormous. Treatment plans need to be rescued from the ideology of the past, the conventional wisdom of what works best. Effective treatments need to be made available to those in need. This means that dollars must be allocated for training and retraining mental health professionals in these newer techniques. Third-party payers need to evaluate which treatments being prescribed for specific disorders actually are effective before approval of payment. Such action will facilitate the move away from the traditions of the past and increase the likelihood of interventions resulting in functional improvement.

4. *Rehabilitation and habilitation.* Treatment goals must extend beyond the remission or reduction of acute symptoms. The onset of severe mental illness is likely to occur at critical times in a person's development, resulting in impairments in educational, vocational, and social achievement. Quality-of-life issues are critical if patients with severe and persistent mental illness are to lead fulfilling and productive lives. Studies comparing patients with and without access to rehabilitative services have demonstrated that those with access have lower hospitalization rates; increased independent living, employment, and social capabilities; and greater satisfaction with life.[86] In brief, the indirect social costs of mental illness decrease substantially with the utilization of rehabilitative services.

5. *Outcome.* Payment systems for mental health services are rapidly moving away from providing incentives for increasing the units of service provided. Fiscal incentives are being developed within managed care firms and capitated systems that provide financial rewards based on outcome. Mental health services need to be evaluated systematically across four outcome domains: (1) clinical symptoms, (2) social and vocational functioning, (3) sense of well-being for the consumer and his or her family, and (4) public welfare benefits (indirect social costs).

Payment systems dependent on outcome criteria may do much to hasten the application of recent scientific advances to the care of mental illness. Managed care systems can supply an incentive for emphasizing quality over quantity in mental health care. However, the unique needs of these patients must be recognized, and the services to them designed sensitively and realistically.

Caring for the mentally ill is costly, but the money and expertise are there for providing a rational and effective system, as long as these resources are channeled wisely. Unfortunately, some recent cases have come to light where chief executive officers and shareholders of for-profit managed care firms have diverted money needed for patient care to such self-serving purposes as seven- and eight-figure compensation packages and private planes. To the extent that our society allows such practices to persist, a portion of our population suffering from severe and chronic mental illness will be denied services and continue to experience homelessness and other dehumanizing conditions."

As the stages of organization of behavioral health care provisions evolve, the critical question will be whether the management of health care money will benefit those in need of care through an outcome-driven behavioral system or whether it will simply be redistributed among the insurers, HMOs, MBHCCs, and providers without substantial benefit to patient care. The need to retrain behavioral health providers to ensure that they possess the knowledge base and skills emerging from cutting-edge research is critical. Ensuring that scarce health care dollars benefit the patients who need mental health services will require creativity and the collaborative work of patient advocates, providers, business, and government if the interests of those suffering from mental illness are to be safeguarded.

■ Need for Further Research

Over the last 10 years, health systems research has increased.[87–91] Considering that health care is the second largest industry in the United States, with total health care costs topping $1.3 trillion for 2000,[92] there still is a strong need for well-designed studies that examine the effects of patterns and modalities of care on both mental and physical outcomes. For the most part, health care continues to be provided on the basis of conventional wisdom,[93] variously modified by incentives targeted toward cost containment. A prominent researcher observes:

> *The major part of health care is based on beliefs and on experience gained by generations, rather than on "scientific" knowledge. Cost and benefits of treatments, interventions, and strategies have only very rarely been established. Recommendations concerning treatments are almost always well-phrased beliefs, for which, however, there is rarely any evidence.*[94]

A variety of systems have evolved to provide mental health services. These systems differ widely in what services are provided, for whom, by whom, and in what setting. Decisions regarding resource allocation rarely are made on the basis of documented need and the distribution of psychiatric illness in U.S. communities. Instead, they are made in our nation's capital or in state assemblies or legislatures. Choices of specific services are based on beliefs held by generations of psychiatrists and other mental health professionals rather than on demonstrated efficacy. The gap between research and practice continues to be considerable. Although cost-containment efforts through managed care have increased the use of effective psychopharmacological agents for treating people with psychiatric disorders, the use of psychosocial interventions with demonstrated efficacy that goes beyond that of pharmacologic agents has been minimal.[95]

The 1999 U.S. surgeon general's report on mental health called for continued efforts to "build the science base" in mental health and illness. Citing developments in the neurosciences and molecular genetics that can offer promising opportunities for research and future treatment applications, the report also highlighted the research challenges inherent in new clinical and health services interventions posed by the evolution of new pharmacologic agents and psychotherapies.[96] Today, scientific research into mental health and illness is referred to as "bottom-up" and "top-down." "Bottom up" refers to research that examines the most fundamental levels of brain functioning such as neurochemical activity and genetics, and their interactions with environmental influences. "Top-down" research refers to research into the broader behavioral context of the brain's cellular and molecular activity and how individual cells communicate to perform mental functions. New, highly sophisticated laboratory methods as well as computer-aided technologies such as magnetic resonance imaging and positron emission tomography are aiding in advanced research. A major challenge in the near future will be to facilitate transfer of new, evidence-based treatments into diverse service delivery settings and systems, while trying to assure better coordination among the elements of the existing delivery system.[97] Given the complex and fragmented nature of the current system, additional research is needed to enlighten policy makers and administrators on the most effective methods of carrying out this transfer in a patient-centered manner.

With the advent of managed care, accusations have been made that financial incentives are driving the market, and that decisions are being based on economic considerations, not patient need. This is a simplistic analysis of a complicated issue. The delivery of mental health care has been driven for years in part by financial incentives that differ from those present under managed care. More research is needed to identify the impact of changing reimbursement systems on the access, quality, and cost benefit of various types of service arrangements in order to more accurately inform policy makers, payers, clinicians, and advocates. In addition, new methods of measuring functional status can make it possible to determine the impact of treatment on the mental health of the general public, with the potential to develop mechanisms to monitor indicators of mental health on a nationally representative sample, similar to studies done for physical illnesses.[98] Additional research on measurement methods and their transfer to the mental health field will be central to accomplishing this goal.

By an executive order issued in 2002, President Bush established the Freedom Commission on Mental Health, whose mission is to conduct a comprehensive review of the mental health service delivery system and "to recommend improvements to enable adults with serious mental illness and children with serious emotional disturbances to live, work, learn and participate fully in their communities."[99] The commission issued an interim progress report six months after its establishment, which stated that, "America's mental health service delivery system is in shambles." Further describing the system as severely fragmented, the report cites needless suffering, frustrated caregivers, and millions of dollars in wasted resources.[100] Referring to the 1999 surgeon general's report, the commission expressed optimism that its final recommendations will clarify how the effective treatments already available can be made accessible to the millions in need through a dramatically reformed mental health delivery system. More time is needed to determine the impact of the Freedom Commission's review and recommendations for system change.

■ Notes

1. J.S. Bockoven, *Moral Treatment in Community Mental Health* (New York: Springer Publishing Co., 1972).
2. J.P. Morrissey and H.H. Goldman, "Cycles of Reform in the Care of the Chronically Mentally Ill," *Hospital and Community Psychiatry* 35 (1984): 785–789.
3. W. Gronfein, "Incentives and Intentions in Mental Health Policy: A Comparison of the Medicaid and Community Mental Health Programs," *Journal of Health and Social Behavior* 26 (1985): 192–206.
4. D. Mechanic, *Mental Health and Social Policy*, 3d ed. (Englewood Cliffs, NJ: Prentice Hall, 1989), 27–46.
5. G.L. Klerman, "The Psychiatric Revolution of the Past 25 Years," in *Deviance and Mental Illness*, ed. W.R. Gove (Newbury Park, CA: Sage Publishing, 1982), 180.
6. D. Mechanic, "Establishing Mental Health Priorities," *The Milbank Quarterly* 72 (1994): 501–514.
7. R.W. Redick et al., "The Evolution and Expansion of Mental Health Care in the United States Between 1955 and 1990," in *Mental Health Statistical Note* 210 (Washington, DC: U.S. Department of Health and Human Services, 1994).
8. G. Norquist and S.E. Hyman, "Advances in Understanding and Treating Mental Illness: Implications for Policy," *Health Affairs* 18, no. 5 (1999): 36.

9. D.A. Regier et al., "The De Facto U.S. Mental and Addictive Disorders Service System: Epidemiological Catchment Area Prospective 1-Year Prevalence Rate of Disorders and Services," *Archives General Psychiatry* 50 (1993): 85–94.

10. D.A. Regier et al., "The Chronically Mentally Ill in Primary Care," *Psychology Medicine* 15 (1995): 265–273.

11. R.C. Kessler et al., "The 12-Month Prevalence and Correlates of Serious Mental Illness (SMI)," in *Center for Mental Health Services, Mental Health United States, 1996* (DHHS Publication No. SMA 96-3098), eds. R.W. Manderscheid & M.A. Sonnenschein (Washington, DC: Superintendent of Documents, U.S. Government Printing Office), 59–70.

12. U.S. Department of Health and Human Services, *Mental Health: A Report of the Surgeon General—Chapter 6* (Rockville, MD: U.S. Department of Health and and Human Services, Substance And Mental Health Services Administration, Center for Mental Health Services, National Institutes of Health, National Institute of Mental Health, 1999), 408.

13. U.S. Department of Health and Human Services, *Mental Health: A Report of the Surgeon General*, 72–73.

14. American Psychiatric Association, *Diagnostic and Statistical Manual*, 4th ed. (Washington, DC: American Psychiatric Press, 1994).

15. P.R. Barker et al., *Serious Mental Illness and Disability in the Adult Household Population: Data from Vital and Health Statistics, no. 218* (Hyattsville, MD: National Center for Health Statistics, 1992).

16. National Advisory Mental Health Council, "Health Care Reform for Americans with Severe Mental Illnesses: Report of the National Advisory Mental Health Council," *American Journal of Psychiatry* 150 (1993): 1447–1465.

17. National Advisory Mental Health Council, "Health Care Reform for Americans with Severe Mental Illnesses."

18. W.E. Narrow et al., "Use of Services by Persons with Mental and Addictive Disorders," *Archives of General Psychiatry* 50 (1993): 95–107.

19. D.A. Regier et al., "Comorbidity of Mental Disorders with Alcohol and Other Drug Abuse: Results from the Epidemiological Catchment Area (ECA) Study," *Journal of the American Medical Association* 264 (1991): 2511–2518.

20. M. Campbell and R.P. Malone, "Mental Retardation and Psychiatric Disorders," *Hospital and Community Psychiatry* 42 (1991): 374–379.

21. U.S. Department of Health and Human Services, *Mental Health: A Report of the Surgeon General*, 409.

22. U.S. Department of Health and Human Services, *Mental Health: A Report of the Surgeon General*, 409.

23. U.S. Senate Special Subcommittee on Aging, *Aging America: Trends and Projections* (Washington, DC: U.S. Department of Health and Human Services, 1998).

24. D.A. Regier et al., "One Month Prevalence of Mental Disorders in the United States: Based on Five Epidemiological Catchment Area Sites," *Archives of General Psychiatry* 45 (1988): 977–986.

25. G.L. Klerman and M.M. Weissman, "Increasing Rates of Depression," *Journal of the American Medical Association* 261 (1989): 2229–2235.

26. U.S. Department of Health and Human Services, *Mental Health: A Report of the Surgeon General—Chapter 5*, 340–341.

27. U.S. Department of Health and Human Services, *Mental Health: A Report of the Surgeon General*, 340.

28. U.S. Department of Health and Human Services, *Mental Health: A Report of the Surgeon General*, 341.

29. D.A. Regier et al., "The De Facto U.S. Mental and Addictive Disorders Service System: Epidemiological Catchment Area Prospective 1-Year Prevalence Rate of Disorders and Services," 85–94.

30. U.S. Department of Health and Human Services, *Mental Health: A Report of the Surgeon General*, 406–407.

31. U.S. Department of Health and Human Services, *Mental Health: A Report of the Surgeon General*, 406.

32. A.P. Blostin, "Mental Health Benefits Financed by Employers," *Monthly Labor Review* 110 (1987): 23–27.

33. U.S. Department of Labor, Bureau of Labor Statistics, "National Compensation Survey: Employee Benefits in Private Industry in the United States, 2000." http://www.bls.gov/ncs/ebs/sp/ebbl0019.pdf (January 2003) Accessed 12 April 2003.

34. C.A. Taube et al., "Medicaid Coverage for Mental Illness: Balancing Access and Costs," *Health Affairs* 9 (1990): 5–18.

35. J.R. Lave and H.H. Goldman, "Medicare Financing for Mental Health Care," *Health Affairs* 9 (1990): 19–30.

36. A. Rupp, "Under Insurance for Severe Mental Illness," *Schizophrenia Bulletin* 17 (1991): 401–405.

37. D. Mechanic and D. Rochefort, "Deinstitutionalization: An Appraisal of Reform," *Annual Review of Sociology* 16 (1990): 301–327.

38. National Alliance for the Mentally Ill, "Facts and Figures about Mental Illness," http://www.nami.org (20 January 2001). Accessed 3 January 2003.

39. U.S. Department of Health and Human Services, *Mental Health: A Report of the Surgeon General*, 412.

40. S.H. Zuvekas, "Trends in Mental Health Services Use and Spending: 1987–1996," *Health Affairs* 20, no. 2 (2001), 218.

41. S.H. Zuvekas, "Trends in Mental Health Services Use and Spending: 1987–1996," 215.

42. U.S. Department of Health and Human Services, *Mental Health: A Report of the Surgeon General*, 417.

43. I. Strumwassen et al., "Appropriateness of Psychiatric and Substance Abuse Hospitalizations," *Medical Care* 29 (1991): AS77–AS89.

44. M.J. England and V.V. Goff, "Health Reform and Organized Systems of Care," in *New Directions for Mental Health Services*, eds. M.J. England and V.V. Goff (San Francisco: Jossey-Bass, Publishers, 1993), 5–12.

45. P.G. Frank and J. Lave, "Economics of Managed Mental Health," in *Managed Mental Health Services*, ed. S. Feldman (Springfield, IL: Charles C Thomas, 1992), 83–99.

46. S.T. Sharfstein et al., "Mental Health Services," in *Health Care Delivery in the United States*, 5th ed., ed. A. Kovner (New York: Springer Publishing Co., 1995), 232–266.

47. S. Feldman, *Managed Mental Health Services* (Springfield, IL: Charles C Thomas, 1992), xiv.

48. J. Gabel, "Job-Based Health Benefits in 2002: Some Important Trends," *Health Affairs* 21, no. 5 (2002), 143.

49. Feldman, *Managed Mental Health Services*.

50. Kaiser Family Foundation and Health Research and Educational Trust, "*2002 Survey of Employer-Sponsored Health Benefits, Chart 11,*"http://www.kff.org/content/2002/20020905a. (Fall 2002) Accessed 10 September 2002.

51. J.K. Iglehart, "Health Policy Report: Managed Care and Mental Health," *New England Journal of Medicine* 334 (1996): 131–135.

52. P.J. Boyle and D. Callahan, "Managed Care in Mental Health: The Ethical Issues," *Health Affairs* 14 (suppl. 3) (1995): 7–22.

53. D. Hodgkin et al., "Make or Buy: HMOs' Contracting Arrangements for Mental Health Care," *Administration and Policy in Mental Health* 24, no. 4 (March 1997): 359–376.

54. R.E. Meyer and C.J. McLaughlin, "The Response of Academic Psychiatry to Managed Care: Clinical Delivery Systems," in *Between Mind, Brain and Managed Care*, eds. R.E. Meyer and C.J. McLaughlin (Washington, DC: American Psychiatric Press, Inc., 1998), 28.

55. M.H. Bailit and L.L. Burgess, "Competing Interests: Public-Sector Managed Behavioral Health Care," *Health Affairs* 18, no. 5 (1999): 112–113.

56. H. Davidson et al., "State Purchase of Mental Health Care: Models and Motivations for Monitoring Accountability," *International Journal of Law and Psychiatry* 14 (1991): 387–403.

57. A. Brotman, "Privatization of Mental Health Services: The Massachusetts Experiment," *Journal of Health Politics, Policy & Law* 17 (1992): 541–551.

58. R.E. Johnson and B.H. McFarland, "Treated Prevalence Rate of Severe Mental Illness among HMO Members," *Hospital and Community Psychiatry* 45 (1994): 919–924.

59. N. Lurie et al., "Does Capitation Affect the Health of the Chronically Mentally Ill? Results from a Randomized Trial," *Journal of the American Medical Association* 267 (1992): 3300–3304.

60. J.J. Callahan et al., "Mental Health and Substance Abuse Treatment in Managed Care: The Massachusetts Medicaid Experience," *Health Affairs* 14 (1995): 173–184.

61. M.H. Bailit and L.L. Burgess, "Competing Interests: Public-Sector Managed Behavioral Health Care," 121.

62. Center for Mental Health Services, "*Mental Health, United States, 2000,*" R.W. Manderscheid and M.J. Henderson, eds., DHHS Pub No. (SMA) 01-3537 (Washington, DC: Supt. Of Docs., U.S. Govt. Printing Office, 2001). http://www.mentalhealth.org/publications/allpubs/SMA01-3537/chapter9.asp. Accessed 12 April 2003.

63. S. Findlay, "Managed Behavioral Health Care in 1999: An Industry at a Crossroads," 118.

64. R. Sturm and R. Liccardo Pacula, "State Mental Health Parity Laws: Cause or Consequence of Differences in Use?" *Health Affairs* 18, no. 5 (1999): 182–183.

65. Findlay, "Managed Behavioral Health Care in 1999: An Industry at a Crossroads," 117.
66. Sturm and Liccardo Pacula, "State Mental Health Parity Laws: Cause or Consequence of Differences in Use?," 182.
67. Sturm and Liccardo Pacula, "State Mental Health Parity Laws: Cause or Consequence of Differences in Use?," 183.
68. National Alliance for the Mentally Ill, "The Mental Health Parity Act of 1996," http://www.nami.org/update/parity96.html (3 January 1998). Accessed 19 August 2000.
69. National Alliance for the Mentally Ill, "The President, Congress, and the Mental Health Parity Amendment: Let's Hold the Leaders Who Killed It Accountable." http://www.nami.org/pressroom/20011218.html (20 December 2002). Accessed 3 January 2003.
70. Sturm and Liccardo Pacula, "State Mental Health Parity Laws: Cause or Consequence of Differences in Use?," 184.
71. The Kaiser Family Foundation and Health Research and Educational Trust, *Employer Health Benefits Survey 1999*, http://www.kff.org/content/1999/1538/KFFexecsum.pdf (1999). Accessed 18 June 2000.
72. The Kaiser Family Foundation and Health Resource and Educational Trust, *Employer Health Benefits 2002 Annual Survey*, http://www.kff.org/content/2002/3251/3251-section9.pdf. Accessed 3 January 2003.
73. D.M. Steinwachs et al., "Data Watch: Patterns of Use and Costs among Severely Mentally Ill People," *Health Affairs* 11 (1992): 178–185.
74. K. Bridges et al., "Psychiatric Rehabilitation: Redefined for the 1990s," *International Journal of Social Psychiatry* 40 (1994): 1–16.
75. National Advisory Mental Health Council, "Health Care Reform for Americans with Severe Mental Illnesses," 1447–1465.
76. National Advisory Mental Health Council, "Health Care Reform for Americans with Severe Mental Illnesses," 1447–1465.
77. National Institutes of Health, *Basic Behavioral Science Research for Mental Health: A National Investment: A Report of the National Advisory Mental Health Council* (Washington, DC: National Institutes of Health, 1995).
78. Blostin, "Mental Health Benefits Financed by Employers," 23–27.
79. Bureau of Labor Statistics, "Employee Benefits of Medium and Large Firms."
80. Taube et al., "Medicaid Coverage for Mental Illness," 5–18.
81. Lave and Goldman, "Medicare Financing for Mental Health Care," 19–30.
82. Rupp, "Under Insurance for Severe Mental Illness," 401–405.
83. U.S. Department of Health and Human Services, *Mental Health: A Report of the Surgeon General*, 2.
84. C.A. Taube et al., *Caring for People with Severe Mental Disorders: A National Plan of Research to Improve Services* (Washington, DC: National Institute of Mental Health, 1991).
85. T.L. Lalley et al., "Caring for People with Severe Mental Disorders: A National Plan to Improve Services," *Schizophrenia Bulletin* 18 (1992): 559–700.
86. National Advisory Mental Health Council, "Health Care Reform for Americans with Severe Mental Illnesses," 1447–1465.

87. National Institute of Mental Health, *The Future of Mental Health Services Research* (Washington, DC: U.S. Department of Health and Human Services, 1989).

88. Taube et al., *Caring for People with Severe Mental Disorders.*

89. Lalley et al., "Caring for People with Severe Mental Disorders: A National Plan to Improve Services."

90. F.L. Newman et al., "Introduction to the Special Section on Seeking New Methods in Mental Health Services Research," *Journal of Consulting and Clinical Psychology* 61 (1994): 667–669.

91. I.I. Stein and E.J. Hollingsworth, *Maturing Mental Health Systems: New Challenges and Opportunities* (San Francisco: Jossey-Bass, Publishers, 1995).

92. K.R. Levit et al., "Inflation Spurs Health Spending in 2000," *Health Affairs* 21, no. 1 (2002): 172.

93. J.K. Galbraith, *The Affluent Society* (New York: New American Library, 1958).

94. D. Schwelfel, "Studies on the Cost-Effectiveness of Managing Chronic Psychiatric Patients," in *Costs and Effects of Managing Chronic Psychotic Patients*, eds. D. Schwelfel et al. (Berlin: Springer-Verlag, 1988), 6.

95. "Side Effects: Managed Care Focus on Psychiatric Drugs—Alarming Many Doctors," *Wall Street Journal* (1 December 1995), B1.

96. U.S. Department of Health and Human Services, *Mental Health: A Report of the Surgeon General*, 2–3.

97. U.S. Department of Health and Human Services, *Mental Health: A Report of the Surgeon General*, 100.

98. G. Norquist and S.E. Hyman, "Advances in Understanding and Treating Mental Illness: Implications for Policy," 37.

99. White House Office of the Press Secretary, "President's New Freedom Commission on Mental Health," http://www.whitehouse.gov/news/releases/2002/04/20020429-2.html (29 April 2002). Accessed 28 December 2002.

100. U.S. Substance Abuse and Mental Health Services Administration, "Interim Report of the President's New Freedom Commission on Mental Health," http://www.mentalhealth.org/publications/allpubs/NMH02-0144/default.asp (29 October 2002). Accessed 4 January 2003.

Chapter 11

Public Health and the Role of Government in Health Care

This chapter presents the history of governmental efforts to prevent or control the problems of health and disease. Efforts to protect the public's health, begun in early European history and transferred to Colonial America, are traced, with emphasis on their purpose, motivation, and success. The rise and decline of America's once elaborate federal, state, and local partnerships in the delivery of public health services are described, as well as the efforts of private and voluntary agencies. Also discussed are the barriers to effective preventive services that result from the lack of a population perspective in the U.S. health care system. The chapter concludes with a discussion of public health challenges and goals, emerging issues, and the changing role of government.

The term "public health" is usually defined broadly as the efforts made by communities to cope with the health problems that arise when people live in groups. Community life creates the need to control the transmission of communicable diseases, maintain a sanitary environment, provide for safe water and food, and sustain people with disabilities and low-income populations.[1]

The world history of public health is a fascinating study of civilized society's attempts to deal with the biological, social, and environmental forces that have contributed to the pervasive problems of morbidity and mortality, and with the unfortunate citizens who have been handicapped by illness, disability, and poverty. Several books on the history of public health by Columbia University's late public health historian, George Rosen, are highly recommended for those interested in in-depth descriptions. The following observations are presented primarily to set the stage for understanding the development of government's role in the evolution of public health in the United States.

Throughout history, public health activities have reflected the state of knowledge at the time regarding the nature and cause of the diseases that afflict mankind, the practices employed for their control or treatment, and the dominant social ideologies of political jurisdictions. From the concepts of spiritual cleanliness and community responsibility codified by the ancient Hebrews for religious reasons, to the systems of personal hygiene practiced by the Greeks in an effort to achieve a perfect balance between body and mind, ancient civilizations learned patterns of individual behavior that they believed promoted health and reduced the risk of disease. It remained for the Romans, however, to develop public health as a governmental matter beyond individual practice. The feats of engineering and administrative accomplishments that provided the Romans with clean water and effective sewage and swamp drainage systems were the forerunners of politically sanctioned environmental protections of the public's health. In addition, the Roman Empire is given credit for establishing a network of infirmaries to treat illness among the disadvantaged populations. These infirmaries are considered to be the first public hospitals.

The medieval period that followed the fall of Rome was characterized by the disintegration of the cities and the return of anarchy. The overpopulated walled towns built to withstand enemy attacks crowded families together in the most unhealthy circumstances. The pest-ridden, unsanitary living conditions and the narrow, dark streets that overflowed with human waste and refuse provided fertile environments for disease epidemics that decimated large segments of those populations. Superstitious, demonic, and theological theories of epidemic disease displaced ancient concerns for personal hygiene and the quality of the environment.

The Renaissance, however, was characterized by a great revival of learning. Along with advances in art, literature, and philosophy and the rise of industry and commerce, there was a renewed interest in science and medicine. From the sixteenth to the eighteenth centuries, public health was shaped by two countervailing trends.[2] Although the administration of rudimentary medical and nursing services continued to be the responsibility of towns and other local units, the concept of the modern state was beginning to emerge. Because only a political jurisdiction that protected and cared for its citizens could reap the continuing economic benefits of production and world trade, healthy laborers and soldiers became valuable commodities. Thus, in the centralized national governments of Europe during the sixteenth and seventeenth centuries, maintaining the health of laborers and soldiers became important economic and political as well as public health concerns.

■ Public Health in England

Poverty, illness, and disability were common problems in the towns and parishes of England during the sixteenth and seventeenth centuries, and most communities responded with some form of publicly supported medical care provided in private homes or at public infirmaries. The Elizabethan Poor Laws of 1601 addressed the issue of the "lame, impotent, old, blind, and such other among them being poor and not able to work" without dealing directly with health matters.[3] The law was expanded subsequently to include the provision of nursing and medical care.

It was also in England that the collection and analysis of national statistics regarding industrial production and demographics began in the seventeenth century. The work of the father of political arithmetic, William Petty (1623–1687), and the statistical analyses of his friend, John Graunt (1620–1674), established the importance of vital statistics and led to such epidemiologic tools as population-specific and disease-specific morbidity and mortality rates, life tables, and the calculus of probability. Study of the vital statistics contained in the Bills of Mortality published weekly in London led to a better understanding of the social phenomena that were factors in the promotion of health and the occurrence of disease.

Of interest, in light of subsequent debates about the merits of national health services, was the proposal of John Bellers, a London merchant and philanthropist (1654–1725). At the turn of the century, he proposed dealing with public health problems on a national scale. In *An Essay Toward Improvement of Physick*, Bellers suggested that the people's health was too important to the community to be left to the uncertainty of individual initiative. He argued that the health of the people was the responsibility of the state, whose task it was to establish and maintain hospitals and laboratories, erect a national health institute, and provide medical care for the sick.

The Elizabethan Poor Laws obligated each parish in England to maintain its own disadvantaged citizens. Despite a variety of schemes to deal with the health problems of the low-income populations, including the widespread development of workhouses to teach the unemployed to support themselves, the fundamental economic and social problems that led to pervasive poverty remained unsolved. By the nineteenth century, the industrialization of England had made poverty and social distress more prevalent than ever. It was in that climate that the drastic Poor Law Amendment Act of 1834 was passed. The dual intent was to reduce the rates of dependency and free the labor market to spur industrialization. The law required that able-bodied people and their families be given aid only in well-regulated workhouses.

The same circumstances that supported the new industrial society, factories, and the congested dwellings of urban environments produced new health problems. As people crowded into burgeoning towns and cities, diseases flourished and spread. It was the Poor Law Commission of 1834 under the leadership of Edwin Chadwick that developed the means to address public health problems. Motivated by the belief that it would be good economy to prevent disease, Chadwick advocated the use of carefully collected data to link population characteristics, environmental conditions, and the incidence of diseases. After many investigations, political debates, and subsequent political compromises, England's Public Health Act became law in 1848, and a General Board of Health was created. Although the subsequent history of public health in England is a chronicle of social change, epidemics, and political machinations, it is evident that the growth of their sanitary reform movement and the creation of the General Board of Health in 1848 established the British as the world leaders in public health philosophy and practice. Public health in early America was heavily influenced by the medical and administrative experience of the British.[4]

■ Public Health and Government-Supported Services

The history of public health in the United States from the early colonial period to the end of the nineteenth century followed the same development pattern as that which had occurred in England. Yellow fever and cholera epidemics stimulated sanitary reforms, and the early cities and towns began to assume responsibility for the collective health of their citizens. Public medical care in the United States, however, bore the stigma of its "Poor Law" legacy. The New York Poor Law of 1788 provided that any town or city could establish an almshouse, and within a few years most towns and cities had done so. Although there was a series of shocking exposés of terrible conditions in many of these facilities, the concept of the almshouse and town-employed physicians remained the mainstay of sick people among the low-income population until the depression of the 1930s.

Lemuel Shattuck, a Massachusetts statistician, conducted U.S. sanitary surveys similar to those of Chadwick in England. In his Report of the Sanitary Commission, published in 1850, he documented differences in morbidity and mortality rates in different locations and related them to various environmental conditions. Consequently, he argued, the city or state had to take responsibility for the environment. Although largely ignored at the time of its release, the report has come to be considered one of the most influential documents in the evolution of public health in the United States.[5]

In 1865, emulating the Shattuck survey in Massachusetts, the New York City Council of Hygiene and Public Health published a shocking exposé of unsanitary conditions in the city. Within a year a public health law was passed creating a city Board of Health. Creating an appropriate administrative structure for local public health efforts became a turning point for public health in the United States.

As in England and other countries, early federal public health initiatives were motivated more by economic and commercial concerns than humanitarian values. For instance, the Public Health Service came into being in 1798 as the Marine Hospital Service when President John Adams signed into law an act providing for the care and relief of seamen who were sick or disabled. Because healthy sailors were a valuable commercial commodity, and because the seaport towns took responsibility only for their own citizens, it was left to the federal government to provide health services to the seamen and passengers of the important shipping industry. Additionally, it was of serious concern to the citizens of seaports that the personnel of foreign ships not transmit to them diseases contracted elsewhere.

Soon thereafter, the first Marine Hospital was set up in Boston Harbor, and seamen were receiving care in port cities along the East Coast. In 1870, the Marine Hospital Service was reorganized as a national hospital system with a central headquarters in Washington, D.C. The medical officer in charge, known at first as the supervising surgeon, was later given the title of surgeon general. It is significant in light of the commercial motivation for its creation that the Marine Hospital Service was established as a component of the Treasury Department.

In 1889, Congress established the Public Health Service Commissioned Corps. Envisioned as a mobile force of physicians to assist the nation in fighting disease and protecting health, the Corps was set up along military lines, with titles and pay corresponding to Army and Navy grades, and physicians subject to duty wherever assigned.[6] In 1891, the bacteriological laboratory of Dr. Joseph J. Kinyuon in the Staten Island Marine Hospital was moved to Washington, D.C., where it was expanded to include pathology, chemistry, and pharmacology. It was the forerunner of the National Institutes of Health, which today provides two-thirds of all the federal support for biomedical research in this country.

Eleven years later, in 1902, a new law changed the Marine Hospital Service's name to the Public Health and Marine Hospital Service. In 1912, the name would be changed again to its present designation: the United States Public Health Service. From this modest start, the Public Health Service underwent a series of reorganizations and expansions until it became a major agency of the United States Department of Health and Human Services and responsible for the largest public health program in the world.[7]

In 1933, it became apparent that state and local governments with limited tax revenues required help from the federal government to provide welfare assistance, and the Federal Emergency Relief Act was passed. It provided federal aid to the states and authorized general medical care for acute and chronic illness, obstetrical services, emergency dental extractions, bedside nursing, drugs, and medical supplies. Because participation by the states was optional, the act was not implemented in many parts of the country.[8] The passage of the Social

Security Act of 1935 ended the era of makeshift federal and state programs to meet the health needs of the sick people among the low-income population. Title VI of the landmark Social Security Act of 1935 was instrumental in the expansion of the Public Health Service. The act delegated to the Public Health Service the authority to assist states, counties, health districts, and other political subdivisions to establish and maintain public health services. Title VI provided the impetus for all political jurisdictions to create public health agencies and services. After 141 years, the Public Health Service was removed from the Treasury Department to become a component of a new Federal Security Agency, created in 1939 to bring together most of the health, welfare, and educational services scattered throughout the federal government.

During World War II, the Public Health Service carried out emergency health and sanitation efforts that contributed substantially to the country's defense efforts. Immediately thereafter, a critical shortage of medical facilities prompted the passage of the National Hospital Survey and Construction Act, called Hill-Burton after its congressional sponsors. The act stimulated the growth of the health care industry by providing federal aid to the states for hospital and health center construction. Since 1946, the Public Health Service has provided national leadership in hospital planning, research, and operation. In 1946, the Federal Security Agency also was expanded to include the Children's Bureau and the Food and Drug Administration.

In 1953, the Public Health Service, with the other components of the Federal Security Agency, became part of the newly created Department of Health, Education and Welfare (HEW). During the next decade, the health care industry faced the multiple challenges of coping with a rapidly expanding U.S. population, rising public expectations for health services, and a host of technological advances in health care with an inadequate supply of health professionals. HEW responded in 1963 with the Health Professions Educational Assistance Act, which provided grants to build health professional schools, and in 1964 with the Nurse Training Act, which authorized federal aid for construction and rehabilitation of nursing schools and provided loans to nursing students.

The National Institute for Occupational Health and Safety, the National Institute on Alcohol Abuse and Alcoholism, the National Health Service Corps, and major initiatives in addressing cancer and heart, lung, and blood diseases were initiated in the early 1970s. In 1979, the education component of HEW was transferred to a new Department of Education, and HEW was renamed the Department of Health and Human Services.[9]

Now, with a 2002 budget of $460 billion and over 65,000 employees, the Department of Health and Human Services (HHS) is the federal government's principal agency concerned with health protection and promotion and provision of health and other human services to vulnerable populations. In addition to administering the Medicare and Medicaid programs, HHS includes over 300 separate programs[10] that encompass activities such as:

■ Medical and social science research
■ Infectious disease prevention and control
■ Assurance of food and drug safety
■ Child support enforcement
■ Improvement of maternal and child health
■ Management of preschool education services (Head Start)
■ Prevention of child abuse and domestic violence
■ Substance abuse prevention and treatment
■ Provision of services for older Americans

HHS carries out these activities through the following 11 Public Health Service Operating Divisions:[11]

1. *National Institutes of Health (NIH)*. Established first as a laboratory in 1887, the NIH is the world's premier medical research organization and includes 18 separate health institutes, the National Center for Complementary and Alternative Medicine, and the National Library of Medicine. The NIH supports over 35,000 research projects on a variety of medical conditions, and in 2002 operated with an annual budget of $20.9 billion. It employs more than 17,400 individuals.
2. *Food and Drug Administration (FDA)*. This agency assures the safety of foods and cosmetics and the safety and efficacy of pharmaceuticals, biological products, and medical devices. The FDA's 2002 budget was $1.3 billion. It employs more than 10,000 individuals.
3. *Centers for Disease Control and Prevention (CDC)*. Established in 1946, the CDC is the primary federal agency responsible for protecting the American public's health through monitoring of disease trends, investigations of outbreaks and health and injury risks, and implementation of illness and injury control and prevention measures. The 2002 budget was $3.7 billion. The agency employs more than 8,600 individuals.
4. *Agency for Toxic Substances and Disease Registry (ATSDR)*. In collaboration with states and other federal agencies, the ATSDR focuses on preventing exposures to hazardous substances from waste sites. The agency conducts public health assessments, health studies, surveillance activities, and health education and training in communities around waste sites on the U.S. Environmental Protection Agency's National Priorities List. The agency, supervised by the CDC, employs more than 400 individuals and has a budget of about $70 million.

5. *Indian Health Service (IHS)*. The IHS operates 38 hospitals, 56 health centers, 4 school health centers, and 44 health stations. Through transfers of IHS services operating authority, tribes also administer an additional 13 hospitals, 160 health centers, 3 school health centers, 76 health stations, and 160 Alaska village clinics. Services are provided to nearly 1.5 million American Indians and Alaska Natives of 557 federally recognized tribes in Alaska and the 48 contiguous states. The service employs about 14,800 individuals and had a 2002 operating budget of $2.9 billion.

6. *Health Resources and Service Administration (HRSA)*. Established in 1982 to provide a coordinated agency for multiple programs serving low-income, uninsured, and medically underserved populations, the HRSA provides funds for comprehensive primary and preventive services through community-based health centers at more than 3,000 sites nationwide. The HRSA also supports maternal and child health programs, programs to increase diversity and numbers of health care professionals in underserved communities, and supportive services for HIV/AIDS victims through the Ryan White Care Act. It employs more than 2,000 individuals and had a 2002 budget of $6.5 billion.

7. *Substance Abuse and Mental Health Services Administration (SAMHSA)*. This agency works to improve the quality and availability of substance abuse prevention, addiction treatment, and mental health services through federal block grants. It provides a variety of grants to states and local communities to address emerging substance abuse trends, mental health service needs, and HIV/AIDS. The agency's 2002 budget was $2.9 billion, and it employs more than 600 individuals.

8. *Agency for Healthcare Research and Quality (AHRQ)*. Established in 1989, AHRQ is the lead agency for supporting research to improve the quality of health care, reduce its cost, improve patient safety, address medical errors, and broaden access to essential services. Major activities include sponsoring and conducting research to provide evidence-based information on health care outcomes with respect to quality, costs, uses, and access. With 294 employees, the agency's 2002 budget was $191 million.

9. *Centers for Medicare and Medicaid Services (CMMS), formerly the Health Care Financing Administration (HCFA)*. This agency administers the Medicare and Medicaid programs. Medicare insures more than 39 million Americans, and Medicaid, a joint federal/state program, provides coverage for over 34 million low-income persons, including 18 million children, and nursing home coverage for low-income older adults. It administers the new Children's Health Insurance Program, currently covering

more than 2.2 million children. The agency employs more than 4,500 individuals and, in 2002, had a budget of $375 billion.

10. *Administration for Children and Families (ACF)*. The ACF administers over 60 programs to promote the economic and social well-being of families, children, individuals, and communities. It administers the state/federal welfare program, Temporary Assistance to Needy Families, national child support enforcement, and the Head Start program. It provides funds to assist low-income families with child care expenses, supports state programs in adoption assistance and foster care, and funds child abuse and domestic violence prevention programs. The agency has more than 1,500 employees and had a 2002 operating budget of $44.6 billion.

11. *Administration on Aging (AOA)*. The federal focal point and advocate agency for older persons, the AoA administers federal programs under the Older Americans Act. Programs assist older persons to remain in their own homes by supporting services such as "meals on wheels." The AoA collaborates with its nationwide network of regional offices and state and area agencies to plan, coordinate, and develop community-level systems of services that meet the needs of older individuals and their caregivers. The agency employs 124 individuals and had a 2002 operating budget of $1.3 billion.

HHS also is the federal government's largest grant-making agency, providing approximately 60,000 grants per year under the aegis of its various operating divisions.[12] National health expenditures for research in 1998 totaled $19.9 billion, of which the federal government financed $15.5 billion, or almost 78%, excluding research and development expenditures of drug companies and other manufacturers and providers of medical equipment and supplies.[13]

Initiated to provide care for Civil War veterans who were disabled, indigent, or both, the Veteran's Health Administration system (VA) has grown to become one of the world's largest health care delivery systems. It currently operates 173 medical centers with approximately 51,000 beds, 391 outpatient and outreach clinics, 131 nursing home care units, and 39 domiciliaries, providing a broad range of medical, surgical, and rehabilitative care.[14] In 2002, the system spent $21.7 billion for veterans' health care.[15] On an annual basis, the VA treats nearly 1 million patients in its hospitals, 79,000 in its nursing homes, and 25,000 in its domiciliaries. The system's outpatient clinics register approximately 27.5 million visits per year. Since 1950, the VA has maintained major affiliations with medical schools throughout the United States. Today, 105 such affiliations are in place. In 1966, federal legislation allowed the VA medical centers to affiliate with other health science schools. Current affiliations total 54 dental schools and 1,140 other schools throughout the United States. Each year approximately 100,000 health professionals receive training at VA medical centers.[16] The VA also conducts a broad array of world-class clinical and health services research.

Originally, the VA provided services only to those with service-related conditions, but by 1970 virtually all restrictions on eligibility were lifted. Any veteran over 65 years of age, regardless of income or relationship of illness to a service-related cause, became eligible. To aid in controlling costs, the system later established a priority ranking for eligibility based on economic need and connection of illness to service. The system has been controversial and ambiguous. In 1996, legislation was passed that made significant changes in veterans' eligibility for medical care and eliminated complicated rules governing eligibility for outpatient services. In 1999, the Veterans Millennium Health Care and Benefits Act was passed by Congress to expand veterans' long-term care services and provide reimbursement for emergency treatment of enrolled veterans. It also clarified priority categories for eligibility.[17]

In 1993, the VA began a systemwide reengineering of its services by focusing on "a continuum of care that balances health maintenance, disease prevention and a population perspective with the episodic treatment of acute disease."[18] In 1999, the VA reorganized its medical system into 22 integrated networks of care in order to "pool and align" resources to best meet local needs and provide improved service access and cost-effectiveness.[19]

Through the Department of Defense Military Health Service program, the federal government provides both direct health care services and support for health care services for 8.1 million U.S. military personnel and their dependents, military retirees and their families, and others entitled to Department of Defense benefits.[20] The Military Health Service operates 98 hospitals and 480 clinics worldwide, primarily servicing active-duty members of the armed forces. The majority of civilian care is purchased through managed care support contracts implemented under a program entitled TRICARE. The 2000 budget for military health services programs totaled $16.2 billion, or 6 percent of the total Department of Defense budget.[21]

The states also play an important financial role in funding health care and health-related services. In 1998, state and local governments contributed $2.8 billion, or 14.1 percent of total national health care expenditures for research, and funded $101.3 billion of personal health care expenditures, or 10 percent of the national total expenditures including hospital, nursing home, or home health care services.[22] Many states also operate and fund state mental institutions, support medical schools, maintain health departments that provide direct preventive and primary care services, and support maternal and child health improvement, infectious disease monitoring and control, and other community health initiatives.

City and county government jurisdictions support and deliver general and specialty health care services through their health departments and over 100 hospitals and health systems that together comprise the infrastructure of many of America's metropolitan health systems.[23] The outpatient and inpatient services of government-supported public hospitals provide a community's "safety net" for individuals who are uninsured or underinsured and cannot access care elsewhere. Public hospitals also are often the sites of major teaching programs for an area's medical school. Frequently, they provide services that are financially unattractive to other community hospitals, such as burn care, psychiatric medicine, trauma care, and crisis response units for both natural and man-made disasters.[24] In addition, city and county health departments may provide direct patient care services in clinics or health centers, referrals for care, and other services to meet community needs of their high-risk, medically underserved populations.

■ Decline in Influence of the Public Health Service

Over the years, public health agencies' many accomplishments have contributed to significant improvements in both the health and life expectancy of Americans. Using population-based strategies for disease and injury prevention, public health has contributed to substantial declines in morbidity and mortality and dramatically changed the profiles of disease, injury, and death in the United States. Yet, despite the centrality of public health in providing the basis for the health of Americans, its funding has always competed with other, more highly valued demands in the health sector.[25]

The several reorganizations of federal public health agencies occurred in response to continuing criticism of their failure to improve access to at least minimally adequate medical care to underserved populations. Pressures emanated from public health professionals, medical care organizations, political leaders, and the popular media. Criticism of the Public Health Service rose in the 1960s when its efforts to provide incentives to state and local agencies for more innovative approaches to meeting these demands through categorical and project grants were judged ineffective. Thus, when several new and important programs for improving access to medical care were passed, agencies other than the Public Health Service were assigned to administer them. Medicare was assigned to the Social Security Administration, Medicaid to the Social and Rehabilitation Services, Head Start and Neighborhood Health Centers to the Office of Economic Opportunity, and the Model Cities Program to Housing and Urban Development.

The end of President Johnson's term of office in 1968 marked the end of an era in federal health policy. The Nixon administration took issue with the three-tiered system of the federal Public Health Service, state health agencies, and local public health departments that was expected to combine local initiative with policy input and national standards for advancing access to adequate health services. In its place, a new policy dubbed the "New Federalism" was initiated. It involved the progressive removal of federal responsibilities for a uniform, cooperative national public health system and the transfer of those responsibilities to the states. It was the beginning, at the federal level, of the Republican strategy of converting federal program support to block grants, reducing the available funds and sending them to the states for administration. Although it was relatively unsuccessful during the Nixon/Ford administrations, it was revived in a new and more extreme form when Ronald Reagan was elected in 1980, and public health became the primary target. The decline of the government's organized system of public health services accelerated thereafter.[26]

■ Responsibilities of the Public Health Sector

In 1990, the Department of Health and Human Services published *Public Health Service: Healthy People 2000: National Health Promotion and Disease Prevention Objectives*. Objective 8.14 of that document calls for 90 percent of the population to be served by local health departments that would effectively carry out the three core functions of public health: assessment, policy development, and quality assurance. These core health department functions are intended to put into operation, within the resource and other constraints extant in each jurisdiction, the following generally accepted health department performance responsibilities:[27]

■ Focus on primary prevention: prevention that occurs before the onset of disease. Identify environmental and behavioral factors that are associated with conditions, such as lung cancer or heart disease, and educate the community or protect it from the risk.

■ Protect communities from infectious and toxic agents through monitoring or surveillance. Gather information to control and, where possible, prevent health problems resulting from these agents.

■ Respond to unanticipated natural and human-generated disasters. Assess health risks posed by contaminated food, water, or air and inform the public and the medical care system of sources of danger and strategies for appropriate response.

■ Promote the well-being of the public through programs to notify and educate people about risks and protective measures that can be applied at the community level.

- ■ Target hard-to-reach populations with clinical services. Create outreach programs to link high-risk populations to medical services to address individual health care needs, as well as to interrupt the spread of disease in the community.
- ■ Maintain diagnostic laboratory services to support diverse monitoring and prevention programs. These facilities permit identification of emerging threats from infectious agents and environmental toxins. Set and enforce standards for new and existing laboratory tests conducted in medical settings.
- ■ Collect information on health outcomes to ensure the quality of services provided through hospitals, nursing homes, and other medical care delivery institutions. Develop referral systems for high-risk perinatal care, and plan regionalization of trauma and cardiac care. Provide aggregate information on health outcomes to inform consumers and medical care professionals about the quality of care being delivered at the community level.

It is through the fulfillment of these public health responsibilities that public health departments protect the public against preventable communicable diseases and exposure to toxic environmental pollutants, harmful products, and poor quality health care. These public health practices promote healthy personal behaviors and risk factor reduction communitywide by identifying and modifying patterns of chronic disease and injury, informing and educating consumers and health care providers about appropriate use of medical services, developing and maintaining comprehensive health programs in schools and child day care facilities, providing occupational safety and health programs, and ensuring that human immunodeficiency virus (HIV) and sexually transmitted disease prevention programs are implemented. These public health practices are the bedrock foundations of modern population-focused health care.

However, in 1993, a team of investigators from the School of Public Health at the University of Illinois at Chicago, working with representatives of the Centers for Disease Control and Prevention, surveyed 208 health departments responding from a random national sample stratified by jurisdiction and population base. The findings suggested that less than 40 percent of the U.S. population was served by a health department that effectively addressed the core functions of public health.[28]

Clearly, with resource support for public health continuing to decline, it is not surprising that the United States failed to meet 85 percent of the challenging goals of *Healthy People 2000*. In a new 10-year plan, *Healthy People 2010*, released by the Department of Health and Human Services in January 2000, the government admitted that the nation had met only 15 percent of the 319 targets established in 1990.

In some areas, particularly obesity, marijuana use, exercise, asthma, and diabetes, the health of Americans either stayed the same or worsened.

Nevertheless, *Healthy People 2010,* the third set of 10-year targets for health improvement in the United States, set two broad goals, supported by 467 objectives that are grouped into 28 focus areas. One major goal is "to increase the years and quality of health life." The other major goal is "to eliminate health disparities."[29]

These goals and their supporting objectives were developed for the new decade by Healthy People Consortium, a group of 650 national, professional, and voluntary organizations, the business community, and state and local public health agencies. Meetings began in 1996, and the first completed draft of 7,704 pages was posted on the Web for public comment in September 1998. More than 11,000 comments were received electronically. The recommendations from a series of public hearings and other Web communications were processed before publication of the final report. Given the dismal failure to meet the multitudinous objectives of the two previous Healthy People reports, one might question whether the extraordinary effort expended in these highly labor-intensive, expensive, and time-consuming exercises might be better spent in more pragmatic and potentially productive efforts.

In 1985, the Institute of Medicine, concerned about the need to protect the nation's health through an effective, organized public health sector, convened a special committee to study the status of public health in the United States. The committee reported its findings and recommendations in 1988. The report concluded "public health is a vital function that is in trouble."[30] In an analysis of the contributing factors, it noted:

> We have observed disorganization, weak and unstable leadership, a lessening of professional and expert competence in leadership positions, hostility to public health concepts and approaches, outdated statutes, inadequate financial support for public health activities and public health education, gaps in the data gathering and analysis that are essential to public health functions of assessment and surveillance, and lack of effective links between the public and private sectors for the accomplishment of public health objectives.[31]

The report linked the poor public image of public health and the public's lack of knowledge and appreciation for the mission and content of public health to those deficiencies and to a number of other problems. Particular emphasis was placed on the failure of sound policy development in public health as evidenced by ambiguous responses to the AIDS epidemic, the "politicalization" of public health agencies, and the lack of clear delineation of the responsibilities between levels of government.

In 1988, the committee made organizational, educational, financial, and political recommendations for addressing these complex and interrelated problems. Unfortunately, its strategies depended on continuing strong financial support for existing public health agencies and stronger, more sharply focused leadership that could build increasingly productive links with the private and voluntary health care sectors. In the ensuing years, the required leadership has not been evident, financial support for public health has continued to decline, and public and political support for government public health agencies has further diminished.

Although the goals and objectives of the Healthy People reports are commendable and their definition gives the agencies involved a sense of accomplishment, it should be obvious that the lack of an effective, well-organized public health sector makes the effort an exercise in futility. Perhaps one of the weaknesses of public health is the propensity of its advocates to set arbitrary and usually unobtainable goals rather than face the much more difficult challenge of developing the leadership, expertise, and political strength to achieve them.

■ Relationships of Public Health and Private Medicine

Public health and clinical medicine have complementary roles in caring for the health of the American people. Although they often address the same health problems, their attention is directed at different stages of disease or injury. Clinical medicine devotes its most intensive resources to restoring health or palliating disease in relatively small numbers of individuals. Rather than targeting individuals, public health uses strategies that promote health or prevent disease in large populations.[32]

Unfortunately, the implementation of these roles has been hindered by the often contentious relationship that has existed for decades between public health leadership and the private medical practitioners and their advocacy organization, the American Medical Association. Although the need for curative medicine administered to individuals and the need for preventive measures for the protection of populations have coexisted in all societies since ancient civilizations, and physicians who specialize in public health or preventive medicine have received the same basic medical education as those who pursue the diagnostic and therapeutic specialties, the ideologic differences between them have produced vigorous debate. J.G. Freymann suggests that the reasons for the persistent discord include the identification of public health by practicing physicians with governmental bureaucracy, the linking of the care of low-income populations with welfare, the focus of physicians toward individuals, and the custom of being paid only for active therapy.[33]

Historically, the different emphases of the two types of practitioners, that is, the population-based orientation of public health professionals and the individual-centered focus of private health providers, has often divided rather than enhanced public and private health services. The scientific advances in medicine since World War II only served to emphasize the value differences between practitioners with a population perspective and those focused on individual patients. Physicians educated and socialized to a biological model of medicine that emphasized sophisticated technologies and practice specialization have shown little appreciation for the simpler organizational measures that reach out to the underserved and provide access to basic health monitoring, preventive care, and primary medical care.

Understandably, individual physicians with the daily responsibility and heavy workloads of caring for waiting rooms full of patients consider that their personal professional efforts fully meet their community or societal obligations. For the most part, they are more than willing to delegate to the public health professionals concerns for the overall health of society and for those who do not have access to their offices.

The history of public health is marked primarily by struggles over the limits of its mandate. Just as the opponents of the several attempts to initiate programs of national health insurance described public health prejudicially as "socialized medicine," special interest groups are threatened by the perception that public health programs represent subversive social change that constitutes an unjustified intrusion of government into the lives of private individuals.

The medical profession had both philosophical and economic reasons for voicing their concerns. P. Starr observed: "Doctors fought against public treatment of the sick, requirements for reporting cases of tuberculosis and venereal disease, and attempts by public health authorities to establish health centers to coordinate preventive and curative medicine."[34] Extending the boundaries of public health was regarded as the opening wedge for usurping the physicians' role. Physicians opposed disease screening and primary care services, even though they were targeted at the populations with the lowest incomes, because physicians feared that public health agencies were expanding into activities that they believed were rightfully their own.

There are, of course, many examples of the synergistic effects of private and public medicine. The immunization of children and adults against a variety of preventable diseases is a good example of how public health and private medical practitioners have worked together effectively. A number of screening programs, such as those for tuberculosis, lung cancer, breast cancer, and hypertension, have linked the personal services of private medicine and the population-oriented practice of public health in productive liaisons.

■ Resource Priorities Favor Curative Medicine

The allocation of U.S. health resources provides persuasive evidence of the public's and the professionals' fascination with dramatic high-technology diagnostic and therapeutic medicine. Despite the centrality of public health in providing basic health programs and the effectiveness and economic advantages inherent in prevention as compared to cure, there is little funding for research or practice for public health promotion or disease prevention. This is in contrast to the large sums that finance the research in and practice of remedial medical care. Less than 1 percent of the over $1 trillion spent annually for health care was allocated to government public health activities. Between 1981 and 1993, there were public health imperatives on the emergence of acquired immune deficiency syndrome (AIDS); the reemergence of tuberculosis and measles; and the escalating problems of substance abuse, violence, and teenage pregnancy. Total U.S. health expenditures during this period increased by more than 210 percent, whereas funding of public health services as a proportion of the health care budget declined by 25 percent.[35]

The major investment in hospital neonatal intensive care units during the last two decades is a dramatic example of the lack of balance in the health care system. Although numerous studies have demonstrated that funds expended for prenatal care of high-risk mothers reduce the number of premature births requiring exceedingly expensive and often futile efforts to save those infants, public subsidies for prenatal care have declined, while more and more costly technology has been introduced to increase the ability to salvage increasingly small and premature infants. For example, the federal Special Supplemental Food Program for Women, Infants and Children (WIC), which provides supplemental food, nutrition, and health education to low-income pregnant and postpartum women, infants, and children, is estimated, after careful studies, to reduce low birth weight rates by 25 percent and very low birth weight rates by 45 percent, with Medicaid savings of $4.21 for every WIC dollar spent on pregnant women. In contrast, neonatal intensive care, although effective in reducing neonatal mortality, is the least cost-effective strategy.[36]

These questionable funding priorities will be of critical importance in determining the effectiveness of health care in the future. Just as the preference for support of costly neonatal intensive care units rather than public health programs of prenatal care contributes to the unacceptably high rates of infant mortality in the United States, the focus on remedial medicine for America's growing elderly population denies the reality of the changing distribution of illness and disability. The major causes of disease and disability among the increasing numbers of elderly are chronic conditions that result from multiple causes that are not usually amenable to technological remedies.

The traditional medical model of clinical practice poorly serves many older individuals. Normal function and the absence of disease characterize the medical definition of health. Health is assumed by the absence of symptoms and signs that the human body is in some state of biological disruption. The accepted medical focus on the biomedical aspects of care with an emphasis on specific diseases and organ systems assumes that nonphysiological malfunction, such as the inability, common to advancing age, to carry out the roles and tasks of one's usual social milieu, is not part of health. That medical model is not appropriate to guide care for most older patients, who may need a multidisciplinary approach that focuses on overall needs. Attention needs to be paid to managing chronic conditions—helping patients adjust to their limitations and maintain daily functioning within the context of their living arrangement and family and social support.

■ Health Care Reform and the Public Health/Medicine Relationship

Important factors in the current effort to reform the U.S. health care system give promise of a more functional future partnership between public health and private practice medicine. The drive by those paying for health care (employers, organized consumers, and governments) for improved measures of health status and system performance and the emphasis on integrated health systems that focus on health improvement for defined populations are creating pressures within the system for more cost-effective, community-driven strategies for combining the resources of public health and networks of personal care services.

Although complementary, if not integrated, systems of public health and medical care services seem like ideal models with which to address the nation's health care problems of the twenty-first century, the longstanding differences in philosophy, values, and assumptions between public health and organized medicine are likely to make cooperative ventures difficult. Nevertheless, in the current era of previously inconceivable health system changes, a new and functional relationship driven by mutual needs could develop between these two sectors.

Both public health leaders and clinicians would need sufficient motivation to improve preventive service rates. Strong external incentives or requirements as well as perceptive internal vision would be required to change organizational commitment. A new emphasis on prevention would have to be seen as important for organizational promotion or financial viability before providers would be galvanized to action. The history of public and preventive health services in the United States illustrates, time and again, that the prestige priorities—and profits—in its remedial medicine system lie with diagnosing and treating already existing disease.

The current medical care system fails to provide effective preventive services even when they are demonstrated to be the most cost-effective procedures available. In contrast, new treatment technologies are implemented despite serious reservations about their efficacy and cost-effectiveness. Thus, with all of its groundbreaking research, talented workforce, and technological know-how, the United States has the distinction of having the world's most costly and inefficient health care system.[37]

Figure 11–1 shows estimates of the deaths per year from preventable causes. Tobacco, diet, and sedentary lifestyles are major contributors to early mortality, yet effective medical interventions are not integrated into the practice standards that drive the delivery of medical services.[38]

Clearly, the medical and public health systems that evolved from the remarkable scientific achievements since World War I placed their emphases on tests, drugs, surgeries, vaccines, and environmental controls. Personal behaviors were considered either outside the scope of the medical care system or immutable to change. Medical insurance companies that rarely reimbursed providers for preventive services in general, and behavioral counseling in particular, reinforced these assumptions.

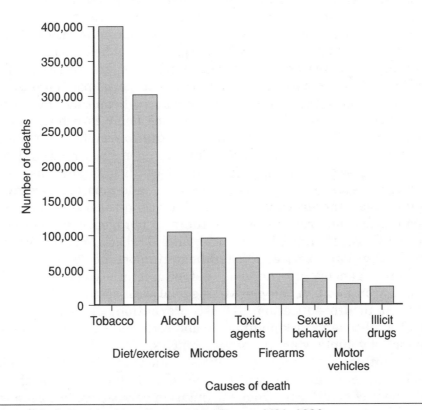

Figure 11–1 Deaths from Preventable Causes, USA, 1990
Source: Reprinted from *Journal of the American Medical Association*, 1993, Vol. 270, 2207–2212.

■ Hospital-Sponsored Public Health Activities

The market forces that have changed the structure and character of hospitals during the last two decades have stimulated them to initiate or expand a variety of outpatient public health–type services, including community-based and work site health promotion. This integration of outpatient medical and public health services is a direct response to the pressure placed on hospitals by third-party payers to reduce inpatient admissions and lengths of stay. In many cases, acute care hospitals have added services such as community education on healthy behaviors and risk factor reduction, comprehensive school health programs, preventive health programs in child day care facilities, community education on chronic disease prevention and management, and occupational safety and health programs. These services have both helped their service populations and provided new sources of much needed revenue.

■ Public Health Services of Voluntary Agencies

The role of volunteerism, voluntary agencies, and institutions as adjunct resources and services to those provided by governments and for-profit practices and corporations is a major theme in the evolution of health care in the United States. Private not-for-profit institutions have been the prevailing mechanism for the provision of health care services in the United States, and with the government, share the responsibilities for meeting the needs of communities and special populations.[39]

In addition to this country's not-for-profit hospitals, there are a host of voluntary agencies providing nursing home care, hospice care, home care, medical and vocational rehabilitation, and other personal health care services. A variety of voluntary agencies serve the special needs of persons with specific medical conditions such as AIDS, asthma, diabetes, cerebral palsy, hemophilia, and muscular dystrophy. Similar organizations support research on conditions such as cancer, heart disease, and respiratory disorders. Others, such as the American Red Cross, Planned Parenthood, and Meals on Wheels, focus on providing specific services. Of significant importance is the fact that voluntary agencies provide many valued and effective services that are not prominent in the private medical care sector. Programs directed at health education, disease prevention, disease detection, health maintenance, rehabilitation, and terminal care have been the province of voluntary not-for-profit agencies.

The influence of large nonprofit foundations, such as the Robert Wood Johnson Foundation and the Pew Charitable Trusts, on the advancement of health care from a population perspective has been considerable. By providing funds on a competitive basis to stimulate research and innovative program demonstrations, these and other foundations have caused hospitals and other agencies, in collaboration with universities and colleges, to engage in progressive health service delivery improvements that may otherwise have been years in development. Particularly commendable is the selection of health care objectives to which those funds are dedicated.

The synergistic effect of government, private, and voluntary efforts has been both a bane and a blessing in the provision of health care in the United States. Our system's disorderly evolution as a combination of the charitable efforts of voluntary and religious organizations, multilevel government responses to community needs, and traditional U.S. free enterprise ensured the development of a complex network that is both inordinately successful in a technological sense and plagued by costly inefficiencies, duplications, and inequities in access and quality. Nevertheless, this pluralistic approach, rather than the types of national health care systems common to other industrial societies, appears, at least for the near future, to be the only health care system strategy acceptable to the U.S. people.

■ Changing Roles of Government in Public Health

For decades, all three levels of government in the United States—federal, state, and local—have played significant roles in financing and regulating public health services and in maintaining agencies and systems that directly or indirectly deliver health care. The federal government surveys the population's health status and health needs, sets policies and standards, passes laws and regulations, supports biomedical and health services research, provides technical assistance and resources to state and local health agencies, helps finance health care through support of programs (such as Medicare and Medicaid), and delivers personal health care services through networks of facilities (such as those maintained by the Department of Defense, the Department of Veterans Affairs, and the Administration on Native Americans).[40]

Public health services in the states are financed, regulated, and delivered through a variety of organizational structures. In some states, public health activities are divided among several entities, including health departments, social service, welfare, aging, and Medicaid. Many states now combine health and social service agencies to create large human service operations that join health and social services for children and youth, for people with developmental disabilities and other special populations, and for special problems such as alcoholism and drug abuse. Most states contribute heavily to the financing of Medicaid, medical education, and public health programs, and to mental health through both community mental health programs and state-operated psychiatric hospitals. States also are involved in regulation through health codes, licensing of facilities and personnel, and supervision of the insurance industry.

Considerable variation exists in the organizational structure of agencies engaged in public health activities in local governmental jurisdictions. Counties, districts, and other local governments may have health, social service, environmental, and mental health departments. They can be independent or divisions of state agencies. Many cities and counties support and operate local health departments, public hospitals, clinics, and various other services. They also establish and enforce local health codes.

Rather than supporting and acknowledging the many benefits of this multilevel configuration of public health agencies that ensure safe food and water; control of epidemic diseases; and programs of care for infants, children, and adults with special needs; and, in general, improve the length and quality of life in the United States, the nation has moved toward increased privatization, withdrawn support from public health activities, and allowed the system to fall into disarray. The United States appears to have lost sight of both the goals and benefits of public health.[41]

■ Public Health in an Era of Privatization and Managed Care

The market forces affecting hospitals, nursing homes, voluntary agencies, and other institutions of the U.S. health care system are also significantly changing the financial base and functions of public health departments. The declines in public health funding and the trend toward privatization of those public health services that could be delivered more efficiently outside of local bureaucracies have left many local health departments with minimal staff focused on only the most essential public health services.

Outsourcing to private providers who often had more comprehensive clinical capacity was one of several organizational strategies to contain or reduce costs while maintaining or improving the quality and efficiency of necessary public health services. Survey findings indicate that those health departments became smaller while cost savings were rare.[42]

With few exceptions, most health departments have maintained their responsibilities for assessing and ensuring the delivery of necessary public health services even though privatized. As might be expected, however, the reduction of health department–delivered services has made it difficult for many departments to maintain a strong community presence. In addition, negotiating with private service entities for the delivery and monitoring of public health services requires staff not customarily employed by public health departments. Health departments now find it necessary to replace service personnel with management staff knowledgeable in contracting and other business-related skills.

■ State Children's Health Insurance Program

The Balanced Budget Act of 1997 includes a program to expand health insurance coverage for children. The Act establishes the State Children's Health Insurance Program (SCHIP) under a new title XXI of the Social Security Act. Forty-eight billion dollars will become available to the states over the next 10 years for providing health insurance to uninsured children in families with incomes up to 200 percent of the poverty level. States will have broad flexibility to establish new programs or expand their existing Medicaid program.

States must submit a plan for program design and implementation to the U.S. Department of Health and Human Services for approval. Outreach, direct health services to children, and other health services initiatives must be described, as well as plans for coverage, delivery systems, eligibility, quality assurance, and coordination with existing programs.

The public health implications of this legislation are significant. Of all of the criticisms of the U.S. health care system, the lack of insurance coverage for the estimated 8.5 to 11.3 million children under age 18 is the least defensible. This legislation reflects the growing consensus among the public and policy makers that it is appropriate for the government to step in and expand the insurance coverage of low-income children.

Federal dollars will enhance the programs already in place in some states and stimulate child health care coverage in states that have yet to develop such programs. Problems exist for the states, however. States must allocate substantial amounts of their own funds to draw their federal allotments. They must also decide to develop a new comprehensive program or expand an existing Medicaid program. Nevertheless, public health experts are almost uniformly positive about the long-term impact of the new legislation on the number of uninsured children.[43]

■ Federal Support to Address Emerging Health Issues

Several new health concerns have attracted the interest of Congress and the president. The following are among the major issues:

■ The national effort to shift as many Medicare recipients as possible from traditional fee-for-service programs to health maintenance organizations (HMOs) is rapidly failing. The intent was to reduce costs and provide Medicare recipients with more complete health care, including prescription drug coverage. The HMOs, however, found the

Medicare reimbursement rates inadequate to cover the costs of treating older adults. One after another of the HMOs have withdrawn from the program, putting over a million Medicare recipients at risk of losing drug benefits. At this time, it appears that the problem will be addressed by either increasing government funding for Medicare HMOs or creating a Medicare drug benefit for older adults and people with disabilities who are covered by the program.

■ Rising numbers of uninsured patients, together with reduced Medicaid coverage and other government reductions, are straining the nation's safety net and putting the most vulnerable populations at serious risk. Public hospitals, community health centers, local health departments, and rural health clinics, as well as school-based clinics, provide a loose collection of services for those without coverage or the ability to pay. Those facilities and the special service providers, such as AIDS services, depend on a patchwork of grants and subsidies to stay in business. With nearly one in five Americans uninsured, Medicaid cutbacks, and provisions in the Balanced Budget Act of 1997 that reduced subsidies to hospitals that serve low-income patients, the government is being urged to develop a new safety net initiative. A March 2000 report of the Institute of Medicine recommends that the government provide competitive grants to support the diverse group of facilities that provide care for low-income populations and the uninsured. The report also calls for a new government oversight body to monitor and assess the effect of federal and state policies on the system.[44]

■ A crescendo of complaints from patients and their physicians about managed care organizations that deny approval of needed but expensive medical services has prompted the introduction of a number of patient protection bills in the United States Congress. Any patient protection legislation enacted by Congress and signed by the president will have been the result of contentious debate and intense lobbying by the stakeholders in the health care system. The insurance industry and employer groups would like a weak patient protection law that continues to protect insurers from litigation for damages resulting from service denials. Patient support groups and physician organizations would like the decision-making process returned to each patient's physician with minimal interference from insurers. Election year posturing strongly influences the debate.

■ The National Academy of Sciences, Institute of Medicine report that concluded that medical mistakes claim the lives of as many as 98,000 people per year drew a swift response from Congress. Legislative proposals were held up, however, by disputes over the recommendation for mandatory reporting of medical errors. The immediate response was to increase the budget of the federal Agency for Healthcare Research and Quality (AHRQ), with the additional funds earmarked for reducing medical errors.

■ The AHRQ has a very broad research agenda that deals with the delivery and outcomes of health care, its quality and effectiveness, and the needs of special populations. New issues are emerging, however, that will require increased research support. Newer research interests involve ethical concerns brought about by changing the system from providing all possible care without consideration of costs to provision of less costly care. In addition, research is needed to clarify the results of trade-offs in the allocation of medical service resources. New research funding will also be required to address the ethical issues brought about by the latest advances in genomics and other high-technology developments.

■ Future Role of Government in Promoting the Public's Health

Because the provision of medical treatment and related services accounts for approximately 99 percent of aggregate national health expenditures, national debate and efforts to reform the U.S. health care system have focused on financing, insurance, and cost containment of treatment. Various estimates suggest that only about 10 percent of all early deaths can be prevented by medical treatment. In contrast, populationwide public health approaches have the potential to help prevent some 70 percent of early deaths in the United States through measures targeted to the social, environmental, and behavioral factors that contribute to those deaths.[45] Clearly, the value placed on high-technology clinical medicine by individuals, societies, and governments within the United States overwhelm consideration of the more cost-effective, but less dramatic, prevention strategies of public health. Unlike pictures of heart transplant recipients, for example, images of the hundreds of thousands of children who have *not* been crippled and have *not* died due to poliomyelitis since successful immunization programs have been instituted cannot be shown by the media.

State and local governments struggling with large deficits have considered it necessary to sacrifice the personnel and services of their public health agencies. The shortsightedness of those decisions, however, is becoming increasingly evident. Although there is continued general unhappiness with tax-supported programs and institutions, pressures for improving state and local public health services are developing outside the community of public health advocates. Leaders in business and industry connect a healthy and educated public to economic growth and development. They, and others concerned about the demise of such programs as school health, maternal and child health, water quality, community nutrition, environmental control, and disease control, are rethinking the wisdom of some of these governmental cost-cutting priorities. Private foundations and voluntary agencies are not able to fill the gaps left by the withdrawal of governmental support.

The people and political leaders of the United States are going through an unprecedented reassessment of guiding principles, core values, and funding priorities. Experience with the democratic process suggests that the voting public will respond to legislative and policy errors only after the untoward effects of faulty decisions touch on them personally and significantly.

Following the terrorist assaults of September 11, 2001, lawmakers, prodded by the public, recognized that a broader public health infrastructure is required to protect Americans against chemical or biological attacks. A number of public health defense programs have been proposed that include stockpiling vaccines against anthrax, plague, and smallpox. Of particular importance is the need to prepare health care professionals, hospitals, and other agencies to respond quickly and effectively to threats or actual disasters.[46]

To that end, the largest reorganization of the federal government since World War II took place in April, 2003 with the establishment of the Department of Homeland Security (DHS). Twenty two new and existing governmental agencies that include 180,000 employees were assembled under the leadership of Tom Ridge, newly appointed Secretary of Homeland Security. The DHS has the broad mission of strengthening this country's borders; improving intelligence analyses; infrastructure protection; and comprehensive response and recovery operations should there be a terrorist attack with chemical or biologic weapons. To help fulfill its mandate, the new department has a host of interlocking governmental relationships with other federal and state units. Among those are liaisons with the National Institutes of Health, the Centers for Disease Control and Prevention, the U.S. Public Health Service, the Federal Drug Administration and other units of the Department of Health and Human Services . In addition, state and local health departments are expected to play important roles in prevention of spread or in response and recovery operations should any attacks occur.[47]

It is unfortunate that it requires a new threat or epidemic to halt the demise of organized public health and restore an effective public health structure. It may not be in the models we know, but it will receive new recognition, new support, and new leadership because, once again, public health has demonstrated its central role in maintaining the health and well-being of the U.S. people.

■ Notes

1. S. Shindell et al., *A Coursebook in Health Care Delivery* (New York: Appleton & Lange, 1976), 304–308.
2. G. Rosen, *A History of Public Health* (New York: MD Publications, 1957), 82–83.
3. Rosen, *A History of Public Health,* 120–129.
4. Rosen, *A History of Public Health,* 219–233.

5. Committee for the Study of the Future of Public Health, Division of Health Care Services, Institute of Medicine, *The Future of Public Health* (Washington, DC: National Academy Press, 1988), 60–61.

6. Department of Health and Human Services, *The Public Health Service: Some Historical Notes* (Washington, DC: Public Health Service, 1988), 1–8.

7. M.W. Raffel and N.K. Raffel, *The U.S. Health System: Origins and Functions,* 4th ed. (Albany, NY: Delmar Publishers, 1994).

8. A.S. Yerby, "Public Medical Care for the Needy in the United States," in *Medical Care, Social and Organizational Aspects,* ed. L.J. DeGroot (Springfield, IL: Charles C Thomas, 1966), 382–401.

9. Department of Health and Human Services, The Public Health Service, 1–8.

10. U.S. Department of Health and Human Services, "HHS: What We Do." http://www.hhs.gov/about/profile.htm (29 June 2000). Accessed 6 July 2000.

11. U.S. Department of Health and Human Services, "Agencies in HHS." http://www.hhs.gov/news/press/profile/html (19 June 2002). Accessed 11 September 2002.

12. U.S. Department of Health and Human Services, "HHS: What We Do."

13. Health Care Financing Administration, Office of the Actuary: National Health Statistics Group, "National Health Care Expenditures by Source of Funds and Type of Expenditure: Selected Calendar Years 1993–98." http://www.hcfa.gov/stats/nhe-oact/tables/t3.htm (10 January 2000). Accessed 12 July 2000.

14. Department of Veterans Affairs, "Veterans Health Administration." http://www.va.gov/About_va/orgs/vha/index.htm (1 January 2000). Accessed 14 August 2000.

15. Department of Veterans Affairs, Veterans Health Administration, "Facts About the Department of Veterans Affairs." http://www.va.gov/pressrel/vafacts.htm (March 2002), Accessed 11 September 2002.

16. Department of Veterans Affairs, "Veterans Health Administration," 1.

17. U.S. Department of Veterans Affairs, Veterans Health Administration, "VA Medical Care Fact Sheet." http://www.va.gov/customer/medcarfs.htm (1 January 2000). Accessed 12 July 2000.

18. J. Tuchschmidt, "Managing Care for Veterans," *Forum* (Washington, DC: VA Office of Research and Development in Conjunction with the Association for Health Services Research, 1997), 1.

19. Department of Veterans Affairs, "Veterans Health Administration."

20. Office of the Assistant Secretary of Defense (Health Affairs), "Strategy for Implementing the High Performance MHS Plan." http://www.tricare.osd.mil/ hcr/downloads/CongRept.doc (September 1999). Accessed 2 August 2000.

21. Office of the Assistant Secretary of Defense (Health Affairs), "Strategy for Implementing the High Performance MHS Plan."

22. Health Care Financing Administration, "National Health Care Expenditures by Source of Funds and Type of Expenditure: Selected Calendar Years 1993–98."

23. National Association of Public Hospitals and Health Systems, "America's Essential Community Providers." http://www.naph.org/welcome.html (March 2000). Accessed 4 August 2000.

24. National Association of Public Hospitals and Health Systems, "America's Essential Community Providers."

25. W. Shonick, *Government and Health Services: Government's Role in the Development of U.S. Health Services, 1930–1980* (New York: Oxford University Press, 1995), 460–464.
26. Shonick, Government and Health Services, 98–101.
27. U.S. Department of Health and Human Services, Public Health Service, *For a Healthy Nation: Returns on Investment in Public Health* (Washington, DC: U.S. Government Printing Office, 1994), 1–13.
28. B.J. Tornock et al., "Local Health Department Effectiveness in Addressing the Core Functions of Public Health," *Public Health Reports* 109, no. 5 (1994): 653–658.
29. U.S. Department of Health and Human Services, *Prevention Report* 14, no. 4 (2000): 1–2.
30. Committee for the Study of the Future of Public Health, *The Future of Public Health*, 17.
31. Committee for the Study of the Future of Public Health, *The Future of Public Health*, 32.
32. U.S. Department of Health and Human Services, Public Health Service, *For a Healthy Nation*, 1–13.
33. J.G. Freymann, "Medicine's Great Schism: Prevention vs. Cure: An Historical Interpretation," *Medical Care* 13, no. 7 (1975): 525–536.
34. P. Starr, "Transformation in Defeat: The Changing Objectives of National Health Insurance," *American Journal of Public Health* 72, no. 1 (1982): 78–88.
35. U.S. Department of Health and Human Services, Public Health Service, *For a Healthy Nation*, 1–13.
36. S. Avruch and A.P. Cackley, "Savings Achieved by Giving WIC Benefits to Women Prenatally," *Public Health Reports* 110, no. 1 (1995): 27–34.
37. T.M. Vogt et al., "The Medical Care System: The Need for a New Paradigm," *HMO Practice* 12, no. 1 (March 1999): 5–12.
38. Vogt et al., "The Medical Care System: The Need for a New Paradigm," 5–12.
39. J.D. Seay and B.C. Vladeck, *Mission Matters: A Report on the Future of Voluntary Health Care Institutions* (New York: United Hospital Fund of New York, 1988), 13–15.
40. Committee for the Study of the Future of Public Health, *The Future of Public Health*, 7–10.
41. Committee for the Study of the Future of Public Health, *The Future of Public Health*, 19–32.
42. *Privatization and Public Health: A Study of Initiatives and Early Lessons Learned* (Washington, DC: Public Health Foundation, September 1997).
43. J. Rovner, "Expanding Health Insurance for Children: Congress Passes Bucks to States," *Advances, The Robert Wood Johnson Foundation Quarterly Newsletter* 4 (1997): 1–2.
44. "America's Health Care Safety Net Intact but Endangered." http://www.news@nas.edu.catalog/9612html (30 March 2000). Accessed 29 July 2000.
45. U.S. Public Health Service, *Prevention Report* (Washington, DC: Department of Health and Human Services, 1995), 1–12.
46. "Suddenly, Public Health Administration Is Seen as Top Priority," *Wall Street Journal*, 28 September 2002, A16.
47. www.govexec.com/homelandHSchart.hbm 15 November 2002, Accessed 30 April 2003.

Chapter 12

Research: How Health Care Advances

This chapter explains the focus of different types of research and how each type contributes to the overall advances in health and medicine. Health services research, a newer field that addresses the workings of the health care system rather than specific problems of disease or disability, is described. The offices and goals of its major funding source, the federal Agency for Healthcare Research and Quality (AHRQ), are listed. Finally, research into the quality of medical care, the problems being addressed, and the research challenges of the future are discussed.

The last half of the twentieth century saw a remarkable growth of scientifically rigorous research in medicine, dentistry, nursing, and the other health professions. The change from depending on the clinical impressions of individual physicians and other health care practitioners to relying on the statistical probability of accurate findings from carefully controlled studies is one of the most important advances in scientific medicine. No longer is the literature of the health professions filled with subjective anecdotal reports of the progress of treatment in one or more individual cases. Now, readers of peer-reviewed professional journals can monitor the progress of basic science or clinical or technological discoveries with confidence, knowing that published findings are, with only rare exceptions, based on research studies that have been rigorously designed and conducted to yield statistically credible results.

In contrast, the ever-growing volume of reports of medical developments that appear in the popular media are often premature, and, depending on the source, may be cause for skepticism. The imprudent publication of inadequately or unproven therapies, the sensationalizing of minor scientific advances, and the promotion of fraudulent devices and treatments create unrealistic expectations among anxious patients and families that often result in crushing disappointments, mistreatment, and costly deceptions.

From both professional and public perspectives, the continuing research yield of new technologies and clinical advances create ongoing challenges of evaluation, interpretation, and potential applications.

■ The Focus of Different Types of Research

Figure 12–1 illustrates the focus of the different types of health care research. There are clear distinctions among researchers in terms of focus, methods, and the nature of their subsequent findings. Although the kinds of information derived from each type of research may be different, each knowledge gain is an essential step in the never-ending quest to create a more efficient and effective health care system.[1]

Research in Health and Disease

Research studies conducted by those in the professional disciplines of health and disease fall into several categories. Basic science research is the work of biochemists, physiologists, biologists, pharmacologists, and others concerned with sciences that are fundamental to understanding the growth, development, structure, and function of the human body and its responses to external stimuli. Much of basic science research is at the cellular level and takes place in highly sophisticated laboratories. Other basic research may involve animal or human studies. Whatever its nature, however, basic science research is the essential antecedent of advances in clinical medicine.

Clinical research focuses primarily on the various steps in the process of medical care—the early detection, diagnosis, and treatment of disease or injury; the maintenance of optimal physical, mental, and social functioning; the limitation and rehabilitation of disability; and the palliative care of those who are irreversibly ill. Individuals in all the clinical specialties of medicine, nursing, allied health, and related

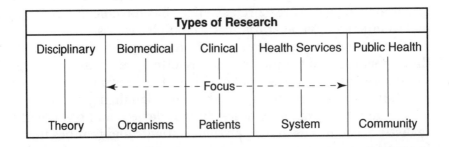

Figure 12–1 Variations in Research Focus
Source: Used with permission from *Evaluating the Medical Care System: Effectiveness, Efficiency, and Equity,* by Lu Ann Aday et al. (Chicago: Health Administration Press, 1993), p. 4.

health professions conduct clinical research, often in collaboration with those in the basic sciences. Much of clinical research is experimental, involving carefully controlled clinical trials of diagnostic or therapeutic procedures, new drugs, or technological developments.

Clinical trials test a new treatment or drug against a prevailing standard of care. If no standard drug exists or if it is too easily identified, a control group will receive a placebo or mock drug to minimize subject bias. To further reduce bias, random selection is used to decide which volunteer patients will be in the experimental and control groups. In a double-blind study, neither the researchers nor the patients know who is receiving the test drug or treatment until the study is completed and an identifying code revealed.

Research studies have a number of safeguards to protect the safety and rights of volunteer subjects. Studies funded by governmental agencies or foundations are subject to scrutiny by a peer review committee that judges the scientific merit of the research design and the potential value of the findings. Then a hospital-based or institutional review board checks for ethical considerations and patient protections. Lastly, volunteer subjects must receive and sign an informed consent form that spells out in clear detail the potential risks or side effects, and the expected benefits of their participation. Volunteers must weigh any potential risks against the likelihood that, by participating in research, they will receive state-of-the-art care and close health monitoring, and will contribute to the advancement of science.

Epidemiology

Epidemiology, or population research, is concerned with the distribution and determinants of health, diseases, and injuries in human populations. Much of that research is observational; it is the collection of information about natural phenomena, the characteristics and behaviors of people, aspects of their location or environment, and their exposure to certain circumstances or events.

Observational studies may be descriptive or analytical. Descriptive studies use patient records, interview surveys, various databases, and other information sources to identify those factors and conditions that determine the distribution of health and disease among specific populations. They provide the details or characteristics of diseases or biological phenomena and the prevalence or magnitude of their occurrence. Descriptive studies are relatively fast and inexpensive and often raise questions or suggest hypotheses to be tested. They usually are followed by analytic studies, which try to explain biologic phenomena by seeking statistical associations between factors that may contribute to a subsequent occurrence and the occurrence itself.

Some analytic studies attempt, under naturally occurring circumstances, to observe the differences between two or more populations with different characteristics or behaviors. For instance, data about smokers and nonsmokers may be collected to determine the relative risk of a related outcome such as lung cancer. Or a cohort study may follow a population over time, as in the case of a Framingham, Massachusetts, study. For years, epidemiologists have been studying a cooperating population of Framingham to determine associations between such variables as diet, weight, exercise, and other behaviors and characteristics related to heart disease and other outcomes. These observational studies are valuable in explaining patterns of disease or disease processes and providing information about the association of specific activities or agents with health or disease effects.

Experimental Epidemiology

Observational studies usually are followed by another major type of research: experimental studies. In experimental studies, the investigator actively intervenes by manipulating one variable to see what happens with another. Although they are the best test of cause and effect, such studies are technically difficult to carry out and often raise ethical issues. Control populations are used to ensure that other, nonexperimental variables are not affecting the outcome. Like clinical trials, such studies may raise ethical issues when experiments involve the use of a clinical procedure that may expose the subjects to significant or unknown risk. Ethical questions also are raised when experimental studies require the withholding of some potentially beneficial drug or procedure from individuals in the control group to prove the drug's or procedure's effectiveness decisively.

Other Applications of Epidemiologic Methods

Because the population perspective of epidemiology usually requires the study and analysis of data obtained from or about large-scale population samples, the discipline has developed principles and methods that can be applied to the study of a wide range of problems in several fields. Thus, the concepts and quantitative methods of epidemiology have been used not only to add to the understanding of the etiology of health and disease, but also to plan, administer, and evaluate health services; to forecast the health needs of population groups; to assess the adequacy of the supply of health personnel; and, most recently, to determine the outcomes of specific treatment modalities in a variety of clinical settings.

Advances in statistical theory and the epidemiology of medical care make it possible to analyze and interpret performance data obtained from the large Medicare and other insurance databases. Many of the findings of inexplicable geographic variations in the amount and cost of hospital treatments and in the use of a variety of health care services resulted from analysis of Medicare claims data and other large health insurance databases.

Health Services Research

Until the last two decades, most research addressed the need to broaden understanding of health and disease, to find new and more effective means of diagnosis and treatment, and, in effect, to improve the quality and length of life. For the two decades after World War II, supply-side subsidy programs dominated federal health care policy. Like other subsidy programs, Medicare and Medicaid were politically crafted solutions rather than research-based strategies. Nevertheless, those major health care subsidy programs were the driving forces behind the rise of health services research. The continuous collection of cost and utilization data from these programs revealed serious deficiencies in the capability of the health care system to efficiently and effectively deliver the knowledge and skills already at hand. In addition, evidence was growing that the large variations in the kinds and amounts of care delivered for the same conditions represented unacceptable volumes of inappropriate or questionable care and too much indecision or confusion among clinicians about the best courses of treatment. Health services research was born of the need to improve the efficiency and effectiveness of the health care system and to determine which of the health care treatment options for each condition produces the best outcomes.

Agency for Healthcare Research and Quality

Ever since John Wennberg documented large differences in the use of medical and surgical procedures among physicians in small geographic areas in the late 1980s, a number of similar studies brought the value of increasingly more costly health care into serious question. Wennberg noted that the rate of surgeries correlated with the number of surgeons and the number of hospital beds, rather than with differences among patients. He found that per capita expenditures for hospitalization in Boston were consistently double those in nearby New Haven.[2-4] Widely varying physician practice patterns provided little direction as to the most appropriate use of even the most common clinical procedures. In addition, adequate outcome measures for specific intervention modalities generally were lacking.

The problem did not escape the attention of the 101st Congress. The development of new knowledge through research has long been held as an appropriate and essential role of the federal government, as evidenced by the establishment and proactive role of the National

Institutes of Health. When it became clear that the indecision about the most appropriate and effective ways to diagnose and treat specific medical, dental, and other conditions was contributing to unacceptably large variations in the cost, quality, and outcomes of health care, federal legislation was passed to support the development of clinical guidelines. The Agency for Health Care Policy and Research (AHCPR) was established in 1989 as the successor to the National Center for Health Services Research and Health Care Technology. It is one of eight agencies of the Public Health Service within the Department of Health and Human Services.

AHCPR was responsible for updating and promoting the development and review of clinically relevant guidelines to assist health care practitioners in the prevention, diagnosis, treatment, and management of clinical conditions. Clinical guidelines are intended to enhance the quality, appropriateness, and effectiveness of health care.[5] The authorizing legislation directed that panels of qualified experts be convened by AHCPR or by public and not-for-profit private organizations. These panels were to review literature that contained the findings of numerous studies of clinical conditions, and, after considering the scientific evidence, to recommend clinical guidelines to assist practitioner and patient decisions about appropriate care for specific clinical conditions.

The agency's priority activities included extramural research through the Medical Treatment Effectiveness Program (MEDTEP). MEDTEP funded two types of research projects: patient outcome research teams (PORTs) and literature synthesis projects or meta-analyses. Both the PORT groups and the smaller literature synthesis projects identified and analyzed patient outcomes associated with alternative practice patterns and recommended changes where appropriate. During its decade-long existence, AHCPR supported studies that resulted in a prodigious array of publications focused on patient care and clinical decision making, technology assessment, the quality and costs of care, and treatment outcomes. Although no longer directly involved in producing clinical practice guidelines, the agency assists private-sector groups by supplying them with the scientific evidence they need to develop their own guidelines.

Within AHCPR there was an Office of the Forum for Quality and Effectiveness in Health Care, which focused on the development and periodic review of practice recommendations. In addition, there were Centers for Intramural and Extramural Research, an Office of Technology Assessment, and an Office for Data Development, among others.[6]

Some changes occurred in the mandate of AHCPR since its 1989 inception. The agency narrowly escaped the loss of funding and possible elimination in 1996 after incurring the wrath of national organizations of surgeons. In keeping with its original mission, AHCPR issued clinical guidelines. One such guideline discouraged surgery as a treatment for back pain on the grounds that it provided no better outcomes than more conservative treatments. Organizations of angry surgeons led a lobbying effort that convinced key members of Congress that the agency was exceeding its authority and establishing standards of clinical practice without considering the expertise and opinions of the medical specialists involved.[7]

The dispute was resolved when AHCPR agreed to function as a "science partner" with public and private organizations by simply assisting in developing knowledge that can be used to improve clinical practice. The agency would no longer produce clinical guidelines, but focus instead on funding research on medical interventions and analyzing the data that would underlie the development of clinical guidelines. The guidelines themselves would be generated by medical specialty and other organizations.

Subsequently, the Healthcare Research and Quality Act of 1999 was passed, which retitled the Agency for Health Care Policy and Research (AHCPR) to the Agency for Healthcare Research and Quality (AHRQ) and changed the title of the administrator to director. The mission of AHRQ is to: (1) improve the outcomes and quality of health care services, (2) reduce its costs, (3) address patient safety, and (4) broaden effective services through establishment of a broad base of scientific research that promotes improvements in clinical and health systems practices, including prevention of disease.[8]

The agency is composed of ten major functional components:

1. Immediate Office of the Director
2. Office of Management
3. Office of Research Review, Education and Policy
4. Office of Health Care Information
5. Center for Practice and Technology Assessment
6. Center for Outcomes and Effectiveness Research
7. Center for Primary Care Research
8. Center for Organization and Delivery Studies
9. Center for Cost and Funding Studies
10. Center for Quality Management[9]

A top priority of AHRQ is getting its sponsored research results and new health information into the hands of consumers. In addition to a number of consumer-oriented publications, the agency provides information to the public over the Internet. Its Web site, www.ahrq.gov, offers a great deal of health care information.

Building on concerns about medical errors and the quality of care, Congress and the president have increased support of the AHRQ. If that support continues during the next decade, the agency's greatest contribution to health care may be in the increases in patient care quality and reductions in costs that will result from provider acceptance of its service quality assessments and evidence-based practice recommendations.

Health Services Research and Health Policy

Health services research combines the perspectives and methods of epidemiology, sociology, economics, and clinical medicine; therefore, its curriculum is broader than the research courses taught in most medical schools. Although the basic concepts of epidemiologic research and associated statistics apply, process and outcome measures that reflect the behavioral and economic variables associated with questions of therapeutic effectiveness and cost benefit also are used. The ability of health services research to address issues of therapeutic effectiveness and cost benefit during this period of fiscal exigency contributed to the field's substantial growth and current value.

The contributions of health services research to health policy within recent years are impressive. Major examples include the Wennberg studies of small area variation in medical utilization, the prospective payment system based on diagnosis-related groups (DRGs),[10, 11] research on inappropriate medical procedures,[12] resource-based relative value scale research,[13-15] and the background research that supported the concepts of health maintenance organizations (HMOs) and managed care.

The RAND Health Insurance Experiment,[16, 17] one of the largest and longest running health services research projects ever undertaken, began in 1971 and contributed vast amounts of information on the effects of cost sharing on the provision and outcomes of health services. Between 1974 and 1977 the project enrolled families in six sites, representing four major census regions, northern and southern rural areas, and a range of city sizes. Participating families were assigned to one of four different fee-for-service plans or to a prepaid group practice. As might have been expected, individuals in the various plans differed significantly in their rate of use, with little measurable effect on health outcomes. Although the reduced use of hospitals and specialized care by those in HMO plans did not affect their health status, those patients new to HMOs were somewhat less satisfied than the fee-for-service patients. The Health Insurance Experiment was followed by two large research studies: the Health Services Utilization Study and the Medical Outcomes Study. The findings of both have given impetus to the federal support of outcomes research.[18]

Determining the outcomes and effectiveness of different health care interventions aids clinical decision making, reduces costs, and benefits patients. If the United States is ever able to build political consensus in support of a national health policy, the findings of health services research will underpin the decisions. In the meantime, the findings related to treatment effectiveness guide the cost-containment efforts of managed care organizations.

Quality Improvement

Until the last few years, health care's impressive accomplishments made it difficult for health care researchers, policy makers, and organizational leaders to publicly acknowledge that poor quality health care is a major problem within the dynamic and productive biomedical enterprise in the United States. In 1990, after two years of study, hearings, and site visits, the Institute of Medicine issued a report that cited widespread overuse of expensive invasive technology, underuse of inexpensive "caring" services, and implementation of error-prone procedures that harmed patients and wasted money.[19, 20]

Although these conclusions from so prestigious a body were devastating in their significance to health care reformers, they were hardly news to health service researchers. For decades, practitioners assumed that quality, like beauty, was in the eye of the beholder and, therefore, was unmeasurable except in cases of obvious violation of generally accepted standards. The medical and other health care professions had promoted the image of health care as a blend of almost impenetrable, science-based disciplines, leaving the providers of care as the only ones capable of understanding the processes taking place. Thus, only physicians could judge the work of other physicians. Such peer review–based assessment has always been difficult for reviewers and limited in effectiveness. Peer review recognizes that only part of medical care is based on factual knowledge. A substantial component of medical decision making is based on clinical judgment. Clinical judgment means combining consideration of the potential risks and benefits of each physician's internal list of diagnostic and treatment alternatives with his or her medical intuition regarding the likelihood of success based on the condition of each patient. Under these complex and often inexplicable circumstances, physicians are repelled by the notion of either judging or being judged by their colleagues.

That is why, until recently, quality assurance, whether in hospitals or by regulatory agencies, was focused only on identifying exceptionally poor care. This practice, popularly known as the Bad Apple theory, was based on the presumption that the best way to ensure quality was to identify the bad apples and remove or rehabilitate them. Thus, during the 1970s and 1980s, quality assurance interventions only followed detection of undesirable occurrences. For example, flagrant violations of professional standards had to be in evidence before professional review organizations required physicians to begin quality improvement plans. Of course, physicians were guaranteed due process to dispute the evidence.

Focusing on isolated violations required a great deal of review time to uncover a single case that called for remedial action. In addition, it was an unpleasant duty for reviewers to assign blame to a colleague, who might soon be on a committee reviewing their records. Most importantly, such an inspection of quality represented a method that implicitly defined quality as the absence of mishap. Clinician dislike of quality assurance activities during the 1970s and 1980s was well founded. The processes were offensive and had little constructive impact.

Specifying and striving for excellent care are very recent quality assurance phenomena in the health care arena. Just as the automobile and other industries were late giving up supervision as a control mechanism and introducing "quality circles" or teamwork, so, too, were hospitals and other health care organizations that had long focused on peer review committees, incident reports, and other negative quality monitoring activities.

Health services researchers had known for decades that health care quality was measurable, and that excellent, as well as poor, care could be identified and quantified. In 1966, Avedis Donabedian[21] characterized the concept of health care as divided into the components of structure, process, and outcomes and the research paradigm of their assumed linkages, all of which have guided quality of care investigators to this day.

Donabedian suggested that the number, kinds, and skills of the providers, as well as the adequacy of their physical resources and the manner in which they perform appropriate procedures, should, in the aggregate, influence the quality of the subsequent outcomes. Although today the construct may seem like a simple statement of the obvious, at the time, attention to structural criteria was the major, if not the only, quality assurance activity in favor. It was generally assumed that properly trained professionals, given adequate resources in properly equipped facilities, performed at acceptable standards of quality. For example, for many years the then Joint Commission on the Accreditation of Hospitals made judgments about the quality of hospitals on the basis of structural standards, such as physical facilities and equipment, ratios of professional staff to patients, and the qualifications of various personnel. Later, it added process components to its structural standards. Aspects of process are the diagnostic, treatment, and patient management decisions and their appropriateness in relation to current knowledge and practice. These quality assessments were directed to process components and did not attempt to determine what happened to the patients as the result of the medical decisions and interventions. Only recently did the Joint Commission on Accreditation of Healthcare Organizations include outcomes in its accreditation assessments.

Yet, as far back as the 1950s when Oscar Peterson and his associates at the University of North Carolina reported on a statewide study of general practice physicians, it was known that the quality of health service processes or practices may not reflect the quality of the underlying structural components of training and experience. Looking primarily at process components and using explicit practice quality criteria established in advance by a committee of general practitioners, researchers made on-site observations of each physician's practice behaviors for approximately one week. Forty-four percent of the physicians observed showed practice behaviors that were assessed as "below average" or "poor" in quality. Actual performance deficiencies may have been even greater because the presence of the observer may have motivated physicians to temporarily improve their usual performance.[22]

Similarly, in the early 1960s, M.A. Morehead conducted a study of the quality of care rendered to members of the Teamsters Union in New York City. At that time, the union was spending about $20 million per year for hospital services for its members and their families, and wondered whether the quality of the services justified that expense. Unlike the North Carolina study, however, the criteria against which performance was measured were implicit, that is, left to the individual judgments of "expert" reviewers. Teams of various kinds of specialists reviewed samples of patient records from the large number of hospitals in New York City. Although an examination of outcomes was not part of the study, the researchers did look at the association between structure and process and found strong relationships. Both the level of specialty training of the physicians and the teaching status of the hospitals were associated strongly with high percentages of appropriate admissions and the provision of optimal care.[23]

It should be noted, however, that the teams of medical experts making the judgments were themselves board-certified specialists associated with teaching hospitals, so that the implicit personal standards they used reflected their own practice styles, values, and beliefs as to what constituted quality care. Clearly, their selection as judges biased the study in the direction of its subsequent findings—an intrinsic problem when standards are personal and not predefined.

Nevertheless, the findings of the Teamsters' study have been replicated in many others since. In another early study by Peterson and associates,[24] the percentage of pelvic surgical procedures with incorrect diagnoses was determined by analyses of the pathologists' examination of the removed tissues. Again, there was a significant difference between major teaching hospitals and other proprietary and not-for-profit institutions. There also was a difference between physicians who were members of the American College of Surgeons and those who were not.

These early landmark quality-of-care studies are noted to illustrate the difference between implicit and explicit normative or judgmental standards. Implicit standards rely on the internalized judgments of the expert individuals involved in the quality assessment. Explicit standards are those developed and agreed on in advance of the assessment. Explicit standards minimize the variation and bias that invariably result when judgments are internalized. More current studies judge the appropriateness of hospital admissions and various procedures, and, in general, associate specific structural characteristics of the health care system with practice or process variations. The previously noted small area variation studies are typical examples of such research designs.

There is another method for assessing the quality of health care practices that is based on empirical standards. Derived from distributions, averages, ranges, and other measures of data variability, information collected from a number of similar health service providers is compared to identify practices that deviate from the norms. A current popular use of empirical standards is in the patient severity-adjusted hospital performance data collected by health departments and community-based employer and insurer groups to measure and compare both process activities and outcomes. These performance "report cards" are becoming increasingly valuable to the purchasers of care who need an objective method to guide their choices among managed care organizations, health care systems, and group practices. The empirical measures of quality include such variables as:

■ Timeliness of ambulation
■ Compliance with basic nursing care standards
■ Average length of stay
■ Number of home care referrals
■ Number of rehabilitation referrals
■ Timeliness of consultation completion
■ Timeliness of orders and results
■ Patient wait times by department or area
■ Infection rates
■ Decubitus rates
■ Medication errors
■ Patient complaints
■ Readmissions within 30 days
■ Neonatal and maternal mortalities
■ Perioperative mortalities

Normative and empirical standards are both used in studying the quality of health care in the United States. For example, empirical analyses are performed to test or modify normative recommendations. Empirical or actual experience data are collected to confirm performance and outcome improvements after the imposition of clinical guidelines derived from studies using normative standards.

Medical Errors

In November 1999, the Institute of Medicine (IOM) again issued a report on the quality of medical care. Focused on medical errors, the report described mistakes occurring during the course of hospital care as one of the nation's leading causes of death and disability. Citing two major studies, estimating that medical errors kill some 44,000 to 98,000 people in U.S. hospitals each year, the IOM report was a stunning indictment of the current systems of hospital care. The report contained a series of recommendations for improving patient safety in the admittedly high-risk environments of modern hospitals. Among the recommendations was a proposal for establishing a center for patient safety within the AHRQ. The proposed center would establish national safety goals, track progress in improving safety, and invest in research to learn more about preventing mistakes.[25] Congress responded by designating part of the increase in the budget for the AHRQ for that purpose.

Evidence-Based Medicine

Evidence-based medicine is defined as "the systematic application of the best available evidence to the evaluation of options and decisions in clinical practice, management and policy-making."[26] Although that statement may appear to be a description of the way physicians and other health care providers have practiced since the inception of scientific medicine, it reflects a spreading concern that quite the opposite is true. The wide range of variability in clinical practice, the complexity of diagnostic testing and medical decision making, and the difficulty that physicians have in keeping up with the overwhelming volumes of scientific literature suggest that a significant percentage of clinical management decisions are not supported by reliable evidence of effectiveness.

Although it is generally assumed that physicians are reasonably confident that the treatments they give are beneficial, the reality is that medical practice is fraught with uncertainty. In addition, the ethical basis for clinical decision making allows physicians to exercise their preferences for certain medical theories or practices that may or may not have been evaluated to link treatment to benefits.[27]

Proponents of evidence-based medicine propose that if all health services are intended to improve the health status and quality of life of the recipients, then:

The acid test is whether services, programs and policies improve health beyond what could be achieved with the same resources by different means, or by doing nothing at all. Evidence is the key to accountability; the decisions made by health care providers, administrators, policy makers, patients, and the public need to be based on appropriate, balanced, and high-quality evidence.[28]

The evidence-based approach to assessing the acceptability of research findings considers the evidence from randomized clinical trials involving large numbers of participants the most valid. Evidence-based medicine advocates dismiss outcomes research that uses large data files created from claim records, hospital discharges, Medicare, or other sources because the subjects are not randomized. "Outcomes research using claims data is an excellent way of finding out what doctors are doing, but it's a terrible way to find out what doctors should be doing," states Thomas C. Chalmers, MD, of Harvard School of Public Health, Boston.[29]

In general, most of the investigations reported in the peer-reviewed medical literature have been preliminary tests of innovations and served science rather than providing guidance to practitioners in clinical practice. Only a small portion of those efforts survive testing well enough to justify routine clinical application.[30]

The situation is changing rapidly, however. Articles on evidence-based medicine are appearing with increasing frequency in the medical literature.[31] (See Figure 12–2.) Cost-control pressures that encourage efforts to ensure that therapies have documented patient

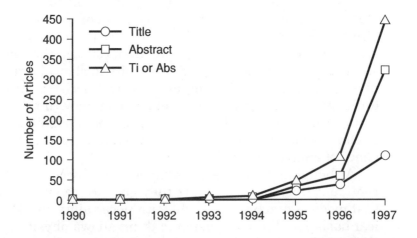

Figure 12–2 Number of Articles Containing Keywords "Evidence-Based" or "Evidence-Based Medicine" in Title (Ti), Abstract (Abs), or Either, by Year
Source: Reprinted with permission from Elsevier (*The Lancet,* 1997, Vol. 349, 1329–1330).

benefit, growing interest in the quality of patient care, and increasing sophistication on the part of patients concerning the care that they receive have stimulated acceptance of the concepts of evidence-based medical practice.[32]

Outcomes Research

Given the huge investment in U.S. health care and the inequitable distribution of its services, do the end effects on the health and well-being of patients and populations justify the costs? Insurance companies, state and federal governments, employers, and consumers are looking to outcomes research for information that will help them make better decisions about what kinds of health care should be reimbursed, for whom, and when.

Because outcomes research evaluates results of health care processes in the real world of physicians' offices, hospitals, clinics, and homes, it contrasts with traditional randomized controlled studies that test the effects of treatments in controlled environments. In addition, the research in usual service settings, or "effectiveness research," differs from controlled clinical trials, or "efficacy research," in the nature of the outcomes measured. Traditionally, studies measured health status, or outcomes, with physiological measurements—laboratory tests, complication rates, recovery, or survival. To more adequately capture health status, outcomes research measures a patient's functional status and well-being. Satisfaction with care also must complement traditional measures.

Functional status includes three components that assess patients' abilities to function in their own environment:

1. Physical functioning
2. Role functioning—the extent to which health interferes with usual daily activities, like work or school
3. Social functioning—whether health affects normal social activities, such as visiting friends or participating in group activities

Personal well-being measures describe patients' senses of physical and mental well-being—their mental health or general mood, their own view of their general health, and their general sense about the quality of their lives. Patient satisfaction measures the patients' views about the services received, including access, convenience, communication, financial coverage, and technical quality.

Outcomes research also uses meta-analysis, a technique to summarize comparable findings from multiple studies. More importantly, however, outcomes research goes beyond determining what works in ideal circumstances to assessing which treatments for specific clinical

problems work best in different circumstances. Appropriateness studies are conducted to determine circumstances in which a procedure
should and should not be performed. Even though a procedure is
proven effective, it is not appropriate for every patient in all circumstances. The frequency of inappropriate clinical interventions is one
of the major quality-of-care problems in the system. Research is also
underway to develop the tools to identify patient preferences when
treatment options are available. Although most discussions about appropriateness stress the cost savings that could be achieved by reducing unnecessary care and overuse of services, it is important to re-
member that outcomes research may be just as likely to uncover
underuse of appropriate services.

It is important to recognize that the ultimate value of outcomes research can be measured only by its ability to incorporate the results
of its efforts into the health care process. To be effective, the findings
of outcomes research must first reach and then change the behaviors
of providers, patients, health care institutions, and payers. The end-
point of outcomes research, the clinical practice guidelines intended
to assist practitioners and patients in choosing appropriate health
care for specific conditions, must be disseminated in acceptable and
motivational ways. With the health care industry in a state of rapid
and generally unpredictable change, the need to make appropriate investments in outcomes research has become increasingly apparent.
The conclusion is now inescapable that the United States cannot continue to spend over $1 trillion a year on health care without learning
much more than is now known about what that investment is buying.

Patient Satisfaction

Patient satisfaction has become an important component of the quality of care. Although the subjective ratings of health care received by
patients may be based on markedly different criteria from those considered important by care providers, they capture aspects of care and
personal preferences that contribute significantly to perceived quality. It has become increasingly important in the competitive market
climate of health care that the providers' characteristics, organization, and system attributes important to the consumers be identified
and monitored. In addition to caregivers' technical and interpersonal
skills, such patient concerns as waiting times for appointments,
emergency responses, helpfulness and communication of staff, and
the facility's appearance contribute to patient evaluations of health
services delivery programs and subsequent satisfaction with the
quality of care received.

A number of instruments have been devised to measure patient
satisfaction with health care, and most managed care plans, hospitals,
and other health service facilities and agencies have adopted one or

more to regularly assess patient satisfaction. Some, like the Patient Satisfaction Questionnaire (PSQ) developed at Southern Illinois University School of Medicine, are short, self-administered survey forms.[33] Others, like the popular patient satisfaction instruments of the Picker Institute of Boston, Massachusetts, may be used as self-administered questionnaires mailed to patients after a health care experience or completed by interviewers during telephone surveys.[34] Whether by mail, direct contact, or telephone interview, questioning patients after a recent health care experience is an effective way to both identify outstanding service personnel and uncover fundamental problems in the quality of care as defined by patients. It not only serves the purpose of providing humane and effective care, but it is also good marketing to do everything possible to increase patient satisfaction, maintain patient loyalty, and enhance patient referrals.

■ Research Ethics

In the over four decades since World War II, the federal government has invested heavily in biomedical research. The ensuing public–private partnership in health has produced some of the finest medical research in the world. The growth of medical knowledge is unparalleled, and the United States can take well-deserved pride in its research accomplishments.

However, many, if not most, of the sophisticated new technologies address the need to ameliorate the problems of patients who already have the condition or disease under treatment. Both the priorities and the profits intrinsic to the U.S. health care system focus on remedial rather than preventive strategies. Only in the case of frightening epidemics, such as that of polio in the 1940s or AIDS in the 1990s, has there been the requisite moral imperatives to adequately fund abundant research efforts that address public health problems. Clearly, much of the recent funding for medical research has failed to fulfill the generally held belief that the products of taxpayer-supported research should benefit not only the practice of medicine, but also the community at large.[35]

The increasing amount of research funding emanating from pharmaceutical companies is of growing concern. Pharmaceutical companies that pay researchers to design and interpret drug trials have been accused of spinning the results or suppressing unfavorable findings. The conflicts that arise in the testing of new drugs and publishing the results are deepened as more and more of these studies are shifted from academic institutions to commercial research firms.[36]

Commercialism, with its accompanying ethical concerns, has invaded the research laboratory in a big way with the unfolding of the human genome. The scientific importance of being able to read the 3 billion DNA "letters" of the human body is being overshadowed by visions of the technology's commercial potential. The completion of the DNA sequence will revolutionize medicine by giving scientists unprecedented insights into the workings of the human body. Although the benefits of these genetic breakthroughs are years away, debates over whether the technology will stay in the public domain and strategies for profiting from the ability to treat medical conditions through gene manipulation are already under way. Clearly, the admirable advances in understanding and technology resulting from sophisticated medical research are increasingly accompanied by less-than-commendable bending of ethical precepts.

■ Future Challenges

Much, if not most, of U.S. health care research has been directed toward improving the health care system's ability to diagnose and treat injury, disease, and disability among those who seek care from the health care providers in the vast and complex array of existing health services. For decades, health care has been a complaint and response system, with most patient and provider interactions initiated by ailing patients. Physicians and other health professionals have maintained the mindset that their major, if not sole, duty was to resolve patient problems as expeditiously as possible. Now, largely because of the influences of managed care, research studies are increasingly focused on identifying and improving the health status of populations. Research priorities are shifting from an individual patient perspective to a population orientation and toward continuous scrutiny of the efficiency and effectiveness of the care delivered.

Basic science research will continue to contribute to the diagnostic and therapeutic efficacy of health care by adding to the knowledge about the human body and its functions. In small but critically important increments, basic science research will unlock many of the secrets of aging, cell growth regulation, mental degradation, and other mysteries of immunology, genetics, microbiology, and neuroendocrinology. The propensity of medicine to use newly obtained knowledge to alter certain physiologic processes, as in the several forms of gene manipulation, will produce new ethical, legal, and clinical issues that then will require further research and adjudication.

Massive databases of gene and protein sequences and structure/function information have made possible a new worldwide research effort called bioinformatics. Bioinformatic research probes those large computer databases to learn more about life's processes in health and disease and to find new or better drugs. It is considered the future of biotechnology.

Of particular interest is research in genomics, the study of genetic material in the chromosomes of specific organisms. The sequencing of the human genome will reshape biology and medicine and lead to significant improvements in the diagnosis of disease and individual responses to drugs.[37]

Similarly, certain advances in clinical medicine and the other health disciplines will result in new and particularly disturbing moral dilemmas. Medical achievements, such as those that permit the maintenance of life in otherwise terminal and unresponsive individuals, or the transplantation of organs in short supply that require choosing among recipient candidates when those denied will surely die, generate extremely complex ethical, economic, religious, personal, and professional issues. Thus, much of the basic and clinical research that solves yesterday's problems relating to individual patient care will create new problems to be addressed in the never-ending cycle of discovery, application, and evaluation.

Medical researchers and clinicians are becoming increasingly concerned that health care in the United States is entering a "postantibiotic" era in which bacterial infections will be unaffected by even the most powerful of available antibiotics. Evidence is accumulating that a growing number of microbes, including strains of staphylococcus and streptococcus bacteria, are becoming resistant to common antimicrobials.[38]

Staphylococcus bacteria are the major cause of hospital infections. According to the Centers for Disease Control and Prevention, these infections are responsible for about 13 percent of the 2 million infections that occur in U.S. hospitals each year. Overall, those hospital infections result in the deaths of 60,000 to 80,000 patients.[39]

Although epidemiologists and clinicians specializing in infectious disease have warned for decades that misuse and overuse of antibiotics would result in a host of deadly drug-resistant pathogens, it appears that neither physicians nor patients took the warnings seriously. Apparently, there was a widespread belief that the constant development of new antimicrobial drugs would keep medicine a step ahead of bacterial resistance. Although the limited development of new antibiotic drugs has failed to keep step with antibiotic resistance, scientists see a promising alternative in bacterial genetics. Introducing synthetic genes into bacteria appears to turn off the bacteria's ability to resist antibiotics.[40]

While researchers address the problems of treatment of these lethal infections, hospitals strive to prevent them. Because bacteria can be transmitted on blankets, clothing, walls, medical equipment, and by hand, hospitals are implementing rigorous infection control and surveillance policies and new education programs for both providers and patients.

Health services research, on the other hand, will continue to focus on the performance of the health care system as the basis for proposing or evaluating health policy alternatives. It is interdisciplinary, value-laden research concerned with the effectiveness or benefits of care, the efficiency or resource cost of care, and the equity or fairness of the distribution of care. As the U.S. health care system goes through its wrenching adjustment to competitive, market-driven reforms, health services research becomes more and more central to the development of a logical, well-documented rationale for future health care policies and delivery systems. At present, clinical uncertainty is pervasive in the health care industry as it defines illness, selects among treatment options, and tries to determine the probabilities of desired and unintended results and to judge the quality of individual outcomes.

Documenting the influence of financial incentives that affect both patient and provider, understanding the important relationships of socioeconomic status to health and health care, determining the effects of the training and experience of the health care team and the ability of the members to work together, and understanding how these many influences interact are basic to improving the quality of care. Reducing the monumental quandaries in medicine and health care about what works well in what situations is the challenge of health services research and the key to a more effective, efficient, and equitable health care system.

Managed care companies and groups of consumers and businesses are supporting an effort to develop national performance measures for health plans that will help consumers and payers compare plans on measures other than cost. Insurers increasingly are using outcomes research results to refine and improve their reimbursement systems. Hospitals, HMOs, and other organized care systems are incorporating results of outcomes research into their quality review and improvement practices. Results not only provide guidance on what is good care, but also form the basis for discussion among providers and managers about ways of designing more efficient delivery systems.

Public health research is a related research arena that deserves to receive higher priority and significantly increased political support. If health care is ever to develop a true population perspective rather than an individual patient perspective and reap the health and economic benefits of preventive rather than curative medicine, then epidemiology and public health research must be charged with finding ways to better understand and resolve the huge differences in health, health behaviors, health care, and health system effectiveness among communities and the population groups within them. Epidemiology, the core discipline of public health research, relates the health problems and use of health care resources to defined populations. It identifies groups that do not present themselves for health care, as well as those that do. Thus, epidemiology can assess the health problems and the provision of health care for the total population rather than just those who are in contact with health services. Surveillance and monitoring of health conditions and assessing the effect of health care measures on the entire population are important factors in formulating health policy, organizing health services, and allocating limited resources.[41] The strategy for identifying and dealing with real or suspected biological attacks on citizens of the United States will depend heavily on the ability of epidemiologists to identify the common source of such outbreaks, the patterns of transmission, and the outcomes of preventive and remedial efforts.

As health care adds to its traditional focus on theories, disease, and individual patient care, the performance of the health care system and the health status of populations, public health, and health services research assume increasing relevance and importance. No matter how well the health care system performs for some of the people, it will never be fully satisfactory until it can provide a basic level of care for all.

■ Notes

1. L.A. Aday et al., *Evaluating the Medical Care System: Effectiveness, Efficiency, and Equity* (Ann Arbor, MI: Health Administration Press, 1993), 4.
2. J.E. Wennberg et al., "Are Hospital Services Rationed in New Haven or Over-Utilized in Boston?" Lancet 1 (1987): 1185–1189.
3. J.E. Wennberg, "Which Rate Is Right?" *New England Journal of Medicine* 314 (1986): 310–311.
4. J.E. Wennberg et al., "Hospital Use and Mortality among Medicare Beneficiaries in Boston and New Haven," *New England Journal of Medicine* 321 (1989): 1168–1173.
5. Agency for Health Care Policy and Research, U.S. Department of Health and Human Services, *AHCPR Program Note* (Rockville, MD: Public Health Service, 1990), 1–5.
6. Agency for Health Care Policy and Research, *AHCPR Program Note,* 1–2.
7. J. Stephenson, "Revitalized AHCPR Pursues Research on Quality," *Journal of the American Medical Association* 278, no. 19 (19 November 1997): 1557.
8. AHRQ Fiscal Year 2003 Budget in Brief, Agency for Healthcare Research and Quality, Rockville, MD. http://www.ahrq.gov/about/cj2003/budbrf03.htm (February 2002). Accessed 28 August 2002.
9. Agency for Healthcare Research and Quality: Offices and Centers, Agency for Healthcare Research and Quality, Rockville, MD. http://www.ahrq.gov/about/offcntrs.htm_(March 2002). Accessed 28 August 2002.
10. R. Mills et al., "AUTOGRP: An Interactive Computer System for the Analysis of Health Care Data," *Medical Care* 14 (1976): 603–615.

11. R. Fetter et al., "Case-Mix Definition by Diagnostically-Related Groups," *Medical Care Supplement* 18 (1980): 1–53.
12. M.R. Chassin et al., "Does Inappropriate Use Explain Geographic Variations in the Use of Health Care Services? A Study of Three Procedures," *Journal of the American Medical Association* 258 (1987): 2533–2537.
13. W.C. Hsiao and W.B. Stason, "Toward Developing a Relative Value Scale for Medical and Surgical Services," *Health Care Financing Review* 1, no. 2 (1979): 23–28.
14. W.C. Hsiao et al., "Results and Policy Implications of the Resource-Based Relative Value Study," *New England Journal of Medicine* 319, no. 13 (1988): 881–888.
15. W.C. Hsiao et al., *A National Study of Resource-Based Relative Value Scale for Physician Services: Final Report to the Health Care Financing Administration* (Boston, MA: Harvard School of Public Health, 1988).
16. J.P. Newhouse, "A Design for a Health Insurance Experiment," *Inquiry* 11, no. 1 (1974): 5–27.
17. J.P. Newhouse et al., "The Findings of the RAND Health Insurance Experiment—A Response to Welch et al.," *Medical Care* 25, no. 2 (1987): 157–179.
18. J.P. Newhouse, "Controlled Experimentation as Research Policy," in *Health Services Research: Key to Health Policy,* ed. E. Ginzberg (Cambridge, MA: Harvard University Press, 1991), 162–194.
19. K.N. Lohr and the Institute of Medicine, *Medicare: A Strategy for Quality Assurance,* vol. 1 (Washington, DC: National Academy Press, 1990), 1–19.
20. R.H. Palmer, "Considerations in Defining Quality of Health Care, Part I," in *Striving for Quality in Health Care: An Inquiry into Policy and Practice,* ed. R.H. Palmer et al. (Ann Arbor, MI: Health Administration Press, 1991), 1–4.
21. A. Donabedian, "Evaluating the Quality of Medical Care," *Milbank Memorial Fund Quarterly* 44 (1966): 166–206.
22. O. Peterson, "An Analytic Study of North Carolina General Practice," *Journal of Medical Education,* Supplement, Part 2 (1956).
23. M.A. Morehead, "The Medical Audit as an Operational Tool," *Journal of Public Health* 57 (1967): 1643–1656.
24. O. Peterson et al., "A Study of Diagnostic Performance: A Preliminary Report," *Journal of Medical Education* 41, no. 8 (1966): 797–803.
25. L.T. Kohn et al., *To Err Is Human: Building a Safer Health System* (Washington DC: Institute of Medicine, 1999), 74–77.
26. J.E. Ware Jr. et al., "Defining and Measuring Patient Satisfaction with Medical Care," *Evaluation and Planning* 6 (1983): 247–263.
27. M. Watanabe, "A Call for Action from the National Forum on Health," *Canadian Medical Association Journal* 156, no. 7 (1 April 1997): 999–1000.
28. C. Marwick, "Federal Agency Focuses on Outcomes Research," *Journal of the American Medical Association* 270, no. 2 (14 July 1993): 164–165.
29. Watanabe, "A Call for Action from the National Forum on Health," 999–1000.
30. Marwick, "Federal Agency Focuses on Outcomes Research," 164–165.

31. F. Davidoff et al., "Evidence-Based Medicine," *British Medical Journal* 310 no. 6987 (29 April 1995): 1085–1086.

32. R.C. Hooker, "The Rise and Rise of Evidence-Based Medicine," (Letter) *Lancet* 349 no. 9061 (3 May 1997): 1329–1330.

33. Marwick, "Federal Agency Focuses on Outcomes Research," 164–165.

34. M. Gerteis et al., *Through the Patient's Eyes: Understanding and Promoting Patient-Centered Care* (San Francisco: Jossey-Bass Publishers, 1993), 1–15.

35. L.M. Constantine, "Healthcare Providers Confront Rise in Resistant Pathogens," *Report of Medical Guidelines and Outcomes Research* 8, no. 21 (Capitol Productions, 16 October 1997): 1–5.

36. R. Stevens, *In Sickness and in Wealth*, (New York: Basic Books, Inc., 1989), 48.

37. The George Washington University Medical Center. http://www.gwumc.edu/bioinformatics (July 2002). Accessed 27 August 2002.

38. T. Bodenheimer, "Uneasy Alliance—Clinical Investigators and the Drug Industry," *The New England Journal of Medicine* 2000, no. 342:1516–1518, 1539–1544.

39. Constantine, "Healthcare Providers Confront Rise in Resistant Pathogens," 1–5.

40. Constantine, "Healthcare Providers Confront Rise in Resistant Pathogens," 1–5.

41. M.A. Ibrahim, *Epidemiology and Health Policy* (Gaithersburg, MD: Aspen Publishers, 1985), 6.

Chapter 13

The Future of Health Care

This concluding chapter provides some forecasts about the future of various components of the U.S. health care system. It outlines the changes that have occurred among health care organizations, services, and facilities, and physicians, nurses, and other personnel, and projects those trends into the future. The chapter also sketches the corporate growth in health care and the impact of technological advances, managed care, academic health centers, and federal and state governmental initiatives and draws conclusions about the future of America's health care system.

In the previous chapters, we have presented a mix of facts, expert opinions, findings of published studies, and historical background. Although the selection of content and the interpretations of historical events undoubtedly reflect our own public health or population perspective, we have tried to provide a balanced view of the health care system and its evolution, strengths, and weaknesses. When discussing the future, however, we are entering uncharted territory, progressing from the current structure and conduct of health care to conjecture about its reformation. Looking ahead is far more hazardous than looking back, and we acknowledge that the predictions that follow represent only our personal educated guesses about the directions our health care system will take in the coming years. Even the most thoughtful forecasts, founded on carefully studied trends and data-based projections by reputable authorities, will be affected by unforeseeable and rapid changes in the health care environment.

Reforms driven by cost-conscious market forces are often complex, chaotic, and disabling to those unable to adapt to continuing uncertainty. According to chaos theory, "a small change in input can quickly translate into overwhelming differences in output,"[1] and, as has been demonstrated already, the health care system is particularly sensitive to input changes. In the past, every tinkering effort to address one of the three basic problems of the health care system—costs, quality, and access—has resulted in significant changes in one or both of the others. Improving access to health care for low-income populations and older adults through Medicaid and Medicare had a significant inflationary effect on costs. Containing costs through managed care now raises questions about quality and access. Similarly, seemingly small changes within a health care institution, such as a leadership response to an outside financial, technological, or market development, may result in unanticipated pressures on the operations within the organization. Thus, many of the recent organizational machinations of the institutions and agencies struggling to cope with health care reforms may, in the long run, turn out to be counterproductive overreactions.

■ The Paradox of U.S. Health Care

It is unfortunate that the extraordinary successes of the U.S. health care system and the technological accomplishments that brought worldwide acclaim to U.S. scientists are offset in the minds of the public and in the opinions of health system analysts by the system's persistent and increasingly evident deficiencies. The policy decisions of health care leadership after World War II are duly credited with medicine's impressive advances, its prestige, and its wealth. Those health care policies led the National Institutes of Health and the National Science Foundation to invest heavily in the potential of our nation's universities and medical schools to develop basic and applied research and to dedicate federal and state funds to the expansion of academic medical centers. The burgeoning health care industry prompted the initiation of federal programs that significantly expanded the number and size of U.S. hospitals and led to an exponential increase in the size of the health care workforce. Those health care policies that produced the financial incentives in the health care reimbursement system encouraged specialization among physicians and other health care practitioners.

Those policies also contributed to the long-standing health care problems of inequitable access, variable quality, and runaway costs. The success of the health care industry (measured by the dollars invested and spent), the growth of its workforce, its astounding physical and technological infrastructure, its impressive outcomes, and its unfettered revenues must be weighed against its failure to recognize a social mission broader than addressing the individual needs of those who accessed its services. Until recently, the technology-oriented, can-do culture that pervades health care, and medicine in particular, appeared to have mesmerized the consuming public and health care providers into thinking that more dramatic medical marvels would solve the ills of the system. For many years, the public that supported the rising costs of health care had equally ascending expectations for what medicine could accomplish.

Now, however, there is growing discontent with a system that cannot deliver even a basic level of health care to significant portions of the public, that cannot control costs that have increased at twice the rate of other commodities, and that provides some services of doubtful necessity and therapeutic benefit. Nothing has shaken the public's previously durable faith in medicine as much as the growing awareness that many of the new technologies that yield economic benefits to providers may be of only marginal value in the diagnosis and treatment of patients.

■ The Major Challenges Facing Health Care

Regardless of widespread criticism of America's system of health care, the public and political clamor for fundamental reform seems to have waned from its peak in the mid-1990s. The competitive managed care systems that followed the demise of national health care reform have been somewhat effective in containing health care costs, but several other very serious problems continue to plague the system. These problems, described as "major forces reshaping the health care system industry," are outlined in Table 13–1.[2]

There were both positive and negative consequences in the decade that followed this enumeration of societal developments that were influencing health care. Both the consumers and the providers of health care are increasingly concerned that the negative consequences of social, technical, and economic forces impacting the health system are resulting in a more disordered and less trustworthy health care system.

■ The Growing Number of Uninsured

The population of uninsured Americans is a constantly changing, heterogeneous group that includes the full range of annual incomes. The sluggish economy, receding governmental budgets, and rising health care costs have dissuaded an increasing number of middle- and upper-income people to forgo health insurance. About 18 million of the 41 million uninsured fall into that category. Many are self-employed or retired early without insurance benefits. Retiree health insurance coverage has declined steadily since 1990.[3]

Two other groups make up the balance of the uninsured. Many low-income uninsured are eligible for Medicaid or State Children's Health Insurance Programs but are either unaware of their eligibility or the enrollment process. The other uninsured group is made up of low-income people who do not qualify for public programs. According to the NIHCM, about nine million people fall into this category. Many of these people are employed full- or part-time in low-paying jobs without health benefits, or in transition after losing a job. Still others have been dropped from Medicaid after moving into the workforce. These transition gaps are the reason for the constantly changing composition of the uninsured population.

Table 13–1 Key Forces Influencing the Health Care System

FORCES	IMPLICATIONS AND ISSUES
• Growing number of uninsured	• Creation of basic benefit package • State-level experimentations • What does the country want to afford?
• Demand for greater accountability —fiscal and clinical	• Search for value (greater quality for a given cost or lower cost for a given level of quality) • What works?
• Technological growth and innovation	• New diagnostic and treatment modalities • Growth of outpatient care • Increased issues involving prolongation of life
• Changing population composition: growth of elderly and ethnically heterogenous population	• Changes in demand for care • Increased number of ethical issues • Increased social morbidity
• Changing professional labor supply	• Shortages of key health professionals • Redefinition of professional roles • Productivity and quality issues
• Globalization of the economy	• Increased scrutiny of health care costs
• Changing composition of the delivery system: consolidations and mergers—horizontal and vertical	• Increased potential for managing a continuum of care • Increased potential for providing care to defined populations
• Information management	• Facilitates accountability • Tool for increased productivity • Direct clinical applications • Opportunity to actively manage clinical care

Source: Reprinted with permission from S.M. Shortell and U.E. Reinhardt, "Creating and Executing Health Policy in the 1990s," in *Improving Health Policy and Management: Nine Critical Research Issues,* pp. 3–36, S.M. Shortell and U.E. Reinhardt, eds. © 1992, Academy of Health Services.

Addressing the huge problem of uninsured Americans always raises the political issues that swirl around the concept of a national health insurance or single payer system. Yet, small segments of the problem have been addressed quite successfully by governments through Medicaid, SCHIP, and a number of innovative state programs. They are limited, however, to low-income groups. The major impediment to insuring most of the 41 million uninsured Americans is affordability. Yet, they do get health care. As might be expected, that care is delayed, episodic, and incomplete. Nevertheless, it amounted to about $35 billion of uncompensated care in 2001.[4] The care is provided by clinics, hospitals, physicians, and other providers who either absorb the costs or receive some general support from government or private funds.

Private health plans recognize that that money is in the system and that the increasing numbers of non-poor uninsured constitute a potential market for new lower cost insurance plans. They also recognize that the uninsured face serious health and financial risks. On a less altruistic note, private plans worry that if the situation continues unabated for too long, the government will finally step in with an intervention that will be unfavorable to the insurance industry.

In response, private health plans have been experimenting with insurance products designed to attract uninsured individuals and small businesses. It is a difficult task to create an insurance product that will appeal to low- and moderate-income persons and still be flexible enough to attract both younger, healthy workers and older, higher risk individuals. Nevertheless, there is general agreement that carefully crafted insurance plans that protect against high medical costs can be affordable and effective.

Although most people would prefer comprehensive health care coverage, it is simply too expensive for most small businesses and low- to moderate-income individuals. If health care costs continue to rise at unacceptable rates, more and more people will find health insurance unaffordable. The concept of medical saving accounts in which people simply set aside money, tax-free, to cover medical expenses and, each year, roll over unspent funds will become more and more attractive.

■ Demand for Greater Accountability, Fiscal and Clinical

Given the many different entrenched interests in health care, it is not surprising that only a few minor changes in the system of care have been allowed to occur. The many professions, employers, employees, and service, financial, and educational institutions have repeatedly demonstrated the capability of exercising the power necessary to maintain the status quo. Thus, the health care system, apart from the advances in clinical practice, has an inbuilt resistance to change. As a consequence, the long and escalating problems of health care costs and unconscionable rates of unacceptable clinical quality have remained unabated for decades. Since there are no single solutions to these complex, interlocking problems, and little likelihood that all or most of the vested interests would support a set of simultaneously applied solutions, the problems continue. Anything more than tinkering with the system would have a negative effect on at least one of the major players capable of nullifying the proposed changes.

The failed attempts to address the issue of the variable quality of clinical care illustrate a facet of the problem. Concerns about the quality of health care, both anecdotally and empirically, have been expressed for decades. Since there were always small numbers of patients involved in any individual hospital, physicians and hospital executives tended to overlook the problems. Finally, in 1999, there was a credible, widely publicized assessment of the problem. The previously cited 1999 Institute of Medicine report, *To Err is Human: Building a Safer Health System,* estimated that as many as 98,000 die in hospitals each year as a result of medical errors. It produced a brief flurry of discussion in Congress and then moved far down on the list of U.S. concerns. When 3,000 people died on September 11th, 2001, the United States went to war. When over 3,000 people die every two weeks as a result of medical errors, the silence is incomprehensible and discouraging.

The lack of response by physicians and policymakers reflects the generally held assumption that the medical profession effectively polices itself. The esteemed position of physicians in society and the confidentiality of the interactions between doctors and their patients have long shielded medicine from the sweeping reforms that corrected abuses in other industries. Yet, the truth is that the medical profession has failed to exercise the leadership necessary to correct the long-standing medical care system deficiencies that the IOM report identified. System improvements occur only after wide public exposure of high risk practice patterns.

Michael L. Millenson, author of the 1997 book, *Demanding Medical Excellence: Doctors and Accountability in the Information Age,* University of Chicago Press, described that shortcoming more recently in "Health Affairs."[5]

The blunt answer is that professionalism alone has consistently failed to protect patients. Rather, it has been professionalism pushed into action by pressure from the press, public, politicians, and the pocketbook. For example, anesthesiologists finally acted to improve patient safety only after a television exposé of anesthesia accidents. Rising malpractice premiums—an economic incentive—provided an extra sense of urgency. Similarly, the "sign your site" protocol came in reaction to a nationally publicized incident in which a Florida surgeon amputated the wrong foot of a diabetic man in 1995. The People's Medical Society, a consumer group, had suggested a "sign your site" initiative a decade before, only to be met by indignation and ridicule on the part of surgeons. In mid-2002, the provider-dominated Joint Commission on Accreditation of Healthcare Organizations (JCAHO) finally proposed rules requiring hospitals to reduce wrong site surgery— seven years after the scandal and seventeen years after the consumer group had suggested such a move. Even with this delay and even with the utter simplicity of the act of signing one's name, 20–40 percent of surgeons continue to resist efforts to get them to sign voluntarily, a past president of the orthopedic academy admitted to the Washington Post.

In fairness, individual providers are beset by so many individual problems that they willingly leave the more global problems of clinical practice to their organizational leadership. Physicians and other providers are caught between patient demands, their own uncertainties as to the best course of treatment, and the need to constrain costs. In addition, the steady production of new drugs, devices, and procedures makes their knowledge quickly obsolete. The time and effort required to remain current with clinical developments place a heavy burden on busy practitioners. They readily admit that they find it impossible to keep up with their voluminous literature and attend even the most relevant continuing professional education courses. That many practitioners become outmoded, despite their best efforts, contributes to the quality chasm.

Although achieving system-wide improvements in health care quality depends on resolving complex, multidimensional issues, there are some hopeful signs on the horizon. Continuously rising health care costs encourage purchasers of health care coverage, individuals, employers, and state and federal governments, to become more involved in assessing and improving the quality of care. Nothing is more expensive nor wasteful the cost of inappropriate or error-prone care and its sequelae.

The federal Agency for Healthcare Research and Quality (AHRQ) is helping to pierce the culture of silence that seems to surround medical errors by establishing the first peer-reviewed, Web-based medical journal, *www.webmm.ahrq.gov.*, to stimulate discussion of medical errors in a blame-free environment.[6] Physicians and other health professionals submit medical errors cases to the site for interactive discussion and analysis. Contributors may remain anonymous if they prefer.

In addition, the Department of Health and Human Services (DHHS) is participating in the Hospital Quality Information Initiative, a joint effort with the leadership of the nation's hospitals to provide the public with information on the quality of care. A similar effort was launched in 2002 that involved providing quality measures of nursing home care. These concepts are different from the contentious issue of a proposed national mandatory, or even voluntary, error reporting system. The federal government's strategy is clearly moving away from assigning blame and towards educating both providers and consumers to function as full partners.

With the capability of the Internet to dispense knowledge that used to be available only to the few "insiders," previously thwarted consumers, purchasers, legislators, and other interested parties will drive the demand for information. When purchasers of health care services have the information and performance measures that allow them to identify high quality, safe medical care based on scientific evidence of effectiveness, poor performing providers and institutions will be forced to shape up or lose their market to higher quality competitors. Clinical practice guidelines, evidence-based medicine, and other mechanisms for improving the practice of medicine will find greater acceptance among service facilities and practitioners.

Like the long-standing and half-heartedly addressed "quality of care" problem, the comparable dilemma of escalating health care costs has received only infrequent and generally ineffective attention. The sweeping take-over of health care in the United States by managed care organizations had only a temporary impact on the rate of national health care spending. There has been a rapid acceleration of health spending since 1998 and no promising measures in sight to curb spending growth.[7]

In fact, no initiatives in the last thirty years, either regulatory or voluntary, have had other than a temporary impact on this nation's health care costs. Unfortunately, the current war on terrorism and its ripple effects on federal and state budgets, and the economy, in general, make runaway health care costs a far more critical problem. On one side, new and costly drugs and procedures continue to proliferate and add to medicine's already impressive capability. On the other, the aging population and others with persistent medical care needs are increasingly finding the high cost of drugs and other medical services beyond their means. The problem intensifies as the economy weakens and governmental support and personal budgets decline.

All of the potential remedies to the problem of health costs are painful. The U.S. health care system has long enjoyed unrestrained demand and exercised every incentive to do all that is possible for every patient regardless of cost. For the most part, patients, unless uninsured, have been protected from any significant out-of-pocket costs associated with those procedures. Employers, the major purchasers of health insurance coverage, have considered that employee benefit a reasonable addition to wages and salaries. Now that health care costs have increased beyond acceptable levels, many people must choose between forgoing other goods and services or living without health insurance and some treatments and drugs. State and federal programs are reducing benefits, and employers are turning more of the costs of employee health insurance back to their workers. In the current environment of unrestrained wartime expenditures, there appears to be little political will to take the drastic actions that would be necessary to curb health care spending. As was evident in the approach to the problems of health quality, governmental initiatives during this period of economic turmoil are likely to be uncoordinated strategies that nibble at the margins of the problem.

Market forces, however, can drive changes that would be impossible to achieve by regulation. As in other areas of the economy, consumers, increasingly sensitive to costs, can hold down spending. They will need help, however, from insurers and government. If the government succeeds in arming the public with easily understood quality of care assessments of providers, facilities, and procedures, and if insurers provide better financial support for preventive services and disease management, patients will make better choices of health resources and services. To do so, consumers will need far more information about the comparative risks and benefits of contemplated procedures and available alternatives then they currently receive. With a better information base and a willingness to exercise more control over their medical care, consumers can reduce the amount of inappropriate, incorrect, and wasteful medical care. Consumers and employers, both, will understand and take into account the costs and benefits of the health insurance plans that they purchase.[8]

The increasing use of the Internet to obtain health information by the public reflects the will and ability of Americans to understand complex issues and make informed decisions about their health care. It is increasingly evident that judgments about the consumption of medical services, formerly the province of providers with compliant patients, will be made in the future by more knowledgeable consumers concerned about the economic consequences of those decisions. If and when assertive users of health care services take charge of their medical care, market forces will begin to function on the basis of cost and quality as they do in other service areas.

The alternative to reducing excessive costs is a single payer system that eliminates the substantial amount of health care dollars that are wasted on the administration of multiple insurance plans and the huge burden of their required paper work. Nothing in the current political environment, however, portends interest in reducing the largess of big corporate insurers with impressive lobbying capability.

■ Technological Growth and Innovation

Growth of Home, Outpatient, and Ambulatory Care

The changes occurring in hospital care and the demographics of aging have produced rapid growth of home care in recent years. In fact, home health care has been the fastest growing segment of the health care industry since 1989. Spending for home health services increased

60 percent between 1993 and 1994, while the health care industry overall increased by only about 8 percent. Lacking any major change in Medicare (which still reimburses home health care on a retrospective basis), growth within the home care industry is expected to continue rapidly over the next few years.[9]

A number of factors are responsible for the most recent extraordinary growth in the number of medical and surgical procedures performed in outpatient and ambulatory settings. Advances in diagnostic technology, anesthesiology, and surgery have combined to make same-day surgery possible for procedures that formerly required hospital inpatient admissions. Third-party payers were quick to recognize the considerable cost savings of ambulatory surgery and began producing an ever-lengthening list of diagnostic and surgical procedures that would no longer be reimbursed if patients were admitted to hospitals as inpatients unless there were extenuating medical circumstances.

With federal and state incentives to encourage the development of more outpatient and ambulatory facilities and broad consumer acceptance, every service possible is now being provided in outpatient or ambulatory settings. These include cancer treatment, kidney dialysis, diagnostic imaging, rehabilitation services, urgent care, wellness and preventive medicine activities, and sports medicine, in addition to surgery. With the care comparable to, if not better than, that received in hospitals and provided at far lower cost, it is clear that ambulatory care will reduce the mission of hospitals to serving only those patients in need of intensive nursing and medical interventions.

Technology

A revealing example of the coercive power of glamorous and expensive technological developments over thoughtful considerations of cost benefit to patients is the medical popularity of magnetic resonance imaging (MRI) scanners. More than 2,000 of these very profitable, high-technology imaging devices have been installed in hospitals and outpatient facilities across the country. At an average cost of about $1.5 million each, the national investment in them is nearly $3 billion. Each of these machines is paid for by charging patients $900 to $1,200 per MRI scan, generating upward of another $3 billion in health care costs. How has this huge investment in admittedly superior diagnostic capability paid off in terms of medical care improvements? An extensive literature search published in the American College of Physicians' *Annals of Internal Medicine* in 1994 could not find a single study that documented a change in patient outcomes. Although the diagnostic information the MRI scan provided to the clinician was considered "better, clearer pictures and a truer demonstration of the disease or the anatomy," not one controlled comparison of diagnostic accuracy or changes in therapeutic choices documented patient benefits.[10] It is particularly discouraging that in many communities the number of MRI scanners installed near each other exceeds any reasonable estimate of population need or service requirement. They are only adding to the costs of health care as redundant entrepreneurial ventures.

Similarly, the technology that permits physicians to save the lives of extremely low birthweight babies (one to two pounds), only to have them suffer from lifelong neurosensory impairments, behavior problems, and learning disorders, raises serious questions about the role of technology in modern medicine. The ability to prolong the life of advanced Alzheimer's patients and other seriously demented and terminally ill patients, in many cases over the objections of family members who would rather their loved ones die peacefully, is another example of the dominant role of technology in medical practice.

It is becoming increasingly clear that technological progress in health care has been a mixed blessing. The impersonal, if not inhumane, imposition of high-technology medicine between patients and practitioners has changed both the image and the mission of the health care enterprise. The complex social problems that affect access to health care; the geographic, economic, and other demographic inequities in the value and availability of care; and the serious discrepancies in the quality of care—these issues cannot be remedied by technological means.

■ Changing Population Composition

As was previously discussed, the U.S. population is growing older and will continue to do so for decades. The older population will not only increase in size relative to younger groups, but a growing number of elderly will survive to very advanced ages. In addition, the number of large, intact families capable of housing and caring for aged relatives has diminished rapidly. Families raise fewer children and those children often migrate to other locations when they attain maturity. Consequently, the health care needs of the larger population of the more frail elderly are expected to place increasing demands on the health care system. Those demands will focus particularly on the chronic care component of the U.S. system, a sector that has not been particularly attractive to health care providers. In addition, much of the long term care capability in the United States is in the hands of the private, for-profit sector, which has an uneven record for the quality of its services.

The health care needs of this growing older population will also be influenced by its changing racial and ethnic diversity. The major changes occurring in the total U.S. population will be reflected in the older population. Minority groups and Hispanics, in particular, will become larger proportions of the elderly. These changes have important implications for medical care. There are significant differences in mortality rates, chronic conditions, service preferences and use, and attitudes toward medical care across racial/ethnic groups. For instance, Hispanics have lower rates of diseases such as hypertension and arthritis than whites and higher rates of conditions such as diabetes. Blacks are more likely to require treatment for hypertension, cerebrovascular disease, diabetes, and obesity than whites and have persistently higher mortality rates.[11]

It is important to note that the increased demands on the health care system posed by population changes coupled with the problems of health care workforce supply portend serious staffing problems ahead. The growth in demand for nurses, nursing aides, various types of therapists and aides in the acute care sector, and the relative unattractiveness of long-term facilities as employment sites for those service personnel, have left many chronic care facilities dangerously understaffed. It is likely that the situation will become even more desperate as the shortage of registered nurses worsens. At the moment, there are neither the funds available in the long-term care system to attract those difficult to recruit service personnel nor alternative plans for meeting the residential needs of the Medicaid-dependent elderly.

The chronically ill who do not require placement in a long-term care facility also have problems with a health care system that retains its historical focus on acute illness or injury and those conditions that are amenable to remediation. The current system does not deal well with the aged chronically ill who present persistent symptoms, increasing disability, psychosocial sequelae, and difficult lifestyle adjustments. Although small gains have been made by managed care organizations addressing specific chronic conditions, effective chronic illness care would require a major change in health service priorities. Simply adding new geriatric services to a system focused on acute care does not solve the basic problem.[12]

In addition to the need to change organizational designs and services, obstacles to improving the care of the chronically ill also include changing the personal values and clinical behaviors of physicians, nurses, and other health professionals. Educated for and trained in acute care facilities, it requires a major shift in mindset and practice behaviors for clinicians to accept the less dramatic, multidisciplinary nature of geriatric practice. As a result, health care reform as it relates to the chronically ill aged will be slow and will not keep pace with the more dramatic advances in other areas of clinical practice.

■ Changing Professional Labor Supply

Health care workers, other than physicians, generally have been ignored in the debates over health care policy and reforms. Yet the economic and other forces reducing the size and services of the hospital industry, shifting inpatient procedures to outpatient settings, and producing other organizational changes are likely to result in significant disruptions in the established employment practices of many classes of health care workers. Although the health care industry always will employ a significant portion of the U.S. workforce, the number and kinds of employees and the sites of their employment will be in transition during the next several years as the health care system adjusts itself.

Health economist Uwe E. Reinhardt lists several reasons why predicting the size or composition of the future health workforce is ill advised.[13] He points out that health care providers are exercising considerable flexibility in assigning tasks to the various health professions. Given this employment latitude and the likelihood that the future health care system will be dominated by competitively bid annual capitation payments, he expects that staffing patterns of health institutions will be sensitive to the relative cost of different types of providers. In the quest for efficiency, Reinhardt expects a great deal of experimentation and variation in staffing patterns across health care systems and regions in the United States. In addition, scientific advances constantly provide new opportunities to substitute technology for human labor. Other technologic advances create needs for new types of health personnel. Under all of these disparate and evolving circumstances, it would be imprudent, indeed, to predict a future surplus or shortage for any type of health professional. It is likely, however, that, whatever health care staffing patterns eventually result, the impact of health care reforms on the health care workforce will be considerable.

Significant reductions in Medicaid and Medicare, which threaten public and other hospitals in inner cities, could result in large minority job losses. Conversely, black women, who now hold a fifth of the nursing home jobs and a larger proportion of home care positions, would benefit from an expanding long-term care sector.[14] Although employment predictions are difficult during a period of major system changes, it is likely that both circumstances will occur. Employment will decrease in acute care hospitals, with disproportionate effects on women and minorities, and increase in the ambulatory and long-term care sectors, with equally disproportionate but positive consequences for the same employee groups. Thus, rather than a total decrease in employment, there probably will be a shift in employment sites. Those with the flexibility to make the transition should find continuing employment.

Physicians

Nothing has been more dramatic during health care reforms than the reduction in power, prestige, and independence of physician specialists. In the 1990s, managed care limitations on the number of specialists that could join their systems and on the frequency and circumstances of their use temporarily altered their positions in the health care hierarchy. In contrast, the demand for primary care practitioners increased as more people enrolled in managed care plans. There was a critical need for physicians who could provide primary care, serve as gatekeepers to limit access to more expensive specialists, and emphasize preventive medicine and health promotion. As the supply of primary care physicians increased and managed care organizations relaxed their more stringent restrictions on specialist care, however, the ratio of specialists to generalists began returning to its former levels.

Clearly, the predictions of the last two decades have not materialized. To the contrary, current market indicators suggest that, rather than a surplus, a shortage of physicians, particularly of specialists, will exist in major regions of the country.

In addition, less desirable practice locations such as inner city and rural areas continue to suffer from an undersupply of both primary care and specialty physicians. It is now apparent that those who believed that physician distribution problems would be solved by producing more physicians did not reckon with the ability of newly trained physicians to start up busy practices and earn satisfactory incomes in areas already well served.

In the absence of medical workforce policies or government intervention, market forces will continue to reconfigure the system on the basis of economic concerns, with little or no regard for considerations of quality or access. Quality and access are public and professional, not market, concerns and are the issues governments and health organizations should be addressing. Even in geographic areas where physicians are in adequate supply, too many individuals remain without access to medical care and too many hospitals depend on graduates of foreign medical schools to provide essential inpatient services.

Major gaps in the availability of primary care physicians have been filled by substitution of nurse practitioners and physician assistants. In addition, the increasing popularity of chiropractors, acupuncturists, and other alternative practitioners reflects public dissatisfaction with the complexity and impersonal nature of today's medical care. The increasing number of substitutes for traditional medical practitioners presents a formidable problem for health policy planners that could have severe economic, public, and professional consequences. Yet, if nothing is done, the profession of medicine is likely to find itself practicing in ever narrower specialty areas while other disciplines fill in the gaps.[15]

New Physician Roles

Two new hospital-based roles have emerged for physicians in the changing health care system. The first is the hospitalist, who provides all of the care to the hospital inpatients of office-based physicians. Because these physicians are constantly in hospitals and are more familiar with their inner workings, they are considered to be more efficient and more capable of continually monitoring and managing inpatient care than are office-based physicians. Employment opportunities for hospitalists are increasing, with well over 4,000 hospitalists estimated to already be in practice.

The second emerging role for physicians is that of medical manager. Physicians, many with additional management or administration training, are entering the medical management area through employment in pharmaceutical companies, managed care organizations, or large group practices. The demand for physicians with advanced training in management or administration is expected to increase as the corporatization of health care increases.

Academic Health Centers

Academic health centers, the country's medical, dental, nursing, and other health professional schools and their teaching institutions, are critically important to the U.S. health care system. They educate and train successive generations of health care personnel, conduct much of the research that advances the capabilities of the system, and provide health care to large numbers of economically disadvantaged people. Yet academic health centers are particularly vulnerable to the current economic strains within the health care system. Their intertwined functions of education, research, and patient care make each of their mission's components more expensive than if they were provided singly. Over the years, state and federal financing for these three functions has been augmented through revenues obtained from the patient care provided in teaching hospitals. Given the impending reductions in financial support from state and federal governments, a generally shrinking market for hospital services, and the high cost of the services of teaching hospitals, the implications for the nation's academic health centers are ominous.

In recognition of these potential problems, a Task Force on Academic Health Centers was convened by the Commonwealth Fund in 1983. After two years of study, it identified three areas for corrective action:

1. The system and costs of graduate medical education
2. The financing of teaching hospitals
3. The role of teaching hospitals in the care of the poor and uninsured

The task force suggested that teaching hospitals should be paid more, that governments should support uncompensated care of the poor and uninsured, and that the professional organizations, hospitals, and medical schools should collaborate in controlling the size, cost, and nature of graduate medical education. In light of subsequent events, these suggestions were unrealistic and inconsequential.

As pressures grow on academic health centers to plan for an impending shortage rather than surplus of physician specialists, to curb the influx of foreign-trained physicians, to modify training sites to recognize the growth of ambulatory care, and to cope with increasing financial difficulties, thorny policy decisions will have to be made. If past performance is an indicator, these decisions will be deferred for as long as possible and then debated hotly.[16]

In the meantime, academic medical centers will have to cope with slow but steady reductions in their Medicare Graduate Medical Education subsidies, and they will have to adjust the number of hospital residencies accordingly. The problems of uncompensated care will increase and Medicare income from outpatient care will decrease. Although most academic medical centers are fairly well positioned to cope with future economic and policy changes, those in poor urban settings or in high HMO penetration areas may find it more difficult to survive.

Health Professions

As noted earlier, the health care reforms taking place are being driven by market forces. Fiscal exigency is forcing reorganizing and restructuring of health care facilities and services. Addressing the social mission of health care is a completely different and far more demanding challenge to health care professionals. For providers to be socially responsive, they have to be broadly educated to identify and understand the needs and workings of society.

Roger J. Bulger, president of the Association of Academic Medical Centers, has urged a major reorientation of health professional education:

> *Health professionals need to understand the anthropology of healing and the social meaning of the whole health enterprise, from primary through the most high-tech tertiary care. Forces have been unleashed over the last decade with which the health professions have collaborated, but which in my view have seriously eroded the public trust in the so-called serving health professions and seem to threaten the very foundations of these professions. Thus our students and faculties must become more sophisticated in their thinking about the nature and role of professions and the proper functions of the university in the post-modern, post-industrial society.*[17]

A significant change in the philosophies of the health professions must occur, however, before the U.S. health care system can understand and adopt a more community health–oriented, less disease-oriented mission and embrace a perspective that is oriented toward populations rather than individuals. The institutions and organizations of the health professions must mature beyond their conservative and self-protective policies and become more effective at leading rather than obstructing the inevitable system changes that will take place. The health professions must make a concerted effort to demonstrate to an increasingly skeptical public that they understand and are concerned about the need to provide more equitable financial access to health care for all. Providers can do much to restore the eroding public trust in the health care enterprise by showing a collective social responsiveness to the best interests of the public as well as the professions. Clearly, clinicians must refocus from their narrow identification with a single profession or specialty to their obligations to the larger community. This means that health professionals must become more deeply involved with helping the political and other societal leaders work through the health policy issues at every level.

This brings us back to how health professionals are educated and socialized to recognize their role in society. As long as health care providers see themselves as highly trained skilled experts in narrow technical fields that are part of a mosaic of narrow health care specialties, they will be unlikely to understand or be capable of applying a population perspective. Thus, there is optimism that the efforts to correct the imbalance between specialists and generalists and the primary care focus of managed care organizations will bring a new community focus and health promotion perspective to health care.

The public perception of the health professions is changing. In the future, it will not be enough for health care providers to serve and comfort one individual at a time. An effort will have to be made to teach and exercise compassion for groups of people, which will have a beneficial impact on the public's health. The education of all health professionals should enhance their potential to address the problems of unequal access to competent care and promote accountability for the effectiveness of their therapies. By virtue of their elite position in society, health professionals are held to a higher standard of performance than the average wage-earner. Health professionals will be expected to contribute to the public good and to perform their professional duties responsibly. They will be expected to bring their salient knowledge and problem-solving skills to bear on relevant social problems. In its highest expression, medicine and health care are a calling to public service irrespective of the patients' economic or political position. It is the exercise of that professional obligation for which health care providers are rewarded, and from which their special status is derived.

Nurses

In many ways, nurses are the most qualified to respond to the changes that have occurred in the health system. Nurses' training focuses more on the behavioral and preventive aspects of health care than does physician education. Their skills are as relevant to outpatient care as they are to inpatient care. Nurses are important members of health care teams and have experience in managing lesser-trained caregivers. Yet, the radical changes occurring in both the organization and delivery of health care are particularly disconcerting to the nursing profession. The displacement of acute care hospitals as the hub of the health care system and the major movements to managed care and integrated health care systems are having profound effects on the approximately 2.1 million registered nurses who constitute the largest component of the health professions. Throughout the last decade, two-thirds of all employed nurses were employed in hospitals.[18]

Increased case-mix severity, decreased nurse–patient ratios, and delegation of traditional nursing duties to lesser-trained personnel have given hospital nurses reason to be concerned over the quality of patient care that has long been their responsibility. That this large proportion of the health care workforce is singularly vulnerable to the staff reductions that must accompany the declining admission and occupancy rates of acute care hospitals is of major concern to nursing leaders and educators.

With mounting evidence that pervasive understaffing of hospital nurses is resulting in preventable complications and patient deaths, provider, public, and governmental pressures to improve the hospital nursing environment and give inpatient nurses reason to, once again, take pride and pleasure in their work are increasing.

Much will have to change, however, to make it happen. Excessive paperwork, inefficient communication systems, managerial responsibilities, and supervision of lesser trained aides require an inordinate amount of time spent in functions other than providing direct patient care. Combined with long work hours, stagnant salaries, and other difficulties, they contribute to low job satisfaction and frustrating work environments. With the number of entrants to schools of nursing declining, an increase in the number of nurses leaving the profession, and an increase in the number of working nurses reaching retirement age, demand is exceeding supply at an accelerating rate.

Nursing is of vital importance to hospitals, and hospitals need to improve their overall relationships with the nursing profession. The future ability of hospitals to serve the needs of the growing population of older patients, to improve the quality of care, and to serve the latest advances in medicine and its technology depend on an adequate workforce of well prepared and competent nurses. Solving the multiple problems presented to nurses by hospitals in times of fiscal constraints will require strong commitment to quality improvement, work redesign, and building strong, respectful relationships between the hospital and its nurses. The future of both hospitals and the nursing profession depends on it.[19]

Nurse Practitioners

Nurse practitioners (NPs) are in great demand. NPs increasingly are providing primary health care for infants, children, and adults in a wide variety of settings. Hospitals, HMOs, schools, ambulatory care clinics, community health centers, and home care organizations have found that NPs deliver quality primary care and score higher than physicians on patient satisfaction, resolution of chronic disease problems, and patient compliance with taking medications, keeping appointments, and following recommended behavioral changes. Most NPs work in clinical specialties such as pediatrics, family practice, obstetrics/gynecology, and geriatrics. Many meet the basic health care needs of inner city and rural populations that are not adequately served by physicians. The future supply of NPs is expected to increase as demand grows and training programs increase. It is estimated that 125,000 NPs will be practicing by 2010.[20]

Physician Assistants

Physician assistants (PAs) are licensed to practice medicine under a physician's supervision. In 1998, there were about 31,000 PAs in clinical practice. Like NPs, PAs were intended to work in primary care settings, but there has been a steady increase in surgical subspecialization. Based on projected job growth and training capacity, it is estimated that 68,000 PAs will be in practice by 2010.[21]

Because the salaries of nonphysician providers are approaching those of newly trained physicians, it is difficult to predict how NPs and PAs will fare if the economic pressures continue and a surplus of physicians becomes a serious problem. An optimistic view is that NPs and PAs, supported by effective practice guidelines and computerized treatment protocols, could become the patient's first point of entry into the health care system.[22]

■ Globalization of the Economy— Increased Scrutiny of Health Care Costs

Nothing in the development of America's system of health care can match the phenomenal growth and gain in influence of managed care in the decade of the 1990s. Beginning on the West Coast and sweeping eastward, managed care organizations captured major segments of patient populations by contracting to provide health care to the employees of the large businesses in each community.

With the managed care "takeover" of a majority of the insured patients in the United States, traditional indemnity carriers that paid each fee-for-service bill were considered too expensive to compete in the new, aggressively competitive markets. In fact, Wall Street considered the traditional insurance cycle of alternate years of rate cutting and premium increases to be dead. Managed care plans were thought to be capable of forecasting patient care costs so precisely that they could avoid the financial ups and downs of conventional insurance plans.[23]

Quite the opposite would turn out to be true. As was the case with many companies that underwent rapid growth in favorable environments, the administrative policies and operational systems that served managed care corporations well in their formative years turned out to be inadequate for their size and business activities as success made them corporate giants. The largest and most successful managed care organizations in the United States—Oxford Health Plans, Aetna, Pacificare Health Systems Corporation, United Health-Care Corporation, Columbia/HCA Healthcare, and even Kaiser Permanente, the not-for-profit grandfather of the managed care movement—all reported millions of dollars in losses for 1997. The rapid growth of the industry at a rate of more than 10 percent per year has exceeded the capabilities of their sophisticated computerized systems, which are supposed to keep track of costs and accurately estimate benefits to new groups of enrollees.[24]

Other factors have contributed to the financial problems of managed care organizations. Their entry into the Medicaid and Medicare markets has been an unprofitable experience and is destined to get worse. Many states have decreased their already low payments to health maintenance organizations (HMOs) for serving Medicaid patients. Rather than take further losses, many managed care organizations are giving up Medicaid contracts. Federal Medicare payments, on the other hand, have allowed managed care organizations to make profits, but rising costs and programmatic cutbacks may make Medicare managed care a questionable venture for HMOs.[25]

Managed care organizations have other problems as well. The competition for market share caused them to keep premiums low while costs were going up. In addition, subscriber dissatisfaction with and mistrust of managed care organizations is producing a shift to more flexible plans that allow access to costlier treatments. With financial projections exceeded and cost-containment strategies exhausted, managed care organizations are forced to resort to double-digit increases in annual premiums. The increased costs of managed care contracts will further encourage subscribers to switch to competing insurance plans.

Physicians, angered by ever more stringent cost-containment tactics that reduced their incomes and autonomy and subjected them to continuing disputes over service decisions, have built public and legislative pressure to correct perceived abuses. In addition, many physicians have changed practice patterns in response to loss of income. They formed coalitions that increased their clout when contracting with managed care organizations and reduced the number of alternative sources of care with which managed care organizations could contract. "Any-willing-provider" laws, which require managed care organizations to open their networks to any physician who wants to join, also increased physician power.

Patients, too, are gaining more control in their relationships with physicians and hospitals due to widespread dissemination of health information about alternative treatments and sources of care in the media and on the Internet. The result has been a more equitable balance of power among managed care organizations, physicians, and patients.[26]

Thus, the future of managed care, once considered inordinately bright, has dimmed. As new and more flexible health insurance schemes evolve to compete in the health care market, the unrestrained power of managed care that led to so much patient and provider dissatisfaction has been replaced by more conciliatory relationships. Health plans are offering less restrictive managed care products and eliminating or relaxing referral and authorization requirements.

By bowing to provider and subscriber complaints, however, managed care organizations have lost some of their control over costs. To compensate, various plans that require patients to share greater percentages of health care costs are being tested. Higher consumer cost-sharing, double-digit increases in premiums, medical inflation, a weakened economy, and competition from innovative indemnity and other insurance plans may seriously erode the dominant role of managed care in America's health care system.[27]

Patients' Rights Legislation

Still other problems are looming for managed care plans. HMOs must respond to a flurry of state and federal legislative initiatives aimed at making them more accountable to the public and providers for decisions about payments and services, for better information about rules, regulations, and benefits, and for independent dispute resolution processes.[28] Legislators at both the state and the federal level are showing a growing interest in protecting consumers from perceived or potential problems with managed care plans. They are concerned, however, with predictions that government involvement will cause managed care plans to increase premium costs and/or ration care.

In 1998, a broadly representative presidential Advisory Commission on Consumer Protection and Quality in the Health Care Industry was appointed to draft a health care consumer's bill of rights. The key features of the commission's recommendation were coverage of emergency care; access to information regarding treatment options; adequate networks of physicians and other providers and direct access to specialists; access to external, impartial appeals of coverage denials; and access to information about health plan restrictions, benefits, physicians, hospital quality, and consumer satisfaction.[29]

Only weak consumer protection legislation could win approval in the Republican-led Congress, however.[30] In 2002, the House and the Senate passed differing versions of the "Patients' Bill of Rights." Although both bills provide key rights such as access to emergency care and to specialists, only the Senate bill provides adequate means for patients to enforce those rights. In addition, only the Senate bill allows states to exceed the basic federal rights. The House bill would prohibit states from setting their own more stringent standards. This is an important difference because over 40 states have already passed some version of a Patients' Bill of Rights, while waiting for federal legislation.

Consumer protection legislation is generally opposed by a coalition of large employers and managed care organizations, so provisions that would allow people covered by work-sponsored insurance to sue their health plans for medical malpractice have been considered too costly. However, it is important to note that advocates of patients' rights legislation take the popular and persuasive position that such protections are necessary to "shift power . . . from managed-care companies, insurance companies, and health care facilities to patients and their physicians."[31] Because patients' rights legislation protects and empowers physicians as much as consumers, the American Medical Association (AMA) is increasing the pressure on lawmakers to pass "real" rights legislation.

More trouble lies ahead for managed care organizations. Like makers of cigarettes, guns, and lead paint, managed care companies are under growing legal attack. Class-action suits that claim cost-saving strategies ignore the best interests of the patients are growing in number. The federal law that has long protected managed care companies has been weakened by a series of judicial decisions, so the litigation could result in huge settlements.

A New Health Insurance Plan

There is a new twist in health insurance that is favored by employers and their employees alike. It is a consumer-controlled health plan that involves both benefits and risks for employees that accept it.

The new plan requires employers to contribute a set amount, say $2,000, into a personal care account for each employee. Workers can then use that money any way they want for health care expenses. Any money that is unspent at the end of the year is carried over into their account for the next year. Employers usually combine a high-deductible insurance policy with the personal care account to cover exceptional costs. The employees would have to pay the deductible before the additional insurance would take effect.

The new plans are expected to reduce medical expenses by providing a strong incentive for employees to avoid minor health care services and make more cost-effective medical decisions. Aware, for the first time, of the true costs of medical procedures, employees are expected to become wiser users of health care services.

Because the Internal Revenue Service allows unspent funds to be carried over into future years, it is possible for healthy workers to accumulate thousands of dollars in their personal accounts. The unspent funds can also be used to purchase additional insurance policies to cover their deductibles.

On the other hand, the new consumer-driven plans penalize older or chronically ill workers who may make substantial use of medical services over the course of a year. They would be better served by remaining in conventional insurance plans.

Consumer-driven health insurance plans have not been in effect long enough to judge their effectiveness in controlling the costs of employer or employee health benefits or satisfaction with the method. The innovation has the potential, however, of making a major change in the health insurance market.

Changing Composition of the Delivery System

In the current unstable health care environment created by increasing market pressures, an organization's ability to respond to change by moving in new directions depends on the flexibility and core competencies of its leaders and employees. It is difficult, therefore, for the more rigid, hierarchical organizational structures that characterize many of this country's health care institutions and organizations to transform themselves into leaner, more adaptive enterprises without significant internal turmoil, if not failure.

Health care has a long history of formally dedicated community entities with management and operating structures that adhere to traditional organizational models. They have boards of trustees and executives in charge of administration, finances, marketing, human resources, and other functions. Roles and responsibilities at every employment level have been traditional, constant, and well defined. Until recently, employment in the health care sector was essentially secure and generated strong loyalties to the employing institution.

The centralist "command and control" model of governance typical of most hospitals and corporations in the United States for the last several decades represents the antithesis of organizational flexibility and adaptability. Even though hospitals and other health service organizations maintain shared missions and values with well-defined purposes, policies, and procedures, either a chief executive or chief operating officer makes all decisions. Efforts to improve the quality, productivity, or profitability of care have involved team-building, cross-training, downsizing, alliances, mergers, joint ventures, and other tactics that appeared likely to result in a competitive advantage. Most of those strategies, however, required that corporate officers, unaccustomed to sharing decision-making power, delegate some decision-making authority to line employees who were then expected to become newly accountable for consequential decisions. Not surprisingly, these efforts have produced mixed and, at best, short-term results.

Some voluntary hospitals have, however, adapted well to the changing environment. They either have not been challenged by the intense cost-competitive forces of managed care or have been successful in reaching equitable arrangements with the insurers of large patient populations. Still other hospital leaderships have been unable to grasp the reality and magnitude of health care reform or have been shortsighted in their accommodations to change.

In an industry in which the average, very well compensated chief executive officers hired by volunteer boards retain their positions for just a few years, long-term thinking and planning is the exception rather than the rule. As economic pressures increase and competitive situations become more desperate, immediate financial remedies become the highest priority. The use of consultants, usually with financial backgrounds, to help in developing quick fixes for economic problems is common among health care institutions.

One strategy that hospitals are employing with great success is the use of subacute care units to get around the diagnosis-related group (DRG) cost controls of Medicare. Instead of discharging older patients at the end of their acute care stay and simply collecting the Medicare-established DRG reimbursement rate, hospitals are now shifting those patients to newly developed subacute care units, where they receive skilled nursing and rehabilitation services. Thus, the hospitals collect both the DRG flat, lump-sum payment for the regular hospital stay and an additional, very profitable, daily rate for the subacute care.

The basic problem is that hospital occupancy rates have fallen from the low 80 percent range to the low 60s in the last decade, but neither beds nor hospitals have closed at a rate equal to the drop in demand. In 1980, there were 5,800 individual hospitals in the United States. Most were voluntary not-for-profit institutions, operating autonomously with their own governing boards, administrations, and community supporters. Despite concerns about excess hospital capacity, there are still about 5,000 hospitals in the United States. Although the number will continue to decline, a variety of business, political, and social reasons will make hospital closings very difficult.[32] More importantly, almost all hospitals are now part of for-profit or not-for-profit corporate networks. Where 20 or 30 separate and competing hospitals once served a particular geographic area, now a somewhat smaller number of institutions divided among a few health care networks are meeting regional needs.

Given the many important relationships of hospitals with the other components of the health care system and the strong community support that most hospitals enjoy, it is unlikely that rapid change will occur in the rate of hospital closures. It will be much easier to close hospital beds and convert the space to other types of service. An increasing number of services can be provided by hospitals without using inpatient beds.

With the relaxation of tightly supervised medical care by managed care organizations, hospitals will be tempted to return to traditional competitive strategies for capturing patients and admitting physicians rather than competing for managed care contracts. Hospital investments in new and more profitable services and associated marketing efforts will contribute to rising health care costs. The effect will be to stimulate policy makers to invoke control mechanisms such as certificate of need laws.

Corporate Growth in Health Care

In the last few years, stakeholders in health care have been scrambling to find the right template of size and service to remain competitive in the rapidly changing health care marketplace. The pervasive influence of managed care, the reductions in state and federal financial support, and the ever increasing sophistication of health care technology have combined to offer remarkable opportunities to break away from outdated traditions and take venturesome risks. The drive to create increasingly integrated and diversified organizations is based on the potential of such service delivery systems to reduce excess capacity and improve the coordination and cost-effectiveness of clinical services.

Although market forces have contained some of the rising costs of health care, there is little evidence to date that many communities have benefited from the service efficiencies and improvements that institutional mergers and acquisitions were supposed to achieve. Rather, such corporate growth has raised the specter of monopoly power, bureaucratic inertia, and depersonalization of relationships between providers and patients.[33] The economies of scale expected of horizontal integration—the merger of similar institutions serving the same market—have yet to be convincingly demonstrated. Rather, there are underlying concerns that, having captured a larger share of a market, merged institutions would be tempted to negotiate raised prices and enjoy monopolistic advantages. Vertical integration, on the other hand, has a more evident potential to enhance the comprehensiveness, coordination, and efficiency of clinical services. In addition to hospitals, vertically integrated systems may include a range of other types of health care facilities and services, such as long-term care facilities, ambulatory diagnostic and surgery centers, home care services, and community-based outpatient services. The aim is to capture and retain market share by creating a seamless system of services at different levels that will allow patients, once in the system, to move up or down the continuum of care without leaving the corporate network. Although the experience to date has been mixed, integrating organizations along the continuum of care and circumventing the fragmentation of services, each owned and managed independently, makes exceedingly good sense. Multi-institutional networks are extremely attractive to managed care organizations that prefer to deal with as few provider administrations as possible while still providing a complete range of services. Integrated networks can be held clinically and financially accountable for the outcomes of care and the health status of the populations they serve and have the potential to provide the members of managed care organizations with the most appropriate care in a seamless continuum at competitive prices.

The market potential of integrated systems of care has sparked a flurry of for-profit and not-for-profit mergers and acquisitions. Beginning with the defeat of President Clinton's health reform proposal in 1994, there was a significant upswing in consolidation activity. The creation of giant investor-owned service networks led a number of not-for-profit hospitals and other institutions to band together and develop continuums of care. In the year 1994 alone, over 10 percent of U.S. hospitals were involved in acquisitions or mergers.[34]

With considerable success, the more entrepreneurial for-profit health care corporations have built their own integrated health service systems to improve their market positions. A good example of this trend is Columbia/HCA Healthcare Corporation, headquartered in Nashville, Tennessee. Responding to the insurers' pressure on patients to seek treatment in less expensive settings, Columbia/HCA acquired 14 ambulatory surgery centers in 1995 and tripled its holdings among home health care agencies and skilled nursing facilities. In the same year, the corporation purchased 143 hospitals to bring its total to 338. Within a few years, the nation's largest hospital chain employed 285,000 employees and received $20 billion in annual revenues.

Like several other large corporations that experienced phenomenal growth and engaged in high finance, however, its executives engaged in fiscal machinations to make good profits even better. Eventually, their aggressive business strategies resulted in intense scrutiny by federal and state agencies. Over the next five years, the corporation contended with federal and state charges that it conspired to defraud government health care programs by making false statements, submitting false bills, and committing other illegalities. The corporation replaced its top executives, divested itself of many facilities, and changed its name to HCA—The Healthcare Co. It subsequently pled guilty to many of the charges and paid millions of dollars to settle claims.[35]

Thus, the introduction of large for-profit conglomerates into the health care arena increases the risk that corporate growth and profit will have higher priority among corporate executives than patient care and community service.

This should not deter the not-for-profit sector from aggressively pursuing more contemporary business and service plans. To survive the health care reformation, voluntary hospital systems must free themselves from the cultural inertia that has made implementing lasting change so time consuming and difficult, and, instead, emulate those highly successful private sector companies that thrive on the flexibility to make strategic choices and redefine corporate goals in opportunistic ways. To cope with new challenges, voluntary hospitals will require the same clarity of purpose, flexibility, and determination to make strategic choices as for-profit companies do. They will need unequivocal plans that spell out the relative importance of competing priorities and guide decisions about personnel, resources, and service delivery. Those hospitals that become essential components of vertically integrated systems will take part in the future of health care. Those that do not will remain part of its past and eventually disappear.

Corporate Alliances

Many hospital systems and physician groups are developing mergers and joint ventures. Within the last two years, the number of physician-hospital organizations (PHOs) is estimated to have reached over 3,000 nationwide and is still growing rapidly. It is evident to both hospitals and physicians that there are mutually beneficial advantages to developing long-term relationships that improve their ability to compete effectively with other integrated delivery systems in negotiating prepaid managed care contracts.

There are also increasing numbers of hospital systems and PHOs forming alliances or joint ventures with managed care organizations. Because the parties in these alliances assume some level of financial risk, they share a common interest in accountable and cost-effective health care and in maintaining the overall success of the system. If the arrangement is carried out equitably, all the parties benefit. With the majority of Americans now enrolled in managed care, even the most recalcitrant providers find it expedient to join these integrated systems or be left behind.

These developments are not without serious legal, ethical, and financial challenges. Along with their proven and, as yet, unproven benefits are a number of significant concerns. Different corporate cultures, mixed financial incentives, increased regulation, difficulty adapting to new provider roles, and antitrust issues are but a few of the hazards. The blending of for-profit and not-for-profit entities in joint ventures, the potential for self-referral abuses, and the proposed any-willing-provider laws that would force insurers to accept any provider willing to met their criteria into their networks all spell potential trouble for managed care companies and their service contractors.[36]

Information Management

The demand for more complete, accurate, and transferable health care data has grown rapidly during the last decade. All health care constituencies, providers, consumers, insurers, employers, governments, and researchers are increasingly seeking information about the processes and outcomes of care. The increasing complexity of diagnostic techniques and therapeutic procedures and growing public awareness of the unacceptable frequency of medical errors have focused attention on the management or lack of management of the huge volumes of information generated by the processes of medical care.

In recent years, the growing numbers of new and efficient technologies for managing and transferring volumes of data allow providers and health plans to replace voluminous and often disorganized medical records with standardized, reliable, and clinically relevant information. Opportunities for transcription mistakes, misinterpretation of hand-writing or medication orders, and other common errors of information transfer are minimized.

While the technology for management of data, once collected, is at a high level of sophistication, there are serious obstacles to obtaining and assembling complete health information about individual patients.

Since most patients obtain health care services from a number of providers and facilities, the information about their care is divided among the various settings and sites. The still unmet information management challenge is dealing with fragmentation of patient information as those patients move through a disorganized treatment system.[37]

Originators of seamless health information systems that allow sharing of patient diagnostic, treatment, and outcome information face other problems as well. There are incredibly complex confidentiality, compatibility, and transferability issues that have challenged system designers for years. Nevertheless, the critical role of advanced information and communications technologies in evidenced based assessments of clinical practice, physician report cards, clinical guidelines, patient education, and a large number of other uses is recognized by everyone concerned with the future of health care. As with other obstacles to health service advances, the growing need to solve those intrinsic system problems will drive information experts to develop acceptable solutions.

In the meantime, the importance of these health information technologies has alerted the business community to the promise of an emerging health information infrastructure. Although much of the current information system development has been the result of the academic medical researchers and developers, a number of private health information technology industries are already engaged in the building of the technical components of that hardware and software infrastructure. Other private companies are working on paperless solutions to recording and monitoring clinical procedures. It appears that the free-enterprise system is augmenting, if not supplanting, the years of information systems development by in-house designers employed by hospitals and academic institutions. Whether harmonious or competitive, it appears that the common interests of the clinical communities and the profit-motivated commercial sector will eventually result in a new era of health care information technology. It will be a giant step forward in advancing the efficacy, efficiency, and safety of medical care.[38]

■ Future Role of the Federal Government

The last few years have been a period of great change for U.S. health care and for the role of government. A health care marketplace dominated by purchasers, customers, and competition has replaced the concept of a health care system shaped and managed to conform to professional values and priorities. Ever since the acrimonious 1994 public debates about health care prompted by President Clinton's failed proposal for health care reform, the long-held tenets about the role of government in society and in health care have been questioned in both the legislative and executive branches. During a period in which Congress, in attempting to achieve a balanced budget, is questioning the utility and effectiveness of many of the federal programs of the last several decades, the private sector's domination of the health care marketplace supports those who would drastically reduce the federal government's financial contributions to health research, education, and regulation.

With marketplace pressures and state-by-state reforms running far ahead of federal legislation in reconfiguring the health care system, containing cost increases, and increasing access to basic primary care services, our society is, in effect, renegotiating the federal government's role in health care. The corporatization of the health care industry has been demonstrated to be far more effective in rapidly achieving important system changes than the bureaucratic implementation of federal legislation. Capitation under managed care unquestionably succeeds in producing more cost-effective care, and driving down discretionary specialist referrals, hospital inpatient days, and diagnostic testing. As a consequence, many assume that the federal government needs only to move Medicare and Medicaid recipients into managed care and let capitation achieve what federal programs have failed to do. It is a simplistic policy solution that would legitimize diverting health care funds to other purposes. Reducing federal support for Medicaid and Medicare along with shrinking state subsidies has the potential for seriously undermining the country's health care safety net. Reducing health care costs at the source is most effective as a local initiative. Strong regional planning and cooperation, rather than competition among regional hospitals, reduces excess and redundant services and ensure a comprehensive network of services.

Managed care has replaced traditional indemnity insurance throughout much of the country, and fears that some patients are being mistreated have prompted Congress and state legislatures to consider an array of patient protection measures. State legislators have established such standards as 48-hour hospital stays for childbirth, access to emergency rooms, and appeal processes for patients denied payments for care.[39]

In 1999, the congressional impasse over passing consumer protection legislation prompted state legislatures to take matters into their own hands. In that year, health care issues made up a large proportion of bills in state legislatures. Prompted by rising prices for prescription drugs and other increases in medical costs, the financial problems of some large HMOs, purported abuses of patients, and other citizen concerns, state legislators introduced an extraordinary 27,000 health care bills.[40] Clearly, the states are not about to wait for the federal government to fix the health care system.

Except for significant patient protection legislation, the federal government has also acted on behalf of patients. The 105th and 106th Congress introduced many bills to benefit patients. Some have been imposed by legislation, and others by executive order. One important piece of legislation that had bipartisan support was the Health Insurance Reform Act, also called the Healthcare Access, Portability, and Renewability Act, which was signed into law in 1996. It ensures the portability of health care insurance for workers who change jobs. The legislation permits individuals to continue insurance coverage after a loss or change of employment by mandating the renewability of insurance coverage except for specific reasons, such as the nonpayment of premiums. The act also regulates the circumstances in which an insurance plan may limit benefits because of preexisting conditions. It also mandates special enrollment periods for individuals who have experienced certain changes in family composition or employment status. The legislation prohibits insurers from declining to offer individual coverage for reasons of health status, medical condition, or other factors, such as the loss of eligibility for group coverage.[41]

That people can switch jobs after being fully covered with one employer and be fully covered under the new employer's policy without any new restrictions on preexisting conditions will be of great help to those who feel locked into a job because they fear losing health care coverage. In addition, people who lose employer-based insurance coverage and are unemployed or employed without coverage will be able to buy health insurance. The breadth and costs of that coverage, however, may make those policies unaffordable.

■ Conclusion

The 1990s marked a major reformation in the U.S. health care system. The social and economic changes affecting society during that decade altered public perceptions and expectations of health care and prepared Americans for sweeping reforms in both the organization and delivery of health care services. Although tensions exist between the advocates of major and immediate system revisions and those who prefer more limited, incremental changes, all agree that the health care industry is in a period of unprecedented instability and transition.

Although concerns about costs are prompting new examinations of the allocation of resources and the assignments of health personnel, there also are new perspectives on the value and quality of health care services. There are strong pressures on providers to analyze and document the outcomes and effectiveness of their health care interventions.[42]

The continuing presence of millions of uninsured Americans reflects the nation's reluctance to decide whether the federal government should assure health coverage for all its citizens or only fill the gaps for those without the means to obtain their own. Other nations have long considered health care a right of citizenship and provide the subsidies necessary to give everyone reasonable access to basic care.

Repeatedly in the history of health care in the United States, however, the public has been persuaded to instruct its representatives that health care is a "good" that should be supplied privately with as few exceptions as possible. That the system costs more, and has large gaps, illogical redundancies, and inexplicable variations in quality and access is countered by the prevailing belief that its scientific and technological superiority makes up for its deficiencies.

The need for industry restructuring to remedy the deficiencies in the health care system, however, is the overriding concern of those who believe the United States should develop a more socially responsible system of health care and end its embarrassing distinction as the only Western democracy that permits a sizable percentage of its population to live without health insurance coverage. Given that health care in the United States evolved out of the professional and economic objectives of providers rather than consumer needs and has been financed by a convoluted system of private insurance augmented by inadequately managed and inflationary public sector programs, it is not surprising that the resulting system is characterized by escalating costs and glaring gaps in coverage. Clearly, the problems cannot be solved satisfactorily without major structural revisions.[43]

Physicians, who historically have been rewarded generously for their work, are already distressed and will be increasingly frustrated by being forced to participate in systems they believe violate their professional prerogatives. To them, their changing role signifies the decline of medicine as a profession. The autonomy that physicians enjoyed in their work and the feeling that their profession constituted a special brotherhood devoted to a higher purpose is diminished. Physicians now see themselves more as workers in the health service machine rather than as occupants of a lofty position in society.[44]

Patients, too, have changed. Keenly aware of the variability in the quality of care, they no longer consider medicine as a kind of mystical art that only physicians and nurses can understand. Patients now educate themselves on health matters, increasingly challenge medical decisions, and turn to alternative providers and treatments if they are dissatisfied with their care. The Internet and other medical information sources have empowered patients and are rapidly turning them into educated consumers. As such, their dissatisfactions with health care can no longer be ignored by either health care providers or governments.

To summarize, the basic questions facing the stakeholders in the health care industry today are:

■ What is society's obligation to ensure access to a basic level of health care for all its citizens, and how can this be accomplished?
■ How can an acceptable quality of health care be ensured?
■ How can the costs of health care be kept affordable for both individuals and society?
■ How can the ethical dilemmas produced by technological advances and limited resources be resolved?

The idealized solutions to the problems of huge variations in costs, treatments, and outcomes; fragmented services; episodic treatment of illness; and badly distributed overcapacity all have general support as concepts, but engender opposing views on how to resolve them. Among the most frequently voiced suggestions are:

■ Alter the health care focus from diagnosing and treating illness to maintaining wellness and preventing illness.
■ Expand the health care system's accountability from the health status of individual patients to that of defined populations.
■ Change the health services' emphasis from acute episodic care to continuous comprehensive care and chronic disease management.
■ Eliminate the financial incentives to provide more services and fill hospital beds, and substitute incentives to provide appropriate care at an appropriate level.
■ Assume universal access to health care.
■ Change from merely coordinating the delivery of services to actively managing the quality of processes and outcomes.
■ Add a serious commitment to the resolution of community and public health issues.

There are some constructive governmental interventions that, combined with market forces, probably are changing the health care system faster and more profoundly than would have occurred had a national health reform plan been enacted. State-by-state reforms are attempting to reduce or contain Medicaid expenditures, some by experimenting with Medicaid managed care and others by simply reducing fee-for-service benefits. It also is important to recognize the national attention brought to outcomes research and cost-effectiveness concerns by the federal Agency for Healthcare Research and Quality. With both purchasers and managed care organizations determined to eliminate the costs of inappropriate services and clinical interventions of no or marginal benefit, the agency's support of studies of cost-effectiveness and subsequent production of clinical guidelines takes on added importance. Reducing some of the clinical uncertainty in health care and guiding practitioners to the most effective treatment modalities for specific conditions can effect significant cost savings as well as prevent unnecessary or inappropriate treatment interventions.

Current trends suggest that the future of health care in the United States will include more reforms at the state level. As individual state experiments show positive results, other states will adopt the changes. Many of those state reforms will support the expansion of managed care. That support, however, will be contingent on a series of patient protection standards that hold managed care organizations responsible for faulty decisions. The ability of managed care organizations to contain costs by limiting expensive and discretionary specialist use and by exercising cost-based oversight of ineffective or marginally beneficial interventions is tremendously attractive to states and other purchasers of health care.

The managed care backlash, however, has made patients more aggressive and less trusting. The wide publicity given to the Institute of Medicine's report on the frequency of medical errors has increased public concerns about patient safety in medical environments. Managed care disputes with physicians over reimbursement for certain procedures have created doubts about the appropriateness of those procedures. Access to ubiquitous medical information on the Internet has given the public a better understanding of the breadth of choice faced by physicians in making clinical judgments and medical decisions. These factors combined with the increasing costs of health care are, once again, producing a surge of interest in increased governmental involvement in health care reforms.

It is now evident that managed care and other insurers, by identifying and then paying for only essential services, along with more widespread acceptance of clinical guidelines, cannot significantly reduce the costly proliferation of redundant technology, control the entrepreneurial development of unnecessary duplications of service, and curb unnecessary clinical interventions.

Although managed care plans have had some success in their mission to reduce the growth in health care costs, certain aspects of that market-driven reform have been painful and unpopular—a consequence of shifting the power from providers to purchasers and limiting consumer options. Thus, once again, the United States Congress is under pressure to legislate patients' rights, rein in drug costs, develop quality controls, and find ways to support the uninsured.

Unfortunately, at this writing, the President and Congress have placed health care reforms behind more pressing international problems in their order of priorities. Although many states have taken the initiative to legislate health care consumer and related protections, such piecemeal efforts are hardly adequate to address a U.S. health care system that is again at a critical turning point. It is increasingly evident that significant reforms are required in both the financing and delivery of health care.

What is yet to be determined, however, is whether the reformed health care system can ensure acceptable quality and access. If the purchasing decision makers, employers, insurers, and consumers remain sensitive to the value or benefits of competing services as well as their relative costs, there is the potential for the quality of health care in the United States to improve as well as become more affordable. Higher-cost services will have to prove that they offer a better service to justify the additional expense, and lower-cost services will have to demonstrate acceptable outcomes.

Health care reforms can make the systems of care different, but they cannot make the care better. Only the providers working in concert with supportive systems can improve health care outcomes. Freed from many of the disincentives of fee-for-service medicine, providers may emphasize wellness and prevention and reduce unnecessary interventions. They may become as effective in improving the health status of whole populations as they have for patients they formerly treated on an individual basis.

It is anticipated that the public and purchasers will be aided in choosing from among competing providers and managed care plans by having access to a great deal of timely performance information. Unlike the selective secrecy that has characterized health care in the past, it is expected that future health care organizations will be required to provide annual quality performance "report cards" for public and purchaser scrutiny. Some institutions and managed care organizations already produce these.

Hospitals face a harsh short-term future. Unrelenting economic pressures in the face of reduced occupancy rates will undoubtedly result in a significant number of closings, and those that survive will be different institutions from those that presently exist. Hospitals are likely to be just one component of a vertically integrated system of care that includes long-term as well as ambulatory care and a variety of community-based services. Because many of the acute care services will be provided in ambulatory settings, the major role of hospitals probably will be in the provision of intensive patient care and, perhaps, the diagnosis and management of the chronically ill. There also will be significant changes in their relationships with physicians. Rather than simply serving as physicians' workshops, hospitals will be active partners with physician groups, negotiating with managed care organizations and sharing financial risk.

The relationship of hospitals to physicians will take on increasing importance as the old assumptions about medical care and surgery continue to undergo profound change. The future of hospitals depends on the future of medicine. The future of medicine is grounded in the scientists and clinicians developing the cutting edge advances in medicine and surgery. Thus, it behooves hospitals to convene and respond to those whose combined expertise and judgment can formulate solutions to deficits in quality and patient satisfaction and can anticipate the service modalities of the future.

The changing demographics in the United States will compel a major expansion of long-term care facilities and services. Long-term care will become an increasingly complex array of services integrated into vertical systems. Of all the problems facing the future health care system, the aging of the population, with its attendant burden of chronic disease and disability, presents the most formidable organizational and economic challenge. Needless to say, those facilities and services striving mightily to survive the more immediate challenges have yet to develop longer-range plans to cope with that future inevitability.

The growing demand for support of chronic care is likely to force a major change in the structure and financing of health care in the United States. Unlike the acute care system, chronic care is unplanned and often insensitive to desperate situations. For example, regardless of type, the insurance coverage for the extraordinary care provided in a hospital to save a life often abruptly ceases when the patient is brought home. Although essential patient services such as feeding, bathing, transferring from bed to wheelchair, and preventing bedsores are considered "medically necessary" when provided by skilled nurses in institutions, those same services are dismissed as "custodial care" when delivered at home.

As more and more middle-aged Americans find themselves faced with the care of aged and functionally limited relatives, the demand for expanded support of chronic care services will increase. Public awareness of the deficiencies of the current system will grow and bring considerable pressure for change in public and private financing mechanisms.

People with chronic conditions already consume almost 70 percent of the nation's expenditures on personal care, mostly for physician and hospital services, a reflection of the system's focus on acute incidents.[45] Clearly, there is a monumental challenge in this era of severe economic constraint to create and finance a chronic care system that meets social as well as medical needs. Until that can be accomplished, the aged and chronically ill and their caregivers will be required to meet their home care, transportation, social support, and other needs however they can.

It is important to recognize that, although the health care system itself is in turmoil, the sciences within health care are making extraordinary progress. Medical technology is a major driver of the health care system, and the system quickly absorbs new devices and pharmaceuticals. Just as clinicians and researchers embraced the use of new imaging techniques, so too will they adopt new devices for minimally invasive surgery, gene mapping and therapy, new vaccines, artificial blood, and other advances that will transform the practice of medicine.

These dramatic advances, however, will be accompanied by new and vexing problems of cost, accessibility, inadequate training, and professional ethics. Practicing physicians are already overwhelmed with the profusion of new knowledge. Currently there are 10 million citations on the computerized scientific literature resource, Medline, and 3,000 more are added to the popular bibliographic database each month. The availability of new knowledge also vastly exceeds the capacity of the institutions that deliver and finance health care to access and use it. It is difficult for these hierarchical organizations to respond to past problems, much less adapt to new developments. The fact that thousands of deaths were reported to occur each year as a result of medical errors in hospitals, and neither the public nor the health care community seemed aware of the magnitude of the problem, is a reflection of the size, complexity, and disorder that characterizes the system. Compare that fact to the response to a single airplane crash, after which every fragment of evidence is collected to determine the cause and prevent its reoccurrence.

Clearly, the enormous potential for good that the U.S. health care system enjoys comes with deep concerns. How will the recipients of new technology be chosen? Who will address the ethical dilemmas that lie behind the ability to genetically alter human beings? When will the need to set stricter standards of competence when people's lives are at stake be faced by the medical profession? When will the government rein in the unlimited profits of pharmaceutical firms that price their drugs beyond the means of those who need them the most? These and similar issues are central to a constructive reformation of the U.S. health care system.

The public and the stakeholders in the health care system have expressed a generalized dissatisfaction with the manner in which health care has been delivered—the inexplicable variation in how patients are treated, the resultant costs, and the increasing number of people without access to at least a minimum level of basic care. Similar dissatisfaction exists among health care providers, but for quite different reasons. Although the causes of the problem are easily identifiable, they do not lend themselves to simple, uncomplicated solutions. Experience has demonstrated that changes in public policy that threaten U.S. commitment to social diversity and the preservation of individual autonomy inevitably fail. The vested interests in the traditional modes of health care delivery have repeatedly demonstrated their ability to generate political opposition to serious legislative challenges to the health care status quo. On the other hand, those same interests, including the powerful health care political lobbies, seem ineffectual in the face of apparently overwhelming market forces. Rather than change occurring as a result of public policy, economic forces are driving a combative health care system reformation that is altering the roles of many traditional health care institutions. The end result, however, is expected to be a more comprehensive, coordinated, and cost-efficient system.

These are exciting times for students of health care. Never has so large a change in so important an industry so intimately affected so many people. It is a time for introspection regarding one's values, circumspection regarding one's advocacy for any one position, and careful inspection of any experimental changes that come about. Will the health care reforms now in progress resolve or worsen the key issues of access, costs, and quality? Can we possibly achieve an ideal health policy scenario, such as that proposed by Stephen Shortell and colleagues, in which there is fiscal and clinical accountability for defined populations, resources allocated according to a region's consumer needs, and up-front negotiations among all relevant parties about what services will be delivered to what people at what price?[46] Only time and skilled leadership will tell.

■ Notes

1. J. Gleick, "Chaos: Making a New Science," in *Corporation on a Tightrope: Balancing Leadership, Governance, and Technology in an Age of Complexity*, eds. J.G. Sifonis and B. Goldberg (New York: Viking, 1987), 1–19.
2. S.M. Shortell and U.E. Reinhardt, "Creating and Executing Health Policy in the 1990s," in *Improving Health Policy and Management: Nine Critical Research Issues for the 1990s*, eds. S.M. Shortell and U.E. Reinhardt (Ann Arbor, MI: Health Administration Press, 1992), 5–6.
3. National Institute for Health Care Management, "The Uninsured: A Study of Health Plan Initiatives and the Lessons Learned," National Institute for Health Care Management Research and Education Foundation, Washington, D.C. www.nihcm.org/UninsuredES.pdf (11 March, 2003) Accessed 1 April, 2003.
4. J. Hadley, J. Holahan, "How Much Medical Care Do the Uninsured Use, and Who Pays for It?," Health Affairs, vol. 22, no. 2. March/April 2003: 23.
5. M.L. Millenson, "The Silence." *Health Affairs,* Vol. 22, No. 2, March/April 2003: 103–112.
6. C.M. Clancy, T. Scully, *A Call to Excellence*, "Health Affairs" vol. 22, no. 2, March/April 2003: 113–115.
7. S. Hefler et al., "Health Spending Projections for 2001-2011: The Latest Outlook," *Health Affairs* March/April 2002: 207–218.
8. S.H. Altman et al, "Ecalating Health Care Spending: Is it Desirable Or Inevitable", *Health Affairs*, Web Exclusive, 3 January 2003. http://healthaffairs.org/WebExclusive/2201Altman.pdf Accessed 7 March 03.

9. *The Comparative Performance of U.S. Hospitals*, 25.

10. D.L. Kent et al., "The Clinical Efficacy of Magnetic Resonance Imaging," *Annals of Internal Medicine* 120, no. 10 (1994): 856–875.

11. D.A. Wolf, "Population Change: Friend Or Foe of the Chronic Care System?" Health Affairs, Nov./Dec. 2001, Vo. 20, No.6, pp. 64–78.

12. E.H. Wagner et al., "Improving Chronic Illness Care: Translating Evidence Into Action," Health Affairs, Nov./Dec. 2001, Vo. 20, No.6, pp. 28–42.

13. U.E. Reinhardt, "The Economic and Moral Case for Letting the Market Determine the Health Workforce," in *The U.S. Health Workforce: Power, Politics, and Policy*, eds. M. Osterweis et al. (Washington, DC: Association of Academic Health Centers, 1996), 3–13.

14. D.U. Himmelstein et al., "Medical Care Employment in the United States, 1968 to 1993: The Importance of Health Sector Jobs for African Americans and Women," *American Journal of Public Health* 86, no. 4 (1996): 525–528.

15. R.A. Cooper et al., "Economic and Demographic Trends Signal an Impending Physician Shortage," *Health Affairs* 21, no. 1 (January/February 2002): 140–154.

16. The Commonwealth Fund, *Prescription for Change, Report of the Task Force on Academic Health Centers* (New York: Harkness House, 1985), 1–35.

17. R.J. Bulger, "If a Rose Is a Rose, Then What Is an Academic Health Center?" (Paper presented at Millard Fillmore Hospitals' Annual Vital Issues in Health Care Symposium, Buffalo, NY, April 18, 1991).

18. Amara et al., "Health and Healthcare 2010: The Forecast, the Challenge," 73–78.

19. P. Buerhaus et al., "Strengthening Hospital Nursing," *Hospital Affairs* 21, no. 5 (September/October 2002), 123–132.

20. R. Cooper et al., "Current and Projected Workforce of Nonphysician Clinicians," *Journal of the American Medical Association* 282 (September 2, 1998): 9.

21. Cooper et al., "Current and Projected Workforce of Nonphysician Clinicians," 9.

22. Amara et al., "Health and Healthcare 2010: The Forecast, the Challenge," 73-84.

23. G. Anders, "Kaiser's Red Ink Spells Trouble for HMOs," *Wall Street Journal*, 17 February 1998, B1, B19.

24. "Managed Care Systems Are Feeling Sick," *Wall Street Journal*, 22 December 1997, A8.

25. "Managed Care Systems Are Feeling Sick," A8.

26. D.E. Grembowski et al., "Managed Care and the U.S. Health Care System: A Social Exchange Perspective," *Social Science & Medicine* 54 (2002): 1167–1180.

27. D.A. Draper et al., "The Changing Face of Managed Care," *Health Affairs* (January/February 2002): 11–23.

28. R.L. Rundle, "HMOs Brace Themselves for Avalanche of New Laws," *Wall Street Journal*, 20 February 1998, B4.

29. G.J. Annas, "A National Bill of Patients' Rights," *New England Journal of Medicine* 338, no. 10 (1998): 695–699.

30. G. Aston, "Employers Oppose House Bill Creating Federal Standards for Managed Care Plans," *American Medical News* (10 November 1997): 3–4.

31. Annas, "A National Bill of Patients' Rights," 695–699.

32. R. Amara et al., "Health and Healthcare 2010: The Forecast, the Challenge," in *The Institute for the Future,* vol. 15, no. 2, ed. J.K. Engehart (San Francisco: Jossey-Bass Publishers, January 2000): 62–67.

33. J.C. Robinson, "The Dynamics and Limits of Corporate Growth in Health Care," *Health Affairs* (Bethesda, MD: Project HOPE, 1996), 156.

34. *The Comparative Performance of U.S. Hospitals: The Sourcebook, 1996* (Baltimore: Health Care Industry Analysts, Inc.; Chicago: Deloitte Touche, 1996), 14–15.

35. "HCA Sews Up Fraud Lawsuit for $95.3M," *Nashville Business Journal.* http://nashville.bizjournals.com/Nashville/stories/2000/12/11/dail (14 December 2000). Accessed 29 August 2002.

36. *The Comparative Performance of U.S. Hospitals*, 22–23.

37. J.D. Kleinke, "Clinical Information Technology In the Real World" *Health Affairs* vol 17, no 6, Nov.–Dec.1998: .23–38.

38. D.W. Moran, "Health Information Policy: On Preparing for the Next War," *Health Affairs* vol 17, no 6, Nov.–Dec.1998: 9–22.

39. M. Stauffer, "Issue Brief: Comprehensive Consumer Rights Bills." http//www.hpts.org (1 April 1999). Accessed 15 August 2000.

40. "For Many States, Health Care Bills Are Top Priority," *New York Times*, 23 January 2000, A1.

41. "Bill Summary and Status for the 104th Congress." http://thomas.loc.gov (21 August 1996). Accessed May 5, 1998.

42. S.B. Jones, "The Health Policy Landscape," in *Health Care Delivery: Current Issues and the Public Policy Debate*, eds. R. Kaufman et al. (Washington, DC: Association of Academic Health Centers, 1991), 1–6.

43. E. Haislmaier, "A Cure for the Health Care Crisis," *Issues in Sciences and Technology* 6, no. 3 (1990): 59–63.

44. R.W. Dworkin, "The Cultural Revolution in Health Care, the Public Interest," *National Affairs, Inc.* (Spring 2000): 35–49.

45. C. Hoffman et al., "Persons with Chronic Conditions, Their Prevalence and Costs," *Journal of the American Medical Association* 278, no. 18 (1996): 1473–1479.

46. S.M. Shortell et al., *Strategic Choices for America's Hospitals: Managing Change in Turbulent Times* (San Francisco: Jossey-Bass Publishers, 1990), 301–327.

Appendix A

Abbreviations and Acronyms

AAFP	American Academy of Family Physicians
AAMC	Association of American Medical Colleges
AAN	American Academy of Nursing
AARP	American Association of Retired Persons
ACEHSA	Accrediting Commission on Education for Health Services Administrators
ACF	Administration on Children and Families
ACGME	Accreditation Council for Graduate Medical Education
ACHE	American College of Healthcare Executives
ACP	American College of Physicians
ACR	Advanced Certified Rolfer
ACS	American College of Surgeons
ACYF	Administration for Children, Youth, and Families
ADAMHA	Alcohol, Drug Abuse, and Mental Health Administration
ADD	Administration on Developmental Disabilities
ADLs	activities of daily living
AFDC	Aid to Families with Dependent Children
AFL-CIO	American Federation of Labor and Congress of Industrial Organizations
AHA	American Hospital Association
AHC	academic health center
AHCPR	Agency for Health Care Policy and Research (former name of the Agency for Healthcare Research and Quality)
AHP	accountable health plan
AHRQ	Agency for Healthcare Research and Quality (formerly Agency for Health Care Policy and Research)
AHSR	Association for Health Services Research (former name of the Academy for Health Services Research and Health Policy)
AID	U.S. Agency for International Development

AIDS	Acquired Immune Deficiency Syndrome
ALOS	average length of stay
AMA	American Medical Association
AMC	academic medical center
ANA	Administration for Native Americans; American Nurses Association
AOA	Administration on Aging
APA	American Psychiatric Association; American Psychological Association
APEX/PH	Assessment Protocol for Excellence in Public Health
APHA	American Public Health Association
APTA	American Physical Therapy Association
ASAHP	Association of Schools of Allied Health Professions
ASH	Assistant Secretary for Health
ASHED	AIDS School Health Education Database
ASHP	Adolescent and School Health Programs
ASIM	American Society of Internal Medicine
ASSIST	American Stop Smoking Intervention Study
ASTHO	Association of State and Territorial Health Officials
ATF	Bureau of Alcohol, Tobacco, and Firearms
ATSDR	Agency for Toxic Substances and Disease Registry
AUPHA	Association of University Programs in Health Administration
BAC	blood alcohol concentration
BBA	Balanced Budget Act of 1997
BC/BS	Blue Cross and Blue Shield
BCHS	Bureau of Community Health Services
BHP	Bureau of Health Professions
BHRD	Bureau of Health Resources Development
BIA	Bureau of Indian Affairs
BLS	Bureau of Labor Statistics
BPHC	Bureau of Primary Health Care
BRFSS	Behavioral Risk Factor Surveillance System
CAH	critical access hospital
CAT	computerized axial tomography (scanner)
CBER	Center for Biologics Evaluation and Research
CCN	community care network; critical care nurse
CCRC	continuing care retirement community
CDC	Centers for Disease Control and Prevention

CDER	Center for Drug Evaluation and Research
CDF	Children's Defense Fund
CDRH	Center for Devices and Radiological Health
CEO	chief executive officer
CEU	continuing education unit
CFO	chief financial officer
CFSAN	Center for Food Safety and Applied Nutrition
CHAMPUS	Civilian Health and Medical Program of the Uniformed Services
CHAP	Child Health Assurance Program
CHC	community health center
CHID	Combined Health Information Database
CHP	comprehensive health planning
CME	continuing medical education
CMHC	community mental health center
COBRA	Consolidated Budget Reconciliation Act
COGME	Council on Graduate Medical Education
CON	certificate of need
CPI	Consumer Price Index
CPR	customary, prevailing, and reasonable (fees)
CPSC	Consumer Product Safety Commission
CPT	Current Procedure Terminology
CPT-4	Current Procedural Terminology—4th Edition
CQI	continuous quality improvement
CRCC	Commission on Rehabilitation Counselor Certification
CT	computed tomography
CTP	Certified Trager Practitioner
CVM	Center for Veterinary Medicine
DC	Doctor of Chiropractic
DHEW	Department of Health, Education, and Welfare
DHHS	Department of Health and Human Services
DME	durable medical equipment
DNR	do not resuscitate
DNS/DNSc	Doctor of Nursing Science
DO	Doctor of Osteopathy
DOE	Department of Education
DOI	Department of Interior
DOJ	Department of Justice

DOL	Department of Labor
DOT	Department of Transportation
DRG	diagnosis-related group
DVA	Department of Veterans Affairs
EACH	essential access community hospital
EAP	employee assistance program
ECA	epidemiologic catchment area
ECF	extended care facility
EMS	emergency medical services
EPA	Environmental Protection Agency
EPO	epidemiology program office
EPSDT	early and periodic screening, diagnosis, and treatment
ER	emergency room
ERISA	Employee Retirement Income Security Act
ESRD	end stage renal disease
FAHS	Federation of American Health Systems
FAS	fetal alcohol syndrome
FDA	Food and Drug Administration
FDIR	Food Distribution Program on Indian Reservations
FEHBP	Federal Employee Health Benefits Program
FEMA	Federal Emergency Management Association
FFS	fee for service
FHSR	Foundation for Health Services Research
FHWA	Federal Highway Administration
FIC	Fogarty International Center
FMG	foreign medical graduate
FNS	Food and Nutrition Service
FQHC	federally qualified health center
FTC	Federal Trade Commission
FTE	full-time equivalent
FY	fiscal year
GDP	gross domestic product
GHAA	Group Health Association of America
GHC	group health cooperative
GHI	group health insurance
GME	graduate medical education
GMENAC	Graduate Medical Education National Advisory Committee

GNP	gross national product
HACCP	Hazard Analysis Critical Control Point
HANES	Health and Nutrition Examination Survey
HBCU	historically black colleges and universities
HBV	hepatitis B virus
HCA	Hospital Corporation of America
HCFA	Health Care Financing Administration
HCV	hepatitis C virus
HDL	high-density lipoprotein cholesterol
HEDIS	Health Plan Employer Data and Information Set
HETC	Health Education and Training Center
HEW	Health, Education, and Welfare
HHS	Health and Human Services (Department of)
HIAA	Health Insurance Association of America
HIP	health insurance plan
HIS	health interview survey
HIV	human immunodeficiency virus
HMO	health maintenance organization
HNIS	Human Nutrition and Information Service
HPDP	health promotion and disease prevention
HPEAA	Health Professions Educational Assistance Act
HRA	Health Resources Administration
HRQL	health-related quality of life
HRSA	Health Resources and Services Administration
HSA	Health Systems Agency
HTPCP	Healthy Tomorrows Partnership for Children Program
HUD	Housing and Urban Development (department of)
IADLs	instrumental activities of daily life
ICD	International Classification of Diseases
ICD-9-CM	International Classification of Diseases, 9th Revision, Clinical Modification
ICU	intensive care unit
IDDM	insulin-dependent diabetes mellitus
IHPO	International Health Program Office
IHS	Indian Health Service
IMR	infant mortality rate
INPHO	Information Network for Public Health Officials

IOM	Institute of Medicine
IPA	individual practice association
IPN	integrated provider network
IPO	independent practitioner organization
Joint Commission	Joint Commission on Accreditation of Healthcare Organizations
LCME	Liaison Committee on Medical Education
LDL	low-density lipoprotein cholesterol
LIHEAP	Low-Income Home Energy Assistance Program
LOS	length of stay
LPN	Licensed Practical Nurse
LTC	long-term care
MBHCC	managed behavioral health care company
MCHB	Maternal and Child Health Bureau
MCN	Migrant Clinicians Network
MCO	managed care organization
MD	Medical Doctor
MDC	major diagnostic category
MDS	minimum data set
MEDLARS	Medical Literature Analysis and Retrieval System
MEDTEP	Medical Treatment Effectiveness Program
MEHP	Minority Environmental Health Program
MHTS	Minority Health Tracking System
MLP	Midlevel Practitioner
MRI	magnetic resonance imaging
MSA	metropolitan statistical area; medical savings account
MSHA	Mine Safety and Health Administration
MSO	Management Services Organization
MVP	Medicare volume performance
NACAA	National Association of Consumer Agency Administrators
NACHM	National Advisory Commission on Health Manpower
NACHO	National Association of County Health Officials
NAHC	National Association for Home Care
NAIEP	National AIDS Information and Education Program
NAM	National Association of Manufacturers
NAMCS	National Ambulatory Care Survey
NAMHC	National Advisory Mental Health Council

NAMI	National Alliance for the Mentally Ill
NAPO	National AIDS Program Office
NCADI	National Clearinghouse for Alcohol and Drug Information
NCAI	National Congress of American Indians
NCCAN	National Center on Child Abuse and Neglect
NCCDPHP	National Center for Chronic Disease Prevention and Health Promotion
NCEH	National Center for Environmental Health
NCHGR	National Center for Human Genome Research
NCHS	National Center for Health Statistics
NCHSR	National Center for Health Services Research
NCI	National Cancer Institute
NCID	National Center for Infectious Diseases
NCIPC	National Center for Injury Prevention and Control
NCPIE	National Council on Patient Information and Education
NCPS	National Center for Prevention Services
NCQA	National Committee on Quality Assurance
NCRR	National Center for Research Resources
NCTR	National Center for Toxilogical Research
ND	Doctor of Naturopathy; Doctor of Nursing
NEI	National Eye Institute
NF	nursing facility
NHDS	National Hospital Discharge Survey
NHE	National Health Expenditures
NHIC	National Health Information Center
NHIS	National Health Interview Survey
NHLBI	National Heart, Lung, and Blood Institute
NHSC	National Health Service Corps
NIA	National Institute on Aging
NIAAA	National Institute on Alcohol Abuse and Alcoholism
NIAID	National Institute of Allergy and Infectious Diseases
NIAMS	National Institute of Arthritis and Musculoskeletal and Skin Diseases
NICHD	National Institute of Child Health and Human Development
NIDA	National Institute on Drug Abuse

NIDCD	National Institute on Deafness and Other Communication Disorders
NIDDK	National Institute of Diabetes and Digestive and Kidney Diseases
NIDR	National Institute of Dental Research
NIDRR	National Institute on Disability and Rehabilitation Research
NIEHS	National Institute of Environmental Health Sciences
NIGMS	National Institute of General Medical Sciences
NIH	National Institutes of Health
NIMH	National Institute of Mental Health
NINDS	National Institute of Neurological Disorders and Stroke
NINR	National Institute of Nursing Research
NIOSH	National Institute of Occupational Safety and Health
NLM	National Library of Medicine
NLN	National League for Nursing
NLTN	National Laboratory Training Network
NMIHS	National Maternal and Infant Health Survey
NMR	nuclear magnetic resonance
NVSS	National Vital Statistics System
OAM	Office of Alternative Medicine
OASIS	Outcomes and Assessment Information Set
OBRA	Omnibus Budget Reconciliation Act
OCS	Office of Community Services
OCSE	Office of Child Support Enforcement
ODPHP	Office of Disease Prevention and Health Promotion
OECD	Organization of Economic Development
OEO	Office of Economic Opportunity
OFA	Office of Family Assistance
OHTA	Office of Health Technology Assessment
OIH	Office of International Health
OMB	Office of Management and Budget
OMH	Office of Minority Health
ORHP	Office of Rural Health Policy
ORT	Operation Restore Trust
OSH	Office of Smoking and Health
OSHA	Occupational Safety and Health Administration
OT	occupational therapy

OTA	Office of Technology Assessment
OWH	Office on Women's Health
PA	Physician Assistant
PAC	political action committee
PACE	Program of All-Inclusive Care for the Elderly
PAR	preadmission review
PCP	primary care provider; primary care physician
PET	positron emission tomography
PGP	prepaid group practice
PharmD	Doctor of Pharmacy
PHO	physician-hospital organization
PHP	prepaid health plan
PHS	Public Health Service
PIRC	Preventative Intervention Research Center
PMPM	per member per month
PMPY	per member per year
POE	point of enrollment
PORT	patient outcomes research team
POS	point of service
PPA	preferred provider arrangement
PCCM	primary care case management
PPHA	Pennsylvania Public Health Association
PPO	preferred provider organization
PPRC	Physician Payment Review Commission
PPS	prospective payment system
PRO	peer review organization
ProPAC	Prospective Payment Assessment Commission
PSO	provider service organization; provider-sponsored organization
PSQ	patient satisfaction questionnaire
PSRO	Professional Standards Review Organization
PT	physical therapy
PTMPY	per thousand members per year
QA	quality assurance
RAPs	radiologists, anesthesiologists, and pathologists
RBRVS	resource-based relative value scale
RMP	regional medical program
RN	Registered Nurse

RPCH	rural primary care hospital
RPP	Registered Polarity Practitioner
RRA	Registered Records Administrator
RRC	residency review committee
RSPA	Research and Special Programs Administration
RUG	resource utilization group
RVS	relative value scale
RVUs	relative value units
SAMHSA	Substance Abuse and Mental Health Services Administration
SCHIP	State Children's Health Insurance Program
SEIU	Service Employees International Union
SHMO	social health maintenance organization
SMI	supplemental medical insurance
SNF	skilled nursing facility
SSA	Social Security Administration
SSI	Supplemental Security Income
STD	sexually transmitted disease
TEFRA	Tax Equity and Fiscal Responsibility Act
Title XIX	Medicaid
Title XVIII	Medicare
TPA	third-party administrator
TPN	total parenteral nutrition
TQM	total quality management
UCR	usual, customary, and reasonable reimbursement
UR	utilization review
USDHEW	United States Department of Health, Education, and Welfare
USDHHS	United States Department of Health and Human Services
USFMG	United States foreign medical graduate
USPHS	United States Public Health Service
VA	Veterans Administration; Department of Veterans Affairs
VNA	Visiting Nurses Association
WHO	World Health Organization
WIC	Special Supplemental Food Program for Women, Infants, and Children

Appendix B

Web Sites

■ ## U.S. Government

Agency for Healthcare Research and Quality: www.ahrq.gov.

Centers for Medicare and Medicaid Services: www.medicare.gov

Department of Health and Human Services: www.HHS.gov

Department of Veterans Affairs, Veterans Health Administration: http://www.va.gov/health_benefits

National Center for Complementary and Alternative Medicine: http://www.nccam.nih.gov

National Center for Health Statistics: http://www.cdc.gov/nchs

National Guideline Clearinghouse: www.guideline.gov

National Institutes of Health: www.nih.gov

National Library of Medicine: http://clinicaltrials.gov and http://www.nlm.nih.gov/medlineplus

Office of Disease Prevention and Health Promotion: www.healthfinder.gov

State Children's Health Insurance Program: http://cms.hhs.gov/schlip

U.S. Administration on Aging: http://www.aoa.dhhs.gov

U.S. Centers for Disease Control and Prevention: http://www.cdc.gov

U.S. Congressional Budget Office: http://www.cbo.gov

U.S. Department of Health and Human Services: http://healthfinder.gov

U.S. Department of Health and Human Services: http://www.hhs.gov

U.S. Department of Labor, Bureau of Labor Statistics: http://stats.bls.gov

U.S. Food and Drug Administration: http://www.fda.gov

■ Other Organizations

Alliance for Quality Health Care: www.nyhealthfinder.com

American Academy of Family Physicians: www.familydoctor.org

American Accreditation Healthcare Commission: www.urac.org

American Association of Health Plans: http://www.aahp.org

American Association of Retired Persons: www.aarp.org/health

American Board of Medical Specialties: www.certifieddoctor.org

American Cancer Society: www.cancer.org

American Health Care Association: http://www.ahca.org

American Heart Association: www.americanheart.org

American Lung Association: www.lungusa.org

American Medical Association: www.ama-assn.org/aps/amahg.htm

Annals of Long Term Care: http://www.mmhc.com

The Commonwealth Fund: http://www.cmwf.org

Families USA: http://www.familiesusa.org

Health Care Careers and Jobs Center: http://www.healthcarejobs.org

Joint Commission on Accreditation of Healthcare Organizations: www.jcaho.org

Kaiser Family Foundation and Health Research and Educational Trust: http://www.kff.org

Long-Term Care Provider.com News and Analysis: http://www.longtermcareprovider.com

Mayo Clinic: www.mayoclinic.com

Medscape: http://www.medscape.com

Modern Healthcare: http://www.modernhealthcare.com

National Alliance for Caregiving: http://www.caregiving.org

National Alliance for the Mentally Ill: http://www.nami.org

National Association for Home Care: http://www.nahc.org

National Center for Assisted Living: http://www.ncal.org

National Committee for Quality Assurance: www.ncqa.org

Index

A

Academic health centers, 71–72, 147-148
  areas for corrective action, 433–434
  Balanced Budget Act and, 72
Academic Medical Centers, 146–148
  cost-saving arrangements, 149
  funding of, 148–149
Accreditation Council for Graduate Medical
        Education (ACGME), 150, 156
Accrediting Commission on Education for
        Health Services Administration
        (ACEHSA), 198
Acquired immune deficiency syndrome
        (AIDS). *See* AIDS
Adams, John, 371
Administration for Children and Families
        (ACF), 375
Administration on Aging (AOA), 375
Administrators of health care, 198–199
Adult day care, 321–323
Advanced certified rolfers (ACRs), 209
Agency for Healthcare Policy and Quality,
        44
Agency for Health Care Policy and
        Research (AHCPR), 166
  clinical guidelines, 400–401
  dispute with surgeons organization,
        400–401
  priority activities, 400
  responsibilities of, 400
Agency for Healthcare Research and
        Quality (AHRQ), 17, 374,
        401–402, 425, 451

center for patient safety, 407
funds earmarked for reducing medical
        errors, 390
need for increased research support,
        391
Agency for Toxic Substances and Disease
        Registry (ATSDR), 373
Aging-in-place services, 323–325
Aging population
  the aging of America, 53–54
  effect on health care employment, 181,
        215
  elderly with chronic physical ailments,
        24–26
  financial coverage for long-term needs,
        27
  growth and diversity of, 23
  percent by race and Hispanic origin, 26*f*
  persons age 65 or older, 24*f*, 54, 298
  projected population by age and sex, 25*f*
  rate of aging, 23
Aging process, natural history and levels
        of prevention, 9, 12*f*
AIDS, 23, 328
  increasing research efforts, 411
  public health imperatives, 383
AIDS Action Council, 50
Alcohol, 23
Allergy and immunology, subspecialty
        certifications, 153*t*
Allied health personnel, 199–209
  allied health programs, students and
        graduates, 206–207*t*

Allied health personnel *(continued)*
  alternative therapists, 208–209
  behavioral scientists, 204
  career advancement in, 207–208
  factors influencing demand for
    changing nature of disease,
      disability, and treatment,
      209–210
    corporatization of health care, 212
    expansion of home care, 211–212
    financing health services, 210–211
    influence of managed care, 211
    physician supply, 210
    technology, 210
  health care workforce in a chaotic
    system, 213–214
  health care workforce issues,
    212–213
  in hospitals, 76–77
  laboratory technologists and
    technicians, 200
  nuclear medicine technology,
    200–201
  occupational therapy, 202
  physical therapy, 201–202
  physician assistant, 203–204
  radiologic technology, 200
  rehabilitation counselor, 204–205
  social work, 204
  speech language pathology, 202–203
  support services, 205–206
  therapeutic science practitioners, 76,
    201
Alternative therapists, 208–209
  amount of money spent on in 1990,
    208
  as health care stakeholders, 14–15
Altman, S.H., 248
Alzheimer's disease, 320, 321, 328
Ambulatory care, 115–142
  community health centers, 134–137,
    136*t*
  continued future expansion, 140
  free-standing services
    number of, 129
    primary care centers, 129–130
    urgery centers, 131–132, 132*f,*
      133*f,* 134
    ent/emergent care centers,
      130–131
  growth of, 427–428
  hospital emergency services, 126–128
    distribution of emergency
      department visits, 126, 127*f*
    for routine care, 127–128
    training of physicians and nurses,
      128
  hospital services, 121–126
    adoption of diagnosis-related
      groups (DRGs), 124
    care for the medically indigent
      population, 126
    expansion and reorganization of
      outpatient clinics, 124–125
    history of, 121–122
    organization and delivery of,
      124–125
    outpatient clinics today, 122–123
    outpatient revenues, 122, 123*f*
    specialty medical clinics, 123–124
    support for the teaching mission of
      the hospitals, 125
  mental health services, 336
  other practitioners, 121
  overview and trends
    capacity, 116
    diagnosis-related group (DRG)
      payment system, 115–116
    expansion of hospital service net-
      works, 116–117
    managed care organizations,
      influence toward ambulatory
      services, 116
    physician involvement, 117
    total number of facilities, 117
  private medical office practice
    malpractice insurance costs, 119
    managed care and, 121
    Medicare reimbursement and, 119
    multispecialties group practice, 120
    shift to group practice, 118–120
    solo-practice model, 118–119
    surgical group practice, 120–121
  public health services, 137–138
  by rural and urban hospitals, 19
  voluntary agencies, 139–140
American Academy of Family
    Physicians (AAFP), 47
American Association of Colleges of
    Nursing, 186

American Association of Medical
Colleges, 184
American Association of Nurse
Anesthetists, 190
American Association of Retired
Persons (AARP), 13, 49
American Board of Dental Public
Health, 193
American Board of Medical Specialties,
152–153, 153–155*t,* 159
American Board of Ophthalmology, 152
American Cancer Society, 13, 50, 208
American College of Healthcare
Executives, 199
American College of Nurse Midwives,
190
American College of Physicians (ACP),
47
American College of Surgeons (ACS), 47
American Dental Association, 16
American Federation of Labor (AFL), 51
American Heart Association, 13
American Hospital Association (AHA),
47–48, 66, 156
approval of insurance plans, 35
reimbursement for low-income
populations, 233
"Statement on a Patient's Bill of
Rights," 81
survey of hospitals offering alternative
medicine treatments, 15
American Managed Care and Review
Association and Group Health
Association of America, 289
American Medical Association (AMA)
begins publication of JAMA, 145
and capitation strategies, 165
code of ethics, 167–168
creates Council on Medical Education,
145
drug evaluations, 43
efforts at reform, 146
endorsement of GMEs, 150
formation of, 144
guidelines for approved residencies,
156
influence of, 46–47
lobbying by, 16
opposition to health insurance, 34, 35
on physician assistant programs, 203

programs to assess ramifications of
medical advancements, 43
on relationship between patient and
his physician, 33
American Nurses Association (ANA),
16, 48
American Physical Therapy Association
(APTA), 201
American Psychiatric Association
(APA), 349
American Public Health Association
(APHA), 16, 52
American Red Cross, 386
American Society of Internal Medicine
(ASIM), 47
American Speech-Language-Hearing
Association, 203
Anesthesia techniques, safety of, 42
Anesthesiology, subspecialty
certifications, 153*t*
Angiography, coronary, appropriateness
and use of study, 107*f*
Antibiotics, misuse of, 413
Arthritis Foundation, 50
Asians, older, 24, 26*f*
Assisted living facilities, 306–308
cost of care in, 307–308
definition of, 306–307
monthly rent and fees, 308, 308*f*
number of facilities and population
in, 307, 307*f*
oversight and regulation of, 307
Assisted Living Federation of America
(ALFA), 306
Association for Home Care and Hospice,
312
Association Medical Care Plans, 232
Association of American Medical
Colleges (AAMC), 145, 156
efforts at reform, 146
endorsement of GMEs, 150

B
"Baby boom" population, 23, 25*f*
Balanced Budget Act (BBA) of 1997
and academic health centers, 72
cost-based reimbursement, 136
decreases in subsidies to teaching
hospitals, 148–149
effect on hospitals, 70

Balanced Budget Act (BBA) *(continued)*
impact on health care financing, 223
and Medicare
CAA's provisions, 255
"Comprehensive Plan for Program
Integrity," 257
created major new policy direction
for Medicare and Medicaid,
250–251
major provisions of
changing provider payment
methods and amounts, 253, 257
conducting demonstration
projects, 253, 257
developing prevention initiatives,
253, 257
establishing a new Medicare
Part C, 252–253
establishing program integrity
provisions, 254, 257
Medicare + Choice, 18, 253,
256–257
providing anti-fraud and abuse
provisions, 254, 257
providing rural hospital
initiatives, 253–254, 257
managed care enrollment initiative,
256–257
Medicare Integrity Program, 257
Medicare Payment Advisory
Commission established, 252
Medicare savings by 2002, 252, 252*f*
Medicare spending pre- and post-
BBA, 255–256, 255*f*, 256*t*
National Bipartisan Commission
on the Future of Medicare,
251–252
need for radical changes in
Medicare system, 249–250
new mandate for reform, 249–250
projected savings, 1998-2002, 251*f*
ProPAC and Physician Payment
Review Commission replaced,
252
reimbursement for "telemedicine,"
20
PACE, 26
provisions affecting nurses, 192
Rural Hospital Flexibility Program,
20

State Children's Health Insurance
Program (SCHIP), 138, 389, 422
Balanced Budget Refinement Act
(BBRA) of 1999, 148–149, 223,
257
Balanced Budget Relief Act, 71–72
Baltimore College of Dental Surgery,
192
Baylor University Hospital plan, 35
Behavioral scientists, 77, 204
Behaviors, high-risk. *See* AIDS
Bellers, John, 369
Bellevue Hospital, 64
Benefits Protection and Improvement
Act of 2000, 257, 260
Beth Israel Hospital, Boston, 93
Bills of Mortality, 369
Biomedical and technological advances,
42–44
during the 1960s, 42
computed tomography CT scan, 43
financial and ethical dilemmas, 43–44
intraocular lens implants, 43
Bipartisan Patient Protection Act of
2001, 284
Birth-control pill, 42
Birth rates, in developed countries, 4
Black populations, older, 23–24, 26*f*
Blue Cross/Blue Shield, 15, 49,
232–234
Depression of 1929 and the birth of
Blue Cross, 34–36
and the hospital industry, 66
Board of Certification of Advanced
Clinical Competence, 201
Bulger, Roger J., 434
Bureau of Labor Statistics, 181
Bush, George, 48, 361
Bush, George W., 48
Bush administration, grant availability
for health centers, 137
Business and labor, influence of, 50–51

C
Cancer
levels of preventive measures against,
11*f*
natural history of, 10*f*
Capitation concept, 22, 165, 274–275
Caregivers, support for, 54

Carnegie Foundation for the
Advancement of Teaching
Flexner Report on medical education,
145–146
report on dental education, 193
Carter, Jimmy, 47, 338
Cataract surgery, appropriateness and
use of study, 107*f*
Catholic Health Association of the
United States, 48
Cedars-Sinai Medical Center, Los
Angeles, 93
Centers for Disease Control and
Prevention (CDC), 138, 373,
392
Centers for Intramural and Extramural
Research, 400
Centers for Medicare and Medicaid
Services (CMMS), 263,
374–375
Certification of health care professionals,
182
Certified trager practitioners (CTPs),
209
Chadwick, Edwin, 369–370
Chalmers, Thomas C., 408
Champy, James, 91
Child Health Insurance Program, 135
Chiropractors, 196–197
Cigarettes, 23
Clinical nurse specialist, 192
Clinical practice guidelines, 166–167
ClinicalTrials.gov, 170–171
Clinton, Bill, 3, 47, 49
Clinton's National Health Security Act.
See National Health Security
Act, 1993
College of Philadelphia (Univ. of
Pennsylvania), 143
Colon and rectal surgery, subspecialty
certifications, 153*t*
Columbia/HCA Healthcare Corporation,
444–445
Columbia University School of Public
Health and Administrative
Medicine study of hospital
care, 101–102
Commission on Rehabilitation
Counselor Certification
(CRCC), 205

Commission on Rehabilitation Facilities,
323
Committee on the Costs of Medical
Care, 1932, 35
Committee on Unproven Methods of
Cancer Treatment, 208
Community ambulatory care health
centers, 134–137, 136*t*
Community Health Accreditation
Program, 312
Comprehensive Health Planning Act,
1966, 39, 242
"Comprehensive Plan for Program
Integrity," 257
Computed tomography CT scan, 43, 77
Congress of Industrial Organizations
(AFL/CIO), 51
Consolidated Omnibus Budget
Reconciliation Act (COBRA),
245–246
Consumer groups, influence of, 49–50
Continuing care retirement and life care
communities (CCRCs), 325–326
Continuous quality improvement
(CQI), 91, 108–109
Coronary artery bypass grafting
(CABG), appropriateness and
use of study, 107*f*
Corporations
corporate alliances, 445–446
corporate growth in health care,
443–445
Costs of U.S. health care, 35, 37–38. *See
also* Financing health care
for alternative therapies, 14, 15
cost containment and the
restructuring of medical
practice, 164–165
cost *vs.* quality of care, 40–41, 111,
314–315
economic incentives that fuel rising
costs, 228
escalating costs, 426–427
forces of reform, 109–111
respite care, 320–321
rising costs and reduction in coverage, 52–53
Council of Medical Specialty Societies,
156
Council on Medical Education, 145

Council on Scientific Affairs, 43
Countries, developed, common trends among, 5–6
Cousins, Lionel, 322
Credentialing and regulating health professionals, 181–183, 323
Critical care nurse (CCN), 187

D
Dartmouth College, opens first medical school, 144
Deaths, medical mishaps, acute care hospitals, 29
Dentistry, 192–194
    demographic composition of, 194
    dental schools, 192–193, 194
    history of, 192
    practice specialties, 194
    public health dentistry, 193
    reorganization of dental education, 193
Department of Health and Human Services (DHHS), 263, 372–375, 389, 392
    Hospital Quality Information Initiative, 425
    regulations for home care, 315
    study of pharmacist workforce, 195
Department of Homeland Security (DHS), 392
Depression of 1929 and the birth of Blue Cross, 34–36
Dermatology, subspecialty certifications, 153t
"Desirable Characteristics of Quality Indicators or Groups of Quality Indicators for Use in Report Cards," 291
Developments in U.S. Health Care
    aging of America, 53–54
    basic issues, 59–60
    biomedical advances, 42–44
        during the 1960s, 42
        computed tomography CT scan, 43
        financial and ethical dilemmas, 43–44
        intraocular lens implants, 43
    dominant influence of government, 36–38

earliest history of, 33–34
economic influences:rising costs, 52
efforts at planning and quality control, 38–40
    Comprehensive Health Planning Act, 1966, 39
    Health Professions Educational Assistance Act, 1963, 39
    Health Systems Agency (HSA), 39
    Maternal Child Health and Mental Retardation Planning Amendments, 39–40
    National Health Planning and Resources Development Act, 1974, 39
    Nurse Training Act, 39
    Public Health Service Act, 1965, 38–39
Great Depression and the birth of Blue Cross, 34–36
Health Insurance Portability and Accountability Act (HIPAA), 58
influence of interest groups
    American Medical Association (AMA), 46–47
    American Nurses Association (ANA), 48
    business and labor, 50–51
    connection between politicians and lobbyists, 46
    consumer groups, 49–50
    insurance companies, 48–49
    other hospital groups, 48
    other physician groups, 47–48
    pharmaceutical industry, 51
    public health focus on prevention, 52
Internet and Health Care, 58–59
managed care organizations, 40–41, 41f
Oregon Death with Dignity Act, 56–57
the Reagan administration, 41–42
roles of medical education and specialization, 44–46
the uninsured and access to medical care, 52–53
values and assumptions that guide priorities, 54–56

Diagnosis-related group (DRG)
  payment system, 85–87,
  243–244, 402
  and ambulatory care, 115–116, 124
Diagnostic and Therapeutic Technology
  Assessment Program, 43
Diagnostic imaging, advances in, 21
Diagnostic services, 77–78
Disease prevention, 8*f*, 9
Doctors of naturopathy (NDs), 209
Donabedian, Avedis, 100, 404
Drugs, illegal, 23
Duke University, physician assistant
  program, 203

E
Economic influences: rising costs of
  health care, 52
Educational Commission for Foreign
  Medical Graduates (ECFMG),
  184
Educational programs, allied health
  professionals, 206–207*t*
  181–183, 323, 434–435
Education and training institutions.
  See also Academic Medical
  Centers; Medical Schools
  as health care stakeholders, 16
Eisenberg, David, 208
Elderly populations, proportion of total
  populations, 6
Elias, P.H., 27–28
Elizabethan Poor Laws of 1601, 369
Eloise Hospital, Michigan, 65
Emergency medicine, subspecialty
  certifications, 153*t*
Employee Retirement and Income
  Security Act of 1974 (ERISA),
  234–235
Employees. *See* Personnel, health care;
  Staff
Employers, as health care stakeholders,
  13
Endarterectomy, carotid,
  appropriateness and use of
  study, 107*f*
Endoscopy, upper GI, appropriateness
  and use of study, 107*f*
England, Mary Jane, 349

Epidemiologic Catchment Area (ECA),
  339
Epidemiology
  analytical observational studies, 398
  defined, 397
  descriptive observational studies,
    397
  experimental, 398
  future challenges for, 414–415
  misuse of antibiotics and, 413
  NIMH priorities for, 357
  other applications, 398–399
Epstein, Arnold, 291
Essential access community hospital
  (EACH), 19–20
Ethics
  in issues of health care, 30–31,
    43–45, 169–170, 455
  in research, 411–412
Euthanasia, 57
Evidence-based medicine, 407–409, 408*f*

F
Family practice, subspecialty
  certifications, 153*t*
Federal Emergency Relief Act of 1933,
  371
Federally Qualified Health Center
  Program, 135
Federal Security Agency, 372
Federation of American Health Systems
  (FAHS), 48
Fee-for-service payment, 98, 164, 165,
  169, 274, 275
Feldman, Saul, 350–351
Financing health care. *See also* Costs of
  U.S. health care; Health
  insurance; Medicaid; Medicare
  future: continuing change, 263–264
  health care expenditures
    changes in health care delivery
      and, 222–223
    components of, 228, 229*f*
    factors resulting in increased costs
      economic incentives that fuel
        rising costs, 228
      growth of specialized medicine,
        225–226
      a labor-intensive industry, 227

Financing health care *(continued)*
    new diagnostic treatment and
        technology, 223–225, 225*f*
    uninsured and underinsured,
        226–227, 227*f*
  government contributions to, 223
  share of gross domestic product,
    221–222, 222*f*
  for public health services, 138
  for qualified health centers, 135–137
  sources of health care payment, 228,
    229*f*, 230–231, 230*t*
  for voluntary health care agencies,
    139–140
Flexner, Abraham, 145, 146
Flexner Report and Medical School
    reforms, 145–146
Food, Drug, and Cosmetic Act, 1962
    amendments to, 37
Food and Drug Administration (FDA),
    373
  proposed changes to, 49–50
Fox, Daniel M., 213
Freedom Commission on Mental
    Health, 361
Freedom of information acts, 167
Freeman, Kay, 165
Funding
  of graduate medical education, 148,
    156–157
  of medical schools, 148
  nursing education, 186

G
Gay Men's Health Crisis, 50
Gene manipulation and therapy,
    ethical issues and, 170
General Education Board, 146
Genomics research, 413
Georgetown University Medical Center,
    economic losses of, 72
Ginzberg, Eli, 2
Gittlesohn, Alan, 102
Goldman, Ronald, 103
Government. *See also* Medicaid;
    Medicare; Public health
  future role of in U.S. health care,
    447–449
  government contributions to health
    care expenditures, 223

as health care stakeholder, 14
  influence on health care industry,
    36–38
Graduate Medical Education Consortia,
    149–150
Graduate medical education (GME),
    148, 156–157, 434
Graham, Robert, 47
Grants-in-aid programs, 37
Graunt, John, 369
Group Health Association of America
    (GHAA), 16, 49
Group Health of Puget Sound, 18

H
Hammer, Michael, 91
Harvard University, 144
Head Start, 377
Health, Education, and Welfare (HEW),
    372
Health Care, future of, 419–458
  accountability, fiscal and clinical
    escalating health care costs,
      426–427
    medical errors, 423–424
    resistance to change, 423
    single payer system, 427
    using the Internet to access medical
      information, 426, 427
  changing population composition,
    429–430
  changing professional labor supply,
    431–437
    academic health centers, 433–434
    health professions, 434–436
    nurse practitioners (NPs), 437
    nurses, 436–437
    physician assistants (PAs), 437
    physicians, 432
    physicians, new roles of, 433
  conclusion, 449–456
    basic questions, 451
    chronic care services, 454
    ethical dilemmas, 455
    governmental interventions,
      451–453
    health care delivery, 455–456
    health care reforms, 453
    hospitals, 453–454
    idealized solutions, 451

long-term care facilities, 454
managed care, 452
medical technology, 454–455
need for industry restructuring, 450
patients, 450
physicians, 450
problems of cost and accessibility,
455
future role of the federal government,
447–449
growth of home, outpatient, and
ambulatory care, 427–428
increased scrutiny of health care
costs, 438–447
changing composition of the delivery
system, 441–443
consumer-controlled health
insurance plan, 441
corporate alliances, 445–446
corporate growth in health care,
443–445
information management, 446–447
managed care plans, 438–439
patients' rights legislation, 439–440
key forces influencing the health
care system, 421, 422*t*
major challenges facing health care,
421
paradox of U.S. health care, 420–421
technological growth and innovation,
428–429
the uninsured, 421–423
Health Care, overview of, 1–32
access to health care, 27–29
the aging population
elderly with chronic physical
ailments, 24–26
financial coverage for long-term
needs, 27
growth and diversity of, 23
percent by race and Hispanic origin,
26*f*
projected population by age and
sex, 25*f*
rate of aging, 23
total number of persons age 65 or
older, 24*f*
commercialization of health care, 1
conflicts of interest, 29–30
ethical dilemmas, 30–31

indexes of health and disease, 5–6
managed care, development of
common features, 17
enrollment of Medicare and
Medicaid recipients in, 18
prepaid plans, 17–18
reimbursement variations, 18
types of plans, 17
natural histories of disease
for the aging process, 8*f,* 9
levels of preventive measures, 8*f,* 9
pathogenesis period, 6, 7*f,* 8, 9
prepathogenesis period, 6, 7*f,* 8*f,* 9
Parson's theories on predictable
behaviors, 4–5
patient-focused, 91–93
percent of U.S. gross domestic product,
1
priorities of
benefits of investing in prenatal
care, 20–21
treatment-oriented *vs.* prevention-
oriented health care, 22
tyranny of technology, 21–22
problems of health care
changes in political philosophies
over last 30 years, 2
governmental goals *vs.* those of the
market, 2
quality of care, 29
rural health networks, 19–20
social choices of health care, 22–23
stakeholders in the U.S. health care
industry, 9, 13–17
alternative therapies, 14–15
employers, 13
governments, 14
health professions education and
training institutions, 16
hospitals and other health care
facilities, 13–14
long-term care, 15
managed care organizations and
other insurers, 15
mental health care, 15–16
other health industry organizations,
16–17
professional associations, 16
providers, 13
the public, 13

Health Care, overview of *(continued)*
  research communities, 17
  voluntary facilities and agencies, 16
  understanding health care
    changing attitudes of the public, 3
    complex issues underlying the problems, 4
    increased cynicism about health care system, 3–4
    lack of public knowledge, 3
Healthcare Access, Portability, and Renewability Act of 1996, 449
Healthcare Co., The (HCA), 445
Health Care Financing Administration (HCFA), 89, 167, 374
Health care proxy legislation, 31
Health care reform proposal of 1993, 3
Health Grades, Inc., 168
Health insurance, 66. *See also specific types of insurers*
  and clinical practice guidelines, 167
  consumer-controlled health plan, 441
  evolution of: third-party payment, 231–234
    "assurance," 233
    Blue Cross/Blue Shield plans, 232–234
    government-sponsored, 231
    historic definition of insurance, 232
    post-World War II, 234
    reimbursement for low-income populations, 233
  government as source of payment (*See also* Medicaid; Medicare)
    health services included, 235–236
    other services funded by government, 263
    vendor/puchaser arrangement, 236
  influence of, 48–49
  long-term care insurance (LTCI), 327
  mental health care (*See under* Mental health services)
  self-funded programs, 234–235
    administrative-only arrangements, 234
    advantages to employers, 234
    exemption from ERISA, 234–235

minimum premium plan, 234
premium increases, 2001-2002, 235
third-party administrator (TPA), 234
Health Insurance Association of America (HIAA), 49, 327
Health Insurance Plan of New York, 18
Health Insurance Portability and Accountability Act (HIPAA) of 1996, 58, 250, 257
Health Insurance Reform Act of 1996, 449
Health Maintenance Organization (HMO) Act, 1973, 18, 40, 94, 275
Health maintenance organizations (HMOs), 17, 94, 164. *See also* Managed care
  costs *vs.* quality of health care, 40–41
  development of, 40
  growth of, 40, 41*f*
  mental health services, 352–353
Health Manpower Act, 1968, 186
Health Plan Employer Data and Information Set (HEDIS), 290–291
Health Professions Educational Assistance Act, 1963, 39, 372
Health Resources and Service Administration (HRSA), 374
Health Systems Agency (HSA), 39, 242
Healthy People 2000: National Health Promotion and Disease Prevention Objectives, 54–55, 378–379, 381
Healthy People 2010, 379–380, 381
Healthy People Consortium, 380
Heart bypass operation made possible, 42
Heart-lung machine, discovery of, 42
Henry Ford Health Center, economic losses of, 72
High-technology home care: hospitals without walls, 326–327
Hill-Burton Hospital Construction Act, 1946, 38, 66, 68
Hispanic populations, older, 23–24, 26*f*
HIV prevention programs, 379
"Hold harmless" clauses, 165–166
Home long-term care, 309–316

BBA provisions to control costs and
   address service quality issues,
   314–315
cost effectiveness, 310, 311*t*
definition of, 309
Dept. of Health and Human Services
   regulations, 315
family members as caregivers,
   313–314, 314*f*
formal and informal systems, 309
growth of, 427–428
Medicare certified home health care
   agencies, 311, 312*f*
need for far-reaching reforms,
   315–316
number of agencies, 310
Operation Restore Trust (ORT), 314
origination of, 309–310
Outcomes and Assessment
   Information Set (OASIS), 315
percentage of home health patients
   by age, 309, 309*f*
sources of payment, 310, 311*t*
state licensure and accreditation, 312
types of caregivers, 312–313
Hospice care, 316–319
   criterion for admission, 316
   historical roots, 316
   licensure/certification/accreditation,
      319
   number of hospice providers, 317
   "palliative care," 316
   payment scales, 318
   percentage of Medicare spending,
      318
   settings for, 317–318
   U.S. hospice movement, 316–317
   volunteerism, 318
Hospital ambulatory care services,
   121–126
   adoption of diagnosis-related groups
      (DRGs), 124
   care for the medically indigent popu-
      lation, 126
   expansion and reorganization of out-
      patient clinics, 124–125
   history of, 121–122
   organization and delivery of,
      124–125

outpatient clinics today, 122–123
outpatient revenues, 122, 123*f*
specialty medical clinics, 123–124
support for the teaching mission of
   the hospitals, 125
Hospital emergency services, 126–128
   distribution of emergency department
      visits, 126, 127*f*
   for routine care, 127–128
   training of physicians and nurses, 128
Hospital groups, influence of, 48
Hospitalists, 163–164, 433
Hospital Quality Information Initiative,
   425
Hospitals, 63–113. *See also* Hospitals,
      structure and organization of;
      Patients in hospitals, types and
      roles of; Quality of hospital
      care
   academic health centers, medical
      education and specialization,
      71–72
   economic losses of academic medical
      centers, 72
   financial condition of, 70–71
   growth and decline of
      hospitals by type of ownership, 69*t*
      numbers of beds according to type
         of hospital, 70
      numbers of hospitals in the United
         States, 68
      types of hospitals, 68–70
   as health care stakeholders, 13–14
   historical perspective
      18th century, 64
      19th century, 65
      early America, 64
      hospitals as almshouses, 65–66
      isolation hospitals, 64–65
      relationship of Protestant and
         Catholic religions with
         hospitals, 65
      women in nursing during the Civil
         War, 65
   offering alternative medicine
      treatments, 15
   rural health networks, 19–20
   sources that shaped the hospital
      industry

Hospitals *(continued)*
    health insurance, 66
    Medicare and Medicaid, 67–68
    structure and organization of, 73–80
        (*See also* Hospitals; Quality of
        hospital care)
      administrative departments, 79
      complexity of the system, 79–80
      diagnosis-related group (DRGs),
        85–87
      discharge planning, 87–88
      hotel services, 79
      market-driven reforms
        integrated health systems,
          93–97
        integrated health systems,
          horizontal integration, 95
        integrated health systems,
          integrated care arrangements,
          97
        integrated health systems, role
          of physicians in, 96–97
        integrated health systems,
          vertical integration, 95–96
        managed care, 90
        market responses to managed
          care, 98–99
        number of hospitals closed since
          1980, 89
        patient-focused care, 91–93
        reengineering, 91
      patient services
        diagnostic, 77–78
        nutritional, 78
        other patient support services, 78
        rehabilitation, 78
      staff
        allied health professionals, 76–77
        medical division, 74–75
        nursing division, 75–76
      subacute care, 88–89, 442
    Veterans Health Administration,
      72–73
Hotel services in hospitals, 79
Housing and Urban Development, 377
Human Genome Project, ethical issues
    and, 170
Human immunodeficiency virus (HIV)
    prevention programs, 379

Hysterectomy, appropriateness and use
    of study, 107*f*

I
Independent practice association (IPA)
    model, 280
Independent practitioner organizations
    (IPOs), 164–165
Indian Health Service (IHS), 374
Infant mortality, in developed countries,
    6
Information management, 446–447
Informed consent, 84–85
Institute of Medicine (IOM), 380–381
    report on medical errors, 29, 103–105,
      110, 390, 403, 407, 424
Insurance. *See* Health insurance
Integrated health systems, 93–97
    horizontal integration, 95
    integrated care arrangements, 97
    role of physicians in, 96–97
    vertical integration, 95–96
Integrated provider networks, 171
Internal medicine, subspecialty
    certifications, 153*t*
International medical school graduates
    (IMGs), 158, 184
Internet and health care, 58–59, 426,
    427
    physicians and, 170–171
Intraocular lens implants, after
    cataract surgery, 43
Investor-owned for-profit hospitals, 69

J
Johns Hopkins Hospital, 64
    cited as "model for medical education,"
      146
    first requires four years of training,
      144
Johnson, Lyndon B., 39, 40, 134, 378
Joint Commission on Mental Illness
    and Health, 336
Joint Commission on the Accreditation
    of Healthcare Organizations
    (JCAHO), 106, 404, 424–425
Joint Commission on the Accreditation
    of Hospitals, 100, 106, 312, 404
Medicare participation, 237

Journal of the American Medical Association (JAMA), 145

K

Kaiser-Permanente Medical Care Program, 18, 277
Kasselbaum-Kennedy Bill. *See* Health Insurance Portability and Accountability Act (HIPAA)
Kennedy, John F., 37
Kennedy, Ted, 284
Kerr-Mills Act of 1960, 258
King's College (Columbia University), 143
Kinyuon, Joseph J., 371
Knowles, J.H., 122
Kongstvedt, Peter, 164, 278

L

Laboratory technologists and technicians, 76, 200
Lathrop, J.P., 109
Legislation. *See also* Balanced Budget Act (BBA) of 1997
  first law concerning medicine, 144
  Healthcare Access, Portability, and Renewability Act of 1996, 449
  health care proxy, 31
  Health Insurance Reform Act of 1996, 449
  medical licensing, first attempts at, 144
  Medicare
    amendments to the Social Security Act, 239–241
    certificate-of-need legislation, 242
    Comprehensive Health Planning (CHP), 242
    Consolidated Omnibus Budget Reconciliation Act (COBRA), 245–246
    efforts at cost containment and quality control, 241
    to form health systems agencies (HSAs), 242
    guarantee of full-cost reimbursement, 241–242
    Omnibus Budget Reconciliation Act (OBRA) 1989, 247–248, 306
    Omnibus Budget Reconciliation Acts, 1980, 1981, 241
    peer review organizations (PROs), 243
    professional standards review organizations (PSROs), 240, 241, 242–243
    Tax Equity and Fiscal Responsibility Act of 1982 (TEFRA), 243
  regional medical program legislation, 146–147
Liaison Committee on Medical Education, 146
Licensed practical nurse (LPNs), 189–190
Licensure of health care professionals, 182, 306, 312, 319
Literature synthesis projects or metanalyses, 400
Living wills, 31
Lobbyists, 46
Long-term care, 297–334
  adult day care, 321–323
  assisted living facilities, 306–308
    cost of care in, 307–308
    definition of, 306–307
    monthly rent and fees, 308, 308*f*
    number of facilities and population in, 307, 307*f*
    oversight and regulation of, 307
  development of services
    almshouses, 300
    communal services, 299–300
    congressional hearings on the nursing home industry, 302–303
    government programs, 300
    home nursing care, 301
    inadequacy of care, 300–301
    nursing home corruption and abuses, 302
    passage of Medicare and Medicaid, 301–302
    percent distribution of facilities by ownership, 300, 301*f*
    Visiting Nurses Association, 301
  financial coverage for, 27
  future of, 328–329
  home care, 309–316

Long-term care *(continued)*
    BBA provisions to control costs and address service quality issues, 314–315
    cost effectiveness, 310, 311*t*
    definition of, 309
    Dept. of Health and Human Services regulations, 315
    family members as caregivers, 313–314, 314*f*
    formal and informal systems, 309
    Medicare certified home health care agencies, 311, 312*f*
    need for far-reaching reforms, 315–316
    number of agencies, 310
    Operation Restore Trust (ORT), 314
    origination of, 309–310
    Outcomes and Assessment Information Set (OASIS), 315
    percentage of home health patients by age, 309, 309*f*
    sources of payment, 310, 311*t*
    state licensure and accreditation, 312
    types of caregivers, 312–313
  hospice care, 316–319
    criterion for admission, 316
    historical roots, 316
    licensure, certification, and accreditation, 319
    number of hospice providers, 317
    "palliative care," 316
    payment scales, 318
    percentage of Medicare spending, 318
    settings for, 317–318
    U.S. hospice movement, 316–317
    volunteerism, 318
  the ideal delivery system, 297–298
  innovations in
    aging-in-place, 323–325
    continuing care retirement and life care communities (CCRCs), 325–326
    high-technology home care: hospitals without walls, 326–327
    insurance, 327
  population 65 and older, 298, 299*f*
  population 85 and older, 298, 299*f*
  providers, as health care stakeholders, 15
  residential care facilities, 303
  respite care, 319–321
    costs of, 320–321
    models of, 320
  and rural health networks, 19
  skilled nursing facilities (SNF), 303–306, 304–305, 305*f*
    risk of nursing home placement, 305
    sources of nursing home payment, 304, 304*f*
    state licensure and federal certification, 306
    typical staffing in, 305–306

M
Macy Foundation conference, 150
Magnetic resonance imaging (MRI), 77, 428–429
Major diagnostic categories (MDCs), 243
Malpractice insurance, 168–169
Managed behavioral health care company (MBHCC), 352–354
Managed care, 271–295. *See also specific organizations*
  capitation strategies, 165, 274–275
  development of
    common features, 17
    enrollment of Medicare and Medicaid recipients in, 18
    prepaid plans, 17–18
    reimbursement variations, 18
    types of plans, 17
  emerging developments in
    American opinions on managed care and other industries, 284, 285*t*
    Bipartisan Patient Protection Act of 2001, 284
    "consumer driven" health plans, 284–285
    performance of MCOs, 1997-2001, 285–286

premium increases, 282–284, 283*f*
surge in employee enrollment, 282
ethical issues and, 169
evolution of
  clinical practice guidelines, 281
  enrollment in 2000, 278, 279*f*
  enrollments by covered workers by
    plan type, 280*f*
  independent practice association
    (IPA) model, 280
  managed care organizations
    (MCOs), 278–281
  number of managed care enrollees,
    1988-20, 278, 279*f*
  physician performance, 281–282
  point-of-service (POS) plans,
    278–279
  preferred provider organizations
    (PPOs), 279–280
  role of the primary care physician,
    282
  shifting of financial risk, 281
  staff models, 280
  "triple option," 281
financial penalties to gatekeepers,
  161, 165
fundamentals
  capitation, 274–275
  concept of prepayment, 274–275
  definition of HMOs, 275
  definition of managed care,
    275–276
  fee-for-service payments, 274, 275
  population basis, 274
  the provider network, 274
the future of, 292
as health care stakeholders, 15
historical perspective, 271–274
  reform attempts, 273–274
  trend in health care expenditures,
    271–273, 272*f*
HMO Act of 1973, 275
  direct contact model, 278
  group or staff model, 277
  group practice model, 278
  individual practice association
    (IPA), 277–278
  mandated services, 276–277
  network model, 278

"hold harmless" clauses, 165–166
impact on the hospital community,
  90
influence toward ambulatory care, 116
market responses to, 98–99
Medicaid
  "carve-outs," 288–289
  enrollment in, *vs.* traditional
    enrollment, 1990-2002,
    287–288, *288f*
  plan models, 288
Medicare + Choice
  Balanced Budget Act of 1997, 286
  enrollment in, *vs.* traditional
    Medicare, 1990-2002, 286, 287*f*
  number of Medicare HMOs, 2003,
    286
  risk adjustment system, 286–287
  trends in premium and benefit
    structures, 287
quality assurance, 289–292
  "Desirable Characteristics of
    Quality Indicators or Groups
    of Quality Indicators for Use
    in Report Cards," 291
  Health Plan Employer Data and
    Information Set (HEDIS),
    290–291
  internal techniques, 291–292
  National Committee on Quality
    Assurance (NCQA)
    accreditation services,
    289–290
and reimbursement to voluntary
  agencies, 139–140
relationship between costs and quality,
  111
utilization reviews, 164
Managed care organizations (MCOs),
  278–281
Management services organizations
  (MSOs), 171–172
Marine Hospital Service, 1798, 370
Massachusetts General Hospital, 66
economic losses of, 72
Maternal Child Health and Mental
  Retardation Planning
  Amendments, 39–40
McCain, John, 284

McManus, G.L., 94

Meals on Wheels, 386

Medex program for physician assistants, 203

Medicaid, 258–263. *See also* Financing health care

for aliens, 259

amendments to Title XIX, 258

Balanced Budget Act of 1997, 260–262

    child health initiative, 261–262, 262*f*

    consumer protection provisions, 261

"carve-outs," 288–289

compared to Medicare, 258

direct reimbursement to providers, 259

enrollment in, *vs.* traditional enrollment, 1990-2002, 287–288, *288f*

federal guidelines, 258

future success of, 263

growth in spending, 259–260

health care for those outside these programs, 53

and the hospital industry, 67

inflationary effects of, 37–38

long-term institutional care, 27, 259

managed care enrollments, 18, 136, 260, 261*f,* 438

mental health services, 336, 337, 338, 354

passage of in 1965, 35, 258

Personal Responsibility and Work Opportunity Reconciliation Act, 259

plan models, 288

public health services, 390

reimbursement, community health centers, 135

state guidelines, 258–259

structure of, 258

Medical Education and specialization, 44–46. *See also* Academic Medical Centers; Medical Schools

demand for specialists, 45–46

effects on hospitals, 71–72

needed educational reforms, 46

producing an oversupply of physicians, 44–45

regional medical program legislation, 146–147

Medical Education in the United States and Canada (Flexner Report), 145–146

Medical errors, 29, 103–105, 104*f,* 110, 390, 403, 407

Medical foundations, 172

Medical genetics, subspecialty certifications, 154*t*

Medical Outcome Studies, 402

Medical practice

cost containment and the restructuring of, 164–165

future of, 172–174

Medical procedures, summary of selected studies, 107*f*

Medical Schools

Academic Medical Centers, 146–148

changing supply of physicians and geographic variation in physician capacity, 157

increases in number of graduates and residents, 157–158

influences on practice specialty decisions, 159–160

international medical school graduates (IMGs), 158

policies and programs to increase number of physicians, 157

ratios of generalist to specialist physicians, 158–160

Flexner Report and Medical School reforms, 145–146

funding of graduate medical education, 156–157

Graduate Medical Education Consortia, 149–150

history of, 143–145

admission requirements, 144

apprentice-trained physicians, 143, 144

attempts to establish national standard, 144–145

first attempts at licensing, 144

first in America, 143–144
first law concerning medicine, 144
preventive medicine, 161–162
residency programs, 150
specialty boards and residency per-
    formance, 152–153, 153–155*t*,
    156
Medical societies, 144–145
Medical Society of Boston, 144
medical specialty societies, clinical
    practice guidelines, 166–167
Medical Treatment Effectiveness
    Program (MEDTEP), 400
Medicare, 236–257. *See also* Financing
    health care
accreditation by Joint Commission on
    Accreditation of Hospitals, 237
"all-payer" rate systems, 246
association with Blue Cross, 237
Balanced Budget Act (BBA) of 1997
    CAA's provisions, 255
    "Comprehensive Plan for Program
        Integrity," 257
    created major new policy direction
        for Medicare and Medicaid,
        250–251
    major provisions of
        changing provider payment
            methods and amounts, 253,
            257
        conducting demonstration
            projects, 253, 257
        developing prevention initiatives,
            253, 257
        establishing a new Medicare
            Part C, 252–253
        establishing program integrity
            provisions, 254, 257
        Medicare + Choice, 253, 256–257
        providing anti-fraud and abuse
            provisions, 254, 257
        providing rural hospital
            initiatives, 253–254, 257
    managed care enrollment initiative,
        256–257
    Medicare Integrity Program, 257
    Medicare Payment Advisory
        Commission established, 252
    Medicare savings by 2002, 252, 252*f*

Medicare spending pre- and post-
    BBA, 255–256, 255*f,* 256*t*
National Bipartisan Commission
    on the Future of Medicare,
    251–252
need for radical changes in
    Medicare system, 249–250
new mandate for reform, 249–250
projected savings, 1998-2002, 251*f*
ProPAC and Physician Payment
    Review Commission replaced,
    252
Balanced Budget Refinement Act of
    1999 (BBRA), 257
Benefits Protection and Improvement
    Act of 2000, 257
coinsurance, 238
deductibles, 238
diagnosis-related groups (DRGs)
    payment system, 87, 243–244
efforts at curtailing fraud and abuse,
    257
enacted in 1966, 237
enrollment in managed care plans,
    18, 389–390
funding for community health centers,
    135
government subsidy of graduate
    medical education, 148, 157
Health Insurance Portability and
    Accountability Act (HIPAA) of
    1996, 250, 257
home health agencies and, 138
home health care services, 245
the hospital industry and, 67
inflationary effects of, 37–38
legislation
    amendments to the Social Security
        Act, 239–241
    certificate-of-need legislation, 242
    Comprehensive Health Planning
        (CHP), 242
    Consolidated Omnibus Budget
        Reconciliation Act (COBRA),
        245–246
    efforts at cost containment and
        quality control, 241
    to form health systems agencies
        (HSAs), 242

Medicare *(continued)*
  guarantee of full-cost
    reimbursement, 241–242
  Omnibus Budget Reconciliation
    Acts (OBRA), 241, 247–248,
    306
  peer review organizations (PROs),
    243
  professional standards review
    organizations (PSROs), 240,
    241, 242–243
  Tax Equity and Fiscal
    Responsibility Act of 1982
    (TEFRA), 243
  major diagnostic categories (MDCs),
    243
  Medicare Economic Index, 247
  Medicare Volume Performance
    standards, 248
  Medi-gap policies, 238
  mental health services, 336
  Part A, 237
  Part B, 237–238
  passage of in 1965, 35
  prospective payment system, 47, 244,
    246
  reasons for increases in hospital
    expenses, 238
  reimbursements
    to hospitals, 238–239
    to long-term care hospitals, 89
  research/studies
    Prospective Payment Assessment
      Commission (ProPAC), 245
    RAND Corporation, 245
  resource-based relative value scale
    (RBRVS), 247–248
  rising costs and reduction in coverage,
    52–53
Medicare, Medicaid, and State Child
  Health Insurance Program
  Benefits Improvement and
  Protection Act, 223
Medicare + Choice, 253, 256–257
  Balanced Budget Act of 1997, 286
  enrollment in, *vs.* traditional
    Medicare, 1990-2002, 286, 287*f*
  number of Medicare HMOs, 2003,
    286
  risk adjustment system, 286–287
  trends in premium and benefit
    structures, 287
Medicare Payment Advisory
  Commission, 252
Medicare Volume Performance
  standards, 248
Mendelson, Mary Adelaide, 302
Mental health care providers, as health
  care stakeholders, 15–16
Mental Health Equitable Treatment
  Act of 2001, 355
Mental Health Parity Act of 1997, 355
Mental health services, 335–366
  ambulatory services, 336
  barriers to accessing service,
    356–357
  diagnostic categories
    adjustment disorders, 342
    anxiety disorders, 341
    cognitive disorders, 340
    disorders due to a general medical
      condition, 340
    disorders first diagnosed in infancy,
      childhood, or adolescence, 340
    dissociative disorders, 341
    eating disorders, 342
    factitious disorders, 341
    impulse control disorders, 342
    mood disorders, 341
    other conditions that may be a
      focus of clinical attention, 342
    personality disorders, 342
    schizophrenia and other psychotic
      disorders, 341
    sexual and gender identity
      disorders, 341–342
    sleep disorders, 342
    somatoform disorders, 341
    substance-related disorders,
      340–341
  government activity in, 335–336
  historical perspective
    deinstitutionalization movement,
      337
    entitlement programs, 336
    federal support for community-
      based services, 336–337
    first biological treatments, 335

increasing costs of, 337–338

National Alliance for the Mentally
Ill (NAMI), 337, 338

National Mental Health Act of
1946, 335

number of people in inpatient
facilities, 1950's, 336

psychoactive medications
introduced, 336

psychosocial programs under
Medicaid expanded, 338

Quaker emphasis on mental illness
as treatable, 335

reallocation of federal money, 338

report of the Joint Commission on
Mental Illness and Health,
336

shift from inpatient to outpatient
services, 338

"war neurosis" and "shell shock,"
335

insurance coverage/managed
behavioral health care

distribution of sources of payment
for mental health/substance
abuse, 349*f*

efforts to control costs, 353–354

employer benefits, 351

evolution of behavioral carve-outs,
352–353

expenditures in the mid-1990s, 351

financial considerations *vs.* clinical
need, 349–350

financial incentives to abuse the
system, 350–351

managed care systems, 351–352

management of service utilization,
353

parity legislation, impact of,
354–355

payment based on units of service,
350

for people with severe and
persistent mental illness,
355–356

need for further research, 359–361

NIMH priorities for

assessment, 357–358

epidemiology, 357

outcome, 358–359

rehabilitation and habilitation, 358

treatment, 358

organization and financing of

cost of psychotropic drugs, 348

cost of U.S. mental health services,
348–349, 349*f*

major components of, 346–347, 347*f*

mental health priorities, 348

recipients of, 338–339, 339*t*

children and adolescents, 345

"comorbidity," 343–344, 344*t*

older adults, 345–346

percentage of adults with mental
disorders receiving services,
342–343, 343*f*

undiagnosed and untreated
individuals, 344–345

severe mental illness, 343

Mental Retardation Facilities and
Community Mental Health
Centers Construction Act, 336

Metropolitan Life, marketing of
industrial policies, 34

Military Health Service, 263, 376

Millenson, Michael L., 424

Minorities, enrolled in U.S. medical
schools, 183

Model Cities Program, 377

Molecular biology, ethical issues and,
170

Morehead, M.A., 101, 405

Mortality, infant and maternal, in
developed countries, 6

Mutual of Omaha, 14

N

Nader Report, 302

National Academy of Sciences, report
on medical mistakes, 390

National Adult Day Services
Association, adult day care
standards, 323

National Advisory Mental Health
Council (NAMHC), 343

insurance coverage for mental health
patients, 356

National Alliance for the Mentally Ill
(NAMI), 337, 338, 357–358

National Association of Blue Shield
Plans, 232
National Association of Manufacturers
(NAM), 50, 51
National Bipartisan Commission on
the Future of Medicare,
251–252
National Center for Complementary
and Alternative Medicine
(NCCAM), 208
National Center for Nursing Research,
187
National Commission on Certification
of Physician Assistants, 203
National Committee on Quality
Assurance (NCQA), 289–290
National Co-Morbidity Study, 339
National Council on Graduate Medical
Education, endorsement of
GMEs, 150
National Federation of Independent
Businesses, 50
National health expenditures (NHE),
222, 222f
National health insurance, Great
Britain, 236
National Health Planning and
Resources Development Act,
1974, 39
National Health Security Act, 1993, 46,
47, 89, 236, 248, 250, 264,
273–274
National Health Service Corps, 372
National Hemophilia Foundation, 50
National Hospital Survey and
Construction Act, 372
National Institute for Occupational
Health and Safety, 372
National Institute of Dental Research
(NIDR), 193
National Institute of Mental Health
(NIMH), 345, 357
National Institute on Alcohol Abuse
and Alcoholism, 372
National Institutes of Health (NIH),
373, 392
competition for grants, 149
government support of, 37
Office of Alternative Medicine, 15

National League of Nurses Community
Health Accreditation Program,
319
National Mental Health Act of 1946, 335
Neighborhood Health Centers, 377
Neonatal intensive care, 383
New Federalism policies, 37, 41–42,
378
Newsday, freedom of information
request, 167–168
New York Hospital, 66
first hospital pharmacist at, 194–195
New York Poor Law of 1788, 370
Nixon, Richard M., 37, 378
Nonteaching hospitals, 68
Nuclear medicine
subspecialty certifications, 154t
technology, 200–201
Nurse anesthetists, 190–191
Nurse midwives, 190
Nurse practitioners (NPs), 190–191
future supply of, 437
Nurses/Nursing, 185–192
during the Civil War, 65
doctoral programs, 187
effect of World War I on profession of,
185–186
effects on nursing employment,
188–189
employment of registered nurses by
setting, 2000, 186, 187t
first training program in the United
States, 185
frustration with role in hospitals, 4
funding for educational preparation
of nurses, 186
future supply of nurses, 436–437
increased workloads, 189
medicare revisions and, 192
number of registered nurses, 186
nursing division in a hospital, 75–76
nursing education, 186–187
nursing research, 187
percentage of male RNs, 188
professions
clinical nurse specialist, 192
critical care nurse (CCN), 187
licensed practical nurse (LPNs),
189–190

nurse anesthetists, 190–191
nurse midwives, 190
nurse practitioners, 190–191
Protestant nursing movement, 65
specialization, 187
staff crisis, creating shortage of,
105–106
supply and demand projections for
FTE registered nurses, 188, 188*f*
Nurse Training Act, 39, 186, 372
Nutritional services, 78

O
Occupational Safety and Health Act
(OSHA), 51
Occupational therapy, 202
Office for Data Development, 400
Office of Alternative Medicine (OAM),
208
Office of Economic Opportunity, 377
Office of Technology Assessment (OTA),
44, 400
Office of the Forum for Quality and
Effectiveness in Health Care,
400
Omnibus Budget Reconciliation Act
(OBRA)
1980, 1981, 241
1989, 247–248, 306
On Lok Senior Health Services, 324
Operation Restore Trust (ORT), 314
Ophthalmology, 154*t*
Optometry, 197–198
Oregon Death with Dignity Act, 56–57
Orthopaedic surgery, subspecialty
certifications, 154*t*
Otolaryngology, subspecialty
certifications, 154*t*
Outcomes and Assessment Information
Set (OASIS), 315
Outcomes research, 409–410
Outpatient care, growth of, 428

P
Pacific Islanders, older, 24, 26*f*
Palmer, B.J., 196
Palmer, Daniel David, 196
Parson, Talcott, theories on predictable
behaviors, 4–5

Pathology, subspecialty certifications,
154*t*
"Patient dumping," 244, 245–246
Patient outcome research teams
(PORTs), 400
Patient protection laws, 390
Patients
as health care stakeholders, 13
proactive roles of, 5
Patient satisfaction, 410–411
Patients' Bill of Rights, 81, 439–440
Patients' Coalition, 50
Patients in hospitals, types and roles
of, 80–85
important decisions, informed consent,
and second opinions, 84–85
patient-focused health care, 91–93
rights and responsibilities of
hospitalized patients, 81–84
dependence on nursing and
hospital staff, 83–84
institutional circumstances that
violate patients' rights, 82–83
patients as active participants in,
their care, 83–84
Patient support services, 78
Pediatrics, subspecialty certifications,
154–155*t*
Peer review organization (PRO), 88
Pennsylvania Hospital, 66
People's Medical Society, 424
Percutaneous transluminal coronary
angioplasty (PTCA), 107*f*
Personal Responsibility and Work
Opportunity Reconciliation
Act, 259
Personnel, health care, 179–220
credentialing and regulating health
professionals, 181–183
distribution of health care
employment by settings, 179,
180*f*
and health care reforms, 180–181
health professions, 179–180
home health care job growth, 181
new employment opportunities, 181
occupations
allied health personnel, 199–209
chiropractors, 196–197

Personnel, health care *(continued)*
  dentistry, 192–194
  health care administrators,
    198–199
  nursing, 185–192
  optometry, 197–198
  pharmacy, 194–195
  physicians, 183–185
  podiatric medicine, 195–196
Peterson, Oscar, 405
Petty, William, 369
Pew Charitable Trusts, 17, 161, 386
Pew Health Professions Commission,
  161
Pharmaceutical industry
  and clinical practice guidelines, 167
  influence of, 51
Pharmaceutical practice, 194–195
  pharmacy education, 195
  predicted shortages of licensed
    pharmacists, 195
Pharmaceutical Research and
    Manufacturers Association, 50
Physical Medicine and Rehabilitation,
    subspecialty certifications,
    155*t*
Physical therapy, 201–202
Physician assistants (PAs), 203–204
  future supply of, 437
Physician groups, influence of, 47–48
Physician-hospital organizations
    (PHOs), 445–446
Physician/hospital relationships,
    162–164
  competition for patients, 163
  financial consequences of clinical
    decisions, 163
  "hospitalists," 163–164
  physician-hospital organizations
    (PHOs), 172
  stresses on, 163
Physician-owned laboratories, 30
Physician performance evaluation, 165,
    167–168
Physicians
  changing supply of
    alternative physician substitutes,
      185
    apprentice-trained, 143–144

Doctor of Medicine (MD), 149
Doctor of Osteopathic Medicine
    (DO), 149
"hospitalists," 163–164, 433
IMGs, 184
and the Internet, 170–171
number of schools awarding MD or
    DO degrees, 183
number of women enrolled in U.S.
    medical schools, 183
primary care ("gatekeepers"),
    160–161, 165, 184
role of in integrated health
    systems, 96–97
shortages in medical specialties,
    184–185
and U.S. Medical Schools
  geographic variation in
    physician capacity, 157
  increases in number of
    graduates and residents,
    157–158
  influences on practice specialty
    decisions, 159–160
  international medical school
    graduates (IMGs), 158
  policies and programs to
    increase number of physicians,
    157
  ratios of generalist to specialist
    physicians, 158–160
  future supply of, 432
  medical manager, 433
Picker/Commonwealth Program for
    Patient-Centered Care, 1987,
    92–93
Planned Parenthood, 386
Plastic surgery, subspecialty
    certifications, 155*t*
Podiatric medicine, 195–196
Point-of-service (POS) plans, 278–279
Poor Law Amendment Act of 1834, 369
Poor Law Commission of 1834,
    369–370
Populations
  changing population composition,
    429–430
  proportion of elderly populations, 6
  services for low-income, 135

Positron emission tomography (PET), 77

Preferred provider organizations (PPOs), 17, 164, 279–280

Prenatal care, benefits of investing in, 20–21

Prepaid health plans, 17–18

Prescription drug coverage, 18

Presidential Commission on Mental Health, 338

Preventive medicine, 8*f,* 9, 161–162

Primary ambulatory care centers, 129–130

Princeton Survey Research Associates, study on health care, 110

Private medical office practice and ambulatory care
  malpractice insurance costs, 119
  managed care and, 121
  Medicare reimbursement and, 119
  multispecialties group practice, 120
  shift to group practice, 118–120
  solo-practice model, 118–119
  surgical group practice, 120–121

Professional standards review organizations (PSROs), 102–103

Program for All-Inclusive Care for the Elderly (PACE), 324–325

Prospective continuing life care community (CLCC), 325–326

Prospective Payment Assessment Commission (ProPAC), 245

Prospective payment system, 402

Provider network contracting
  customizing the models, 172
  integrated provider networks, 171
  management services organizations (MSOs), 171–172
  medical foundations, 172
  physician-hospital organizations (PHOs), 172

Providers of health care, as health care stakeholders, 13

Prudential Insurance Company of America, 14, 34

Psychiatry and Neurology, subspecialty certifications, 155*t*

Public health, 263, 367–394
  and ambulatory care, 137–138
  in an era of privatization and managed care, 388–389
  changing roles of government in, 387–388
  deaths from preventable causes, 385, 385*f*
  decline in influence of, 377–378
  defense programs, 392
  in England
    Bills of Mortality, 369
    Elizabethan Poor Laws of 1601, 369
    Poor Law Amendment Act of 1834, 369
    Poor Law Commission of 1834, 369–370
    proposal of John Bellers, 369
  federal support to address emerging health issues, 389–391
  focus on prevention, 52
  future role of government in promoting, 391–392
  government-supported services
    Department of Health and Human Services (DHHS), 372–375
    Federal Emergency Relief Act of 1933, 371
    Health, Education, and Welfare (HEW), 372
    Marine Hospital Service, 1798, 370
    metropolitan health systems, 377
    Military Health Service, 376
    National Hospital Survey and Construction Act, 372
    New York Poor Law of 1788, 370
    Public Health Service, 371–372
    Public Health Service Commission Corps, 1889, 371
    Public Health Service operating divisions, 373–375
    Shattuck's Report of the Sanitary Commission of 1850, 370
    Social Security Act of 1935, 371–372
    state-sponsored services, 376–377
    TRICARE, 376
    Veterans Health Administration (VA), 375–376

Public health *(continued)*
  health care reform and public
      health/medicine relationship,
      384–385
  hospital-sponsored activities, 386
  "public health" defined, 367
  relationships with private medicine,
      381–382
  resource priorities favor curative
      medicine, 383–384
  responsibilities of the public health
      sector
    *Healthy People 2000: National
        Health Promotion and Disease
        Prevention Objectives,* 54–55,
        378–379, 381
    Healthy People 2010, 379–380
    Healthy People Consortium, 380
    Institute of Medicine, 380–381
  services of voluntary agencies,
      386–387
  State Children's Health Insurance
      Program (SCHIP), 389
  world history of, 367–368
Public Health Service, operating
    divisions, 373–375
Public Health Service Act, 1965, 38–39,
    135
Public Hospital of Baltimore, 64
Public hospitals, 69

Q
Quality improvement research,
    403–407
  Bad Apple theory, 403
  clinical judgment, 403
  empirical standards, 406–407
  implicit and explicit standards, 406
  Institute of Medicine report, 1990,
      403
  peer review-based assessment,
      403–404
  performance proficiencies, 405
  process components, 404–405
  structural criteria, 404–405
  Teamsters' study, 405
Quality Management Office, Depart-
    ment of Veterans Affairs, 103
Quality of hospital care, 99–111
  current research efforts in quality
      improvement, 106–108, 107*f*
  definition of quality, 100
  forces of reform: cost/quality/access,
      109–111
  hazards of hospitalization, 103–105
  incremental quality improvement,
      108–109
  landmark studies, 101–102
  outcomes of care, 101
  peer review technique (chart audits),
      100
  process components of care, 100–101
  responsibility of governing boards,
      108
  shortage of nurses creating staffing
      crisis, 105–106
  structural criteria, 100
  types of errors, 104*f*
  variations in medical care, 102–103
"Quicker and sicker," 244

R
Radiograph technology, 21
Radiologic technology, 200
Radiology, subspecialty certifications,
    155*t*
RAND Corporation
  health services, insurance, and
      medical outcomes studies, 402
  medical procedures study, 107*f,* 166
Reagan, Ronald, 41–42, 47, 378
*Reengineering the Corporation: A
    Manifesto for Business
    Revolution,* 91
Registered polarity practitioners
    (RPPs), 209
Registered Records Administrator
    (RRA), 205
Registration of health care professionals,
    182–183
Regulations
  assisted living facilities, 307
  for home care, 315
Rehabilitation counselor, 204–205
Rehabilitation services, 78
Reinhardt, Uwe E., 431
Research: how health care advances,
    395–417

communities, as health care
stakeholders, 17
epidemiology
analytical observational studies,
398
defined, 397
descriptive observational studies,
397
experimental, 398
other applications, 398–399
evidence-based medicine, 407–409,
408*f*
future challenges, 412–415
basic science research, 412
bioinformatic research, 412
genomics research, 413
in health services research, 414
managed care, 414
misuse of antibiotics, 413
new moral dilemmas, 413
public health research, 414–415
research priorities, 412
health and disease
basic research, 396
clinical research, 396–397
clinical trials, 397
research studies, 397
volunteer subjects, 397
health services
Agency for Health Care Policy and
Research (AHCPR)
clinical guidelines, 400–401
dispute with surgeons
organization, 400–401
priority activities, 400
responsibilities of, 400
Agency for Healthcare Research
and Quality (AHRQ), 401–402
research and health policy,
402–403
subsidy programs, 399
medical errors, 407
outcomes research, 409–410
patient satisfaction, 410–411
quality improvement, 403–407
Bad Apple theory, 403
clinical judgment, 403
empirical standards, 406–407
implicit and explicit standards, 406

Institute of Medicine report, 1990,
403
peer review-based assessment,
403–404
performance proficiencies, 405
process components, 404–405
structural criteria, 404–405
Teamsters' study, 101–102, 405
research ethics, 411–412
variations in research focus, 396*f*
Residency programs, 150, 183–184
guidelines for approved residencies,
156
Residency review committee (RRC),
156
Resource-based relative value scale
(RBRVS), 247–248
Respite care, 319–321
costs of, 320–321
models of, 320
Restructuring Health Care, 109
Ridge, Tom, 392
Robert Wood Johnson Foundation, 17,
386
Rosen, George, 367
Rural primary care hospital (RPCH),
19–20

S
Sabin and Salk vaccines, discovery of,
42
Sade, R.M., 27, 28
Sammons, James S., 47
Saunders, Dame Cicely, 316
School of Public Health, U. of Illinois,
379
Service Employees International Union
(SEIU), 51
Sexually transmitted disease prevention
programs, 379
Shattuck, Lemuel, 370
Shortell, Stephen, 456
Silver, George, 59–60
Single payer system, 427
Social and Rehabilitation Services, 377
Social Security Act of 1935, 37, 102
Title VI, public health services,
371–372
Title XVIII, Medicare, 67, 237

Social Security Act of 1935 *(continued)*
  Title XIX, Medicaid, 67, 258
  Title XXI, health insurance coverage
    for children, 389
Social Security and Disability Insurance,
    336
Social work, 204
Specialist support service personnel, 77
Specialization, 151–152
  ratios of generalist to specialist
    physicians, 158–160
Special Supplemental Food Program for
    Women, Infants, and Children
    (WIC), 383
Specialty boards and residency perfor-
    mance, 152–153, 153–155*t,*
    156
Speech language pathology, 202–203
Staff. *See also* Personnel, health care
  frustration of, 4
  in hospitals
    administrative department, 79
    allied health professionals, 76–77
    medical division, 74–75
    nursing division, 75–76
Stanford University Hospital, economic
    losses of, 72
Starr, P., 382
State Children's Health Insurance
    Programs (SCHIPs), 138, 250,
    262
Stevens, Rosemary, 56, 67–68, 233, 237,
    238
Subacute care, 88–89, 442
Substance Abuse and Mental Health
    Services Administration
    (SAMHSA), 374
Suicide, physician-assisted, 30–31,
    56–57
Supplemental Security Income (SSI),
    258, 259, 307
  mental health services, 336, 338
Support services personnel, 205–206
Surgery, subspecialty certifications,
    155*t*
Surgery centers, for ambulatory care,
    131, 132*f,* 133*f,* 134
Sweeney, John J., 51

T
Task Force on Academic Health Centers,
    433
Tax Equity and Fiscal Responsibility
    Act of 1982 (TEFRA), 243
Teaching hospitals, 68–69
Teamsters' study of hospital care,
    101–102, 405
Technology
  advances in
    during the 1960s, 42
    assessing the value of, 21–22
    computed tomography CT scan, 43
    ethical issues and, 43–44, 169–170
    intraocular lens implants, 43
  effect on health care employment,
    215
  financial dilemmas, 43–44
  future of medical technology,
    454–455
  growth of, 428–429
  high-technology home care, 326–327
  increased costs from, 223–225, 225*f*
  technological growth and innovation,
    428–429
  tyranny of, 21–22
Technology Assessment Act, 1972, 44
Tender Loving Greed, 302
Therapeutic science practitioners, 201
Third-party administrator (TPA), 234
Thoracic surgery, 155*t*
Todd, James, 47
*To Err is Human: Building a Safer
    Health System,* 424
Total quality management (TQM), 91,
    108–109
Tranquilizers, introduction of, 42
Treatment-oriented *vs.* prevention-
    oriented health care, 22
TRICARE, 376
Tympanostomy, appropriateness and
    use of study, 107*f*

U
U. of Connecticut Health Center,
    economic losses of, 72
U. of Pennsylvania Health System, eco-
    nomic losses of, 72

UCLA Medical Center, economic losses of, 72

Urgent/emergent ambulatory care centers, 130–131

Urology, 155*t*

U.S. Chamber of Commerce, 50–51

U.S. National Institutes of Health Web site, 170–171

U.S. Public Health Service, 69, 392

Utilization reviews, 164

V

VA Health Services Research and Development Service (HSR&D), 73

Veterans Affairs medical centers, 14, 69

Veterans Health Administration (VA), 72–73, 263, 335–336, 375–376

Veterans Integrated Service Networks (VISNs), 73

Veterans Millennium Health Care and Benefits Act of 1999, 376

Voluntary facilities and agencies for ambulatory health care, 139–140 as health care stakeholders, 16

Voluntary not-for-profit hospitals, 69

W

Wallack, S.S., 248

Wennberg, John, 102, 402

Women, enrolled in U.S. medical schools, 183

Women, Infant, and Children (WIC) supplemental nutrition program, 135

World Health Organization (WHO), definition of health, 5